MURDER INCORPORATED

empire \ genocide \ manifest destiny

A Three Book Series

BOOK TWO:

"America's Favorite Pastime"

BOOK ONE: **"Dreaming of Empire"**

BOOK THREE: **"Perfecting Tyranny"**

Mumia Abu-Jamal & Stephen Vittoria

PRISON RADIO
San Francisco
2019

Published by Prison Radio
San Francisco

First Published in 2019

Prison Radio, P.O. Box 411074, San Francisco, CA 94141

Edited by Justin Lebanowski

Cover Design by Robert Guillory

Interior Design by Rocco Melillo

First Edition Softcover / January 2019

LIBRARY OF CONGRESS CATALOGING-IN-PUBLICATION DATA

Abu-Jamal, Mumia – Vittoria, Stephen. Murder Incorporated: Empire,
Genocide, and Manifest Destiny/Book Two—1st ed. p. cm.

Includes bibliographical references and index.

1.History—American Empire.
2. History—War.
3.History—Manifest Destiny.

ISBN: 978-0-9989600-6-7

Printed in the USA

It was our original desire to dedicate *Murder Incorporated—Book Two, America's Favorite Pastime* to an actual murder victim in one of America's many wars of imperial vanity. But it's not that easy. Who do we embrace? Who do we pick? There are millions of victims. How about the throngs of children, like ten-year-old Ha Mi, who ran for her life as a Boeing B-52 Stratofortress dropped precision-guided ordnance from a silent and invisible 45,000 feet above Hanoi?

Or maybe Mamana Bibi, a grandmother in Pakistan who was out in the family field picking vegetables when a Hellfire missile hit her flush on? USA! USA! God bless the CIA or USAF or whichever murder outfit pulled the cowardly trigger in their air-conditioned trailer in Florida or the Nevada desert or wherever they house their cute joystick video games. But wait, we almost forgot, because two minutes later, after they whacked the grandmother, her eighteen-year-old grandson, Kaleem, ran out to help her, not knowing she was killed on impact. As he arrived, the drones returned with more U.S. taxpayer-funded Hellfire missiles—and now Kaleem gets fucked up real bad, wounded and riddled with shrapnel. (Note: the drones returning is a clever little strategy called a "double-tap" strike—here's how this shit works: After the initial strike, the drones wait a few minutes while people in the area rush into the scene, obviously to help the victims, but then wham-bam, here come the drones for act two, striking again, this time killing the rescuers and other poor bastards who wandered into the bull's-eye.)

Then there was six-year-old Takato Michishita who lived in Nagasaki, Japan, in the middle of the American Century. On 9 August 1945 his mother decided to keep Takato and his sister home from school. She said she had "a bad feeling." Takato said this never happened before, but good thing for them it did because around noon on this bright sunny summer day, an American B-29 bomber piloted by Massachusetts native Charles Sweeney dropped a plutonium implosion nuclear bomb on Nagasaki. The bomb, nicknamed "Fat Boy" because of its wide, round shape, detonated over the helpless Japanese city. Takato's school was wiped out—including every child and teacher inside. We could have dedicated this book to all of them.

Or what about the one hundred or so "merciless savages," also known as the Pomo People in Northern California, who were wiped out by Nathaniel Lyon and his U.S. Army cavalry on 15 May 1850 in what was called the Bloody Island Massacre? Let's dedicate the book to them. We could also dedicate this work to the murdered tens of thousands at the hands of Reagan-era U.S. covert killing sprees in Central America, bolstered (to this day) by the vicious training of Latin American torturers and assassins inside the U.S. Army's School of the Americas (now repackaged as the "Western Hemisphere Institute for Security Cooperation").

You get it. The beat goes on, and on, and on...

Let's try this... let's dedicate this book to the future brothers and sisters who do not become murder victims, who are not slaughtered by the American Empire, who live long and fruitful lives because this nation finally wakes up to its violent DNA and says "no—not in my name," a nation that is woke ("If You're Woke You Dig It"), and stays woke, and learns to love rather than kill.

Maybe says Don Quixote. Probably not says Sancho Panza.

—MAJ & SV

Postscriptum: Ten-year-old Ha Mi actually survived the Christmas bombings of Hanoi, part of Richard Nixon's *Operation Linebacker II*, during which the U.S. Air Force flew more than 700 nighttime sorties over North Vietnam, dropping more than 20,000 tons of killing force. Please note that Washington suspended the vicious and devastating murder spree on Christmas Day—in honor of Jesus' birthday.

ACKNOWLEDGMENTS

Who births a book? Who gives it blood, sinews, limbs, brain, and spine? Books are born, more often than not, by other books, which light flames in the psyche, passing light to those flung far into the river of time.

When I think of great books, it is hardly or ever the official Canon. It is often little known people who wrote against the storm, their minds ablaze by fires from another era—like J.A. Rogers, a self-taught historian who appeared in a slew of Black newspapers, like the *Pittsburgh Courier*, the *Afro American*, and who also wrote numerous books, filled not only with texts, but photographs to affirm his theories. He traveled across continents to salvage some tidbit, some morsel of knowledge that would amaze readers, of Black names, Black nations, Black princes who emerged in worlds we had never known.

This work, therefore, was sparked when a curious teenager found more fun in a bookstore than on a baseball diamond. For, there he read Yosef Ben-Jochannon, Ivan Van Sertima, Herbert Aptheker, C.L.R. James, George Nash, Ishakamusa Barashango, Runoko Rashidi, Ward Churchill, Du Bois, et al.

Often the works of these historians were emblazoned with deftly drawn dark figures in majestic poses, speaking to us across eons, saying softly, almost imperceptibly: "I am Here. I am Here."

Many, if not most of these historians were (a term few would use themselves) "outlaw" historians—rebels, who turned their backs on the Guild, for their work was so disruptive of the accepted Canon.

They searched and searched and unearthed Canons from Antiquity that preceded the works of Europe by centuries. For example, who knows that the phrase "Black is Beautiful!" so evocative of the proverbial '60s, was echoed in spirit more than a thousand years before that era? As a man of that era (really, a teen), I thought we were breaking new ground, speaking thoughts that bubbled in our breasts for the first time.

Well, Dr. Ben (as Yochannon was affectionately known by his students) certainly knew, for in many of his typewritten texts, he cited Al-Jahiz's *Book of the Glory of the Black Race*, written by a Black Arab of Basra, Iraq, decades after Islam's founding. This work, written between 776–868 A.D., reads as if it were written at the height of the Black Power Movement, circa 1968!

These writers dared to break new ground, and to not only learn new things, but to unlearn old canonical verities that were as traditional as they were misleading.

Of course, this work is inspired by the remarkable Howard Zinn, who, burned by the savagery of World War II, and inspired by the true courage of civil rights activists (many of whom were his students, like the acclaimed novelist, Alice Walker), learned not from the classics, but from his students, among them men and women who marched on the front lines of history.

This work is dedicated to all of them, who, by their works, made this one possible.

Mumia Abu-Jamal

The idea for this project emerged from dust during a late evening conversation I had with Gore Vidal in the parlor of his home in the Hollywood Hills. His grasp of history, all history, was only surpassed by his grasp of the evils unleashed by the ruling elite that he knew so well, the robber barons who own the club—own it lock, stock, and smoking barrel. Our back and forth tête-à-tête jumped from TR to FDR, Caesar to Camelot, Foggy Bottom to Langley, and of course from Italian to California wine. And in the crevices and fissures, feeling wholly out of my league with this legendary mind, I stumbled upon the genesis of *Murder Incorporated*—some rudimentary concept that I actually verbalized aloud (thinking, of course, what gibberish did I just set free). But to my great surprise Gore acknowledged the idea with that devious twinkle he sometimes offered and then consecrated my embryonic suggestion by pronouncing "Exactly." That's all I needed.

This project started as a feature documentary film. But after thirty-plus hours of filmed interviews, I slowly realized that it was near insanity to try and tell the five-hundred-year saga of the American Empire in an hour and a half. That's when I turned to my brother with an amazing mind and rock solid will to tell the truth, the whole truth, and nothing but the truth, Mumia Abu-Jamal, and said, "Mu, whaddaya say we..." His immediate fire jettisoned our ship into orbit.

There are a few other writers and soothsayers that delivered me to that night with Mr. Vidal, starting with Dick Gregory (a prophet), Muhammad Ali (the people's champion), Jim Bouton (fire-balling right-hander and unheralded revolutionary), Hunter S. Thompson (with those "right kind of eyes"), Arthur George Rust, Jr., Howard Zinn and Noam Chomsky, Norman Mailer and Bob Dylan, Stanley Kubrick and Dalton Trumbo, George Carlin and Lenny Bruce, the Man in Black, as well as the man wearing white linens and seersucker, Samuel Langhorne Clemens.

There are some folks who helped immensely with stewarding this project along the way: our savage editor Justin Lebanowski, who I still feel like punching every now and then (and then hugging because he was usually right); literary agent Morty Mint who never stopped supporting this project; Jim Kelch who read every word and offered invaluable counsel; Robert Guillory remains a constant pillar of strength and designed killer covers; Rocco Melillo and Julia Sarno-Melillo for their inspired hand and eye designing the interior of these books; Riva Enteen for her tireless work clearing all the potent voices we weaved throughout;

proofreader Jennifer Grubba for making sure everything was punctuated and sppellled correctly, and that at least something from our grade school teachers/ grammaticians sunk in to Messrs. Abu-Jamal and Vittoria; and to Catherine Murphy for her invaluable help on Che and Cuba.

And, of course, to Noelle Hanrahan of Prison Radio for her ongoing heroic and Herculean efforts of producing thousands of broadcasts, delivering Mumia Abu-Jamal's voice around the world... and for embracing this book series and the authors with unbridled enthusiasm.

And finally, to a mother and father who didn't teach their son hate... to my daughter Shannon, art historian extraordinaire and a woman who continues to amaze me every moment of every day, offering great hope for the future... and to my lifelong partner and BFF, Ellen Mary Vittoria, whose love keeps my blood pumping for all these sunrises.

Stephen Vittoria

EDITOR'S NOTE

The book series you have in your hand, be it paper or pixels, is the result of an unusual collaboration between two men who met in unusual fashion, but who communed as we always have, since the origin of thought yielded not only "like-mindedness" but the deeper affinities of friendship, solidarity, and love. When filmmaker Stephen Vittoria set out to make a documentary about the "500 year Euro-American march of Empire," he made two valuable discoveries: first, that such a story could not be properly told in a feature length film; second, that one of his interviewees could be, in fact would be, the subject of his next film. *Long Distance Revolutionary* (2013) tells the life story of journalist and imprisoned dissident Mumia Abu-Jamal, whose fascinating life both before and after incarceration had been largely backgrounded by the publicity of his case and its connection to the Death Penalty debate that raged in the late 1990s.

The kinship kindled during the making of that film has yielded this book, written collaboratively through correspondence between Vittoria and Abu-Jamal, the former composing on a MacBook in Los Angeles and the latter composing on a Swintec clear cabinet electronic typewriter (manufactured especially for prisoners) in the Pennsylvania State Correctional Facility at Mahanoy. (*Murder Incorporated: Empire, Genocide, and Manifest Destiny,* will in fact be the ninth volume penned solely or in collaboration by Abu-Jamal from within prison.) It's worth noting that since the life of this book began as a film, a number of interviews were already conducted (with the likes of Gore Vidal, Noam Chomsky, Tariq Ali, Michael Parenti, and others), excerpts of which you'll find peppered throughout. And much like a documentary film, this book includes a colorful choir of trenchant voices, many of them an inspiration to the authors, underscoring that history must be told by the many and, often, the many unheard, and not by the few armed with bullhorn and bully pulpit.

Some readers may take affront at this book, as they might others like it that seek to stridently criticize the American nation, or perhaps more pointedly, the American government and its position and conduct in the world, throughout its brief and productive history. But for the muted and muffled to be heard, their gestures must be bold and their voices loud. Some may take affront at the ironic humor and fiery, sometimes vulgar characterizations. But what is a vulgar word employed to describe vulgar acts of treachery, thievery, slavery, and murder? And ultimately, this book is intended to be informative, insightful, inspiring, and compelling. And if it pisses you off, I can tell you—it's meant to.

J. Alan Lebanowski, Editor

Fall, 2017
New York City

Book Two Note:

As the lives of slaves paid for the early growth of the new American nation, so were more lives sacrificed to advance the expanse of empire in the 20th century. Book Two in this three-part series is a damning account of war—and the selling of war in America. How the getting of riches, imperial expansion, and consolidation of power have been the true aim of American wars and covert actions, abroad and at home. The seeds of exceptionalism and divine entitlement whose planting was detailed in Book One, "Dreaming of Empire," yield "America's Favorite Pastime" and the nightmare side of the American Century.

J.A.L., Editor

Winter, 2019
New York City

CHANGES

FOREWORD

The past never leaves us, and the future is already here.
—Lewis Mumford, *The Myth of the Machine*, 1967

The Presence of the Past

History repeats itself when we refuse to embrace its inconvenient lessons and especially its demonstrative patterns. Psychologist Carl Jung has described individual and societal defense mechanisms of "projecting one's shadow" onto others to avoid acknowledging painful qualities within oneself, or one's society. He describes a "psychology of war" in which "everything our own nation does is good, everything which the other nations do are wicked. The center of all that is mean and vile is always to be found several miles behind the enemy's lines." The collective American shadow of U.S. imperialism blinds us from seeing our own chronic pattern of arrogant, aggressive global behavior.

Today, the U.S. Department of War operates on an explicit policy of Full Spectrum Dominance (see Joint Vision 2020 DOD). The concept is to dominate all life on land, water, air, outer space, cyberspace, as well as the inner space between our ears. But this policy is consistent with and the logical extension of the founding of the American nation—established on the forceful dispossession and murder of Indigenous Peoples in North America and of kidnapped and terrorized labor from the African continent. All of this carried out with virtual impunity. As Jung understood so well, our individual and collective lives have been conditioned by shared denial of the ugly and unspeakable suffering caused by this systematic dispossession, enabling the collective fantasy called "American Exceptionalism." A boiling cauldron of lies now preserves the original lie, producing our pretend society living in historical mythology and amnesia.

This upside down version of reality was incorporated into Jefferson's Declaration of Independence: "(The King) has excited domestic insurrections amongst us, and has endeavored to bring on the inhabitants of our Frontiers, the merciless Indian Savages, whose known Rule of Warfare is an undistinguished destruction of all Ages, Sexes, and Conditions."

As I will discuss later from my Vietnam experiences, I discovered who the real merciless savages were, and I was one of them, along with hundreds of thousands of other American soldiers as we engaged in the abhorrent slaughter and destruction of the Vietnamese.

But it's imperative to understand that the behavior of the earliest settlers in the 1600s formed the basis for a militarized culture. Violence of settler vigilante groups regularly tracked down Indigenous communities with the distinct goal of annihilating them. It was considered civilization versus savagery, using the equivalent of paramilitary units, who now would be described as "special forces." The same military tactics were soon to be used as slave patrols tracking down for capture and oftentimes killing resistant runaway slaves, enforcing the plantation economy based on enforced slave labor.

Three years after the signing of the Declaration of Independence, the so-called "Father of our Country," land speculator and slaveholder, George Washington, was serving as the Supreme Commanding General of the Colonial Army during the Revolutionary War. In 1779, he ordered more than one-quarter of his Continental Army (4,500 soldiers) to clear out the Iroquois Indians in upstate New York who were attacking invading settler inhabitants. His explicit orders reveal lasting U.S. military policy: "total destruction and devastation" of the Indigenous settlements, to "ruin their crops" and to "lay waste" to the whole lot. Washington's orders concluded that the soldiers were not to entertain any peace proposals before the "the total ruinment of their settlements" in order that they will have an "inability to injure us" and we will be secured by the "terror" you will inflict upon them.

Thus, was established the policy of total war, or genocide, including killing all human beings encountered, destruction of stored food and crops, preventing peace, pre-emptive war, terror of scorched earth, and revenge against those participating in their own self-defense.

The campaign was "successfully" carried out, with all forty Seneca villages destroyed (including the Seneca capital of Kanadesaga, or present-day Geneva, New York, the city of my birth), all dwellings looted and torched, cornfields and fruit orchards burned. Indigenous not able to safely flee, including women and children, were slaughtered. Washington proudly described this hunt of "wild beasts" as a war of "extermination."

From the American Revolution to the year 1902, the Continental Army engaged in 1,240 battles against Indigenous Peoples—aka manifest slaughter. And between 1798 and today, the U.S. overtly intervened with its military into dozens of nations nearly 600 times. And since World War II, the U.S. has conducted thousands of covert interventions around the world, while bombing some thirty countries. Additionally, by 1930, the U.S. sent military gunboats into Latin American ports almost 6,000 times, while aggressively moving on Cuba, Puerto Rico, Mexico, Guatemala, Honduras, Panama, Columbia, Nicaragua, and Haiti. And the beat down goes on and on.

War & Murder. Ubiquitous. Omnipresent. Pervasive. Universal.

Total Genocidal Terrorist War
(Vinh Long Province, Mekong Delta, Vietnam, April 1969)

As a United States Air Force First Lieutenant, I accompanied a South Vietnamese officer on an extra duty assignment to personally assess the success (or failure) of a target bombed within the hour. It was my sixth week in country. Up to that moment I didn't have a clue as to what kind of military target we would find, or what was typical in Vietnam. We reached our destination in my jeep, then disembarked and cleared our way through some tall vegetation, what we commonly called elephant grass, to observe the smoke visible beyond, the supposed target.

I heard the intense bellowing of wretched pain. To our right was a large water buffalo lying on its right side with a three foot gash in its abdomen, and a third of its skull was missing—an absolute bloody mess. I immediately vomited and was in shock. How that animal was still alive was beyond me. To this day, I wish I had the clear mind to have killed it, ending its miserable pain.

As we walked further, I saw the main target—smoking ruins of what had been modest dwellings, with bodies strewn everywhere, virtually all napalmed, some still moaning, but most presumed dead as they lie in their stillness. I estimated one hundred and fifty bodies, the vast majority small children. Of course, I quickly realized, the only targets in Vietnam were the people themselves and their modest village structures. Oh, fuck, I get it! Body counts. A dead Vietnamese from infant to old age was a "VC"—the belittling name we gave to the so-called enemy—the Viet Cong. Later the same week, we assessed four additional targets, all of them inhabited by Vietnamese, undefended fishing and farming villages totally destroyed in low-level daylight bombings aka "turkey shoots." Just that one week I calculated that we had witnessed somewhere between 700 and 900 murdered Vietnamese, again the overwhelming majority being small children, all counted as "VC" in Seventh Air Force bombing reports. The U.S. was giddy that all "targets had been successfully destroyed." Body counts and Vietnamese villages!

I haven't been the same since.

During the course of America's direct assault on Southeast Asia (1964 to 1973), the United States destroyed 13,000 of the 21,000 villages (more than 60 percent), murdering at least four million Vietnamese, not counting perhaps an additional two million Cambodians and Laotians. This means that for every one of the more than 58,000 American soldiers killed, 100 Southeast Asians were butchered. The U.S. left 26 million bomb craters in one of the poorest nations on earth. And the U.S. used the most intensive chemical warfare in human history as it sprayed 21 million gallons of toxic herbicides to defoliate vast swaths of forest while destroying rice and other precious food crops, leaving many poisoned Vietnamese as well as U.S. troops.

During my 2016 visit to Vietnam, I witnessed the presence of countless third generation birth defects in children. The chemicals had contaminated the genetic structure of the Vietnamese people, continuing the killing and maiming decades later. And for what? To ensure that the humble people of Vietnam be prevented from achieving their basic human rights of self-determination and autonomy, and to ensure their continued neo-colonization for the benefit of western-style capitalism. Fuck! All this unthinkable pain and abject suffering hammered down on the Vietnamese in their own land (as well as American soldiers) was for the sole and vain benefit of a terribly destructive and predatory economic ideology.

As I wrote earlier, my Vietnam experiences—both viscerally as well as intellectually—defined for me who the real "merciless savages" are (no thanks to Mr. Jefferson and his Declaration). For centuries we had it upside down. As Pogo said in Walt Kelly's 1970 comic strip: "We have met the enemy and he is us."

Hit and Run Terrorist War: "Low Intensity Conflict" (LIC)
(January 1986, Esteli, Nicaragua—in the mountains 90 miles north of Managua)

I was in my first week studying Spanish in a language school, living with a local family. Early on Sunday evening, I watched members of my host family earnestly doing their reading and writing homework with chalk on a blackboard as part of Nicaragua's revolutionary literacy campaign. We heard a loud but distant explosion and immediately our lights went out. Without missing a beat, they resumed their studies old school with candlelight.

We quickly received word that Reagan's wandering bands of ruthless terrorists, called Contras, seeking to overthrow the revolutionary Sandinista government, had blown up one of the electric distribution towers near Esteli after attacking three nearby farming cooperatives, murdering eleven campesinos.

The next morning, Monday, I stood next to my Nicaraguan mother, Alejandra, on the street leading to the cemetery, soberly watching two horse drawn wagons carrying handmade open caskets with six of the bodies killed in the farming cooperatives, including several small children (there's always small children). I could not hold back my tears as I began to sob, holding my mother's hand. Fuck, I've been here before. Vietnam. Funny—so was America.

Within fifty days after Reagan's inauguration in January 1981, he had begun preparations to overthrow the newly created Sandinista revolutionary Nicaraguan government after the Sandinistas had overthrown Washington's all-time favorite dictator, Somoza, in 1979. To this day, the U.S. has never forgiven the Sandinistas, as is being demonstrated in the latest 2018 soft coup attempt against the current successful, *democratically-elected* Sandinista government.

During the ten-year, one-billion-dollar Reagan Contra War (1981 to 1990), much of Nicaragua's infrastructure was destroyed with more than 30,000 campesinos murdered, not to mention thousands of hacked-maimed-amputees created. Vast numbers of schools, health clinics, farming cooperatives, government buildings, bridges, roads, and other foundational infrastructure were destroyed during the war, including much of the national electric grid system. In 1986, the World Court ordered the U.S. to cease all Contra activities and make appropriate reparations, later determined to be $17 billion dollars. Reagan and his cronies arrogantly refused to abide by the Court's ruling, ignoring it completely. Plain and simple, all war is terror, but this type of hit and run attacks from the sanctuary of their Washington-funded training camps in Honduras and Costa Rica are what U.S. military planners and strategists describe as "Low Intensity Conflict," which, of course, is anything but low intensive for its victims. Nonetheless, this is a very popular style of military intervention employed by the U.S. as it sees fit in many countries around the world.

Nation of Shoppers and Bombers

We in the United States live in a culture of war. Video games, movies and television, comic books, military recruitment commercials, sporting events that require a puppet-like National Anthem and God Bless America, media lapdogs cheering on American exceptionalism with severe xenophobic fervor—all of it glorifying war without serious question. The direct and indirect military budget is now trending toward one trillion dollars, the very essence of the American economy. The U.S. is currently at war, including bombing, in at least seven nations—Libya, Niger, Afghanistan, Somalia, Yemen, Syria, and Iraq—designed to preserve America's shopping habits and, of course, the obscene profits for the warmongers. Special Operations Forces are deployed to more than 70 percent of the world's countries drumming up "terrorists," oblivious to the fact that Washington is the wholesale terrorist force in the world. In fact the U.S. has nearly 1,000 military bases in dozens of countries dotting the planet, with combat troops in fifteen of them. And now the Pentagon and CIA use regular drone strikes to target cell phones in the possession of those dangerous *retail* terrorists that somebody in the U.S. military-intelligence network arrogantly identified as a threat to the "American Way of Life" (AWOL). Every administration operates weekly with kill lists. This is insane and it's criminal. It's almost as if the country needs a new name, maybe something like "Murder Incorporated."

"It Never Happened"

How to explain remaining a citizen of the world's most dangerous country without going mad? To block out the killing fields of our government's global bombings each day, and the violent actions of our Special Ops forces shooting up the world's so-called "dangerous" people, we keep shopping. We have fallen into a kind of drugged state of standardized and homogenized thought, starved of genuine wide-ranging ideas and serious political discourse, such that our innate sense of empathy and justice as humans is submerged into ruthless and rapacious economics. Nobel Prize-winning British playwright Harold Pinter has described the American denial regarding its chronic and violent foreign policy that murders hundreds of thousands, if not millions, this way:

"It never happened. Nothing ever happened. Even while it was happening it wasn't happening. It didn't matter. It was of no interest."

This Orwellian/Pinteresque immorality play has all been facilitated by the corporate-owned mass media, think tanks funded by big, sloppy monied interests, sophisticated public relations firms crafting master and redundant messages, along with an education system (read: indoctrination system) designed to guarantee obedient citizens and compliant workers. And ultimately, this manipulated and targeted behavior creates a designed lack of genuine knowledge regarding America's unspeakable militarized history. In other words, the body politic owns no authentic historical context, such that its cultural DNA of getting whatever it wants without consequence leads to evermore violence and war. The U.S. populace and its oligarchic government operates with virtual impunity, never having been held to account for its murderous sins.

More than fifty years ago, the Reverend Martin Luther King, Jr., proclaimed that the "greatest purveyor of violence in the world is my own government." Nothing has changed. Our collective minds have been systematically colonized to accept the totally unacceptable.

S. Brian Willson
South of Managua, Nicaragua
Fall, 2018

PROLOGUE

"History," Edward Gibbon (1737-1794) wrote in his classic *The Decline and Fall of the Roman Empire*, is "little more than the register of crimes, follies, and misfortunes of mankind." Gibbon is writing of Rome here, but the same might be said of another empire: the American Empire.

The readers who have read *Murder Incorporated—Book One: Dreaming of Empire* have some inkling of the American origins of empire, born in the blood, tears, and sorrows of genocide, slavery, and mass death. Much of Book One is a vast panorama of how imperial America came to be and how it grew into the Leviathan that later emerged.

This volume takes that leap and engages our readers in "America's Favorite Pastime," revealing the malevolent hand of the Empire in its waging of war, and its hidden, muffled militarism behind its spycraft as practiced by the Central Intelligence Agency and other assorted thugs, miscreants, and degenerates roaming Washington's house of horrors. The bloodthirsty warmonger and war criminal, John Bolton, is emblematic of these swamp creatures.

It is more than a little ironic that, as these words are being penned, the U.S. nation is now embroiled in the question of Russian interference in American elections. The U.S. media and its chattering classes are up in arms that another antagonistic nation (Russia) has dared to interfere with U.S. internal elections. Guess how many countries have experienced American interference in their elections? (Careful, it may be easier to select the countries that Washington has not interfered with!)

We have now made note of Rome, the greatest empire of European antiquity. But Great Rome, at its height, didn't have the hundreds upon hundreds of military bases boasted of by the American Empire. The late, noted foreign affairs analyst, Chalmers Johnson, author of the Blowback trilogy, made much of the 700-plus U.S. military bases that envelop the planet and he established (rather easily) that this level of foreign military presence has no historical precedent. Nonetheless, this suffocating presence is a hallmark of empire and its complement: imperialism.

What is imperialism, Grandpa?

British noble Robert Lowe (1811-1895), living during the height of the British Empire, expressed the following: "What does imperialism mean? It means the assertion of absolute force over others." *Absolute force over others.*

What Lowe, the Viscount of Sherbrooke, was saying, in essence, was war—state terrorism and murder as a tool of conquest and domination "over others" in order to exploit their resources and to bend them to (British) imperial will.

Just like Rome. *Just like the Roman Empire.*

The Reader might rightly ask, "C'mon, Jamal and Vittoria—why are you guys on this Rome kick? I didn't get this book to read about ancient history!" To which we'd doubtless reply: *But how do you think America came to be an empire, if not modeling itself after other empires? Why do you think the new nation's first political organizers voted for a Senate, instead of a Parliament?*

The very term "Senate" arrives from Rome—not from London. The economic and political elites who were lovingly christened the Founding Fathers of the American State dreamed of empire—of New Rome—of the American Empire.

Hackneyed as it is, but equally precise as it is, "War," said the former U.S. General, William Tecumseh Sherman, "is hell." And it is there to which we must turn as we examine "America's Favorite Pastime"—which = war, which =

HELL ON EARTH

From the so-called Indian Wars waged to lay claim to the indigenous continent, to the American wars that devoured Europe and the deserts of North Africa, of the Middle East, to the island nations in the Caribbean, marching on through Central and South America, and of course its trek westward into Asia's tropical cities and forests, America has been in a fever to fight, to conquer, to demonstrate and verify that it is, in fact, the Master of the Hill. And now, the final frontier—space. *"Look, up in the sky, it's a bird! It's a plane! It's Super—err, it's Space Force!"*

Soldiers sang songs to give them strength to kill for their economic class masters; songs that continue to resonate well over a century after they were penned. Consider this 1847 ditty meant to bolster the courage of the Marines:

> *From the halls of Montezuma*
> *To the shores of Tripoli;*
> *We fight our country's battles*
> *In the air, on land, and sea . . .*

Montezuma—Emperor of the Aztecs, ca. 1502-1520 CE, in what is today known as Mexico; *shores of Tripoli*—the capital city of Libya, a nation in North Africa. Even in these simplistic cheerleader songs, we hear the rhythms of imperialism and the hammer of conquest, and always the stark naked hubris of martial power. This was, is, and today remains a global endeavor of capital über Alles. Of $$$ ruling armies, nations, regional blocs, and the world entire. From World Wars to so-called regional conflicts... from proxy wars to cold war(s)... the American Empire has flown its global flag to enrich, to exploit, and to dominate—especially those who refuse to bow.

History stands on the sidelines, witnessing the spectacle as Washington marches over its dominions, carrying its atomic murder weapons, its plutonium-loaded murder missiles, its poison gases and Agent Oranges, and perhaps worse, its spies (spooks, moles, rat finks, agent provocateurs).

A simple fact we all know: virtually every nation has spies—even though every nation outlaws spies under the crime called espionage. Which means, when you think about it, every nation opposes spies—unless, of course, they work for your nation. The CIA has worked to undermine, corrupt, remove, and topple governments around this pale blue dot—and of both enemy nations and allies. They have paid off leaders, turned a blind eye when their lapdog client states have committed heinous crimes... and when they felt the need, the Central Intelligence Agency has exterminated such leaders with (as the saying goes) "extreme prejudice."

The 20th century was awash in American regime change—in the epoch's twilight in Iraq under Saddam Hussein. But did you realize that Saddam (and the entire post-colonial government) was a CIA asset? Because in the off-center world of espionage, this murky-polluted-cesspool of espionage, today's asset is but tomorrow's target.

In South Vietnam, President Ngo Dinh Diem, praised in the American press as an ally, dared to say NO to his American masters—and then in the clear and cooperative sight of the Kennedy Administration, the CIA bribed his generals, who swiftly exterminated the puppet leader and his brother in the back of a truck. Events such as this have happened unceremoniously on every continent (with the possible exception of Antarctica), not to mention from sea to shining sea.

Is this mere hyperbole? We think not.

One need only read *The CIA's Greatest Hits* by Mark Zepezauer, which chillingly recounts the integration of the Gehlen Organization into the CIA, a body composed of high-ranking Nazi officers and officials (named after Hitler's intelligence chief and Nazi General, Reinhard Gehlen). In fact, the CIA's Greatest Hits unfurl like an endless magic carpet ride: continuous post-World War II American infiltration into countless sovereign nations—from dirty tricks in national and local elections, to cold-blooded assassinations of friend and foe alike, including dirty wars exterminating populations on almost every continent. One need only read *The Devil's Chessboard* by David Talbot to experience the abject corruption and dark depravity of Allen Dulles and his long thuggish shadow over American policy and actions.

Or, how about *Legacy of Ashes: The History of the CIA* by Tim Weiner, which recounts President Harry Truman's deep disease with the paramilitary conversion of the CIA under the rubric of "intelligence." In fact, this metamorphosis triggered its handy role in the overthrow of Iran's first democratically elected leader, Mohammad Mossadegh, followed by the CIA's almost total control over Middle Eastern leaders, many who owe their thrones to CIA defenses.

These are some of our published sources, which provide color and clarity whenever we examine U.S. affairs abroad. All of it underscoring the historic fact that the agency is a tool, an instrument, a vital mechanism of imperial power—no less so than every branch of the United States Armed Forces.

Fortress America

We began this Prologue by examining the curse of war, and then delved into espionage. Was this mere happenstance? Hardly, for the nexus between these two subjects is clear: both practices attack the sovereignty of nations—the power of nations to live free of foreign intervention, cross border attacks, and international violence. If one country corrupts, buys off, or executes another country's leaders—isn't that an Act of War? If a foreign nation removes one leader to put in its own preferred puppet—isn't that really an Act of War?

We continuously use a word that isn't really used in daily conversation: *Imperialism.* But by doing so, we only reveal what is happening around the world, despite the lack of conversation either among ourselves, or in the corporate media because if something isn't normally discussed openly is surely not a reason to reject it, for we believe that U.S. imperialism is central and predominant to international relations, as well it is to domestic relations, as it dramatically impacts both—economically, psychologically, and historically. Let's never lose sight of this bottom line: the wealth of the U.S. nation is used to create Fortress America, instead of addressing the needs of its citizenry and, of course, the poor and dispossessed.

To illustrate how imperialism works in the real world, we quote a conversation between a former U.S. president and his foreign underlings, for it illustrates what we are reporting with unusual clarity. We turn to Mark Zepezauer—who quotes the 36th President of the United States, formally known at Southwest Texas State Teachers College as "Bullshit Johnson"—as he launches into a tirade against Greek nationalists, who dared to protest U.S. actions:

> When the Greek Ambassador objected to Johnson's plan for settling a dispute concerning Cyprus, LBJ said, "Fuck your Parliament and your constitution. America is an elephant. Cyprus is a flea. Greece is a flea. If these two fleas continue itching the elephant, they may just get whacked by the elephant's trunk, whacked good… If your prime minister gives me talk about democracy, parliament and constitutions, he, his parliament and his constitution may not last very long."[1]

Whoa. Does that sound like an American President—or a Mafia don? (Answer: Both). Until the ignorant atrocity "elected" as Murder Incorporated's 45th CEO, this truthful utterance, this political trash talk, would not see the light of public day—it would be in the shadows, behind closed doors. In public the dialogue would be the usual spit-shined American bullshit, some hollow banality about liberty, freedom, and God's hand moving in exceptional ways. But what we're actually witnessing in Bullshit Johnson's diatribe is imperialism in action, ground floor right off the assembly line imperialism: *Do what we want—or else!*

If you're a teenager in high school, this book will bear no similarity to the children's books provided you by a deferential, cringing history teacher, whose job it is to drug you with false patriotism and subservience to political leaders. For here you will find no paeans to the once-living gods of American myth, like Washington and cherry trees, Jefferson on liberty or Adams and the rights of women. We present no myths, fables, or fabled glories of empire. Our work throughout this enterprise is raw. Hard. Real.

True.

We do not feed pabulum to the young. We give them energy—real food to grow on, food for thought, food to open their eyes—to empire, specifically to this killing empire.

It's for young men and women in college; for workers on the job; for kids in the 'hood and el barrio, to all who wish to share the real history of America's Empire.

For Americans aren't children—they are sons and daughters of hellraisers—people so radical that they exceeded the wants of their leaders—so-called Founding Fathers. They didn't bow to their leaders; they whipped their asses! They pulled down the mansions of the rich! (See pp. 142-181 of Book One).

Learn your history. Embrace it. Then work to create a new one!

We love you all.

—**Mumia Abu-Jamal & Stephen Vittoria**
Parts Unknown

1 The Great Meat Grinder

"What's so noble about being dead?"
—Joe Bonham from Dalton Trumbo's *Johnny Got His Gun*

Throughout the 20th century, historians proudly called it "The Great War." But this so-called "great war" was nothing more than another gruesome human spectacle—a monstrous meat grinder. In the years leading up to the outbreak of hostilities in 1914, the technology of war grew in leaps and bounds. Killing was made significantly easier thanks to the advent of the machine gun, as well as the effectiveness of gas and chemical weaponry. Rapid-fire artillery and tank warfare were lethal beyond anything ever seen before, making hamburger meat out of once living and breathing human beings. And then there was the ghastly reality of trench warfare with the iconic barbed-wire emplacements, where thousands upon thousands would die within hours for the mere advancement of a few yards. This display of futility—which created a grinding battlefield stalemate—was almost comical if not for the horrifying bloodshed. As an example, the vast majority of the British Army was killed in just the first three months of the war. In order to quickly replenish the ranks with new raw meat, the British government loosened their restrictions on volunteer requirements. Had he still been alive, even Joseph (aka John) Merrick (the Elephant Man) would have fit nicely into their ranks.

"Ten million were to die on the battlefield," Howard Zinn reminds us in *A People's History of the United States*. Add to the ten million another twenty million souls who died from war-related disease and starvation. "And no one since that day has been able to show that the war brought any gain for humanity that would be worth one human life," Zinn writes, "The rhetoric of the socialists, that it was an 'imperialist war,' now seems moderate and hardly arguable."[1]

The War To End All Wars: A Primer

Triggered by the assassination of archduke Franz Ferdinand of Austria in June of 1914, war erupted across Europe. Unprecedented in its slaughter, this international clash was groundbreaking in that it was being fought by industrial nations mass-producing weapons and drafting armies from entire populations. The war raged until 1918 and set Germany, Austria-Hungary, and Turkey against France, Britain, Italy, Russia, Japan, and finally in 1917, the United States. Although fought early in the 20th century, World War I proved to be a defining and watershed moment in the political landscape of a world gone wrong: the inferno greatly destabilized Europe and set in motion the necessary puzzle pieces that would soon launch World War II.

The European theatres of war included the Eastern Front (which extended from the Baltic Sea in the north to the Black Sea in the south and cut deep into Central Europe) and the Western Front (which ran for more than 400 miles from the Swiss border to the Belgian coast).

Not to be left out were the oil riches of Mesopotamia. The West already had their sights set on the jackpot: massive amounts of black gold sitting just beneath desert sands. Great Britain occupied Basra—the Turkish port at the entrance of the Persian Gulf—and their goal was to shelter southern oil wells and defend the giant Abadan refinery in Iran. In fact, the British advanced north along the Tigris River toward Baghdad but were beaten back and finally surrendered to the Turks. As you can no doubt see a century later, the same battle continues to rage over control of that black gold.

The so-called "Great War" (like most wars) was being fought for the acquisition of treasure; in this case we find the industrialized countries of Europe scheming and slaughtering for greater control over their colonies and the associated big time booty sitting at the end of rainbows that touched down in the Balkans, in Alsace-Lorraine, throughout Mesopotamia, and deep into Africa. As Helen Keller wrote during her steadfast stance against World War I:

> Every modern war has had its roots in exploitation. The Civil War
> was fought to decide whether the slaveholders of the South or
> the capitalists of the North should exploit the West. The Spanish-
> American War decided that the United States should exploit Cuba
> and the Philippines. The South African War decided that the

British should exploit the diamond mines. The Russo-Japanese War decided that Japan should exploit Korea. The present war is to decide who shall exploit the Balkans, Turkey, Persia, Egypt, India, China, Africa. And we are whetting our sword to scare the victors into sharing the spoils with us.[2]

In May of 1915, W.E.B. Du Bois wrote a prescient essay entitled "The African Roots of War." This in-depth piece defined the struggle between the Allied Forces and the Germans as nothing more than an imperial battle for empire: "...in a very real sense Africa is a prime cause for this terrible overturning of civilization."[3] Du Bois then reminded his readers why the bodies were piling up in frightening numbers: it was all about the endgame of seizing the ivory and rubber and cocoa and palm oil throughout the motherland, and of course the gold and diamonds buried in South Africa.

Journalist John Silas "Jack" Reed reported from Europe on the war. In an article entitled "The Traders' War" for *The Masses* magazine, Reed writes:

> The Austro-Serbian conflict is a mere bagatelle—as if Hoboken should declare war on Coney Island—but all the Civilization of Europe is drawn in. The real War, of which this sudden outburst of death and destruction is only an incident, began long ago. It has been raging for tens of years, but its battles have been so little advertised that they have been hardly noted. It is a clash of Traders.[4]

It was Reed, in the midst of the Bolshevik Revolution, who wrote the historic journal of revolution, *Ten Days That Shook The World*. It was Reed who Warren Beatty immortalized in his epic film *Reds*. And it was Reed who passionately attempted to warn his readers—like I.F. Stone after him and John Pilger and Jeremy Scahill more recently—that governments lie and they lie most about war. "The Great War" was no exception; it was no preposterous "Struggle for Existence" as was advertised to win hearts and minds. Later in "The Traders' War," Reed writes:

> The situation in short is this. German capitalists want more profits. *English and French capitalists want it all.* This War of Commerce has gone on for years, and Germany has felt herself worsted. Every year she has suffered some new setback. The commercial "smothering" of Germany is a fact of current history.

This effort to crowd out Germany is frankly admitted by the economic writers of England and France. It comes out in a petty and childish way in the popular attempts to boycott things "Made in Germany" [flash forward to "Freedom Fries"]. On a larger scale it is embodied in 'ententes' and secret treaties. Those who treat of the subject in philosophical phraseology justify it by referring to the much abused "Struggle for Existence."[5] [Emphasis added]

Reed then emphatically cautioned: *"But we must not be duped by this editorial buncombe about Liberalism going forth to Holy War against Tyranny."* Buncombe indeed. Utter nonsense. Just like "weapons of mass destruction," imaginary "Tonkin Gulfs," and all the other lies the masters of war invent and construct on their way to kingdom come.

If there was an official "birth" of aggressive modern-day American imperialism with war as the locomotive, one that stepped out from behind continental colonialism and its co-dependent genocide of America's original inhabitants, it was the so-called Spanish-American War of 1898. These belligerent incursions "marked the entrance of the United States into the worldwide scramble for colonies among advanced powers,"[6] writes political author Lance Selfa. Laying the foundation that Reed and Keller would dramatically echo, the great feminist and radical warrior Emma Goldman wrote of America's imperial adventures and ensuing plunder throughout Latin America and Asia, including its colonial conquests in Cuba, Puerto Rico, and the Philippines:

> [W]hen we sobered up from our patriotic spree—it suddenly
> dawned on us that the cause of the Spanish-American War was
> the consideration of the price of sugar; or, to be more explicit, that
> the lives, blood, and money of the American people were used to
> protect the interests of American capitalists.[7]

This grand muscle-pumping foray by Washington into other lands emboldened America's embryonic dreams of empire and was religiously carried forward by Theodore Roosevelt and William Howard Taft during the first decade of the 20th century, but as Lance Selfa explains:

> No Democrat put a presidential stamp on U.S. empire until
> Woodrow Wilson became president in 1913; Wilson ordered
> military interventions in more countries and stationed more troops

for longer periods than either Roosevelt or Roosevelt's Republican successor, William Howard Taft. In particular, Wilson turned the Caribbean Sea into an American lake.[8]

The Patron Saint of American Liberalism

Woodrow Wilson threw the U.S. Marines on the back of his intrusive foreign policy and ordered invasions throughout the Caribbean and Latin America, followed by an all-out occupation of Haiti that lasted until 1934—the consequences of which have reverberated into the 21st century and continue to hammer the Haitian people to this day. Woodrow Wilson—a man lionized by mainstream historians and presidential scholars as the patron saint of American liberalism and a great humanitarian—has a clear-cut record of violent and unadulterated imperial ventures. In fact, beyond these imperial "skirmishes," mythical "Wilsonian idealism" also included hurling America into World War I to allegedly "make the world safe for democracy." The son and grandson of Presbyterian ministers, Wilson naively expected this "Great War" to be the war that would somehow end all wars. In his book *The Irony of Manifest Destiny: The Tragedy of America's Foreign Policy*, political historian William Pfaff underscores Wilson's magical trip to the moon:

> The American intervention in the First World War was an event of lasting consequence because of the meaning assigned to it by Woodrow Wilson... convinced that the American nation, and he personally, were bearers of a divine commission to reform civilization by abolishing war and extending to the globe the benevolent principles of American democracy and religion.
>
> He believed that the world "will turn to America for those moral aspirations which lie at the basis of all freedom... and that her flag is the flag not only of America, but of humanity." He reinterpreted the world war as an ideological war... [It] would be the war "that would end war," producing permanent peace. "[America's world role has come] by no plan of our conceiving, but by the hand of God who led us into this way... It was of this that we dreamed at our birth."[9]

Pfaff then extended Wilson's foundation straight through the 20th century:

> With Woodrow Wilson the Manifest Destiny of the United States ceased to be continental expansion and national power and

progress, and was reimagined as a divinely ordained mission to humanity, as American statesmen have interpreted all the nation's subsequent wars. The idea became essential to the American national myth.[10]

"Wilsonian idealism" also included his grandiose plan known as "The League of Nations"—what author Justin Raimondo refers to as "Wilson's stillborn brainchild."[11] William Pfaff describes Wilson's chilling vision:

> Wilson offered a plan for postwar security which would rest upon new international institutions based on American conceptions and values, so as to end what eight decades later Secretary of State Condoleezza Rice, echoing his 1916 rhetoric, would call "the destructive pattern of great power rivalry."
>
> Wilson proposed the creation of a League of Nations, that (as he privately acknowledged) would eventually become an American-dominated world government.[12]

"We are all God's children... This is God's vision... Our country has borne a special burden in global affairs... Our cause is just, our resolve unwavering."[13] Woodrow Wilson? Teddy Roosevelt? Nope—enter Barack Hussein Obama. "In Cairo, at West Point, at Oslo," writes author and filmmaker Tariq Ali, "Obama has treated the world to one uplifting homily after another, each address larded with every euphemism that White House speechwriters can muster to describe America's glowing mission in the world."[14] As discussed in a previous chapter, every president and ruling CEO of the American Empire née republic channels the spirit of John Winthrop and his "City upon a Hill" to underscore American exceptionalism. Ali draws the rock-solid connection between Obama and one of his predecessors:

> Historically, the model for this variant of imperial presidency is Woodrow Wilson, no less pious a Christian, whose every second word was peace, democracy or self-determination, while his armies invaded Mexico, occupied Haiti and attacked Russia, and his treaties handed one colony after another to his partners in war. Obama is a hand-me-down version of the same, without even Fourteen Points to betray. But cant still goes a long way to satisfy those who yearn for it, as the award to Obama of what Garcia Márquez once called the Nobel Prize for War has graphically shown.[15]

But long before Wilson visualized himself as Captain America, chosen by God to hand-deliver American liberty to all corners of the planet, he professed his firm belief in the almighty dollar ruling the roost. "Writing as a Princeton political scientist more than a decade before he was elected president," writes Lance Selfa, "he concluded that the 'flag followed commerce.'"[16] Wilson wrote these telling words from behind the walls of his privileged and safe ivy-covered Princeton confines:

> Since trade ignores national boundaries and the manufacturer insists on having the world as a market, the flag of his nation must follow him, and the doors of the nations which are closed against him must be battered down. Concessions obtained by financiers must be safeguarded by ministers of state, even if the sovereignty of unwilling nations be outraged in the process. Colonies must be obtained or planted in order that no useful corner of the world may be overlooked or left unused.[17]

Holy shit. The patron saint of American liberalism had unknown demons living beneath his flesh, fiendish imps that resembled Attila the Hun on a bad hair day. In fact, Wilson's thoughts on economic control resembled those of Vito Corleone, proprietor of the Genco Pura Olive Oil Company, who ascribed to the same philosophy when discussing plunder with his associates, only he said it with fewer words and was much more to the point: "I'm gonna make him an offer he can't refuse."

The US would never have gone into World War I had it not been for Wilson. He was a compulsive interventionist. Prior to the world war, he sent troops to Mexico, Haiti, and the Dominican Republic. An unreconstructed southerner, he made Jim Crow law in Washington.[18]
—Gore Vidal

Wilson earned much of his so-called liberal reputation early in his presidency: he helped create progressive income taxes, lobbied for decent working conditions for railroad workers and merchant seamen, fought to limit child labor abuses, and he attempted to (somewhat) restrict corporate power. He even advocated public ownership of the giant American railroad business. But then, of course, the demons emerged: Wilson was raised in the Deep South and Jim Crow was a dear friend of his. In his essay, "Race and Nation in the Thoughts and Politics of

Woodrow Wilson," Gary Gerstle concludes that Wilson was ultimately "deeply racist in his thoughts and politics, and apparently he was comfortable with being so."[19]

His actions as president bear this out; in fact, Wilson "did not object when two of his cabinet appointees re-segregated their departments,"[20] reports Michael Kazin of *The New Republic*. It wasn't long before Wilson's racist foundation influenced his aggressive foreign policy, particularly belligerent on brown people. It was an all too familiar policy that embraced the white man's burden of American exceptionalism. Kazin continues: "A crusading Presbyterian, he vowed to 'teach the Latin American republics to elect good men' and dispatched troops to Mexico and Haiti when they didn't follow his advice."[21]

In 1916, Wilson ran for reelection as a candidate ostensibly opposed to American entry into the First World War. William Pfaff characterizes Wilson during this period as a "splendid isolationist."[22] In fact his infamous campaign slogan was "HE KEPT US OUT OF WAR." But, lo and behold, just months after his reelection, Wilson launched the United States (and of course its expendable flesh and blood) into the great meat grinder. The ex-president of Princeton University and ex-Governor of New Jersey used the significant American antiwar sentiment to ensure his second term, while at the same time paving the economic highway that would eventually ensure America's involvement in the war—something American big business was euphoric about as it waited anxiously in the wings.

Officially, the United States remained neutral during the first three years of the war, but this was a PR façade whitewashing what was actually transpiring behind the closed doors of power in Washington and in the mahogany boardrooms of various U.S. corporations and banks. In fact, the U.S. was anything but neutral if we use war profits as a yardstick. By 1915, orders for American war materials were actually stimulating a moribund American economy. "Wilson lifted the ban on private bank loans to the Allies," writes Howard Zinn. "[J.P.] Morgan could now begin lending money in such great amounts as to both make great profit and tie American finance closely to the interest of a British victory in the war against Germany."[23] In fact, by April of 1917, more than two billion dollars worth of goods were purchased by the Allies. "America became bound with the Allies in a fateful union of war and prosperity," writes Pulitzer Prize-winning historian Richard Hofstadter.[24]

All Quiet on the Western Front

Opposition to the war was strong as conscientious objectors from many nations refused to fight. In Great Britain some 16,000 men requested conscientious objector status including philosopher Bertrand Russell. Mutinies were commonplace in the French army, of which Zinn writes: "out of 112 divisions, 68 would have mutinies; 629 men would be tried and condemned, 50 shot by firing squads. American troops were badly needed."[25] Obviously, the young men being fed into the war pigs' meat grinder were starting to take it personally. And who could blame them? One battle on the Somme cost the British Army 300,000 dead and wounded soldiers. The third battle at Ypres in Belgium during the second half of 1917 cost the British army another 400,000 men. The territorial gain for the Allies: five miles.

As discussed, the practical reality that allowed the slaughter to continue and the casualties to grow so dramatically was the technology of killing—the machine-gun, rapid-fire artillery, along with chlorine and mustard gas. But another, more sinister reason was the combatants' ability—on both sides—to control the message and the news (read: lie through their teeth). And this included control of the truth regarding the horrors transpiring on the battlefield as well as controlling the message and propaganda regarding the so-called dire necessity to go to war. The British, French, and American public knew very little about the horrendous body counts piling up throughout Europe. The German population suffered similar ignorance under the same type of information blackout, as exemplified by Erich Maria Remarque in his novel *All Quiet on the Western Front*—the title of his masterpiece being the official message regularly sent back home by the German hierarchy as hundreds of thousands died.

Sauerkraut... is now LIBERTY CABBAGE

> *Johnny, get your gun, get your gun, get your gun*
> *Johnny, show the "Hun" you're a son-of-a-gun*
> *Hoist the flag and let her fly*
> *Yankee Doodle do or die...*
>
> —George M. Cohan, *Over There* (1917)

Wilson and Washington influence peddlers knew it was time to turn around the antiwar tide sweeping across America—and they knew it was going to be a monumental task. The socialist movement was growing strong, proclaiming the war was nothing more than an exercise to bolster Wall Street. The Industrial Workers of the World (the Wobblies) were likewise expanding their influence and many of their rank and file members were steadfastly against the war. Nevertheless, as Noam Chomsky explains in his book *Media Control*, the Wilson administration was able to whip the American public into crazed wartime frenzy:

> The population was extremely pacifistic and saw no reason to become involved in a European war. The Wilson administration was actually committed to war and had to do something about it. They established a government propaganda commission, called the Creel Commission, which succeeded, within six months, in turning a pacifist population into a hysterical, war-mongering population which wanted to destroy everything German, tear the Germans limb from limb, go to war and save the world.[26]

Even before Woodrow Wilson tapped the muckraking newspaperman George Creel as his propaganda Svengali, American spinmeisters were hard at work on the truth. On 7 May 1915 a German U-Boat sank the *RMS Lusitania* off the coast of Ireland. The ocean liner, owned by Cunard Line, sank in a matter of minutes. More than sixty percent of the people onboard died and the attack turned world opinion dramatically against Germany. "The United States claimed the Lusitania carried an innocent cargo, and therefore the torpedoing was a monstrous German atrocity," writes Howard Zinn. "Actually, the Lusitania was heavily armed: it carried 1,248 cases of 3-inch shells, 4,927 boxes of cartridges (1,000 rounds in each box), and 2,000 more cases of small-arms ammunition. Her manifests were falsified to hide this fact, and the British and American governments lied about the cargo."[27] Zinn concludes that, "It was unrealistic to expect that the Germans should treat the United States as neutral in the war when the U.S. had been shipping great amounts of war materials to Germany's enemies."[28]

Under the heading "there's a sucker born every minute," the anti-German campaign was spreading through the American population like wildfire. Super-patriotism reached near hysterical levels. Literature and newspapers of the day began attacking German-American groups in all walks of life as being agents of German rule. Right-wing xenophobic groups lobbied strenuously for the burning of German language books and pressured municipalities to change the German-sounding names of their towns. Beethoven, Bach, and Mozart were scratched from community orchestras. And then the real nuttiness started: changing sauerkraut to "liberty cabbage" and hamburger to "liberty steak." In fact, the President of the United States did not hold back from throwing gasoline on the fire, as Wilson offered this bit of fiction during his Flag Day address:

> The military masters of Germany denied us the right to be
> neutral. They filled our unsuspecting communities with vicious
> spies and conspirators and sought to corrupt the opinion of our
> people in their own behalf. When they found that they could not do
> that, their agents diligently spread sedition amongst us and sought
> to draw our own citizens from their allegiance...[29]

Not to be outdone, Elihu Root, former Secretary of State under Teddy Roosevelt, speaking at New York City's Union League Club, warned America that "there are men walking about the streets of this city tonight who ought to be taken out at sunrise tomorrow and shot for treason."[30] Damn—Teddy must have jizzed in his pants.

Indeed, it was a monumental task, but the budding Empire was "able to drive a reluctant population into a war by terrifying them and eliciting jingoist fanaticism,"[31] Chomsky explains. In fact, nightmarish images were conjured up to shock the acquiescent American public. "For example, there was a good deal of fabrication of atrocities by the Huns," writes Chomsky, "Belgian babies with their arms torn off, all sorts of awful things that you still read in history books. Much of it was invented by the British propaganda ministry, whose own commitment at the time, as they put it in their secret deliberations, was 'to direct the thought of most of the world.'"[32] The British also destroyed the telegraph cable from Germany to the U.S. so that all war "news" would be generated from London. Chomsky then emphasizes the objectives of the misinformation campaign spearheaded by Great Britain: "[T]hey wanted to control the thought of the more intelligent members of the community in the United States, who would then disseminate the propaganda that they were concocting and convert the pacifistic country to wartime hysteria... It worked very well."[33]

The historical lesson, Professor?

> State propaganda, when supported by the educated classes
> and when no deviation is permitted from it, can have a big effect.
> It was a lesson learned by Hitler and many others, and it has been
> pursued to this day.[34]

And, of course, the American press walked lockstep with Washington's wishes. Editorials abounded in the lead-up to war. This one from *The New York Times* was representative of the ongoing witch-hunt: "The time has come for strict interpretation and prompt enforcement of the laws of this country relating to treason, sedition, and conspiracy against the government... It is the duty of every good citizen to communicate to proper authorities any evidence of sedition that comes to his notice."[35]

When selling war and imperial notions, the fishing net must be large, casting far and wide, beyond the standard government propaganda and expected media consent to gain approval. The sales pitch also needs academia and the guild historians. "The state must spin an elaborate web of illusion and deceit," argues Chomsky, "with the cooperation of the ideological institutions that generally serve its interests."[36] The game becomes fantasy: the semblance of a free market of ideas. A term was concocted for this process: "historical engineering," coined by Pulitzer Prize-winning historian Fredric Logan Paxson, a former president of the Organization of American Historians and professor at the University of California. He explained that "historical engineering" defined the work he accomplished revising textbooks during wartime to fit the prevailing temper of the period. In fact, he casually called his actions "mere historical engineering."[37]

Conscription: The Selective Service Act of 1917

> *"Somebody said let's go out and fight for liberty and so they went out and got killed without ever once thinking of liberty... What the hell does liberty mean anyhow? It's a word like house or table or any other word. Only it's a special kind of word. A guy says house and he can point to a house to prove it. But a guy says come on let's fight for liberty and he can't show you liberty. He can't prove the thing he's talking about so how in the hell can he be telling you to fight for it? No sir anybody who went out and got into the front line trenches to fight for liberty was a goddamn fool and the guy who got him there was a liar."*
>
> —Joe Bonham from Dalton Trumbo's *Johnny Got His Gun*

In April of 1917 the United States entered the hostilities, declaring war on Germany. Woodrow Wilson and his War Department desperately needed at least a million bodies to shove into the trenches of Europe as well as his divine war to end all wars. But a funny thing happened on the way to Mr. Wilson's war: only 73,000 Americans volunteered. "Fuck this shit," Congress bellowed (or something like that), and then quickly voted for a draft. Once again, it was time for the robber barons to seize your children, your flesh and blood—not theirs, yours—and then go bowling for dollars. In fact, this feeble response verified for Wilson and his administration how unpopular this war was and triggered the aforementioned massive public relations (anti-German) campaign unleashed on the American public and aimed at military recruitment, as Howard Zinn illustrates:

> George Creel, a veteran newspaperman, became the government's
> official propagandist for the war; he set up a Committee on Public
> Information to persuade Americans the war was right. It sponsored
> 75,000 speakers, who gave 750,000 four-minute speeches in five
> thousand American cities and towns.[38]

Created by Creel and strongly backed by Wilson, these "Four Minute Men" were employed as human recruitment commercials in movie theatres across the nation. In the time it took to change reels during a picture show (four minutes), these guys would stand up and offer harrowing warnings—bold-faced lies created in laboratories and dripping with fear:

> While we are sitting here tonight enjoying a picture show, do
> you realize that thousands of Belgians, people just like ourselves,
> are languishing in slavery under Prussian masters?… Prussian
> "Schrecklichket" (deliberate policy of terrorism) leads to almost
> unbelievable besotten brutality. The German soldiers… were
> often forced against their wills, they themselves weeping, to carry
> out unspeakable orders against defenseless old men, women, and
> children… For instance, at Dinant the wives and children of 40 men
> were forced to witness the execution of their husbands and fathers.[39]

Other stories conjured up by American and British propaganda masters included Germans hacking off the hands of children and boiling their own dead troops to produce glycerin. No doubt, Germans committed atrocities during World War I. Every army in every war since man crawled out of the sea has committed atrocities. It's now known that these wild stories of Prussian barbarism—the ones used to demonize and motivate revenge—were fabricated. A popular propaganda and recruitment poster during the time depicted Jesus wearing khaki and staring down the barrel of a gun. In his book, *War is a Lie,* David Swanson offers this thought after acknowledging that Germans and Americans primarily belong to the same religion: "How much easier it is to use religion in wars against Muslims in the twenty-first century."[40]

With the memory of a weak Civil War draft still alive in Washington, Congress wrote the new conscription act to include almost every able bodied male. The Selective Service Act of 1917 determined a "liability for military service of all male citizens" between the ages of 21 and 31. Regardless of limitations, everyone would at least be eligible for a job in this man's army—everyone except those men in certain economic sectors that Wilson and his draft administrator, Judge Advocate General Enoch Crowder, deemed too valuable to America's industrial power.[41] By late 1917, ten million Americans were registered for the draft. Military leaders didn't think this was enough cannon fodder, so the range was expanded from 18 to 45 years of age. What was next? Gun-toting toddlers and the infirm? Hello grandpa.

Local draft boards administered the bureaucracy of the draft and their decisions were clearly based on social class and race. The poor (as is the case now with a de facto poor peoples draft) were habitually selected first. Why? They were categorized as the expendable ones. When it came to race, well, this was a godsend to the sons of the wealthy and influential. It was a chance to "rid" their communities of young African Americans.[42] In fact, many local draft boards made it mandatory for black recruits to tear off a corner of their application forms to make their registration easily identifiable. These systematic procedures ensured that the poor as well as the young Black male population were disproportionately drafted.[43]

Not much has changed.

At first glance, one might think that draft evasion was far greater during the Vietnam War than in "The Great War." Not true by a country mile. In fact, draft evasion during World War I dwarfed that of Vietnam, where figures cite the more recent war at about 571,000 men, in comparison to the war to end all wars where draft evasion was close to 3,000,000 men.[44]

The U.S. military used the court martial as a battering ram to beat back dissent in the new ranks. With dodging and desertion common among recruits, military tribunals sentenced many dissenters and conscientious objectors to long prison terms, penal labor camps, life imprisonment, and some even to death (although these sentences were modified to long stints at hard labor). Stories abounded of communities across the country sheltering local draft dodgers as political heroes.

Fueled by the fear and hate propaganda initiated by Washington, vigilante groups, like the America Defense Society, rose up around the country and took matters into their own hands. Along with their government enablers, they were hell-bent on suppressing dissent—violently if necessary. Typical tactics by these groups included rounding up draft-age men and forcing them to prove their status. Here's an example of a flyer printed in Kansas warning of retribution:

A WARNING

Those inclined to tantalize a community by holding out against the Red Cross, refusing to buy Liberty bonds and declining to sign Loyalty Pledge cards are advised that they are placing themselves on dangerous ground... Indignation will develop to such an extent that "due process of law" will not be a feature in the punishment handed out to them.
R. B. Quinn, Chairman
Harvey County Council of Defense, 1918[45]

Ben Salmon was a pacifist, a devout Catholic, a conscientious objector, as well as being an outspoken critic of "Just War" theology. For his beliefs during World War I, Ben Salmon was denounced by Roman Catholic honchos and portrayed as a "spy suspect" by *The New York Times*. In June 1917 he wrote Wilson a letter stating his complete aversion to war.

> If the parent orders the child to do wrong, the child should disobey. If the State commands the subject to violate God's law, the subject should ignore the State. Man is anterior to the State, and God is supreme. Both by precept and example, the lowly Nazarene taught us the doctrine of non-resistance, and so convinced was he of the soundness of that doctrine that he sealed his belief with death on the cross. When human law conflicts with Divine law, my duty is clear. Conscience, my infallible guide, impels me to tell you that prison, death, or both, are infinitely preferable to joining any branch of the Army.[46]

Ben Salmon was never inducted into the U.S. military but nonetheless they court-martialed him for desertion and spreading propaganda. He was then sentenced to death, later changed to twenty-five years hard labor.[47] In response to the notorious "Palmer Raids" and the subsequent egregious civil liberties abuses unleashed on dissenters and radicals throughout the country, a tiny band of citizens and lawyers started fighting back. They became known as the American Civil Liberties Union with the primary objective of defending the law and spirit enshrined in the United States Constitution. They fought for Ben Salmon and on 26 November 1920 he was pardoned and released. Ben was homeward bound but in very bad health—appalling maladies caused by the force-feedings and cruel beatings he absorbed in prison.

Ben Salmon: another young man that courageously embraced peace and nonviolence, only to be stomped on by a cowardly country defined and motivated by brutality.

Emma

She was no pacifist. Emma Goldman (1869–1940) remained on the frontlines of radical political action her entire life, battling the forces of government and corporate (shall we say) "intemperance" with uncompromising punch. Piss and vinegar. Goldman had no problem throwin' down on the mean streets of any political battlefield.

Born in Russia and emigrating to New York City, Goldman became associated with the anarchist movement on the heels of the Haymarket Riot in Chicago. Goldman did battle with the growing socialist movements of the time for being too subservient to the majority, their ranks too bourgeois to ever acquire genuine influence, let alone gain control of anything. In her early 20s she was involved in an assassination plot on industrialist Henry Clay Frick during the Homestead Steel strike—a failed attempt carried out by her political partner Alexander Berkman; later in life she was entrenched in the Russian and Spanish revolutions. But it was her opposition to America's build-up toward active involvement in World War I, followed by her anti-conscription organizing, that set the U.S. government on tilt.

In fact, it got her deported.

Just weeks after Woodrow Wilson and the U.S. declared war on Germany in April of 1917, Emma Goldman and others launched the "No-Conscription League," dedicated to encouraging and supporting conscientious objectors in their fight for freedom. The movement was growing, attracting some 8,000 participants to one particular meeting.[48] But the general whiplash against the draft reached far wider than just radical anarchists and included a broad coalition of antiwar groups including mainstream liberals, rank and file union memberships, as well as most socialist movements across the country. Goldman strongly believed that Wilson's draft challenged the essence of liberty as defined by American history and law. She wrote:

> In these days when every principle and conception of democracy
> and individual liberty is being cast overboard under the pretext
> of democratizing Germany, it behooves every liberty loving man
> and woman to insist on his or her right of individual choice in the
> ordering of his life and action.[49]

But the growing antiwar movement ran smack into the headwinds of a storm churning hard, fueled by histrionic nationalism as well as a ravenous anti-left crusade coordinated directly from the Oval Office. For all intents and purposes, the movement was wiped out and large numbers of foreign-born dissidents were deported.

Goldman, along with Berkman, were arrested, charged, and convicted of conspiring against the draft—a court case author Lance Selfa described as "a foregone conclusion."[50] Both were sentenced to two-year prison terms. When Goldman left the Missouri State Penitentiary in September of 1919, she was arrested again, this time by a young and rambunctious Justice Department juggernaut named J. Edgar Hoover. The soon-to-be law and order legend was building his junior G-Man career on the backs of radicals like Goldman and wrote the actual case briefs against her, lobbying the courts to deport this anti-American back to whence she came.[51] Hoover wrote, "Emma Goldman and Alexander Berkman are, beyond doubt, two of the most dangerous anarchists in this country and return to the community will result in undue harm."[52] (Decades later, and countless times in between and after, Hoover—that pillar of American justice—would play the same tired, illegal, and murderous game, as evidenced by another of Hoover's famous fear-mongering warnings: "The Black Panther Party, without question, represents the greatest threat to the internal security of the country.")

Emma Goldman addressed the jury directly at her trial. Her courage that day was palpable—and who in their right mind could gainsay the rightness of her cause?

> [A] democracy conceived in the military servitude of the masses, in
> their economic enslavement, and nurtured in their tears and blood,
> is not democracy at all. It is despotism—the cumulative result of

a chain of abuses, which according to that dangerous document, the Declaration of Independence, the people have the right to overthrow.[53]

Two months later and heavily guarded by government storm troopers, Emma Goldman and hundreds of other foreign-born radicals boarded a ship called *The Buford* that cut through the North Atlantic and back to Mother Russia.

The attack on Goldman, Berkman, and the No-Conscription League marked the beginning of the aforementioned Palmer Raids—a series of government thug assaults aimed at destroying progressive and radical groups throughout America, raids orchestrated by Wilson's attorney general A. Mitchell Palmer. In fact, the office of *Mother Earth*—Emma Goldman's publication—was one of the first to be targeted by AG Palmer. The Goldman Exhibition at UC Berkeley reports that, "Rumor has it that J. Edgar Hoover used her confiscated library and manuscripts to educate himself on the radical Left... most of the material was later destroyed."[54]

In a fitting postscript to Goldman's historic battle against Woodrow Wilson's "Great War" and his subsequent effort to recruit raw meat to fight for his robber baron buddies' bank accounts, we flash-forward to 2003 where we find University of California–Berkeley officials blocking their own Emma Goldman Papers Project from sending out a fundraising letter that quoted Goldman railing against war from eighty-plus years before. "University officials said the appeal was too 'political' to appear during the Bush administration's ramp-up to war in Iraq,"[55] writes the Project's own archivist. But the researchers at Berkeley's Emma Goldman Papers Project did not give in to administration threats. In fact, the research group and others publically protested Berkeley's decision to suppress free speech (right in the shadow of Mario Savio); their courageous efforts pressed the university to back down.

"When one man says, 'No, I won't,' Rome begins to fear."
—Kirk Douglas as *Spartacus* (from Dalton Trumbo's screenplay)

From Alcatraz to Leavenworth: Seeking Shelter from the Storm

Along with the Amish and Mennonites, the Hutterites evolved through history from Martin Luther's 16th century Radical Reformation as absolute pacifists. Hutterites faced harsh persecution in numerous countries for their steadfast beliefs against war that included the traditional trappings of war, like wearing a uniform and paying war taxes. Duane C.S. Stoltzfus, a professor at Indiana's Goshen College, explains the pacifist back-story of Hutterites' living in 20th century America:

> Soldiering was most assuredly not in their DNA. The communal church to which they belonged had been resolutely set against all warfare for 400 years. Their grandparents had immigrated to the United States decades earlier, leaving their farms in Russia to travel thousands of miles, all to avoid having their men drafted into a newly expanded Russian military.[56]

Emigrating from throughout Europe, the Hutterites experienced similar harassment in the U.S. as they did elsewhere: they were reclusive, followed their strict own dress code, rejected war bonds, and here's the zinger—many of them spoke German.

In May of 1918, three brothers—David, Michael, and Joseph Hofer, along with Jacob Wipf (Joseph's brother-in-law)—left their 4,000-acre farm at the Rockport Hutterite Colony in South Dakota and boarded a train for the great northwest and Camp Lewis in Washington. For tens of thousands of west coast recruits, this was the first step toward the jaws of the great meat grinder. These four Hutterite farmers were drafted into Woodrow Wilson's perverted vision of a lasting peace through blood sport, wanting "to cooperate as long as they could, hoping for an assignment they could accept,"[57] Stoltzfus explains.

With Mount Rainier looming just beyond the camp, and less than one day after their arrival at Camp Lewis, the four farmers were thrown into the stockade for refusing to fill out the "Statement of Soldier" on the grounds that they were not soldiers and therefore could not make statements as soldiers. In fact they were conscientious objectors. Stoltzfus explains that, "The Hofer brothers and Jacob Wipf had the misfortune of arriving at Camp Lewis just as commanders across the country appeared intent on using trials to send a message to conscientious objectors like [these four Hutterites]."[58]

Getting ready for trial, the government needed to make the case that the men were insincere in their beliefs. The government argued that, "anyone of sound mind who refused the military's fair offer of noncombatant service must be insincere." Clearly, the military was setting them up for a monkey trial with an ironclad and trumped-up case. The pacifist farmers had no chance. "They saw themselves as Christians, not soldiers," writes Stoltzfus, "and as Christians their refusal to obey military orders was a sure sign of sincerity. The Hutterites and military officials were talking to one another across kingdom walls."[59]

In fact, to the United States of America, this vaguely familiar phrase—"Congress shall make no law respecting an establishment of religion, *or prohibiting the free exercise thereof"* —didn't mean a goddamn thing. David, Michael, Joseph, and Jacob were found guilty and condemned to twenty years of hard labor on Alcatraz.

Imagine the state of mind of these four young men as they cut across San Francisco Bay toward "The Rock"—at the time a military prison. (It wasn't until 1933 that Alcatraz became the federal penitentiary that made Al Capone, Machine Gun Kelly, and Robert "the Birdman of Alcatraz" Stroud legendary inmates.) The four Hutterites were immediately thrown into the hole: pitch-black dungeons sodden with water, sans toilets. Warm uniforms were left for the men, enticing them to embrace the warmth as a way to concede to wearing the military garb. There was no food for almost a week, only a few ounces of water each day. Their hands were chained to the cell-door bars—chained high so their feet barely touched the floor. For four months straight, David, Michael, Joseph, and Jacob would spend two weeks in the hole and two weeks in a general population cell. In the letters the men wrote home to their families they suggested that their death could be imminent. God bless the divinely inspired vision of Woodrow Wilson and God bless America.

On 29 September 1918, allied troops broke through the German fortifications at the Hindenberg Line, marking the beginning of the end of World War I. Less than two months later Kaiser Wilhelm II relinquished his power and the Weimar Republic was founded—and then two days later, at eleven o'clock on the eleventh day of the eleventh month of 1918, the war ended as Germany and the Allies ceased hostilities. A few days later, the four Hutterite farmers—pacifists and conscientious objectors who wanted nothing to do with America's or the world's killing machine—were transferred in chains to Fort Leavenworth, Kansas, where two of the brothers, Joseph and Michael, were immediately hospitalized in critical condition from months of deprivation. The prison bureaucracy called the families back in South Dakota and their wives headed for Kansas. When they arrived, Stoltzfus writes:

> Joseph was barely able to communicate. He died at 8:35 the following morning, Nov. 29. The guards said that family members could not see him. But Maria, Joseph's wife, was forceful. The head officer relented. With tears in her eyes, she approached the coffin, which was set on two chairs. When the lid was opened, she found Joseph in death dressed in a military uniform that he had steadfastly refused to wear in life. Michael Hofer died a few days later.[60]

David Hofer, the surviving brother, was released and traveled back home with the bodies. Jacob Wipf remained at Leavenworth in solitary confinement for another five months before his release. When he returned to South Dakota, many of the Hutterite colonies were deserted—his fellow Hutterites having fled to Canada. Soon, the Rockport colony that Joseph, Michael, David, and Jacob called home and had worked the land was also abandoned. Left behind in a small cemetery were two headstones marked for two dead brothers—ironically, both men driven to early graves by the same machine that they refused to join with as fellow murderers.

The Espionage Act

They have always taught and trained you to believe it to be your patriotic duty to go to war and to have yourselves slaughtered at their command. But in all the history of the world you, the people, have never had a voice in declaring war, and strange as it certainly appears, no war by any nation in any age has ever been declared by the people.[61]
　　　　　　　　　　　　—Eugene Debs, 16 June 1918 (Canton, Ohio)

With Woodrow Wilson's propaganda campaign working wonders on the American people, Washington power left no stone unturned. It was time for Congress to enact legislation that would target Americans with the temerity to challenge the government's drumbeat to war—and in most cases that meant Socialists, people like Eugene V. Debs. In fact, because of his antiwar speech that June day in 1918, Debs was arrested and prosecuted under the Espionage Act and sentenced to ten years in a federal penitentiary. He served two and half years at Woodstock Prison in Atlanta and also ran for president from this federal facility, garnering nearly one million votes. His sentence was then commuted by Wilson's successor, Warren Gamaliel Harding. (The Espionage Act lives on, used against Daniel Ellsberg and more recently deployed by Barack Obama against Chelsea Manning, Edward Snowden, and John Kiriakou, former CIA analyst and whistleblower who contends that, "Obama's use of the Espionage Act is modern-day McCarthyism... It is meant to send a message to anybody else considering speaking truth to power: challenge us and we will destroy you."[62])

Once again, under the heading of "law is politics by other means," the Wilson administration, along with large majorities in Congress passed the Espionage Act (along with the 1918 amendment called the Sedition Act) to obliterate any and all dissent. In classic fashion, most of the legislation reflected typical overblown governmental paranoia about traitors obtaining codebooks, signal books, and blueprints with intentions of handing them over to the enemy. But the devil was in the details of the autocratic aims of Wilson and his divine mission of unbridled American power.

> [To] cause... or incite... insubordination, disloyalty, mutiny, or
> refusal of duty, in the military or naval forces of the United States...
>
> [To] utter, print, write, or publish any disloyal, profane, scurrilous,
> or abusive language about the form of government of the United
> States, or the Constitution of the United States, or the military or
> naval forces of the United States, or the flag... or the uniform of
> the Army or Navy of the United States, or any language intended
> to bring the form of government... or the Constitution... or the
> military or naval forces... or the flag... of the United States into
> contempt, scorn, contumely, or disrepute...
>
> [To] willfully display the flag of a foreign enemy...
>
> [To] urge, incite, or advocate any curtailment of production in
> this country of any thing or things... necessary or essential to the
> prosecution of the war...

The original language of the Espionage Act included what would be referred to as the press censorship provision, which declared it unlawful for any person during this time of war to publish any information that the president *"in his judgment"* considered "of such character that it is or might be useful to the enemy." Although this particular provision was struck from the act after heated debate in Congress, nevertheless it reveals the fervor with which Wilson was attempting to silence the press and squelch dissent.[63] [Emphasis added]

Besides their childish obsession with "the flag" (Carlin: *I consider them to be symbols and I leave symbols to the "symbol-minded"*), this obviously unconstitutional claptrap was designed to intimidate and bury American dissent six feet under (take a knee Colin K). Even the Supreme Court went along for this joyride in 1919 with a unanimous decision upholding the act in *Schenck v. U.S.*

Charles Schenk was a well-known socialist who was distributing flyers to U.S. servicemen recently drafted for the war. Schenck and his flyers claimed that conscription was nothing more than "involuntary servitude" as defined by the 13th Amendment to the U.S. Constitution. Schenck's flyer also stated that the war was motivated by wanton capitalist avarice. It strongly urged the soldiers to fight to repeal the illegal draft. Schenck was charged and found guilty under the Espionage Act of conspiring "to cause insubordination" within the ranks of the U.S. military. On appeal, the case was reviewed by the Supreme Court and apparently the Court believed that certain legislation trumps the Constitution—specifically the First Amendment, which is abundantly clear in its language:

> **Congress shall make no law** respecting an establishment of religion, or prohibiting the free exercise thereof; or **abridging the freedom of speech,** or of the press; or the right of the people peaceably to assemble, and to petition the Government for a redress of grievances.

Congress shall make no law abridging the freedom of speech.

NO law abridging freedom of speech.

Where's the loophole? Where's the wiggle room for interpretation?

Well, we'll tell you. Nowhere—except in the realm of the power elite's personal ongoing circle jerk. And the guy with the biggest member in this 1919 get-together was Oliver Wendell Holmes, the famous and revered "liberal" justice who wrote the unanimous opinion in *Schenck v. U.S.* The Court found that "the character of every act depends on the circumstances in which it is done." Ain't that convenient?

NO LAW ABRIDGING FREEDOM OF SPEECH.

Then Holmes offered this beauty: "[T]he most stringent protection of free speech would not protect a man in falsely shouting fire in a theatre and causing a panic."

Essentially, Holmes and the Court determined that limitations on the constitutional protection of free speech (i.e., what constitutes a "panic") could be determined at will by the Executive Branch.

With this decision, the Court shot down the simplicity and the genius of the First Amendment and then built a house of cards on the flimsy foundation of an impossible to determine "clear and present danger" test. The Constitution, written in language and spirit that **limits the behavior of the government,** was once again subverted by corrupt power—the very thing the Framers (sort of) feared. Howard Zinn offers the perfect rebuttal:

> Few people would think free speech should be conferred
> on someone shouting fire in a theater and causing a panic.
> But did that example fit criticism of the war? Zechariah Chafee,
> a Harvard law school professor, wrote later (Free Speech in the
> United States) that a more apt analogy for Schenck was someone
> getting up between the acts at a theater and declaring that there
> were not enough fire exits. To play further with the example:
> was not Schenck's act more like someone shouting, not falsely, but
> truly, to people about to buy tickets and enter a theater, that there
> was a fire raging inside?
>
> Perhaps free speech could not be tolerated by any reasonable
> person if it constituted a "clear and present danger" to life and
> liberty; after all, free speech must compete with other vital rights.
> But was not the war itself a "clear and present danger," indeed,
> more clear and more present and more dangerous to life than any
> argument against it? Did citizens not have a right to object to war, a
> right to be a danger to dangerous policies?[64]

(It should be noted that fifty years later in 1969, the Supreme Court somewhat amended the Schenck decision in *Brandenburg v. Ohio*, replacing the previous ruling with the "imminent lawless action" test, which allows the government to limit speech that might incite illegal actions before authorities can arrive to prevent the action.)

But for Woodrow Wilson and the makers of war (as well as wartime hysteria), the 1919 Court went along for the joyride. In fact it's crystal clear that as time has marched down the long and winding road of this country's history, both in the era of Republic and the age of Empire, the rights of individuals in the American experiment have been whittled away—some by covert action, some by corporate and economic terrorism, and others right out in the light of day, under the so-called rule of law and with the patronage of those learned men and women in long black robes who protect New Rome—not with the scales of justice—but with the anvil of repression.

"War is a Racket"

Smedley Darlington Butler joined the United States Marine Corps during the Spanish-American War. He earned the Brevette Medal during the Boxer Rebellion in China. He was awarded two Congressional Medals of Honor—one for the capture of Vera Cruz, Mexico in 1914 and the other for the capture of Fort Riviere in Haiti in 1917. He fought in Central America and then again in World War I when he was promoted to the rank of Major General. He was also awarded the Distinguished Service Medal in 1919.

In 1933, two years after he retired, he delivered a speech entitled "War is a Racket." This historic public address remains one of the great and bold antiwar statements of all time as Butler eviscerates the masters of war from the inside out. Very similar to the passion found pulsating in Vietnam Veterans Against the War and Iraq Veterans Against the War, Butler came out swinging, landing titanic body blows like a young Joe Louis on American war makers. He was no longer the soldier blindly following orders. Rather, he was a soul transformed by the ugly, perverted, and bloody truth. It was the early 1930s and Butler sensed the "international war clouds gathering" once again and clearly felt radically motivated to warn his fellow earthlings about their impending doom. "There are 40,000,000 men under arms in the world today," Butler intoned, "and our statesmen and diplomats have the temerity to say that war is not in the making. Hell's bells! Are these 40,000,000 men being trained to be dancers?"[65]

The racket, as Butler defines it, always begins and ends with the accrual of gold: wealth, capital, money, riches, dead presidents, moolah…

> War is a racket. It always has been… In the World War a mere handful garnered the profits of the conflict. At least 21,000 new millionaires and billionaires were made in the United States during the World War. That many admitted their huge blood gains in their income tax returns. How many other war millionaires falsified their tax returns no one knows.[66]

Using World War I as his proving grounds, Butler followed the money, followed war profiteering (not liberty or democracy) to the heart of darkness:

> The normal profits of a business concern in the United States are six, eight, ten, and sometimes twelve percent. But war-time profits—ah! that is another matter—twenty, sixty, one hundred, three hundred, and even eighteen hundred per cent—the sky is the limit. All that traffic will bear. Uncle Sam has the money. Let's get it. Of course, it isn't put that crudely in war-time. It is dressed into speeches about patriotism, love of country, and "we must all put our shoulders to the wheel," but the profits jump and leap and skyrocket—and are safely pocketed. Let's just take a few examples:
>
> …the du Ponts… Bethlehem Steel… United States Steel… Anaconda [and] Utah Copper… International Nickel Company… American Sugar Refining Company… meat packers… cotton manufacturers… garment makers… coal producers… the shoe people… the munitions manufacturers and armament makers, they also sold to the enemy… mosquito netting… Airplane and engine manufacturers… shipbuilders… And let us not forget the bankers who financed the Great War. If anyone had the cream of the profits it was the bankers… And their profits were as secret as they were immense. How the bankers made their millions and their billions I do not know, because those little secrets never become public—even before a Senate investigatory body.[67]

The list is actually considerably longer; and the amount of wealth amassed in World War I—*and all wars*—is staggering. Major General Smedley Butler then asks the next most important question: "Who pays the bills?" Asked and answered:

Who provides the profits—these nice little profits of 20,
100, 300, 1,500 and 1,800 per cent? We all pay them—in
taxation. We paid the bankers their profits when we bought
Liberty Bonds at $100.00 and sold them back at $84 or $86 to
the bankers. These bankers collected $100 plus. It was a simple
manipulation. The bankers control the security marts. It was
easy for them to depress the price of these bonds. Then all of us—
the people—got frightened and sold the bonds at $84 or $86.
The bankers bought them. Then these same bankers stimulated a
boom and government bonds went to par—and above. Then the
bankers collected their profits.[68]

To this very moment, the price of war—including all the associated accoutrements,
all the salivated-over hardware (giving the brass giddy-hard excitement that even
Pfizer would be proud of), as well as their exciting and futuristic "Buck Rogers
in the 21st Century" space toys (playthings that the Military-Industrial Complex
holds so dear)—disembowels the people of the United States and the world of a
better life: healthcare, elder care, education, food, housing, infrastructure, clean
air, clean water, a chance at economic equality, and above all, peace.

But the ultimate price of war is borne and absorbed primarily by the young men
and women that the old men first steal and then send to kill, get maimed, or die in
their skirmishes for profits and power. Butler told his captive audience:

But the soldier pays the biggest part of the bill. If you don't
believe this, visit the American cemeteries on the battlefields
abroad. Or visit any of the veteran's hospitals in the United
States… I have visited eighteen government hospitals for veterans.
In them are a total of about 50,000 destroyed men—men who
were the pick of the nation eighteen years ago. The very able chief
surgeon at the government hospital at Milwaukee, where there are
3,800 of the living dead, told me that mortality among veterans is
three times as great as among those who stayed at home.

Boys with a normal viewpoint were taken out of the fields
and offices and factories and classrooms and put into the ranks.
There they were remolded; they were made over; they were made
to "about face," to regard murder as the order of the day. They were
put shoulder-to-shoulder and, through mass psychology, they were

entirely changed. We used them for a couple of years and trained
them to think nothing at all of killing or of being killed.

In the government hospital in Marion, Indiana, 1,800 of these
boys are in pens! Five hundred of them in a barracks with steel
bars and wires all around outside the buildings and on the porches.
These already have been mentally destroyed. These boys don't even
look like human beings.

That's a part of the bill. So much for the dead—they have
paid their part of the war profits… They paid for it in the trenches
where they shot and were shot; where they were hungry for days at
a time; where they slept in the mud and the cold and in the rain—
with the moans and shrieks of the dying for a horrible lullaby.[69]

Butler goes on to duly accuse his brethren and his country of willfully lying
through their teeth, using propaganda to manipulate their minds and steal their
souls:

So vicious was this war propaganda that even God was
brought into it. With few exceptions our clergymen joined
in the clamor to kill, kill, kill. To kill the Germans. God is on
our side… it is His will that the Germans be killed. And in Germany,
the good pastors called upon the Germans to kill the allies… to
please the same God.[70]

At the time the term "chicken hawk" did not yet refer to the politician, industrialist,
banker, preacher, or anyone who used other people's children as human props in
their geopolitical and economic passion play. No doubt had the term been in use
back in World War I, Smedley Darlington Butler would have applied the word
generously in his speech. Nevertheless, the concept, the charge still existed to be
laid at the feet of these degenerates:

How many of these war millionaires shouldered a rifle? How many
of them dug a trench? How many of them knew what it meant to
go hungry in a rat-infested dug-out? How many of them spent
sleepless, frightened nights, ducking shells and shrapnel and
machine gun bullets? How many of them parried a bayonet thrust of
an enemy? How many of them were wounded or killed in battle?[71]

Butler then offers the only fair and equitable solution, one that most assuredly would have the warmongers rioting in the streets:

> The only way to smash this racket is to conscript capital and industry and labor before the nation's manhood can be conscripted. One month before the Government can conscript the young men of the nation—it must conscript capital and industry and labor. Let the officers and the directors and the high-powered executives of our armament factories and our munitions makers and our shipbuilders and our airplane builders and the manufacturers of all the other things that provide profit in war time as well as the bankers and the speculators, be conscripted—to get $30 a month, the same wage as the lads in the trenches get.

> Let the workers in these plants get the same wages—all the workers, all presidents, all executives, all directors, all managers, all bankers—yes, and all generals and all admirals and all officers and all politicians and all government office holders—everyone in the nation be restricted to a total monthly income not to exceed that paid to the soldier in the trenches!

> Why shouldn't they? They aren't running any risk of being killed or of having their bodies mangled or their minds shattered.[72]

"All men are enamored of decorations," Napoleon Bonaparte once quipped, "they positively hunger for them." The handing out of medals like Halloween candy to school kids didn't appear in America until the Civil War. The Napoleonic system taught governments—the U.S. included—that being in the medal business could attract young soldiers for less money, "because the boys liked to be decorated," suggests Major General Butler.

Why Fight? "Maintaining Preeminent Trade"

In his essay, "A Question of Hegemony," William Pfaff notes that, "Woodrow Wilson… regarded the outbreak of World War I as a fit of madness among the Europeans."[73] In public, Wilson said things like "There is such a thing as a man too proud to fight. There is such a thing as a nation being so right that it does not need to convince others by force that it is right." The established history suggests that Wilson's hand was finally forced into war because of Germany's escalating and murderous submarine campaign. ("Enough, goddamnit, damn the torpedoes!

America's on the way!") But in addition to this convenient knee-jerk reaction by America to destroy the out-of control murderous Huns was Wilson's earnest, albeit delusional, altruistic motivations to finally join the festivities. "He did so," Pfaff continues, "in order to fight a war to end wars, to make the world safe for democracy, and to end 'power politics,' after which the U.S. would lead the way into a new international order in which war would be abolished."[74]

Pfaff is correct to a certain point about Wilson and his motives for war as well as America's motives for entry into World War I. His analysis helps to explain the burgeoning empire's early attempt at control of the global community. It also helps to paint an accurate portrait of Wilson's lifelong arrogant, religious, and narcissistic (Pfaff calls it "megalomaniacal") embrace of Manifest Destiny, as evidenced by Wilson's statement after the American and allied victory in the war, a statement that suggests America's role as one of divine intervention: "It was of this that we dreamed at our birth. America shall in truth show the way... [The world turned] to America for those moral inspirations which lie at the base of all freedom... [The world] shall know that she puts human rights above all other rights, and that her flag is the flag not only of America, but of humanity."[75]

As outlined earlier in the chapter, this analysis is only part of the narrative; it's the more personal and plot driven story, living for the most part on the surface and for the benefit of pristine appearances and stale history books. The core essence of this story—the soft-center truth of why governments and empires fight wars— exists at the base and in the foundation and is rarely, if ever, mentioned as the driving force of war. Major General Smedley Butler concludes:

> Woodrow Wilson was re-elected president in 1916 on a platform that he had "kept us out of war" and on the implied promise that he would "keep us out of war." Yet, five months later he asked Congress to declare war on Germany. In that five-month interval the people had not been asked whether they had changed their minds. The 4,000,000 young men who put on uniforms and marched or sailed away were not asked whether they wanted to go forth to suffer and die.
>
> Then what caused our government to change its mind so suddenly?
>
> Money.[76]

In fact, one month before Washington declared war on Germany, Wilson received a cable from Walter Hines Page, his ambassador to England, who wrote:

> The pressure of this approaching crisis, I am certain, has
> gone beyond the ability of the Morgan financial agency for
> the British and French governments. The financial necessities
> of the Allies are too great and urgent for any private agency to
> handle, for every agency has to encounter business rivalries and
> sectional antagonism. It is not improbable that the only way of
> maintaining our present preeminent trade position and averting a
> panic is by declaring war on Germany.[77]

Weeks later the United States dove headfirst into the trenches of Europe. Page didn't discuss democracy, liberty, German atrocities, or German submarines torpedoing everything on the high seas. Page simply underscored the real motivation: *money*.

The Aftermath

With Europe overwhelmed and devastated by war, Russia was rocked with two revolutions that destroyed Czarist rule and led to the subsequent creation of the Soviet Union. In fact the Russian Revolutions marked the first wave of communism to wash across Europe. The March 1917 Revolution forced the abdication of Czar Nicholas II and was the first demonstrable class struggle as predicted by Karl Marx. The November 1917 Revolution was led by Vladimir Lenin who instituted "the dictatorship of the proletariat," adopted the Communist Party, and then withdrew Russia from World War I. Lenin also positioned the Soviets as the supreme power in Russia.

But Washington and its other capitalist allies were not about to sit back and casually let the Bolsheviks run rampant and "overthrow all existing governments and establish on the ruins a despotism of the proletariat in every country,"[78] as Wilson's Secretary of State Robert Lansing warned in a confidential communiqué. No doubt, fear was beginning to spread as rebellion rumbled just under the surface of a world heretofore owned and operated by the wealthy ruling class. In fact, American labor leaders were showing strong signs of solidarity with Lenin and his revolutionary forces. Political historian Michael Parenti observes:

> The plutocracy's worst nightmare was coming true: here
> was a successful socialist revolution by the unlettered and

unwashed masses against the natural leaders of society, the persons of talent and property. Unless drastic measures were taken, might not other countries follow suit?[79]

Drastic measures began in August of 1918 as fourteen nations—spearheaded by the U.S., France, England, and Japan—invaded Soviet Russia with the aim of overthrowing the Bolsheviks. The allied invasion bolstered the intransigent pro-czarist White Guard armies with significant aid as well as boots on the ground. History books and American commentators, as they are apt to do, have whitewashed and watered-down Washington's involvement in the assault on revolutionary Russia. America's role is usually minimized as nothing more than a Boy Scouts' expedition in the snow. Parenti writes, "American and other allied troops participated regularly in atrocities. Widespread pillaging and killing of civilians, including the massacre of thousands of Jews, were carried out by the reactionary White Guard armies."[80]

Parenti also reports that one dissenting American serviceman made his feelings known regarding his White Guard confederates, those "lying, thieving, murdering, tsarist army officials who keep their people in this ignorance and poverty." The American sergeant believed the vast majority of the Russian population was sympathetic with the revolutionaries, concluding "and I don't blame them."[81]

American presidents have also failed to remember this incursion on Soviet soil, a precursor to the Cold War that started long before the post-World War II cotillion dance that presented the warring debutantes to the world stage. On Soviet television in 1972, Richard Nixon declared, "Most important of all, we have never fought one another in war."[82]

WRONG.

In 1984, during his State of the Union address, Ronald Reagan echoed the same: "[I]t's true that our governments have had serious differences. But our sons and daughters have never fought each other in war."[83]

WRONG.

Once again, the myth of American history stomps its cloven hoof down on reality. A 1985 *New York Times* poll reported that only 14% of Americans were aware that American troops invaded Russia in 1918. But by contrast, when Nikita Khrushchev was in Los Angeles in 1959, he said (this time with both shoes on his feet) that America's "armed intervention in Russia was the most unpleasant thing that ever occurred in the relations between our two countries, for we had never waged war against America until then; our troops have never set foot on American soil, while your troops have set foot on Soviet soil. You see how it is, ladies and gentlemen."[84]

CORRECT.

Chalk another one up for the old double standard: American Exceptionalism. Or possibly it might be more apropos to say: American Denial.

Back to the trenches. The initial smokescreen conjured up by the invading allied force suggested that the goal of the incursion was to re-harness Russia's might against Germany in the still ongoing World War. But as Parenti reminds us, "the World War ended shortly after the invasion, yet the allies continued in their military campaign against the Bolshevik government for almost another two years."[85] Then why did it continue, we ask rhetorically? Parenti draws the only logical conclusion with this age-old fact of political life in the land of capital:

> In truth, the allied leaders intervened in revolutionary Russia for the same reason conservative rulers have intervened in revolutionary conflicts before and since: to protect the existing social order. Recall how various European monarchs colluded against the French Revolution... Likewise, after the 1918 armistice, the victorious Western allies allowed the German militarists to retain 5,000 machine guns to be used against German workers "infected with Bolshevism." The allies made clear that they would not tolerate a socialist workers' government in Germany nor permit diplomatic relations between Berlin and the newly installed Soviet government in the Kremlin.[86]

This is exactly why U.S. Secretary of State Robert Lansing was whispering in Woodrow Wilson's ear as Wilson contemplated committing at least 40,000 American troops to help lead and bolster the allies' Russian invasion. Lansing and his fellow American policymakers saw Bolshevism as the "most hideous and monstrous thing that the human mind has ever conceived."[87] Apparently, Lansing didn't live long enough to the see the '61 Mets play.

A Fragile Peace

The "War to End All Wars" left the people of Europe and the world shocked and stunned. The Allied Victory marked the end of the German, Russian, Ottoman, and Austro-Hungarian Empires. It was against this backdrop that Wilson and the victorious powers attempted to bring permanent peace to Europe. But the victors were quick to blame Germany for initiating the war and vowed immediate punishment and castigation, which was drafted and codified in the subsequent Treaty of Versailles—a fiasco of imperialist stupidity that officially ended the war and enacted harsh retribution on Germany. The Treaty forced the Germans to take sole responsibility for the war along with economic and territorial concessions that were clearly punitive and devastating—concessions that would later lead directly to the rise of an Austrian mad man and the Second World War.

The total number of casualties—both military and civilian—during World War I will be debated forever, but regardless of the exact numbers, the carnage was astounding, beyond belief, shocking. Estimates vary, but the consensus suggests there were 16 million deaths as well as 21 million wounded. The masters of war on all sides really outdid themselves: 37 million casualties. Goddamn, we're good at killing each other.

"The Robber League of Nations"

On the surface, the creation of the "League of Nations"—the forerunner of the U.N.— appears to be a selfless and humane move toward what Woodrow Wilson deemed "a just peace." Wilson's Fourteen Points, which outlined his god-like calling to end war and create a safer world, fit perfectly into his "divinely ordained mission" of Manifest Destiny: forcing the world (for its own good) to "turn to America for those moral aspirations which lie at the basis of all freedom."

Established in 1919, after the end of World War I, the League was assembled by the victorious allied nations to enforce the terms of the castigatory Treaty of Versailles. With all of Europe still smoldering and the stench of death still rank in the air, Russian leader and recent revolutionary Vladimir Lenin called this new diplomatic body "the robber League of Nations."[88] Brown University professor Bill Keach writes, "[Lenin] argued that Woodrow Wilson's great plan for international peace and cooperation was really an extension of the very imperialist forces that had created the war in the first place."[89] Obviously, Lenin clearly understood the direct connection between the ravenous desires of predatory capitalism and its insatiable need to wage wars of plunder and control. Lenin argued that:

Socialists have always condemned wars between nations as barbarous and brutal. We understand the inevitable connection between wars and the class struggle within a country; we understand that wars cannot be abolished unless classes are abolished and socialism is created.[90]

The Russian leader "was acutely aware that socialism had not yet been fully created after the First World War, either in Russia or internationally," writes Keach. "Because of this he understood that 'The League of Nations and the entire postwar policy' coming out of the Treaty of Versailles were in fact agreements among the winners in the Great War about how to assure their continued domination."[91]

"Impressive" can only describe the revolutionaries of the time, as their critical analysis of capitalism's kinship with war was nothing short of prescient, prophetic, and damn near clairvoyant when looking at the current intrigues of the American Empire. Called by some "[T]he best brain after Marx,"[92] fiercely independent Rosa Luxemburg was no shill for dogma of any kind and spent a lifetime defining the natural connection between capitalism and war. Standing on the eve of World War I, she clearly understood that "Militarism in both its forms—as war and as armed peace—is a legitimate child, a logical result of capitalism."[93] Her deeper analysis reads like a spot-on contemporary critique of Western hegemony:

> [For Social Democrats] to endeavour to make it clear to
> the people that militarism is closely linked up with colonial
> politics, with tariff politics, and with international politics,
> and that therefore the present Nations, if they really seriously
> and honestly wish to call a halt on competitive armaments,
> would have to begin by disarming in the commercial political field,
> give up colonial predatory campaigns and the international politics
> of spheres of influence in all parts of the world. In a word, in their
> foreign as well as in their domestic politics they would have to do
> the exact contrary of everything which the nature of the present
> politics of a capitalist class state demands.[94]

Shortly before his death and right in the midst of the U.S.-led fourteen nation blockade and assault on the young Bolshevik government, journalist John Reed wrote stirring words warning of American promises of aid, which Reed translated as nothing more than Washington and its allies gaining an imperial foothold on various anti-capitalist movements, thereby asphyxiating the possibility of additional revolutions. Reed's extraordinary but undelivered 1920 speech at the Azerbaijan's Baku Congress put the international march of the budding U.S. Empire in the crosshairs:

> You, the peoples of the East, the peoples of Asia, have not yet experienced for yourselves the rule of America. You know and hate the British, French and Italian imperialists, and probably you think that "free America" will govern better, will liberate the peoples of the colonies, will feed and defend them. No. The workers and peasants of the Philippines, the peoples of Central America and the islands of the Caribbean, they know what it means to live under the rule of "free America."

> Take, for example, the peoples of the Philippines. In 1898 the Filipinos rebelled against the cruel colonial government of Spain, and the Americans helped them. But after the Spaniards had been driven out the Americans did not want to go away. Then the Filipinos rose against the Americans, and this time the "liberators" started to kill them, their wives and children: they tortured them and eventually conquered them. They seized their land and forced them to work and make profits for American capitalists.

> This has also happened in Cuba, which was freed from Spanish rule with the help of the Americans. It is now an independent Republic. But American millionaire trusts own all the sugar plantations... And the moment that the workers of Cuba try to elect a government which is not in the interests of the American capitalists, the United States of America sends soldiers into Cuba to compel the people to vote for their oppressors.

> Or let us take the example of the republics of Haiti and San Domingo, where the peoples won freedom a century ago. Since this island was fertile and the people living on it could be put to use by the American capitalists, the government of the U.S. sent soldiers and sailors there on the pretext of maintaining order and smashed these two republics, setting up in their place a military dictatorship worse than the British tyrants.[95]

Reed candidly encapsulated America's growing imperial résumé. Then, in a twist that boldly underscores Reed's understanding that imperial oppression knows no bounds, he connects the dots of empire back to the American homeland:

> In North America itself there are ten million Negroes who possess
> neither political or civil rights, despite the fact that by law they
> are equal citizens. With the purpose of distracting the attention
> of the American workers from the capitalists, their exploiters, the
> latter stir up hatred against the Negroes, provoking war between
> the white and black races. The Negroes, whom they lawlessly
> burn alive, are beginning to see that their only hope lies in armed
> resistance to the white bandits.[96]

Clearly seeing through the hegemonic designs of Wilsonian idealism (Wilson's Fourteen Points), as well as the controlling ambition of the League of Nations, Reed offered this bare naked observation:

> But there is also another very important reason: the American
> capitalists, together with the other capitalist nations, united in the
> League of Nations, are afraid that the workers and peasants...will
> follow the example of Soviet Russia and Soviet Azerbaidzhan, will
> take power and their country's resources into their own hands, and
> will work for themselves, making a united front with the workers
> and peasants of the whole world against world imperialism. The
> American capitalists are afraid of a revolution in the East.[97]

Leon Trotsky was many things: incredible journalist, orator, revolutionary leader, and visionary who clearly described a future where most men and women could be empowered to bolster the common good. Trotsky was also a ruthless son of a bitch with a concurrent history of trampling on human rights and killing god-knows how many people. But early on, he had the essence of imperialist war down cold. He truly understood, probably more than anything else, the enslavement of the weak by the actions of the strong. As a major revolutionary player during the tectonic shifts of power after World War I, his cautionary words bear repeating here:

> Capitalism has transferred into the field of international relations
> the same methods applied by it in "regulating" the internal
> economic life of the nations. The path of competition is the path of
> systematically annihilating the small and medium-sized enterprises
> and of achieving the supremacy of big capital. World competition
> of the capitalist forces means the systematic subjection of the small,

medium-sized and backward nations by the great and greatest capitalist powers.[98]

Ironically, the United States never joined the League of Nations. After Wilson championed the new allied-controlled diplomatic body, internal debate between Wilson and Massachusetts senator Henry Cabot Lodge forced a congressional stalemate. At the time, Lodge was the chairman of the Senate Foreign Relations Committee and was demanding specific changes to the League's charter. Wilson refused to budge and then suffered a massive and debilitating stroke, which ended his presidency. Warren Harding followed Wilson in the Oval Office and was steadfastly opposed to the League, which ended up spelling doom for what would become a very ineffectual body.

As the 1920s unfolded, pacifism and isolation were the prevalent attitudes for the majority of European citizens. By the 1930s the League was powerless to halt the aggressive moves underfoot by Italy and Germany. And then, as a result of the Great Depression, fringe movements such as fascism became more appealing to the general population and grew in strength, which further weakened the League's feeble attempts.

In the end, Wilsonian idealism, with its sugarplum fairy designs on American conquest and rule, was shoveled onto the garbage heap of history. But grand imperialists had no reason to fear for the Empire would storm back in short order.

Paths of Glory

In 1957, legendary filmmaker Stanley Kubrick made what is arguably one of the greatest, if not *the* greatest antiwar film of all time: *Paths of Glory*. The plot (based on actual events) is simple: a vainglorious and ruthless general orders French soldiers mired in the death trenches of World War I to engage in a suicidal attack on a German fortification. The death toll proves devastating. The attack is so stark raving mad that the French general in command orders French artillery to fire on their own troops in a deranged attempt to drive the men forward, deeper into the meat grinder. But the artillery commander refuses to fire without a written order and the assault ends as an unmitigated disaster. The demented general is beside himself, and along with his superior officers, they decide that cowardice runs rampant through the ranks and demand immediate courts-martial. The high command resolves to execute one man from each company. Their reasoning? "One way to maintain discipline is to shoot a man now and then."

What makes *Paths of Glory* so strikingly different from other antiwar films is that the gore and brutality of the battlefield is juxtaposed against the cold and calculating sterility of corporate-like boardrooms populated by old men who habitually send young men off to kill and die. Kubrick underscores the barefaced and chilling business decisions that are made without remorse or contrition. The film and its message are timeless because the madness and psychosis of war, as well as the base reasons why wars are fought, remain the same... the pawns remain the same... and the kings remain the same. Only the dates and the paymasters change.

Some may say, "Hell, it's only a movie. Kubrick, this master manipulator, weaved his own twisted piece of propaganda, his own piece of revisionist history." Well, judging by the reaction of the French government, who banned the film in France until 1975, Kubrick was dead solid perfect with his evaluation and ultimate indictment of the deceit, hubris, and fear that has unfailingly fueled all war machines since time immemorial.

Pawns, indeed. Like feeding bodies into a wood-chipper. Millions upon millions upon millions upon millions... and the beat goes on. World War I was a bloodthirsty fiasco, as are all wars—the ultimate expression of human failure. For the American Empire, there was a chance to possibly sidestep this particular meat grinder, but alas the ghosts of Manifest Destiny, that goddamn city on a hill, the feel-good expansionist years of the American Holocaust, as well as the economic success of American slavery (aka three hundred years of outright terrorism), welled up in Woodrow Wilson's chest and presented itself in a bizarrely naïve notion of waging war to end war. In fact, this crazed notion by the godhead

Wilson was the uninspired forerunner of the equally insane American notion in Vietnam: *you must burn the village in order to save it.*

Are we surprised by Wilson's twofold failure—a historic gaffe energized by gullibility and theophany? Hardly, especially after you factor in his White House sessions with psychic and clairvoyant Edgar Cayce.[99] Mysticism, medieval religious fervor, and flag-waving "last refuge of a scoundrel" patriotism all rolled into another imperial adventure. Wilson, like so many other so-called leaders before him and after, believed he was an oracle envisioning his own private new world order. What delusion to think that through vicious war and economic plunder he would achieve lasting peace? Wilson forgot about, didn't care, or possibly didn't know German philosopher Walter Benjamin's denunciation of his folly (and all others like it): "There is no document of civilization which is not at the same time a document of barbarism."

In a mere 88 minutes, *Paths of Glory* slices and dices all of this and more. If we had one wish it would be to tie every living American president, ex-president, senator, congressman, medal-wearing Pentagon stooge, as well as anyone associated with the war machine—including the SOBs who build, order, and deliver the death toys—to a steel chair in a dark room. The room is empty except for these items: one of the abovementioned bastards is duct-taped to the chair… right in his or her face is a giant flat-screen television flanked by two monster JBL speakers turned up to eleven… their heads are locked into a contraption that ensures their eyes never budge from the screen (yes, just like Kubrick's other dagger *A Clockwork Orange*). Eddie the engineer blows a deafening boat horn and then hits play on the BluRay machine. Multiple viewings may be required.

In Kubrick's masterful celluloid work, Colonel Dax, portrayed with righteous fury by Kirk Douglas, addresses the brass:

> *"Gentlemen of the court, there are times that I'm ashamed to be a member of the human race and this is one such occasion."*

Yeah.

2 The War After the War to End All Wars

Just so you know, we're about to tread on some legendary terrain. An American protectorate that is holy, sacred, anointed, and glory be to God sanctified.

This terrain is also a state of mind emblematic of what novelist Philip Roth deemed the "American Pastoral." It is, of course, the sanctity that renders this seemingly serene and unquestioned territory a danger zone where body armor is required, especially for the non-believers, those heathens who refuse to swallow the dogma sheltered on this consecrated island—a bucolic kingdom protected by the high priests of propaganda, backed to the max by their chieftains gazing down from high atop Corporate HQ. To the heathen this land of milk and honey is a fetid swamp.

It's also a landscape replete with short-tempered land mines designed to detonate under the feet of any loony tunes stranger who has the audacity to question the unquestionable—the gospel that rests cosseted beneath this hallowed ground—and that is to interrogate the absolute veracity of the 11th Commandment: that World War II was the good war, the people's war, or the war that simply could not be avoided.

Well, don your helmets and slip on your Kevlar®, we're gonna take on World War II.

Triumph of the Will
~meets~
Saving Private Ryan

In 1935, German cinema screens lit up with the words *Triumph des Willens*—translated to the King's English: Triumph of the Will, "produced by order of the Führer."

In the opening shots of this classic propaganda film, Adolf Hitler's plane floats through heavenly peace on its way back to Nuremberg where he was to preside over a military display. "Twenty years after the outbreak of World War… sixteen years after the start of the German suffering… nineteen months after the start of Germany's rebirth… Adolf Hitler flew again to Nuremberg to review the columns of his faithful followers…" So begins Leni Riefenstahl's narrative of the God-like leader's arrival to an adoring and loving populace, his plane appearing as a cruciform over the city, soaring past cathedral spires pointing skyward—to paradise. And below, his devoted subjects anxiously and obediently await his much anticipated arrival. It's a ridiculous and embarrassingly silly display of manipulation. Church bells ring throughout the entire film as the narrative paints a messianic vision of the very righteous Führer ready to lead the Homeland to glory, to triumph.

The Nazi monster machine was ready to roll.

"This is the plot of Shane, *Triumph of the Will*, Saving Private Ryan and practically every western every made," writes Justin Lewis-Anthony, Rector of St. Stephen's Church in Canterbury. "It is the founding myth of our politics and our society. It tells us that violence works, and that leadership only comes from the imposition of a superman's will upon the masses, and preferably those masses 'out there,' not us."[1]

Historian Howard Zinn builds on this sentiment through a personal recollection of seeing the film:

> I watched Private Ryan's extraordinarily photographed battle scenes, and I was thoroughly taken in. But when the movie was over, I realized that it was exactly that—I had been taken in. And I disliked the film intensely. I was angry at it because I did not want the suffering of men in war to be used—yes, exploited—in such a way as to revive what should be buried along with all those bodies in Arlington Cemetery: the glory of military heroism.[2]

As so-called American Century came to a close, one of the great hustles of American propaganda was hoisted on the American people by the Hollywood myth-making machine, orchestrated by one of its chief mythmakers Steven Spielberg, whose films regularly reinforce the white, suburban, comfortable status quo. After all, that's who Spielberg is—a conservative filmmaker hell-bent on protecting the hopes and dreams of Baby Boomers without ever suggesting that their comfort is bought and protected by the poverty and pain of those who find themselves on the wrong end of empire and its never-ending thirst for capital. *Saving Private Ryan* is what happens when an amusement park mentality is at the creative trigger of a narrative depicting a very complex reality.

Born in 1946, Spielberg experienced two and half 1950s and then leapfrogged into 1975, selling Americans (and the world) on ridiculous fish stories, aliens eating candy, and then a tale of the Marlboro Man beating the Nazis to the Ark of the Covenant. Clearly from studying his box office success, which seems to be his true motivation, the man who would cement America's munificence in the good, noble, and righteous World War of Rosie the Riveter was never influenced by the carnage of Vietnam—a "bad" war that happened right under his nose during his most formative years. *Saving Private Ryan* was made by a propagandist who views the BIG ONE, WWII, not through the dark prism of Vietnam but rather through feel-good fairytales like *God is my Co-Pilot*, *Twelve O'Clock High*, and Frank Capra's overt indoctrination series *Why We Fight*. In fact, Capra, working closely with U.S. Military guru George C. Marshall, took umbrage when his work was characterized as "propaganda," similar to the work produced by his German and Japanese counterparts. Instead Capra considered his Why We Fight series as "informational films" explaining why the boys are, in fact, in uniform. Zinn continues:

> "The greatest war movie ever made," the film critics say
> about Saving Private Ryan. They are a disappointing lot,
> the film critics. They are excited, even exultant, about the
> brilliant cinematography, depicting the bloody chaos of the
> Omaha Beach landing. But they are pitifully superficial.[3]

More than superficial, they are active participants in the promotion and support of WAR as a viable and constructive answer to solving conflict between people and nations. "The admiring critics of the movie give their own answer to that," explains Zinn, "It is a war movie, they say, not an anti-war movie."

The cheerleaders for this bloodshed and bravado "fail to ask the most important question: Will this film help persuade the next generation that such scenes must never occur again? Will it make clear that we must resist war, even if it is accompanied by the seductive speeches of political leaders saying that this latest war, unlike other bad wars we remember, will be another 'good' one, like World War II?"[4] Human entrails swashing around the shallow Atlantic along with separated limbs, mangled torsos, and severed heads will not stop future generations from embracing war as a solution—especially if Spielberg and his partner in war propaganda, Tom Hanks, have their way. No matter what temporary lesson is absorbed by the masses about the horrors and failure of war, the drumbeat and excitement for new wars can easily be generated by political leaders waxing on patriotically about eliminating demons (or "the Other"). This is followed by instilling the necessary dose of fear—and then all of it is sold and solidified by the sycophantic media and the so-called Hollywood liberal establishment (a right-wing manufactured myth about the entertainment industry that's so misguided and ill-defined as to be drop dead laughable).

Christ on a Stick

Spielberg's infomercial is so chock-full of Christian imagery that it borders on an outright Crusade, beginning with the sea of crosses engulfing the returning veteran "Ryan" in the Normandy American Cemetery and Memorial overlooking Omaha Beach and continues right through to the decisive battle where Hanks' squad fights from a steeple high atop a church, picking off Nazis. The great actor, Barry Pepper, as Private Jackson, audibly prays before pulling the trigger:

> My goodness, and my fortress; my high tower, and my
> deliverer; my shield, and He in whom I trust. *BANG.*

Now, staring down the scope of his rifle before another kill:

> O my God, I trust in thee: let me not be ashamed, let not my
> enemies triumph over me. *BANG.*

Throughout the film, moments of Christian iconography, including the kissing of cross necklaces, remind us of a compassionate and caring God just moments before someone is iced or does the icing.

The powerful manipulation continues in the film as Spielberg opens the crypt and rolls out Abraham Lincoln and his dusty old (dare we say empty) words to the mother of five dead sons during the Civil War who "died gloriously on the field of battle." The venerable character actor, Harve Presnell, portraying General George C. Marshall, delivers Lincoln's earlier attempt at absurdist dark comedy in a letter to Private Ryan's mother informing her that her son is coming home safe. Lincoln's words, as narrated by Presnell, play over the astonished and stunned matinee kisser of Matt Damon (Private Ryan) as he gazes down in awe at the hero Hanks who saved his life:

> "I pray that our Heavenly Father may assuage the anguish of your bereavement, and leave you only the cherished memory of the loved and lost, and the solemn pride that must be yours to have laid so costly a sacrifice upon the alter of freedom. Abraham Lincoln." Yours very sincerely and respectfully, George C. Marshall, General, Chief of Staff.

Private Ryan, in typical Spielberg fashion, now becomes the personal manifestation of a grateful and indebted nation—symbolism 101.

Ultimately, the film is a prayer, an intercession on behalf of simpler times when America resembled the nostalgic order of a Rockwell painting and not the chaos expressed in the tempest of Jackson Pollock. In fact, Saving Private Ryan is a veiled critique of an American society that Spielberg and Hanks believe has fallen from grace and neglected the courage and patriotic zeal necessary to protect the greatness of a great nation. Spielberg's mythmaking goes to enormous lengths to dispel the harsh realities and severe lessons of his generation, the Vietnam generation, who learned all too well that war is brutality, that war is state-sponsored terrorism, that war is mass murder, and finally, that war is the ultimate expression of collapse between living beings. *War is not Thirty Seconds Over Tokyo*, rather it's *All Quiet on the Western Front*. War is not Stephen Ambrose's *The Wild Blue*, rather it's Dalton Trumbo's *Johnny Got His Gun*.

Even those who concede that war is hell will say that some wars are good and just wars and World War II—according to Steven Spielberg and apparently Jesus—was one of those wars, despite what Mr. Franklin of Philadelphia once said: "There never was a good war, or a bad peace."

In his extraordinary rebuke of Spielberg's party line ("Private Ryan Saves War"), Zinn concludes:

> The audience is left with no choice but to conclude that this one [WWII]—while it causes sorrow to a million mothers—is in

a good cause. Yes, getting rid of fascism was a good cause. But does that unquestionably make it a good war? The war corrupted us, did it not? The hate it engendered was not confined to Nazis. We put Japanese families in concentration camps. We killed huge numbers of innocent people—the word "atrocity" fits— in our bombings of Dresden, Hamburg, Tokyo, and finally Hiroshima and Nagasaki. And when the war ended, we and our Allies began preparing for another war, this time with nuclear weapons, which, if used, would make Hitler's Holocaust look puny.

We can argue endlessly over whether there was an alternative in the short run, whether fascism could have been resisted without fifty million dead. But the long-term effect of World War II on our thinking was pernicious and deep. It made war—so thoroughly discredited by the senseless slaughter of World War I— noble once again. It enabled political leaders—whatever miserable adventure they would take us into, whatever mayhem they would wreak on other people (two million dead in Korea, at least that many in Southeast Asia, hundreds of thousands in Iraq) and on our own—to invoke World War II as a model.

Communism supplanted Nazism as a reason for war, and when we could no longer point to Communism as a threat, a convenient enemy, like Saddam Hussein, could be compared to Hitler. Our leaders used glib analogies to justify immense suffering. The presumed absolute goodness of World War II created an aura of rightness around war itself.[5]

Blowback in Deutschland

As is always the case with armed conflict, the seeds of aggression are planted long before the rallying cry and long before the first shots are ever fired. This was clearly the case regarding the rise of fascism in Germany and the subsequent hostilities of World War II, which began years prior to Hitler's September 1939 march into Poland and the December 1941 Japanese attack on Hawaii—America's colony in the Pacific.

In actuality, in Europe, World War II began with the World War I armistice in 1919 and the subsequent Treaty of Versailles, which placed the full blame and responsibility for the war squarely on Germany along with Austria-Hungary. The treaty called for severe political sanctions as well as heavy-duty war reparations against Germany. Treaty Article 232 demanded Germany pay "compensation for all damage done to the civilian population of the Allied and Associated Powers and to their property during the period of the belligerency." This amounted to approximately $63 billion (later reduced to $33 billion, about $402 billion today). The last payment was made, believe it or not, in 2010.[6] The treaty also forced Germany to relinquish large parcels of land and to surrender its colonies. Further, the German army was limited to 100,000 personnel.

From the outset, many critics of the treaty—including German citizens and politicians across the political spectrum—were up in arms over what they believed to be ruthless demands by the Allies, demands designed to further destroy Germany. In fact, German Chancellor Philipp Scheidemann resigned rather than sign the take-it-or-leave-it document. Believing that Woodrow Wilson's more constructive "Fourteen Points" would actually dictate the terms, many Germans also felt betrayed. Caught between a diplomatic rock and a hard place—and with no military force to resist the stranglehold—the new Weimar Republic (soon to be the German Reich) signed the treaty.

With what the Germans viewed as an unyielding, austere, and cruel treaty in force, super-inflation wrecked the German economy. Other variants contributed to the collapse (strikes, work slowdowns, as well as passive resistance by the German government), but ultimately it was the weight of economic sanctions and war reparations that tore the German economy apart.

Historians and economists have argued the "fairness" of the treaty for decades, but British economist John Maynard Keynes, who attended the Versailles Conference as a delegate (and resigned in frustration), strongly advocated for a more generous peace that would not penalize Germany so harshly. In fact, Keynes hoped the treaty would support economic recovery throughout all of Europe. Keynes, one of the most influential economists of his century, wrote the original fundamental analysis entitled *The Economic Consequences of the Peace*. This work, based on Keynes' first-hand experiences and insight, suggested that the Treaty of Versailles was a "Carthaginian" peace—one that forced a merciless and punitive "peace" on Germany by further devastating the beaten foe. The spiral down and failure of the Weimar Republic through the 1920s and into the early 1930s was finally rendered complete by the onset of the Great Depression.

But regardless of the changing and contradictory examinations surrounding the Treaty of Versailles and its ultimate impact on devastating German society, the bitterness and antipathy triggered by the Allies' hammerlock created fertile psychological ground for the rise of the demagogue Hitler and his monstrous Nazi engine. The German people were ripe and ready for a nationalistic trance. Add fear, vengeance, and powerful (yet dangerous) messages like Riefenstahl's *Triumph of the Will*, and it's not hard to see how Nazi Germany was born and bred. #MakeGermanyGreatAgain.

But could the so-called "unavoidable war" actually have been avoided? Not if you listen to the guild historians or the binary claptrap of America's right-or-wrong drum beaters. But, if you consider those viewing history through the lens of historical analysis rather than red, white, and blue blinders—those who consider war an utter and complete failure of human creative thought and compassion—then yes, the possibility existed. Antiwar activist David Swanson, author of the courageous and much-needed tome, *War is a Lie*, strongly argues that it could have been avoided, or at the very least delayed, to give the possibility of a negotiated settlement a fighting chance. But many, like Winston Churchill, were chomping at the bit. Swanson writes:

> In 1939, when Italy tried to open negotiations with Britain
> on behalf of Germany, Churchill shut them down cold: "If
> Ciano realizes (sic) our inflexible purpose he will be less likely
> to toy with the idea of an Italian mediation." Churchill's inflexible
> purpose was to go to war.[7]

Like the marionette George W. Bush decades later, and the blustery gasbag Lyndon Baines Johnson before him, *war WAS the goal, war WAS the desire*. The empty attempts to allegedly avoid war were nothing more than theatrical embroidery to give the illusion of trying. Swanson continues:

> Of course, Hitler was not particularly trustworthy. But what
> if the Jews had been spared, Poland had been occupied, and
> peace had been maintained between the Allies and Germany
> for some minutes, hours, days, weeks, months, or years? The
> war could have begun whenever it began, with no harm done
> and some moments of peace gained. And every moment of peace
> could have been used to negotiate a more permanent peace, as well
> as independence for Poland.[8]

As we know, Britain's Lord Halifax and Neville Chamberlain were advocating peace with Germany in 1940. Churchill again said no. Shortly thereafter, in a public speech, Hitler again proposed peace with the Allies. Churchill once again said "Nope."

Clearly, Winnie the British Bulldog wanted war. His entire career is littered with gruesome examples of the use of violence and slaughter as a way to maintain Britain's control and dominion over, well, over just about everybody. Starting as a young Member of Parliament, Churchill "charged through imperial atrocities... based on his belief that 'the Aryan stock is bound to triumph.'"[9] Winnie's resume reads more like Attila the Hun's rather than the false historic narrative of Churchill as diplomatic orator and seeker of peace that surrounds this western icon. In the 1920s, when Churchill was Britain's Colonial Secretary and the Kurds rebelled against British rule, he supported the horrors of chemical terror: "I am strongly in favour of using poisoned gas against uncivilised tribes... [It] would spread a lively terror."[10] Shortly thereafter, Britain used mustard gas against the Kurds.[11]

In December of 1900, at New York's Waldorf-Astoria, Churchill—then a war correspondent—was introduced by none other than Mark Twain, who in the great Twain tradition, cloaked his skewering of the young Churchill in a clever and devious way, as reported by *The New York Times*:

> The lecture began at 8:30, Samuel L. Clemens (Mark Twain)
> being in the chair. Mr. Clemens, introducing the speaker, said
> Mr. Churchill knew all about war and nothing about peace.
> War might be very interesting to persons who like that sort of
> entertainment, but he had never enjoyed it himself. During
> the civil war [Twain] remembered visiting a battlefield once,
> but he had never felt comfortable there. One cannot carry an
> umbrella when it rains, for when shells are flying they might get
> tangled up with the umbrella.[12]

The *Times* went on to report Twain's wrap up: "England and America were kin in almost everything; now they are kin in sin." A century later, journalist Johann Hari reports in the UK's *The Independent*, Churchill's thoughts on peace as an alternative to war and it seems Twain's dagger to the heart was spot on:

> When Mahatma Gandhi launched his campaign of peaceful
> resistance, Churchill raged that he "ought to be lain bound
> hand and foot at the gates of Delhi, and then trampled on by
> an enormous elephant with the new Viceroy seated on its back."

As the resistance swelled, he announced: "I hate Indians. They are a beastly people with a beastly religion."[13]

From the moment Churchill left the Royal Military College (Sandhurst), he was looking to brawl. "All his life he was most excited—on the evidence, only really excited—by war," writes historian Ralph Raico. "He loved war as few modern men ever have—he even 'loved the bangs,' as he called them."[14]

In an article for *The New York Times*, Richard Burton expressed his visceral thoughts about portraying Winston Churchill in a television film. The seven-time Oscar nominee wrote:

> In the course of preparing myself... I realized afresh that I
> hate Churchill and all of his kind. I hate them virulently. They
> have stalked down the corridors of endless power all through
> history... What man of sanity would say on hearing of the atrocities
> committed by the Japanese against British and Anzac prisoners of
> war, "We shall wipe them out, every one of them, men, women, and
> children. There shall not be a Japanese left on the face of the earth."
> Such simple-minded cravings for revenge leave me with a horrified
> but reluctant awe for such single-minded and merciless ferocity.[15]

But the abovementioned snapshots of Churchill's career are a mere sampling of his violent political motivations. (Shortly, Sir Winston will burst back into these pages as we discuss the saturation firebombing of Dresden, sanctioned by Churchill in February of 1945, murdering thousands upon thousands of Germans, mostly civilians.[16]) This war-lusty point man made decisions that led to absolute brutality, an inferno that cost between 60 and 70 million lives—the deadliest military abortion in history.

This is not to minimize the inherent malignancy and dangerous growth of Nazism and, of course, the moral insanity that was Adolf Hitler and his devout followers, rather this narrative underscores the age-old lesson that violence begets violence, war begets war. The cycle continues as one thug recognizes a worse thug and engages battle—and in the crosshairs we find millions upon millions of lives—or, more appropriately, corpses. "Whenever you peer too closely at the goals and conduct of the 'good war,'" Swanson reminds us, "that's what you tend to see: Churchillian eagerness to exterminate enemies en masse."[17] Swanson concludes:

World War II killed 70 million people, and that sort of outcome could be more or less foreseen. What did we imagine was worse than that? Who knows? What we do know is the unmatchable horror of what did happen.[18]

The Neophyte Empire Sets the Stage for War in the Pacific

I wish to see the United States the dominant power on the shores of the Pacific Ocean.
> —Theodore Roosevelt, 1900[19]

Clearly, Mr. Roosevelt, the 26th President of the United States, with visions of empire dancing in his head, understood the importance of the vast Pacific Rim when it came to geo-political control and empire building. "Our future history," Roosevelt declared, "will be more determined by our position on the Pacific facing China than by our position on the Atlantic facing Europe."[20]

History books and the professed official narrative of America's imperial escapades throughout the Pacific bubble will not indicate in much detail the actions and deeds of Teddy Roosevelt and his sidekick William Howard Taft. You sure as hell won't find it in a milquetoast Ken Burns' documentary. Historian James Bradley dramatically documented the wicked kickoff to America's relationships throughout Asia during the 20th century with the 1905 diplomatic cruise that sailed through all the exotic hot spots: Honolulu, Manila, Tokyo, Beijing, Seoul, and more. Bradley titled it *The Imperial Cruise*. It was a diplomatic journey that set the unholy groundwork for TR's enabling of Japan's imperial aims that planted the roots for the Second World War and beyond. Bradley writes, "...behind [Roosevelt's] whispers that critical summer of 1905 was a very big stick—the bruises from which would catalyze World War II in the Pacific, the Chinese Communist Revolution, the Korean War, and an array of tensions that inform our lives today."[21]

During the Seoul portion of this diabolical cruise, Teddy's daughter Alice toasted the Korean leaders who had recently opened their closed and secretive country to the U.S., signing treaties and warmly interacting with their new western friends—leaders who referred to America as an "Elder Brother," leaders who were told that America would firmly back them from aggressive Asian powers, leaders who trusted their new American allies.[22] These were also leaders who should have first consulted with American Indians, who knew a thing or two about treaties and agreements with the United States government. The Korean leaders "had no idea that back in Washington, Roosevelt often said, 'I should like to see Japan have Korea.'"[23]

Just weeks later, Japanese troops moved into Korea and according to a top American diplomat in Seoul, the U.S. escaped Korea "like a stampede of rats from a sinking ship."[24] Bradley writes:

> America would be the first country to recognize Japanese control over Korea, and when Emperor Gojong's emissaries pleaded with the president to stop the Japanese, Teddy coldly informed the stunned Koreans that, as they were now part of Japan, they'd have to route their appeals through Tokyo. With this betrayal, Roosevelt had green-lighted Japanese imperialism on the Asian continent. *Decades later, another Roosevelt would be forced to deal with the bloody ramifications of Teddy's secret maneuvering.* [25][Emphasis added]

Provocateurs

Four decades later, the other Roosevelt to which Bradley refers, had this to say:

> Yesterday, December 7, 1941—a date which will live in infamy—the United States of America was suddenly and deliberately attacked by naval and air forces of the Empire of Japan.

If we were to poll the average American regarding the Japanese Empire's attack on America's distant Pacific naval outpost at Pearl Harbor in the early morning hours of 7 December 1941, it would be described as an abrupt and unprovoked act by madmen who arbitrarily woke up one morning about a week before the assault and decided to destroy the U.S. Pacific Fleet in one sudden burst of immorality. "Immoral it was," writes Howard Zinn, "like any bombing—but not really sudden or shocking to the American government."[26]

FDR's dramatic opening line to a joint session of Congress was technically correct—but oh so deceptive and historically misleading. Among countless other historians and critics who have strenuously challenged the simplistic yarn of Japan's unprovoked actions over Hawaii is Yale University professor Bruce Russett. In his classic book, *No Clear and Present Danger*, Russett explains:

> The evidence, however, shows quite a different picture both of intent and capability. Nor is it enough simply to assert that, because

Japan attacked the United States at Pearl Harbor, America took no action to begin hostilities.[27]

Gore Vidal remembers—as he was apt to do in gloriously biting language—the trigger of war with Japan:

> As a member of The Greatest American Generation, I served in the Pacific Theater of Operations in World War II where one was marinated in propaganda about the essential subhuman bestiality of the Japanese, a savage race who *for no reason whatsoever* took time off from their reasonably successful conquest of mainland Asia to sink, almost idly one Sunday morning, the American fleet based at Pearl Harbor. Why? No reason was ever given us, the innocent victims, other than we were ever so *good* and they were ever so *bad*.[28]

Vidal, at the time, writing in *The New York Review of Books* from his home in Ravello, Italy, also reminds us of the gross manipulation of history by "court historians" wiping the slate clean:

> Although Charles A. Beard, our leading historian in those far-off days, wrote *President Roosevelt and the Coming of War, 1941* (1948), in which he made the case that the Japanese attack was the result of a series of deliberate provocations by FDR, he promptly underwent erasure at the hands of the court historians in place, as always, to demonstrate that what ought not to be true is not true.[29]

Like most auspicious and timely flashpoints in America's long history of making war (i.e. James Polk using "Thornton's Defeat" in 1846 to justify the United States' invasion of Mexico; Lyndon Johnson using the 1964 "Gulf of Tonkin incident" to justify the official onslaught in Southeast Asia; and George W. Bush using the "9-11 attacks" to justify the invasion and destruction of Iraq, which has spread like a poisonous algae bloom into the perpetual, so-called, war on terror), Franklin Roosevelt seized the opportunity to take his itchy administration somersaulting into World War II.

Author and decorated U.S. Naval photographer Robert Stinnett (who served under Lt. George Bush in WWII), spent 17 years investigating the lead-up to the attack on Pearl Harbor—an attack that plunged the emergent American Empire into World War II. His research and exposure of U.S. government documents released under the Freedom of Information Act—much of it damning—paint an odious and manipulative picture regarding the provocation of war with Japan.

> Despite his pleadings and persuasions, powerful isolationist forces prevented Roosevelt from getting into the European war. Roosevelt's advisors included patriots such as General George Marshall, Rear Admiral Walter S. Anderson, and Commander Arthur H. McCollum who understood the need to arouse the United States from its isolationist position.[30]

Stinnett writes that Roosevelt's "fingerprints" are found everywhere on Commander McCollum's 1940 memo advocating eight actions that would drive Japan into an attack on the United States. Stinnett stresses that throughout 1941, "provoking Japan into an overt act of war was the principal policy" fueling Roosevelt's ongoing actions.[31] In fact, communiqués sent to Pacific commanders contained the directive "overt act." Stinnett writes:

> Roosevelt's cabinet members, most notably Secretary of War Harry Stimson, are on record favoring the policy, according to Stimson's diary. Stimson's diary entries of 1941 place him with nine other Americans who knew or were associated with this policy of provocation during 1941.[32]

One of McCollum's actions seemed to be FDR's favorite, one he called "pop-up cruises"—the calculated placement of American warships "within or adjacent to the territorial waters of Japan."[33] At a secret White House meeting, the 32nd President from Hyde Park, New York, quipped:

> I just want them to keep popping up here and there and keep the Japs guessing. I don't mind losing one or two cruisers, but do not take a chance on losing five or six.[34]

"I don't mind losing one or two cruisers." Besides the naval hardware, apparently FDR didn't mind using the American sailors on board those cruisers as expendable cannon fodder in his "Marco Polo-like" war games with the "Japs." But we'll never know for sure since they didn't seem to be on his mind anyway at the time. Maybe that's harsh, maybe in his quiet moments when he rolled himself out to the White House Rose Garden, FDR prayed fervently for their souls… Nah.

In his book, *Dreaming War*, Gore Vidal agrees that Roosevelt consciously provoked the Japanese. Vidal answers the all-important question: Why? "He wanted us in the war against Hitler, but 80 percent of the American people wanted no European war of any kind after the disappointments of 1917. He could do nothing to budge an isolationist electorate."[35]

Stinnett reports that the Pacific fleet commander, Admiral Husband Kimmel, objected to sending cruisers into the region: "It is ill-advised and will result in war if we make this move."[36] The admiral got that right. But the all-important question remains: why did Japan wipe out a U.S. naval base? Professor Bruce Russett—who also edited the Journal of Conflict Resolution from 1972 through 2009—decided to actually dissect the historical markers leading up to Japan's violent actions rather than embrace jingoistic platitudes.

> The Japanese attack would not have come but for the American, British, and Dutch embargo on shipments of strategic raw materials to Japan. Japan's strike against the American naval base merely climaxed a long series of mutually antagonistic acts. *In initiating economic sanctions against Japan the United States undertook actions that were widely recognized in Washington as carrying grave risk of war.*[37] [Emphasis added]

What Prompted Japan's Imperial Conduct?

There were two main motives that prompted their aggression. First, general expansion; Japan was a tiny island empire with a rapidly growing population—one that needed more room and infinitely more raw materials for its existence. Second was Japan's desire to achieve the status of a major player on the world's stage, a player who could strenuously compete with western powers—especially the Soviet Union, who were making their Asiatic imperial ambitions well known.

But throughout the decades leading up to Japan's attack on Pearl Harbor, U.S. policymakers took little issue with Japan's machinations and abuse of China as well as their ongoing intrigues across most of the Asian mainland. Howard Zinn stresses that, "So long as Japan remained a well-behaved member of that imperial club of Great Powers who—in keeping with the Open Door Policy—were sharing the exploitation of China, the United States did not object."[38] In fact, during the first quarter of the 20th century, the United States passively condoned Japan's aggressive economic and oftentimes violent political posture with the Chinese.

American diplomats in China even "supported the coming of Japanese troops."[39]

One of the earliest and strongest U.S. provocations aimed at Japan was "FDR's famous Chicago address (October 5, 1937)," writes Vidal, "asking for a quarantine against aggressor nations." He concludes wryly, of course never forgetting the not-too-distant past: "Certainly, Japan in Manchuria and north China qualified as an aggressor just as we had been one when we conquered the Philippines and moved into the Japanese neighborhood at the start of the twentieth century."[40] But it wasn't until the Japanese "threatened potential U.S. markets by its attempted takeover of China"[41] that the U.S. started to play hardball, as evidenced in 1939 when Washington terminated the long-standing 1911 commercial treaty in force with Japan.

Staying with Vidal's abovementioned baseball metaphor, the U.S. continued the hardball approach and went headhunting with bean-balls as Japan—desperate for natural resources and raw materials depleted by their long, entrenched war with China—turned their attention south, coveting all the tin, nickel, and rubber in British Malaya, oil in the Dutch East Indies, and rice in Thailand. Japanese leaders knew full well that their expansion into Southeast Asia risked a military war with Washington since the U.S. itself depended on Indochina for massive amounts of materials and resources.[42]

The game escalated. In 1940, FDR signed the Export Control Act, used to prohibit usual exports to Japan of necessary melting irons, scrap iron, aviation and motor fuels, as well as other essentials. Then at the end of July 1941, the Roosevelt administration froze Japanese assets in the United States and halted oil exports, which for all intents and purposes ended commercial relations between both countries. Gore Vidal writes, "When Undersecretary of State Sumner Welles was asked by the Japanese if some compromise might be worked out, Welles said there was not the 'slightest ground for any compromise solution.'"[43] That same summer the U.S. tightened their embargo on Japan and was followed by the Dutch and British, who embargoed exports from their colonies in the South Pacific.

"In large part," Russett explains, "[the U.S.] decided that Japanese ambitions in China posed a long-term threat to American interests, and so they forced a confrontation."[44] The mounting pressure applied by FDR, along with his inner circle, pushed the Pacific nation to the brink of retaliatory war with the U.S. This was July of 1941, only months before Pearl Harbor. But as we've outlined above, the relationship between the U.S. and Japanese empires was deteriorating for some time, dating precariously back to the infamous "Imperial Cruise." Many writers, critics, and historians have cited Franklin Roosevelt's Sinophile tendencies as the root of his antagonism toward Japan (along with the fact that his family benefitted financially from the China trade). "When Franklin D. Roosevelt became president in 1933," writes Robert Higgs, a visiting scholar at Oxford and Stanford Universities and the Editor of *The Independent Review*, "the U.S. government fell under the control of a man who disliked the Japanese and harbored a romantic affection for the Chinese."[45] Gore Vidal concurs and further observes that FDR's administration "was aiding and abetting the Chinese warlord Chiang Kai-shek."[46]

On numerous occasions, Japan offered olive branches, attempting to avert a war with America—a war this small island nation knew they could not win against a vast continental power thousands of miles away, especially after their long-drawn-out and draining battle with China. Japanese Prime Minister, Prince Fumimaro Konoye, looked for cracks in this stalemate to forge a peaceful compromise. Vidal writes:

> Pointedly, FDR refused to meet Konoye, whose government
> was then replaced by that of General Hideki Tojo... In November
> 1941 they made a final attempt at peace. We now know—thanks
> to our having broken the Japanese diplomatic code—the contents
> of Hirohito's in-box. Japan looked for a compromise. We looked
> for war.[47]

Clearly, for both economic and geo-political war strategies, Washington avoided any compromise that would lead to peace. FDR's Secretary of War, Henry Stimson (who also held the same position under the corpulent imperialist and "TR" lackey William Howard Taft), "was a lion of the Anglophile, northeastern upper crust and no friend of the Japanese."[48] Together with Roosevelt and other Washington powerbrokers, they were salivating with desire that Japan would react recklessly to the U.S. provocateurs and attack somewhere and somewhere soon. In fact, Secretary of War Stimson wrote in his diary on 25 November 1941, just twelve days before the attack on Pearl Harbor, "The question was how we should maneuver them into firing the first shot without allowing too much danger to ourselves."[49]

By late 1941, the provocation of war with Japan was clear and it was multi-pronged: it began and continued based on economics but later became the much desired entrée into World War II.

On November 26, Washington offered Japan's ambassadors a list of ultimatums that "concluded... with the following order: 'The government of Japan will withdraw all military, naval, air and police forces from China and Indo-China' as well as renounce the tripartite Axis agreement," writes Gore Vidal. Poetically, he concludes, "It was then, as Lincoln once said on a nobler occasion, the war came."[50]

Yes it came, at 7:48am Hawaiian time. The U.S. Pacific Fleet was destroyed by two waves of fighter and torpedo planes along with bombers, all 353 Japanese planes launched from six aircraft carriers. 2,402 Americans were killed along with nearly 1,300 wounded. Japanese casualties were light. Secretary of War Stimson picked up his diary again after the attack and wrote, "my first feeling was of relief... that a crisis had come in a way which would unite all our people."[51]

Yale historian and political scientist Bruce Russett sums up Japan's final action as a "Hobson's Choice"—the proverbial illusion of choice in which only one alternative is really proffered.

> Having decided against withdrawal from China, failed to
> negotiate a settlement with America, and decided on the
> necessity of seizing supplies from Southeast Asia, they were
> faced with the need to blunt what they regarded as the inevitable
> American response... For all the audacity of the strike at Hawaii,
> its aims were limited; to destroy existing United States offensive
> capabilities in the Pacific by tactical surprise.[52]

Japan wanted to buy time to expand, exploit, and control the Pacific southwest, thereby creating an "impregnable line of defense which could long delay an American counteroffensive and mete out heavy casualties when the counterattack did come."[53] To reiterate: the Japanese hierarchy fully realized they could not fight and win a long and distant war with the Americans. Russett maintains that the Japanese "fully recognized" that attacking Pearl Harbor was a gargantuan risk. In fact "Japanese strategists calculated that America's war potential was seven to eight times greater than their own."[54] Russett's exhaustive research brings him to this conclusion:

> The Japanese attack on Pearl Harbor, and for that matter on
> Southeast Asia, is not evidence of any unlimited expansionist
> policy or capability by the Japanese government. It was the

consequence only of a much less ambitious goal, centering on an unwillingness to surrender the position that the Japanese had fought for years to establish in China. When that refusal met an equal American determination that Japan should give up many of her gains in China, the result was war.[55]

The day after the attack on Pearl Harbor, former U.S. President Herbert Hoover, whose administration was also confronted with the Japanese Empire's aggression throughout Asia—especially China, wrote a personal letter in which he stated:

> You and I know that this continuous putting pins in rattlesnakes finally got this country bitten. We also know that if Japan had been allowed to go on without those trade restrictions and provocations, she would have collapsed from internal economic reasons within a couple of years.[56]

Gore Vidal asks the operative question to those "in denial" that Washington was an agitator:

> Why is it, if we were not on the offensive, that so small and faraway an island as Japan attacked what was so clearly, already, a vast imperial continental power? You have now had over sixty years to come up with a plausible answer. Do tell.[57]

"The United States had to go to enormous lengths," writes *War is a Lie* author David Swanson, "to provoke Japan into attacking it."[58] And the collateral damage, and the murder, began early that Sunday December morning, the murderous exchange continuing on both sides for almost four years, culminating with the firebombing of Tokyo and the greatest war crime ever perpetrated in recorded history—the atomic commercial dropped on Nagasaki and Hiroshima in August of 1945.

War Pigs and their Collateral Damage

Generals gathered in their masses
Just like witches at black masses
Evil minds that plot destruction
Sorcerers of death's construction
In the fields the bodies burning

As the war machine keeps turning
Death and hatred to mankind
Poisoning their brainwashed minds
Oh Lord Yeah!

English heavy metal band Black Sabbath released "War Pigs" in 1970. It was the first song on their album *Paranoid*. As the air raid siren echoes under the grinding Gibson SG of southpaw Tony Iommi, ushering in Ozzie's voice, chills run up and down your spine—if you have even an ounce of feeling in your body. Decades later, American rocker Steve Earle wrote another antiwar song entitled "Rich Man's War." Both of these courageous songs sing out against the massive, heartless, and bloody acts of war that shove our bodies into the human food processor and pour our flesh back into the earth, a woeful libation to an evil god.

Among the many slain that infamous December day in 1941, we found three human beings chopped up and eliminated that Sunday morning, three human beings who represent the tragic result of these plotters' destruction: two soldiers used, abused, and wiped off the face of the earth because corrupt, wealthy, old men in Washington and Tokyo had some business to transact. The third, a child, was caught in the crossfire because, as Steve Earle sings:

Somebody somewhere had another plan. She was...

—— *Nancy Masako Arakaki* ——

a Japanese American, who was attending Sunday school that fateful December morning. Her brother David ran when the bombing started and made it home safely, but Nancy did not, gravely wounded and dead by the time she reached the hospital. She was eight, killed by friendly American fire. Oops. Tragedy continued for the family under the heading, "adding insult to injury." Nancy's father—who owned a trucking company that delivered fresh vegetables to American army bases on the island, was arrested and interned at Camp Honolulu. The U.S. Army thought he might be a spy, but along with his family, he was never charged or officially told why he was held prisoner, interned, and kept in captivity until 1947. Sound familiar? And then when the full war commenced, three of the Arakaki children were trapped in Japan. In 1945, the Arakakis' horror continued still when the United States Air Force firebombed Tokyo with napalm. Nancy's brother Henry was severely burned, spending three excruciating months in a hospital recovering. Earle continues:

— *Frank John Annunziato* —

was born in New York City on 11 January 1922. His father, Venturo, was a fruit dealer born in Italy. His mother, Fannie, also born in Italy, was busy raising Frank, his brother Tony, and six sisters—Matilda, Julia, Susie, Adeline, Rose, and Marie. The Annunziato Family lived at 26 Highland Avenue in Yonkers. Frank attended two years of college and was a shipping and receiving clerk before he enlisted in the United States Navy ("for the duration of the War or other emergency, plus six months, subject to the discretion of the President"). As Seaman First Class, he was stationed on Oahu on the USS Shaw, an American destroyer that became the subject of an iconic photograph of the surprise attack when the forward magazine exploded as the ship sustained multiple bomb hits during the Japanese raid. Frank was in for two months before he died on the USS Shaw. He was just a few weeks short of his twentieth birthday. Frank never returned to Yonkers. He stayed in paradise, buried at the National Memorial Cemetery of the Pacific in Honolulu.

— *Japanese pilot Takeshi Hirano* —

flew his Mitsubishi-built A6M2-type O-model 21 "Zero" in the first wave of Japanese attack planes over Pearl Harbor. At 8:10 that clear morning, just a few minutes after the attack commenced, his plane was shot out of the sky by anti-aircraft fire from the USS Helm and from Fort Kamehameha. Hirano was the wingman to the leader of the first wave escorts, Lieutenant Commander Shigeru Itaya. Their mission was to strafe Hickam Field and the Ewa Marine Corps Air Station. "AI-154" crashed into Building 52 at Fort Kam. Japanese Naval Air Pilot First Class Takeshi Hirano was killed along with four U.S. servicemen taking cover behind the building: Cpl. Claude Bryant, Pvt. Eugene Bubb, Pvt. Donat George Duquette, Jr., and Pfc. Oreste DeTorre. American servicemen in the area immediately stripped the fighter plane of souvenirs, including Hirano's pistol. The Japanese pilot was taken to the Fort Shafter morgue and he was buried two days later at Scofield Barracks Cemetery.

Look the Other Way

One of the great chapters in the annals of "the myth and reality of American history" is that persistent myth that America's involvement in World War II was primarily to save the Jewish people from extermination at the hands of the Nazi meat grinder and Adolf Hitler. Once again, antiwar activist David Swanson offers the facts and the boldness to declare World War II unnecessary and misbegotten. In fact, Swanson considers all wars not just unnecessary but criminal. "The most sacred and unquestionable war in U.S. history," writes Swanson, "is World War II... justified because of the degree of evilness of Adolf Hitler, and the evilness is to be found above all in the holocaust...

> But you won't find any recruitment posters of Uncle Sam saying "I Want You... to Save the Jews."[59]

From 1933 until the very early 1940s, the Nazi government was determined to ensure that Germany was "Judenrein"—or cleansed of Jews. The general "spirit" of their plan was to make life so unbearable for the more than 600,000 German Jews that the population would flee the country.[60]

In 1934, when a resolution was proposed in the United States Senate denouncing Germany's treatment of the Jews—a resolution noting "surprise and pain" at Germany's actions (the resolution also strongly suggesting that Germany restore all rights), the U.S. State Department disregarded the clarion call and ensured that the resolution would "be buried in committee."[61] America was the obvious asylum for an oppressed people to look toward for relief, a beacon shining in the dark—the land of the free and home of the brave. Well, not for the Jews, in the year of our Lord, 1938. "Tens of thousands of Jews sought to enter the United States," reports the Simon Wiesenthal Center, "but they were barred from doing so by the stringent American immigration policy. Even the relatively small quotas of visas which existed were often not filled."[62] In fact, this stringent policy can be traced back to 1924 when the United States Congress implemented legislation that greatly limited immigration "and discriminated against groups considered racially and ethnically undesirable."[63]

Numerous plans existed to move a large segment of the Jewish population out of Germany in the late 1930s. Poland and Germany drafted plans to move significant numbers of Jews to Madagascar—at the time a French colony. The Dominican Republic also offered their country as a sanctuary for refugees. In

1938, reacting to increasing domestic and world pressure, FDR organized an international conference to theoretically work on the growing Jewish refugee issue. More than thirty countries gathered in Evian, France on Lake Geneva. (As a harbinger of things to come, "Evian" is "naïve" spelled backwards.) But FDR's conference turned out to be little more than a bone tossed to the barking dogs that demanded action. Historian Ronnie Landau, in his book *The Nazi Holocaust*, frames the Evian Conference:

> The conference was held ostensibly to address the plight of Jewish refugees from persecution. However, as an internal American State Department memorandum declared, the purpose of this American initiative was "to get out in front [of liberal opinion] and attempt to guide the pressure [to increase Jewish immigration] primarily with a view of forestalling attempts to have the immigration laws liberalized."[64]

Historian Arthur Morse, author of *While Six Million Died: A Chronicle of American Apathy*, concurs:

> On this noble note the Evian Conference was born. It would be months in planning, would silence the critics of apathy and, if all worked well, would divert refugees from the United States to the other co-operating nations.[65]

Making his disdain and utter hatred of the Jews readily apparent, the Führer also chimed in regarding the necessity of the conference to take the Jews—or else.

> I can only hope and expect that the other world, which has such deep sympathy for these criminals, will at least be generous enough to convert this sympathy into practical aid. We, on our part, are ready to put these criminals at the disposal of these countries, for all I care, even on luxury ships.[66]

By the end of the conference, the obvious inaction by every, dare we say, cowardly and anti-Semitic country (except the Dominican Republic), proved that the entire exercise was a sham, more public relations than earnest intent. The utter failure of these world leaders—especially the U.S. and Great Britain—offered the suffering Jewish people no safe haven, paving the way for Hitler's diabolical "Final Solution"—the horrific extermination of more than six million human beings, or as holocaust survivor Abel Herzberg so candidly said:

There were not six million Jews murdered; there was one
murder, six million times.[67]

Landau sums up the gross failure of the conference and places the lion's share of
the blame at the feet of the United States, citing its "unwillingness to alter its own
immigration policy," which "sent an unmistakable message to the other nations
assembled at Evian."[68] Landau quotes historical sociologist Helen Fein, author of
extensive works on human rights and genocide:

> Interested and disinterested spectators alike saw the Evian
> Conference as an exercise in Anglo-American collaborative
> hypocrisy.[69]

Fein also argues that policymakers in the U.S. State Department as well as
the British Foreign Office were "anti-Semitic and/or anxious to disavow Nazi
allegations about Jewish influence and to deny any positive identification with
the Jews."[70] Fein makes clear the blown opportunity:

> The western world had been given a prolonged opportunity to
> help the Jews evade victimization before the Holocaust when
> Germany's policy was to expel, not exterminate, German Jews;
> nation after nation refused to alter their immigration policy.[71]

**It was a cumulative and collective failure. The press was ultimately as
culpable as the government.**
—Professor Deborah Lipstadt

One might ask: *Where the hell was the press? Why weren't they acting as a beacon,
rallying a chorus of vehement outrage from citizens everywhere?* These obvious
questions must be asked. Indeed, how could a worldwide cadre of scribes—many
investigative in nature—miss the lead-up to the extermination of six million
people and then miss the preponderance of the actual extermination? In some
instances it was a case of under-reporting or under-estimating the seriousness of
the situation throughout Europe.

Reporting on the build-up to Hitler's "Final Solution" as well as the genocidal years
of the early 1940s, the American press (along with their government for various
reasons cited) was AWOL, and as a case study one newspaper stands out above
all others. Clearly, *The New York Times* was (and remains) the purported paper of
record—especially in the U.S. So how does the alleged "paper of record" miss this

monstrous historical event—a miss from its beginning almost to its conclusion? And because the shocking news was, for all intents and purposes, hidden from sight by the paper that influences all the other papers, the build-up, the camps, the experimentations, the gas chambers, and the ghastly piles of bodies—all of it was hidden from America's consciousness.

In her deep study of this phenomenon, *Buried by The Times: The Holocaust and America's Most Important Newspaper,* journalist Laurel Leff details the almost unbelievable and abject failure of the *Times* and its Jewish-American publisher, Arthur Sulzberger, to truly report on the Holocaust. The failure by the *Times* can't be neatly explained with one reason filling in the blank because a number of reasons emerge as to how this mass murder was grossly underreported and callously tossed to the side. And when you factor in the immensity of the crime, it is legitimate to say that this historically gargantuan, maybe the largest story in modern human history, went basically unreported. In fact, early in the war the *Times* spinelessly buried a story reporting the murder of one million Jews in Europe on page seven. What, the number wasn't big enough?

"True, the *Times* circulation area included almost 3 million Jews, nearly half the Jews in America," writes Leff, "but they preferred the New York Post or Yiddish-language papers."[72] The paper would sporadically cover a domestic or international incident involving a "Jewish" story, but Leff emphasizes, "For the most part, however, Jews were not important to the Times as readers or subjects."[73] Leff reports that the *Times'* scant reporting on the genocide is "self-evident" and clearly backed up by the scarcity of stories. Throughout this entire time period "only 44 front-page stories had anything to do with Jews, a little more than half of which directly concerned their fate in Europe,"[74] writes Leff, who concludes that the *Times* simply did not believe that the accounts—as hard as this is to comprehend—were as important as the other 24,000+ stories that ran on page one during the same time period. While the *Times* ran some stories about Jewish death counts, Leff makes clear that hundreds of stories concerning Jewish suffering (economic deprivation, state-sponsored discrimination, filthy and disease-ridden ghettos, and more) ran buried on the back pages, but all of this was seen as the "unfortunate, but not unusual, collateral damage of war.[75][76] Leff wonders:

> Within a journalistic framework, that seems almost as
> difficult to understand as why the murder of millions would
> not be on the front page.[77]

Which again brings us dramatically back to the "unavoidable" and "Good War" fist-pounding pronouncements that surround World War II, especially in the European Theatre. If the extermination of the Jewish people at the hands of escalating Nazism is at the core of WHY this "good war" was being fought, then how come this wasn't front and center? How and why did the ones that knew about the horrors unfolding (namely certain elite segments of the government and press) remain so silent, so unapologetically apathetic?

Similar to media coverage today, much of what the press covered during World War II—in both Europe and the Pacific—dealt with military news, the battles, the body count, and the football-game-like reporting on the ever-changing line of scrimmage. Even during lulls in combat, big front-page stories about the ongoing genocide were, for the most part, nonexistent.

Buried by the Times also underscores Jewish owner Arthur Sulzberger's driving assimilation desires that pushed editors and writers to avoid emphasizing the distinctly Jewish makeup of the German atrocities. Indeed, what Sulzberger's vigorous assimilation motives reveal is the level of anti-Semitism that was alive and well in America during World War II (and clearly continues in America to this very moment). Stuart Eizenstat, a former senior official in the Clinton Administration specializing on Holocaust-era issues, connects the dots between the American press and its government during the war when commenting on Leff's exposé: "It is part and parcel with the same mindset of the Roosevelt Administration. One can only wonder in great sorrow at how many lives might have been saved if the nation's and world's conscience had been touched by full and complete coverage by the Times of what remains the greatest crime of world history."[78]

In her book, *Beyond Belief: The American Press and the Coming of the Holocaust*, Deborah Lipstadt, professor of Modern Jewish History and Holocaust Studies at Emory University, concurs wholeheartedly regarding government and press accountability:

> The most efficacious thing for the Allies to do was to try and
> ignore the tragedy and make sure that those whose responsibility
> it was to disseminate information did the same. And the press,
> having convinced itself that there was nothing that could be done
> and having inured itself to the moral considerations of what was
> happening, followed suit.[79]

In fact, the long shadow of allegations continue to fall on FDR and his administration about their knowledge of the Führer's specific designs and actions to systematically wipe out all the Jews in Europe—and the administration's subsequent inaction. As we've seen, asylum was denied early on and the possibility of later bombing raids on the rail lines to Dachau or Treblinka or Buchenwald never happened.

In his controversial, but what *The New York Times* itself calls an "exemplary" analysis entitled *The Abandonment of the Jews*, David Wyman, history professor from the University of Massachusetts-Amherst, strenuously argues that the Roosevelt administration ducked into alleyways of flaccidity and took a back seat approach to revealing the carnage perpetrated against the Jews as well as downplaying the extreme need for rescue actions. And all of it was because the Administration believed that "government aid to European Jews might increase anti-Semitism in the United States," as Wyman paraphrases Samuel Rosenman, Special Counsel to FDR and his principal adviser on Jewish matters.[80]

Better to turn a blind eye.

Henry Morgenthau, Jr., Secretary of the Treasury, was the lone Jew in FDR's cabinet. Morgenthau was no closet-radical—he was a dyed-in-the-wool protector of Wall Street treasure. But in early 1944, Morgenthau released a statement that was highly critical of Washington's response (or lack thereof) regarding Nazi genocide[81]—he wrote:

> One of the greatest crimes in history, the slaughter of the Jewish people in Europe, is continuing unabated. This Government has for a long time maintained that its policy is to work out programs to serve those Jews of Europe who could be saved.
>
> I am convinced on the basis of the information which is available to me that certain officials in our State Department, which is charged with carrying out this policy, have been guilty not only of gross procrastination and willful failure to act, but even of willful attempts to prevent action from being taken to rescue Jews from Hitler.
>
> Unless remedial steps of a drastic nature are taken, and taken immediately, I am certain that no effective action will

be taken by this government to prevent the complete extermination of the Jews in German controlled Europe, and that this Government will have to share for all time responsibility for this extermination.[82]

Lipstadt reveals a significant antagonism toward Jews in the U.S. and UK that continually dictated the anemic Allied response. "While no one among the Allies or in the press wanted to see Jews killed," she writes, "virtually no one was willing to advocate that steps be taken to stop the carnage."[83] Power structure policymakers in both Washington and London "were tired of hearing about Jews." Lipstadt quotes Allied officials who were describing eyewitness accounts of mass slaughter as "familiar stuff. The Jews have spoilt their case by laying it too thick for years past."[84] She goes on to report that U.S. State Department officials restrained the War Refugee Board from rescue efforts just in case Hitler decided "to embarrass the United Nations at this time by proposing to deliver thousands of refugees."[85]

Bottom-line: it was bad politics. Forget humanity, forget the truth, and forget saving millions of lives that multiplied excruciating pain decades into the future— it was a debased political calculation to basically do nothing. And once again the leaders in the American government and their "embedded" press acted against the best interests of the people. Lipstadt stands in utter disbelief:

> The press had access to a critically important and unprecedented story. Yet it reacted with equanimity and dispassion... That indifference may be part of the history of the Holocaust which, despite the efforts of scores of historians, will remain unfathomable. We still cannot answer the question that (Detroit Free Press editor) Malcolm Bingay's colleagues asked one another as they saw the remains of the Nazis' work—"how creatures, shaped like human beings, can do such things." Nor can we explain how the world of bystanders—particularly those with access to the news—were able to treat this information with such apathy. Both the Final Solution and the bystanders' equanimity are beyond belief.[86]

Hitler's Angels

In 1997, Switzerland settled with Jewish Holocaust survivors to the tune of $1.25 billion dollars for their financial dealings that helped fund Nazi Germany's build up and subsequent war effort. In the same dark shadows, American corporations aided, developed, and worked with Nazis well into the 1940s. Standard Oil of New Jersey supplied fuel for German U-Boats. Ford built tanks for Hitler. ITT built rocket bombs. Chase moneymen bankrolled the Nazi machine in Paris.[87] And then there was General Motors—a major cog in Germany's ability to run roughshod over Europe.

"General Motors was far more important to the Nazi war machine than Switzerland," explains U.S. Senate Judiciary Committee attorney Bradford Snell, who spent a lifetime investigating and researching GM. "Switzerland was just a repository of looted funds. GM was an integral part of the German war effort. The Nazis could have invaded Poland and Russia without Switzerland. They could not have done so without GM."[88] Snell's revelations about the mammoth car maker was part of his excoriation of GM's subversion and sabotage against clean-running electric public transit in more than forty American cities, a selfishly vicious business plot in the 30s, 40s, and 50s that became known as "the Great American Streetcar Scandal." In fact, it was this kind of avarice that drove certain powerhouses in corporate America to choose profits over patriotism, evil over—well, a lesser evil. Nazi Germany didn't rise to its ugly pinnacle of power simply because of one madman's "magnetic" personality. The insatiable monster needed bankers and industrialists to create the violence, the plunder, and the historic genocide perpetrated by the Third Reich. Who better than American capitalists? Capitalists like Henry Ford, whose portrait hung on Hitler's office wall in Munich.[89]

Buchenwald = 003
Homosexual = 3
Jew = 8

International Business Machines aka IBM, the giant American technology company, was a trusted business partner of Nazi Germany and enjoyed a twelve-year alliance with Hitler's government. Edwin Black, the bestselling author and well-respected investigative journalist, and a name that surely sends shudders through IBM's steel and glass edifice in Armonk, New York, has revealed over the past decade the astonishing and pivotal role of IBM—and its founder and first president, Thomas Watson—in the build up to and actual execution of the Holocaust. Black identifies IBM's direct involvement in all six phases of the hideous process: identification, expulsion from society, confiscation, ghettoization, deportation, and finally extermination. "The documents portray with crystal clarity," writes Black, "the personal involvement and micro-management of IBM president Thomas J. Watson in the company's co-planning and co-organizing of Hitler's campaign to destroy the Jews."[90]

Before he undertook the daunting task of exposing to the world IBM's direct complicity in the extermination of Jews, Edwin Black remembers:

> I was haunted by a question whose answer has long eluded historians. The Germans always had the lists of Jewish names. Suddenly, a squadron of grim-faced SS would burst into a city square and post a notice demanding those listed assemble the next day at the train station for deportation to the East. But how did the Nazis get the lists? For decades, no one has known. Few have asked.[91]

Absolutely haunting—especially when you factor in that the horror didn't happen overnight. It was an evolving process—one of bureaucracy, information, and data.

Strategic planning and immense data.

In fact it was incredibly detailed data that was necessary to identify Jews throughout Germany and eventually throughout all of Europe—and the Nazis didn't simply classify Jews by who went to Temple, "but those of Jewish blood," explains Black, "regardless of their assimilation, intermarriage, religious activity, or even conversion to Christianity."[92]

Hitler first employed a methodical and organized campaign to economically disenfranchise the Jews. This campaign was aimed at the colossal movement of human cargo from their homes into ghetto environments. Hitler then needed to physically transport the Jews via trains from these ghettos to the concentration camps, "with timing so precise the victims were able to walk right out of the boxcar and into a waiting gas chamber."[93]

Clearly, the data mining, cross-indexing, auditing, and sheer volume of complex information demanded a computer. But that was then and there were no computers. "However, another invention did exist," Black explains, "the IBM punch card and card sorting system—a precursor to the computer." Black continues: "IBM, primarily through its German subsidiary, made Hitler's program of Jewish destruction a technologic mission the company pursued with chilling success."[94]

The record also shows the amoral narcissistic behavior at the heart of IBM's operation: they were blinded by their own technological wizardry ("if it can be done, it should be done") as well as "by the fantastical profits to be made at a time when bread lines stretched across the world."[95]

Throughout this entire revelatory period of IBM's involvement and partnership with Nazi Germany made possible by Black's efforts, the behemoth conglomerate has remained mum on their actions. But back in the day, the Justice Department wasn't silent. During their investigation of IBM for trading with the enemy, a chief investigator's memo made clear IBM's involvement with Hitler's Final Solution:

> What Hitler has done to us through his economic warfare, one
> of our own American corporations has also done... Hence IBM
> is in a class with the Nazis... The entire world citizenry is hampered
> by an international monster.[96]

Chilling is the only word that can describe the recent release of the IBM concentration camp codes. Black offers the breakdown:

> IBM maintained a customer site, known as the Hollerith
> Department, in virtually every concentration camp to sort or
> process punch cards and track prisoners. The codes show IBM's
> numerical designation for various camps. Auschwitz was 001,
> Buchenwald was 002; Dachau was 003, and so on. Various prisoner
> types were reduced to IBM numbers, with 3 signifying homosexual,
> 9 for anti-social, and 12 for Gypsy. The IBM number 8 designated
> a Jew. Inmate death was also reduced to an IBM digit: 3 represented
> death by natural causes, 4 by execution, 5 by suicide, and code 6
> designated "special treatment" in gas chambers. IBM engineers had
> to create Hollerith codes to differentiate between a Jew who had
> been worked to death and one who had been gassed, then print
> the cards, configure the machines, train the staff, and continuously
> maintain the fragile systems every two weeks on site in the
> concentration camps.[97]

In fact, IBM technology not only enabled Nazi Germany to maximize its efforts in carrying out the "Final Solution," but also enabled all organizational efforts in the Fatherland and later Nazi Europe. IBM offered complex data solutions—charging exorbitant fees and often foreseeing the Führer's punch card needs. It was a well-oiled system and the bottom line is this: the historical record shows, without a shadow of a doubt, that IBM and their American and international executives—led by Thomas Watson—not only aided and abetted Adolf Hitler's Third Reich, but by doing so were complicit in the genocide of European Jews (and others)—as defined by the Treaty on Genocide.

Edwin Black and others, including Messrs. Abu-Jamal and Vittoria, acknowledge that the Holocaust would have happened with or without IBM. But the giant and powerful corporation, a willing accomplice, helped greatly, enabling the Third Reich to commit genocide so efficiently and on such an astounding scale. Black sums up this dark chapter in the annals of Murder Incorporated:

> International Business Machines, and its president Thomas J. Watson, committed genocide by any standard. It was never about the antisemitism. It was never about the National Socialism. It was always about the money. Business was their middle name.[98]

Executive Order 9066

The headline of the *San Francisco Examiner* in February of 1942 made it all too clear: OUSTER OF ALL JAPS IN CALIFORNIA NEAR!

With the stroke of his pen on Executive Order 9066, Franklin Roosevelt added another harrowing moment to American history, one that would have to be processed through the nationalistic

Photo: Clem Albers, U.S. War Relocation Authority

delusion to avoid tainting the legend of the so-called "good war." Between 110,000 and 120,000 men, women, and children of Japanese ancestry were rounded up and imprisoned in what were officially designated "War Relocation Camps."

Approximately two-thirds of this incarcerated population were American citizens—incarcerated without warrants, indictments, or hearings. The west coast of the United States—identified by FDR's executive order as an "exclusion zone"—was targeted the heaviest. People of Japanese ancestry were excluded (*excluded!*)

from the region; unless, of course, you were already locked up inside internment camps and then you were allowed to continue enjoying the temperate west coast weather, living in ramshackle dwellings and grotesque environs, stripped of your possessions, your homes, and your jobs. Many had their bank accounts frozen. Many were forced to leave their homes with nothing but the clothes on their backs. Many in power embraced this obviously illegal and immoral operation, including California Attorney General (and soon-to-be Chief Justice of the U.S. Supreme Court) Earl Warren, who strongly lobbied the Feds to eliminate all persons of Japanese heritage from the West Coast.

The massive attempt to reposition and whitewash this sad chapter in American history can be easily detected by exploring the ongoing struggle of various groups to rename the facilities used—an act of "spin" on this cruel, illegal, and inhuman treatment of Japanese Americans during those first dark days of the 1940s. The most contentious of the identifying names is "concentration camp," which interestingly enough was the term first used by FDR, Eisenhower, and Harold Ickes, who was then Secretary of the Interior. Of course that designation was quickly banished to the scrap heap because of its obvious link to the Nazi's grand plan. "Damn, all the good names are taken!"

The most commonly used appellation is "internment camp," which softens the culpability a bit, and Americans, especially the gatekeepers (the historians and the press), love to soften America's culpability. But the best euphemism for the forced military round-up and incarceration of the Japanese people is currently used by the good folks at the National Park Service, who prefer to sanitize and spit-shine these prison camps, framing them as "relocation centers." Sounds harmless enough.

Let's call them what they really were: prison camps—and these prison camps were set up across the country and their names still wreak pain and havoc in the hearts and minds of your fellow citizens to this very day; honorable people corralled like beasts in places like Manzanar in California and Minidoka in Idaho. In fact, the prison camps dotted the landscape, stretching east as far as Arkansas, Wisconsin, and even Florida. The stench of death was on the doorstep at many of these camps: Japanese Americans died in these prisons due to extremely bad or nonexistent medical care as well as the extraordinary emotional stress encountered by the innocent "inmates" who were ripped from their lives and suddenly tossed into cages. Others were shot and killed by guards for supposedly resisting orders.[99]

Decades later the United States Congress created the Commission on Wartime Relocation and Internment of Civilians to conduct a "study" of Executive Order 9066 and its impact on Japanese Americans. Even under the heading of the "fox guarding the henhouse," the Commission still issued a rather stinging review of this human rights travesty. Among many things, the 1982 report, entitled "Personal Justice Denied," determined the following:

> This policy of exclusion, removal and detention was executed against 120,000 people without individual review, and exclusion was continued virtually without regard for their demonstrated loyalty to the United States. Congress was fully aware of and supported the policy of removal and detention; it sanctioned the exclusion by enacting a statute which made criminal the violation of orders issued pursuant to Executive Order 9066. The United States Supreme Court held the exclusion constitutionally permissible.[100]

Once again, we find that law is simply politics by other means. Then the commission thoroughly demolishes the preposterous foundation of this entire sad and racist escapade:

> All this was done despite the fact that not a single documented act of espionage, sabotage or fifth column activity was committed by an American citizen of Japanese ancestry or by a resident Japanese alien on the West Coast.[101]

This statement of fact from the Commission's report is a stake in the heart of American delusion regarding the imprisonment of their fellow citizens. This dose of reality is followed by the damnable double standard that:

> No mass exclusion or detention, in any part of the country, was ordered against American citizens of German or Italian descent.[102]

Years of Infamy

Regarding conditions in the camps, the Commission found that "families lived in substandard housing, had inadequate nutrition and health care, and had their livelihoods destroyed: many continued to suffer psychologically long after their release."[103] Now let's roll back the videotape and play "bowling for euphemisms."

Regarding conditions in the camps, the Commission found that:

- families lived in substandard housing (*rank shitholes*)
- had inadequate nutrition (*fed them like dogs*)
- and health care (*who cares if you die*)
- and had their livelihoods destroyed (*we own your ass now*)
- many continued to suffer psychologically long after their release (*the long range effects of terrorism*)

In 1976, Michi Nishiura Weglyn wrote the landmark book *Years of Infamy: The Untold Story of America's Concentration Camps*. She was imprisoned herself at the age of fifteen in the Gila River, Arizona camp—a desert location about thirty miles southeast of Phoenix. Weglyn spent three years incarcerated in Block 66, Barracks 12. At the core of her narrative is a rock-solid detail/reality that clearly obliterates the U.S. Government's (and their apologists') pathetic argument regarding the need (military or otherwise) to conjure up and pull the trigger on Executive Order 9066, which was implemented to protect the trembling and defenseless American public, who we're sure were vomiting in toilets driven by utter and absolute fear. Weglyn stresses:

> Most of the 110,000 persons removed for reasons of
> "national security" were school-age children, infants and
> young adults not yet of voting age.[104]

Kids.

Ah, but the strawberries, that's, that's where I had them, they laughed at me and made jokes...
—Captain Queeg in *The Caine Mutiny*

The officially stated military need for the incarceration of 120,000 Japanese via the shredding of the U.S. Constitution was almost as ludicrous as throwing school kids in jail. General John DeWitt—who was doing his best paranoid Captain Queeg impersonation—was hunkered down in San Francisco's Presidio yelling and screaming from his bunker that, *"the Japs are coming! the Japs are coming!"* ("A Jap's a Jap and that's all there is to it" is what he actually said.)[105]

DeWitt, an early and vocal proponent of incarcerating every "Jap" on the west coast, was a loud voice that greatly influenced FDR to initiate Executive Order 9066. DeWitt and other high-ranking American military leaders nervously expected an almost impossible invasion on the American west coast—an invasion that would be supported by "Nip" spies facilitating acts of espionage up and down the left coast.

Here's how it was supposed to go down: crazed giant-toothed Japs would descend into the contiguous forty-eight, raping and pillaging every city, town, and hamlet from San Ysidro, California, to Clearbrook, Washington. Supposedly, they envisioned—and then more importantly, they sold—this fairytale of a Japanese bombardment from the air over Los Angeles and amphibious landings in San Francisco Bay. History and serious military analysts have concluded nothing could be farther from the actual and reasonable truth. Sure, certifiable lunatics like Michele Malkin (neo-con pundit on the Cartoon Network and author of the book/paperweight *In Defense of Internment)* argue vehemently regarding the absolute military necessity for the violation of life, liberty, and property rights for more than 120,000 peaceful, innocent, and uncharged people—most of them kids, and most of them American citizens.

But the facts suggest a much different reality.

First, let's dismiss the espionage and sabotage claims: Civil rights attorney and legal scholar Peter Irons has investigated and written extensively on the incarceration of Japanese Americans during World War II. In his essay, "Politics and Principle: An Assessment of the Roosevelt Record on Civil Rights and Civil Liberties," Irons details how General DeWitt (aka Captain Queeg), in his final report to the War Department, and staying true to form, charged Japanese Americans "with the commission of acts of espionage, including the transmission of visual and radio signals to Japanese submarines off the West Coast."[106] Except official U.S. Government reports contradicted and rejected DeWitt's wild claims. Irons writes:

> Two Justice Department lawyers, suspicious of DeWitt's claims, persuaded Attorney General Biddle to order investigations by the FBI and the Federal Communications Commission. The reports of these agencies to Biddle conclusively refuted DeWitt's *unsupported allegations.*[107] [Emphasis added]

In fact, in their report, the Justice Department lawyers labeled the DeWitt report "lies" and "intentional falsehoods."[108]

Now, let's dismiss the claims regarding the impending invasion of America by the Japanese Empire—and to do that it takes nothing more than a comparison of the military wherewithal needed to traverse the 5,500 miles from Tokyo to Los Angeles (11,000 miles roundtrip) with the practical reality of what it took Allied Forces to mount Operation Overlord on D-Day. In some circles it's called common sense.

The D-Day "Overlord" invasion utilized 7,000 amphibious vessels that were led by a 12,000 plus airborne aircraft assault, supported on the ground by a troop force of approximately 155,000 soldiers. Shortly thereafter, another 850,000 men, 148,000 military vehicles, and 570,000 tons of supplies bolstered this massive invasion over the next three weeks.

At the beginning of 1942, a month after the attack on Pearl Harbor, the most the Imperial Japanese Navy could possibly muster would have been a fraction of these D-Day invasion numbers. Japanese troop capacity at the time was approximately 42,000. Needless to say, the combined numbers of the Japanese navy and armed forces were laughably inadequate for an invasion of the United States. As well, reinforcement and resupply was at the mercy of an 11,000-mile roundtrip trek. Another important fact is this: America's "war-making" potential was many times higher—that is the ability of a country's workforce to produce and sustain productivity of all necessary armaments and hardware. In 1937, even with the U.S. mired in the quicksand of the Great Depression, its per capita war-making potential was at 41.7% as compared to 3.5% for Japan.[109]

Don't you think Franklin Roosevelt and his military brass knew this? Do you think they were quaking in their boots?

Clearly, the incarceration and removal of American citizens from their homes, jobs, and life was prompted and "motivated by wartime hysteria, racial prejudice, and failure of political leadership," writes Frank Wu of *Criminal Justice Magazine*, "not military necessity."[110] In fact, Wu is paraphrasing the exact same conclusion reached by the U.S. government's own aforementioned appointed commission on "Wartime Relocation and Internment of Civilians." Let's remember, these actions by the U.S. government are a mere 44 years after the *Plessy v. Ferguson* decision (1896) that bolstered the "separate but equal" doctrine, a doctrine still very much in force during the war years, particularly in the Jim Crow south. "Even the United States Army was explicitly segregated," writes Wu. "The pro-internment sentiments fit into the same pattern."[111]

As violence begets violence, so do gruesome actions based on hate and fear mongering. The ghosts live on. In their research for the documentary *Children of the Camps*, PBS researchers unveiled "the mental and physical health impacts of the trauma of the internment experience." They found that the suffering continued for tens of thousands of Japanese Americans long after the camps (read: prisons) were closed.

> Health studies have shown a 2 times greater incidence of heart disease and premature death among former internees, compared to noninterned Japanese Americans.[112]

Like a dog
I am commanded
At bayonet point.
My heart is inflamed
With burning anguish.
—Keiho Soga

There were three types of detention centers: (1) "Civilian Assembly Centers" were temporary camps usually set up at racetracks and stables and primarily housed second-generation Japanese known as "Nisei." These makeshift cages covered California north and south: Stockton, Salinas, Sacramento, Fresno, Pomona, Merced, Marysville, Arcadia, Pinedale, San Bruno, Tulare, Turlock, Woodland, as well as in the Owens Valley. The vast majority of the inmates were then sent to (2) "Relocation Centers" also known as "Internment Camps"—the largest population incarcerated in Tule Lake, right on the California-Oregon border. Finally, there were (3) the "Department of Justice Detention Camps" and these camps housed those Japanese considered to be disruptive by the U.S. government.

Keiho Soga was a Japanese journalist and poet who immigrated to Hawaii and wrote for the Japanese language paper *Hawaii Shimpo* and later became the editor of *Yamato Shimbun* (the newspaper later known as *Nippu Jiji*). Immediately after the Japanese attack at Pearl Harbor, Soga was interned on Oahu, followed by stints in the Lordsburg and Santa Fe camps in New Mexico. In his personal memoir, *Life Behind Barbed Wire*, Soga offers us a glimpse of the personal and family suffering endured by Japanese and Japanese Americans who committed no crime other than being Japanese. Soga's firsthand account of his four years incarcerated "like a dog" offers the reality of physical dislocation, severe economic hardship, horrific conditions, and a forced dramatic restructuring of the Japanese family.

In many instances, the so-called "housing" was nothing more than tarpaper wrapped around wooden floors. They were primitive structures that offered no protection from wind, rain, dust, and temperatures. "Wintertime temperatures in the camps sometimes fell to 30 degrees below zero," writes Soga, "and the buildings were uninsulated. The 'apartments' consisted of a single drafty room, averaging 16 by 20 feet, shared by an entire family. Nine members of Marge Tanwaki's extended family lived in a single room in the Amache Relocation Center in southeastern Colorado."[113] Soga quotes a young Japanese American remembering his family's camp:

> The apartments, as the Army calls them, are stables...
> mud is everywhere... We have absolutely no fresh meat,
> vegetables, or butter. Mealtime queues extend for blocks;
> standing in a rainswept line, feet in the mud, for scant portions...
> Food poisoning, measles, and pneumonia were rampant.[114]

Traditional roles for males and females within the Japanese family were blurred by transposable and menial labor paying a whopping $12 to $19 per month. Important cultural mores and Japanese customs were stripped away by the lack of privacy and forced communal life in the camps.[115] And, of course, as would be expected, the quality of education offered in the camps was crude and debasing. "Violent upheavals" were also, not unexpectedly, prevalent throughout the camps.[116]

"Jewel of the Desert"

The Central Utah Relocation Center—also known as "Topaz"—was the incarceration camp used to house 9,000 plus Japanese American citizens from the San Francisco Bay Area. It could only be an absurd form of real estate advertising that led to the camp's newspaper boldly announcing to the new "residents" that they had arrived at "Topaz—The Jewel of the Desert."[117]

This "jewel" of a camp in Utah's Sevier Desert—once described as a "barren, sand-choked wasteland"[118]—did not experience or report the same kind of ongoing violence and resistance experienced at the other camps, but one 63-year-old man faced the ultimate act of violence; the same act of violence experienced by the disenfranchised and disempowered, especially non-whites, since Europeans invaded paradise 500 years ago. James Wakasa was standing near the barbed wire fence that encaged him on 11 April 1943. According to the military cop who shot and killed the unarmed Wakasa, the elderly "Issei" (first-generation émigré) was trying to escape at the fence. But the autopsy determined that James Hatsuaki Wakasa was shot in the chest while facing the guard tower.[119]

Japanese American leaders demanded that they have a significant role in the investigation of Wakasa's murder and that the funeral be held right on the spot of the slaying. At first, the War Relocation Authority flatly turned down their demands, but the camp's population went on strike and operations at the 20,000-acre camp ceased immediately. Eventually, the funeral took place, but the military cop was found not guilty (once again, sound familiar?). In fact, as one report states, "news of the acquittal was censored from the camp newspaper to avoid further strikes or massive rioting."[120]

American Pie

As American as apple pie, and as tired and hackneyed and historically worn-out as it can possibly be (albeit still lethal and dangerous), overt virulent racism played a major role in the demonization of Japanese Americans as they were herded into cages during World War II. "As a young man," writes *The Economist* in a piece covering Greg Robinson's book *By Order of the President: FDR and the Internment of Japanese Americans*, "FDR had been influenced by Admiral Mahan and his school, who taught in terms richly dipped in racism and eugenic theory, that the Japanese were destined to be America's enemy and could never be assimilated."[121] Propaganda posters depicted

THIS IS THE ENEMY

prone white women under attack from animalistic Japanese mad men. The campaign—executed in obvious, Neanderthal, and cartoon-like fashion—was nonetheless incredibly effective.

The hatred and propaganda was everywhere—from hand-painted signs hanging outside grocery stores that read "JAPS KEEP MOVING—This is a WHITE MAN'S NEIGHBORHOOD" to an article in LIFE Magazine on 22 December 1941 with the headline: "HOW TO TELL JAPS FROM THE CHINESE." The article goes on to illustrate how Americans can distinguish the safe and friendly Chinese from the alien, creature-like Japs. Clearly, both the Japanese and Chinese people are objectified, but one group was demonized like dangerous wild animals and the other depicted as friendly household pets.

The American leaders and the American people held the Germans (and to a lesser degree the Italians) in a dark and scornful light, but as limited enemies and viewed simply as misguided victims of tyrannical leaders. But the Japanese (often called "yellow vermin," "mad dogs," and "monkey men"[122]) were held in a much darker place, one of fanatical hatred. "I'm for catching every Japanese in America," bellowed Congressman Rankin of Mississippi, "and putting them in concentration camps... Damn them! Let's get rid of them now!"[123] This virulent strain of racism was obvious and ubiquitous, and the American press never missed a beat to bang that drum hard, as evidenced by *Time* magazine's war correspondent Robert Sherrod's racist portrait demonizing Japanese soldiers (and by extension all Japanese) on the island of Attu in the Aleutians:

> The results of the Jap fanaticism stagger the imagination. The
> very violence of the scene is incomprehensible to the western
> mind... The ordinary unreasoning Jap is ignorant. Perhaps he is
> human.Nothing on Attu indicates it.[124]

This behavior by the dominant Anglo powers created a culture of fear that underscored one of the most repressive and illegal civil liberty violations ever perpetrated by the United States government.

The Firebombing of Dresden, Tokyo, et al ("Tons of Human Bone Meal")

The Dresden atrocity, tremendously expensive and meticulously planned,
was so meaningless, finally, that only one person on the entire planet got
any benefit from it. I am that person. I wrote this book, which earned a lot
of money for me and made my reputation, such as it is. One way or another,
I got two or three dollars for every person killed. Some business I'm in.[125]

—Kurt Vonnegut, Jr., author of *Slaughterhouse-Five or*
The Children's Crusade: A Duty-Dance with Death, 1969

On page one of Vonnegut's forever controversial and forever knockout novel *Slaughterhouse-Five*, he discusses returning to the German city of Dresden forty-some-odd years after living through an orgy of murder and barbarism as a U.S. soldier and prisoner of war, and calmly suggests that, "There must be tons of human bone meal in the ground." Indeed. In fact, Vonnegut called it "the greatest massacre in European history."[126] So it goes.

February 1945. For all intents and purposes the war in Europe against Nazi aggression and the hell unleashed by Adolf Hitler was over. By January of 1945 Dresden was a defenseless city; anti-aircraft capabilities were nonexistent, and by most accounts the city offered no military or strategic value. In fact, Dresden was known as a hospital city and became a harbor of safety for refugees fleeing from the onslaught of the Red Army and the crumbling of Europe. Many estimates suggest the city's actual population at the time was far greater than the official calculation of 650,000.

Bombing human beings is a dirty business and bombing civilians is a really dirty business. Both fascist powers, Italy and Nazi Germany, bombed civilians—Italy in Ethiopia in the mid-thirties and the Nazis in England and Holland early in World War II. The Japanese Empire was also proficient at bombing Chinese civilians in various Chinese cities. Again, carnage is a dirty business. FDR went on the record condemning the practice (read: murder) by characterizing the bombing as "inhuman barbarism that has profoundly shocked the conscience of humanity."[127] Great words, Mr. Roosevelt, but quickly thereafter Washington and London were knee-deep in the same dirty business.

In 1943, two years before the bloodbath began, the walking dead of Dresden were oblivious to their fate, but their names were already etched into eternity when Allied leaders met in Casablanca. They agreed that a massive bombing campaign over Germany would destroy, by example and attrition, the German people's will to resist. It was an early version of shock and awe. "The saturation bombing of German cities began with thousand-plane raids on Cologne, Essen, Frankfurt, (and) Hamburg," writes Howard Zinn. "The English flew at night with no pretense of aiming at 'military' targets; the Americans flew in the daytime and pretended precision, but bombing from high altitudes made that impossible."[128] In Germany, the culmination "of this terror bombing"[129] was the utter and complete destruction of Dresden.

The campaign was known as "area bombing" and Churchill passed the dirty baton to Arthur Harris, head of the RAF's Bomber Command. His directive was clear: "focus attacks on the morale of the enemy civil population, and in particular, of the industrial workers."[130] For good measure underline <u>civil population</u>.

Centuries before, during the Seven Years War, the King of Prussia attempted one last cannon bombardment of Dresden. His main target: the Church of Our Lady or "Frauenkirche," the spectacular Baroque church with a giant dome that glistens on the cityscape. Cannonballs thumped into the edifice but to no avail—the church survived, at least until the night of 15 February 1945. After two days of massive apocalyptic carpet and saturation bombing by American and British air power, and with the city in complete fiery ruins from the tonnage of death dropped from above—a nonstop barrage of high explosive bombs and incendiary devices hot-packed with napalm as the fuel—the dome and structure collapsed as a result of the "feuerstrum" or firestorm that literally engulfed the city, temperatures boiling flesh at 1,200 degrees Celsius.

Historian Marshall De Bruhl, in his book *Firestorm: Allied Airpower and the Destruction of Dresden*, writes that, "the people of Dresden were lulled into a false sense of security that is often a prelude to great disaster."[131] Ain't that the truth. Because when "feuerstrum" was unleashed on Dresden by the God-fearing Anglo-Americans, "the destruction and death were on a scale not hitherto imagined in warfare."[132]

Controversy still rages over how many Germans were crushed, incinerated, suffocated, blown to bits, or simply disappeared in the hurricane-force winds and flames that consumed the city and its inhabitants. Numbers range from 25,000 to 35,000 to 100,000—with some as high as 250,000 or more. Frankly, the numbers are impossible to count. Political agendas and moral tap dancing have blurred the truth, not to mention the firestorm that ate everything in its path. RAF pilots reported smoke plumes at 15,000 feet, creating turbulence that rocked the hell out of their aircraft. One pilot remembered, "I could still see the fires 500 miles away from Dresden."[133] Couple those blinding realities with the fact that Dresden's population at the time was so bloated and inflated that it's easy to see why the numbers fluctuate so dramatically. But the numbers are almost meaningless when the murder is that rampant and that unabashed—no matter which side is doing the killing and claiming the moral high ground.

As a prisoner of war, Kurt Vonnegut Jr. remembers the job of gathering and removing the corpses:

> A typical shelter, an ordinary basement usually, looked like a
> streetcar full of people who'd simultaneously had heart failure.
> Just people sitting there in their chairs, all dead... The Germans
> got funeral pyres going, burning the bodies to keep them from
> stinking and from spreading disease. One hundred thirty thousand
> corpses were hidden underground.[134]

Lest we forget—the firebombing of Dresden was at the end of the "area bombing" campaign. The saturation bombing of German cities and their civilian populations had already devastated Hamburg, Berlin, Cologne, and other smaller areas with murder estimates for the campaign nearing one million. In his book, *The Bomb*, Zinn frames the bottom line:

> In November of 1942, the chief of the British Air Staff,
> Sir Charles Portal, suggested that in 1943 and 1944 1.5 million
> tons of bombs could be dropped on Germany, destroying six
> million homes, killing 900,000 people, and seriously injuring a
> million more. British historian John Terraine, writing about this
> in his book "The Right of the Line," calls this "a prescription for
> massacre, nothing more nor less."[135]

The atomic evaporation of Hiroshima and Nagasaki have greatly overshadowed similar destruction by more conventional methods, "and the result," suggests De Bruhl, is a "tolerance of bombing as long as it is not nuclear." But regarding the firestorm that devoured Dresden, De Bruhl insists that the murder spree was "as awesome and dreadful as any raid of the war. Both the physical destruction and the casualties were truly horrific."[136]

In an interview with historian Douglas Brinkley for Rolling Stone in 2006, Kurt Vonnegut remembers, "There were too many corpses to bury. So instead the Germans sent in troops with flamethrowers. All these civilians' remains were burned to ashes."

"Tokyo Calling Cards"

About one month later in 1945, a fleet of 300-plus Superfortress bombers dropped almost one half-million M-69 incendiary cylinders over Tokyo. The attack reduced the city to ashes, completely destroying sixteen square miles. Nicknamed "Tokyo Calling Cards" by Collier's magazine and developed by the good folks at Harvard University, Dow Chemical, DuPont, along with a host of other guilty universities and corporations, as well as numerous mad scientists like Harvard's own Louis Fieser. This collection of degenerate mercenaries willfully created instruments of death that were unleashed on civilians who were incinerated in wholesale fashion. Showing no remorse whatsoever, the good professor Fieser told *Time* magazine in 1968: "I have no right to judge the morality of napalm just because I invented it."[137]

Enter "whiz kid" Robert McNamara. Before he was president of the Ford Motor Company and later Secretary of Defense and a major architect of America's long and bloody butchering of Southeast Asia, Bobby-boy cut his teeth working with bat-shit crazy General Curtis LeMay as they worked up the statistical analysis for the fire-bombing and destruction of Tokyo. "We burned to death 100,000 Japanese civilians in Tokyo—men, women and children," McNamara recalled in Errol Morris' film *The Fog of War.* McNamara continued his mea culpa, "LeMay said, 'If we'd lost the war, we'd all have been prosecuted as war criminals.' And I think he's right. He—and I'd say I—were behaving as war criminals."[138]

Bob, you were not "behaving as war criminals," you are war criminals. If David Berkowitz was a serial murderer, so were you. Only your numbers soar majestically past the piker, the Son of Sam.

M-69 incendiary devices were wicked executioners jam-packed with naphthemic acid, palmitic acid, aluminum soap, oleic acid, and gasoline. When this bomb detonated about a hundred feet above the ground the contents blasted out like flaming aerosol and wrapped itself around anything in sight. A researcher explains how it works:

> It burned more furiously than any other incendiary device,
> exhausting as fuel whatever flammable thing it contacted. It
> could also be dropped all the way to the ground, where it would
> lay for some number of seconds before exploding, sending
> dozens of flaming fragments (embedded in cheesecloth) flying
> in all directions, for a hundred yards or more, looking for flammable
> things to eat. One such bomb—a 6-pound unit—could start dozens,
> if not hundreds, of fires.[139]

As in Dresden, the terror was unimaginable. Joseph Coleman, a longtime foreign correspondent for the Associated Press and now a professor of journalism at Indiana University, wrote about the effects:

> The M-69s, which released 100-foot streams of fire upon
> detonating, sent flames rampaging through densely packed
> wooden homes. Superheated air created a wind that sucked
> victims into the flames and fed the twisting infernos. Asphalt
> boiled in the 1,800-degree heat. With much of the fighting-age
> male population at the war front, women, children and the elderly
> struggled in vain to battle the flames or flee.[140]

Coleman goes on to stress that the U.S. firebombing of Tokyo "brought the mass incineration of civilians to a new level in a conflict already characterized by unprecedented bloodshed."

The American firebombing of Tokyo was a milestone achievement for Murder Incorporated. Writing on the 50th anniversary of the campaign, Noam Chomsky (along with Stephen Herman) captures the veracity of the moment:

> [T]he U.S. fire-bombing of Tokyo… killed some 80,000-200,000 people, leaving over a million homeless in the ruins of the largely undefended city and removing it from the list of potential atom bomb targets because further destruction would hardly be impressive, merely piling rubble on rubble, bodies on bodies. The 300 bombers dropped oil-gel sticks and then napalm "on the tightly knit neighbourhoods of wooden houses," Stephen Herman recalls in the Far Eastern Economic Review, in Hong Kong. "The resulting inferno unleashed hell on earth" as people tried to escape by jumping into boiling ponds, planes "hunted down fleeing civilians to deliberately drop bombs on them," and napalmed the river to cut off an escape route. The U.S. Strategic Bombing Survey concluded that *probably more persons lost their lives by fire at Tokyo in a six-hour period than at any time in the history of man.* Herman quotes Richard Finn of American University, one of the American authors of Japan's postwar Constitution, who describes the bombing as "a bloody stain on the pages of American history" that stands alongside the atom bombs.[141] [Emphasis added]

And then, just when you think it can't get any worse, it gets worse.

Shadows and Lies

*The intense heat of the atomic bomb explosion caused this
haunting impression of a victim burned into the steps of a bank.*

This isn't pretty. Let's set the stage with a passage from Truman Nelson's
The Right of Revolution, written in 1967:

> There was a blinding flash; the fireball dropped to the
> ground. A wind blew furiously through the streets of the city.
> It was a wind that could be seen, a wind of solid flame, dense
> enough to liquefy the stones of its channel. Everyone it touched
> died instantly, people a mile away felt their skins peel off and
> hang down like strips of cloth.
>
> Some 200,000 people were killed in a matter of minutes, and
> the President was sent an enthusiastic cable saying: "Operated
> on this morning, stop, diagnosis not yet complete but results
> exceed expectations, stop, interest extends great distance."
>
> Three days later, on August 9, 1945, the President of the United
> States ordered another bomb dropped, this time on Nagasaki.
> There was now a predictable pattern; first tremendous heat, about
> 50,000,000 degrees centigrade... About 100,000 people were killed
> at once... But another 200,000 of Hiroshima and Nagasaki have
> been dying slowly and painfully for the last twenty-two years.

Here then are two primitive bombs, which killed 300,000 people rather quickly and kept another 200,000 in a lifelong concentration camp in which the daily tortures of pain and nausea are inflicted upon them without the necessity of guards, dogs, torture chambers, planned starvation, or uncounted miles of barbed wire.[142]

Also in 1967, some 22 years after the two days that will truly live in infamy, investigative journalist and filmmaker John Pilger visited the Japanese city of Hiroshima. He recently wrote about his experience:

When I first went to Hiroshima in 1967, the shadow on the steps was still there. It was an almost perfect impression of a human being at ease: legs splayed, back bent, one hand by her side as she sat waiting for a bank to open. At a quarter past eight on the morning of August 6, 1945, she and her silhouette were burned into the granite. I stared at the shadow for an hour or more, then walked down to the river and met a man called Yukio, whose chest was still etched with the pattern of the shirt he was wearing when the atomic bomb was dropped.

He and his family still lived in a shack thrown up in the dust of an atomic desert. He described a huge flash over the city, "a bluish light, something like an electrical short," after which wind blew like a tornado and black rain fell. "I was thrown on the ground and noticed only the stalks of my flowers were left. Everything was still and quiet, and when I got up, there were people naked, not saying anything. Some of them had no skin or hair. I was certain I was dead." Nine years later, when I returned to look for him (Yukio), he was dead from leukemia.[143]

Like a boxer absorbing titanic blows in the fifteenth round, blows that have long ceased to register on the giant numbness of pain, the American and global public were ready to accept a healthy new dose of creative destruction. "The Others" were evil incarnate. "Whatever we did was morally right," explains Zinn. "Hitler, Mussolini, Tojo, and their general staffs became indistinguishable from German civilians, or Japanese school children."[144]

Here's another defining moment from the great mind of General Curtis "Bomb Them Back Into The Stone Age" LeMay as he justified the atomic act: "There is no such thing as an innocent civilian."[145]

Hiroshima & Nagasaki:
America's Bright Shining Commercial to the World

Imagine you're in the midst of a nightmare—one of those paralyzing, gruesome hallucinations when terror grips every ounce of your being. Those chilling nightmares when you try to scream but can't, nightmares when your knowledge of the incomprehensible becomes conscious and horrifyingly tangible. Those eerily real nightmares when you wake up howling at the moon.

For hundreds of thousands (if not millions) of people, this nightmare is not hyperbole but stone cold reality, another instance when the masters of war who wield immense power make the unthinkable normal, the diabolical ordinary. And for many, this nightmare lasted for more than a generation. For some, the nightmare is still very much alive.

Welcome to *The Twilight Zone* because you're standing face-to-face with what is possibly America's most grisly sin—an unspeakable crime that takes on freakish forms, an aberration that is at once part Hitler, part Stalin, and part Pol Pot. It is the barbarians at the gate and, almost as hideous as the crime, is the cover-up of the crime, the big "PR" spin—a propaganda blitz of epic proportion; a campaign of great mendacity, one that turns night into day, and it's all been skillfully directed by American policymakers (and their historian and media lapdogs) who sell the giant lie with the audaciousness and balls-to-the-wall brutality of Alec Baldwin's "Blake" in *Glengarry Glen Ross*.

Once you recognize the carnage as truth and acknowledge the accepted history as propaganda and fairytale, only then will you begin to confront America's great abomination—the dark and macabre decision to unleash the dawn of the dead on hundreds of thousands of Japanese civilians in the early days of August 1945.

The shocking truth of murdering hundreds of thousands of what these advertisers considered expendable human beings cannot seriously be explained by the Empire's historians, or government officials, or talking heads on the left or right, or raging ideologues, or pacifist hippies, or anybody for that matter (including your two authors). The raw truth can only be delivered by the dead, the Japanese dead, those unsuspecting innocents who gazed into the face of a wicked messenger and instantaneously became as John Pilger wrote, a "silhouette... burned into the granite," a shadow on the wall.

The dead never knew they were actors in a giant American commercial to the world (particularly aimed at the Soviet Union). Unfortunately, in the dark recesses of this oftentimes-dark planet, "snuff" films exist. Equally unfortunate, this American message to the world was a "snuff" commercial—one hell bent on sending this cable, this telegram to the world:

American exceptionalism. Stop. We rule the roost. Stop. Message sent and received. Stop. Cold War begins. Stop. Fuck you. Stop.

So, let's visit the set of this commercial production, shot on location in mysterious and exotic Japan.

In the dark of night, 2:45am, from the small Pacific island of Tinian, 1,500 miles south of Japan, a B-29 lifted off the runway with its 12-man crew. The pilot, Colonel Paul Tibbetts, nicknamed the plane "Enola Gay"—in honor of his mother. The Superfortress bomber was a modified aircraft bolstered to carry the weight of the atomic bomb. Tibbett's plane and crew were escorted by two other bombers that carried cameras and scientific measuring devices. The bomb itself was nicknamed "Little Boy" and it took $2 billion worth of research to reach this momentous occasion. Four cities were selected as targets: Hiroshima, Nagasaki, Kokura, and Niigata. This was not random. The Target Committee had a plan: select cities that were basically undamaged by the war, cities where the destruction would be obvious and dramatic, ensuring that the first uranium bomb dropped would be "sufficiently spectacular for the importance of the weapon to be internationally recognized when publicity on it was released."[146]

That morning, a quiet and sunny August day, the people of Hiroshima went about their normal business. Shortly after eight o'clock, the American bomber approached its target. The bomb doors swung open and Little Boy tumbled toward earth. Two thousand feet above an area near the Aioi Bridge the world changed forever, as expressed a month earlier in the New Mexico desert by the "father of the atomic bomb," Julius Robert Oppenheimer, who famously quoted the Bhagavad-Gita at the moment he saw the utter destructive force of his terrible creation: *"I am become death, the shatterer of worlds."*

In his Pulitzer Prize-winning book, *The Making of the Atomic Bomb*, journalist and historian Richard Rhodes takes us into Hiroshima that morning, which was the verity of hell:

People exposed within half a mile of the Little Boy fireball were seared to bundles of smoking black char in a fraction of a second as their internal organs boiled away... The small black bundles now stuck to the streets and bridges and sidewalks of Hiroshima numbered in the thousands. At the same instant birds ignited in midair. Mosquitoes and flies, squirrels, family pets crackled and were gone.[147]

In his diary, Dr. Michihiko Hachiya (Director of the Hiroshima Communications Hospital), remembered his vision: "Hiroshima was no longer a city, but a burnt-over prairie. To the east and to the west everything was flattened... How small Hiroshima was with its houses gone."[148]

The grisly stories are too many to count but they all define utter terror. A grocer recalls images of people, walking dead, right after the blast: "At a glance you couldn't tell whether you were looking at them from the front or in back... Wherever I walked I met these people... Many of them died along the road... They didn't look like people of this world."[149]

The walking dead, the "unlucky ones" who weren't killed immediately, existed in a netherworld, roaming toward death, their bodies swollen beyond comprehension, their eyes hanging out of their sockets. A man in grade school at the time remembers: "The river became not a stream of flowing water but rather a stream of drifting dead bodies. No matter how much I might exaggerate the stories of the burned people who died shrieking and of how the city of Hiroshima was burned to the ground, the facts would still be clearly more terrible."[150]

Some had other visions, like "Give 'Em Hell" Harry Truman, 33rd President of the United States and the resident murderer at 1600 Pennsylvania Avenue when the mass execution occurred. Floating back to Washington from Europe onboard the USS Augusta after his Potsdam meeting with Churchill and Stalin, Truman was hanging out with a cadre of ecstatic sailors. The plainspoken, no bullshit, buck-stops-here madman from the Show Me state, exclaimed: "This is the greatest thing in history!"[151]

Well damn! Hug Susie Rottencrotch! See the USA in your Chevrolet! Ice cream sodas for everyone! God bless America, Biff! USA! USA! USA!

And guess what? Uncle Harry liked the outcome of the first uranium bomb so much he decided to drop a second one—this atomic toy was a plutonium bomb named "Fat Man," dropped on the city and people of Nagasaki. Once again, instant mass murder. Immediate carnage. More cheering, Susie and Biff.

It is unabashed, uncensored, brash, raw, and forthright fucking insanity.

Unbridled and Mad

The Reverend Malcolm Boyd, a hero on the frontlines of peace and justice since he was able to stand upright, authored an iconic book of poetry in 1965 titled *Are You Running With Me, Jesus.* This stanza from "Prayers for the Free Society" remains dramatically evocative some fifty years later:

> What was Hiroshima like Jesus when the bomb fell? What went
> through the minds of mothers? What happened to the lives of
> children, what stabbed at the hearts of men when they were
> caught up in a sea of flames… Save us from ourselves. Spare
> us the evils of our heart's good intentions unbridled and mad.[152]

Immoral, mind-numbing defenses continue to this day regarding Truman's decision to drop the bombs and engage in this final act of mass terrorism. "Only with these scenes in our mind can we judge the distressingly cold arguments that go on now, sixty-five years later, about whether it was right to send those planes out those two mornings in August of 1945," exclaims Howard Zinn, one historian not afraid to deal with this harsh reality:

> That this is arguable is a devastating commentary on our
> moral culture.[153]

John Pilger positions this brutal chapter in American history where it belongs—out of the shadows and into the light:

> The atomic bombing of Hiroshima and Nagasaki was a
> criminal act on an epic scale. It was premeditated mass
> murder that unleashed a weapon of intrinsic criminality. For
> this reason its apologists have sought refuge in the mythology
> of the ultimate "good war," whose "ethical bath," as Richard
> Drayton called it, has allowed the west not only to expiate its
> bloody imperial past but to promote 60 years of rapacious war,
> always beneath the shadow of The Bomb.[154]

"Destroy the town in order to save it"

Writer Mikki Smith termed it "How the bomb saved lives and other fables."[155] The company line out of Washington as well as Truman's high command, which was cemented as gospel by the American press and attending suck-up historians, was that the Japanese would never surrender. NEVER. They were a race of extreme fanatics who were blinded by incoherent rage. Every last one of them, babies and children included, had the Kamikaze gene, willing to commit mass suicide until there wasn't a drop of blood left.

So, in order to save Japanese lives, and more importantly to these myth-makers, exceptional American lives, during an epic ground invasion and subsequent Asian apocalypse, the decision was to drop these newfangled mysterious super bombs that would create so much carnage that even these Japanese mad men would succumb to the obvious.

A few days after "Little Boy" and "Fat Man" changed the course of human existence, Winston Churchill, who knows a good deal about mass murder and butchery, was selling and spinning the myth to his House of Commons that the alternative to dropping the bombs and forcing a quick end to the war was sacrificing "a million American, and a quarter million British lives in the desperate battles and massacres of an invasion of Japan."

Destroy the town in order to save it.

Violence on a heretofore-unseen scale will deliver peace. This myth must be well-sold and swallowed whole so that the ultimate lie of World War II being the "good war" is protected through the ages: "we" defeated fascism, fought back fanatical Japanese aggression, and ushered in a worldwide epoch peace and prosperity.

House of Cards

On the surface, to the historical passerby, it seems that dropping the bombs worked. Of course, if we look just a little closer, their case is the quintessential house of cards.

Let's first peg the events chronologically. In early May of 1945, the war ended in Europe. One month later, in mid-June, the almost three-month Battle of Okinawa concluded. This victorious but bloody marathon battle for Allied Forces cleared the way for using Okinawa (only a few hundred miles away) as the launching pad for an invasion of mainland Japan—already codenamed "Operation Downfall."

At the same time, Josef Stalin and Soviet Russia were preparing its massive troop strength for an invasion of Japanese-Manchuria in accordance with the terms of the Yalta agreement. Japan was now alone in the war and wanted desperately to remain neutral with Stalin for obvious reasons. In fact, since the Yalta Conference, the Japanese tried to enlist the Soviets help in negotiating a peace with the Allies.

Professor, author, and a founding Fellow of Harvard's Institute of Politics, Gar Alperovitz has spent decades researching and revealing an alternative narrative to the widely accepted reasons for unleashing the atomic monster. Along with others, his findings are based on exhaustive research along with the release of invaluable classified documents. Putting aside the moral imperative regarding the dropping of the bombs, the findings clearly support two conclusions: (1) that the Japanese were trying to create a platform for peace for almost a year, and (2) that there was no urgent military necessity to drop the bomb—either to force Japan's hand or to save untold lives. Alperovitz writes:

> Although Japanese peace feelers had been sent out as early as September 1944 (and Chiang Kai-shek had been approached regarding surrender possibilities in December 1944), the real effort to end the war began in the spring of 1945. This effort stressed the role of the Soviet Union.[156]

Give Peace a Chance

In late June, "the Japanese Supreme War Council authorized Foreign Minister Togo to approach the Soviet Union,"[157] writes Howard Zinn. They urged Togo to seek a way to end the war by September, which would have been only three weeks after Hiroshima and Nagasaki. In fact, Togo wired back home: "Unconditional surrender is the only obstacle to peace... It is His Majesty's heart's desire to see the swift termination of the war."[158]

Besides the various documented overtures and attempts through the Soviet Union to negotiate a peace with Washington and London, Alperovitz uncovers (after a long campaign for their release) another "smoking gun" found in a giant stack of cables intercepted by the National Security Council. In these pages, it's revealed that at least three months prior to the bombing of Hiroshima and Nagasaki, President Truman himself was advised of Japanese peace proposals through the Portuguese and the Swiss.[159]

In late July, after the joint U.S.–British Potsdam declaration that threatened the "prompt and utter destruction" of Japan if they didn't unconditionally surrender, the only negotiating point that the Japanese held firm on was the protection of their emperor Hirohito, whom the people regarded as a living god. As the Allies demanded nothing short of this "unconditional surrender," the Emperor's future was the only condition. The ironic postscript to this "negotiation" is that after the atomic bombing, and after the mass murder of hundreds of thousands of Japanese, the U.S. allowed the Emperor to retain his status as they needed cohesion and continuity for their postwar occupation. Many wanted Hirohito tried for war crimes but a figurehead was needed and a figurehead they retained. "After the war, His Majesty the Emperor still sat on his throne," writes William Blum, "and the gentlemen who ran the United States had absolutely no problem with this. They never had."[160]

Military Necessity?

With the war over in Europe, the Japanese knew full well that the U.S. would direct the full fury of American firepower solely against Japan. In fact, the destruction of Japan—as evidenced by the massive firebombing of Tokyo in March 1945—was already well underway. The Japanese infrastructure was in a shambles, oil supplies were scarce, manufacturing was almost at a standstill, and food was in short supply. Clearly, Truman's inner circle as well as his military brain trust knew Japan was a beaten country. "In mid-April the Joint Intelligence Committee reported that Japanese leaders were looking for a way to modify the surrender terms to end the war," Alperovitz writes, "The State Department was convinced the Emperor was actively seeking a way to stop the fighting."[161]

When Secretary of War Henry Lewis Stimson whispered to future president and Supreme Commander of the Allied Expeditionary Force, Dwight Eisenhower, that Truman was dropping the bomb, Eisenhower boldly expressed his opposition:

> During his recitation of the relevant facts, I had been conscious of a feeling of depression and so I voiced my grave misgivings, first on the basis of my belief that Japan was already defeated and that dropping the bomb was completely unnecessary, and secondly because I thought that our country should avoid shocking world opinion by the use of a weapon whose employment was, I thought, no longer mandatory as a measure to save American lives. It was my belief that Japan was, at that very moment, seeking some way to surrender with a minimum loss of "face."[162]

Navy Admiral William Leahy, who was also Chief of Staff to FDR and Truman, emphatically wrote that:

> The use of this barbarous weapon at Hiroshima and Nagasaki was of no material assistance in our war against Japan. The Japanese were already defeated and ready to surrender because of the effective sea blockade and the successful bombing with conventional weapons.[163]

General Curtis LeMay—the cigar-chomping military warrior, a real life Dr. Strangelove and madman who could never be confused with a left-wing radical peacenik—stated categorically at a press conference after the atomic slaughter:

> LeMay: *The war would have been over in two weeks without the Russians entering and without the atomic bomb.*

> The Press: *You mean that, sir? Without the Russians and the atomic bomb?*

> LeMay: *The atomic bomb had nothing to do with the end of the war at all.*[164]

Fleet Admiral Chester Nimitz, Commander in Chief of the Pacific Fleet at the time, and whose name and legacy lives on as the USS Nimitz—a supercarrier in the Empire's naval strike group—also issued a public statement regarding the decision to drop the bombs, bombs of instant genocide: "The Japanese had, in fact, already sued for peace. The atomic bomb played no decisive part, from a purely military standpoint, in the defeat of Japan."[165]

As time passed and the truth became safe, it was clear that a large percentage of America's military brass did not believe in the military necessity formula and were against what Admiral William Leahy called "this barbarous weapon." After studying the record, author Mikki Smith called the list of top U.S. military honchos who were against the use of the bomb as a military necessity "staggering."

Shortly after the war, The U.S. Strategic Bombing Survey group, directed by Truman himself to scrutinize the air assaults on Europe and Japan during World War II, released this conclusion on Hiroshima and Nagasaki in July of 1946:

> Based on a detailed investigation of all the facts and supported
> by the testimony of the surviving Japanese leaders involved, it
> is the Survey's opinion that certainly prior to 31 December 1945,
> and in all probability prior to 1 November 1945, Japan would have
> surrendered even if the atomic bombs had not been dropped, even
> if Russia had not entered the war, and even if no invasion had been
> planned or contemplated.[166]

Cover-Up

In what journalists Amy and David Goodman call, "one of the great journalistic betrayals of the last century,"[167] we now know how the U.S. military, along with General Douglas MacArthur and his censors, killed and buried the gruesome aftermath accounts of Hiroshima and Nagasaki as witnessed by two courageous journalists.

Of course, the first thing MacArthur did was bar the western press from the southern regions of Japan. He secured the crime scene and the press dutifully marched in lockstep with military orders. But two men were hell-bent on getting the story: the independent Australian journalist Wilfred Burchett and American George Weller of the *Chicago Daily News*. Burchett ventured into Hiroshima one month after the detonation. David and Amy Goodman write, "Mr. Burchett sat down on a chunk of rubble with his Baby Hermes typewriter. His dispatch began: 'In Hiroshima, 30 days after the first atomic bomb destroyed the city and shook the world, people are still dying, mysteriously and horribly—people who were uninjured in the cataclysm from an unknown something which I can only describe as the atomic plague.'"[168]

"Atomic plague." Radiation. And it was radiation, or the supposed lack thereof, that was at the heart of the giant American lie, the cover-up, this pathetic attempt at mythmaking. "The official U.S. narrative of the atomic bombings downplayed civilian casualties," the Goodmans report, "and categorically dismissed as 'Japanese propaganda' reports of the deadly lingering effects of radiation."[169] Burchett's revelations were published on 5 September 1945 in the *London Daily Express,* grabbed world attention, much to the chagrin of U.S. watch-keepers, and became "a public relations fiasco for the U.S. military."[170]

Now it was George Weller's turn, the *Chicago Daily News'* Pulitzer Prize-winning journalist. His 25,000-word epic feature covering his harrowing discoveries in Nagasaki had to first go through U.S. military censors and, just as Douglas MacArthur ordered the death of so many so-called enemies on planet Earth, so did he order Weller's story killed as well. But Burchett's exposé was still out there in black and white, so it was time for the U.S. government to go into the journalism business. And why not? They already had a *New York Times* reporter on the payroll, one William Laurence, who was not only the science reporter for the *Times* but collected a check from the Department of War. Laurence was pulling double duty: crafting press releases for Truman and Stimson while still filing stories for his New York employer. "He was rewarded by being given a seat on the plane that dropped the bomb on Nagasaki," David and Amy reveal, "an experience that he described in the Times with religious awe."[171]

Three days after Burchett's story rocked the world, the *Times* ran Laurence's "story" on the front page—a story that emphatically rejected Burchett's claim that radiation was killing people. The text of Laurence's story reads like any PR release circulated as damage control after a corporate catastrophe. (Think Exxon Valdez or the BP Deepwater Horizon spills, or even Fukushima Daiichi.)

Now, here's the ugliest part: Laurence and his newspaper won the Pulitzer Prize for this pile of dung; and the worst aspect of their actions as co-conspirators in perpetrating this treacherous government cover-up is that it kept the lie alive and the truth buried regarding the ghastly aftereffects of atomic (and by extension nuclear) weapons. David and Amy Goodman conclude, "It is time for the Pulitzer board to strip Hiroshima's apologist and his newspaper of this undeserved prize."[172]

George Weller died in 2002 but his son finally found a newspaper (*Mainichi Shimbun* in Japan) courageous enough to publish his father's "searing indictment" of what actually happened to the people and the city of Nagasaki.

Under the heading of "even a broken clock is right twice a day," one *New York Times* military correspondent, Hanson Baldwin, was not jumping for joy as a fourth-estate cheerleader enthusiastically framing a pro-government narrative. Instead he wrote:

> We are the inheritors to the mantle of Genghis Khan and of all those in history who have justified the use of utter ruthlessness in war.[173]

The Reason Why

As the atomic mist clears—and the great American myth regarding the bomb's use becomes transparent (and even laughable)—it's time to ask the most important question: *why?* If not to force Japan's hand into surrender, *then why?* If not to avoid a massive land war that would cost hundreds of thousands, if not a million hypothetical Allied lives, *then why?*

Japan was beaten, destroyed, and down for the count. They knew it and they were attempting to bring about peace for at least 18 months prior to Truman dropping the bomb. The imaginary mass invasion was not a reality, and even if it was, U.S. military estimates with regard to "body count" were dramatically lower—the highest ever found in any actual military planning report was between 40,000 and 46,000. In 1985, two separate independent studies scrutinized the casualty estimates and both concluded that the maximum would be 20,000 deaths but probably far lower.[174]

Then why? The subjugated truth is now both clear and liberated, as detailed by Gore Vidal:

> Our great Augustus, Franklin Roosevelt had died... and was succeeded by a no-brainer called Harry Truman, who didn't know what he was doing... Roosevelt had never told him about the Atomic bomb... and his advisors, all the people connected with the bombs, wanted to drop them, show they'd spent their money well. Truman thought it was a good idea because he thought that we needed an enemy. We'd had Hitler and Nazism. Stalin and communism, even better. And while he was at Potsdam with his first meeting with Stalin, he gets news from Alamogordo, New Mexico that the atom bomb works, so he's over excited 'cause he's gonna give it to Stalin... he's looking at Stalin, "Here's the enemy,

just made for us. We can militarize the economy..." Every last one of [Truman's military commanders] said, "Don't do it... Japan is defeated. Everybody knows it..." But... Truman went on with this grotesque adventure... and the Cold War begins.[175]

The premeditated use of the atomic bomb's destructive dexterity and "impressive" killing power allowed the U.S. hierarchy to elevate "gunboat diplomacy" to new and audacious levels. Since the Bolshevik Revolution back in the early part of the 20th century, followed by the U.S. assault on the Soviets in 1918, American policymakers were in a constant do or die battle with the communist menace. Out of necessity, World War II was a respite in this ideological and economic brawl. In his essay "Hiroshima: Needless Slaughter, Useful Terror", William Blum writes, "According to Manhattan Project scientist Leo Szilard, Secretary of State Byrnes had said that the bomb's biggest benefit was not its effect on Japan but its power to 'make Russia more manageable in Europe.'"[176]

In May of 1945, an attaché from Venezuela conveyed a conversation he had with Assistant Secretary of State Nelson Rockefeller. The diplomat said that Rockefeller "communicated to us the anxiety of the United States Government about the Russian attitude." He said that the U.S. government is "beginning to speak of Communism as they once spoke of Nazism and are invoking continental solidarity and hemispheric defense against it." In fact, Winston Churchill knew full well about the Manhattan Project and even knew about the bomb before Truman. Churchill understood the real benefit of dropping the bombs: "We now had something on our hands which would redress the balance with the Russians."[177]

Also in May of 1945, a cable from the German ambassador in Japan was intercepted by U.S. officials and now lives in the National Archives. The cable "dispels any doubt that the Japanese were desperate to sue for peace," reports John Pilger, "including 'capitulation even if the terms were hard.'"[178] Pilger then concludes that instead of pursuing a negotiated peace, Secretary of War Stimson told Truman "he was 'fearful' that the US Air Force would have Japan so 'bombed out' that the new weapon would not be able 'to show its strength.'" There had to be a "Super Bowl" commercial for the world in general and the Russians in particular. The director of the Manhattan Project, General Leslie Groves, later stated bluntly:

> There was never any illusion on my part that Russia was our enemy, and that the project was conducted on that basis.[179]

There's the why. And if there's any lingering doubt, listen to Secretary of War Henry Stimson right after wiping out Nagasaki:

> In the State Department there developed a tendency to think of the bomb as a diplomatic weapon. Outraged by constant evidence of Russian perfidy, some of the men in charge of foreign policy were eager to carry the bomb for a while as their ace-in-the-hole... U.S. statesmen were eager for their country *to browbeat the Russians with the bomb held rather ostentatiously on our hip.*[180] [Emphasis added]

Historian Charles Mee distilled down Russia's two-fold psychological reaction to America's bright shining commercial in stark fashion, proposing: "The Americans had not only used a doomsday machine; they had used it when, as Stalin knew, it was not militarily necessary. It was this chilling fact that doubtless made the greatest impression on the Russians."[181]

Once the long-standing fairy tales as to why the bombs were dropped on Hiroshima and Nagasaki are dispelled, the bitter pill must be swallowed: the fission reaction in several kilograms of uranium and plutonium that instantly wiped out two Japanese cities and more than a quarter million people of color (and caused ongoing debilitating health issues in the Japanese for decades) was executed to put Stalin and the Soviet Union on notice about America's determination, resolve, and strategic superiority as the new and ever-growing world superpower. American power will dictate the end of the war with Japan, not the massive Russian troop advancement through Manchuria. American power will dictate what Asia will look like over the next fifty years, not Soviet expansion. And most importantly, American power will be dictating how Europe will be re-shuffled, not the sleeping bear.

Conservative British statesman and viceroy of India, Lord Curzon, knew a thing or two about international imperialism when he candidly remarked in 1898 that countries are "pieces on a chessboard upon which is being played out a great game for the domination of the world." Underscoring this geo-political reality we find American general and military icon, George C. Marshall, who was quoted frequently as saying that the use of the bomb was not a military decision, but rather a political one.[182]

In 1963, Truman wrote a letter to *Chicago Sun Times* reporter Irv Kupcinet (Truman's opening salutation read "Dear Kup"), who had just penned a very positive piece on the 33rd American president's decision to exterminate 250,000 plus Japanese citizens. The man from Missouri wrote:

> All you have to do is to go out and stand on the keel of the
> Battleship in Pearl Harbor with the 3,000 youngsters underneath it
> who had no chance whatever of saving their lives. That is true of
> two or three other battleships that were sunk in Pearl Harbor.
> Altogether, there were between 3,000 and 6,000 youngsters killed
> at that time without any declaration of war. It was plain murder.[183]

Clearly, for Harry, revenge is a dish best served cold. We're not sure where Truman pulled those figures out from (we can guess) but official U.S. casualties at Pearl Harbor numbered between 2,380 and 2,410. Truman finished strong:

> I have no regrets and, under the same circumstances, I would
> do it again—and this letter is not confidential. Sincerely yours,
> Harry S Truman[184]

Interestingly enough, even after writing "this letter is not confidential," Truman instructed his secretary not to send the letter to Kup.

Eyes Wide Shut

Using Truman's memoirs as a final point of reference, we can "move the debate beyond both the heroic and tragic narratives by suggesting a third narrative," proposes American University professor Peter Kuznick. Truman's own hand wrote a narrative conclusion that is apocalyptic. Kuznick, one of the foremost scholars on the subject, suggests that Truman moved forward with eyes wide shut:

> Ponder the implications of Harry Truman's realization that,
> by using atomic bombs against Japan, he was opening the
> door to the potential annihilation of all species—what he
> described as "the fire destruction prophesied in the Euphrates
> Valley era, after Noah and his fabulous arc" *and chose to use the*
> *bombs anyway.*[185] [Emphasis added]

And remember, Truman still pulled the trigger on this carnage and slaughter knowing full well that the Japanese leaders were desperately looking for surrender terms to end the war—especially before the mass Soviet invasion throttled to full power.

MAD

The apocalyptic threat unleashed over Hiroshima and Nagasaki increased swiftly at the tabernacle of thermonuclear destruction, setting the stage for the destruction of the planet—the very real threat of which continues, hard-core, to this very moment. The Americans unleashed the final dogs of war and the Soviets, by 1949, were in lockstep with their Cold War partners in crime. It was, as Chomsky once so aptly put, "international gangsterism."[186] This partnership between the Soviets and Americans formed the balancing act of nuclear terror this planet has lived under for decades upon decades, aka MAD—Mutual Assured Destruction. And all of this has taken place in the period establishment historians call "the great American century," when in plain fact it was just another cruel century defined by the terror of war, only this time the annihilation of the human species could be glimpsed on the horizon.

World War II, the so-called "good war" enabled the American Empire to grow large and dangerous as it continued to seek world domination—the exact same insane behavior that the American power structure condemned Hitler for attempting during his reign of terror. Today, more than two generations later, the U.S. remains the only country to ever use nuclear weapons on a human population. Couple that harsh reality with constant military bombardment, deadly interventions, economic terror, as well as the constant flow of violent and illegal diplomatic threats (the "everything is on the table" euphemism) and it's clear why many believe the United States of America to be the most dangerous rogue power in the world today.

In 1941, the radical pacifist, Abraham Johannes "A. J." Muste offered this solemn warning: "The problem after a war is with the victor. He thinks he has just proved that war and violence pay. Who will now teach him a lesson?"[187] Muste's prescient words underline American behavior during and since World War II.

Was it the good war?

Well, if this was a good war, if fifty to seventy million dead is the scorecard of a good war, if this terror-ridden path is considered "good" then we unequivocally, categorically, and emphatically must disagree. The masters of war walked down the dirtiest possible path—and then called it "good."

The Reverend A. J. Muste also calls out this hypocrisy: "There is no way to peace, peace is the way."

3 Interventions "R" Us
Building Empire One Dirty Covert Action at a Time

When the good doctor, Hunter S. Thompson, dedicated his book *Gonzo Papers, Volume 1—The Great Shark Hunt*, he wrote: "To Richard Milhous Nixon, who never let me down." Well, we feel the same way about these dangerous clowns in the CIA—they've never let us down. The material that their nefarious, reprehensible, and ridiculous actions generate is incredible silage for comedians and political critics alike. The only people not laughing are the innocents over the last half-century plus who've been unfortunate enough to get caught in their crosshairs.

The question is often asked and debated: *Is the Central Intelligence Agency a fortification of freedom against dangerous enemies or a malevolent scheme to spread American imperialism?*

Let's find out.

> *The CIA is made up of boys whose families sent them to Princeton but wouldn't let them into the family brokerage business.*
> —Lyndon Johnson

Harry Truman & The National Security State

As we know it today, the National Security State was born in the dark recesses of the Truman Administration and, as Gore Vidal writes, "without any national debate or the people's consent, (it) replaced the old American republic with a national security state very much in the global empire business."[1]

As World War II drifted into the recent past, President Harry Truman—fresh off his massive murder spree from high above Hiroshima and Nagasaki—left his dirty fingerprints on American history as he facilitated the end of the American republic and helped to initiate, and then cement in its place, the National Security State: a well-designed plan that elevated and positioned the U.S. military (and the ubiquitous "military industrial complex") as the highest authority in the land. Some of you may remember the political thriller *Seven Days in May*, written by Fletcher Knebel and Charles W. Bailey II—the novel later adapted as a motion picture by screenwriter Rod Serling and director John Frankenheimer. The film stars Burt Lancaster as the treacherous and treasonous General James Mattoon Scott and Kirk Douglas as the hero, Colonel Jiggs Casey. The novel and the film posit the possibility of a military coup over civilian authority—this fictional account clearly influenced by America's virulent right-wing anti-communist fervor of the 1950s. In this case, fiction be damned because the reality occurred just a few years before *Hollywood's noir*-ish tale of a military takeover.

In 1947 to be precise.

Throughout American history there have been various occasions when boilerplate protections of the U.S. Constitution were suspended and the people's power and will were summarily usurped by executive action. Pulitzer Prize-winning journalist Garry Wills writes in his book *Bomb Power: The Modern Presidency and the National Security State* about this historical foundation:

> Suspected aliens were imprisoned in the Quasi-War of the 1790s.
> Lincoln canceled habeas corpus in the Civil War. Roosevelt
> interned Japanese-Americans in World War II. These were seen as
> temporary measures, and the Constitution was generally restored to
> integrity after the crisis was over. But since the inception of World
> War II we have had a continuous state of impending or partial war,
> with retained constitutional restrictions. World War II faded into
> the Cold War, and the Cold War into the war on terror, giving us
> over two-thirds of a century of war in peace, with growing security
> measures, increased governmental secrecy, broad classification of
> information, procedural clearances of those citizens able to know
> what rulers were doing in secret... Normality never returned, and

the executive power increased decade by decade, reaching a new high in the twenty-first century.[2]

In 1947 there was what many believe to be a silent coup underfoot, one that aimed to slowly obliterate FDR's New Deal social spending and replace it with a full-time military junta also known as the National Security State—unelected and operating in the shadows. Officially formulated with the passage of the National Security Act in July of 1947 and as part of Washington's unofficial Cold War strategy, the act restructured the United States military and intelligence apparatus and placed vast powers in the executive branch—with no real oversight. The act created the Joint Chiefs of Staff as well as the sphinx-like National Security Council and the Central Intelligence Agency. From the U.S. government's standpoint, that is to say the heavy-duty policymakers in Washington, there were justifiable reasons to pursue a severe, iron-fisted, and monumental shift in the power structure and operation of the American corporation—a shift away from (at least the appearance of) democratic traditions and toward a modern-day empire that would operate as part plutocracy and part oligarchy.

Gore Vidal concurs: "Since 1950 the United States has fought perhaps a hundred overt and covert wars. None was declared by the nominal representatives of the American People in Congress Assembled; they had meekly turned over to the executive their principal great power, to wage war. That was: the end of that Constitution."[3]

Ultimately, the new paradigm would govern as a totalitarian regime masquerading as the greatest democracy the world has ever seen. This rush to shred the Constitution and consolidate vast power in the hands of a few unelected elites can be traced to what American policymakers at the time began to embrace as the concept of "total war," necessitated, of course, by the modern terror of atomic weaponry (unleashed by them!) and perpetuated by the daunting task of preventing nuclear, species-ending, weapons from bursting free on the horizon. Mr. Kubrick framed the insanity as *Dr. Strangelove or: How I Learned to Stop Worrying and Love the Bomb*. More recently, Mr. Chomsky framed the insanity as *Hegemony or Survival.*

> *You that never done nothin'*
> *But build to destroy*
> *You play with my world*
> *Like it's your little toy*
> —Bob Dylan, "Masters of War"

The historically evolving concept of "total war" came to fruition on the heels of "the good war" and spawned the emergence of the National Security State. In fact, a "total war" state of mind, which has been the American modus operandi since the end of World War II, is an all-consuming system where a belligerent and aggressive super force employs the complete mobilization of every available resource that a society has to offer in order to kill for complete political and economic control on a massive scale—and there is no distinction between enemy combatants and civilians.

One of the great literary hoaxes in American history was the dark and satirical *Report from Iron Mountain*, written by Leonard Lewin in 1967. This brilliant satire offered conclusions from a U.S. government panel of prominent thinkers who determined in detail what would happen if "peace broke out." Despite the fact that the book is a hoax and a biting black comedy, the conclusions are still deadly serious regarding the dangerous directive U.S. policymakers intended for U.S. policy, namely that war was a necessary and ongoing reality to maintain the status quo for global elites. "The organization of a society for the possibility of war is its principal political stabilizer,"[4] the report states. "The basic authority of a modern state over its people resides in its war powers."[5]

This is the acceptable worldview of those who created the necessity for the National Security State. Along with their hired henchmen, they will stop at nothing—and if the historical record proves anything, they will never hesitate to intervene, intimidate, overthrow, destroy, assassinate, disappear, torture, and terrorize with extreme prejudice in order to protect the Holy Grail.

In his study, *A Cross of Iron: Harry S. Truman and the Origins of the National Security State, 1945-1954*, which details the intense internal battle of American policymakers regarding America's post-war role in the world, historian Michael Hogan outlines the dawn of what Gore Vidal termed the "global empire business" as well as the subsequent emergence of the National Security State. Hogan traces the dramatic machinations of unifying the American armed forces, exploiting hard science for military purposes, as well as the drive to control the mass mobilization of military manpower. But, of course, you need massive amounts of ongoing and never-ending money for an operation of this scale—and that's where the American taxpayer comes in. Enter stage left. In the end, this aggressive plan distributed the astronomical cost of "defense" across the entire U.S. economy. The practice continues to this moment. Hogan writes:

The question was whether the organizational framework appropriate to such a program was also appropriate to the way Americans saw themselves, or whether it would undermine their democratic traditions, subvert their Constitution, and transform their country into a modern-day Sparta.[6]

"The Russians are coming! The Russians are coming!"

To fully understand the origins of the National Security State (and thereby the origins of the CIA), which so drastically curtailed whatever reality of a republic did exist in America, one must understand America's obsession with communism, socialism, and the Soviet Union—an obsession rooted in the desire to consolidate power, resources, wealth, and even the very definition of governance; America will define liberty and America will define the ideological menace of communism, socialism, and anything else perceived as a threat to American superiority.

The drive toward bolstering the new security apparatus was spearheaded by the visionaries and architects of empire who waged the Cold War for nearly half of the 20th century. This included George Frost Kennan, who greatly inspired Harry Truman and the foundational texts that defined both the Truman and Eisenhower administration's anti-Soviet policy.[7] There was James Forrestal—America's first Secretary of Defense—who either committed suicide or was abruptly tossed out of a Bethesda Naval Hospital window to his untimely and gruesome death. Forrestal, whose name adorns 1,600 acres of Princeton University's campus as well as a quaint corporate village and an adjacent Marriott hotel, was a pernicious anti-Soviet advocate and a major participant in the development of the National Security Act of 1947.[8] And then, of course, there is the impact of Harry Truman's controversial Secretary of State Dean Acheson, who was arguably the major driving force behind the creation of what many have termed the post-World War II "Pax Americana"—a foreign policy reality energized and dictated by the so-called Truman Doctrine.

Acheson was a protégé of Supreme Court Justice Felix Frankfurter, a close advisor to General George Marshall (the namesake for America's plan of economic imperialism in Europe), as well as a close friend and confidant to Winston Churchill. His access, position, and virulent anti-Soviet stance greatly influenced and helped to shape the dangerous post-WWII world. He was a major player pulling the strings on the Marshall Plan—America's economic "relief plan" for a war-battered Europe, the true aim of which was to curtail Soviet aggression.

The Marshall Plan also set the stage for major U.S. investments throughout Europe, which helped to establish a stranglehold of multinational corporations on populations everywhere. Acheson has also been widely defined as a major architect of the abovementioned Truman Doctrine, which was designed to greatly limit Soviet expansion in the 1950s through treacherous and dangerous saber rattling. He was a driving force and major administration proponent of the North Atlantic Treaty Organization (NATO), designed to ensure an ongoing military confrontation in Europe with the Soviet Union.

In the 2005 collection, *Conversations with Gore Vidal*, the American writer and critic, who enjoyed carte blanche entrée to Washington's power elite, recalled the on-the-ground impression of the burgeoning Evil Empire following the Second World War:

> Nobody was afraid of the Russians. Their omnipotence is one of the great myths. I knew Washington in those days; nobody took them seriously. They were a bunch of clowns. Everybody knew that they had lost 20 million people, they had no technology to speak of, what industrial capacity they had had been knocked out, we had the atom bomb. And yet this scare campaign was put on.[9]

Vidal continues with an overview of post-World War II capitol-think:

> Officially it began in 1947... as a determination at the end of World War II not to disarm and to continue high government spending. There were legitimate reasons for that—a fear of going back into the Depression... For the purposes of teaching I would start with '47, when the National Security Council, CIA, etc. were invented. Then in 1950 the NSC was set in motion with NSC order number 68, a blueprint for the state in which we still live, where 86 percent of the federal revenue goes for war, and the rest supports the largely irrelevant cosmetic government of Congress and Judiciary and the never-ending issues-less presidential elections. Ollie North gave the game away on TV. In effect, he told the Senate, the Chorus, "We are the government of the United States and what are you clowns doing getting in the way."[10]

In his 1991 book of essays, *Deterring Democracy*, American dissident and political critic Noam Chomsky chronologically pegs the emergence of the full-fledged American security state:

The orthodox version is sketched out in stark and vivid terms in what is widely recognized to be the basic US Cold War document, NSC 68 in April 1950, shortly before the Korean War, announcing that "the cold war is in fact a real war in which the survival of the free world is at stake..." The basic structure of the argument has the childlike simplicity of a fairy tale. There are two forces in the world, at "opposite poles." In one corner we have absolute evil; in the other, sublimity. There can be no compromise between them. The diabolical force, by its very nature, must seek total domination of the world. Therefore it must be overcome, uprooted, and eliminated so that the virtuous champion of all that is good may survive to perform his exalted works.[11]

Along with many others, Chomsky views the Cold War and the subsequent materialization of the National Security State as an ongoing historical process but also as an ideological construct. As is the case with any "official" history, there can be a wide chasm between fact and fantasy—and this is never more apparent than when digging deep into the dark and misty dynamics of the Cold War and the creation and so-called "need" for the Central Intelligence Agency (along with other intelligence gathering organizations). Chomsky articulates the black-and-white/good-vs-evil nature of the American Cold War mentality:

The "fundamental design of the Kremlin," NSC 68 author Paul Nitze explains, is "the complete subversion or forcible destruction of the machinery of government and structure of society" in every corner of the world that is not yet "subservient to and controlled from the Kremlin."[12]

Stillborn from the bellicose and combative mentality that permeated Washington in the late 1940s, came strident Cold War policy initiatives as set in motion by the National Security Act of 1947. This was quickly followed by the National Security Agency, the National Security Council, and the Central Intelligence Agency, or—

Capitalism's Invisible Army

—as well as various governmental edifices throughout the District of Columbia that housed brand new giant bureaucracies: a network of minions dedicated to ensuring the Empire's control over domestic and foreign security operations. New shadows were lurking everywhere. Individual freedoms be damned... the Garrison State was complete.

"It was a kind of tacit approval…"

Both the U.S. and Soviet Union used the Cold War as a way to sell policy initiatives to their respective populations: the Soviets in order to "entrench its military-bureaucratic ruling class in power," and for the U.S. to give Washington "a way to compel its population to subsidize high-tech industry." Both superpowers used FEAR to shove the game plan down their throats. "No matter how outlandish the idea that the Soviet Union and its tentacles were strangling the West," Chomsky points out, "the 'Evil Empire' *was* in fact evil, *was* an empire and *was* brutal."[13] Then, in pure Chomsky fashion, he distills down the hard truth that historically keeps him off the pages of America's papers of record:

> In crucial respects, then, the Cold War was a kind of tacit
> arrangement between the Soviet Union and the United States
> under which the US conducted its wars against the Third World
> and controlled its allies in Europe, while the Soviet rulers kept an
> iron grip on their own internal empire and their satellites in
> Eastern Europe—each side using the other to justify repression
> and violence in its own domains.[14]

The Roman Empire lived by this credo: *oderint dum metuant.* So do powerbrokers everywhere: *"Let them hate so long as they fear."*

Are there communists in your toilet?

The next major step involved in the coronation of the National Security State came at the hands of the vast government propaganda machine and their two best partners in crime: the American press and those drunken rubes on Madison Avenue, the "mad men." Paranoia was the story—fear was the product. In fact, fear in this country reached levels so absurd as to be preposterous and downright laughable, as evidenced by a magazine ad for Scot Towels with the headline: *Is Your Washroom Breeding Bolsheviks?*

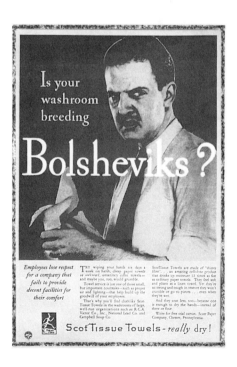

The dangerous Lenin/Trotsky-like dude drying his hands with a Scot paper towel—along with the word "Bolsheviks" screaming in a color Crayola would probably call "red menace"—remains priceless, as is the subhead: *Employees lose respect for a company that fails to provide decent facilities for their comfort.*

Overall message cemented and delivered: Dirty fucking commies.

This message of fear was delivered in ubiquitous fashion to every man, woman, and child living in every city, town, and hamlet in America. And it was delivered like the mail: over and over and over again. It was delivered in newspapers, magazines, movies, textbooks, advertisements, and on television every day for decades—and that message is still being delivered. In fact, the message has been distributed in ways so numerous and universal as to now be part of the American DNA. The message has also been used as a weapon by the U.S. government in countless ways—the early crowning glory being the diabolical House Un-American Activities Committee (HUAC) along with the U.S. Senate's version named the Permanent Subcommittee on Investigations and chaired by the loveable Senator Joe McCarthy who later hired Robert Kennedy as a senior staff member and fellow accomplice. Careers were scorched and lives destroyed by a ruthless red-baiting witch-hunt, all in the name and spirit of "National Security," with its tentacles reaching far into the future, setting the stage for CONINTELPRO and other secret government surveillance programs aimed at spying on, infiltrating, and ultimately destroying (or to use the FBI's term—"neutralizing") groups and individuals deemed by the government to a be a clear and present danger to the "internal security of the United States." These groups included socialists, communists, civil rights and antiwar groups, the Black Panthers, the Nation of Islam, Malcolm X, Martin Luther King, Jr., John Lennon, rogue Boy Scout troops, and of course the raging radical herself, Eleanor Roosevelt. But this is nothing new in American history—just ask John Adams about his Alien and Sedition Acts.

Before his death, Gore Vidal sat down with us for this book and we asked him about Harry Truman, the Russians, and the advent of the modern security state. In his inimitable way, Vidal framed the conversation with biting wit:

> Truman, of course, is the villain. But now he's being depicted as a matinee idol. Corporate America wants him as a hero but he really started the Cold War. He kept it going by terrifying the people, *"The Russians are coming. The Russians are coming. They've got the bomb. They've got the super bomb."* And from then on, presidents say, "Oh,

terrorism. That's the way. The great enemy is going to hit you in the night, without warning…" And if you're in school, you know, get under your desk and you won't get blown to bits. So our rulers, who are now plutocrats, rule entirely by terror, mostly invoked by them. They've got the people terrified of mysterious Fu Manchu figures hiding in the hills of Afghanistan. So, the Russians were never coming. Even now people faint when you say that because they've been infected with this dreaded poison.[15]

This poison that Vidal references runs deep, like radium waste from an old clock factory seeping beneath the soil and into the groundwater of a New Jersey community—toxic waste with a radioactive foundation boasting a half-life of 1,600 years. It just doesn't disappear. In fact, the community needed a Superfund to remove this subterranean infection, and the Fourth-Estate should have been the American people's Superfund, but it wasn't and never will be if it continues its lock-step allegiance with government and corporate power. Vidal concludes, "It has been no secret that Corporate America openly and generously pays for our presidential elections; they also own the Media, which is kept well-nourished by disinformation from executive-controlled secret agencies like the CIA."[16]

Ten Days That Shook The World

The potent anti-Soviet bloc of western powers led by the U.S. and their red scare campaigns did not simply materialize after World War II, but first took root during World War I as the Bolshevik Revolution led to Russia's early exit from the war and the subsequent toppling of the powerful tsar known as "Bloody Nicholas"—also known as "Nikolay Alexandrovich Romanov, Emperor and Autocrat of All the Russias." What followed was an Allied Invasion into the Russian Civil War on the side of the pro-Tsarist White Army. Ostensibly, at first, the American, British, French, and other forces in the fourteen-nation operation were concerned that munitions and arms stored in Russian ports would fall into the hands of the Germans or worse, the Bolsheviks. The Allies were also hell-bent on reestablishing the Eastern Front. But beneath it all, the subtext, as they say in theater, was something else. So, let's ask the question: What was the driving force that moved a young Winston Churchill, Great Britain's Minister of War and Air at the time, to direct the invasion of Russia, heretofore Britain's ally? Well, as Deep Throat instructed Bob Woodward in *All the President's Men*, "follow the money." In this case it was that wretched nine-letter word: *socialism*. Historian and longtime critic of U.S. foreign policy, William Blum, in his book *Killing Hope*, explains why Red October set off fire alarms in the hallways of western power:

> What was there about this Bolshevik Revolution that so alarmed the most powerful nations in the world? What drove them to invade a land whose soldiers had recently fought alongside them for over three years and suffered more casualties than any other country on either side of the World War? The Bolsheviks had had the audacity to make a separate peace with Germany in order to take leave of a war they regarded as imperialist and not in any way *their* war, and to try and rebuild a terribly weary and devastated Russia. But the Bolsheviks had displayed the far greater audacity of overthrowing a capitalist–feudal system and proclaiming the first socialist state in the history of the world. This was uppityness writ incredibly large. This was the crime the Allies had to punish, the virus which had to be eradicated lest it spread to their own people.[17]

The alleged "virus" of socialism continued to threaten western powers (especially the government of the United States and their corporate masters) throughout the 20th century and remained the economic essence of the Cold War. In fact nothing has changed: this reprehensible disease of socialism threatens the same corporatocracy in place today.

Clearly the die was cast with the Allied Invasion of Russia, setting early precedent for later imperialist and super-cop interventions by the new Empire's "Gendarme," "Federales," or, as we've come to affectionately know them in Hollywood propaganda pieces like the TV series *Homeland*, "the Agency." Sometimes operating undercover in what is termed a "covert action" (or as Reagan Executive Order 12333 re-defined it: "special activities"), or as a paramilitary action (think drones), or, when none of that shit works, operating as an all-out military bombardment (think blood for oil), these interventions are nothing more than the United States conducting business as usual. We digress…

Unable to defend his government against the Bolshevik takeover, interim Russian Prime Minister Alexander Kerensky fled to France while Lenin, Trotsky, and others initiated the new Soviet state, and this "red-peril–red-menace–and-red-babies being-eaten-by-their-red-parents" virus scare became the great Satan. In fact, there always has to be a great Satan to rally the masses (think Saddam Hussein and his weapons of mass distraction, or bin Laden, or just about anything Muslim).

William Blum outlines how early and ongoing interventions—bolstered and supported by anti-communist propaganda—kept the socialist state in the crosshairs of capitalism and its bidders:

> History does not tell us what a Soviet Union, allowed to develop in a "normal" way of its own choosing, would look like today. We do know, however, the nature of a Soviet Union attacked in its cradle, raised alone in an extremely hostile world, and, when it managed to survive to adulthood, overrun by the Nazi war machine with the blessings of the Western powers. The resulting insecurities and fears have inevitably led to deformities of character not unlike that found in an individual raised in a similar life-threatening manner. We in the West are never allowed to forget the political shortcomings (real and alleged) of the Soviet Union; at the same time we are never reminded of the history which lies behind it. The anti-communist propaganda campaign began even earlier than the military intervention. Before the year 1918 was over, expressions in the vein of "Red Peril," "the Bolshevik assault on Civilization," and "menace to world by Reds is seen" had become commonplace in the pages of the New York Times.[18]

Clearly, this anti-communist mania became part and parcel of the American psyche throughout the 20th century, only to be replaced after the fall of the Soviet Union by a new and improved boogeyman: terrorism—now one of the double-stranded helices of America's DNA. Blum concludes:

> Literally no story about the Bolsheviks was too contrived, too bizarre, too grotesque, or too perverted to be printed and widely believed—from women being nationalized to babies being eaten (as the early pagans believed the Christians guilty of devouring their children; the same was believed of the Jews in the Middle Ages). From the Red Scare of the 1920s to the McCarthyism of the 1950s to the Reagan Crusade against the Evil Empire of the 1980s, the American people have been subjected to a relentless anti-communist indoctrination. It is imbibed with their mother's milk, pictured in their comic books, spelled out in their school books; their daily paper offers them headlines that tell them all they need to know; ministers find sermons in it, politicians are elected with it, and Reader's Digest becomes rich on it.[19]

"Sophie's Choice"

The idea of "socialism" has been strenuously argued, from dark and smoky 19th century pubs in Marx's adopted home of London to the 21st century New York studios of *Fox News,* which chirps on and on about this dreaded disease—more infectious than Bubonic Plague and AIDS wrapped in a blanket. But the definition is really simple enough: it's the workers themselves controlling production—not predatory economic or political rulers—and this is true in a capitalist structure or in an absolutist paradigm. Dissident and historian Noam Chomsky illustrates the dogma that has mangled and manipulated the term:

> To refer to the Soviet Union as "socialist" is an interesting case of doctrinal doublespeak. The Bolshevik coup of October 1917 placed state power in the hands of Lenin and Trotsky, who moved quickly to dismantle the incipient socialist institutions that had grown up during the popular revolution of the preceding months—the factory councils, the Soviets [popularly elected legislative assemblies], in fact any organ of popular control—and to convert the workforce into what they called a "labor army" under the command of the leader. In any meaningful sense of the term "socialism," the Bolsheviks moved at once to destroy its existing elements. No socialist deviation has been permitted since.[20]

This manipulation, as well as the subsequent propaganda that followed, ensured that power would remain in the hands of the ruling state party. Chomsky then underscores how both superpowers skewed "socialism" for their own power play:

> The Bolsheviks called their system socialist so as to exploit the moral prestige of socialism. The West adopted the same usage for the opposite reason: to defame the feared libertarian ideals by associating them with the Bolshevik dungeon, to undermine the popular belief that there really might be progress towards a more just society, with democratic control over its basic institutions and concern for human needs and rights.[21]

Chomsky concludes with a political "Sophie's Choice"—

> If socialism is the tyranny of Lenin and Stalin, then sane people will say: not for me. And if that's the only alternative to corporate state capitalism, then many will submit to its authoritarian structures as the only reasonable choice.[22]

Both sides of the Cold War poisoned minds for generations regarding "socialism." It was this fascistic mugging and battering—for very disparate reasons—that once again wiped the people's natural rights off the table. Oh, and by the way, this Cold War chess game also nearly wiped the human race off the planet.

Wild Thing

Norman Mailer, the great novelist and journalist, spent a lifetime searching for answers to explain the mystery of America. In his 1991 opus and masterpiece, *Harlot's Ghost*, about life in the Central Intelligence Agency, the story seems to be the classic spy novel—the timeless battle between the forces of good (the U.S.) against the evil and destructive will of the Soviet Union. But as the story unfolds, Mailer's narrative reveals the true enemy: the soul-consuming Cold War itself. And never was this more apparent than at the outset of the Truman Administration's desire to create a means for coordinating intelligence gathering from around the world. Shortly after the 33rd President of the United States assumed power in 1945, he realized he was in an information vacuum, placing his ability to operate from the White House at a severe disadvantage. In his 2008 book, *Legacy of Ashes: The History of the CIA*, Pulitzer Prize-winning author and *New York Times* reporter Tim Weiner frames the early days of Truman's development of his intelligence operation with a brilliant introductory line, "All Harry Truman wanted was a newspaper."[23] FDR's Office of Strategic Services (OSS), the precursor to what became the Central Intelligence Agency, was a wartime outfit and not built to last.[24] Truman knew this and quickly realized he needed vast amounts of information to maximize his presidential power. Weiner writes:

> When the new Central Intelligence Agency arose from its ashes
> [the OSS], Truman wanted it to serve him solely as a global news
> service, delivering daily bulletins. "It was not intended as a Cloak
> & Dagger Outfit!" he wrote. "It was intended merely as a center
> for keeping the President informed on what was going on in
> the world." He insisted that he never wanted the CIA "to act as
> a spy organization. That was never the intention when it was
> organized."[25]

Weiner concludes, "His vision was subverted from the start."[26] It began with a cowboy soldier left over from World War II, General William Donovan, "a bold, charismatic, prescient, sometimes ridiculous, and potentially dangerous man,"[27] writes Louis Menand in his *New Yorker* piece about Douglas Waller's biography entitled *Wild Bill Donovan: The Spymaster Who Created the OSS and Modern American Espionage.* His nickname "Wild Bill" was either given to him by his soldiers because of his war-like bravado or it was borrowed from the original "Wild Thing," the Detroit Tigers and New York Yankees pitcher of the same name who had a tough time finding the plate with any of his pitches (think Bob Ueuker as Harry Doyle: "Juuuust a bit outside...").

History wishes to remember Donovan as the fearless leader of United States intelligence during World War II when he headed up the Office of Strategic Services. Throughout his tenure under FDR, Wild Bill had dreams of a post-war peacetime intelligence juggernaut. Weiner explains:

> The OSS had never been stronger than thirteen thousand members,
> smaller than a single army division. But the service Donovan
> envisioned would be its own army, a force skillfully combating
> communism, defending America from attack, and serving up secrets
> for the White House. He urged the president to "lay the keel of the
> ship at once," and he aimed to be its captain.[28]

There's no doubt that Wild Bill saw this new intelligence entity as the Empire's super cop, its own agile and unencumbered swat team. The statement he is most known for sums up his legacy as well as his impact on plotting the course for the CIA: "In a global and totalitarian war, intelligence must be global and totalitarian."[29] The current CIA website identifies Donovan as "the father of Central Intelligence," and although he never led the CIA nor held an official position, his fingerprints are everywhere on its launch and early endeavors.[30] But his oftentimes rogue behavior made many in Washington nervous about his involvement in a post-war American world. "Very few generals and admirals trusted him," Weiner writes. "They were appalled by his idea of making a spy service out of a scattershot collection of Wall Street brokers, Ivy League eggheads, soldiers of fortune, ad men, news men, stunt men, second-story men, and con men."[31]

Wild Bill's imagination (some might call it a "Looney Tunes" imagination) clearly lives on in the heart and soul of the CIA as they continue to hatch their infamous and criminal actions deep inside the bowels of their citadel in Langley. In fact, the history of the CIA is defined by behavior that runs the gamut from treacherous and odious to sophomoric and batty, as evidenced by some of Wild Bill's greatest hits, starting with the idea of "air-dropping pictures of succulent food into

Germany to provoke hungry inhabitants to rise up against the Nazis."[32] Louis Menand in *The New Yorker* continues:

> Under Donovan, the O.S.S. hatched a scheme to inject Hitler's food with female sex hormones. Following up on a suggestion passed along by F.D.R. himself, it pursued a plan that involved strapping incendiary devices to bats, which would be dropped from airplanes over Japanese cities, on the theory that the bats would nest in the wooden houses in which most Japanese lived and set them on fire.[33]

Fortunately for the Japanese (but not for the bats), when the flying mammals were unleashed from a test plane, the winged marauders fell back to the planet like tiny barbells. This harebrained Wile E. Coyote plan was scrapped, but not U.S. designs on setting Tokyo and other Japanese cities ablaze, which was finally accomplished (as we detailed in the World War II chapter) by dropping M-69 incendiary cluster bombs filled with napalm on densely populated neighborhoods, incinerating 80,000 and 100,000 Japanese civilians.[34] Wild Bill must have been green with envy.

According to Weiner in *Legacy of Ashes*, FDR harbored serious doubts about Wild Bill Donovan and his methods. Toward the end of World War II, Roosevelt ordered a secret investigation of Donovan's OSS. Leaks of the investigation hit papers around the country with even the arch conservative *Washington Times-Herald* calling Donovan's vision a "super spy system"[35] and framing it as an American Gestapo.[36] This was clearly the beginning of the end for Wild Bill's drive to be at the helm when America's postwar intelligence organism took root; and when Roosevelt died in April of '45, Donovan knew it was indeed the end. His defender and his protector flew the coop. And then on the same day, which added insult to injury, FDR's top-secret investigation report was presented to the new president Harry Truman and the report eviscerated Donovan personally as well as the overall effectiveness of the OSS. In painstaking detail, the report offers failure after miserable failure of the OSS during the war—one fumble costing 1,100 French troops their lives on the island of Elba. Ultimately, the fifty-nine pages accused Donovan of "running what amounted to a rogue operation, plagued throughout the war by intelligence failures and all manner of hidden scandal."[37] "The report," Weiner concludes, "was a political murder weapon, honed by the military and sharpened by none other than J. Edgar Hoover."[38] Of course Hoover had his own lollipop dreams of one day running a worldwide spy network.

Donovan and his Office of Strategic Services was dead on arrival as the postwar American Empire dawned, still basking in the explosive bright lights of "Fat Man" and "Little Boy." Less than two years later, in July of 1947, Harry S. Truman signed the National Security Act, which created the Central Intelligence Agency. Section 102 (a) set the monster in motion:

> There is hereby established under the National Security Council a Central Intelligence Agency with a Director of Central Intelligence, who shall be the head thereof. The Director shall be appointed by the President, by the advice and consent of the Senate, from among commissioned officers of the armed services or from among individuals in civilian life. The Director shall receive compensation at the rate of $14,000 a year.[39]

Wild Bill may never have realized his own dreams of running a postwar intelligence agency—his own clandestine spy cabal carrying out covert military actions, bribing scumbags, and of course spreading disinformation like horse manure—but his printer's mark remains imbedded in the Empire's secret imperial police. The Roman Empire also had their secret police or *frumentarii* ("a heavy-handed instrument of imperial power"[40]), and now the U.S. had theirs: the CIA. And General William Donovan and his OSS were "the Petri dish for the spies who later ran the CIA," concludes Douglas Waller. "Allen Dulles, Richard Helms, William Colby, Bill Casey—men who cut their teeth under Donovan—became future directors." Indeed, these future spymasters, these Cold War warriors, these men who delivered murder and mayhem in Southeast Asia, East Timor, Central and South America, were all recruited by "Wild Bill," a force in Washington seen by many as "a power grabber as dangerous as Adolf Hitler."[41] Even early on, Truman himself held grave reservations and "had decided that Donovan's plan had the earmarks of a Gestapo." Waller goes on to paint a clear picture of the new and evolving CIA as little more than a duplicate of its defunct predecessor:

> The daring, the risk taking, the unconventional thinking, the élan and esprit de corps of the OSS would permeate the new agency. The failings of the OSS would, too—the delusions that covert operations, like magic bullets, could produce spectacular results, that legal and ethical corners could be cut for a higher cause, infected the CIA as well.[42]

"Donovan," writes Waller in his final analysis, "was one of the men who shaped modern warfare."[43]

A postscript on Donovan: In 1953, Eisenhower appointed Wild Bill as Ambassador to Thailand and of course, living up to his name, Ambassador Donovan stirred the shit-pot good, including the advocacy of the catastrophic career of Ngo Dinh Diem, who became America's puppet dictator and first president of South Vietnam. Diem, a militant Roman Catholic in an overwhelmingly Buddhist country, was famously unpopular, incredibly paranoid, and ruthless in his role as president. By 1960, South Vietnamese insurgents were in open revolt against Diem's repressive regime. These insurgents were communists and non-communists—the so-called Vietcong or National Liberation Front. The internal rebellion prompted the U.S. to significantly build up its military and economic presence in South Vietnam. By the time Ike leaves office, the United States has poured several billion dollars into Diem's regime and American military "advisors" are multiplying like rabbits, and by the fall of '63, John Kennedy has increased American "advisors" to 16,000— with economic and military aid skyrocketing. On November 3rd, three weeks before Kennedy is murdered in Dallas, Diem and his brother are assassinated in a coup orchestrated by the CIA and South Vietnamese General Duong Van Minh.

Clearly, Donovan's rancid legacy jettisoned itself right into the heart of the Vietnam War.

Soldiers for Christ, Protectors of Christendom

No other historic reality sums up the Central Intelligence Agency more than the ongoing narrative of their attempts to change the world without bothering to understand the world—or more importantly never bothering to understand the people who inhabit the world. But to understand the surreptitious spirit and behavior of the CIA, one must first understand the people who dream of one day calling the unincorporated community of Langley, Virginia, home—that's where you'll find CIA Headquarters overlooking the banks of the Potomac, hard between the George Washington Memorial Parkway and Dolley Madison Boulevard.

Earlier in this chapter we referenced Norman Mailer's masterwork novel on the CIA, *Harlot's Ghost*—a chronicle of the Cold War as well as a parallel and meticulous deconstruction of the American psyche that allows for, consecrates, and ultimately nourishes the men and women who make up "the Agency."

Mailer's seven-year journey writing his 1,300-page tome—one that combines real and fictional characters—is legendary in its details and nuances of the spook-coup-and-assassination business. So much so that Mailer, the iconic scribe of the American left, was invited to speak at Langley and was warmly embraced by senior officials.[44] His epic work, highly critical of the Agency's motives as well as its operations, was lost on the bureaucratic enforcers and executioners who lauded his exposé. (Under the heading of WTF, one has to wonder what Mailer was even doing at Langley!) But journalist Saul Landau, who Gore Vidal once described as "a man I love to steal ideas from," detailed the power of Mailer's half-century spanning indictment of the CIA's murky and bloody history. Among many things, he writes:

> [Mailer's characters adore] criminal behavior and will commit almost any bizarre act to make money… episodes that cover decades of personal and national misalliances and betrayals… the leaders of U.S. "intelligence" lack any ideological foundation except to their own capricious pleasures. The top CIA dogs helped create the myth of Soviet power while politicians and media flaks sold their bullshit to the public… major CIA fiascos carried out in the name of advancing freedom or gathering advantages in the Cold War: In the 1950s, they dug the Berlin Tunnel under KGB headquarters only to discover they had fallen into a KGB trap; they launched the invasion of Cuba after convincing themselves Cuba would fall like Guatemalan President Arbenz did in 1954 in a similar "invasion." The inventors of these plans really don't care about consequences—then or now… assassination plots—and the bizarre set of assassins the Agency chose—to kill Castro. We meet the top dogs, like Allen Dulles and the psychopathic planners of hits, like, E. Howard Hunt. The history of the CIA is after all the abbreviated nuts and bolts of Cold War history… all this nonsense in the name of defending freedom.[45]

The history of the Agency's growth and subsequent recruitment for personnel is one that is entwined with the privilege of the WASP establishment. Let's return to the 36th President of the United States, Lyndon Baines Johnson, and his assessment of the CIA: "The CIA is made up of boys whose families sent them to Princeton but wouldn't let them into the family brokerage business." The man from Stonewall, Texas, got a lot of things wrong, but not his remark about the "boys" of the CIA. Charles Michaud, writing the *Library Journal*'s review of

Harlot's Ghost, cannot help but critique the Agency's religious-like zeal when he states, "It is a spirit born of militant Christianity and buccaneering rapacity, of noblesse oblige and authoritarian devotion, a spirit believing itself tuned in to God without worrying if it's heeding the devil."[46]

Ultimately, the agents cum spooks cum assassins are convinced to forfeit their souls to serve at the pleasure of the Agency. They are hypnotized by covert action. No passage in Mailer's tome better captures this perversion than this exchange (more like "a sermon on the subtleties of evil in the realm of Communism") between Harry Hubbard, the main character and CIA agent, and his mentor Harlot—a top ranking CIA officer:

> "I would remind you," said Harlot, "that the true force of the Russians has little to do with military strength. We are vulnerable to them in another way… For the Russians are able to get their licks in on whatever is left of the Christian in many a rich swine. It goes so deep—this simple idea that nobody on earth should have too much wealth. That's exactly what's satanic about Communism. It trades on the noblest vein in Christianity. It works the great guilt in us. At the core, we Americans are even worse than the English. We're drenched in guilt. We're rich boys, after all, with no background, and we're playing around the world with the hearts of the poor. That's tricky. Especially if you have been brought up to believe that the finest love you will ever come near goes back to the sentiments of Christ washing the feet of those same poor people."
>
> "How would you feel," I asked, "if I said these things? Wouldn't you wonder which side I was working for?" My thwarted curiosity still lay like lead on my stomach.
>
> "If I thought I was on the wrong side," he answered, "I would feel obliged to defect. I do not wish ever to work for evil. It is evil to recognize the good, and continue to work against it. But, make no mistake," he told me, "the sides are clear. Lava is lava, and spirit is spirit. The Reds, not us, are the evil ones, and so they are clever enough to imply that they are in the true tradition of Christ. They are the ones who work at kissing the feet of the poor. Absolute poppycock. But the Third World buys it. That's because the Russians know how to merchandise one crucial commodity:

Ideology. Our spiritual offering is finer, but their marketing of ideas proves superior. Here, those of us who are serious tend to approach God alone, each of us, one by one, but the Soviets are able to perform the conversion en masse. That is because they deliver the commonweal over to man, not God. A disaster. God, not man, has to be the judge. I will always believe that. I also believe that even at my worst, I am still working, always working, as a soldier of God."[47]

Not Just an American 'Thang'

Clearly, the covert and clandestine operations of the CIA—along with the fierce violence associated with these worldwide operations—is not just an American malady. The idea and practice of a secret police force operating outside the law is as old as the nation state itself. Hell, even the Vatican runs their own underground subversive and secretive force known as the "Holy Alliance" or later known as the "The Entity," also the title of Spanish journalist Eric Frattini's expose on five centuries of secret Vatican espionage that has included kidnapping, colonization, persecution, and yes, assassination. Their motto might also hang proudly over the grand doorway entrance to Langley: *With the Cross and the Sword.*

History is littered with examples—some more brutal than others. Iran under Shah Mohammad Reza Pahlavi employed the vicious SAVAK (formed under the direct guidance of United States and Israeli intelligence officers in 1957),[48] infamous for their brutal torture and executions of challengers to the U.S.-backed Pahlavi regime. In fact, as their power grew, SAVAK became the law itself. This secret police force had the legal authority to arrest and detain Iranians indefinitely. SAVAK even operated its own prisons.[49] Sound familiar?

Reporter Craig Smith, writing in *The New York Times*, describes Romania's Securitate—one of the Soviet-era's largest secret police forces: "Under the oppressive regime of Nicolae Ceausescu," Smith recalls, "it was also among the most brutal. An estimated 11,000 agents and a half-million informers watched millions of Romanian citizens, hundreds of thousands of whom were imprisoned for political reasons."[50]

And many were killed. But the sad fact remains: this reprehensible and violent behavior exists at the very core of all spy organizations (with the possible exceptions of CONTROL and KAOS)—and it exists whether that organization operates as a government entity or as a private corporation and contractor like Academi aka XE Services aka Blackwater USA aka Blackwater Worldwide—a sadistic organization that answers to no one except its patron and partner in murder, the U.S. State Department. Just ask one of the 17 Iraqis massacred in Nisour Square (near Baghdad's Green Zone) by a Blackwater USA "security unit" how they feel about Christian (white) supremacist ex-Navy SEAL Erik Prince, the founder and ideological foot soldier of Academi and his mercenary band of murdering thugs. (Prince is the kind of cat that whispers sweet nothings into the Trump Administration's eardrums like they "should recreate a version of the Phoenix Program, the CIA assassination ring that operated during the Vietnam War, to fight ISIS."[51])

Former *New York Times* correspondent and Pulitzer Prize-winning author Chris Hedges sketches the reality and exposes the ugly cynicism of these underhanded operatives from all countries and organizations: "men and women who lie and deceive for a living, who betray relationships, including between each other, who steal and who carry out murder. One knows them immediately."[52] Hedges goes on to make a strong case that beliefs, ideas, and principles mean little to these miscreants, ultimately drawing the inevitable connection to the archetypical crime syndicate. Enter the fictitious Corleones, the Sopranos, or the very real Gambinos—all defined by diabolical murder and mayhem. Hedges continues:

> Their ideological allegiances do not matter. They have the faraway eyes of the disconnected, along with nebulous histories and suspicious and vague associations. They tell incongruous personal stories and practice small deceits that are part of a pathological inability to tell the truth. They can be personable, even charming, but they are also invariably vain, dishonest and sinister. They cannot be trusted. It does not matter what side they are on. They were all the same. Gangsters.[53]

If there's a profile of an individual that longs to be free from moral and legal strictures, who longs to indulge in violence and coercion, this individual has a strong tendency, Hedges suggests, to "gravitate to intelligence agencies, terrorist cells, homeland security, police departments, the special forces and revolutionary groups... Right and wrong are banished from their vocabulary. They disdain the constraints of democracy."

Hedges concludes:

> They have no interest in diplomacy and less in peace. Peace would put them out of business; for them it is simply the temporary

absence of war, which they are sure is inevitable. Their job is to use violence to purge the world of evil. And in the United States they have taken as hostages our diplomatic service and our foreign policy establishment. The CIA has become a huge private army.[54]

"Making the World Safe for the Fortune 500"

With the Soviet Union now a historical footnote, the engine of capital roams the planet like a Tyrannosaurus Rex on steroids. Aided and abetted by the International Monetary Fund, the World Bank, the World Trade Organization, and sweetheart neoliberal assault deals like NAFTA, CAFTA, GATT, and TPP, the current day robber barons are licking their chops all the way to their unregulated banks—in the U.S. and abroad. The American Military-Industrial Intelligence Complex continues to grow in leaps and bounds, unfettered from Moscow's opposition or the weak constraints of a crumbling and ineffectual republic. Plainly and unmistakably, the Central Intelligence Agency has been at the center of an Empire that resembles rolling thunder.

In fact, the CIA utilizes numerous operations to gain their desired result and it's not always secret bombing missions or torture or even those James Bond-like missions that Hollywood loves to extol. Sometimes, as John Perkins revealed in Chapter Two of Book One, it's just good old fashioned extortion, underscoring the fact that "The CIA has played a very, very active role in spreading this empire" through "jackals" and "economic hit men" carrying out the dirty work for the elite emperors and veiled corporatocracy.

As discussed, the clandestine nature of the spook business paints the actions of the CIA with a wide brush stroke—one that's defined by a cloak and dagger burlesque act all motivated by a selfless, humane, and altruistic mission: the innate thirst for freedom, democracy, and Jesus on Sundays. Nothing could be farther from the truth. What about Skull and Bones, you ask? The Freemasons? The Illuminati? You could also include Humpty Dumpty and Tom Thumb on that list. It's not about fairytales—it's about hard cold capital. "The CIA has a role of making the world safe for the Fortune 500; that's its goal," explains political scientist and historian Michael Parenti. "The CIA is not a power unto itself; it's not some sinister, mysterious power. To think that the CIA creates these policies, or this Empire, or this intervention, is like crediting the horse with a horse race."[55]

Plain and simple, the CIA is an instrument of imperialism, and by natural extension, an instrument of the ruling class, protecting their financial interests in every nook and cranny that American corporations manage to bulldoze their way into. "And when you get a president who might want to chart a mildly more liberal course, more conciliatory course, like John F. Kennedy," says Parenti, "the CIA then goes into hostile opposition. But when you get a president like George W. Bush, who represents the ascendant, reactionary interests of the ruling plutocracy of this country, the CIA rolls over and does whatever he says."[56]

William Blum, the former State Department official, is also the author of the 2005 indictment of U.S. interventionist policy entitled *Rogue State: A Guide to the World's Only Superpower*. This searing denunciation by the one-time insider is an antidote to the myths and lies of the American orthodoxy. In fact, Blum's incredibly well researched condemnation begins with the essential and ugly truth: "This book could be entitled: Serial chain-saw baby killers and the women who love them."[57] Or, as we surmise, "Murder Incorporated."

Blum continues his clarion call for truth regarding American foreign policy—a policy stimulated not by ethics and high moral values but rather by base requisites to support and bolster the ever-growing treasure of the one-percent. Blum's four commandments of the CIA's imperatives are as follows:

1. Making the world safe for American corporations.

2. Enhancing the financial statements of defense contractors at home, who have contributed generously to members of Congress.

3. Preventing the rise of any society that might serve as a successful example of an alternative to the capitalist model.

4. Extending political and economic hegemony over as wide an area as possible, as befits a "great power."[58]

The CIA's Greatest Hits

Out of all the government agencies that follow me around, you know the ones I dig the most? The CIA. They're so stupid... I can look out into any audience and spot 'em. Always the cat sittin' there with the brand new beard—price tag hanging down, hippie beads all tangled up in his dog tags.[59]
　　　　　　　　　　　　　　　　　　　　　　　　—Dick Gregory

In the music biz, especially back in the day, greatest hits albums were a shortcut to the market: jam on ten or twelve of an artist's most popular tunes, pop a great image on the cover, and then wordsmith a catchy title like *Don't Fear the Reaper: The Best of Blue Oyster Cult*, or *The Immaculate Collection* from Madonna. But most greatest hits albums are straightforward: *Marvin Gaye's Greatest Hits*, or *Greatest Hits by Cat Stevens*. We will also keep it simple because the CIA, while they create convoluted hot messes around the globe, have always been fueled by a straightforward motivation. In fact, their track list has always been a 4/4 rhythm marching to the beat of empire.

Also, a large dose of gratitude belongs to William Blum for his decades of research. His reckoning sets the stage:

> If you flip over the rock of American foreign policy of the past century, this is what crawls out… invasions… bombings… overthrowing governments… occupations… suppressing movements for social change… assassinating political leaders… perverting elections… manipulating labor unions… manufacturing "news"… death squads… torture… biological warfare… depleted uranium… drug trafficking… mercenaries… It's not a pretty picture. It's enough to give imperialism a bad name.[60]

Blum focused his seasoned eye on Washington's scheming over the last sixty-plus years during the post-World War II period. In fact, he offers a scorecard and that's very apropos for a government and its people (including its media) who view war and politics like the Super Bowl, World Series, and the Stanley Cup all rolled up into one machismo scrum.

U.S. SCORECARD (1945 to 2003*)[61]	
Foreign governments U.S. has attempted to overthrow:	*40+*
*Populist-nationalist movements** U.S. has attempted to crush:*	*30+*
Countries bombed in the process:	*25+*
People murdered in the process:	*>Several Million*
People condemned to a life of agony and despair:	*>Millions More*

*Post-2003, we can now add even more (Haiti, Somalia, Honduras, Libya, Syria, etc.)
**Struggling against intolerable regimes

Guy walks into a D.C. bar, orders a shot, and asks the bartender: "Hey Mac, you know why there will never be a coup d'état in Washington?" The bartender wipes the bar and shrugs no. The guy downs his shot, slides the empty toward Mac and says, "Because there's no American embassy there."

A rigorous and detailed examination of the more prominent "chart-topping" U.S./CIA interventionist hits over the past seventy years reveals a staggering narrative of imperial hubris on the part of American power. Starting with the brutal, coldblooded, and attention-grabbing "commercials" dropped on Hiroshima and Nagasaki in 1945, the first ten years for the new superpower were the decisive and formative years that shaped the American Empire. After the licentious subversion and successful toppling of the Iranian government headed by Mohammad Mossadegh in 1953, American policymakers began to fully appreciate that no country was exempt from U.S. intervention—whether by covert and subterranean actions or by blatant military assault and bombardment. Everything and everybody was on the table.

Chinese Civil War, 1945 to 1949

Historian James Bradley defines him as "ruthless."[62] Historian Howard Zinn defines his regime as a "corrupt dictatorship."[63] Historian Noam Chomsky argues that under his rule China was "rapidly becoming a military-fascist country."[64] In fact, before he left his ancestral home in Xikou, Zhejiang province, one of his tutors called him "stubborn, jealous, tactless, bad-tempered and egotistical."[65] Throughout his rule, his persistent demands for Western support and subsidy also earned him the sound-alike nickname "General Cash-My-Check." But the United States, along with their newly-minted Central Intelligence Agency, called him their pal—Generalissimo Chiang Kai-shek—and then go on to intervene on his behalf in China's celebrated internal struggle.

In fact, the United States strongly supported Kuomintang forces, led by Chiang as he battled the Communist Party of China led by Mao Zedong in their bloody civil war. More than 50,000 U.S. Marines guarded strategic positions while more than 100,000 U.S. troops and military personnel remained on the Chinese mainland after WWII.[66] Along with boots on the ground, Washington equipped and trained a half-million Kuomintang troops under Chiang's control and facilitated their movements throughout China. By the end of the civil war, with Mao Zedong claiming victory with the creation of the People's Republic of China and Chiang Kai-shek on the run to Taiwan, American taxpayers had funneled $2 billion in hard cash and $1 billion in military hardware to Chiang's defeated Nationalists.[67] As per usual, Washington instinctively intervened against the dreaded communist menace. Howard Zinn frames Washington's wrong-headed, knee-jerk judgment:

> According to the State Department's own White Paper on China, Chiang Kai-shek's government had lost the confidence of its own troops and its own people. In January 1949, Chinese Communist forces moved into Peking, the civil war was over, and China was in the hands of a revolutionary movement, the closest thing, in the long history of that ancient country, to a people's government, independent of outside control.[68]

During the anti-communist free-for-all that permeated the American consciousness in the 1950s, the great pejorative question was repeated ad infinitum: *"Who lost China?"* It's a question that still reverberates to this day. Factions on the right as well as on the left in America used the question as a battering ram to bludgeon each other to death. *"Who lost China?"* Well, the only true answer is this: It was never America's to lose.

This is your brain... This is your brain on drugs... And this is the CIA.

In my 30-year history in the Drug Enforcement Administration and related agencies, the major targets of my investigations almost invariably turned out to be working for the CIA.[69]
—Dennis Dayle, former chief of the DEA's Central Tactical Unit

In 1996, Pulitzer Prize-winning investigative journalist Gary Webb wrote a series of articles for the *San Jose Mercury News* entitled "Dark Alliance," which uncovered the CIA-sponsored sale of crack cocaine on the streets of Los Angeles, San Francisco, and beyond to help fund the CIA-backed Contras in Nicaragua for their fight with the Sandinistas. But this wasn't the first time the CIA made a foray into drug running for dollars. In fact, this CIA fundraising strategy has been accepted knowledge for years and was meticulously documented by University of Wisconsin Southeast Asian history professor Alfred McCoy in his eviscerating study, *The Politics of Heroin: CIA Complicity in the Global Drug Trade*, which underscores the CIA and U.S. government's complicity in global drug trafficking. "It seems that the American government has learned nothing from its war on drugs," writes Wilda Williams in *Library Journal*. "In 1972, the CIA attempted to suppress McCoy's classic work, 'The Politics of Heroin in Southeast Asia,' which charged CIA complicity in the narcotics trade as part of its cold war tactics."[70] McCoy states:

> During the 40 years of the cold war, from the late 1940's to this year, the CIA pursued a policy that I call radical pragmatism. Their mission was to stop communism and in pursuit of that mission they would ally with anyone and do anything to fight communism... During the long years of the cold war the CIA mounted major covert guerilla operations along the Soviet-Chinese border. The CIA recruited as allies people we now call drug lords for their operation against communist China in northeastern Burma in 1950, then from 1965 to 1975 [during the Vietnam war] their operation in northern Laos and throughout the decade of the 1980's, the Afghan operation against Soviet forces in Afghanistan.[71]

The roots of this dirty operation first appear in the late 1940s when the CIA facilitated and supported Chiang's Kuomintang forces as they smuggled opium from China and Burma to Bangkok using the CIA's proprietary airline (Civil Air Transport) to haul the load across Chinese air space to Thailand and deliver the payload to General Phoa Siyanan, "head of the Thai secret police and a long-time CIA asset."[72] Civil Air Transport was the "forerunner to the notorious Air America which figured so largely in the Agency's activities in Vietnam, Laos, and Cambodia."[73]

Italian Elections, 1947 to 1948

In a 1998 documentary broadcast on CNN, CIA agent F. Mark Wyatt had this to reveal regarding the CIA's role in an election clearly influenced by the Cold War titans: "We had bags of money that we delivered to selected politicians, to defray their political expenses, their campaign expenses, for posters, for pamphlets."[74] Wyatt, who joined the brand new agency courtesy of the National Security Act, was thrust into action to make sure the Christian Democrats came to power over the Communist Party. Tim Weiner writes that declassified records also reveal that "The CIA's practice of buying political clout was repeated in every Italian election for the next 24 years, and the agency's political influence in Rome lasted a generation."[75]

Taking a page from the future practice in Vietnam of burning the village in order to save it, policymakers in Washington along with their cohorts running American corporations perverted democracy in Italy and elsewhere "in the name of saving democracy" along with unleashing "much psychological warfare to block the specter (communism) that was haunting Europe."[76]

Flash-forward to the 2016 American election and its dumpster-fire aftermath: congressional and senate mouthpieces along with their media cronies all in Willy Loman's blue suit screaming incredulously about "Russian intervention in our sacred vote" and "The Russians successfully meddled in our democracy." Umm...

Greece, 1947 to 1949

"Murder Inc in Greece." It's the actual title of an actual pamphlet written by Olive Sutton in April of 1948 regarding American and British intervention into the Greek Civil War that broke out across that country shortly after World War II. Washington, as it is apt to do, embraced the neo-fascists over the Greek left—a gutsy movement in Greece that fought Hitler and his Nazi regime with everything they could muster. Under the heading "Americans are killing Greeks," Sutton poetically writes that, "Not a single dawn is broken by the clump of heavy boots outside the door without the approval of President Truman's representatives in Greece."[77]

Oppression needs hardware and hardware was no problem for the Greek Royalist Army, who were equipped with untold millions of dollars worth of American military playthings that were then turned on the Greek people. Of course the neo-fascists prevailed and the CIA was instrumental in creating and implementing the KYP—Greece's new security agency, modeled closely on the sadistic spooks working out of Washington and Athens. Greek-Americans in the CIA helped greatly, led by Thomas Karamessines, who later rose through the ranks and was promoted to Deputy Director of Plans in Richard Helms' CIA (in fact later in Karamessines' career his fingerprints were embossed all over "Operation Chaos," a CIA covert program that targeted a wide array of antiwar activity during Vietnam including infiltrating newspapers as well as Students for a Democratic Society, the Black Panther Party, Women Strike for Peace, and Ramparts Magazine).

"Karamessines saw to it that the CIA not only financed but also controlled the Greek military secret service KYP, despite the fact that the latter repeatedly engaged in torture," writes Ganser Daniele in *NATO's Secret Armies: Operation GLADIO and Terrorism in Western Europe*.[78] Ganser quotes a former CIA agent stationed in Greece at the time who recalls, "(the) KYP were good at noodling out Greek Communists and those who flirted with the Soviets."[79] Once "noodled" out, Olive Sutton described what happened next:

> A top U.S. Army official, Lieutenant General James Van Fleet, passes out the orders for the attacks and offensives and raids on villages from his place at the War Council table in Athens. You have seen the pictures of their victims in the newspapers: straggling lines of men and women facing the firing squads of the American-supported Greek government. Gray men and young men, girls with rough long hair. Some with faces lifted, singing, some with arms raised in last defiance. By fours and sixes and eights, decent people are being shot every day in the week.[80]

Noodled. So much for the cradle of democracy.

Philippines—The "HUK" Rebellion, 1945 to 1953

The Hukbalahap Rebellion was a significant peasant revolution that originated in the lowlands area of central Luzon, the largest and most populated island in the Philippines. The Sierra Madres along with the Zambales loom in the distance and envelop the region. "Hukbalahap" is a Tagalog acronym for Hukbo ng Bayan Laban sa Hapon—which translates to "People's Anti-Japanese Army"—and clearly the peasants of this agrarian uprising fought against and despised the Japanese occupation during World War II as well as the next occupation—this one led by the U.S. and the U.S.-backed government forces in Manila. The peasant rebels almost achieved victory in 1950 but soon fell to the Philippine authority bolstered by advanced U.S. weaponry and support. Washington-friendly Philippine president Ramon Magsaysay was putty in U.S. hands as he greatly assisted American handling of the Philippine population. Through the lens of CIA abuse and exploitation, William Blum takes a closer look at Magsaysay:

The most insidious part of the CIA operation in the Philippines was the fundamental manipulation of the nation's political life, featuring stage-managed elections and disinformation campaigns. The high point of this effort was the election to the presidency, in 1953, of Ramon Magsaysay, the cooperative former defense department head.[81]

But this was nothing new in the Philippines—a country that the United States had been using as an imperial playground since the Spanish Empire left in 1898 and sold the islands to the Americans for $20 million. In 1899, U.S. President William McKinley famously said to a Methodist group about the Filipino people that, "We could not leave them to themselves—they were unfit for self-government—and they would soon have anarchy and misrule over there."[82] McKinley, conjuring up as much Manifest Destiny as he could, took it upon himself to "uplift and civilize and Christianize them... for whom Christ also died."[83] Of course, not to be undone, McKinley's successor Theodore Roosevelt—ever the Christian hatchet man—hijacked a giant swath of land at the 1904 St. Louis World's Fair for his Philippine "reservation," where fairgoers could gawk at how the Philippine natives were being reprogrammed and civilized by good, god-fearing disciples of the Jewish carpenter.[84] No doubt that by 1950 the colonial and imperial foundation was deep and it was rock-solid.

As history illustrates, U.S. President Harry Truman was tap dancing for the hard-line Cold Warriors in Washington throughout his time in the White House and authorized large shipments of military supplies to the Manila government to destroy the Huks. Of course, the newly-minted Central Intelligence Agency was lurking in the dark dank shadows in the person (giving him the benefit of the doubt) of Edward Lansdale, who later achieved infamy in Southeast Asia as Chief of the CIA's Saigon Military Mission; his crowning "glory" (besides his legendary political-psyops during the war) was helping the tyrannical Ngo Dinh Diem form his fledgling U.S.-financed and U.S.-controlled puppet government in South Vietnam—an act that precipitated America's longest, bloodiest, and, without a doubt, most murderous war. (Lansdale was also JFK's guy to head Operation Mongoose—the covert plot to overthrow Cuba and assassinate Fidel Castro).

But it was Lansdale's great successes with black ops against the Huks in the Philippines that launched his resume to the top of the Vietnam pile. Marc Bernstein, in his piece "Ed Lansdale's Black Warfare in 1950s Vietnam," writes about the CIA's giant pat on the back for their boy Colonel Ed and his classic "white man's burden" performance in the Philippines:

> The CIA was willing to give Lansdale, a San Francisco advertising executive before World War II, great latitude based on his success in black operations in the Philippines from 1950-53. A U.S. Army officer who transferred his commission to the Air Force after the war, he had helped the Philippine army put down the Hukbalahap rebellion. Philippine Communists formed the guerrilla group originally to fight the Japanese in World War II. After Huk efforts to participate in the postwar government were rebuffed and a reportedly fraudulent election took place in 1949, the Huks began their guerrilla war to overthrow the U.S.-backed government. In waging war against the Huks, Lansdale wielded a wide array of counterinsurgency and psywar tools, some playing upon Filipino superstitions. One such successful unconventional tactic exploited villagers' belief in vampires, another on ghosts of dead Huks. In Lansdale's "Eye of God" campaign, suspected guerrillas living in a village were targets of psywar teams that surreptitiously painted a menacing eye on a wall facing the suspect's hut.[85]

After the U.S. successfully defeated the communist peasant farmers who were looking to take over the world, Washington propped up a succession of marionettes masquerading as Philippine leaders, all "culminating in the dictatorship of Ferdinand Marcos."[86] Perhaps historian Jonathan Nashel, in his book *Edward Lansdale's Cold War*, best frames the schizophrenic reality of America's foreign policy as a "Manichean vision."[87]

> Although the CIA's internal analysis noted that "the appeal of the Huks has been based on the legitimate grievances of tenant farmers," this awareness did not prevent the United States from viewing them as a threat to its national security interests. As noted by John F. Melby, a State Department official overseeing Philippine relations during this time, "They didn't really know much about what Marxism was all about… But [our mission] was to do what had to be done to save the Philippines from its own follies."[88]

"The Good War" was over. The America that teetered between the myth of sweet innocence and the reality of violent shame offered a glimmer of hope, as captured by the lion in winter, Gore Vidal, shortly before his passing:

> There was a cultural burst that Americans had never known before: we became number one for things like ballet. We had dozens of first-rate poets, several not so bad novelists, wonderful music, Lenny Bernstein and Aaron Copland. It was a great moment, and it lasted for five years. Then the Korean War came, and we've never stopped being at war since.[89]

The U.S. Congress never declared war in Korea. Once again, the cowardly body shirked their constitutional responsibility. Truman defined the war as a "police action" conducted under the aegis of the United Nations. The war began on 25 June 1950 but many Americans—who were very busy building suburbs from Levittown, Long Island to Milpitas, California—sort of missed this so-called police action, helping to give the "conflict" its nickname: *The Forgotten War*. Yet this alleged police action claimed the lives of more (perhaps many more) than a million human beings. That's one helluva conflict to forget.[90]

Though the Korean War officially began in June of 1950, the path to war began as soon as the Japanese surrendered and beat feet off the Korean peninsula following World War II, with Japan replaced by the victorious United States and Soviet Union as overseers of this conquered land. A line was drawn in the sand—the 38th Parallel, not to create two separate countries but to demarcate occupation responsibilities. The stated goal of the U.S. and the Soviet Union was to unify the north with the south. But then the all-encompassing Cold War "state of mind" threw a monkey wrench into the best-laid plans of mice and men.

During much of the Cold War years, Colonel L. Fletcher Prouty, a man with incredible access to brothers Allen and John Foster Dulles, as well as the entire nerve center of the expanding Military-Industrial Complex, reports that prior to the dropping of the Atomic Bombs on Hiroshima and Nagasaki, "supplies and equipment for an invasion force of at least half a million men began to be stacked up, fifteen to twenty feet high, all over the island (Okinawa)."[91] The professed and purportedly essential mass invasion of Japan never materialized thanks to Washington's convenient disregard of Japan's overtures for surrender. Instead, American leaders opted for the mass destruction of Hiroshima and Nagasaki as the way to bring the Japanese Empire to its knees and, of course, take a giant step forward in the race for superpower stardom. Shortly thereafter, U.S. Navy transport vessels delivered the unused massive shipments of supplies and equipment to ports in Korea and Indochina. Starting in 1945, Pacific OSS units were working closely with U.S. allies Syngman Rhee in Korea and Ho Chi Minh in Vietnam to organize and manage these massive military shipments "into those two Japanese-devastated countries."[92] Prouty continues:

> Those shipments forecast that in these two locales would be fought
> the two greatest conflicts of the Cold War to date and that both
> would be fought "Cold War style," without a military objective and
> to no victorious conclusion.[93]

Prouty concludes his insider assessment of the Empire's strategy on the Pacific Rim:

> By the end of WWII the great financial powers of the Western
> world, aided by their omnipotent Wall Street lawyers, had decided
> it was time to create a new world power center of transnational
> corporations and, in the process, to destroy the Soviet Union and
> socialism. To achieve this enormous objective they chose as their
> principle driving force the covert power and might of the CIA and
> its invisible allies.[94]

But as the OSS transformed itself into the CIA, their first significant forays into the internal struggles on the Korean peninsula as well as inside the newly formed People's Republic of China were anything but successful. The CIA's own classified histories reveal a bumbling and inept operation. Pulitzer Prize-winning author Tim Weiner details a litany of CIA failures in his national bestseller *Legacy of Ashes*. Citing the agency's own internal review of actions, Weiner reveals, "the agency's paramilitary operations were 'not only ineffective but probably morally reprehensible in the number of lives lost.'"[95] *Morally reprehensible...* the CIA's own review of itself. Weiner continues:

> Thousands of recruited Korean and Chinese agents were dropped
> into North Korea during the war, never to return. "The amount

of time and treasure expended was enormously disproportionate to attainments," the agency concluded. Nothing was gained from "the substantial sums spent and the numerous Koreans sacrificed." Hundreds more Chinese agents died after they were launched onto the mainland in misconceived land, air, and sea operations. "Most of these missions weren't sent for intelligence. They were sent to supply nonexistent or fictitious resistance groups," said Peter Sichel, who saw the string of failures play out after he became station chief in Hong Kong. "They were suicide missions. They were suicidal and irresponsible."[96]

And then there was the U.S. military.

The record shows that a year before war broke out along the 38th Parallel, U.S. puppet leader, President Syngman Rhee was ordering raids into the north. He even publicly declared his objective to invade the north as he repositioned divisions of troops right up to the imaginary 38th Parallel. Each side blamed the other for attacking first but clearly this was a civil war. "The Soviet Union was not involved, and the United States ought not to have been," writes David Swanson, author of *War is a Lie*.[97] Look at a map—Korea is nowhere close to the U.S. "Nonetheless," Swanson concludes, "we entered another 'defensive' war."[98]

"Once upon a time," Blum writes, "the United States fought a great civil war in which the North attempted to reunite the divided country through military force. Did Korea or China or any other foreign power send in an army to slaughter Americans," Blum asks, "charging Lincoln with aggression?"[99] Not that we remember.

U.S. General Douglas MacArthur, itching to get back into battle and start killing Asians again, was "drooling for a war with China and threatening it... Attacking a power plant in North Korea that supplied China, and bombing a border city, was the closest MacArthur got to what he wanted,"[100] writes Swanson.

The Korean War ensued—a vicious fight with each side accusing the other of barbaric and unspeakable atrocities. Both sides dabbled in the use of mind-altering drugs, psychological torture, hypnosis, and brainwashing (see *The Manchurian Candidate*), but most experts agree that this aspect of the war was probably overstated. (However, in other instances the CIA at least was quite active in this diabolical practice of mind tampering. In 2006, Colin Ross published *The C.I.A. Doctors: Human Rights Violations by American Psychiatrists*, which presents evidence based on thousands of CIA documents released through the Freedom of Information Act that underscore systemic and wide-ranging human rights violations by American shrinks over the last 65 years.)

During the Korean War, the cities of Seoul and Pyongyang were both reduced to ruins. Estimates place U.S. deaths at more than 37,000 with total Korean deaths (civilian and armed forces) soaring well beyond a million. "What every North Korean knows is that a family member was killed during the Korean War," write journalists Amy Goodman and Juan Gonzalez, "and usually by incendiary bombing that the US carried out with no limits."Clearly, American military strategists shifted the insidious firebombing used to decimate Japanese and German cities in the Second World War to North Korea, "which had 15 or 16 cities of modest size, and they were all just wiped off the face of the Earth." Goodman and Gonzalez stress that official U.S. Air Force statistics place the percentage of destruction ("sometimes 100 percent") in North Korean cities higher, on average, than the percentage of destruction in German and Japanese cities during World War II.[101]

But it wasn't just death from above. "Many of the dead had been killed at close range," writes Swanson, "slaughtered unarmed and in cold-blood by both sides. *And the border was right back where it had been.*" [Emphasis added]

Ah yes, the border between North and South Korea—just where it remains today more than six decades later—and the same can be said for the hatred between the north and the south. Another war, another lie, and another very predictable failure. So why fight the damn thing? Christ, it was just three years after a complete global conflict. Blum offers the only plausible answer:

> Only a year earlier in 1949, in the Arab-Israeli fighting in Palestine and in the India-Pakistani war over Kashmir, the United Nations, with American support, had intervened to mediate an armistice, not to send in an army to take sides and expand the fighting. And both these conflicts were less in nature of a civil war than was the case in Korea. If the US/UN response had been the same in these earlier cases, Palestine and Kashmir might have wound up as the scorched earth desert that was Korea's fate. What saved them, what kept the US armed forces out, was no more than the absence of a communist side to the conflict.[102]

There it is, communism, the great Satan. America's soft spot—like jelly donuts to a donut-loving diabetic.

Operation MOCKINGBIRD—or Agitprop American Style

It all started in 1949 with the creation of Radio Free Europe—a CIA funded propaganda machine masquerading as a broadcaster dedicated to transmitting "uncensored news and information to audiences behind the Iron Curtain."[103] This instrument of the Cold War faceoff was created by the National Committee for a Free Europe, an anti-communist organization based in New York City that was formed by many powerful U.S. elites including their centerpiece powerbroker, CIA Director Allen W. Dulles. In fact, most of Radio Free Europe's funding for the first two decades was furnished by—you guessed it—the Central Intelligence Agency.[104] One of the stars of Radio Free Europe, the CIA's own Edward R. Murrow, was Jozef Swiatlo, a high-ranking official in Poland's Ministry of Public Security under the auspices of Joseph Stalin.[105] Swiatlo was aptly nicknamed "The Butcher" by prisoners who were rounded up by the Polish secret police. Shortly after "The Butcher" defected to the West, he ended up as a mainstay on the airwaves of Radio Free Europe.

In 1977, *Rolling Stone* magazine published an explosive exposé entitled "The CIA and the Media," written by Carl Bernstein after he left *The Washington Post*. The 25,000-word cover story detailed the gory relationship between America's spy agency and the press during the Cold War years. "The CIA's use of the American news media has been much more extensive than Agency officials have acknowledged publicly or in closed sessions with members of Congress," the famed Watergate reporter writes. "The general outlines of what happened are indisputable; the specifics are harder to come by."[106]

Bernstein contends that when the Church Committee ("United States Senate Select Committee to Study Governmental Operations with Respect to Intelligence Activities," chaired by Senator Frank Church, D-Idaho) investigated these sordid covert activities between the CIA and America's powerful news organizations, the Congressional body covered up significant portions of the operation. Even then the report, published in 1976, was still incredibly damning:

> The CIA currently maintains a network of several hundred foreign
> individuals around the world who provide intelligence for the

CIA and at times attempt to influence opinion through the use of covert propaganda. These individuals provide the CIA with direct access to a large number of newspapers and periodicals, scores of press services and news agencies, radio and television stations, commercial book publishers, and other foreign media outlets.[107]

Through what was first labeled "Operation MOCKINGBIRD" by former Village Voice reporter Deborah Davis in her controversial biography *Katharine the Great: Katharine Graham and Her Washington Post Empire*, the CIA recruited major domestic U.S. news outlets and their reporters to become agency "assets" and disseminators of junk news, misinformation, and the dreaded "P" word—propaganda. America wanted—and the Empire needed—their own "Department for Agitation and Propaganda."

The effort was launched and headed by Allen Dulles, along with undercover State Department official Frank Wisner, and *Washington Post* publisher Philip Graham—Katharine Graham's husband.[108] (Under the heading "Where there's smoke, there's fire," it should also be noted here that Katharine Graham's father, Eugene Meyer, was the *Post*'s publisher until 1946 when he left the paper to become the World Bank's first president.) Shortly thereafter the *Post* became a major player. Bernstein reports that, "Further investigation into the matter, CIA officials say, would inevitably reveal a series of embarrassing relationships in the 1950s and 1960s with some of the most powerful organizations and individuals in American journalism."[109] In fact, as Bernstein's report reveals, more than 400 American journalists over a twenty–five year period "secretly carried out assignments for the Central Intelligence Agency, according to documents on file at CIA headquarters."[110]

The roster of journalistic icons involved in Operation MOCKINGBIRD from America's so-called Fourth Estate reads like a top-ten list of press/media tycoons: William Paley of *CBS*, Henry Luce of *Time*, Arthur Hays Sulzberger of *The New York Times*, Barry Bingham Sr. of the *Louisville Courier–Journal*, and James Copley of the Copley News Service.[111] The Pulitzer Prize-winning Bernstein continues: "Other organizations which cooperated with the CIA include the American Broadcasting Company, the National Broadcasting Company, the Associated Press, United Press International, Reuters, Hearst Newspapers, Scripps–Howard, Newsweek magazine, the Mutual Broadcasting System, the Miami Herald and the old Saturday Evening Post and New York Herald–Tribune."[112] But then Bernstein underscores and reiterates the major players:

By far the most valuable of these associations, according to CIA
officials, have been with the New York Times, CBS and Time Inc.[113]

Is this just the tip of the iceberg? Judging by the various investigative reports
released by Bernstein, Blum, Constantine, and others—it probably is. In the
motion picture, *The Matrix*, Morpheus could have been speaking about the
American press and their active complicity in this daunting "through the looking
glass" nightmare when he warned: *"This is your last chance. After this, there is no
turning back. You take the blue pill - the story ends, you wake up in your bed and believe
whatever you want to believe. You take the red pill - you stay in Wonderland and I show
you how deep the rabbit-hole goes."*

Albania, 1949 to 1953

After World War II, Britain and the United States developed an elaborate plan
to overthrow Albania's communist regime headed by Enver Hoxha, who ruled as
a suspicious and fearful leader, forever threatened by Western advances, ever on
the prowl for the reversal and control of the newly-minted socialist state. In fact,
Albania evolved into a rock-hard isolationist country—Hoxha feeling threatened
from both Cold War superpowers: threatened geographically by Washington's
"vicious capitalist-revisionist encirclement,"[114] as well as being threatened by
the Soviet Bloc who he felt never lived up to the true spirit of Marxist-Leninist
gospel.[115]

Double agent and super-spook Kim Philby (liaison officer between British
intelligence and the CIA who defected to the Soviet Union and was the basis for
John le Carré's wealthy traitor in *Tinker, Tailor, Soldier, Spy*[116]) leaked details of the
U.S./UK overthrow plan to his bosses in Moscow. The breach in security led to the
death of hundreds of "assets" or western infiltrators/agents throughout Albania,
most at the hands of the Albanian security service known as the Sigurimi.[117]

Germany in the 1950s

Declassified in 2002, the National Security Archive reveals the CIA's secret
documented history of the U.S. Government's relationship with General Reinhard
Gehlen, Adolf Hitler's intelligence chief for the Eastern Front during World War

II. The report details how the U.S. Army, followed by the CIA, sponsored Gehlen's clandestine espionage network in which he employed numerous "former" Nazis and well-known war criminals.[118] "The CIA has defied the law," states former congresswoman Elizabeth Holtzman who was a member of the Working Group investigating CIA recruitment of Nazis and war criminals. "In so doing," she continues, "(the CIA) has also trivialized the Holocaust, thumbed its nose at the survivors of the Holocaust and also at the Americans who gave their lives in the effort to defeat the Nazis in World War II."[119]

"Operation GLADIO" was a classic "stay-behind" operation run throughout Europe by NATO and the CIA. Sometimes referred to as "Super NATO," these secret operatives were basically sleeper cells and spy networks created and trained to form resistance movements in the event of a Warsaw Pact takeover of a country or if the communist party came to power through democratic elections. Often, stay-behind operatives strayed from their supposed dormant existence and became very proactive in subversive actions within their own countries. "The CIA orchestrated a wide-ranging campaign of sabotage, terrorism, dirty tricks, and psychological warfare against East Germany," writes William Blum. "This was one of the factors which led to the building of the Berlin Wall in 1961."[120]

Citing various publications in the early 1950s (*Der Spielgel, Newsweek, Saturday Evening Post, The Nation, The New Yorker,* and *The New York Times* among others), Blum describes violent terrorist attacks by CIA-sponsored forces that targeted power stations, shipyards, canals, a dam, public transportation, and more. They blew up railway bridges, roads, and derailed freight trains. Kidnapping of leftists was commonplace. Many people were wounded, many killed.[121]

Clearly, and at the people's expense (always at the people's expense), these subversions were designed to agitate internal rebellion and to hinder eastern bloc countries from rebuilding their economies after the devastation of World War II. From Washington's perspective, it was not permissible for a socialist or communist state to succeed in any way, shape, or form.

Iran, 1953: "Operation Ajax"

It is not far-fetched to draw a line from Operation Ajax through the Shah's repressive regime and the Islamic Revolution to the fireballs that engulfed the World Trade Center in New York.

— *New York Times* correspondent Stephen Kinzer

The West, as spearheaded by Washington and London, are quick to dispatch history to the proverbial garbage heap. But Iranians may be a bit more reticent when it comes to the last seventy years of their own Cold War battle with American-led western powers. In fact, "the United States has been tormenting Iranians for more than fifty years, ever since a U.S.-UK military coup overthrew the parliamentary government and installed the Shah,"[122] writes Noam Chomsky, who is apt not to forget. Nor do the Iranians, who lived under the hellish tyranny of the Shah's twenty-six-year vicious jackhammer approach to population control, racking up "an atrocious record of human rights violations, ignored by the media, which became deeply outraged over such violations after the U.S.-backed tyranny was overthrown."[123]

In 1951, British influence and control began to wane in the Middle East, starting with its expulsion from Iran as the Majlis (Iranian parliament) passed the Naturalization Act, which stripped the British of their control over the Anglo-Iranian Oil Company. Earlier that year, Mohammad Mossadegh ran for Prime Minister promising to liberate his country from the grip of British imperialism and British ownership of Iranian natural resources, namely oil. This kind of independence is the very thing that fuels American (and western) interventionist behavior everywhere. In *How the World Works*, Chomsky elaborates:

> We've consistently opposed democracy if the results can't be controlled. The problem with real democracies is that they're likely to fall prey to the heresy that governments should respond to the needs of their own population, instead of those of US investors. A study of the inter-American system published by the Royal Institute of International Affairs in London concluded that, while the US pays lip service to democracy, the real commitment is to "private, capitalist enterprise." When the rights of investors are threatened, democracy has to go; if all these rights are safeguarded, killers and torturers will do just fine.[124]

With Mossadegh and the Iranians fighting for control of their own oil resources, the henchmen back in Washington were plotting their coup—in collusion with the resident warmonger at 10 Downing Street, Winston Churchill. It was clear that the British government had no intention of meekly walking off into the sunset. Stephen Kinzer, author of *All the Shah's Men: An American Coup and the Roots of Middle East Terror*, describes the newly-appointed British Foreign Secretary, Herbert Morrison, as "colossally unprepared for the job," and that Morrison "considered the challenge from Iran a simple matter of ignorant natives rebelling against the forces of civilization."[125]

The major player running the oil industry in Iran was the Anglo-Iranian Oil Company (later changing its name to British Petroleum aka BP). They fought the will of the Iranian people tooth and nail—every self-inflicted detrimental move was designed to cripple Iran's oil production (especially at the massive Abadan oil refinery) and thereby coerce Mossadegh and Iran back into privatization. The Anglo-Iranian Oil Company refused audits, making it impossible for the Iranian government to determine if they were receiving proper royalties and payments. Then in a move aimed at creating a stalemate, the company finally halted oil production and of course exports dropped dramatically. And when Iran attempted to export what oil they could, as they did with the Italian tanker *Rose Mary*, the Royal Navy intercepted the tanker and forced it into the British protectorate of Aden on the grounds that the ship's oil was stolen property. This news created a panic among buyers and shippers alike and it brought Iranian exports to a standstill. This strong-arm response by the Anglo-Iranian Oil Company and their muscle in the British government had the desired affect: Mossadegh's political coalition began to unravel. He's accused of being a communist based on his push to nationalize the oil industry. He's further accused of falling under the spell of the Soviet Union—and for Washington this is red meat for the Cold War beast, especially considering that Iran shares a border with the USSR. But the popular Iranian prime minister refused to back down.

At first, Eisenhower wasn't biting, hoping for a compromise with Mossadegh, but his Secretary of State, the always-scheming and clearly paranoid John Foster Dulles, envisioned communists (who else) overrunning the entire Middle East with perfect domino-like precision. As transcribed by the official National Security Council note-taker on March 4, 1953:

> The probable consequences of the events of the last few days,
> concluded Mr. Dulles, would be a dictatorship in Iran under
> Mossadegh. As long as the latter lives there was little danger, but
> if he were to be assassinated or removed from power, a political
> vacuum would occur in Iran and the Communists might easily take
> over. The consequences of such a takeover were then outlined in
> all their seriousness by Mr. Dulles. Not only would the free world
> be deprived of the enormous assets represented by Iranian oil

production and reserves, but the Russians would secure these assets and thus henceforth be free of any anxiety about their petroleum situation. Worse still, Mr. Dulles pointed out, if Iran succumbed to the Communists there was little doubt that in short order the other areas of the Middle East, with some sixty percent of the world's oil reserves, would fall into Communist control.[126]

Even before Eisenhower agreed, the end game was set: overthrow the democratically elected Mossadegh and return the Pahlavi dynasty to the Peacock Throne in the person of Shah Mohammed Reza Pahlavi. The architects of the coup plot were two veterans of western political action in and around Tehran: the CIA's Donald Wilber (Princetonian old school CIA) and his British co-conspirator from MI6, Norman Darbyshire. Kinzer details a meeting in Dulles' office at the State Department once the blueprint for the coup was complete:

> When the plotters had assembled, Dulles picked up the report Wilber and Darbyshire had written and said, "So this is how we get rid of that madman Mossadegh!"[127]

Once Eisenhower signed on, albeit without great passion, the gathering storm was rumbling on the horizon. Unlike his boss, Secretary of State John Foster Dulles was wholeheartedly pumping the operation (and giddy Churchill was wetting his pants in anticipation). Resources (read: money) for Operation Ajax were plentiful and, with his brother Allen and his CIA mobilizing their anti-Mossadegh Iranian agents inside Iran, bedlam reigned all around Mossadegh. The hammer was about to fall... and who was the CIA's main operative on the ground? Kermit Roosevelt, the grandson of Theodore "T.R." Roosevelt, Jr. himself—that great rough-riding imperial force who passed along the burning bright Anglo-Saxon torch whose flame proclaimed the Aryan as God's highest creation.

The young Roosevelt and his CIA assets were ready to strike. "They had pushed Iran to the brink of chaos," Kinzer writes. "Newspapers and religious leaders were screaming for Mossadegh's head. Protests and riots organized by the CIA had turned the streets into battlegrounds. Antigovernment propaganda, in Donald Wilber's words, 'poured off the Agency's presses and was rushed by air to Tehran.' Mossadegh was isolated and weaker than ever."

When the smoke settled on August 19, 1953, the government of Mohammad Mossadegh was toppled in a coup d'état planned, orchestrated, and executed by the Central Intelligence Agency. Back home in Washington, in the dark mausoleums of power, jubilation reigned, praise Jesus. Outside there were blue skies, a gentle breeze, and it was a comfortable 80 degrees—a perfect day for empire myth making: that the U.S. could overthrow governments anytime and anywhere on the planet. In fact a year later Guatemala became another notch on the sheriff's belt. As a result of Washington's successful intervention in Iran and subsequent coup d'état, the U.S. dictated the business model for Iran's oil exports: BP would share the pie with a consortium of new vultures, which now included Gulf Oil, Royal Dutch Shell, Compagnie Fraçaise des Pétroles, Standard Oil of California (Chevron), Standard Oil of New Jersey (ExxonMobil), and Texaco.[128]

Happy Motoring!

In 2000, *The New York Times* published segments of a still classified document on the secret history of the 1953 coup written by none other than the "Gentleman Spy" Donald Wilber. In this article, "Secrets of History: The C.I.A. in Iran," James Risen writes that Wilber's assessment of Washington's involvement in the coup is that "(it) stirred up considerable unrest in Iran, giving Iranians a clear choice between instability and supporting the shah."[129] Not much of a choice. Describing the final day of the coup, 19 August 1953, Wilber writes: "It was a day that should never have ended, for it carried with it such a sense of excitement, of satisfaction and of jubilation that it is doubtful whether any other can come up to it."[130]

That is history written by the winners—the maniacal ones that possess the wealth and own the guns. Once in awhile, history can also written by the victims— the oppressed ones who absorb the beating and live with the consequences. In his passionate article "What Kermit Roosevelt Didn't Say," professor Sasan Fayazmanesh writes about how one person's day of glory is another person's day of infamy. We will end this "greatest hit" with Fayazmanesh's passionate rebuttal of another American myth of liberty:

To those who still believe in the fairytale of a righteous US government wanting to spread democracy around the world such revelations might sound shocking. But to us, whose lives were forever changed as a result of this cheap, "$1 million" coup, none of this was news. Like bedtime stories, we had heard them all a hundred times from our parents. The only difference was that where Wilber saw a glorious day, we saw a day of infamy; where he wished the day had never ended, we wished it had never begun; and where he saw a dazzling picture of his majesty's restoration to power, we saw grotesque pictures of a brutal dictatorship, informants, dungeons, torture, executions and 52 blindfolded Americans marching up and down the steps of the "nest of spies." Perhaps Wilber did not see what we saw or, perhaps, he just did not say.

It is, of course, meaningless to write an iffy history. However, one can't help but imagine how things might have been different had it not been for the Kermits and Wilbers of the world. Would the Islamic Revolution of 1979 have taken place? Would Americans have been held hostage for 444 days in exchange for the shah and frozen assets? Would the US have helped Saddam start the Iraq-Iran war? Would over a million people have died as a result of the war? Would the US have imposed numerous unilateral sanctions against Iran for over two decades and made the captains of industry lose billions of dollars? Would Saddam have invaded Kuwait? Would the US have invaded Iraq twice and be in the mess that it is in right now? I guess a better question is this: Will the US ever learn that the Kermits and Wilbers of the world are not that clever, have no foresight, and, in the long-run, do more damage to this country than good? Or, to put it differently, will there ever be an enlightened US government in which there is no room for the likes of Kermits and Wilbers?[131]

Tragically, Donald Wilber's dream of "a day that should never have ended" in fact never did end. His dream continued to come true for the American Empire throughout the remainder of the 20th century, the so-called "American Century," and his dream continues unfettered to this very second. Washington's success in Iran was catalyst and catapult for U.S. intervention everywhere on the planet.

Guatemala, 1954: "Journey to Banana Land"

US planners from Secretary of State Dean Acheson in the late 1940s to the present have warned that "one rotten apple can spoil the barrel." This "rotten apple theory" is called the domino theory for public consumption. The version used to frighten the public has Ho Chi Minh getting in a canoe and landing in California... Maybe some US leaders believe this nonsense, it's possible, but rational planners certainly don't. They understand that the real threat is the "good example."[132]

—Noam Chomsky

Journey to Banana Land[133] was the title of a corporate film produced in 1950 by the United Fruit Company about their paternalistic, "White Man's Burden" vision of Central America and its banana business when the natives were threatening United Fruit's empire. Enter the big time banana eaters from Estados Unidos de América.

The CIA-sponsored coup ousted the democratically elected and liberal government of Jacobo Arbenz, setting in motion forty years of Latin American killing fields: death-squads, torture, and mass executions. William Blum describes it as "unimaginable cruelty, totaling well over 100,000 victims... indisputably one of the most inhuman chapters of the 20th century."[134] Once again, Arbenz committed the cardinal sin of nationalizing industry coveted by foreign corporations backed by first-world governments: in this case the United Fruit Company. Of course, Arbenz's actions set Washington in motion, claiming that Guatemala was about to be swallowed up by the Soviets (even though Moscow didn't even maintain diplomatic ties with the Central American country).[135] So, setting aside the transparent myth of communists hiding in the Sierra Madres ready to pounce on Guatemala City, let's ask the real question regarding U.S. intervention: Why? And, as usual, the answer is rooted in money. The agrarian reforms set forth by Arbenz for the advancement of the Guatemalan people threatened American business interests and, at the same time, planted the seeds of social democracy and liberation—movements that might spread throughout the region. Can't have that shit going on. Once again, the threat of a "good example."

In fact, policymakers are VERY aware of the concept. Like Kryptonite to Superman, good examples threaten business, imperil the Empire. The following statement, made just before the coup by the Inter-American Bureau regarding their allies in the State Department, defines the heart and soul of the good example:

> Guatemala has become an increasing threat to the stability
> of Honduras and El Salvador. Its agrarian reform a powerful
> propaganda weapon; its broad social program, of aiding the workers
> and peasants in a victorious struggle against the upper classes and
> large foreign enterprises, has a strong appeal to the populations of
> Central American neighbors, where similar conditions prevail.[136]

And wherever you find a good example threatening American "bizness" interests, even in the least, you can be sure that the CIA and/or the U.S. Marines are not far behind—and as Chomsky unflinchingly illustrates, the actions used against the so-called natives are methods designed to devastate resistance:

> What the US-run contra forces did in Nicaragua, or what our
> terrorist proxies do in El Salvador or Guatemala, isn't only ordinary
> killing. A major element is brutal, sadistic torture—beating infants
> against rocks, hanging women by their feet with their breasts cut off
> and the skin of their face peeled back so that they'll bleed to death,
> chopping people's heads off and putting them on stakes. The point
> is to crush independent nationalism and popular forces that might
> bring about meaningful democracy.[137]

The Middle East: Egypt in the Mid-1950s

The Eisenhower Doctrine, not unlike the Monroe Doctrine, suggested that the U.S. was prepared to use force in the Middle East to thwart communist aggression (or: how our oil got under your goddamn country is anybody's guess, but we will whack you good if we even smell the hint of nationalism underfoot). And smell they did in the person of Egyptian President Gamal Abdel Nasser—a nationalist who was (naturally) undesirable to American and British oil companies as well as their partner banks. Nasserists emerged from the Egyptian Revolution of 1952 and the movement—watched ever so closely by Washington—combined strong Egyptian nationalism with socialism and was virulently anti-imperialist.

Late in 1956, the Suez War broke out over Egypt's nationalization of the Suez Canal Company. In this conflict, the combined force of France, Britain, and Israel (spearheaded by Great Britain) completely failed to reverse Nasser's nationalization program. Eisenhower and his Secretary of State, John Foster Dulles, believed Britain's defeat left a vacuum of power in the region—one that would be quickly exploited by the Soviet Union. This catapulted the U.S. into action, beginning with Eisenhower's Doctrine, which held the Soviet Union square in its crosshairs. The doctrine authorized the commitment of American forces "to secure and protect the territorial integrity and political independence of such nations, requesting such aid against overt armed aggression from any nation controlled by international communism."[138] Starting with their move to control and defeat the Nasserists, the Eisenhower/Dulles Doctrine attempted to define Washington's emergence as the prevailing power in the region, something the U.S. continued to embrace—*and continues to embrace to this day*—long after Eisenhower is dust in the wind.

> Others also found Nasser undesirable, namely the Muslim Brotherhood who clearly didn't dig his secular rule. Throughout the ensuing years, numerous assassination attempts failed, ushering in a long deadly chess game between Nasser, the Brotherhood, and of course the CIA—a chess game that witnessed the CIA using the Brotherhood ("the grandfather of the Islamic right") against the sovereignty of the Nasser government.[139]

Indonesia, Late 50s with a Mid 60s Redux: Sukarno & Suharto

On August 17, 1945, after decades of struggle against imperialism and foreign capital, the Indonesian people declared their independence from long-standing colonial rule by the Netherlands and a short-lived occupation by the Japanese during World War II. It wasn't until 1949 that the Dutch finally hit the bricks and acknowledged Indonesian independence. Sukarno was a leader in this struggle for independence and the first president of Indonesia. Like Nasser and Mossadegh, Sukarno nationalized Indonesian resources and businesses, heretofore owned and operated by the Dutch. Sukarno was also allowing the PKI (Indonesia's Communist Party) to exist and grow within the political structure. "Such policies could easily give other Third World leaders 'wrong ideas,'" William Blum explains. "The CIA began throwing money into the elections, plotted Sukarno's assassination, tried to blackmail him with a phony sex film, and joined forces with dissident military officers to wage a full-scale war against the government," Blum concludes.[140]

In their seminal book on the CIA entitled *The Invisible Government* (published in

1964), Washington insiders and journalists David Wise and Thomas Ross revealed for the first time the workings of the U.S. intelligence network and espionage operation. This included wings of the Armed Forces as well as the Defense and State Departments, but the head honcho and driving force was clearly the Central Intelligence Agency. In fact when the book was about to be published, the CIA obtained copies of the galleys and Director John McCone demanded wholesale deletions. Random House refused and published the book in its entirety. "The CIA considered buying up the entire printing of *Invisible Government*," reports Spartacus Educational, "'but this idea was rejected when Random House pointed out that if this happened they would have to print a second edition. McCone now formed a special group to deal with the book and tried to arrange for it to get bad reviews.'"[141] So apropos for these CIA spooks, their plan sounding like the plot for a bad sitcom.

When Wise and Ross turn their investigation on Indonesia, they uncover the CIA supplying right wing rebel forces with a makeshift air force of B-26 bombers to assist in overthrowing Sukarno and his government. "Eisenhower had emphatically denied charges that the United States was supporting the rebellion against President Sukarno. 'Our policy,' he said at a press conference on April 30, 'is one of careful neutrality and proper deportment all the way through so as not to be taking sides where it is none of our business.'" We'll let Izzy Stone answer Ike:

All governments are run by liars and nothing they say should be believed.

A short time later, the new U.S. president, John Kennedy, invited Sukarno to Washington and was strangely candid. "During the visit Kennedy commented to one of his aides," writes Wise and Ross, "'No wonder Sukarno doesn't like us very much. He has to sit down with the people who tried to overthrow him.'"[142]

Flash-forward to 1965 and 1966: Southeast Asia is already aflame from the South China Sea to Jakarta. The Indonesian Communist Party (PKI) had grown substantially and was closely tied with Sukarno, who was still president. The Indonesian parliament had passed land reform legislation and the peasants and farmers were demanding realization. In fact, by 1965, the PKI had some 3.5 million members with supportive affiliations totaling 20 million more.[143] Waiting in the wings was Indonesia's next leader, a brutal cat by the name of Suharto, described by Edward S. Herman, Professor Emeritus of Finance at the Wharton School of the University of Pennsylvania, as "a ruthless dictator, a grand larcenist and a mass killer with as many victims as Cambodia's Pol Pot."[144] Anticipating and suspecting a U.S.-backed coup with Suharto lurking in the shadows, lower-ranking army officers aligned with Sukarno attempted to head off the revolt and kidnapped the suspected military leaders. But Suharto, along with his military command and U.S. assistance, took advantage of the opening, and overthrew the Sukarno government. Herman outlines the takeover:

> Suharto's overthrow of the Sukarno government in 1965-66 turned Indonesia from Cold War "neutralism" to fervent anti-Communism, and wiped out the Indonesian Communist Party—exterminating a sizable part of its mass base in the process, in widespread massacres that claimed at least 500,000 and perhaps more than a million victims. The U.S. establishment's enthusiasm for the coup-cum-mass murder was ecstatic; "almost everyone is pleased by the changes being wrought," New York Times columnist C.L. Sulzberger commented (4/8/66).[145]

After the bloodshed, Suharto turned his country into a country club for foreign investment—"Pleasure Island" with enticing natural resources like oil, minerals, and timber, all reaped by subjugated, cut-rate labor. Suharto's family and close buddies brokered the deals. Which brings to mind the late rocker Lou Reed's classic line about political vice, *"Does anyone need yet another politician caught with his pants down and money sticking in his hole?"*

A number of years before, FDR's famous line about Nicaraguan despot Anastasio Somoza fit the new Indonesian leader Suharto perfectly: "He might be a son of a bitch, but he's our son of a bitch."

British Guiana, 1953 to 1964: "The Specter of Columbus"

"For 11 years," William Blum observes, "two of the oldest democracies in the world, Great Britain and the United States, went to great lengths to prevent a democratically elected leader from occupying his office."[146] For the Arawak-speaking Taino people, the ghost of Columbus and his European sledgehammer returned to the scene of the crime—this time in the 20th century—to continue the rape, pillage, and plunder of their existence in the Caribbean. Situated on the northern coast of South America, bordering Venezuela, the British wrestled colonial responsibility for the native people away from the Dutch at the outset of the 19th century and then quickly imported African slave labor to exploit the sugar cane fields. More than a century later, an indigenous leader emerged from the same sugar plantations in British Guiana—Cheddi Jagan, a passionate socialist who experienced first-hand his parents exploitation manuring fields for sugarcane. He was intent on eradicating poverty in his country and saw socialism as the only viable vehicle. But Winston Churchill saw Jagan as a crypto-closet communist and a tool of the Soviet Union. Cheddi Jagan also set off alarms in Washington and London as another possible "good example."

Not often, but every once in awhile, a great truth is uttered by an American leader. One such historic instance was in 1967 when Senator Robert Kennedy visited Peru. He desperately wanted to visit the coalmines against the vehement opposition of the U.S. Embassy. The miners' union was overwhelmingly communist, and once there, Kennedy now wanted to personally travel deep into the mineshaft, which stretched a mile or so under the ocean. Mine representatives implored him not to go, but Bobby went in—for a fairly long time. When he emerged, Kennedy told a reporter, "If I worked in this mine, I'd be a communist too."[147]

Cheddi Jagan also understood this basic truth regarding the exploitation of workers and the human spirit, but he remained a target of U.S. and British efforts to oust him from power—replaced, of course, by a "leader" more acceptable to western business interests. "Using a wide variety of tactics—from general strikes and disinformation to terrorism and British legalisms," writes Blum, "the U. S. and Britain finally forced Jagan out in 1964. John F. Kennedy had given a direct order for his ouster."[148]

Vietnam, 1945 to 1973: Genocide & Terrorism, Cowboy Style

When identifying the basic currency of the American Empire, whether a 19th century budding empire finding its way or one entrenched in 21st century global dominance, murder persists as America's method of ultimate control—and no other period in the nation's history, with the possible exception of the American Holocaust of indigenous people (that continues to this day), defines this murderous method more than America's long, brutal killing spree in Southeast Asia. And the murder (terrorism) has no specific bounds—leader, soldier, civilian—it makes little difference.

Ngo Dinh Diem was the first president of South Vietnam and a stooge puppet leader for his U.S. masters until he outlived his usefulness and was slaughtered, along with his brother, in the back of a truck just three weeks before JFK's fateful trip to Dallas. Diem's tyrannical regime—aided, supported, built, and managed by Washington—was out of control for years. In fact, Kennedy's "advisors" had a ringside seat when Buddhist monks, responding to Diem's cruel regime, immolated themselves on the streets of Saigon.

Think these people were committed?

In a taped conversation between President Lyndon Johnson and Senator Eugene McCarthy in 1966, Johnson casually acknowledges Washington's assassination apparatus in Southeast Asia:

> They started on me with Diem, you remember, "he was corrupt and
> he ought to be killed." So we killed him. We all got together and got
> a goddamn bunch of thugs and we went in and assassinated him.
> Now we've really had no political stability since then.[149]

Take a listen to Johnson's demeanor, chilling in its laid-back, blasé, and nonchalant manner—as if he's talking about the Orioles opening day lineup or one of Lady Bird's new hats. Why? Because for "The Corporation" murder is commonplace. It's natural. It's what they do.

Phoenix Program

When you navigate around on the CIA's website (which is always good for a few laughs), you will stumble onto their mythical narrative regarding the "Phoenix Program" aka "Operation Phoenix." When you hear them tell it, the massive and well-documented assassination program was simply a rural pacification exercise designed to "neutralize" Vietcong political structure. The term "neutralization" is bureaucratese for outright assassination or capture followed by torture. Operation Phoenix was the CIA's counterinsurgency program unleashed in Vietnam by the Agency, along with South Vietnamese military personnel, to eradicate the National Liberation Front's (Vietcong's) infrastructure. It was soon-to-be CIA Director William Colby ridding the countryside of those gadfly communists and their goddamn infrastructure. "'Pacification' became a term drenched in blood," reports Colonel L. Fletcher Prouty. "Borrowed from the French commandos in Algeria by U.S. Army Special Forces activists, it meant to hit an area as hard as possible in order that it would be reduced to rubble—that is, 'pacified.'"[150] This archetype became the mission statement of Operation Phoenix.

"Central to Phoenix," writes historian Douglas Valentine, "is the fact that it targeted civilians, not soldiers."[151] Valentine suggests that the Phoenix Program was the "scalpel" created to replace the "bludgeon" of American B-52 strikes and massive on-the-ground firepower just obliterating villages and hamlets. The scorched earth policy was doing little to win hearts and minds. In fact, these "neutralizations" were usually carried out in the middle of the night while the target or targets were asleep. Valentine concludes:

> The scalpel cut deeper than the U.S. government admits. Indeed,
> Phoenix was, among other things, an instrument of counterterror—
> the psychological warfare tactic in which VCI members were
> brutally murdered along with their families or neighbors as a means
> of terrorizing the neighboring population into a state of submission.
> Such horrendous acts were, for propaganda purposes, often made to
> look as if they had been committed by the enemy.[152]

The current debate regarding America's crusade in the Middle East is replete with masturbatory deliberations on what is torture and what American actions constitute terror. It's a shell game perpetrated by a complicit media embedded with the torturers/terrorists. Operation Phoenix set the gold standard for brutality and the U.S. has been "refining" their efforts ever since. Valentine interviewed retired CIA agent John Patrick Muldoon, known in country as "Picadoon," who was the first director of the PIC (Province Interrogation Center) in Vietnam. Valentine itemized his description of torture methods:

Rape, gang rape, rape using eels, snakes, or hard objects, and rape followed by murder; electrical shock ("the Bell Telephone Hour") rendered by attaching wires to the genitals or other sensitive parts of the body, like the tongue; "the water treatment"; "the airplane," in which a prisoner's arms were tied behind the back and the rope looped over a hook on the ceiling, suspending the prisoner in midair, after which he or she was beaten; beatings with rubber hoses and whips; and the use of police dogs to maul prisoners. All this and more occurred in PICs.[153]

Bart Osborn joined the U.S. Army in 1966. According to Valentine, Osborn "was trained at Fort Bragg and Fort Holabird, and was classified an intelligence area specialist."[154] In 1971, he testified before Congress:

I never knew in the course of all those operations any detainee to live through his interrogation. They all died. There was never any reasonable establishment of the fact that anyone of those individuals was, in fact, cooperating with the VC, but they all died and the majority were either tortured to death or things like thrown out of helicopters.[155]

Bill Colby was actually quite proud of his tenure as a mass murderer in Southeast Asia. "In open congressional testimony," Prouty explains, "William Colby, the CIA's top man in the Phoenix program, claimed, with some pride, that he had eliminated about sixty thousand 'authentic Vietcong agents.'"[156] Prouty then builds up to using the "G" word.

In a war where "body count" seemed to be the primary objective of the fighting forces, one must not lose sight of the great significance of underlying factors that establish a climate of legitimacy for murder, or "neutralization." In fact, these underlying beliefs serve to promote genocide.[157]

In the 2006 documentary film *One Bright Shining Moment*, the Democratic Party's nominee for president, staunch antiwar candidate and longtime authority on America's slaughter in Southeast Asia, George McGovern, made the horrific numbers infinitely clear:

We probably killed two million Vietnamese in that war and a similar number of Cambodians and Laotians. None of those people wanted a quarrel with the United States, and the great tragedy is that we stumbled into that war on the wrong side.[158]

Millions.

The reality of that number seems incomprehensible and probably why certain regimes have gotten away with murder-holocaust-genocide. But it's not so incomprehensible when it's distilled down to a graphic reality. U.S. Navy Seal Elton Manzione, who shared his experiences as a twenty-year-old in Vietnam with historian Douglas Valentine, remembers one such graphic reality:

> The village is very quiet. There are some dogs. They're sleeping.
> They stir, but they don't even growl. I go into the hooch, and I spot
> my person. Well, somebody stirs in the next bed. I'm carrying my
> commando knife, and one of the things we learned is how to kill
> somebody instantly with it. So I put my hand over her mouth and
> come up under the second rib, go through the heart, give it a flick;
> it snaps the spinal cord. Not thinking! Because I think "Hey!" Then
> I hear the explosion go off and I know the gun is out. Somebody
> else in the corner starts to stir, so I pull out the sidearm and put it
> against her head and shoot her. She's dead. Of course, by this time
> the whole village is awake. I go out, waiting for Swetz to come,
> because the gun's been blown. People are kind of wandering around,
> and I'm pretty dazed. And I look back into the hooch, and there
> were two young girls. I'd killed the wrong people.[159]

(Disregarding the Genocide) The Ultimate Tragedy of Vietnam

During World War II, Ho Chi Minh worked closely with the CIA's forerunner—the OSS— in the battle against Japanese occupation. Among many things, the revolutionary leader helped rescue downed American pilots during World War II. Then in the fall of 1945, Ho Chi Minh proclaims as independent the "Democratic Republic of Vietnam" with his Declaration beginning this way: *"All men are created equal; they are endowed by their Creator with certain inalienable rights; among these are life, liberty, and the pursuit of happiness."*

Really? Yeah, he did.

In 1946, Ho Chi Minh, the Communist prime minister, writes Harry Truman a series of letters looking for U.S. aid and assistance. He doesn't turn to the Soviet Union for help against his colonial oppressor, nor to the Chinese, but to the United States—the country with the best historic ideals and rhetoric when it comes to self-determination. Ho Chi Minh legalizes labor unions, he establishes voting rights for men and women. He was attempting to mount a nominal democracy within the confines of Marxist ideology. William Blum explains how Washington regarded these noble pursuits:

> But this would count for nothing in Washington. Ho Chi Minh was
> some kind of Communist. Most people say that the U.S. lost the
> war. But by destroying Vietnam to its core, and poisoning the earth
> and the gene pool for generations (Agent Orange), Washington had
> achieved its main purpose: preventing what might have been the
> rise of a good development option for Asia. Ho Chi Minh was, after
> all, some kind of communist.[160]

In point of fact, Ho Chi Minh was progressive compared to what the Vietnamese experienced under French colonial rule. *Surely, the United States could see this.*

Cambodia, 1955 to 1973: "Sideshow"

Sideshow is the title of William Shawcross's definitive book on Washington's decimation of Cambodia. The book's subtitle underscores the narrative: "Kissinger, Nixon, and the Destruction of Cambodia." The British journalist's full-scale investigation rips open the bloody wound (at the time so marginalized by the American press) and reveals Kissinger and Nixon's secret but massive carpet-bombing of Cambodia, their own little sideshow.

CIA shenanigans in Cambodia began to unfold in the mid-1950s when the country was under the rule of Prince Norodom Sihanouk—a popular leader who wanted to keep his country neutral and out of the growing storm in Vietnam. Sihanouk criticized both U.S. policy as well as communist strategies and also accepted aid from both sides.[161] The title of Sihanouk's memoir is *My War with the CIA*, which should give you some idea of the path this guy had to walk down.

It's clear that Sihanouk's battle with the CIA began when John Peurifoy showed up in neighboring Thailand as the new U.S. ambassador, succeeding William "Wild Bill" Donovan in Bangkok. Of course, U.S. and CIA officials denied there were any hijinks underfoot in Cambodia but only a moron locked in a box could possibly buy their denial, especially with Donovan and Peurifoy's resumes floating around.

In a declassified 2007 CIA report regarding the overthrow of the Arbenz government in Guatemala, it is documented that Peurifoy—then U.S. Ambassador and CIA liaison/station head—was instrumental in orchestrating the coup and used large doses of psychological warfare to bamboozle the people.[162] Sihanouk writes in his memoir that when Peurifoy is assigned to Cambodia, the CIA starts pouring money into the Khmer Serei, a domestic group dedicated to the toppling of the current government. The CIA's fingerprints are everywhere, as evidenced by so-called spontaneous demonstrations in the streets where rebellious placards written in English (basically an unknown language in Cambodia) are moving the plot forward—messages designed to help western journalists depict the story quickly and in the "correct" manner.[163]

Sihanouk identifies at least two assassination attempts by the CIA that were uncovered by Chinese intelligence and thwarted by the Prince. Foreign agents (Thai nationals) were arrested carrying U.S. military-grade weapons, communication devices, and documents that tied them to CIA activities through an advisor to CIA puppet Lon Nol, who later assumed power when Sihanouk was finally overthrown in March of 1970. Lon Nol "immediately began committing Cambodian troops to the war in Vietnam."[164]

Back in August of 1959, a bomb detonated inside the royal palace. It killed numerous servants and staff, but the royal family was not harmed. A few days later, the Indian government was in possession of an intercepted communiqué from a U.S. diplomat (Sam Sary) in Phnom Penh to a CIA operative (Edmund Kellogg) in Southeast Asia saying that Sary regretted the failure to eliminate Sihanouk and will await further instructions. Later it's revealed that a fifth of the U.S. diplomatic staff in Cambodia were trained and/or working closely with the CIA.

While Sihanouk worked hard and briefly succeeded at keeping both the U.S. and National Liberation Front relegated to the border regions, as he desperately tried to stop the war from spreading deep into Cambodia, nevertheless it failed in the end. In his book, *The CIA's Greatest Hits*, Mark Zepezauer outlines the consequences of the CIA-sponsored coup:

> With Sihanouk out of the way, war quickly engulfed Cambodia. US bombing intensified near the Vietnamese border, driving North Vietnamese and NLF troops deeper into Cambodia. From 1969 to 1975, US bombing killed 600,000 Cambodians and created a full-scale famine.[165]

Newly released records documenting the American air assault on Cambodia, as the CIA was toppling the neutral kingdom on the ground, are staggering. In 2000, the Clinton Administration and the United States Air Force released classified data on all American bombing campaigns over Vietnam, Laos, and Cambodia between 1964 and 1975. The database not only reveals far more bombing than was previously reported but also that the bombing actually began under orders from Lyndon Johnson.

> *We heard a terrifying noise which shook the ground; it was as if the earth trembled, rose up and opened beneath our feet. Enormous explosions lit up the sky like huge bolts of lightning; it was the American B-52s.[166]*
> —Cambodian bombing survivor

The most shocking part of this "sideshow" murder spree are the black and white numbers, because cold hard facts on paper paint a gruesome picture of what was happening daily to the population—mostly peasants and farmers—on the ground; the flesh and blood, the dismemberment and death, that leaders of any military assault from any country are so good at whitewashing over.

Sites Bombed by the U.S. Air Force in Cambodia, 1965—1973[167]

- 113,716 sites
- 230,516 sorties
- 2,756,941 tons of ordnance (dump bombs, cluster bombs, phosphorous, napalm)

(The bomb-tonnage dropped on the Cambodian people during this period amounts to more than one-third of that dropped by the Allies during all of World War II.)

U.S. and South Vietnamese ground incursions into Cambodia to snuff out North Vietnamese strongholds failed to garner the results Washington was looking for, so Nixon decided to up the ante and go plunging into the jungles of the neutral country with B-52 "Big Belly" payloads carpet-bombing the landscape—a landscape, mind you, where people still tilled the soil using water buffaloes. "They have to go in there and I mean really go in," Nixon declared (probably with his jowls jiggling like Jell-O), "I want everything that can fly to go in there and crack the hell out of them. There is no limitation on mileage and there is no limitation on budget. Is that clear?"[168] On the other end of the phone, Henry Kissinger heard him loud and clear. Kissinger then relayed the order to General Alexander "I'm in control here" Haig. Kissinger:

> He wants a massive bombing campaign in Cambodia. He doesn't
> want to hear anything. It's an order, it's to be done. Anything that
> flies, on anything that moves. You got that?[169]

Haig's response, on the tape, was simple laughter. So much fun, in fact, that the American Empire—from the leaders tickling their toes in the Potomac, to the brass in the Pentagon, to the commanders on the ground, to the pilots cowardly dropping bombs from the skies above, war criminals and murderers each and every one of them—killed an estimated 600,000 Cambodians.[170]

600,000. Some "sideshow." In fact, the U.S. "secret" bombing campaign directly created the *reign of terror* that followed the American *rain of terror*—this one at the hands of Pol Pot and the Khmer Rouge as the U.S. bombing drove the communist forces and population deeper into Cambodia, "bringing them into greater contact with Khmer Rouge insurgents," write Taylor Owen and Ben Kiernan in their article "Bombs Over Cambodia."[171] Owen, a journalism professor at Columbia, and Kiernan, a history professor at Yale, outline how the bombing, which thundered on the heels of the CIA-sponsored coup, became the rallying cry for Al-Qaeda— excuse us—the Khmer Rouge:

> The bombs drove ordinary Cambodians into the arms of the Khmer
> Rouge, a group that seemed initially to have slim prospects of
> revolutionary success. Pol Pot himself described the Khmer Rouge
> during that period as "fewer than five thousand poorly armed
> guerrillas… scattered across the Cambodian landscape, uncertain
> about their strategy, tactics, loyalty, and leaders." Years after the war
> ended, journalist Bruce Palling asked Chhit Do, a former Khmer
> Rouge officer, if his forces had used the bombing as anti-American

propaganda. Chhit replied: "Every time after there had been bombing, they would take the people to see the craters, to see how big and deep the craters were, to see how the earth had been gouged out and scorched... The ordinary people sometimes literally shit in their pants when the big bombs and shells came. Their minds just froze up and they would wander around mute for three or four days. Terrified and half crazy, the people were ready to believe what they were told. It was because of their dissatisfaction with the bombing that they kept on cooperating with the Khmer Rouge, joining up with the Khmer Rouge, sending their children off to go with them. Sometimes the bombs fell and hit little children, and their fathers would be all for the Khmer Rouge."[172]

First, the Central Intelligence Agency overturned the apple cart and installed Lon Nol as their new puppet. This was followed by a massive and shocking American bombing campaign that completely erased the Cambodian economy. The trifecta was complete when Pol Pot and his Khmer Rouge filled the vacuum left by American death from above with even more genocidal horrors—horrors, William Shawcross reminds us, "that were born out of the inferno that American policy did much to create."[173]

The Congo/Zaire, 1960 to 1965: "Project Wizard"

According to The Church Committee's investigation of CIA plots to assassinate foreign leaders, the findings published in 1975, it's clear that Dwight Eisenhower ordered the assassination of Congo leader Patrice Lumumba at a National Security Council meeting on 18 August 1960. The CIA's "capo" Allen Dulles took the order from his "boss" to his "crew" in the streets. "The following day, Dulles cabled a CIA Station Officer in Leopoldville, Republic of the Congo," the congressional report states, "that 'in high quarters' the 'removal' of Lumumba was 'an urgent and prime objective.' Shortly thereafter the CIA's clandestine service formulated a plot to assassinate Lumumba."[174]

Now, the Belgians also had their own plot to ice Patrice Lumumba called "Operation Barracuda." And, of course, the British also wanted a piece of Lumumba. *Why?* Well, you know why. It's the same exact story over and over again: Lumumba was the Congo's first democratically elected leader after their hastily crafted independence from Belgium, a colonial monarchy that handed the country back but not its vast mineral wealth. Writing in *The New York Times* about "An Assassination's Long Shadow," Adam Hochschild relays Belgian King Baudouin's condescending imperial comment to the African nation: "'It is now up to you, gentlemen,' he arrogantly told Congolese dignitaries, 'to show that you are worthy of our confidence.'"[175]

Patrice Lumumba did not sit idly by. He gave a rousing and raging address that demanded economic and political independence from their colonial oppressors, citing the violence and theft perpetrated by their white tyrants. Lumumba also cited the humiliation of how "French-speaking colonists talked to Africans as adults do to children, using the familiar 'tu' instead of the formal 'vous.' Political independence was not enough, he said; Africans had to also benefit from the great wealth in their soil," Hochschild concludes.[176] Interested not only in checking the effrontery of this independent-minded thinking, Washington was also Cold War nervous about Lumumba's ties with the Soviet Union for aid and military assistance. Hochschild, also the author of *King Leopold's Ghost: A Story of Greed, Terror and Heroism in Colonial Africa,* describes Patrice Lumumba's final and sad demise:

> The C.I.A., with White House approval, ordered his assassination and dispatched an undercover agent with poison. The would-be poisoners could not get close enough to Lumumba to do the job, so instead the United States and Belgium covertly funneled cash and aid to rival politicians who seized power and arrested the prime minister. Fearful of revolt by Lumumba's supporters if he died in their hands, the new Congolese leaders ordered him flown to the copper-rich Katanga region in the country's south, whose secession Belgium had just helped orchestrate. There, on January 17, 1961, after being beaten and tortured, he was shot. It was a chilling moment.[177]

Chaos in the African nation ensued and led to the rise of a CIA favorite son: Joseph Mobutu aka Mobutu Sese Seko, an anti-Lumumba military man who assumed power four years after the brutal assassination. "Mobutu went on to rule the country for more than 30 years," William Blum reports, "with a level of corruption and cruelty that shocked even his CIA handlers."[178] During these thirty plus years of ruthless rule, Mobutu grew spectacularly rich while, of course, the people existed in abject poverty, giving rise to the term "kleptocracy," or rule by thieves.

But as is all too common, Cold War politics locked-in U.S. and western support, no matter how corrupt or violent the "friend" is. "Mobutu was showered with more than $1 billion in American aid and enthusiastically welcomed to the White House by a succession of presidents," writes Hochschild.[179] In fact, George Herbert Walker Bush dubbed Mobutu "one of our most valued friends."[180]

Brazil, 1961 to 1964

Washington was very uneasy about Brazilian President João Goulart's ties to the Brazilian Communist Party as well as his opposition to sanctions against Cuba. The Kennedy Administration knew that Brazilian military leaders were planning a coup. JFK sent his brother, Attorney General Robert Kennedy, to Brazil to strong-arm Goulart into abandoning his communist ties, ties to labor unions and student groups, and to start embracing American and foreign investors.[181] Basically, Kennedy told the democratically elected leader to cut the bullshit with his nationalization of business and in-country resources and jump onboard the big capitalist money train rumbling in the north—or you'll be under the train as it passes through.

After JFK was whacked in what many believe was another CIA-sponsored coup d'état, Lyndon Johnson picked up the ball on ousting Brazilian President João Goulart, as evidenced by White House audiotapes released by the Lyndon Baines Johnson Library, recorded on 31 March 1964. Johnson is chatting with Undersecretary of State George Ball and the newly installed American president instructs Ball to actively support the coup if U.S. collaboration is needed. Johnson: "I think we ought to take every step that we can, be prepared to do everything that we need to do," he directs Ball. Then, regarding the coup moving forward, Johnson charges: "I'd put everybody that had any imagination or ingenuity... (CIA Director John) McCone... (Secretary of Defense Robert) McNamara... we just can't take this one. I'd get right on top of it and stick my neck out a little."[182]

During the first few days of April 1964, the Brazilian military moved to depose Goulart. He contemplated resistance to the military coup but then on April 4 decided it was futile and escaped Brazil for a life in exile. He boarded a plane for Montevideo and was gone—and with him on that plane was his opposition to the U.S. noose around Cuba's neck, his support for labor, and the idea that multinational corporations could not rape the Brazilian people and their resources.

William Blum concludes:

> Yet the man was no radical. He was a millionaire landowner and
> a Catholic who wore a medal of the Virgin around his neck. That,
> however, was not enough to save him… he was overthrown in a
> military coup, which had deep, covert American involvement. The
> official Washington line was… yes, it's unfortunate that democracy
> has been overthrown in Brazil… but, still, the country has been
> saved from communism.[183]

Brazil: Postscript

Once Goulart was history, courtesy of Washington's enthusiastic support of the
coup, the next two decades in Brazil are defined by "a neo-Nazi-style national
security state with torture (and) repression," writes Noam Chomsky. "That
inspired a rash of similar developments in Argentina, Chile and all over the
hemisphere, from the mid-sixties to the eighties—an extremely bloody period."[184]
In fact, shortly after the coup, the CIA and FBI set up shop Brazil to teach, share,
and experiment "with sophisticated torture techniques."[185] Similar to the purpose
of the U.S. Army's School of the Americas (Assassins), the Brazil operation
focused on teaching anti-communist counterinsurgency training to Brazil's
military personnel, who proved to be excellent students, graduating into bands
of secret police that viciously hunted down communists for political and "moral
rehabilitation,"[186] "not to mention torture, murder and other devices of 'population
control.'"[187] In her distinguished study, *Masters of War*, Clara Nieto agrees, clearly
suggesting that America's road to perdition in Latin America started here:

> The era of neofascist dictatorships of the National Security doctrine
> and the so-called dirty wars began after the military coup in Brazil.
> Most of the armed forces of Latin America adopted this doctrine.[188]

 **Dominican Republic, 1963 to 1966**

As the first troops land and step into the sand
The flags are weeping
The marines have landed on the shores of Santo Domingo
> —Phil Ochs, "The Marines Have Landed on the Shores of Santo Domingo"

It's been said that you are known by the company you keep. Once again, enter Washington, who strongly supported Rafael Trujillo, the brutal and long-time dictator of the Dominican Republic, primarily because of his staunch anticommunist actions. Trujillo was assassinated in 1961, his car blasted by machine gun fire on a quiet road between Santo Domingo and San Cristobal, where "El Jefe" kept a young mistress. Tim Mansel of the BBC frames Trujillo's cruel and violent reign:

> Those who dared to oppose him were imprisoned, tortured and
> murdered. Their bodies often disappeared, rumoured to have been
> fed to the sharks.[189]

Not long after Antonio Imbert finished Trujillo off ("Trujillo was wounded but he was still walking, so I shot him again," he says[190]), policymakers in Washington were already contemplating sending in the Marines. "Many Americans having invested $250 million in the Dominican Republic believe that Generalissimo Trujillo was the best guarantee of American interests in the country," warned Florida Senator George Smathers, a good friend to JFK as well as to powerful American business interests. "Open intervention must now be considered to protect their property and to prevent a communist coup."[191]

In 1962, Juan Bosch—a major leader of the Dominican opposition to Trujillo, who lived in exile throughout the Caribbean—returned to his country following Trujillo's demise. A liberal reformer, Bosch was very popular among the poor and the farmers and was elected president. Just months after assuming power, Bosch offered a new constitution that embodied freedoms the Dominicans never knew—including labor rights, farmers' rights, and protection for children. It wasn't long after Bosch was sworn in that the conservative Dominican business sector and the Catholic Church—with rigorous propaganda support from the CIA and the U.S. Information Agency—unleashed an anti-Bosch campaign.[192] Just a mere seven months after taking office, a right-wing military coup toppled the Bosch government with Juan Bosch returning to exile in Puerto Rico. "Not surprisingly," writes Howard Zinn, "the overthrow of the Bosch government by a military coup in 1963, according to Time correspondent Sam Halper, followed 'a wink from the U.S. Pentagon.'"[193]

Needless to say, the new military junta was not warmly embraced by Dominicans, and by 1965, a revolution to return Bosch to power was well underway. Special

U.S. Envoy John Bartlow Martin reported that the revolution posed "a serious threat of communist takeover."[194] But Washington had been edgy about the Dominicans for some time, therefore the revolution was met head-on by Lyndon Johnson and 22,000 U.S. Marines, who landed in Santo Domingo and quickly crushed the rebellion. The U.S. action reminded many of America's "gunboat-diplomacy" so popular in the early years of the 20th century. Howard Zinn puts the Marine invasion under the historical microscope:

> The rebellion was defeated in the name of "stopping communism," but the operating factor was American money and American power. Once the rebels were defeated, and a regime palatable to the United States was again in power, [Richard] Barnet [in his book *Intervention and Revolution*] reports that "Private U.S. investment in housing and tourism began to flow into the island once more. The shooting had scarcely stopped before new Hilton Hotels, Holiday Inns, and housing projects sponsored by IBEC, a Rockefeller-family company, were being planned. The South Puerto Rican Sugar Company, now merged with Gulf and Western Industries, decided to diversify, and use some of its beachfront property for a new tourist center." The Dominican Republic was "stable" once more.[195]

Cuba, 1959 to ???—"America's Castro Fixation"

The tragedy and folly of America's behavior toward Cuba over the past half century, this tiny island nation just ninety miles from Florida, is not only a grotesque embarrassment, it's criminal. From the moment Fulgencio Batista fled to Spain on 1 January 1959 and the 26th of July Movement marched into Havana with Che Guevara and Camilo Cienfuegos at the vanguard, the United States of America strangled and terrorized (through invasion, sanctions, embargoes, assassinations and assassination attempts, bombings, an invasion at the Bay of Pigs, as well as full-scale worldwide agitprop) this small island nation. Fidel Castro, Celia Sanchez, and a host of other Cuban revolutionaries committed the great sin: they established the foundation of a "good example" to be followed throughout the Americas—right in the Empire's backyard.

Our revolution is endangering all American possessions in Latin America. We are telling these countries to make their own revolution.
—Che Guevara

It became real on Friday, 8 September 1960 when Cuba's new premier, Fidel Castro (in diplomatic attendance at the UN General Assembly), visited Harlem, USA and met with Malcolm X. That is when the neighborhood bully went into full fixation mode, especially after news articles like this feature story from the *New York Citizen-Call,* just after Castro's tour of Harlem, presented tangible evidence and a charismatic face representing the dreaded "good example":

> Some 2,000 brown New Yorkers stood in the rain Monday night waiting for Cuba's Premier Fidel Castro to arrive at Harlem's famous old Hotel Theresa… from the conversations among this rain soaked mass of humanity, the idea began to build that Castro would come here to stay because he had found out, as most Negroes found out, the nasty ways the underdog was treated downtown.

> To Harlem's oppressed ghetto dwellers, Castro was that bearded revolutionary who had thrown the nation's rascals out and who had told white America to go to hell.[196]

The confrontation between the new Cuba and the American Empire fills volumes upon volumes of study. The struggle between ideologies, propaganda, and political will has been titanic—a classic match to the death between David and Goliath. From the moment Eisenhower was planning the Bay of Pigs Invasion while Castro, Guevara, and Celia Sánchez were orchestrating the rebellion from high in the Sierra Maestra, the writing was on the wall. The physical reality of the first socialist state existing in the American hemisphere—a revolutionary state with compelling leaders and backed by the Soviet Union—was earth shattering to American policymakers and ideologues. It was in their face. "Fidel had virtually expelled the United States from the island," explains Clara Nieto. "(He) expropriated and nationalized all American enterprises and large land holdings."[197]

From Kennedy's trigger finger on the failed "Playa Giron" Invasion, through the Cuban Missile Crisis, to Cuba's ongoing and public defiance at the United Nations and elsewhere, along with all the failed attempts to kill Castro with poison, exploding cigars, and other James Bond, cartoon-like operations, Cuba and the Cuban people have survived. Not well, but they have survived. In fact, Castro and the Cuban people's dedicated will forced an intransigent Washington to let loose the covert dogs of war (counterinsurgency and guerilla operations) throughout the hemisphere as a warning and in response to the Cuban revolution and resolve. The Cuban example—as shaky as it is because of the constant interference and the ongoing stranglehold by the neighborhood bully—remains a historic and courageous battle against American imperial might.

William Blum offers a tragic conclusion:

> The saddest part of this is that the world will never know what kind of society Cuba could have produced if left alone, if not constantly under the gun and the threat of invasion, if allowed to relax its control at home. The idealism, the vision, the talent were all there. But we'll never know. And that of course was the idea.[198]

Chile, 1964 to 11 September 1973

I don't see why we need to stand by and watch a country go communist due to the irresponsibility of its own people. The issues are much too important for the Chilean voters to be left to decide for themselves.
—Henry Kissinger

Shortly after the mass murderer, war criminal, and Nobel Peace Prize-winning American policymaker Henry Kissinger uttered those words, poet, teacher, and Chilean folk singer Victor Jara was abducted from a university in Santiago by madmen loyal to the American-backed coup against President Salvador Allende, a coup spearheaded by General Augusto Pinochet. Along with thousands of his fellow Chileans, Jara was taken to a stadium, then tortured, electrocuted, and, for good measure, had his wrists and hands broken by his captors to make a "statement" about Victor's membership in the Communist Party and his songs of protest that railed against the ruling elite of his country. Victor Jara was then machine-gunned to death, his body dumped on the streets of Santiago. He was shot forty-four times.

"Salvador Allende was the worst possible scenario for a Washington imperialist," William Blum points out.[199] Indeed, Allende was a democratically elected Marxist who fervently embraced the constitution and was very popular among the masses. Christ, that's a goddamn train wreck in the eyes of the *norteamericanos*.

Allende was a physician who helped build the Socialist Party in Chile. Before his election as president in 1970, he ran three times and lost. Allende once joked that his epitaph would eventually read: "Here lies the next President of Chile."[200] In 1964, according to the Central Intelligence Agency themselves, a series of covert actions were undertaken by the CIA to ensure Allende's defeat. (You throw up in your mouth a little more each time you hear a U.S. president utter perfunctory gibberish about the sanctity of democracy.) Here's the CIA's overview of their covert actions:

> At the direction of the White House and interagency policy coordination committees, CIA undertook the covert activities described below. There were sustained propaganda efforts, including financial support for major news media, against Allende and other Marxists. Political action projects supported selected parties before and after the 1964 elections.[201]

Nevertheless, six years later, in 1970, Salvador Allende won the presidency. The celebrated Chilean writer and relative of the Chilean president, Isabel Allende, wrote in her memoir:

> The CIA orchestrated a plan to prevent Allende from assuming the presidency. First it tried to bribe members of Congress not to designate Allende... since the bribes didn't work, the CIA planned to kidnap the commander in chief of the armed forces, General Rene Schneider; although the plot would be carried out by a neo-Fascist group, it would appear to be the work of a leftist commando unit. The idea was that this action would provoke chaos and a military intervention.[202]

Once again, from the CIA's own report:

> **Support for Coup in 1970.** Under "Track II" of the strategy, CIA sought to instigate a coup to prevent Allende from taking office... CIA was working with three different groups of plotters. All three groups made it clear that any coup would require the kidnapping of Army Commander Rene Schneider, who felt deeply that the Constitution required that the Army allow Allende to assume power. CIA agreed with that assessment.[203]

General Rene Schneider was in fact shot to death in the ensuing clash and the CIA's plan backfired as the Chilean people pulled together and Congress unanimously voted for Allende's installation as president, reaffirming the actual election results. "From that moment on," Isabel Allende writes, "the right and the CIA plotted together to oust the government of the Unidad Popular [Chile's leftist coalition], even at the cost of destroying the economy and Chile's long democratic tradition."[204]

The CIA, along with their cohort right wing extremists, failed in 1964 and then failed again in 1970, despite being hell-bent on installing a regime contrary to the will of the Chilean people. By 1973, "the CIA and the rest of the American foreign policy machine left no stone unturned in their attempt to destabilize the Allende government... paying particular attention to building up military hostility," Blum writes.[205]

Along with the Chilean military, Washington led this surge to topple and remove Allende with millions of well-placed dollars, major propaganda and disinformation campaigns, CIA-instigated sabotage, as well as CIA-instigated labor strikes throughout the country—all of it designed to weaken Allende's government and leadership. Chile's political right, along with the super wealthy and their friendly foreign corporate interests—especially Kennecott Copper, Anaconda (copper), and International Telephone and Telegraph (ITT)—were all set in opposition to Allende. Clara Nieto stresses that, "Nixon—personally—authorized the CIA to blockade Allende's government. He was convinced that Chile was going down the Cuban road and that the Revolution would spread to the rest of the continent."[206]

Thanks to the Wikileaks release of the "Kissinger Cables," it becomes readily apparent that the Vatican and Catholic Church also turned a blind eye to the manipulation and destruction of their flock and supported Pinochet's U.S.-backed coup.[207]

On the first infamous 11 September, this one in 1973, with television cameras poised and General Augusto Pinochet doing his best Napoleon Bonaparte, tanks rolled into Santiago with the blessing, support, and facilitation of the United States of America. Pinochet ordered a full military assault on the capital city. Allende died in the presidential palace. Many believe he committed suicide as his government fell. Under Pinochet's orders, air force jets then bombed the palace. The successful coup ended Chile's long history of constitutional rule.

One of the first actions undertaken by the new U.S.-backed Pinochet regime was the dispatch of a death squad that crisscrossed Chile by helicopter charged with eliminating (read: murdering) the political opponents of Pinochet's coup. The death squad became well known as the "Caravan of Death."[208] Kissinger, as a fellow mass murderer, must have been rock-hard with excitement as reports surfaced of at least 72 executions—brutal executions not unlike the vicious death of Victor Jara.

Unfortunately for the people of Chile, the coup was just the beginning as Pinochet's junta redefined large swaths of the population as the ideological enemy—targeting these individuals as "subversives" and "terrorists." In 2004, a Chilean presidential investigation released a powerful indictment of the Pinochet military government's systematic use of torture and death. Headed by Bishop Sergio Valech, a clergyman who supported and defended victims throughout the onslaught, the "Valech Report on Political Imprisonment and Torture" found that at least 27,000 Chileans were tortured between 1973 and 1990, and that 2,603 Chileans were murdered or "disappeared," with another 1,000+ still unaccounted for and missing.[209]

The United States was not alone in their support of Pinochet's brutal dictatorship for almost two decades. America's client-state partner in crime, Great Britain, under the watchful eye of Margaret Thatcher, was an unabashedly steadfast defender of Augusto Pinochet. "She visited Pinochet in 1999 during his house arrest in England, saying that her country 'owed' him 'a great debt' of gratitude for his help during the 1982 Falklands War," recalls Nima Shirazi, an independent researcher and political analyst.[210] "Without any sense of irony," Shirazi continues, "Thatcher added, 'I'm also very much aware that it is you who brought democracy to Chile.'"[211]

Thatcher wasn't through spewing her pompous gibberish. A short time later, during a Conservative Party Conference, the British prime minister saluted the vicious tyrant as Britain's "staunch, true friend in our time of need" and a man "who stopped the communists taking Chile."[212]

In his book, *The Condor Years: How Pinochet and His Allies Brought Terrorism to Three Continents*, Columbia University journalism professor John Dinges, former correspondent for *Time*, *The Washington Post*, and *ABC News* in Latin America, frames an ugly U.S. legacy in Chile and throughout the Americas:

> The political tragedy of this story is that the military leaders who

carried out the assassinations and mass murders looked to the United States for technical assistance and strategic leadership... The tragedy is that the United States acted not to promote and nurture democracy, but to encourage and justify its overthrow. Even more tragic, and arguably criminal, were the cases in which U.S. officials were directly involved in plots and liaison relationships with those engaged in political assassination and mass murder.[213]

Pop Quiz

Here's the quote:

> *"It is best to remain silent and to forget. It is the only thing to do: we must forget. And forgetting does not occur by opening cases, putting people in jail."*

Who said this? Former Chilean General Augusto Pinochet in 1995 regarding those dark days beginning 11 September 1973, or U.S. President Barack Obama regarding the equally dark days of the Bush/Cheney regime (and later his own)?

Answer: The words are Pinochet's, but the spirit is shared by both, evinced by Obama's refusal to even acknowledge the obvious torture and war crimes of his predecessor, let alone to prosecute. The whitewashing of horrors occurs all the time, by all leaders, everywhere.

Greece, 1964 to 1974: "Shoot the motherfucker"

In *60 Minutes* producer George Crile's book, *Charlie Wilson's War*—the exposé about how Texas congressman Charlie Wilson and his CIA-sidekick, Gust Avrakotos, bamboozled the U.S. Congress into supporting the Mujahideen—Crile retells an exchange between Avrakotos (aka "Dr. Dirty" for his "willingness to handle ethically ambiguous tasks"[214]) and the military men orchestrating another CIA-sponsored coup. Just weeks before a national election that experts believed would return the Papandreou political dynasty back to power in Greece, Andreas Papandreou—the son of former Greek prime minister Georgios Papandreou and outspoken critic of American intelligence and military presence in Greece, who suggested a more neutral Cold War stance by pulling Greece out of NATO—was arrested at gunpoint, along with his father, by the right-wing military junta who seized power on 21 April 1967. CBS producer Crile writes that Washington took the "unusual step of issuing the Greek leader an American passport" and wanted the military strongmen to let them leave the country. Crile then recounts what "Dr. Dirty" Avrakotos suggested:

> "That's the official position. You should let him go," the young CIA man told the colonels. "But unofficially, as your friend, my advice is to shoot the motherfucker because he's going to come back to haunt you."[215]

9 October 1967: "The Murder of Ernesto Che Guevara"

I knew that when the great guiding spirit cleaves humanity into two antagonistic halves, I will be with the people. I see it printed in the night sky that I, eclectic dissembler of doctrine and psychoanalyst of dogma, howling like one possessed, will assault the barricades or the trenches, will take my bloodstained weapon and, consumed with fury, slaughter any enemy who falls into my hands.
—Che Guevara, *The Motorcycle Diaries: Notes on a Latin American Journey*, 1952

The CIA has whacked many foreign leaders and political adversaries over the years, individuals that Washington wanted out of the picture in order to eliminate the dreaded "good example" and therefore protect American and western business interests. But there was one "motherfucker" they wanted dead more than any other motherfucker—and that motherfucker was Ernesto Guevara. Charismatic, enigmatic, as well as iconic, Che was also unflappable, tougher than nails, vastly intelligent, and couldn't be bought. But above all else, and this is what shook the Empire's foundation: he could see through America's imperial mask—and he helped others see through it as well. TAKE HIM OUT!

> *There was no person more feared by the company (CIA) than Che Guevara because he had the capacity and charisma necessary to direct the struggle against the political repression of the traditional hierarchies in power in the countries of Latin America.*
> —CIA officer Philip Agee, who later defected to Cuba

In April of 1965, Fidel Castro was questioned by reporters about Guevara's whereabouts. The Cuban leader tells the foreign scribes that Guevara "will always be where he is most useful to the revolution."[216] By the end of the year, Che readies himself for an expedition to Bolivia.

After the 1959 Cuban Revolution that dispensed with the American-friendly regime of Fulgencio Batista, Che Guevara helped to build the new government. He was first assigned as the head of La Cabana Fortress, a prison-like compound where Batista's counter-revolutionaries and torturers were held after capture. Guevara was in charge of organizing and overseeing the trials and reports emerged that Che was conscientious and meticulous when ensuring objectivity. It should be noted that 55 prisoners at La Cabana were found guilty of torture or murder and subsequently executed.[217] Guevara was then in charge of the new agrarian reform measures that swept the country. Authorized by international law, the new government nationalized huge tracts of land heretofore owned by American corporations who were informed that they would be reimbursed for the land in the amount of the exact value they listed on tax filings. The Americans turned down the offers. Shortly thereafter, in retaliation, Washington implemented the infamous blockade designed to choke Cuba off from the world.[218]

In 1965, Che headed a secret Cuban operation aiding the rebels in the Congo. Just months before his African journey, on 11 December 1964, Che made a historic speech to the United Nation's General Assembly in New York City. In the belly of the beast, on the world's largest stage, Guevara illustrated his ability to undress Washington's motives:

> Our free eyes open now on new horizons and can see what
> yesterday, in our condition as colonial slaves, we could not observe:
> that "Western Civilization" disguises behind its showy facade a
> picture of hyenas and jackals. That is the only name that can be
> applied to those who have gone to fulfill such "humanitarian" tasks
> in the Congo. A carnivorous animal that feeds on unarmed peoples.
> That is what imperialism does to men. That is what distinguishes
> the imperial "white man."[219]

In 1964, Bolivian president Victor Paz Estenssoro was removed from office by a military coup supported and orchestrated once again by Washington powerbrokers who were less than thrilled with his independent thoughts and actions. Two years prior, Estenssoro opposed America's demand of kicking Cuba out of the Organization of American States. The Bolivian president continued diplomatic relations with Cuba and refused to take part in the sanctions leveled against the small Caribbean nation just 100 miles from Miami. The U.S. was also very aware of the potential powerful threat posed by Bolivia's tin miners, who "were seen as a force potentially more radical than the president," writes William Blum in *Killing Hope*.[220] And the miners were getting stronger by the day.

Indeed, Bolivia was ripe for socialist revolution and the Cubans knew it; Che Guevara knew it; and, of course, the United States knew it. It's why Washington worked overtime after the success of the Cuban Revolution to fortify counter-insurgency capabilities throughout Latin America: JFK bolstered U.S. Special Forces fivefold with the Green Berets training local forces everywhere—especially in Bolivia.

But... *"There was music in the cafes at night and revolution in the air..."* and that was unacceptable to American hegemony. "Che and Castro hoped that the Andes would become the Sierra Maestra of all of Latin America," write Michael Ratner and Michael Steven Smith in *Who Killed Che?*[221] They envisioned "a training ground for guerillas who would then spread the revolution from Bolivia to Chile, Argentina, Brazil, Ecuador, Peru, Venezuela, and throughout the entire subcontinent."[222] In fact, Guevara saw the chance to create "two, three, many Vietnams,"[223] and stretch colonialism to the point where it weakens and breaks. In his diary, Che explained:

> The example of our revolution and the lessons it applies for
> Latin America have destroyed all coffee house theories; we have
> demonstrated that a small group of men supported by the people
> and without fear of dying can overcome a disciplined regular army
> and defeat it.[224]

Lyndon Johnson, along with his cadre of White House policymakers and National Security Advisors, his military brass at the Pentagon, as well as his spooks out at Langley, all knew Che was right. They were still smarting from the Cuban failure at the Bay of Pigs and Vietnam wasn't going much better with Ho Chi Minh making imperial life miserable for the invaders. Dick Gregory could have had this casual conversation with Che and both men would be in complete solidarity:

> America has always had a nigger with us and would kick us: "Boss,
> did I do something wrong? Excuse me, boss." So America went
> over there and thought it was a nigger and kicked at him—but that

Vietnamese grabbed his foot. Now, he never had his foot grabbed before. Damn if Uncle Sam ran across some niggers that weren't scared of him. General Giap wrote a book years before the war called "People's War People's Army," and in it he said, "Give me an army that's willing to die and I'll defeat any army that's willing to kill."[225]

"Thus, for Washington, defeating Che was crucial," conclude Ratner and Smith. In fact, the pressure was mounting against U.S. imperialism everywhere: "Vietnam, Cuba, El Salvador, Guatemala, Nicaragua, and, above all, the Union of Soviet Socialist Republics."[226] The prospects of armed socialist rebellions dotting the landscape were terrifying to the American government as well as to American business leaders. Once again in *Killing Hope*, William Blum defines the CIA as "obsessed... with tracking down the legendary guerrilla."[227] When the U.S. determined that Che was leading a revolutionary force in the southern mountains of Bolivia, the CIA sharpened their focus: Vast amounts of American military supplies begin to arrive; Green Berets arrived to provide crash training to Bolivian forces; state-of-the-art communication, intelligence, and reconnaissance technology was put into play, including infrared detection systems; in short order, thousands and thousands of square miles are captured on aerial photography; exiled Cubans are flown in by the CIA to oversee and conduct interrogations (read: torture) of locals who are suspected of aiding and abetting the guerrilla forces. Blum characterizes the operation as "overkill."[228]

> *On October 9th, 1967, Ernesto "Che" Guevara was put to death by Bolivian soldiers, trained, equipped and guided by U.S. Green Beret and CIA operatives. His execution remains a historic and controversial event.*
> —Peter Kornbluh, *The Death of Che Guevara: Declassified*, National Security Archive, George Washington University

The Cover Story. As first reported by the Bolivian high command, Che Guevara was killed in battle. This lie was quickly dispelled and the basic truth surfaced: Guevara was captured and then executed the following day. What remains in question is who actually ordered the execution. As is always the case with operations run by the White House through the Central Intelligence Agency, we witness the formulation of "plausible deniability." In 1948, just after Truman set the National Security Council in motion, they approved a secret order (NSC 10/2), which authorized a long list of covert operations that positioned the Agency as a paramilitary force operating outside international law, and since these NSC 10/2 activities are clearly illegal, this operational paradigm demands that government and elected officials are protected from culpability. "The national security doctrine of 'plausible deniability' combined lying with hypocrisy," writes Jim Douglas, author of *JFK and the Unspeakable: Why He Died and Why It Matters*. "It marked the creation of a Frankenstein monster."[229]

The Johnson Administration strongly stated that the kill order came from Bolivian officials and not the CIA or anybody in Washington. In fact, Johnson's staff insisted that they wanted Che alive. These statements not only fly in the face of what happened on the ground but also fly in the face of history.

The History. Washington wanted the Castro brothers (Fidel and Raul) "eliminated" along with Guevara right after the revolution in 1960. During the Church Committee investigations in 1975, a report comes to light. Allen Dulles asked J.C. King—the CIA Chief of Western Hemispheric Operations—to investigate the plausibility of "eliminating" Fidel Castro. King looked into it and then reported back. "At a March 1960 meeting," writes historian H.W. Brands, "King told the CIA task force in charge of policy toward Cuba that assassination didn't appear promising. 'Unless Fidel and Raul Castro and Che Guevara could be eliminated in one package—which is highly unlikely—the operation can be a long, drawn-out affair and the present government will only be overthrown by the use of force.'"[230] One week later, Eisenhower signs off on a plan to invade Cuba using Cuban exiles (Bay of Pigs). But the assassination plans continue. The CIA recruits Chicago Mafia superstar "Handsome Johnny" Rosselli to poison the Castro brothers and Che. Rosselli is happy to help his adopted country in their enduring struggle for democracy and liberty. In fact, Rosselli testified about the plot loud and clear during the Church Committee investigation on alleged assassination plots.[231] Although "Handsome Johnny" tried and tried hard, the poison pills never ended up in Che's rice and beans, nor Castro's. But just one year after the Church Committee investigations, in 1976, possibly as part of America's Bicentennial Celebration, Johnny Rosselli wound up in a fuel drum floating off the coast of Miami. Rosselli had been strangled, shot, and his legs were sawed off. *Happy Birthday, America.*

ON THE GROUND

In their book *Who Killed Che?*, constitutional attorney and President Emeritus of the Center for Constitutional Rights, Michael Ratner, along with author and human rights attorney, Michael Steven Smith, make an incredibly well documented and compelling case that turns the cover story—that Che was murdered by the Bolivian military dictatorship—into a work of fiction. They set up the case this way:

> Documents which have recently been obtained from the
> U.S. government lead to a different conclusion: that the U.S.
> government, particularly its Central Intelligence Agency, had Che
> murdered, having secured the participation of its Bolivian client
> state.[232]

In the early afternoon of 9 October 1967, in a tiny mountain village in Bolivia, a sergeant in his country's army downed some booze and walked into the rural schoolhouse where the wounded revolutionary Ernesto Che Guevara was in custody and shot him to death. "It was murder," conclude Ratner and Smith. "Under the laws that govern warfare, including guerrilla war, the killing of a prisoner is murder and constitutes a war crime. It is not just the actual shooter who is guilty of a war crime. Those higher-ups that ordered, acquiesced to, or failed to prevent the murder are guilty as well." They emphasize: "There is no statute of limitations for this crime."[233]

Two CIA agents who were on the ground in Bolivia hold the keys to the box marked "Truth" regarding the murder of Che Guevara. First there is Cuban ex-pat Gustavo Villoldo, head of the CIA in-country team. Despite the fact that the so-called historical record indicates that the CIA team (plugged into the Bolivian army doing battle with Guevara and his guerrillas) had very specific orders to "do everything possible to keep him (Che) alive,"[234] Villoldo informs the president of Bolivia, Rene Barrientos, at his home, "that if Che were captured he personally would do everything in his power to have him executed."[235] This is a complete contradiction by the head of the CIA's in-country team, clearly countermanding the so-called "keep him alive" order. In fact, despite Villoldo's seemingly rogue, if not insubordinate behavior, he kept working for the CIA and the Empire until 1970—another three years.

Then there is the CIA agent, Felix Rodriguez, who actually gave the kill order right inside the small schoolhouse. In fact, Rodriguez claims he was the highest-ranking officer on the scene—disguised as a Bolivian army captain. He was waiting for the radio call. The code was simple: "500" identified Guevara; "600" meant dead—kill him; "700" meant keep him alive. The order came—"500, 600." Rodriguez had the order repeated—"500, 600." Rodriguez passed the order on to the Bolivian soldier designated to do the kill. A few minutes later Che Guevara was dead.

Ratner and Smith offer the obvious conclusion:

> In [Rodriguez's] book, Shadow Warrior: the CIA Hero of a Hundred Unknown Battles, he insists that he had been told by the CIA that if Che were captured alive he was to "do everything possible to keep him alive—everything!" Rodriguez says he could have countermanded the murder order and saved Che's life, but he chose not to, leaving Che's fate in the hands of the Bolivians. This story makes little sense. Rodriguez was working for the CIA and would continue to do so for many years. If his bosses and paymasters wanted Che kept alive, he surely would have done so. If he had disobeyed the CIA's avowed wishes to "do everything" to keep Che alive, would he have been allowed to continue as a CIA operative? The obvious conclusion is the CIA wanted Che dead and that the story was crafted to give the White House "plausible deniability."[236]

As a postscript to this obvious conclusion, the BBC's Will Grant conducted an interview with Felix Rodriguez in his Miami home. The interview re-hashes the long ago story and offers nothing new except for this, which bolsters the above claim: "If he had disobeyed the CIA's avowed wishes to 'do everything' to keep Che alive, would he have been allowed to continue as a CIA operative?" In Rodriguez's home, Grant describes a small CIA museum—memorabilia from Rodriguez's CIA past: photographs of a distinguished career, a CIA medal for exceptional service to the Agency, a blood-soaked North Vietnamese flag, and then the coup de grace—a photograph of Felix Rodriguez talking with President George Bush, Sr. in the White House.[237]

In March of 1968, Ramparts magazine published a story by Michèle Ray. A month after the death of Che Guevara, she traveled to Bolivia on assignment for Paris Match. She spent seven weeks investigating the killing of the guerrilla leader. She titled her piece "The Execution of Che by the CIA." Here is a passage from her piece about an encounter between the wounded Guevara and the teacher in the village on the morning of the day Che was executed:

After having tried vainly to interrogate the prisoner, [Colonel] Selnich decides to leave him alone. He has the guard outside reinforced. On Monday morning Che asks to see the *maestra,* the schoolmistress of the village.

Twenty-two-year-old Julia Cortez told Father Schiller: "I was afraid to go there, afraid he would be a brute. But instead I found an agreeable-looking man, with a soft and ironic glance... It was impossible for me to look him in the eye."

"Ah! you are the *maestra.* Do you know that there is no accent on the *'se'* of *ya se leer?"* he says as a preface, pointing at one of the drawings that hangs on the wall. "You know that in Cuba there are no schools like this one. We would call this a prison. How can the children of the *campesinos* study here... It's antipedagogical."

"We live in a poor country," the schoolmistress replies.

"But the government officials and the generals have Mercedes cars and plenty of other things... *¿Verdad?* That's what we are fighting against."

"You have come a long way to fight in Bolivia."

"I am a revolutionary and I've been in a lot of places."

"You have come to kill our soldiers."

"You know, a war is either lost or won."

The maestra repeated this conversation to Jorge Torrico. "I had to look down while I talked to him... his gaze was unbearable. Piercing... and so tranquil."[238]

Shortly after her visit "with the famous Che Guevara," Julia Cortez, the *maestra,* was back in her home some 50 meters away from the schoolhouse in La Higuera—a poor town of 400 people living in tiny adobe huts with tile roofs. There were no cars, just a few small stone streets and a mule path. As usual, it was very quiet. Peaceful. Then suddenly, the serenity is broken. Julia Cortez hears a burst of gunshots. The *maestra* knows Ernesto Che Guevara, the revolutionary, the man she found so tranquil, is dead.

Operation CHAOS

Beginning as a nascent domestic intelligence operation in 1959 and in direct violation of the National Security Act (which assigned legal responsibility to the FBI), the Eisenhower Administration illegally ordered the CIA to keep tabs on Cuban exiles and other émigrés living on U.S. soil. In force until 1973 and under the control of the White House, Operation CHAOS charged the CIA with spying on thousands upon thousands of Americans. But it wasn't until 1967—as the Vietnam War roared from the jungles of Southeast Asia—that the program hit full stride under LBJ. Ostensibly, the agents were looking for ties between the antiwar movement and foreign governments. CIA Director Richard Helms placed the program under the auspices of the obsessive and paranoid Soviet-spy hunter James Jesus Angleton.[239]

By the time Nixon was talking to the presidential portraits on the wall, Operation CHAOS was a bloated three-headed monster. Nixon's own paranoia was like throwing gasoline on Angleton's fire. The CIA operated at least sixty agents overseas, who were spying, eavesdropping, and collecting data on American citizens. At home, CHAOS was infiltrating numerous groups including Students for a Democratic Society (SDS), Women Strike for Peace, and the Black Panther Party. "The purview of Operation CHAOS quickly spun out of control," writes Paul Pierpaoli, "and the CIA began conducting surveillance on groups and individuals who did not have any direct links to the antiwar movement." The groups included the Women's Liberation Movement as well as (believe it or not) B'nai B'rith and the Israeli Embassy.[240]

In a move of comic genius, the CIA created their own "bogus" trash company in order to sift through mail, correspondence, and paperwork tossed away by the Israeli Embassy. When Helms presented LBJ with the Agency's first report in 1967, the CIA found no substantial links between the antiwar movement and agitators from foreign governments. In fact, the next five reports offered the same conclusion. A big zero—yet Operation CHAOS grew faster and larger. By the time Operation CHAOS was tossed onto its own trash heap, "the CIA compiled 7,000 files on individual Americans and 1,000 files on various groups and organizations," Pierpaoli reports in *The Encyclopedia of the Vietnam War*. The CIA, along with the White House collected another list of more than 300,000 Americans listed as "persons of interest," even though the so-called damning information collected added up to nothing.[241]

We wonder if they still have the garbage truck out at Langley.

Into the Seventies... *The Song Remains the Same*
(With apologies to Page, Bonham, Plant, and Jones)

What should be painfully evident by now is that this ongoing interventionist history by the CIA is ugly and vicious, and at the same time, very predictable: Communism and socialism... *bad*; leaders in sovereign countries who attempt to nationalize internal resources as well as the production of these resources... *bad*; leaders and populations in sovereign countries who do not obey the demands or wishes of the United States of America and their associated corporate partners... *bad*.

But those in-country forces—no matter how corrupt or sadistic—ready to brandish the sword against the people's best interests and do their paymaster's bidding... *good*.

For the American Empire, this independent behavior by foreign countries (usually countries filled with poor brown populations) must be dealt with and dealt with swiftly. First, there needs to be a cover story that somehow threatens American sensibilities and America's sense of exceptionalism, so the intervention becomes a matter of "national security," or "national defense," or as a way to maintain stability in a foreign land that America suddenly cares a great deal about. The cover story is also very necessary for theatrical purposes: the U.S. can't simply use the obvious tenets of imperialism as the rationale for commandeering the land, the resources, the labor, and the markets of a foreign people. It needs a good dose of bullshit to spread around the O.K. Corral.

The Empire's interventions to "remedy" the situation can take various forms: rigged elections; a plethora of economic manipulations and pressure; various and sundry covert operations; sophisticated media and propaganda campaigns including disinformation, misinformation, and of course outright lies; and when all of that doesn't work or the situation is deemed too complex for these measures, the U.S. will then turn to the process they love most and conduct best: military intervention on various scales.

In his essay "Murder Is Our National Sport," journalist Chris Hedges holds nothing back as he defines the ugly march of U.S. interventionist history:

> The United States believes in regeneration through violence. We have carried out blood baths on foreign soil and on our own land for generations in the vain quest of a better world. And the worse it gets, the deeper our empire sinks under the weight of its own decay and depravity, the more we kill.[242]

Underscoring Hedges' somber reality is the likewise ugly march of U.S. interventionist policy through the end of the 20th century. A few more of the "greatest hits" include:

East Timor, Ongoing Since 1975

We made a decision.

U.S. actions in East Timor were so foul, so treacherous, and went so underreported that we dedicated an entire chapter later in this book ("East Timor: Empire's Playground (Or Kissinger Strikes Again)") to this ugly and largely ignored rotten enterprise.

Nicaragua: Carter, Reagan, Cocaine, Crack, Contras, and the CIA

Anastasio Somoza, nicknamed "Tachito," was the last of the Somoza family dynasty to rule Nicaragua until his dictatorship was overthrown by the Sandinistas in 1979—the political resistance movement that fought against the longtime U.S. occupation of Nicaragua throughout most of the 20th century and specifically against the U.S. Marines in the late 1920s and early 1930s. Somoza was re-elected in 1974 but by 1978 the Sandinistas' resistance grew much stronger, bolstered by internal and external pressure: many in the Catholic Church throughout Latin America, who embraced liberation theology, strongly criticized the Somoza regime and this support helped to rally the population; various human rights groups also strongly criticized Somoza's brutal dictatorship along with his "vicious national guard."[243] Rape, torture, and unbridled executions were commonplace extensions of Somoza's regime.[244] Historian Howard Zinn frames American support:

In Nicaragua, the United States had helped maintain the Somoza dictatorship for decades. Misreading the basic weakness of that regime, and the popularity of the revolution against it, the Carter administration continued its support for Somoza until close to the regime's fall in 1979.[245]

Placed under the paranoid historical microscope of the White House and Washington policymakers, Nicaragua began to resemble another "long-dreaded beast," i.e. Cuba—and that was simply not acceptable. Uncle Sam was apoplectic: *"Hell, we've got Cuba choking to death, that spic Che is rotting in hell, Allende blew his goddamn brains out, and now these cockroaches are coming out of the friggin' woodwork. Get a tourniquet on this sonuvabitch!"*

In the late 1970s, with Jimmy Carter at the helm, Washington's interference and outside disruption of the Sandinistas' revolution was done by economic and diplomatic means. Then came Reagan, whose "regime was one of murder, brutality, and violence, which devastated a number of countries and probably left two hundred thousand people dead in Latin America, with hundreds of thousands of orphans and widows,"[246] concludes Noam Chomsky. In fact, Raygun's reign of terror came down on the heads of the Nicaraguan people by way of their proxy army, the Contras (Contrarrevolución Nacional or National Counterrevolution), recruited from Tachito's ruthless National Guard, and who the gentlemen Ronnie eloquently referred to as "the moral equivalent of our Founding Fathers."[247]

The game was on: the Contras received enormous financial and clandestine support from Washington. "It was all-out war, aiming to destroy the progressive social and economic programs of the government," Blum points out, "burning down schools and medical clinics, raping, torturing, mining harbors, bombing and strafing. These were Ronald Reagan's "freedom fighters."[248]

Reagan's point man carrying out the dirty work in Latin America was John Negroponte, U.S. Ambassador to Honduras (he was kind of like how Charles "Tex" Watson helped out Charlie Manson). While in Honduras, Negroponte was in control of the largest CIA station on the planet. The base served as the launching pad for U.S./Contra attacks inside Nicaragua, which is right next-door—attacks that severely hampered the gains of the revolution. In fact, the ravages of war were consuming the country, the economy, the leadership, and most importantly the people. In 1990, after a decade of American economic and violent interference that never allowed reforms and initiatives to evolve and take hold, the Sandinistas suffered a major election defeat effectively ending the revolution.

Gary Webb owns the Nicaraguan postscript

Gary Webb rocked the foundation of myth in America with his courageous and astounding 1996 exposé "Dark Alliance." This profoundly researched investigative sledgehammer reveals that a San Francisco/Bay Area drug mob sold and distributed tons of cocaine to street gangs, especially in Los Angeles, and then funneled millions in profits to finance the CIA-sponsored Nicaraguan Contras. Webb reported that this pipeline was protected by the CIA while the Reagan Administration was sheltering street dealers from arrest and prosecution. Webb's story further detailed how U.S. law enforcement protested the CIA's quashing of their case investigations into drug kingpins Oscar Danilo Blandon and Norvin Meneses—two cornerstones of the vile scheme to finance the CIA's dirty little war in Latin America while simultaneously wreaking crack havoc in Los Angeles and other American cities.

As expected, Webb's scorching investigation produced a ferocious firestorm of controversy. "Shoot the messenger" is the classic kneejerk reaction from the American media—the gatekeepers of what is holy and unholy in their perverted, embedded club (see Ellsberg, Assange, Manning, Snowden, et al). In fact, the press attacked Webb unmercifully, especially the holy trinity of big boys: *The New York Times*, *Los Angeles Times*, and *Washington Post*. For example, Howard Kurtz, the Post's influential media critic ridiculed Webb and his reporting, sniggering, "Oliver Stone, check your voice mail."[249] But sanity and courage did speak up. Author and historian Mike Davis framed the mendacious attack by writing, "Gary Webb was the epitome of journalistic guts, but instead of winning a Pulitzer he was betrayed by his employers and slandered by his profession. (He was a) reporter who unmasked one of the most evil conspiracies in American history."[250]

The *Mercury News* cowered away from its reporter and Webb's career waned. In 2004 he was found dead—the victim of his own messy gunshot wounds. The Sacramento County coroner's office determined his death a suicide. Many have questioned the finding.

Jeff Cohen, founder of the media watch group F.A.I.R., was blunt in his indictment of the "hit pieces" attacking the veracity of Webb's reporting. "The Post and others criticized Webb for referring to the Contras of the so-called Nicaraguan Democratic Force as 'the CIA's army,'" Cohen writes, and then stresses, "an absurd objection since by all accounts, including those of Contra leaders, the CIA set up the group, selected its leaders and paid their salaries, and directed its day-to-day battlefield strategies."[251]

Tom Hayden points out that just two years after Gary Webb broke the story, the CIA copped to even more than he reported. "By then," Hayden continues, "Webb was discredited, disrespected, and destroyed by his own journalism community."[252]

On the evening of 16 January 1999, investigative reporter Gary Webb spoke to an audience at the First United Methodist Church in Eugene, Oregon. He stressed the point that the reality of the U.S. government's culpability infecting inner cities with crack was far greater than he ever reported:

> I do not believe—and I have never believed—that the crack cocaine
> explosion was a conscious CIA conspiracy, or anybody's conspiracy,
> to decimate black America. I've never believed that South Central
> Los Angeles was targeted by the U.S. government to become the
> crack capitol of the world. But that isn't to say that the CIA's hands
> or the U.S. government's hands are clean in this matter. Actually, far
> from it. After spending three years of my life looking into this, I am
> more convinced than ever that the U.S. government's responsibility
> for the drug problems in South Central Los Angeles and other inner
> cities is greater than I ever wrote in the newspaper.[253]

Ultimately, Gary Webb's penetrating work has only been further vindicated in most quarters. Twenty-five year veteran of the Drug Enforcement Agency, Michael Levine, wrote about CIA-drug smuggling: "I witnessed it. The Agency operatives were drug smugglers, and Gary found that out... you are owed a huge apology. But I doubt that you'll get it. Not in this lifetime."[254]

But the strongest vindication of Gary Webb's daring exposé comes from the Central Intelligence Agency itself. In early 1998, CIA Inspector General Frederick Hitz released the findings of his investigation into the Contra mess. "Hitz's Volume One admitted that not only were many of Webb's allegations true," writes investigative journalist Robert Parry, "but that (Webb) actually understated the seriousness of the Contra-drug crimes and the CIA's knowledge."[255] Investigative journalist George Sanchez paints a picture of an "agency so obsessed with promoting the government's ideological agenda that harm done to citizens of the United States of America, was overlooked in an Orwellian ends-justify-the-means operation."[256]

Robert Parry, the George Polk Award-winning journalist who uncovered Oliver North's connection in the Iran-Contra scandal, put this miserable story—one that defines a sad and criminal legacy—in its proper light:

> On this second anniversary of Webb's death it should be
> remembered that his great gift to American history was that he,
> along with angry African-American citizens, forced the government
> to admit some of the worst crimes ever condoned by any White
> House: the protection of drug smuggling into the United States as
> part of a covert war against a country, Nicaragua, that represented
> no real threat to Americans.[257]

Robert Parry's last statement appears to sum up the sad and criminal legacy of the Central Intelligence Agency; along with their military brass comrades that "build all the guns, build the death planes, build the big bombs, hide behind walls, hide behind desks"—all of them guilty of hideous crimes against humanity. The carnage left in their wake is astounding when studied individually, shocking when absorbed in a cumulative revelation. But again, Parry's words seem to summarize their ongoing actions (more like *Groundhog Day*) and offer us consistent historical threads: crimes that are condoned by the White House as part of a covert war against a country that represents no real threat.

Once again, the song remained the same and, as the clock wound down on the so-called "American Century," the same tired story of U.S. intervention continued unabated, unbroken, and punishing to those who dared to think or act independently.

But in the end, under the standard of "Truth crushed to earth will rise again," you can tattoo this on a billboard: *GARY WEBB WAS RIGHT.*

Grenada: "It's the nutmeg, stupid"

Grenada is a small island nation that produces about 20 percent of the world's supply of nutmeg. In fact, many refer to this island in the Caribbean near Venezuela as the "island of spice" as they also produce significant amounts of cinnamon, ginger, cloves, and mace. In the 1980s, the island's population was roughly 90,000 with more than 80 percent of Grenada's population descended from African slaves. In 1983, when the most powerful nation in the history of mankind invaded the "island of spice" there was not one stoplight in the country. Grenada's "naval fleet consisted of about 10 fishing trawlers."[258] So it begs the question: why would Reagan and his über empire invade an agrarian people and their tiny country with a population the size of Van Nuys, California? You guessed it... at the time, the people of Grenada were initiating a political and social revolution of their own—one that began amidst corruption and tyranny in 1979 with the ouster of Eric Gairy and his "Mongoose Gang" (secret police backed by the U.S.-supported Pinochet regime) and replaced by the very popular socialist movement known as New Jewel. Educator and author Bill Bigelow remembers his first trip there in 1982:

> When I first visited the island, a literacy campaign was under
> way, new schools had been built, and unemployed youth in
> the countryside benefited from new agricultural cooperatives.
> Grenada welcomed Cuban aid: teachers, health professionals,
> and construction workers on the new international airport who
> aimed to replace the antiquated and dangerous airstrip up in the
> mountains. In just four years, unemployment was cut from 49
> percent to 14 percent. Instead of advertising cigarettes and booze,
> colorful billboards throughout the island promoted education: "Each
> One Teach One," "If You Know, Teach; If You Don't, Learn," and
> "Education Is Production, Too."[259]

By October 1983, the New Jewel Movement was in a shambles; the well-liked Prime Minister Maurice Bishop was arrested and executed and replaced by a trigger-happy military government. Bigelow concludes, "This violence was the culmination of sectarian infighting whose origins are still murky—a flammable concoction of ambition, ideological rigidity, and leadership isolation, made more volatile by the ever-present threat of U.S. intervention."[260] In fact, the Reagan administration had been conducting menacing invasion exercises in Puerto Rico as "a not-so-veiled threat" with Reagan claiming at the time "that Grenada's construction of the international airport was a ruse for 'Soviet-Cuban militarization.'"[261]

There it is! Could be another Cuba. Another dreaded good example. "Fuck no," says the piss-poor actor and former president of the Screen Actors Guild who turned names of commie sympathizers over to the FBI during Hollywood's blacklist period. So Ronald Wilson Reagan launches "Operation Urgent Fury" as another do-or-die chapter in America's battle with COMMUNISM. The explanation by Reagan and his henchmen was ludicrous if not downright goofy: in the event of a Soviet attack (on what we're not sure), an unfriendly Grenada could be used as a beachhead helping interdict oil and other supplies, hampering the U.S. war effort against Mother Russia's imaginary invasion of nowhere. You simply cannot make this shit up. In fact, the United Nations General Assembly condemned the invasion as a "flagrant violation of international law" by a margin of 108-9, but Reagan still had no problem defending his imperial actions, defining Grenada as "a Soviet-Cuban colony being readied as a military bastion to export terror and undermine democracy. We got there just in time."[262] Reagan concurrently claimed that the U.S. was trying to rescue some 800 American medical students "even though the medical school's chancellor denounced the invasion and said it posed a greater risk to students than the turmoil then wracking the island."[263]

Bill Bigelow, the co-editor of educational publisher Rethinking Schools and the co-director of the Zinn Education Project, returned to Grenada ten months after the invasion amidst the U.S. occupation. Under the heading of "adding insult to injury," Bigelow reports:

> Driving from the airport to St. George's, the first thing I noticed was that the popular education billboards had been chopped down. And it wasn't only these symbols of the Revo [affectionate Grenadian name for the revolution] that had been eliminated. The U.S.-installed interim government had abolished the agency to aid cooperatives; eliminated the Centre for Popular Education, the literacy program; shuttered a government-owned agro-industries plant; and returned land from farmers' cooperatives to absentee owners.[264]

As the 1980s unfolded and the blatant aggressiveness of the Reagan regime became readily apparent, it was obvious that the spinmeisters and mythmakers manufacturing consent needed more than the evils of communism to rally support.

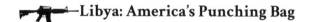

Libya: America's Punching Bag

Terrorism.

A very durable successor to the communist "threat" and "Right from the start," Noam Chomsky reminds us, "they used Libya as a punching bag."[265] In fact, relations between the U.S. and Libya immediately worsened with Reagan's election in 1980 followed by his regime's obsession with removing Muammar el-Qaddafi from power—an obsession mostly fueled by the new administration's close ties with their oil industry cronies.[266] Relations were already strained when rebels in Libya attacked and burned the American embassy in Tripoli the year before his election, but Ronnie, Bush I, and CIA Director William Casey took the relationship to a whole new level, attempting various assassination attempts and covert actions against the Libyan leader and his command. "Every time they had to rally support for aid to the Contras or something," Chomsky continues, "they'd engineer a confrontation with Libya. It got so ludicrous that, at one point, the White House was surrounded with tanks to protect poor President Reagan from Libyan hit squads. It became an international joke."[267]

Tanks. Around the White House. Give 'em balls for theatrics.

Most folks connect the take down of Pan Am Flight 103 (270 casualties) as a Libyan terrorist attack, "blaming Libya for being behind the bombing without any good evidence."[268] This tragedy happened six months after the U.S. Navy shot down Iran Air Flight 655, killing 290 Iranians, mostly pilgrims. "The link between the two events was quickly seen and the likelihood that the Pan Am 103 event was an act of vengeance by Iran was a working hypothesis," notes Edward Herman. He writes that the connection is "supported further by an unproven claim of Western security forces that Iran had offered a $10 million reward for a retaliatory act."[269] As the investigation continued, the primary target for guilt was the Popular Front for the Liberation of Palestine-General Command led by Ahmed Jibral, "based in Syria, and responding to the Iranian offer."[270] But as Herman correctly points out:

> [A]s relations with Saddam Hussein deteriorated in 1989 and
> 1990, and the United States sought better relations with Syria and
> Iran in the run-up to the first Persian Gulf War, Western officials
> became quiet on the Syria-Iran connection... As Paul Foot noted,
> "The evidence against the PFLP which had been so carefully put
> together and was so immensely impressive was quietly but firmly
> junked."[271] Libya provided a suitable new culprit, as it was already
> on the US-UK hit list and had been subjected to a series of efforts
> at "regime change," a hostility based on its independence, support

of the Palestinians and other dissident forces (including the ANC and Mandela in their resistance to the apartheid regime), as well as occasional support of anti-Western terrorists. So Libya it was.[272]

And deservedly so, Qaddafi was the perfect villain or "punching bag" for the transition to terrorism as evil foe. But then, as Qaddafi watched the U.S. literally turn Iraq to rubble over their so-called "weapons of mass destruction," he began to re-think his tenuous stance with the West and turned over his useless diagrams to build WMDs and quickly became "rehabilitated," soon to be in business with George W. Bush's crime operation—and this included, of course, the CIA.

> *I would never want to belong to any club that would have someone like me for a member.*
> —Groucho Marx

All of this came to light after the fall of Qaddafi in 2011 as Human Rights Watch discovered a treasure trove of documents in Libya clearly linking the Bush Administration and the CIA with Qaddafi's intelligence operation. The documents also link Great Britain's MI6 with the furtive process of sending people the U.S. "kidnapped ('rendition') to Libya to be 'questioned' by Libya's goons, and almost certainly to be tortured," explains historian Juan Cole. "Qaddafi also gave permission to the CIA from 2004 to establish a formal presence in the country."[273] Documents also reveal that the CIA and MI6 captured Libyan dissidents in other countries and returned them to Libya for interrogation aka torture. One of these CIA-captured individuals was Abdel Hakim Belhadj, a military commander, who reported that he was first tortured by the CIA, then shipped back to Libya to be tortured at the notorious Abu Salim prison in Tripoli.[274]

Regarding the disclosure of these cozy ties between the U.S./CIA and Qaddafi's regime, Peter Bouckaert of Human Rights Watch called the relationship, "A very dark chapter in American intelligence history."[275] Indeed, another glaring example of Washington's collaboration with authoritarian regimes to further dubious U.S. policy.

Libya: from foe to ally in the time it takes to say "extraordinary rendition." And then back again—

"We came. We saw. He died." (Chuckle. Chuckle. Argh. Argh.)

Arguably the worst presidential candidate to ever be the Democratic Party's standard-bearer uttered that callous and arrogant imperial gloat as Secretary of State (when *CBS News* interviewed her in October of 2011) following the sodomizing and public murder of Muammar el-Qaddafi. Hillary Clinton was downright gleeful about the brutality—an obvious erotic extension of her warmongering that rallied and ignited the US-NATO bombing of Libya—an all-too-familiar western military intervention that resulted in the African country's destruction.

HILLARY CLINTON:
"We came. We saw. He died." (chuckle-chuckle-argh-argh)

JULIUS CAESAR:
"Veni. Vidi. Vici. (not sure if he giggled like a circus clown, too)

Clearly, enemies and friends or villains and good guys can change at a moment's notice—not because of past evils or current atrocities, but rather by political expediency and their perceived effectiveness. Justice, along with an honest read of history, be damned.

Sex, Drugs, and Devil Worship...
America's Love Affair with Manuel Noriega

Let's review Manuel Noriega's sparkling resume:

- During the late 1950s and into the 60s, the young Noriega was already working with the U.S. Defense Intelligence Agency and CIA, spying on Panamanian leftists as well as fellow students at his Peruvian military academy.[276] [277]

- In the 1960s, he continued his covert relationship with the CIA and, at the same time, improved his police interrogation skills by supervising sexual torture of prisoners using Coke bottles and splintered sticks.[278]

- Without a doubt, he is the most famous graduate of the U.S. Army's "School of the Americas" (also known as the "School of the Assassins"). His instructors rated him "outstanding." The list of his fellow alumni reads like a who's who of Latin American despots.[279]

- Washington knew that their important asset in Panama was a major player in drug trafficking since at least 1972—including later deals with Pablo Escobar and the Medellín Cartel.[280] In fact, the Nixon administration considered assassinating him but passed on the opportunity.[281]

- In the 1970s, CIA Director George Herbert Walker Bush ignored the drug-dealing elephant hanging around Noriega's neck and put him on the official CIA payroll at $100,000 per year.[282]

- In 1976, Noriega and his chum, George Herbert Walker Bush, hung out at CIA Headquarters in Langley; Bush gives Noriega a VIP guided tour.[283]

- In the 1980s, the tin-pot dictator remained tight with his U.S. paymasters; Noriega actively spied on Fidel Castro and Daniel Ortega for the CIA; he let the U.S. establish listening posts in Panama aimed at all Central American countries; he allowed the U.S. to base spy planes in Panama in violation of canal treaties; he helped to funnel money and arms to the Contras in Nicaragua and allowed the U.S. military and CIA to train the Contras in Panama.[284]

- He remained on the CIA payroll until 1988[285]—the year before the American invasion of Panama (with its Orwellian code name: Operation Just Cause), when contrary to the "official" military body count of 500 dead Panamanian civilians, thousands were killed and tens of thousands left homeless. Twenty-three U.S. soldiers were killed and 324 wounded.

A few days before Christmas 1989, more than 27,000 U.S. troops, bolstered by the deployment of heavy duty U.S. air assault, including AC-130 Spectre gunships, Super Tweet Dragonfly attack aircraft, F-117A stealth fighters, as well as AH-64 Apache helicopters, pulverized the small, defenseless country (filled with brown people). The destitute barrio of El Chorillo is burnt to the ground and earns the unfortunate nickname "Little Hiroshima." Panamanians as well as independent studies (Commission for the Defense of Human Rights in Central America) place the casualty figure somewhere between 2,000 and 6,000.

PRESIDENTIAL PRESS CONFERENCE, DECEMBER 21, 1989
THE WHITE HOUSE

> TERRENCE HUNT (ASSOCIATED PRESS): *Are you frustrated that he got away?*

> BUSH: *I've been frustrated that he's been in power this long— extraordinarily frustrated. The good news: He's out of power. The bad news: He has not yet been brought to justice.*

> HELEN THOMAS (UPI): *You did mention the casualties. Did you expect them to be so high on both sides? And also, is it really worth it to send people to their death for this, to get Noriega?*

> BUSH: *We had some estimates, Helen, on the casualties ahead of time, but not in numbers... every human life is precious. And yet I have to answer: Yes, it has been worth it.*

This kind of American hubris is astounding and downright deplorable—especially with the ease in which it's stated as well as how readily it's accepted by the press and body politic. In 1997, as Bill Clinton's Secretary of State, Madeleine Albright was painfully clear when interviewed on *60 Minutes*:

> LESLEY STAHL (CBS): (Regarding Iraq) *We have heard that half a million children have died. I mean, that's more children than died in Hiroshima. And, you know, is the price worth it?*

> ALBRIGHT: *I think this is a very hard choice, but the price—we think the price is worth it.*

Clearly, the U.S. invasion of Panama had little to do with Noriega's drug trafficking. Washington knew about his extracurricular activity for years and always looked the other way. The former "outstanding" U.S. Army assassin student and Bush pal had simply "outlived his usefulness," writes William Blum. "Bush wanted to send a clear message to the people of Nicaragua, who had an election scheduled in two months, that this might be their fate if they reelected the Sandinistas," Blum continues. "Bush also wanted to flex some military muscle to illustrate to Congress the need for a large combat-ready force even after the very recent dissolution of the 'Soviet threat.'" Add to Blum's criteria the habitual

American interest in maximum control over the Panama Canal (which defines its business penetration into Central America and Asia), and you can witness the newly crowned, world's-only superpower, flexing its muscle.

Drugs? What drugs?

Throughout Noriega's rise to power and rule, there were stories of sexually deviant behavior, rape,[286] as well as hints of the occult and devil worship. In fact, two days after the invasion in 1989, the *Los Angeles Times* reported that when U.S. troops broke into Noriega's fortified house and office they found signs of a hectic exit along with vats of blood and animal entrails.[287]

There is a somewhat infamous photograph of George H. W. Bush sitting comfortably with Noriega as they chat. The photograph is so bizarre that one wonders if Photoshop moles are involved. But they're not, and the photo is real, and the image, like the old adage says, is worth a thousand words. The caption should read: Former CIA Director and current U.S. Vice President shares a warm private moment with the multi-talented Manuel Noriega: dictator, drug dealer, sexual deviant, rapist, and devil worshiper.

Vice President George H. W. Bush and then General Manuel Antonio Noriega in a 1983 meeting.

Strange bedfellows? Nah, perfect bedfellows.

Blowback

Most of the time, if you treat people right, you don't have to be afraid of them.
—Kathy Kelly, *Other Lands Have Dreams: From Baghdad to Pekin Prison*

In July of 1979, six months before the Soviet Union invaded Afghanistan, the Carter administration along with a huge assist from the CIA, began to arm and support the rebels (the Mujahideen) in their battle with the pro-Soviet government in Kabul. The official story at the time was that Washington began their support *after* the Soviet invasion, but this myth has been completely dispelled, most notably by former CIA Director Robert Gates and Jimmy Carter's National Security Advisor Zbigniew Brzezinski.[288]

When the invasion actually happened, Carter threw out the usual gibberish about how the incursion jeopardized American interests in the Persian Gulf, and then feigned outrage at the evil superpower's belligerence toward Afghani lives and liberty. But in reality, Washington powerbrokers and their CIA cohorts actively planned and ultimately helped to lure the Soviets into a long, expensive, and drawn out war—a final giant "bear trap" to take them down for the count. In the words of Brzezinski, the idea was to give "the USSR its Vietnam War." In fact, that line became the mantra throughout Washington.

For the next twelve years, "the CIA spent $3 billion training and arming Islamist radicals to fight the Soviets in Afghanistan (an amount matched by the Saudis bill for bill, according to a CIA official)," report Amy and David Goodman. "It was the largest covert U.S. operation since World War II."[289]

Sometimes "blowback" has a very distinct face and for Americans that face arose from the CIA's machinations in Afghanistan in the visage of public enemy number one, Osama bin Laden. In 1980, as a twenty-three-year-old Saudi national, Osama bin Muhammad bin Awad bin Laden left the safe and cushy confines of a lavish lifestyle to fight back the Soviet Army. He didn't see much action, possibly one battle. His main job was funneling money—some of it his family's—into the anti-Soviet struggle. By 1984, bin Laden was instrumental in creating Maktab al-Khidamat, an organization that directed funds and fighters to the Mujahideen. In many ways, Maktab al-Khidamat is the forerunner to al-Qaeda.

Many claim that the CIA directly funded bin Laden and that he was an official CIA asset or contract agent. There is little if any evidence to back up those claims.

However, as NBC news correspondent Michael Moran writes, "What (his) CIA bio conveniently fails to specify (in its unclassified form, at least) is that the [Maktab al-Khidamat] was nurtured by Pakistan's state security services, the Inter-Services Intelligence agency, or ISI, the CIA's primary conduit for conducting the covert war against Moscow's occupation."[290] Throughout the 1980s, Washington continued to fund and support the Afghan fighters with loads of money, weapons, and advanced military strategy. Clearly, Washington was drunk on their own Cold War elixir; giddy and reckless as they hurdled every which way with their rebel contingent of anti-Soviet fighters, who later transformed into al-Qaeda, GIA, and other fierce Islamic insurgents—and Bin Laden went to the head of the class. "It should be pointed out that the evidence of bin Laden's connection to these activities is mostly classified," Moran concludes, "though its hard to imagine the CIA rushing to take credit for a Frankenstein's monster like this."[291]

So on the morning of Tuesday, 11 September 2001, the Battle of Maravar Pass in eastern Afghanistan, near the city of Asadabad, the capital city of Kunar Province, a battle fought in 1985, came roaring back to the streets of Lower Manhattan, to Arlington County, Virginia, hard by the Potomac, and finally back to Shanksville, Pennsylvania. The monster breaks free and vows revenge on Victor. Soon Elizabeth is dead.

In an interview in 1998 with the French publication *Le Nouvel Observateur*, Zbigniew Brzezinski cements forever the corrupt and perverse essence of American foreign policy since the end of World War II—the obsession with the advancement of predatory capitalism over the perceived evils of socialism and communism. The astronomical expenditures in war and death (your money by the way) are only outdone by the cost of human life and misery. Ultimately, the obsession defines the rank insanity of the Cold War.

Interview with Zbigniew Brzezinski, *Le Nouvel Observateur*, January 1998:

> *Q: When the Soviets justified their intervention by asserting that they intended to fight against a secret involvement of the United States in Afghanistan, people didn't believe them. However, there was a basis of truth. You don't regret anything today?*
>
> *B: Regret what? That secret operation was an excellent idea. It had the effect of drawing the Russians into the Afghan trap and you want me to regret it? The day that the Soviets officially crossed the border, I wrote to President Carter. We now have the opportunity of giving to the USSR its Vietnam War. Indeed, for almost 10 years, Moscow had to carry on a war unsupportable by the government, a conflict that brought about the demoralization and finally the breakup of the Soviet empire.*

Q: And neither do you regret having supported the Islamic fundamentalism, having given arms and advice to future terrorists?

B: What is most important to the history of the world? The Taliban or the collapse of the Soviet empire? Some stirred-up Moslems or the liberation of Central Europe and the end of the cold war?[292]

Well, "Brzezinski got his answer on 9/11"—Amy and David Goodman's simple but robust rejoinder to Brzezinski's arrogant response.[293] The additional reply to Brzezinski and his boss, Jimmy Carter, would be a number: 1,250,000—the estimated civilian casualties[294] murdered by the Soviet and American chess game played out over the ancient land of the Silk Road.

"The Dulles Brothers were traitors"

Like we mentioned pages before—when it comes to interventions, coup d'états, assassinations, rigging elections, bribing scumbags, and/or outright shoot 'em up cowboy occupations, *the song remains the same*: drunken blind hubris rules and at any cost. This is the core essence of American exceptionalism, as evidenced and preached by ex-CIA Director and President George H.W. Bush's infamous and oft-repeated statement regarding the USS Vincennes shooting down of Iranian Flight 655, killing 290 passengers—"I'll never apologize for the United States. Ever. I don't care what the facts are."

Bush was brutally candid, because when it comes to American history, facts have never been important: it is history for those devoid of soul or memory. Whether it was the whitewashing of reality in El Salvador during the 1980s when Archbishop Oscar Romero was viciously gunned down while saying mass... or in the island nation of Haiti when Washington supported the vile dictatorship of "Baby Doc" Duvalier (because he was ardently anti-communist) over the popular former priest Jean Bertrand Aristide... or intervening in Iraq and Yugoslavia during the 1990s with devastating bombing campaigns... or back to Iraq, Iran, and Afghanistan with more myths and violence laying waste to populations, cultures, and families—the United States of America (along with their client states) has been relentless in its pursuit of complete hegemony and dominion over the international capitalist state. "U.S. policy is to make the world safe for the Fortune 500 and its global system of capital accumulation," writes Michael Parenti in his classic book *Against Empire*:

> Governments that strive for any kind of economic independence

or any sort of populist redistributive politics, who have sought to take some of their economic surplus and apply it to not-for-profit services that benefit the people—such governments are the ones most likely to feel the wrath of U.S. intervention or invasion.[295]

By necessity, the American people will never know the full story of your courage.
—President Bill Clinton (in a speech before the CIA celebrating its 50th anniversary)

Indeed, Bill. We all know that "courage" is your middle name. In fact, when studying the history of the Central Intelligence Agency, nothing jumps out more than the concept of "courage." But we prefer another quote, this one from former Supreme Court justice Arthur Goldberg: "The Dulles brothers were traitors."[296] Goldberg collected his own intelligence on the Dulles brothers' moneyed interaction with, and protection of, their Nazi industrialist clients and German banking colleagues who continued to work with Hitler and the Nazi war machine throughout World War II. Many historians conclude that Allen Welsh Dulles jumped at the opportunity to direct the newly minted agency as a way to cover up their association with the Nazi monster, "giving aid and comfort to the enemy."[297]

"You Think the NSA Is Bad? Meet Former CIA Director Allen Dulles"

So blared a *Mother Jones'* headline in 2015 upon the publication of author David Talbot's extraordinary tome, *The Devil's Chessboard: Allen Dulles, the CIA, and the Rise of America's Secret Government,* an in-depth chronicle that solidifies Dulles as the dark overlord central to the creation and subsequent cementing of America's modern (and bloody) shadow government. And Talbot, the founder of Salon.com, does his own cementing of Dulles, documenting beyond a shadow of a doubt how the CIA under his sledgehammer reign became a remarkable and effective killing machine in duty to American hegemony—as well as Dulles' own personal power.

Allen Dulles, the younger of the Dulles brothers, was "the knight-errant who enforced America's imperial will," writes Talbot. "As director of the CIA, Allen Dulles liked to think he was the hand of the king, but if so, he was the left hand—the sinister hand. He was master of the dark deeds that empires require."[298] In fact both Dulles brothers were not intimidated whatsoever by their bosses, namely Franklin Roosevelt, Harry Truman, and Dwight Eisenhower. Earlier in Allen Dulles' career as a superstar spook in World War II Europe, "he blatantly ignored Roosevelt's policy of unconditional surrender and pursued his own strategy of secret negotiations with Nazi leaders."[299] It was boilerplate for FDR and the Allied winners: the Nazi hierarchy would pay for their heinous crimes—and pay dearly. Instead, Dulles was orchestrating his own "get out of jail free" card for surrender. "It was a stunningly cynical and insubordinate gambit," Talbot concludes. "The pact that Dulles envisioned not only dismissed the genocide against the Jews as an irrelevant issue, it also rejected the president's firmly stated policy against secret deal making with the enemy."[300]

Once the war was over in Europe, Dulles then greased the escape hatch through Nazi ratlines that paved the way for his stable of demented madmen to find gainful U.S. employment elsewhere, places and assignments where their hatchets and chemicals could still be useful. Talbot explains why:

> The staggering sacrifice made by the Russian people in the war
> against Hitler meant little to Dulles. He was more interested in
> salvaging the Third Reich's security apparatus and turning it against
> the Soviet Union—which he had always regarded as America's true
> enemy.[301]

In fact, Dulles' partners in crime spanned the globe from Nazi German war criminals and Nazi-controlled cartels to Mafia chieftains and corrupt henchmen slithering in soggy catacombs everywhere. Along with his brother John Foster Dulles, Secretary of State through much of Eisenhower's presidency, the Dulles Brothers put pedal to metal on Washington's aggressive interventionist foreign policy—one of them overt, the other covert. Talbot distills down their dangerous and dark legacy:

> During the Eisenhower administration, the Dulles brothers would
> finally be given full license to exercise their power in the global
> arena. In the name of defending the free world from Communist
> tyranny, they would impose an American reign on the world

enforced by nuclear terror and cloak-and-dagger brutality. Elevated to the pinnacle of Washington power, they continued to forcefully represent the interests of their corporate caste, conflating them with the national interest.[302]

Their relentless black and white canon—a classic Manichean world view—can best be understood when absorbing this infamous statement by John Foster Dulles:

> *For us there are two kinds of people in the world. There are those who are Christians and support free enterprise, and there are the others.*[303]

Hey, Bill... Hey, Bubba... tell us another bedtime story about courage.

Conscience

He was patriotic and planned on becoming a Foreign Service Officer. He was going to dedicate himself to slaying "the beast of the International Communist Conspiracy." But then a funny thing happened on the way to the Empire: the bloodthirsty horror of Vietnam. "It was making me sick at heart," William Blum remembers. "My conscience had found its cause."

We end this chapter with the words of a man who has dedicated himself to revealing the appalling and inexcusable behavior of the American Empire—behavior that grieves him deeply. William Blum implores the beast to "Stop the bombings, the invasions, the endless wars, the torture, the sanctions, the overthrows, the support of dictatorships, the unmitigated support of Israel; stop all the things that make the United States so hated."[304] Bill Blum has the last word:

> The boys of Capital, they also chortle in their martinis about the death of socialism. The word has been banned from polite conversation. And they hope that no one will notice that every socialist experiment of any significance in the twentieth century—without exception—has either been crushed, overthrown, or invaded, or corrupted, perverted, subverted, or destabilized, or otherwise had life made impossible for it, by the United States. Not one socialist government or movement—from the Russian Revolution to the Sandinistas in Nicaragua, from Communist China to the FMLN in Salvador—not one was permitted to rise or fall solely on its own merits; not one was left secure enough to drop its guard against the all-powerful enemy abroad and freely and fully relax control at home.

It's as if the Wright brothers' first experiments with flying machines all failed because the automobile interests sabotaged each test flight. And then the good and god-fearing folk of the world looked upon this, took notice of the consequences, nodded their collective heads wisely, and intoned solemnly: Man shall never fly.[305]

4 The Military-Industrial Complex
Or Empire's Wet Dream

Let's dispose with the bullshit straightaway. From Ike's nationally televised farewell address on 17 January 1961:

> *In the councils of government, we must guard against the acquisition of unwarranted influence, whether sought or unsought, by the military-industrial complex. The potential for the disastrous rise of misplaced power exists, and will persist.*

Good words. Even great words. Words that have been deified, sanctified, consecrated, and made holy by antiwar disciples of all stripes and colors. In fact, those words, as historian David Greenberg writes, "entered the political lexicon almost immediately."[1] But in reality, the earnestness of these words was utter and unadulterated, 100% good old-fashioned, American bullshit.

And the deification is understandable: an American military legend walks off into the sunset warning his beloved nation of a gathering storm on the horizon, one that will shake the very foundation of American democracy itself. Oliver Stone opened his film *JFK* with Ike's famous Oval Office swan song as the initial shot across the bow in the iconic director's reenactment of the epic battle between his dark antagonist (the military-industrial complex) and his bright and shining protagonist (Camelot)—a battle Stone posits ended in tragedy on 22 November 1963 as spectral forces protecting military capital had Kennedy whacked... *back and to the left.*

Greenberg distills down Eisenhower's parting shot succinctly, writing that the admonition signified "the notion that a permanent ruling class, encompassing the Pentagon and its corporate suppliers, was on the verge of controlling the American government, even in peacetime."[2] Ike's warning suggested that over time this stranglehold on the country's vision, resources, and collective soul would tighten to the point where America operated more like a garrison state instead of a republic. It is the belief of your authors that the U.S. is there—and has been for a very long time.

Lo and behold, Ike's bullshit proved prophetic (even a broken clock is right twice a day). But how could his dire words not prove true? The lid to Pandora's box had long been ripped off its hinges—and Ike was one of the main caporegimes handing out crowbars during the operation. It was an inside job like the '78 Lufthansa heist at JFK. But then this unexpected and odd left-hand turn generated by Ike's farewell speech created an altered Eisenhower persona, one that has been glorified to the brink of Gandhi-like sainthood. Progressive politicos, left-wing radicals, and pacifists everywhere have embraced Ike and his seemingly trenchant distress signal much as Jesuits embrace Jesus and his Sermon on the Mount.

But Dwight David Eisenhower was no Pete Seeger nor did he evolve into some rogue and heroic figure defiantly standing outside of America's massive killing machine saying "No, not in my name." Greenberg concludes that "Eisenhower's speech itself has come to be romanticized all out of proportion to its merit… while Ike has implausibly morphed from martial hero and hard-line anti-Communist into a prophet of peace, a cousin of Norman Cousins."[3]

A decorated World War II general crowned king, Eisenhower was, in reality, an essential and inseparable constituent of the mushrooming military-industrial complex. As General of the Army and "Supreme Commander Allied Expeditionary Force" (D-Day), the West Point graduate and 5-star general led the massive invasion of Normandy on 6 June 1944, catapulting his already festooned military legend to superhuman status.

In 1946, while still the Army Chief of Staff, General Eisenhower wrote a detailed memo to his brethren in the War Department essentially outlining the components and necessity for an all-encompassing military complex. Ike stressed a peacetime paradigm that was a synthesis of minds and resources from the military, the government, science, academia, and, of course, his golfing buddies in big business and industry:

The armed forces could not have won the war alone. Scientists and businessmen contributed techniques and weapons, which enabled us to outwit and overwhelm the enemy. Their understanding of the Army's needs made possible the highest degree of cooperation. This pattern of integration must be translated into a peacetime counterpart, which will not merely familiarize the Army with the progress made in science and industry, but draw into our planning for national security all the civilian resources, which can contribute to the defense of the country... The Army as one of the main agencies responsible for the defense of the nation has the duty to take the initiative in promoting closer relations between civilian and military interests. It must establish definite policies and administrative leadership which will make possible even greater contributions from science, technology, and management than during the last war.[4]

After the war, Eisenhower became the commander of NATO forces in Europe. He was an unabashed, dyed-in-the-wool, hard-nosed Cold Warrior perched on the frontline struggle against the Soviets and international communism. It was the thunderous emergence of a perilous and deadly Cold War faceoff between the two armed-to-the-teeth superpowers that would last for half a century and would cost both combatants untold amounts of treasure, resources, and lives. For decades, there would be historic proxy wars, political assassinations, and bloody coups. Both nations would engage in massive and nefarious intelligence and surveillance gamesmanship—CIA and KGB hijinks that covered the gamut from the ridiculous and trivial to outright, cold-blooded murder. And lest we forget, all of this was conducted while both combatants had their nervously twitching finger on the nuclear trigger.

In fact, Eisenhower, the president peace activists love to quote, was not shy when it came to toying with the idea of using nuclear weapons. The old warrior was a virulent anti-Soviet, anti-communist, pragmatic taskmaster and believed Russia was out "to communize the world" and that the U.S. was facing "a battle to extinction." Ike also wrote in his diary that liberal Democrats were ushering the nation "toward total socialism."[5] Dwight... put down the diary, drink your cocoa, and go to bed.

Ira Chernus, Professor of Religious Studies at the University of Colorado, has studied Ike's presidency in great detail, penning three books on America's 34th

President. His research reveals a man and a presidency that viewed the planet and its inhabitants as nothing more than a giant military game board where wealthy old white men in costumes push toy soldiers and tanks and nukes around the globe with big sticks—Stratego with real-life consequences.

> Eisenhower's plans always assumed that the U.S. would somehow survive the war. In 1959, when he was well aware that a nuclear war would kill 100 million or more Americans, he still approved NSC 5904/1, the official U.S. policy for global war, which made the nation's first objective "to prevail, and survive as a nation capable of controlling its own destiny" by planning for a "quick recovery." "We are simply going to have to be prepared to operate with people who are 'nuts,'" he told his Cabinet, to "preserve some common sense in a situation in which everybody is going crazy."[6]

Serious preparations to survive a nuclear winter. Crazy sure do know crazy. Then the old man got his nose into the details. Chernus explains:

> Exploring plans for widespread bomb shelters, Ike told his Cabinet that he wanted to "get private industry active on many of the little 'practical' problems as perhaps designing a small air purifier for use by individuals." When he realized that the "little 'practical' problems" of shelters could not be solved, the president turned to the evacuation of cities as the key to survival. He wanted simulated evacuations to continue "until they became a regular part of our lives."[7]

Chernus believes that Eisenhower drifted between fantasy and reality, planning for World War III while at the same time he worried about raising finances in a post-holocaust America to fight the next war.

As the sun set on Ike's eight years in office, he was more aware than ever of the true destructive force of the species-ending arsenals housed by both superpowers, but he remained unwavering in his nuclear strategy, writing that "the only practical move would be to start using them from the beginning without any distinction whatever between them and conventional weapons."[8]

He's a great humanitarian, he's a great philanthropist
He knows just where to touch you, honey, and how you like to be kissed

He'll put both his arms around you
You can feel the tender touch of the beast
You know that sometimes Satan comes as a man of peace
                                                    —Bob Dylan

In the early 1990s, General George Lee Butler was the main guy running STRATCOM (U.S. Strategic Command), the military's control mechanism overseeing nuclear weaponry and the strategy associated with using them. Butler surveyed the historical minefield that perambulated through the last half century of nuclear insanity and pondered the miraculous fact that humanity still walked the earth, suggesting that, "We escaped the Cold War without a nuclear holocaust by some combination of skill, luck, and divine intervention, and I suspect the latter in greatest proportion."[9]

This was—this is—the end-times eight ball these two superpowers shoved the human race behind, and Ike was right in the thick of things, a prime architect of the madness.

"It was the best of times, it was the worst of times...

> *...it was the age of wisdom, it was the age of foolishness, it was the epoch of belief,*
> *it was the epoch of incredulity, it was the season of Light, it was the season of Darkness,*
> *it was the spring of hope, it was the winter of despair, we had everything before us,*
> *we had nothing before us, we were all going direct to Heaven, we were all going direct*
> *the other way..."*

The 1950s can surely be described with Dickensian prose. It was in this early fifties environment that the Republican hierarchy convinced the aging gladiator to run for president against a "commie sympathizer" named Adlai Stevenson. David Greenberg writes that one of Ike's biggest achievements "was to drag the rank and file into the age of internationalism with his triumph over Robert Taft for the 1952 presidential nomination, which isolated the isolationists in the GOP." In fact, Eisenhower's eight years at the helm plays out like a handbook for "internationalism," also known as blatant imperial intervention—with the Pentagon and military swelling into a behemoth and the CIA running roughshod all over the planet. Eisenhower's curriculum vitae of CIA-orchestrated coups and assassinations is quite impressive, including covert capers in Iran, Guatemala, British Guiana, Indonesia, Cambodia, and the Big Kahuna known as "Invasión de Bahía de Cochinos" or the Bay of Pigs—the failed military invasion of Cuba that Eisenhower set into motion and then dumped into Kennedy's lap.

Then there was the "Eisenhower Doctrine"—articulated by Ike in a major policy speech before a joint session of Congress in January of 1957. Nothing more than an extension and reheated re-dishing of the Monroe Doctrine, Eisenhower defined the Middle East as "the most strategically important area in the world."[10] The Doctrine plainly offered American military muscle to any Middle Eastern country that requested "such aid, against overt armed aggression from any nation controlled by International Communism."[11] It would take an annual convention of Village Idiots not to see that Washington was circling the wagons around the vast petroleum reserves so coveted by Western economies, particularly the U.S. and Great Britain. The American Empire needed to make sure that the massive Black Gold treasure gushed straight to the West, strategically bypassing the actual inhabitants of the region.

Eisenhower made it clear that the United States would use necessary armed force to help any country in the Middle East stave off the aggression of international communism. Historian and former State Department employee, William Blum, offers this assessment of Ike's doctrine:

> The English translation of this was that no one would be allowed to dominate, or have excessive influence over the Middle East and its oil fields except the United States, and that anyone who tried would be, by definition, "Communist." In keeping with this policy, the United States twice attempted to overthrow the Syrian government, staged several shows-of-force in the Mediterranean to intimidate movements opposed to U.S.-supported governments in Jordan and Lebanon, landed 14,000 troops in Lebanon, and conspired to overthrow or assassinate Nasser of Egypt and his troublesome middle-east nationalism.[12]

This was the Eisenhower Doctrine. But the rose-colored glasses of American mythology prefers a mnemonic embrace for this era as those warm and fuzzy days of sock hops, drive-in roller-skating burger joints, and the birth of *Leave It To Beaver*, as remembered by Scottish singer-songwriter Al Stewart:

> *You're on your way back home in a brand new station wagon*
> *A pile of rolling chrome, ten miles to the gallon*
> *Your mother puts her makeup on, you watch her crunch the gears*
> *It's a child's view of the Eisenhower years*[13]

The Set-Up

After Harry Truman dropped his big bombs on Japan—gruesome destruction that sent the extraordinary and intended warning shots to the Soviets—Truman & Co. followed with the implementation of top-secret National Security Council Memorandum 68, which proved to be America's "imperial blueprint"[14] for the unfolding Cold War: a lethal inferno that was burning and spreading fast. The thrust of American policy articulated in NSC-68 fully embraced State Department guru and future U.S. Ambassador to the Soviet Union George F. Kennan's principles of "containment" regarding Washington's ability to box in and suppress alleged Soviet and communist expansion—a somewhat delusional belief and a political scarecrow that envisioned an evil, omnipresent, and elephantine creature swallowing God's children alive. The core essence of this aggressive policy was clear: the premeditated use of military actions and coercion rather than diplomatic actions seeking compromise and peace. The U.S. State Department's Office of the Historian concurs, writing that, "NSC-68 concluded that the only plausible way to deter the Soviet Union was for President Harry Truman to support a massive build-up of both conventional and nuclear arms."[15]

And, of course, this shit was gonna cost beaucoup bucks.

How much? Well, according to the State Department, it started with a bang: "[T]he Truman Administration almost tripled defense spending as a percentage of the gross domestic product between 1950 and 1953."[16] And Washington, along with their valued partners in private industry—especially in aviation and weapons manufacturing—has never looked back.

Enter Mr. Eisenhower

So by the time Ike put his hand on the Bible and said "I do," American policymakers were already in full gear, implementing plans hatched in Washington during World War II for the U.S. to control and dominate what was defined as "the Grand Area"—which included the Western Hemisphere, the Far East, and the former British Empire along with their aforementioned vast Middle Eastern energy reserves. Washington's elite powerbrokers made it clear that in this newfangled postwar world, "the US would maintain 'unquestioned power,'" writes Noam Chomsky, quoting official American policy, "with 'military and economic supremacy,' while ensuring the 'limitation of any exercise of sovereignty' by states that might interfere with its global designs. The careful wartime plans were soon implemented."[17]

These plans added up to one word: global empire. (Well, that's two.)

And global empires need *massive amounts of force* to implement their designs, followed by the same *massive amounts of force* to ensure an iron grip on the people, resources, and/or geopolitical regions in their servitude. Let's be clear: operations of this size are not served by factories accepting purchase orders. They are maintained instead by a vast conglomerate, a leviathan, and one that is fueled by enormous piles of cash along with an incalculable amount of indoctrination. For success, an operation of this magnitude demands a vast abundance of propaganda, a steady stream of disinformation, and strategic agitprop that when tallied together will buy a hushed and god-like reverence to the altar of power.

In *Unwarranted Influence,* James Ledbetter's in-depth look at Eisenhower and the Military-Industrial Complex, the journalist makes clear that, "it is either ironic or contradictory or hypocritical that the man who first sounded a warning against a 'military-industrial complex' was, by any definition, a leading figure in that complex."[18] And the numbers clearly belie the idea that Eisenhower was anything less than an American combatant hell-bent on dragging the human species to the edge of extinction through catastrophic nuclear power. It was all executed in service to the demands of reckless imperialism aimed at total domination. America or bust.

When Ike was elected in 1952, the American stockpile of nuclear warheads hovered around 1,000. Eight years later, when this lifelong military man left office looking and sounding like everyman's genial grandpa, American nuclear warheads had soared beyond 23,000—on its way to a high of 31,000. Seems like Ike's golfing buddies really got their way.

Clearly, a massive U.S. military apparatus along with aggressive nuclear diplomacy was the bedrock of Eisenhower's "New Look" foreign policy, the guiding principles of which were dutifully carried out by Secretary of State John Foster Dulles. One of these guiding principles was the attempt to wage a belligerent Cold War in what today would be termed a "cost-effective manner." Simply put: *more bang for the buck.* Fresh off the crippling expense of the Korean War, Ike desperately wanted to prevent the U.S. economy from crumbling under the weight of an open-ended superpower struggle with the Soviet Union. David Greenberg paints an interesting portrait of Eisenhower, one that conjures up an executive sitting in the Oval Office clipping coupons out of the Sunday paper:

What united all these parts of Eisenhower's foreign policy was not any pacifistic streak but a cramped, green-eyeshade parsimony—a desire to wage the Cold War on the cheap. Reared with old-fashioned values about thrift, Eisenhower tried to cut the Defense Department budget not because he wanted to scale back America's military profile or role in the world but because he wanted to save money.[19]

As American (that is "white American") prosperity skyrocketed throughout the fifties, Grandpa Dwight supervised Washington's "massive retaliation" strategy—a policy that embraced immense airpower as its focal point. Greenberg argues that "Eisenhower was a Cold Warrior nonpareil," and that his Secretary of State, John Foster Dulles, "belittled containment and talked with George W. Bush-like braggadocio of what he called 'liberation' or 'roll back'—an active program to free countries under Soviet domination."[20] Dulles' attempted bludgeoning of the Soviet Union never matched his swagger, but along with Ike, "he did create a new American foreign-policy doctrine of 'massive retaliation,'" Greenberg writes, "the readiness to use nuclear weapons against conventional attacks."[21] Boston University history professor Andrew Bacevich further explains:

> Eisenhower had established "massive retaliation"—the threat of
> a large-scale nuclear response to deter Soviet aggression—as the
> centerpiece of U.S. national-security doctrine. Yet even as this
> posture was intended to intimidate the Kremlin, the president
> expected it to offer Americans a sense of security, thereby enabling
> him to rein in military expenditures. In that regard, he miscalculated
> badly.[22]

Bacevich goes on to chronicle the economy of America's "Ozzie & Harriet" years:

> During the Eisenhower years, military outlays served as a seemingly
> inexhaustible engine of economic well-being. Keeping the Soviets
> at bay required the design and acquisition of a vast array of guns and
> missiles, bombers and warships, tanks and fighter planes. Ensuring
> that U.S. forces stayed in fighting trim entailed the construction of
> bases, barracks, depots, and training facilities. Research labs received
> funding. Businesses large and small won contracts. Organized labor
> got jobs. And politicians who delivered all these goodies to their
> constituents hauled in endorsements, campaign contributions, and

votes. Throughout the 1950s, unemployment stayed tolerably low and inflation minimal, while budget deficits ranged from trivial to non-existent. What was not to like?[23]

Indeed, especially for the Dr. Strangelove-like phantoms meandering the halls of that five-sided foxhole in Virginia. Clearly, the two-term Eisenhower presidency boasted soaring military budgets, "figures without precedent in the nation's peacetime history," writes Bacevich.[24] In fact, military and Pentagon budgets averaged more than fifty percent of all federal spending, which made Eisenhower's pipedreams of fiscal responsibility laughable.

In fact, it was this fiscal and power imbalance, in which the avarice of private industry was taking over as conductor of the military train, at least in terms of pushing expenditure and expansion, that lead to Ike's "regret" about the swelling Military-Industrial Complex. For Ike, it wasn't about the fact that the American military machine was growing into a behemoth, but rather that the defense industry (i.e. private business) was appropriating the process and calling the shots, relegating the Executive Branch and especially Congress to a backseat position, one rolling out of town, south, toward Oblivion in a '57 Ford Country Squire station wagon sheathed in wood paneling.

***The men who possess real power in this country
have no intention of ending the cold war.***
—Albert Einstein

The successful launch of Sputnik 1 (the first artificial satellite) into low earth orbit by the Soviets on 4 October 1957 hit Americans like a two-by-four to the unsuspecting face of a rosy-cheeked, wide-eyed cherub. "The success of Sputnik," writes historian David Halberstam, "seemed to herald a kind of technological Pearl Harbor, which was exactly what Edward Teller [Father of the Hydrogen Bomb] said it was."[25] Ike and those in the military establishment were well aware of the Soviet's technological capabilities and the administration tried to nonchalantly play it off with a shrug. But the American public remained startled and shocked by the Soviet's dramatic success, and with the assistance of the Democratic Party, began to imagine a distinct missile gap between the two arm wrestling superpowers with a clear-cut advantage suddenly going to the Evil Empire. Al Stewart once more:

> *There's a beep in the sky in 1957*
> *A metal ball that flies through Soviet heaven*

Papers shout the headlines, politicians fan the fears
It's a child's view of the Eisenhower years

It also didn't help Ike that only days after the second Soviet launch (Sputnik 2), a top-secret report entitled "Deterrence and Survival in the Nuclear Age" (or the "Gaither Report") was delivered to the Oval Office by the Security Resources Panel of the President's Science Advisory Committee. Chaired by H. Rowan Gaither (who helped create the military-friendly RAND Corporation think tank), the panel made it abundantly clear: the Soviet Union was speeding past the U.S. in nuclear technology and development, making U.S. defenses vulnerable to Soviet capabilities.

The report, which author James Ledbetter suggests was "exceptionally well-timed," sent shockwaves through Washington's corridors of power and put great political pressure on the Eisenhower administration to alter their course (empty the coffers). It was also frustrating for Ike and his officials because, based on secret U-2 spy plane intelligence, they simply didn't agree with the report but were not about to release the classified U-2 data to counter the findings. Not surprisingly, the Gaither Report went on to make recommendations that would help solve U.S. susceptibility. "They proposed a massive military spending program," Ledbetter writes, "that would not only match the alleged Soviet offensive capabilities, but commit more than $20 billion to a nationwide system of nuclear fallout shelters."[26] Yeah, that'll work. (Messrs. Abu-Jamal and Vittoria will stay under our grade-school wood desks, thank you very much.)

And who were the main voices behind the Gaither Report's "economic" recommendations? "There could be no hiding the fact that the billions in increased military spending called for by the panel would benefit many of the very people making the recommendations," Ledbetter reports. "Two of the report's principal directors were Robert C. Sprague, who headed his own business of military electronics, and William C. Foster of the Olin-Mathiesen Chemical Company, a producer of gunpowder and ammunition."[27] Cozy and all-too-familiar some sixty years later? One can imagine Smedley Butler clawing his way back from the grave wanting to wreak havoc on these war racketeers.

As the 1950s drew to a close, Eisenhower became increasingly frustrated with defense contractors, as well as his own Defense Department, and how easily both were able to manipulate Congress into approving massive military expenditures.

"He resented the skill with which Defense Department brass finagled congressional leaders," Greenberg suggests. "Even his obsession with balancing the books, though a product of a pre-Keynesian worldview, had the virtue of keeping him alert to Pentagon bloat."[28] It was clear that the Commander-in-Chief, a career military giant, knew beyond a shadow of a doubt that political machinations designed at creating huge fortunes for a few contractors was driving the military train forward into the budgetary stratosphere, not actual defense or military rationale. "The period following the Sputnik-Gaither crisis," Ledbetter concludes, "demonstrates Eisenhower's military-industrial-complex critique in its early stages."[29] Ike saw the handwriting on the wall and it read: *unwarranted influence.*

Sure, unwarranted—but by who? Those who have historically lionized Ike's words as a call for arms reduction as well as a curtailed military establishment (or god forbid peace) have done so with a very bad read of history, misconstruing his alleged warning, which was sounded as saber-rattling on behalf of those in government hell-bent on a grandiose and omnipresent military versus those in private boardrooms equally hell-bent on a grandiose and omnipresent military. It was two junkyard dogs fighting over the same bone.

Will the Real Dwight Eisenhower Please Stand Up!

Regardless of Ike's de rigueur nods in his farewell speech to truth, justice, liberty, diplomacy, peace, God, and apple pie (the requisite affirmation every CEO of the American corporation is obliged to offer), Eisenhower's most telling words from the Oval Office on that cold January night were a crystal clear and ringing endorsement of prevailing Cold War insanity and the lockstep military madness that continues to mushroom evermore gargantuan, threatening the continuation of life on this planet. Forget Ike's words fêted by history, they are dust in the wind. But do remember these words from the same flawed and duplicitous speech, words that have great traction, words that remain bright and guilty:

> We face a hostile ideology global in scope, atheistic in character, ruthless in purpose, and insidious in method... We have been compelled to create a permanent armaments industry of vast proportions... A vital element in keeping the peace is our military establishment. Our arms must be mighty, ready for instant action, so that no potential aggressor may be tempted to risk his own destruction.

Professor Chernus, author of *Apocalypse Management: Eisenhower and the Discourse of National Insecurity*, concurs that Ike became "a terrific poster-boy for peace,"[30] but that this image of Mamie's husband is false pretense, that the lesser known and more belligerent passages in his famous farewell "was not merely rhetoric for public consumption. Eisenhower never saw any hope of rapprochement with the Soviets. He always saw them as irredeemably treacherous, 'implacably hostile and seeking our destruction,' as he wrote to Winston Churchill. 'Where in the hell can you let the Communists chip away any more? We just can't stand it.'"[31]

In 1958, Eisenhower executed NSC document 5810/1 that redefined nuclear weapons "as conventional weapons; and to use them whenever required to achieve national objectives." His signature made this insanity official U.S. policy. Ike told his National Security Council that, "The only sensible thing for us to do was to put all our resources into our hydrogen bombs."[32] This is the leader peace activists love to embrace. Chernus stresses that, "The president who planned to fight and win a nuclear war, saying 'he would rather be atomized than communized,' reminds us how dangerous the cold war era really was, how much our leaders will put us all at risk in the name of 'national security,' and how easily they can mask their intentions behind benign images."[33]

But Ike's perceived warning on the evening of 17 January 1961—a warning that shares a place on the mantle of American history with George Washington's admonishment of entangling "our peace and prosperity in the toils of European ambition"—was not, we contend, a caution against a colossal and unequaled military, but rather who would be running (and profiting from) the big show. Greenberg reminds us that Ike's "warnings about military overreach were couched, *it's usually forgotten*, in passages insisting on the need for a *military of unprecedented size*, which Eisenhower called 'a vital element in keeping the peace.'"[34] [Emphasis added]

Ike believed the rise of communism was to blame for escalating the Cold War, not the military, or its subsequent growth and actions. The good general even supported America's Vietnam fiasco, a vicious and mind bogglingly expensive jungle war that helped to define the Military-Industrial Complex as real and tangible and dangerous. "We do know that Ike, a staunch believer in the domino theory," writes Greenberg, "supported the Vietnam War under both John F. Kennedy and Lyndon Johnson."[35] In 1964, a scant three years after his legendary "peaceful" farewell, and during the time "his ideas about the military-industrial complex were starting to gather their cultlike following," private citizen Dwight Eisenhower "said that to quit the war would mean 'a tremendous loss of prestige—the loss of the whole subcontinent of Southeast Asia.'"[36] In 1965, as the U.S. was unveiling Operation Rolling Thunder (LBJ's sustained bombing campaign over North Vietnam), Citizen Dwight offered this endorsement of the American murder spree: "In Vietnam, the way the president is conducting operations is very good indeed for the United States."[37] Law professor Marjorie Cohn also reports (citing Daniel Ellsberg) that former President Eisenhower recommended to then President Johnson that the U.S. use nuclear weapons in both North and South Vietnam.[38] In fact, Eisenhower and Johnson talked frequently on the telephone during the war and it's chilling to hear them nonchalantly discuss the possible use or non-use of atomic weapons in Vietnam—calm, cool, calculated, and right before a pleasant chat about Mamie visiting Lady Bird for tea just the day before.[39] Frightening enough already, the ominous impact of their casual demeanor deepens when one hears little change in tone as the conversation shifts from atomic weapons to tea.

Let's adjourn this opening salvo on Dwight Eisenhower's famous farewell speech, one that has been galvanized by the political left as Abbie Hoffman's last will and testament. It was not. It was nothing more than political legerdemain. Artful chicanery. To draw a parallel to recent hocus-pocus, let's think Barack Obama. Like the liberal bourgeoisie embracing his laughable healthcare plan as "reform," or their misguided belief that Mr. Obama is a transparent defender of civil liberties and Constitutional aegis. Or this great Orwellian masterpiece: with "great humility," Obama accepting the Nobel Peace Prize. It's masterful sleight of hand: the wizard says one thing and then orchestrates another.

Plain and simple, Dwight David Eisenhower was a major architect and builder of the largest and most vicious killing machine that has ever graced this pale blue dot. His words on that cold January evening in 1961 could just as easily have been "abracadabra."

Back to "That City on a Hill"

In *Hoax*, journalist Nicholas von Hoffman's unblinking critique of American foreign policy, its propaganda, as well as its citizens' gullibility to buy into this "hoax," draws an initial and direct line back to John Winthrop's goddamn 17th century "City upon a Hill," the original hoax that set in motion America's ability to swallow enormous buckets of bullshit at a single sitting. Ultimately, it is the "religion of Americanism," the fevered belief "that America was to be the cynosure of the world."

> The city on a hill is a place established by God. The conviction that the United States is God-based, faith-based, and chosen of heaven persists undiminished. It gives Americans that special *oomph* they have whenever they tell anyone and everyone "we are right and you are wrong." It cannot be otherwise, for Providence has chosen America to work through human history.[40]

This quasi-secular religion of America, the granting of manifest destiny by God Almighty, has given Americans and their government the claim to pretty much do whatever they damn well want: conquer, enslave, dispossess, shoot, kill, bomb, maim, refinance, reload, repeat. This consecrated exceptionalism, this righteous particularism has been "running in the background, supplying rationalizations for all manner of public acts which reeked of everything but the odor of sanctity."[41]

This is the kind of deep-seated, God-anointed nonsense that must magically become gospel for the rulers to get away with the lies and corruption that they do: hoodwinking the masses into a state of imagined grace, one that ensures their hallucinatory state while the thugs whistle for their wheel-man, ransack the people's treasury, use their children's flesh and blood as cannon fodder, and then retreat back behind the walls of their seaside estates, belly-laughing all the way to their Swiss banks. Our familiar friend, General Smedley Butler, the great American bullshit detector, implored the soldiers of his day to stop being "suckers," and reminded his fellow World War I veterans that the real war was between them—

> ...and all the lying, over-stuffed, sleek and slippery customers who send soldiers off to war with cheers and welcome them home again—what's left of 'em—with kicks! It's war with that little, tight, close-fisted bunch of Tories who think that God made the United States for about two hundred of them and created the rest of us to make their money for them and guard it against foreign danger and lie down in the mud or jump through hoops or do anything else under heaven they want us to do.[42]

Many have referred to it as "the religion of America," the idea that American political traditions and foundations are steeped in the dark tea of religion and blessed with unadulterated goodness. The Constitution and Declaration of Independence, two documents crafted in the 18th century by enlightened slave-owning land barons, "have been turned into Holy Writ," von Hoffman writes, "treated as sacred writings, the material on which shoals of Talmudist professors and lawyers feed and use to instruct the multitudes about the immutable religious truths of a political system which must be ever revered and never changed, not by one Biblical jot nor proverbial tittle."[43] Like jihadists drunk on the elixir of distant and imaginary virgins, Americans—for centuries—have embraced with zeal "America as a religious edifice," von Hoffman argues. The multitudes, kneeling at the altar of America, are promised "the dream," the American Dream, just as long as their American leaders—who sit at the right hand of the Father—remain in control of everything. For America is Jesus and Jesus is America. What America decides is right, and how America acts, regardless of what actions it pursues, is always basked in the sweet halo of warm light. "For the millions, high- and low-income, this set of ideas has become more than a metaphor," von Hoffman concludes, "It's as real as church on Sunday."[44]

This delusional fantasy is what allows the masters of war free rein in the marketplace of ideas and in the souk of death. Armed with the people's money (and their flesh), the military mandarins create, expand, and control their lucrative hell on earth.

Signposts Along the Way: Overview

The Goliath military complex that exists today did not start with Dick Cheney, Donald Rumsfeld, Halliburton, and Boeing. It began at the very spark of the American republic, circa 1783, when 28-year-old Alexander Hamilton lobbied the Continental Congress to consider a military peace establishment that would help the new government increase national security by lessening their dependence on foreign arms. Eight years later, in his *Report on Manufactures*, Hamilton strongly pushed for the expansion of domestic industrial wherewithal to once again strengthen national security. Also from the very beginning, there was a constant debate between two schools of thought: reliance on the private manufacture of weapons versus the government building its own weaponry. As the 19th century unfolded, legislation as well as the practical need for large shipments of arms on a constant basis opened up massive opportunities in the private sector. This expanding policy of the U.S. government contracting with private arms manufacturers built the foundation for a permanent arms industry.[45]

Over the next two hundred plus years, constant war fueled the arms industry forward. Here are the most significant markers along the way:

- The Civil War was America's first full-scale industrial mobilization. It was a national effort that bordered on total war. The keen and eager demand produced massive profits for the private sector and was clear-cut prophesy to what lay ahead.

- In the 19th and early 20th centuries, America embarked on numerous imperial adventures—including but not limited to the annexation of Hawaii, the invasions of Cuba, Puerto Rico, Panama, and the Philippines. These armed incursions created a mounting and ongoing demand for considerable military hardware. Weapons manufacturers couldn't build the toys fast enough. Imperialism proved great for business and vice versa.

- World War I was a short but key watershed moment for the burgeoning American defense industry. Modern technology, like the machine gun and chemical warfare, along with fighter planes, long-range bombers, and reconnaissance aircraft greatly increased demand and volume, with price tags skyrocketing. But after the war there was a kneejerk reaction to the horrific carnage in Europe and many Americans demanded isolation from world hostilities and pushed hard for disarmament—and this included a chorus of condemnation against war profiteering by the "merchants of death." It was an outcry that clearly dampened their exciting and robust industry.

- World War II reignited the defense industry and proved to be the moment when many current-day weapons manufacturers began historic production. In fact, the postwar years proved to be the exact opposite of the business-killing boomerang years that followed "The Great War." The Second World War also sparked U.S. government-sponsored research on a mammoth scale. Government funding of academic and private development became a key factor in the explosive growth of the MIC.

- In 1939, Italian physicist Enrico Fermi met with U.S. Navy brass at Columbia University to discuss fission or splitting a large atomic nucleus in two. Later the same year, Albert Einstein informed

FDR that he supported the theory of a nuclear chain reaction and its capability as a weapon of mass destruction. Six years later, in the early morning hours of 16 July 1945, the United States successfully detonated the first atomic bomb in the New Mexico desert. Human history changed forever. The original $6,000 pre-war budget for research on the atomic bomb ballooned to more than $2 billion once the Manhattan Project ended. Then in August of '45, Harry Truman dropped his greeting card on the inhabitants of Hiroshima and Nagasaki. The macabre cheers of joy still reverberate throughout the MIC as the aftershocks of this ghoulish moment still lights-up their cash register to this very day.

- In 1947, when Bernard Baruch said, "Let us not be deceived: We are today in the midst of a cold war,"—thereby coining the term "Cold War," an apt description of the strained and ice cold relationship between the newfangled superpowers—he was not factoring in the defense industry that experienced a rather red hot Cold War, one that was chock-full of breathtakingly huge government contracts. In fact, nothing fueled the MIC more than the belligerent arms race, both conventional and nuclear, between Washington and Moscow. Both superpowers offered massive military aid to their client states, which generated additional and substantial arms production. Materializing on the heels of World War II, this massive build-up created a perpetual and immutable juggernaut, one that was running amok with the American people's money. "The Pentagon," writes labor leader, activist, and author Sidney Lens, "wastes the taxpayer's money like the proverbial sailor on a drunken binge."[46] Lens cites a Brookings Institution report that reveals, "during the 1950s virtually all large military contracts…ultimately involved costs in excess of original contractual estimates of from 300 to 700 percent." Anybody want to buy a coffee pot for $7,000.00?

- Korea, Vietnam, and the Persian Gulf—Guns & Butter Forever: The economic model that offers society a choice between defense (guns) and civilian programs (butter) was conjoined together through the Cold War and persists at the heart of current U.S. aggression in the Middle East and Africa. Americans withstood an expensive adventure in Korea as well as a much longer and much more costly war in Vietnam ($170 billion, almost $1 trillion by today's standards as calculated by the Congressional Research Service). This was followed by the now-familiar perpetual war cry in the Persian Gulf and surrounding Middle East—recent American adventures swelling the national deficit to ludicrous heights. Delivering guns and butter has been like juggling bowling balls while perched along a wire strung between two skyscrapers. And for the model to work, it must allow for a robust and *permanently growing* defense industry while maintaining domestic spending at a level just high enough to keep the natives from burning the entire town down (where do we sign up?). To keep this model working, the United States has recklessly mortgaged its future.

What this all adds up to is this (and, of course, "this" depends on who you are and what side of the street you're ambling down): If you're John Q. Public, like we're John Q. Public, part of the axiomatic "99 percent," then your money and treasure—your birthright of democracy, your flesh, spirit, and soul, as well as your future and your children's future—has been sold down the river by shady and corrupt American leaders in all three branches of government, men and women who Lou Reed summed up so well when he sang this in his song "Strawman":

> *Does anyone need yet another politician*
> *Caught with his pants down and money sticking in his hole*

But if you're a corporate executive or shareholder in the defense industry, as well as one from the myriad of associated defense industries, or if you're a defense lobbyist spreading millions around Washington on behalf of Lockheed Martin, United Technologies, etcetera, or one of the legions of blue collar workers employed by the defense industry, or a congressperson who ensures (for a sweet price tag) that defense jobs stay in your district, or if you're a member of the military brass sauntering on one of the Empire's many, many, many, *many* bases around the globe, or if you're a military officer or bureaucrat guarding the gates of hell that sit under the largest office building in the world, the one built hard between Arlington and the Potomac, then, quite frankly, the Military-Industrial Complex is your daddy.

Signposts Along the Way: A Detailed History

War against a foreign country only happens when the moneyed classes think they are going to profit from it.

—George Orwell

Long before the close of World War II and the "official" escalation of what is commonly referred to as the Military-Industrial Complex (better described today as the Military-Industrial-*Intelligence* Complex), this violence-ready bureaucratic nightmare was seeded in a barbaric history—well more than a century of perpetual terror, plunder, and extermination of the indigenous population across the North American continent, followed by imperial battles of conquest, expansion, and aggression against, among others: Mexico, Hawaii, Spain, Cuba, the Philippines, and China during the Boxer Rebellion. Indicative of Washington's attitude during this period were the sentiments of Rushmore-chiseled Teddy Roosevelt. Journalist David Talbot writes, "Granting freedom to Philippine rebels or backing down from the Boxers in China, shouted Roosevelt, 'would be precisely like giving independence to the wildest tribe of Apaches in Arizona.'"[47] Clearly, conquest and empire building was the perfect union of American control, power, and exceptionalism with the bank of big business. And the more omnipresent the Empire, the larger the windfall for big business—and, of course, the less resources there are for the general welfare. It's a simple formula.

From Mark Twain's *The Battle Hymn of the Republic, Updated*:

In a sordid slime harmonious Greed was born in yonder ditch,
With a longing in his bosom—and for others' goods an itch.
As Christ died to make men holy, let men die to make us rich
Our god is marching on.

From the beginning of America, newly minted weapons manufacturers were at the forefront of the young nation's drive for dominion. Early American conquests, whether it was the wiping out of the indigenous population (who Lincoln's General John Pope termed "wild beasts"), or the disposal of the Spanish Empire by the American army and navy, weren't accomplished with sticks and stones. Technology may not have been anywhere near as sophisticated as the armaments we witness today, but heavy-duty weaponry was still needed and big money was still to be made; and there was a new nation with imperial urgings to feed.

World War I, which drove the fevered acceleration of mechanized warfare, propelling the arms and killing industry to never before seen levels, generated weapons research and technologies that demanded significant financial wherewithal to underwrite a massive and ever-growing arsenal of war, one that achieved new and creative ways to mutilate and kill people.

As the 20th century unfolded, domestic and world financial markets were recruited and enticed, and they gladly became willing partners (read: merchants of death) in underwriting and then profiting beyond their wildest dreams in the lucrative business of war. For instance, Percy Rockefeller—who sat on too numerous to mention boards of major American corporations including Bethlehem Steel— purchased Remington Arms in 1914, right on the precipice of war and then raked in barrels of blood money. His buddy, Samuel Bush, grand pappy to George Herbert Walker Bush and a prominent industrialist sitting on the government's War Industries Board, made sure Rockefeller and Remington enjoyed no-bid contracts, enabling them to supply almost 70 percent of all Allied weapons. But of course he didn't just make his friends money. Samuel Bush's company, Buckeye Steel Castings, built all the gun barrels for Remington.[48] Voila. See how that shit works?

Classic and reprehensible behavior by these war racketeers was on display as well in the person of Pierre DuPont, the kingpin behind the giant chemical company that has grabbed mountains of profit from death. Years after the "Great War," in 1932, DuPont continued to lobby heavily against bonus payments owed to the mangled, broke, and terrorized WWI veterans who were petitioning the government for recompense. These brutal actions by DuPont and other war racketeers led directly to President Herbert Hoover inflicting the iron fists of General Douglas MacArthur and General George S. Patton, along with their battery of American troops, on their fellow U.S. veterans who were gathered in Washington demanding what was rightfully theirs. When the 12th Infantry and 3rd Cavalry regiments descended on the Hooverville campsite on the banks of the Anacostia River, they did so with fixed bayonets, vomit-inducing tear gas, and six battle tanks loaded for bear. The U.S. Army ran the veterans back across the river. These vicious attacks, orchestrated by the war racketeers and carried out by their Army goons, embraced the spirit set forth by President Calvin Coolidge in 1924, when he vetoed a Congressional bill granting the payments to the more than four million veterans, mockingly adding, "Patriotism which is bought and paid for is not patriotism."[49] And who was MacArthur's junior aide during this American military operation against U.S. veterans? None other than Dwight

David Eisenhower. Needless to say, the retreating "Bonus Army" of American vets did not like Ike.

Former U.S. Senator Mike Gravel, the man responsible, along with Daniel Ellsberg, for the release of the Pentagon Papers, writes that, "Private businessmen emerged from the First World War actively participating in government decision making about arms production."[50] No doubt this cozy relationship encouraged private business to "influence foreign policy toward an arms race and war."[51] But it took some time during the interwar years for this relationship to evolve. In fact, following World War I, there was a significant lag in U.S. military spending and growth. Between 1922 and 1939, budgets averaged $744 million, which was about 1 percent of the Gross National Product.[52] At the time, military contracts and purchases were still subject to very strict legal guidelines. "The military purchaser publicly advertised its demand for a definite quantity of a specific item," reports Robert Higgs of *The Independent Institute*. The military then "accepted sealed bids, and automatically awarded the contract to the lowest bidder."[53]

In fact, during the 1930s, American manufacturers and contractors steered clear of business associations with FDR's New Deal government. In 1940, *Fortune* magazine polled business execs about conducting military business with the United States and the survey revealed that 77 percent had serious fears and were uncertain about contracting rearmament work. The reason? Captains of industry believed FDR's administration was "strongly anti-business" and couldn't rely on their cooperation.[54] Based on the prevailing and general attitude of the times that "the arms industry helped create the conditions for war," FDR responded with a straightforward critique of this relationship, saying "This grave menace to the peace of the world is due in no small measure to the uncontrolled activities of the manufacturers and merchants of engines of destruction."[55]

Under the heading of "love the one you're with," these captains of industry, despite being rebuffed by FDR, were nevertheless finding buyers elsewhere. For years, Germany, Italy, and Japan were aggressively building their own military-industrial complexes as well as their own "advanced war machines with the help of American industry"[56]—and this allowed American munitions manufacturers, the aeronautics industry, as well as American industry up and down the assembly line to cash in from all angles, enemies and allies alike.

Regardless of the concerns of industry and their duplicitous dealings, a meeting took place in the White House in 1939 necessitated by the emergence of a new global war that would plant the seeds for a massive uptick in government contracts. It was a fifteen-minute get-together between FDR and Vannevar Bush (no relation to the Bush Crime Family). Bush was the Dean of Engineering at MIT during the 1930s, where he spearheaded the early development of computer sciences, and by 1939 he was president of the Carnegie Institution for Science. With war rumbling in Europe, Bush advocated a "National Defense Research Committee" that would oversee the scientific research necessary for a potent American military. At the end of this constructive fifteen minutes, Roosevelt appointed Bush the head of this new entity. And make no mistake about it: in that meeting lay the origins of the current-day military leviathan, for the National Defense Research Committee brought together all the major entities necessary for this fraternity to operate on high octane—government, industry, science, university research, and obviously the military itself. Also under Bush's command was the Manhattan Project and the development of the atomic bomb. "All the participants," Gravel writes, "in what [Eisenhower] would later call the military-industrial complex. Bush is considered its father."[57]

Another moment, lasting just fifteen minutes, that will live in infamy.

Washington was now on the fast track toward military preparedness but it was almost as if they were starting from scratch. When FDR visited an Ogdensburg, New York, military exercise by the Army and Air Force, General Clifford Powell informed the president that during tank maneuvers the soldiers would be using "drain pipes to simulate mortars and broom sticks to simulate machine guns."[58] Shortly thereafter, FDR asked General Marshall for a tally of bombers in America's arsenal. Marshall informed the Commander in Chief that there were only forty-nine serviceable bombers in the American fleet. Secretary of War Henry Stimson wrote in his diary that FDR's "head went back as if someone had hit him in the chest."[59] By 1940, Franklin Roosevelt was still publicly saying that America would not enter the war in Europe but, as Gravel writes, "he was secretly preparing for war."[60]

> *If you are going to try to go to war, or to prepare for war, in a capitalist country, you have got to let business make money out of the process or business won't work.*[61]
>
> —Henry Stimson, Secretary of War

With the Nazi war machine churning in Europe, and FDR's ongoing tête-à-tête with the Japanese about ready to come to a head, Congress unlocked the dam and the floodwaters began to flow. In fact, between 1940 and 1941, the War Department received more funding than during all of World War I. "Tightening the military-industrial nexus," writes Mike Gravel, "the War and Navy departments dropped sealed-bid contracts in favor of negotiated deals."[62] This under-the-radar procedural change altered the playing field forever. Gravel reports that:

> During the Second World War an astounding $300 billion went into the pockets of contractors and their employees. General Motors got the most: 8 percent of the total. What was good for America was good for General Motors, including, apparently, war.[63]

From the Ashes of World War Rises an Empire

With Europe in ruins, Japan incinerated, and the world's economy badly broken, the smoke began to clear—and emerging from the smoldering ashes we find the American Empire: intact, unspoiled, and with military bases, installations, and soldiers all over the planet. "America's hegemony lasted exactly five years," writes Gore Vidal, "Then the cold and hot wars began."[64] Post-World War II American rhetoric sounded identical to American rhetoric throughout the ages: the charitable dissemination of life, liberty, and the pursuit of happiness. Sidney Lens writes that, "America's goal in the postwar world, it seems, was not quite as eleemosynary as its public proclamations pretended; a dollar sign lurked in the shadows."[65] And one of America's most prominent carnival barkers was Harry Truman, who made it abundantly clear that "the Russians would soon be put in their places" and that America would finally be running the world "in a way that the world ought to be run."[66] Truman went on to proclaim (during a speech at Baylor University) that freedom trumped peace and that "free enterprise" was the key. Truman (as well as many others) sold the idea that "regimented economies" were the natural enemy of free enterprise and that "the whole world should adopt the American system." Truman concluded that this precious American system of free will "could survive in America only if it became a world system."[67] Talk about sowing the seeds of fear. In his essay, *Decline of the Empire*, Gore Vidal explores this fear mongering:

> Our masters would have us believe that all our problems are the fault of the Evil Empire of the East, with its Satanic and atheistic religion, ever ready to destroy us in the night. This nonsense began at a time when we had atomic weapons and the Russians did not. They had lost 20 million of their people in the war, and 8 million

of them before the war, thanks to their neoconservative Mongolian political system. Most important, there was never any chance, then or now, of the money power (all that matters) shifting from New York to Moscow.[68]

Fear was then, as it remains today, the prime motivator used by the rulers to persuade the masses (read: taxpayers) to go along with colossal military budgets during peacetime. Fear is also a handy motivator when the rulers become trigger-happy and need to get physical in some foreign and sovereign land. Fear fed to the people, feeds the monster. Gore Vidal agrees: "Well, World War II made prosperous the United States, which had been undergoing a depression for a dozen years; and made very rich those magnates and their managers who govern the republic, with many a wink, in the people's name."[69] Vidal continues:

> In order to maintain a general prosperity (and enormous wealth for the few) they decided that we would become the world's policeman, perennial shield against the Mongol hordes. We shall have an arms race, said one of the high priests, John Foster Dulles, and we shall win it because the Russians will go broke first. We were then put on a permanent wartime economy.[70]

Regardless of America's Cold War psychosis and the howls of "red menace" that reverberated throughout the 1950s (and well beyond), dreaded communism grew very little after 1949. In fact it was American power that stepped into "the vacuums that were left after the decline of the European influence in Asia, Africa, and even Latin America."[71] It was a sweeping and comprehensive exchange of power that took place, dramatically expanding the U.S. Empire and their heavyweight military presence in foreign lands. "Americans devoted much attention to the expansion of communism," writes Harvard political scientist Samuel Huntington, "and in the process they tended to ignore the expansion of the United States influence and presence throughout much of the world."[72]

As we've seen, the spectacular growth of the Military-Industrial Complex during the 20th century, particularly during the 1950s and into the 1960s, was a direct result of insatiable avarice on the part of the defense industry, both the governmental and private sectors. Cold War paranoia (real and manufactured) was utilized skillfully as gasoline heaved on a bonfire. The American public was (and still is) quaking in their boots, and this resignation by the masses allowed their leaders and their leaders' business accomplices to run hog-wild with their tax dollars as well as their conscience and morality. Alas, Gargantua lives.

But Gargantua must also exist and expand on foreign shores for its power and profits to evolve and grow. Sidney Lens identified two basic paradigms that the MIC utilized to enlarge their existence in the postwar world:

1. A system of aid and loans aimed at stabilizing the economies of our allies, but also at keeping them moored to the "American way."

2. A system of military alliances, military training and support, as well as the use of the CIA and AFL-CIO labor leaders, to assure that governments we consider friendly remain in power.[73]

And lest we forget, this American military and economic aid came with major conditions attached to its acceptance—conditions that were always harshly detrimental to the economies and people in these nations, conditions that would give Tony Soprano professional envy. But these aggressive policies worked like a charm. In the aftermath of World War II, from 1949 to 1966, the U.S. Defense Department sold more than $16 billion dollars worth of death toys to U.S.-aligned countries and conditionally gave away another $30 billion worth of weaponry to governments friendly with the U.S.[74] And, of course, always quid pro quo. The propaganda disseminated to the American people during this period washed over them like baptismal holy water: the U.S. was spreading freedom and liberty to the people of the world. The American public—and we must continue to underscore the fact that American taxpayers finance these fiendish operations, all of them—actually believes and embraces the fairytale that their government is spreading freedom and goodness, while at the same time keeping them safe by arming themselves and the world to the teeth. It calls to mind John Steinbeck's reflection that, "It is in the things not mentioned that the untruth lies." Sociologist and scholar, Herbert Irving Schiller, identified the "success" of America's sleight of hand:

> The association of the objectives of American expansionism with
> the concept of freedom, in which the former are obscured and the
> latter emphasized, has been a brilliant achievement of American
> policy. Rarely has a word, "freedom," produced so much confusion
> and obtained so much misdirected endorsement.[75]

"Lord Cecil Rhodes," writes Lens, "who conquered much of Africa for the British, suggested that the simplest way to achieve peace was for England to convert the rest of the world to its colony."[76] Clearly, the American Empire has ripped that page out of Britain's playbook and stapled it to their chest. But instead of achieving peace, the Empire has driven the world to the edge of nuclear destruction and, during the post-WWII Cold War years, made fortunes for the tentacles of the MIC. It's just like what Garrett Morris' fictional Mets ballplayer, Chico Escuela, used to say: "Baseball been berra berra good to me." The Cold War, like all wars, was berra berra good for business.

Arsenal of Horror

In the visiting room at SCI Mahoney, the prison where one of your authors remains incarcerated, both authors have discussed the Vietnam War in great depth… and (obviously) we've never identified one single positive attribute regarding the war except when we discussed the unintended historical intersection of that gruesome murder spree with the military monster fueling it from afar. The positive attribute? The public's ability to finally glimpse the monster.

Up to that point (1964) on the continuum gauging the growth of America's garrison state, the Pentagon was infallible in the eyes of the American press, and by extension, the American people—the group of silent partners financing the entire shebang. But the war unraveled so wrong, and so fast, and for so many reasons that in the blowback that ensued Washington lost control of almost everything associated with their messy foreign entanglement: they lost control of the message and the already-shaky reason why they were fighting this distant jungle war; they lost control of the usually complicit press; they lost control of the war itself, via their poor underestimation of the resolve of the so-called "enemy" who were ferociously fighting back for their own land and sovereignty; and finally, they lost control of their own soldiers, their own pawns in the game.

In fact, the ensuing and rampaging shit-storm that churned from all quarters pinned the war racketeers under their desks, making the once untouchable military cyclops ripe for criticism and eventual cutbacks. Sidney Lens describes it as "Unmasking the Goliath." Lens argues that until the war in Southeast Asia became untenable and indefensible, "the Pentagon wore a halo." It didn't matter what the masters of war touched: weaponry, strategy, or their all-important massive sinkhole budgets, everything was "sacrosanct." Lens writes that, "its judgment was accepted like a message from Mount Sinai, and the nation followed it from one weapons system to another, from one enlarged budget to another, with humble awe."[77]

Senator J. William Fulbright, Southern Democrat from Arkansas, released figures in the late 1960s that documented federal spending from 1947 to 1967—the decisive years of growth for the U.S. military whale. $904 billion (or 57%+ of its budget) was handed over by Washington lawmakers to the defense industry and their associated private contractors for military procurement. During the same period only 6 percent was allocated to health, education, housing, labor, and community development. "Convincing the American people that they ought to spend nine times as much on guns as on human welfare," Lens writes, "was an act of mesmerism by the military establishment without parallel."[78] Lens identifies the collaborators in this gangland operation:

> Both the people and Congress rubber-stamped an arsenal of
> horror… Except for a handful of pacifists, radicals, and,
> periodically, a few members of Congress, no one questioned
> the utility or sanity of all this.[79]

A Pot of Gold at the End of the Ho Chi Minh Trail

The country and the people of Vietnam hold a very special place in the extraordinary expansion that led to the current hammerlock of Washington's Military-Industrial Complex on the flesh, spirit, and treasure of the American people (as well as the MIC's clutch on its partners and victims around the world). It was in this land, 9,000 miles away from the safe confines of Foggy Bottom, that American military masters fashioned a thirty-year assault that jettisoned the Pentagon, the Department of Defense, and their soul mates in the powerful defense and aeronautics industries, to vertiginous new heights. And for the most part, this obscene growth continues unencumbered this cold, dark, red, white, and blue 21st century day.

Early in World War II, the Japanese booted the French out of their distant colony, but when Japan surrendered in 1945, of course the French wanted their colony back. But things didn't go well for continued European colonialism as the French experienced another Waterloo with an overwhelming military defeat at Dien Bien Phu—this one at the hands of a Vietnamese peasant army. The American government also shared greatly in this loss as Washington was financing a majority of France's imperial actions in Southeast Asia. So with their tails between their legs, the French packed up the Beaujolais and scurried back to Europe in 1954, marking the end of French colonialism in Indochina. But in that moment, the baton was passed to the Americans for what would soon become Washington's long, bloody, and abhorrently expensive war in Vietnam. From the smoldering ashes of Dien Bien Phu to Uncle Sam's ratcheting up to a shooting war, is a tale John Prados describes as one "of desperate men and hubris."[80] Prados, historian and Senior Fellow at The National Security Archive, describes Washington as "trapped within the policy framework they themselves had created, and convinced they could do better than the French, these men put America on the march to war in Viet-Nam."[81] But it goes further than the expected beating of the proverbial drums of war. They also helped to orchestrate gigantic profit margins for the MIC, subsidized—as always—by the American taxpayer. It became a two-decade raid on the American treasury, one that carries on to this cold, dark, red, white, and blue 21st century day. (Why not? It's a good line.)

But the MIC's maneuverings underfoot then (as now) for unquestioned power designed to manufacture buckets of gold, were a complex labyrinth of intertwined stratagems—the work of expert alchemists blending xenophobia, fear-mongering, racism, military machismo, and geopolitical psychobabble into one potent cocktail. So as the French retreated and the Americans settled into Indochina's underbrush, it was the muscle-flexing, iron-pumping military that offered up insanity as an immediate course of action. Under the rubric of "Talk about hubris, talk about the Empire and the MIC operating rogue and with a fuck you attitude," Prados reveals that during this crisis period of transition between the two Western powers, U.S. leaders and planners seriously considered the use of nuclear weapons in Vietnam.

TEXT:
Far East U.S. Air Force Staff Study K720.04-8 (April 12, 1954)

TITLE:
Recommend an Effective Course of Action to Achieve US Objectives in Indochina

PLANNERS RECOMMENDED:
All types of weapons and devices, including atomic bombs, should be made available and used whenever a militarily profitable target is discovered. In order to gain maximum psychological benefit from the decision to use atomic weapons where profitable in a localized

war, the decision should be generally announced. Its subsequent employment would not then create world-wide opinion that the US is about to embark on a global war.[82]

In his book, *Operation Vulture*, Prados meticulously details how "U.S. Navy aircraft carriers conducted nuclear weapons drills on their way to patrols off the Vietnamese coast."[83] Luckily, some diplomatic progress was made with the Geneva Accords in 1954, enough at least so Eisenhower didn't take the advice of his Far East U.S. Air Force Staff, since, as Prados points out, "the warriors were edging closer and closer to battle." But once again, Eisenhower is no angel here: he worked overtime "to keep the lid on his conversations about nukes," writes Prados, and "Ike's action should be seen as the cover up it was, and the absence of open acknowledgement of the nukes in memoirs and so on should no longer be taken as evidence that none were involved."[84]

Moreover, as we've noted earlier, Ike rekindled the nuclear option with LBJ, which in turn recalls some biting wit from *Dr. Strangelove or: How I Learned to Stop Worrying and Love the Bomb*. And if this movie dialogue wasn't written by Stanley Kubrick and Terry Southern, one might believe that it was Oval Office reality:

> PRESIDENT MERKIN MUFFLEY
> I will not go down in history as the greatest mass-murderer since Adolf Hitler.
>
> GENERAL "BUCK" TURGIDSON
> Perhaps it might be better, Mr. President, if you were more concerned with the American People than with your image in the history books.

And clearly from the outset of American involvement in Vietnam, right through to the reign of Nixon and Kissinger (as also evidenced on Nixon's tapes), massive American firepower was the norm while nuclear weapons remained a serious option if shit got too far out of hand—this madness echoed by General Curtis LeMay, who famously suggested bombing Vietnam back into the Stone Age. It was American exceptionalism hurtling through space and time, a true harbinger of things to come.

The lead-up to and final execution of America's attack on the people of Vietnam was a time of remarkable imperial insolence in Washington, an era of astonishing gall. American political leaders and policymakers, along with their trigger-happy and bellicose military leadership, exhibited no restraint nor remorse when dropping untold tons of ordnance on the peasant population of Indochina—or as the 1st Battalion, 8th Cavalry, Charlie Company called themselves: *Death from Above.* When Boeing's B-52 Stratofortresses dropped their immense payloads during the ongoing carpet-bombing of Vietnam, one might imagine the gruesome screams of death and dismemberment on the ground. One might also imagine that when these B-52s opened their bomb bays and let fly 60,000 pounds of massive destruction, screams of joy accompanied by a ringing cash register could be heard in boardrooms throughout the MIC.

And the most dangerous aspect to all of this? Despite the massive antiwar tempest that was whipping up both inside and outside the American government, Washington powerbrokers and the MIC held their own, continuing to exhibit the financial wherewithal—of course driven by immense profit incentive—to keep building, strafing, and bombing. But by the late 1960s, the American death count began to seriously outdistance their powerful propaganda machine. Then stimulated by a vibrant and vocal antiwar movement, significant segments of the American population joined in opposition to the war, and by extension, in opposition to the vast military machine. "Just when the power of the militarist alliance seemed unstoppable in the late 1960s," writes investigative historian Gareth Porter, "the public turned decisively against the Vietnam War, and a long period of public pressure to reduce military spending began. As a result, military manpower was reduced to below even the Eisenhower era levels."[85]

The Paris Peace Accords were signed in January of 1973, with American combat troops and B-52 strikes gone by March of 1973. This was followed by a major North Vietnamese offensive that led to the fall of Saigon in April of 1975, culminating with the final unification of North and South Vietnam in July of 1976. By the time this unification took place, some thirty years of imperial "management" had ruled in Southeast Asia. With that much control, one would expect to see some major accomplishments, right? Here's a checklist:

- Did the U.S. finally achieve its objective of freeing the South Vietnamese people from the evils of communist rule? *Nope.*

- Did the U.S. finally set up a thriving democratic government in South Vietnam? *Nope.*

- Were any long-range Cold War ideological issues settled? Communist versus anti-communist? ***Nope.***

- What about the dreaded domino theory? Did the dominos fall hard and fast as predicted by American leaders? Asia, Africa, Antarctica? ***Nope.***

So what the hell was accomplished? Probably best to ask a soul of Vietnamese descent since white men in suits rarely ask the victims. In the 2016 novel *The Sympathizer*, Viet Thanh Nguyen sums up the only conceivable value of the decades-long butchery:

> Our country itself was cursed, bastardized, partitioned into north and south, and if it could be said of us that we chose division and death in our uncivil war, that was also only partially true. We had not chosen to be debased by the French, to be divided by them into an unholy trinity of north, center, and south, to be turned over to the great powers of capitalism and communism for a further bisection, then given roles as the clashing armies of a Cold War chess match played in air-conditioned rooms by white men wearing suits and lies.

"White men wearing suits and lies." Booyah.

Strategically Staged Genocide

At the height of American bombing in 1966, pacifist philosopher Bertrand Russell organized a citizens' action coalition known as the International War Crimes Tribunal. In an effort to underscore America's vicious crimes against the people of Vietnam, Russell and the Tribunal argued that the Nuremberg Principles also applied to U.S. actions in Vietnam—victorious or not. In his book, *Story of a Death Foretold* (on the Chilean coup of 1973, another vicious action supported by the same Washington criminals operating in Vietnam), University of London senior lecturer and author, Oscar Guardiola-Rivera, details the essence of the argument as articulated by French philosopher and playwright Jean-Paul Sartre:

> Sartre stated that US military strategy in Vietnam amounted to a strategically staged genocide. He also pointed out that this strategy was being applied with the intention of imposing a one-world model in the interest of big world powers... "The ties of the 'One-

World' model on which the United States wants to impose its hegemony, have grown tighter and tighter," he wrote. "The group which the United States wants to intimidate and terrorize by way of the Vietnamese nation is the human group in its entirety."[86]

The Losers

In a war this misguided and tragic, there are bound to be losers—lots of them. Here's another checklist,[87] albeit partial, that encapsulates one set of victims. When you peruse this list, imagine how much money—*your money by the way*—that it takes to produce this much death and destruction. Author Michael Yates rightly calls the extent of America's carnage "mind-boggling."

- Close to four million Southeast Asians killed
- More bombs dropped on Southeast Asia than were dropped by all combatants in all previous wars throughout history
- 19,000,000+ gallons of herbicide unleashed to poison the land
- Of 15,000 hamlets dotting the countryside in the south of Vietnam, 9,000 were obliterated
- In North Vietnam, all six industrial cities were utterly destroyed
- In North Vietnam, twenty-eight of their thirty provincial towns were leveled by U.S. bombing
- In North Vietnam, ninety-six of their one hundred and sixteen district towns were leveled by U.S. bombing
- American leaders threatened to unleash nuclear weapons thirteen times
- Once U.S. troops left Southeast Asia, unexploded bombs and land mines claimed an additional 42,000 lives (in fact, live explosives still exist on millions of acres)
- Defoliants like "Agent Orange" infected millions of Vietnamese, causing horrific health complications, birth defects, genetic disorders, and of course death; the U.S. spread almost 12 million gallons of the liquid mixture containing the 2,4-D and 2,4,5-T herbicides over 25 percent of the countryside where more than 3,000 villages were in the spray zone; the toxin dioxin remains in soil, water, and human bodies for long periods of time; in underground aquifers, the dioxin can last for more than 100 years[88] (thanks Monsanto and Dow Chemical, choke on the fucking money)

- Washington dropped nearly a half-million tons of napalm on the people of Vietnam for ten years. Napalm B is a gel that consists of plastic polystyrene, hydrocarbon benzene, and gasoline. The mixture burns at between 1,500° and 2,200° Fahrenheit. Napalm gel sticks to everything including human beings. Nearby victims not engulfed by the immediate flame also suffered greatly, including carbon monoxide poisoning. Roughly 60% of the Vietnamese people targeted by napalm bombing suffered fifth-degree burns, which means the flame burned down to bone.[89] The major U.S. supplier of napalm during the Vietnam War was Dow Chemical.

The list goes on and on (and the destruction and death crossed the border into Cambodia and Laos), but you get the idea: the American power structure spent unimaginable amounts of booty on the prosecution of their slaughter; and, as we know, unimaginable amounts of booty generates inconceivable amounts of profit. Blue-chip dividends. Elephantine and long-term paydays for all the major players in both the private and public sector of the "defense" industry—the border between each sector amorphous and always shape-shifting depending on who's in power and who's a consultant or CEO. Case in point: Dick Cheney (more soon).

Many historians and journalists have written extensively about how America "lost" the Vietnam War. Well that depends on who you're speaking to. If you're chatting with a surviving Vietnamese victim on the streets of Ho Chi Minh City or an American mother whose son returned in pieces in a body bag, you're probably not going to find many individuals who feel like winners and losers. Rather, you're going to find people who were maimed, shredded, and terrorized for life—and that's if you were lucky. Clearly, there were many American losers:

- 58,220 dead American soldiers (11,465 under 20 years old)

- 303,644 wounded American soldiers

- Untold numbers of American soldiers rotated back to the States with serious mental illnesses; the Research Triangle Institute estimates that 830,000 Vietnam veterans have full-blown or partial Post-Traumatic Stress Disorder

- Many of the 3 million U.S. soldiers who had tours of duty in Vietnam were exposed to Agent Orange and other herbicides used in combat; the U.S. Department of Veterans Affairs has identified

14 presumptive diseases associated with this exposure including Chronic B-cell Leukemia, Type 2 Diabetes, Hodgkin's Disease, Ischemic Heart Disease, Parkinson's Disease, Prostate Cancer, Respiratory Cancers including lung cancer, and Soft Tissue Sarcomas (cancer)

- Count the families and friends of every fatality and casualty above as a victim—do the math: mothers, fathers, siblings, lovers, best friends, and so forth… the number grows exponentially when determining who lost a loved one or has had to deal with the trauma associated with a host of horrendous wounds and suffering.[90]

The Winners

From the early 60s to the early and mid 70s, Washington let loose an unprecedented torrent of firepower throughout Indochina. Adjusted for current-day dollars, direct costs for the Vietnam War for the ten-year period between 1965 and 1975 was $738 billion dollars.[91] And this number does not account for U.S. dollars pumped into the massive nation-building campaign below the 17th parallel that began in 1954 and continued right through the imaginary Tonkin Gulf incident in 1964. It was a staggering and costly mission that included major infrastructure projects: building roads and bridges, airfields, seaports, as well as dredging canals. It consisted of substantial military and economic aid flowing into the south to subsidize agriculture, public administration, police and counterespionage, as well as supplying a host of specialists and technicians in almost every walk of life, not to mention the so-called military "advisors" that ballooned to 16,000 by 1964. Also, the $738 billion dollar price tag doesn't include any "black budgets," those hidden buckets of money that magically appear for CIA and clandestine operations—and the Vietnam War was a watershed moment for deadly CIA buffoonery. American taxpayer dollars flowed like water into the jungles and destruction of Vietnam, which sets the stage for opening the big envelope.

And the winners are...

Not surprisingly, the winners in the Vietnam War were the corporations and kingpins that populate the Military-Industrial Complex: a syndicate of wide-ranging defense contractors, sub-contractors, aerospace companies, and, of course, their licentious bankers on the most corrupt street in America—Wall Street. Corporate winners include Bell Helicopter, Boeing, General Electric,

Union Carbide, Grumman, General Dynamics, Raytheon, Lockheed, AT&T, Hughes Aircraft, IBM, Sperry Corp., and the list goes on and on and on...

The winners also include various institutions of higher learning—colleges and universities that receive lucrative grants for military research and development, schools like MIT, Stanford, Cal Berkeley, Caltech, Michigan, and so forth, schools that specialize in strategic disciplines: electronics, engineering, aeronautics, materials science, and of course physics. These famous schools prime the pump for recruitment right into the Pentagon and the defense industries, feeding the MIC with "the best and the brightest" advisers, scientists, and consultants—the brain trust that creates unique and efficient ways to kill people. Johns Hopkins history professor, Stuart Leslie, underscores the impact:

> Their faculty members literally wrote the books for particular specialties and through those texts reshaped their disciplines across the country. Their faculty and students started the companies, most of them defense-oriented, around which Silicon Valley and Route 128 (themselves largely a by-product of defense spending) crystallized.[92]

Let's also not forget the congressional, senatorial, and cabinet members who populate the boards and power structures of these companies before and after they serve their country in public service. Actually, it's more like "serving up their country on a silver platter."

Nixon's "X-File"

For some, like Richard Nixon and his personal Wall Street cronies, extending the Vietnam War was a realistic option to keep the gravy train rolling. Investigative journalist Robert Parry (who broke many an Iran-Contra story for AP and *Newsweek*) revealed what the archivists at Lyndon Johnson's presidential library refer to as their "X-File," which details how Nixon helped to sabotage the peace talks in 1968, an act LBJ labeled as "treason."

The file chronicles how in October of 1968, during the presidential campaign against Democrat Hubert Humphrey, Nixon worked to "block" the proposed peace settlement. In fact, Nixon's behind-the-scenes maneuvers were offered as a secret inside "tip" designed to help his Wall Street cronies hedge their moves on stocks and bonds. "These investment bankers were colluding over how to make money with their inside knowledge of Nixon's scheme to extend the Vietnam

War," Parry writes. "Such an image of these 'masters of the universe' sitting around a table plotting financial strategies while a half million American soldiers were sitting in a war zone is a picture that even the harshest critics of Wall Street might find hard to envision."[93]

Like clockwork, the Johnson Administration was suddenly faced with South Vietnamese President Nguyen van Thieu's abrupt hesitation at the Paris Peace Talks—a hesitation engineered by the Republican presidential campaign, which convinced Thieu he would get a much better deal with "President" Nixon. Parry concludes that Nixon's campaign "was colluding with [Thieu] to derail the Paris peace talks."[94] In fact, "Candidate" Nixon was manipulating a two-pronged strategy by stalling the peace process: one, if Johnson achieved a settlement before the November election, Humphrey stood a much greater chance of winning the presidential vote; and two, by extending the war, Wall Street insiders could manage the highs and lows of the stock and bond markets based on battlefield and political developments. More war = more defense contracts = continued enhanced piles of profit. Lieutenant Colonel William Astore (USAF-Retired) refers to perpetual war as "the eternal marriage of combat and commerce" and that the people need to be constantly reminded "of the degree to which war as disaster capitalism is driven by profit and power."[95]

Johnson ordered an FBI investigation into Nixon's actions, which "uncovered the framework of Nixon's blocking operation."[96] Tricky Dick pulled it off as his swine on Wall Street reveled. Upon leaving the presidency, LBJ instructed his National Security Advisor, Walt Rostow, to remove the file from the White House. The "X-File" wasn't opened until 1994. Parry concludes:

> After Johnson's peace initiative failed, the Vietnam War dragged
> on another four years, leading to the deaths of an additional 20,763
> U.S. soldiers, with 111,230 wounded. An estimated one million
> more Vietnamese also died.[97]

War is commerce… nothing more, nothing less

You may not be interested in war, but war is interested in you.
—Leon Trotsky

Sure, America's thirty-year incursion into the jungles of Southeast Asia was mistakenly motivated by and linked to ongoing Cold War battles with the Soviet

Union, and sure, it was about the U.S. containing China. And, sure, it was, as Gore Vidal told us, "a war of imperial vanity." But ultimately, it was a war—like all wars—for profit, one that fed the beast that Eisenhower hinted at, a beast that was growing completely beyond democracy's grip.

As the 1970s pulled away from Vietnam, there was a knee-jerk public and political reaction against military spending. Goliath was momentarily down for the count, like Howard Cosell screaming "Down goes Frazier! Down goes Frazier! Down goes Frazier!" Indeed, the Vietnam experience left a cold metallic taste of blood in the mouths of most Americans. "Militarism's defeat in Vietnam led to a rare but brief period of national self-examination," explains former U.S. Senator Mike Gravel. The country asked itself groundbreaking questions: "What kind of a nation have we become? How could we have been so blindly led into the outrage of Vietnam? Are we using our tremendous power and wealth for progress at home and abroad, or simply to multiply that wealth and power for its own sake?"[98] Gravel reminds us that, as unbelievable as it may seem in today's complicit country club climate, it was a period of tough Congressional committees that took on the CIA and exposed their assassinations, questioned the assassination of JFK, and wasn't afraid of holding the military's feet to the fire. Even the American press, who were "partly humbled and partly triumphant" during Vietnam, got tough. It was a time when the bastards were exposed.

But it didn't last long. Serious efforts were afoot to reverse the decline in spending, efforts orchestrated by the winners of the Vietnam War—the defense industry along with their allies in the Pentagon and on Capitol Hill. They employed diehard right-wing groups, like the Committee on the Present Danger, to help turn the tide. Hell, just a couple of years before, the so-called left-radical prairie statesman from South Dakota, the antiwar and Pentagon budget slashing U.S. Senator, George McGovern, was the Democratic nominee for president. Had Watergate broke sooner, had the Democratic leadership of Hubert Humphrey, George Meany, and Richard Daley not wanted their party back from the wild-eyed hippies and feminists and didn't sabotage their own candidate, George McGovern and his commie co-conspirators could very well have been setting up shop at 1600 Pennsylvania Avenue. The entrenched and growing stronger by the day corporate oligarchy was not about to let this shit ever happen again. Day in and day out, they were taking their lumps, so they dug in deep and went on the warpath—and they've been playing for keeps ever since.

"On the fourth day, I'd be assassinated"

To illustrate the point, we turn to Bill Blum, the historian and ex-State Department official who knows a thing or two about the protective nature of the American power structure. In January of 2006, Osama bin Laden released an audiotape suggesting that if Americans have a sincere "desire for peace and security" then they should read the opening paragraph of Blum's book *Rogue State*. Osama bin Laden then quotes Blum's words:

> If I were the president, I could stop terrorist attacks against the United States in a few days. Permanently. I would first apologize— very publicly and very sincerely—to all the widows and the orphans, the impoverished and the tortured, and all the many millions of other victims of American imperialism. I would then announce that America's global interventions—including the awful bombings— have come to an end. And I would inform Israel that it is no longer the 51st state of the union but—oddly enough—a foreign country. I would then reduce the military budget by at least 90% and use the savings to pay reparations to the victims and repair the damage from the many American bombings and invasions. There would be more than enough money. Do you know what one year of the US military budget is equal to? One year. It's equal to more than $20,000 per hour for every hour since Jesus Christ was born.
>
> That's what I'd do on my first three days in the White House. On the fourth day, I'd be assassinated.[99]

Blum's predicted demise at the crescendo of his dream underscores what is at stake when sanity and even a hint of egalitarian behavior threaten the status quo and the unilateral domain of the MIC and their wealthy benefactors—and that's exactly what was transpiring in the 1970s.

And then James Earl Carter walked into town, elected to the White House campaigning on reducing arms sales and focusing on human rights. This follow-up to McGovern's ascendency triggered an immediate response from the wounded hard right in the lobbying snake pit known as the American League for Exports and Security Assistance. "ALESA was explicitly designed to thwart Carter's efforts on this front,"[100] reports William Hartung, the Director of the Arms & Security Project at the Center for International Policy. Then history started rolling in favor of those anxious to rekindle the glory days of the military

Goliath. In 1979, the U.S.-supported Shah of Iran and his Pahlavi dynasty was overthrown in the Iranian Revolution and replaced by an Islamic republic and the Ayatollah Khomeini, and then just across the border to the east, the Soviet Union invaded Afghanistan in December and stayed for ten years.

"Gooooooooooooood morning, Afghanistan."

These major developments bolstered the hawks in Carter's White House, and combined with outside agitprop, newspeak, and right-wing evangelism, Carter was painted into a corner reserved for the weak and infirm, never getting a second term as Reagan and his band of merry men went for the jugular. And who was standing in the winner's circle once again? Hartung explains:

> The [arms] industry as a whole cashed in, as Reagan pursued the largest peacetime military buildup in U.S. history, while specific companies got special favors. Rockwell International was able to restore funding for the B-1 bomber, combining White House support with a pork barrel campaign that placed subcontracts for work on the plane in nearly every Congressional district. Boeing benefited from the administration's all-out support for a multi-billion sale of AWACS radar planes to Saudi Arabia, while General Dynamics reaped the rewards from a relaxation of the Carter administration's limits on sales of combat aircraft to Latin America to squeeze in a sale of F-b fighters to Venezuela.[101]

But it wasn't all wine and roses for the so-called Reagan Revolution when it came to military procurement. There was the Pentagon's "Spare Parts" corrupted buying practices of paying hundreds of bucks for toilet seats and thousands for coffee pots, a new 80s reality Hartung defines as "an entire procurement system run amok." There was also an inside the Pentagon corruption scandal that the FBI investigated for three years known as "Operation Ill Wind"—revealing a massive bribe operation between Defense Department officials and the largest military contractors looking to win lucrative deals to build their murder toys, usual suspects like United Technologies, Boeing, Hughes, General Dynamics, Lockheed, and General Electric—a fine organization that brings "good things to life." During this investigation, the FBI prosecuted more than sixty contractors, consultants, and government officials.[102]

There were other setbacks to the MIC trying once again to reach the Promised Land. The Reagan administration's attempt at lifting Goliath back up into the clouds of Mount Olympus with its development of the Strategic Defense Initiative (known by its fairytale name as "Star Wars") was met with stiff opposition from organized dissent, namely the Union of Concerned Scientists. Coupled with the Soviet's demise and the end of the Cold War, "the Star Wars missile defense system was unceremoniously thrown onto the back burner."[103] William Hartung then encapsulates one of America's most famous dirtbags:

> And, in the most dangerous scandal of all, a National Security Council staffer named Oliver North was caught running an illegal gun-running operation out of the basement of the Executive Office Building, using a network of front companies and unsavory characters to override the will of Congress and subvert the Constitution while arming the government of Iran and the anti-government contra "rebels" in Nicaragua.[104]

God Bless America.

I'm running out of enemies. I'm down to Castro and Kim Il Sung.
—General Colin Powell, Chairman, Joint Chief of Staff

In 1987, political journalist and peace advocate Norman Cousins wrote *The Pathology of Power*, a chilling look at America's military kingdom. The preface, written by an unlikely source, Cold War architect and U.S. diplomat George F. Kennan, is candid in its evaluation of Washington's garrison state on the eve of the Soviet Union's collapse:

> Were the Soviet Union to sink tomorrow under the waters of the ocean, the American military–industrial complex would have to remain, substantially unchanged, until some other adversary could be invented. Anything else would be an unacceptable shock to the American economy.[105]

Invent an adversary, indeed—in fact, it was already well underway. Throughout the 1980s in Latin America, as Reagan carried out his covert wars in El Salvador, Nicaragua, Costa Rica, and Honduras, the comfortable old enemy "communism" faded seamlessly into the new kid on the block: "terrorism." Both were used as precepts for American action as well as to fuel fear and its subsequent byproduct—obedience—by the mainstream American media and therefore by the American public. The 1980s transition from enemy communism to enemy terrorism was also a mix of old and new school ideas: a lingering Cold War mentality merging with new themes and a new bogeyman who was somehow going to take down the mighty American juggernaut. "This is an eternal war against terrorism," railed Gore Vidal. "It's like a war against dandruff. There's no such thing as a war against terrorism. It's idiotic. These are slogans. These are lies. It's advertising, which is the only art form we ever invented and developed."[106]

The Reagan administration did not unveil an official or comprehensive "war on terror," but rather laid the strategy, foundation, and building blocks for the current "war on an abstract noun"—one that was implemented full bore by the cowboy buffoon, George W. Bush, and then carried on with sinister grace by Barack Obama, the white-coated waiter on the Pullman car of empire.

The Reagan administration also inspired the current notion of preemptive military action against countries or entities thought to be terrorist supporters or sympathizers, as evidenced by their strikes on Libya in 1986. "Terrorism has replaced Communism as the rationale for the militarization of the country," writes Howard Zinn, "for military adventures abroad, and for the suppression of civil liberties at home. It serves the same purpose, serving to create hysteria."[107]

It also served another purpose: the war on terror instigated the necessary groundswell for a massive resurgence and perpetual windfall for the Pentagon and their "'arms merchants'—an older, more honest term than today's 'defense contractor,'"[108] Lieutenant Colonel Astore reminds us.

Reagan's legacy remains one of great polarization—which side of the truth you're standing on determines one's view. If you're standing on the side that embraces "America: love it or leave it" and feel no remorse when American firepower, inspired by American Exceptionalism, slaughters in the name of American business, then Reagan is your guy. But if you look at the eight years of Ronald Reagan as the era when "the militarists were restored to full power,"[109] then Reagan's eight years were a crime against humanity. Mike Gravel, tossed out of the Senate during Reagan's sweeping victory, chronologically pegs the evolution from Reagan toward what Chris Hedges deems is now a time "We Americans speak to the world exclusively in the language of force."[110] Gravel writes:

> The victors in that reactionary triumph started with small probes:
> a landing on Grenada here, an invasion of Panama there, working

themselves up to a limited ground campaign in Iraq in 1991. By 2003—just twenty-three years later [from Reagan's election in 1980]—the resurgent militarists, with support from their courtiers in Congress and the press, felt bold enough for a Vietnam-sized invasion.

The old monster that I had tried to slay was back, more ferocious than ever.[111]

As the Soviet Union passed into history, leaving the U.S. as the sole remaining superpower, and with budget deficits soaring in the early 1990s, the defense industry went fishing for business overseas to help beef-up their bottom line and they were quite successful tapping into the wealth of countries like Saudi Arabia and Taiwan. Bubba Clinton's 90s experienced pockets of spending that kept the military contractors chugging along, including resumption of the Star Wars missile defense program, "helped along by the findings of the Rumsfeld Commission," writes William Hartung, "another classic exercise in threat exaggeration headed up by former Ford (and future George W. Bush) Secretary of Defense Donald Rumsfeld."[112]

But nothing—NOTHING—invigorated, re-energized, restored, re-animated, strengthened, delivered, or quickened the most recent meteoric rise of the Military-Industrial Intelligence Complex like nineteen crazed Kamikaze pilots slamming commercial jetliners into office buildings, the Pentagon, and a field in Pennsylvania. It was a classic case of blowback, the ugly boomerang consequences of American hubris and violence in the Middle East. It was what Ward Churchill was viciously vilified for defining as "On the Justice of Roosting Chickens," a nod to Malcolm X's 1963 speech "God's Judgment of White America (The Chickens Come Home to Roost)."

The truth hit American shores like a tidal wave, the rhetorical question reverberating, "Why do they hate us?" But you don't have to be a true detective to have seen blowback bristling in the wind, especially if one honestly surveys 20th century Western colonialism and treachery in the region. After decades of Western resource plunder, regime change, overt and covert intervention, and, of course, death, it was all topped off by Bush I's first Gulf Massacre, followed by the genocidal US/UK sanctions (ostensibly labeled UN sanctions) that directly killed or caused the murderous death of hundreds of thousands of Iraqi children while continuing to decimate the Iraqi population and infrastructure. In fact, the severe sanctions "caused more deaths," writes Noam Chomsky in *Failed States*, "than 'all the so-called weapons of mass destruction throughout history,' two hawkish military specialists estimate."[113]

Those are the facts. Not a polarized political point of view or skewed anti-American rant. Facts. Years of terror, years of wanton death. Did the neighborhood bully really believe that no one would ever swing back? Of course someone was going to swing back and they did, and Americans didn't like it. Not one bit. Terror is terror. Violence is violence. It's gruesome.

So Americans were scared shitless, they were ripe, and they were ready to accept and sign-off on anything… and the policymakers in Washington and throughout the Military-Industrial-Intelligence Complex knew it, rejoiced in it, and then acted upon it tooth and nail, hammer and tongs—and went for the kill. With the American corporate media in full war paint, beating the drums and cheerleading for lockstep consent, the American Empire invaded Afghanistan, and then Iraq, and they started killing people. Lots of them. The Crusades were back and this time in service to Manifest Destiny. And that's when…

The Flood Gates Burst Wide Open

In 2000, the reactionary hawks from the Reagan-Bush regime were back in power under the puppet presidency of the marionette from Crawford, Texas, and his handler, the real fixer, shoot 'em in the face Dick Cheney. Former Secretary of Defense (during the first Gulf Massacre) and former Chairman and CEO of Halliburton (parent company to Kellogg, Brand, and Root—the #1 recipient of Iraq War contracts at $39.5 billion), Richard Bruce Cheney was like a sixteen-year-old stud prancing around a whorehouse with a fistful of fifties. "Major weapons contractors," Hartung stresses, "hit the jackpot with the presidency of George W. Bush." Journalist Gareth Porter concurs:

> The 9/11 attacks were the biggest single boon to the militarist
> alliance. The Bush administration exploited the climate of fear
> to railroad the country into a war of aggression against Iraq. The
> underlying strategy, approved by the military leadership after 9/11,
> was to use Iraq as a base from which to wage a campaign of regime
> change in a long list of countries.[114]

But let's make it clear: the war on Iraq didn't just happen, thought up on the spot by some enterprising villains sipping martinis in exclusive D.C. clubs as a response to the 9/11 attacks. "Although the majority of Americans believe the 2003 attack on Iraq was a direct response to the 2001 Al Qaeda attack on the World Trade Center and the Pentagon," writes peace activist and physician Dr. Helen Caldicott, "in fact the Iraq war was in the planning stages at least eleven years earlier."[115]

In 1992, toward the end of Pappy Bush's presidency, a cadre of privileged white guys known as "defense intellectuals" (aka war pigs for cash) gathered as architects for something called "Project for the New American Century." The roster reads like a prosecutor's list of war criminals looming in Iraq and Afghanistan's future (if such a list ever materialized, but it won't). Wolfowitz, Perle, Feith, and Woolsey were the big fish. "They began to publish a series of letters in *The Weekly Standard*," Caldicott reports, "calling for another U.S. invasion of Iraq, as well as advocating support of Israel's campaign against the Palestinians and warning about the rising power of China."[116] Cheney, who was still Secretary of Defense, then tapped his underling Wolfowitz to pen a policy document that argued for a new invasion of Iraq so the U.S. would lock up "access to vital raw material, primarily Persian Gulf oil." It's also well known that in 1998, a PNAC contingent that included Wolfowitz, Perle, and then three more future war criminals—Bolton, Abrams, and Rumsfeld—lobbied Bill Clinton to remove Saddam Hussein from power.

Lest anyone still believes that the military mastodon and its subsequent wars are anything but corrupt economics, a slice of Richard Perle's story should eliminate all doubt. There's an "advisory committee" to the Department of Defense known as the "Defense Policy Board." Perle was the Board's chairman during the early years of Bush II and during the invasion of Iraq. He answered directly to Secretary of Defense Donald Rumsfeld. The individuals who sit on this board have major relationships with the top defense contractors. In fact, at the time, nine of the board members had, according to Dr. Caldicott, "significant affiliations with companies that collectively took 76 billion dollars in military contracts during the years 2001—2002."[117] And here's the beauty part: the American people have no access to this information.

During Perle's tenure, he was on the payroll of the infamous Goldman Sachs. His job? Advise and consult Goldman Sachs' clients regarding investment opportunities in postwar Iraq. Trireme was Perle's venture-capital corporation, which raised some $45 million to invest. Almost 50 percent came from MIC favorite son, Boeing. Perle was also on the board of Autonomy Corporation—a

British high-tech company that boasts massive contracts with the Department of Homeland Security, the NSA, and the Secret Service. Perle was the proud owner of 75,000 shares in a company charged with monitoring email correspondence and phone conversations in a so-called free society.

This kind of inside cronyism and collusion adds up to nothing less than coercive Black Hand tactics, an operation that can only be defined as an extortion racket. The operation in play here is eerily similar to any other violent and oppressive criminal syndicate. Call it what you want—Cosa Nostra, the mob, the Mafia, the Five Families, it's all the same: organized crime.

> *We will export death and violence to the four corners of the earth in defense*
> *of our great country.*
>> —George W. Bush (quoted by Bob Woodward in
>> his book *Bush at War* - 2003)

> *How does he do it? How do they do it?*
> *Uncanny and immutable*
> *This is such a happening tailpipe of a party*
> *Like sugar, the guests are so refined*
> *A confidence man, but why so beleaguered?*
> *He's not a leader, he's a Texas leaguer*
> *Swinging for the fence, got lucky with a strike*
> *Drilling for fear makes the job simple*
> *Born on third, thinks he got a triple*
> —Eddie Vedder, "Bu$hleaguer"

When Bush and Cheney completed the neocon coup of the American government in 2000, the PNAC group was waiting in the wings with their well-defined strategy for a never-ending and massive Persian Gulf military presence, one ready to strike "preemptively" at a moment's notice. "A 2000 PNAC report dolefully noted," explains Caldicott, "that 'the process of transformation, even if it brings revolutionary change, is likely to be a long one, *absent some catastrophic and catalyzing event.*'"[118] [Emphasis added]

You mean like "Remember the Alamo," "Remember the Maine," or the rant about Germans ruthlessly killing defenseless Americans on the Lusitania, or FDR's "a date which will live in infamy," or Lyndon Johnson's Gulf of Tonkin incident? Well, in 2001, they were handed "9-11." Indeed, the cold and calculated atrocities carried out by Osama bin Laden and Al-Qaeda provided the *"catastrophic and catalyzing event"* that the neocons were hoping for and dreaming about—it was just what the doctor ordered.

Speaking of doctors, one of your authors spent some time with Dr. Hunter S. Thompson out at Owl Farm in snow-covered Woody Creek, Colorado, and at other times on the telephone reading out loud, yelling out loud, and laughing out loud. Hunter was a man with many weapons; his best and most effective was a red IBM Selectric typewriter. He was a genius, a maniac, a sweet man, a bastard, but above all he was an author and journalist who could take you to parts simultaneously known and unknown, like "that place where the wave finally broke, and rolled back."

On 12 September 2001, one day after the day that shook America to its core, Thompson wrote an article that somehow, miraculously, appeared on the ESPN website. It's entitled "Fear & Loathing in America" and the commentary remains chilling in its psychic relevance:

> The towers are gone now, reduced to bloody rubble, along with all hopes for Peace in Our Time, in the United States or any other country. Make no mistake about it: We are At War now—with somebody—and we will stay At War with that mysterious Enemy for the rest of our lives.
>
> It will be a Religious War, a sort of Christian Jihad, fueled by religious hatred and led by merciless fanatics on both sides. It will be guerilla warfare on a global scale, with no front lines and no identifiable enemy.
>
> This is going to be a very expensive war, and Victory is not guaranteed—for anyone, and certainly not for anyone as baffled as George W. Bush. All he knows is that his father started the war a long time ago, and that he, the goofy child-President, has been chosen by Fate and the global Oil industry to finish it Now. He will declare a National Security Emergency and clamp down Hard on Everybody, no matter where they live or why. If the guilty won't hold up their hands and confess, he and the Generals will ferret them out by force.[119]

It started on 7 October 2001 as "the goofy child-President" launched Operation Enduring Freedom on the war-weary people of Afghanistan. It then dangerously escalated on 20 March 2003 as we witnessed Boy Bush's and Cheney's Nazi-like invasion, occupation, rape, and butchery of an already terrorized and annihilated country—Iraq.

The Gonzo journalist was right: "This is going to be a very expensive war." And that was the plan all along: allow the vast array of arms merchants, private defense contractors, private mercenary armies and military firms (like Blackwater, G4S, and Aegis), along with more than 2,000 private companies (like Booz Allen Hamilton) to filch your tax dollars on counterterrorism, intelligence, and the now well-entrenched Gestapo-like homeland security. Years after the initiation of PNAC, Bush and Cheney, along with their merchants of death, were making a killing—on death. On destruction. On pushing a somewhat successful "free" and constitution-driven republic toward a Draconian police state, both at home and abroad.

And the really sad part? The country was simply handed over to the militarists, who didn't even "have to pursue the hard sell," Lieutenant Colonel William Astore (Ret.) emphasizes, "not when war and preparations for it have become so permanently, inseparably intertwined with the American economy, foreign policy, and our nation's identity as a rugged land of 'warriors' and 'heroes.'"[120] Astore reminds us that when it comes to war and the economics of war—

> Some pay a high price. Many pay a little. A few gain a lot. Keep an eye on those few and you'll end up with a keener appreciation of what war is actually all about.

> No wonder our leaders tell us not to worry... just support those troops, go shopping, and keep waving that flag. If patriotism is famously the last refuge of the scoundrel, it's also the first recourse of those seeking to mobilize customers for the latest bloodletting exercise in combat as commerce.[121]

The build-up to the Iraq invasion centered on Washington's fairytale about big bad Saddam developing weapons of mass destruction, and if he wasn't wiped out immediately, together with Al-Qaeda, these maniacs were close to pulling the nuclear and biological triggers. Then Colin Powell got jiggy with it, putting on a (now infamous) high school level PowerPoint presentation at the United

Nations with photographs of ice cream trucks masquerading as mobile chemical labs, revealing a little vial filled with anthrax or Kryptonite or maybe both—and then the ex-general predicted the end of the world. Condoleezza Rice did her part with the lapdog media, sharing scary doomsday visions of "mushroom clouds" dotting the landscape. The play-acting worked as Americans bought these fantastic scenarios hook, line, and sinker. Europeans not so much, and for the most part they remained skeptical, and rightly so.

When the so-called weapons of mass destruction never materialized, the U.S. strategy changed in mid-sentence. The war quickly became about protecting the Iraqi people and delivering Santa Claus-like presents of democracy, freedom, and full voting rights. America was sharing its wealth and liberty. Jefferson gazed down on Baghdad from the clouds above and said it was so.

That's a beautiful bedtime story except that some journalists, like Greg Palast, got their hands on a one-hundred-page secret State Department document detailing the "Iraq Strategy" and U.S. plans for a "post-conflict" economy. Best of all, the document was written long before the Iraq invasion. "There's nothing in the 'Iraq Strategy' about democracy and voting," writes Palast, "but there's plenty of detail about creating a free-market Disneyland in Mesopotamia, with all state assets… sold off to corporate powers." The strategy made special mention of one asset: "especially those in the oil and supporting industries."[122]

When Bill Clinton left office in early 2001, the U.S. boasted a $230 billion dollar surplus (this was before the dastardly effects of Clinton's repeal of the Glass-Steagall Act took hold and greatly helped to demolish the U.S. economy). When Bush, Cheney, and their band of neocon operators left office in 2009, and with the MIC securely back in the saddle, U.S. taxpayers were left with a $1.3 trillion dollar deficit.[123] Mortgaging the future, and possibly bankrupting future generations, to build the obscene fortunes of the very few is not unlike organized crime running roughshod over a neighborhood Brooklyn business and then picking it clean like vultures on a carcass.

Clearly, the entire Middle East military operation, from start to finish, was a double barrel shotgun heist. First, the Military-Industrial Intelligence Complex raided the U.S. Treasury and made off with trillions, while at the same time setting their sights on the Middle East for further plunder through regional control and regime change: oil, corporate contracts, and of course, perpetual war—for perpetual war means perpetual gouging and uninterrupted profits.

New Math

When one digs into the actual budget numbers, it becomes clear how devastatingly destructive (pun intended) military spending is to the general welfare and health of a society. And when you dig deeper, even the economic experts have a hard time following the money in this labyrinthine shell game. For example, in 2015, the "official" Pentagon budget was approximately $495 billion (down from the "official" number the year before). In fact, war hawks railed at this paltry number and the supposed cuts, crying about the dire threat this so-called reduction in military funds would pose to U.S. security. (This was of course coupled with cries about bleeding heart wasteful spending on public services like education, nutrition, housing, Head Start, the environment, job training, and low-income assistance programs.)

But here's the rub: the $495 billion doesn't even come close to the actual military budget and dollars spent. The Department of Defense (along with the White House and Congress) employs their battery of master illusionists, armed with diversionary shells aplenty, to go to work on the U.S. Treasury and taxpayers' dollars. Immediately upon factoring in "mandatory spending" (military retirement and other DOD-only spending) and what's called "placeholder spending" or Overseas Contingency Operations (funding for American wars in Afghanistan and elsewhere), the DOD total jumps from $495 billion to $581.2 billion.

And we're just warming up. Now it's time to factor in what's determined to be "National Defense." This includes nuclear weapons activities, international FBI hijinks, Selective Service, and other "miscellaneous" defense-related proceedings. This category further includes something called "Opportunity, Growth and Security Initiative." Winslow Wheeler, the director of the Straus Military Reform Project, writes that this bucket of cash is "a slush fund if ever there was one."[124] So, for those of you keeping score, the subtotal after National Defense: $636.6 billion (with a "b").

Next we find a long list of direct costs that are never factored in to the military or national security budget. They include more military retirement costs, military health care costs, Veterans Affairs, international affairs, Homeland Security, and finally the whopping interest on the U.S. national debt. Let's see, add $82.7 billion, carry the six, and there you have it, the grand total is $1 trillion and 9 billion dollars.

Or $1,009,000,000,000.[125]

The number is basically incomprehensible. And that's for ONE year. Raed Jarrar is a policy coordinator for the American Friends Service Committee, a Quaker organization dedicated to fostering peace and justice everywhere. He acknowledges that we can all comprehend a million. But what about a billion? "Think about it this way: a million minutes ago [from February 2015] was March of 2013. A billion minutes ago was just after the time of Jesus."[126] But that's billions, chump change. What about this trillion number up above? "While a million seconds adds up to less than two weeks, a trillion seconds ago is almost 32,000 years to date. This is right around the time Neanderthals were discussing their national security (no offense to creationists)."[127]

War Whores

The subhead belongs to Nicholas von Hoffman and represents his stake-to-the-heart critique of American pseudo-journalism, especially war correspondents. The gritty journalist (about whom *Washington Post* publisher Katharine Graham once wrote: "My life would have been a lot simpler had Nicholas von Hoffman not appeared in the paper") argues that when it comes to television news, "anybody who's anybody has some sort of combat experience." CBS reporter Jim Axelrod, who was embedded with U.S. troops in Iraq, believes that, "anybody who is trying to make a career for one's self [knows] what war can mean."[128] Von Hoffman states the simple conclusion: "the oil companies and munitions makers are not the only ones who have a material interest in the shooting."

Turn on the networks or cable news outlets, or read print journalism. It doesn't take an extensive examination to see that the American mainstream media is enamored with the American military and their missions. Very few, if any, voices of dissent are sought out and offered as a counterbalance to the avalanche of White House and State Department officials, Pentagon spokesmen, military and intelligence analysts, and, of course, the never-ending parade of retired generals. Many, if not most, of these ex-generals profit handsomely off of America's ongoing wars, but corporate media outlets *never* reveal their economic ties. One shining example of this is retired four-star Army General Jack Keane. Speaking on Fox News in 2014, Keane was given the pulpit to preach:

> JACK KEANE: I do believe that the air campaign that's taking
> place in Iraq now will be expanded. But also we should expand

immediately into Syria. He [Obama] does not need congressional authorization for that. I'll leave it to him whether he thinks he should get that or not, but the fact of the matter from a military perspective, we should be bombing Syria and Iraq simultaneously now.

Critiquing this type of blatant cheerleading and propaganda model—this unpaid infomercial for the MIC—journalist Amy Goodman on *DemocracyNow!* revealed what any serious journalist would:

> AMY GOODMAN: That's retired General Jack Keane, speaking on Fox News Sunday. He is introduced simply as a think tank leader and a former military official. Again, what's not disclosed is the range of his affiliations with Pentagon contractors. Keane is a special adviser to Academi, the contractor formerly known as Blackwater, and a board member of the military contractor General Dynamics. He's also a venture partner to SCP Partners, an investment firm that works with military contractors. Keane's think tank has also provided data on ISIS used by The New York Times, the BBC, and other major outlets.[129]

Keane is the tip of the iceberg. As an example, between 2009 and 2011, during which 108 three- and four-star admirals and generals retired from the U.S. military, 70 percent grabbed lucrative jobs with defense contractors and defense consultants.[130]

Investigative hound dog journalist Jeremy Scahill, author of *Dirty Wars* and *Blackwater: The Rise of the World's Most Powerful Mercenary Army*, illustrates the absurdity of the American media's love affair with their military masters:

> ...on NBC News... Brian Williams, when he was announcing the new, latest, greatest threat [Syrian Khorasan Group]... had a graphic next to him that just said "the new enemy." We could just take a picture of that, and every year or so—apparently now it's going to be every two or three months—we can just have Brian Williams there with "the new threat." It could become an annual holiday in this country where we just celebrate whatever new war is going to give Lockheed Martin and Boeing and all these companies tremendous profits.[131]

We cannot underscore General Smedley Butler's iconic pronouncement enough: *war is a racket.* John Steinbeck knew it. As a war correspondent in the Second World War, the great American writer wrote:

> We were all part of the war effort. We went along with it, and not only that, we abetted it. Gradually it became a part of us that the truth about anything was automatically secret and that to trifle with it was to interfere with the war effort.[132]

The derogatory term "war whores" applies to many, but it has a special meaning for the United States Congress—the elected representatives of the People, the men and women charged with the general welfare of the People, the senators and congresspersons entrusted with the People's future. Except this sacred bond means absolutely nothing to these elected representatives. Congress is bought and sold with an ease that's astounding. For instance, in 2013 alone, defense contractors spread around $65 million on Capitol Hill to buy influence and ensure that decisions go their way. The big three, Boeing, Lockheed Martin, and United Technologies, stuffed the most payola in the legislators' pockets—$43 million.[133]

You work your ass off and pay a hefty tax debt to Uncle Sam. Then your representatives turn around and jettison huge amounts of your money into the Military-Industrial Intelligence Complex, which is used to build weapons and ordnance that kills and terrorizes people you don't know, people who have never done anything to harm you. In turn, the defense contractors amass fortunes, the Empire grows evermore brutal, and the Congress of the United States, the body responsible for representing your wellbeing when it comes to the rights of man, sells it all for 30 pieces of silver. "Capitalism breeds the venal perpetrators and rewards the most unscrupulous among them," declares Michael Parenti. "And they, in turn, do the system's dirty work."[134]

Survival

> *Jesse, you asked me if I was in the meth business or the money business. Neither. I'm in the empire business.*
>
> —Walter White to Jesse Pinkman, *Breaking Bad*

We note elsewhere and throughout this book series, the centrality of wealth accumulation to the machinations of empire. For global fortunes and the global consolidation of power and influence are the dual principles of empire. The ultimate goal is the cumulative effect of achieved domination. It's about achieving monopoly status or being "the" cartel of the planet.

In this chapter, we've literally only scratched the surface of the role played by the all-pervading military complex, this monster syndicate, this gang of thugs, that has tentacles that stretch every which way but loose. The perpetual war syndrome (or as the Army calls it: "the era of persistent warfare") has become like the air we breathe—omnipresent. The Executive acts as sheriff, judge, jury, and executioner. The CIA and Special Ops function in basic secrecy with little or no congressional oversight—a posse galloping out of Yuma with a never-ending bounty and the firepower to get it done. This "Permanent War State," writes Gareth Porter, is "a set of institutions with the authority to wage largely secret wars across a vast expanse of the globe for the indefinite future."[135] Former Congressman and presidential candidate, Dennis Kucinich, encapsulated this nasty cycle of perpetual war when offering some insight into Obama's war with ISIS:

> Nothing better illustrates the bankruptcy of the Obama administration's foreign policy than funding groups that turn on the U.S. again and again, a neo-con fueled cycle of profits for war makers and destruction of ever-shifting "enemies."[136]

American bases dot the planet like a thousand points of light. Drones crisscross the skies over the Middle East, Africa, and Asia as American presidents play video games with teenage pilots jerking their joysticks. Soon, these same drones might be strafing a town or city near you. The U.S. government and their crony defense partners sell weapons, and also utilize weapons as military aid, all over the globe. The weapons turn a lucrative profit for contractors, while securing submissive behavior on the part of America's client states. And all of it, when added together, expands the Empire's reach. The U.S. has also been very adept at arming despots and kooks, like Saddam Hussein and the Saudi Royal Family, as well as a host of other current and old school favorites. Let's also add to this roll call what some have dubbed the military-academic complex—colleges and universities who ingest government grants whole like a python ingests rats. These bright and ambitious scientists turn from work aimed at enhancing life on the planet to work that's dedicated to death and destruction. Defense contractors may build the killing machines, but they're conceived and developed by the best schools in the country. "Napalm," Sidney Lens points out just one example, "was developed at Harvard by a Harvard professor."[137]

Domestically, the economy of the United States would crumble without the military Goliath. In just the ten years from 1998 to 2008, the military budget doubled, and the national debt, well, you know how that's going. And as the U.S. moves into the third decade of this century, the hawkish and bellicose Trump administration—fueled by the likes of (former) Defense Secretary James "Mad Dog" Mattis—is (surprise, surprise) escalating military spending well beyond recent budgetary increases. The reason? A revitalized U.S. military strategy that centers on counterbalancing and potentially going to war with China and/or Russia.

"In the Middle Ages wars were fought by the military class exclusively," writes Lens, "the general population was virtually uninvolved." But this current military syndrome (there's really no other word for it) has engulfed and swallowed up American society. It's always been in the American DNA but now *it is* the American DNA. Religious-like zealotry embraces this martial takeover like Christ entering Jerusalem. The American press, the American sports world, the American corporate environment, the American branches of Christianity and Judaism, as well as the Hollywood myth machine—EVERYTHING & EVERYBODY welcomes the blood libation of war, and for what? This is why the truth-tellers looking to upset the apple cart, like Julian Assange, like Edward Snowden, and back in the day, Daniel Ellsberg, have been so vilified by the entirety of Murder Incorporated, including the Fourth Estate. "In times of turmoil the military always seems to be a good alternative. It presents the facade of order," Chris Hedges explains. "But order in the military, as the people of Egypt are now learning again, is akin to slavery. It is the order of a prison. And that is where [James] Clapper and his fellow generals and intelligence chiefs would like to place any citizen who dares to question their unimpeded right to turn us all into mindless recruits. They have the power to make their demented dreams a reality."[138]

In his book *Imperial Delusions: American Militarism and Endless War*, professor and author Carl Boggs writes:

> The United States has become the domain of virulent militarism in
> defense of an expanding Empire, the dynamic agency of a system
> of economic, political, and military domination without parallel in
> human history.[139]

Boggs gives us the necessary political dynamic. But the syndrome is also personal. Back in 1969, at the height of the Vietnam War, Nobel Prize-winning professor

George Wald made a much fêted and celebrated speech, making it crystal clear that the Pentagon "is corrupting the life of the whole country." Chris Hedges echoes Wald's spirit and delves into the perversion of the nation's soul:

> The U.S. military has won the ideological war. The nation sees human and social problems as military problems. To fight terrorists Americans have become terrorists. Peace is for the weak. War is for the strong. Hypermasculinity has triumphed over empathy. We Americans speak to the world exclusively in the language of force. And those who oversee our massive security and surveillance state seek to speak to us in the same demented language.[140]

But what have the militarists won? It seems to us, say it again, absolutely nothing.

> *Lost in a Roman wilderness of pain*
> *And all the children are insane...*
> *Desperately in need of some stranger's hand*
> *In a desperate land...*
> *This is the end, beautiful friend*
> —Jim Morrison

Chomsky called America's quest for global dominance "Hegemony or survival."

There it is: survival.

Lieutenant Colonel William Astore warns, "Just remember: in the grand bargain that is war, it's their product and their profit. And that's no bargain for America, or for that matter for the world."[141]

Survival.

Sidney Lens points out that, "Sanity is the application of intelligence to the need for survival." The militarists build to destroy. The sane people, instead, suggest survival. "The first step in that direction," Lens concludes, "is the dismantling of the military-industrial complex."[142]

Survival.

Bertrand Russell, the British philosopher and dedicated pacifist, studied the distant past of this planet, which enabled him to clearly identify the current nightmare, and then he gazed into the future and finally understood peace on Earth.

Our own planet, in which philosophers are apt to take a parochial and excessive interest, was once too hot to support life, and will in time be too cold. After ages during which the earth produced harmless trilobites and butterflies, evolution progressed to the point at which it generated Neros, Genghis Khans, and Hitlers. This, however, is a passing nightmare; in time the earth will become again incapable of supporting life, and peace will return.[143]

Survival.

5 The Big Muddy

Where to start? How about here? In the pain we both share.

> *We sacrifice our sons like Abraham*
> *on distant orders from unknowns on high,*
> *offerings from a media that maddens us*
> *inflames our passions*
> *and perverts our natural empathy*

Writing these lines calls to mind words Leonard Cohen wrote in 1968 about Isaac, the son of Abraham, in protest of the Vietnam War.

> You who build these altars now,
> to sacrifice these children,
> you must not do it anymore.
> A scheme is not a vision
> and you never have been tempted
> by a demon or a god.
> —"The Story of Isaac"

In the openly imperial 1850s, America's most famous naval officer, Commodore Matthew Perry, would, in a speech, explicate his view of Asia's future with a certainty that seems rare for either a military man or a politician:

> It requires no sage to predict events so strongly foreshadowed to
> us all: "still Westward will the course of empire take its way."…
> The people of America will, in some form or other extend their
> dominion and their power, until they shall have brought within

their mighty embrace the islands of the great Pacific, and placed the Saxon race upon the eastern shores of Asia.[1]

Vietnam: The Domino Theory

7 April 1954—Dwight Eisenhower explains the "falling domino" principle during a presidential news conference:

> You have a row of dominoes set-up, you knock over the first one, and what will happen to the last one is the certainty that it will go over very quickly. So you could have a beginning of a disintegration that would have the most profound influences... The possible consequences of the loss are just incalculable to the free world.

For Americans who lived in America during the '50s, '60s, and early 1970s, they heard, *ad infinitum*, that Vietnam could not be allowed to "fall" to the Communists, for by doing so it would create a "domino effect" whereby neighboring states would all fall in line, as Asia would become a red continent of Communism. The brightest minds in the land lobbed this theoretical hand-grenade into the minds of millions of Americans, sending primal fear to erupt from the limbic systems of the multitude. *"No! Not that! All of Asia will fall like dominoes—we cannot lose Asia!"*

(Forget for a moment that the U.S. never "owned" Asia, but that was the tenor of American news broadcasts for decades, sending intellectual and journalistic elites into a national dither.)

The politicians, fearing being seen as "weak" on Communism, began the long slog into Indochina to relieve the frustrated and bedraggled French—who had taken a beating by the Indochinese (later called Vietnamese) nationalists—at the Battle of Dien Bien Phu (8 May 1954). Initially, Washington sent military "advisers" to take up the white man's burden that fell from French shoulders after so ignominious a defeat at the hands of the Asian peasant fighters. Where the effete, faulty French had fallen, the beefy, well-muscled American Aryans would surely prevail. For were not Americans "the good guys?"

There is actually amazingly strong scholarly and psychological data supporting precisely this effect in American war planning. According to some psychologists practicing abnormal psychology, the apparent ease with which Americans could enter into a conflict with the harrowing dimensions of the Vietnam War could be reduced to two primary errors: 1) heuristics; and 2) groupthink.

By heuristics we mean mental shortcuts of thinking (i.e., an educated guess or common sense) that frame our ways of perceiving the world, sometimes unconsciously so. In the Vietnam context, it can be seen in the highest levels of American military and political planning, where any man (and in that age, it was surely all men) thought, *"Of course we can beat these little yellow men who eat rice and wear black pajamas. We're Americans! We eat beef!"* (It's what's for dinner!)

This sounds somewhat glib, of course, but it expresses, in a nutshell, the "common sense" that governed the initiation of the Vietnam War—for there was little serious question but that "we" could kick their little pansy asses with ease.

Groupthink refers to the manner with which small and insular groups come to conclusions that seem to make sense within the group, only because any real discussion or dissent is muted. This was especially so in the military-spy-government circles of the 1950s, where the mere mention of "communism" sent people into fits of rage. Because these thoughts permeated the highest levels of government thinkers, it allowed policy planners and other military people to escalate things fairly easily, despite serious counseling otherwise. *"Why certainly these no good gooks can't beat us. Don't worry, we just need more _____"* (and fill in the blank).

A Little Matter of History

Clearly, the Vietnam "conflict" was raging for some time before Washington rolled up its sleeves and got dirty in the late 1950s and early '60s. In fact, the long and tragic story of Vietnam begins well before Hollywood's history lesson— years before Sergeant Joker and Rafterman and centuries before "Charlie don't surf!" By the time America barrels into Southeast Asia, we find a country and a people whose narrative has been shaped and defined by the colonial adventures of distant imperial masters. In the beginning, a Chinese general by the name of Zhao Tuo conquers the monarchy of Au Lac, just south of China (what is now northern Vietnam) and names it "Nam Viet." For more than two thousand years, this chunk of southern Asia remained in a constant state of turmoil: a battle between independence and Chinese rule.

Americans, and before their arrival, Europeans, have had a hypnotic, fetishistic fascination with Asia—a culture that drew them forth, like bats out of hell, looting the old places, the cities of vast wealth that were old when Europe was young. The West may have originally come as explorers and merchants, centuries ago—but in recent history, more often than not, they are merchants of death.

By the dawn of the 20th century, the British, the Germans, the Russians, the Japanese, as well as the French all took their colonial drill bits to the people and lands of Vietnam, all attempting to carve out a fertile extension to their empires in Southeast Asia. France—continuing their long colonial intervention—went in hammer and tongs and seized Cambodia, Laos, and Vietnam and christened it "French Indochina," and then milked it for all the tin and tungsten, rice and rubber that it was worth.

Flash forward to World War II: the Japanese kick the French out, but then the Japanese lose the war, surrender, and of course the French want their colony back. But it's not going to be that easy because a very effective nationalist movement is underway, one spearheaded through a Vietnamese patriot by the name of Ho Chi Minh—tenacious in his pursuit of Vietnamese independence and rather adept at blending nationalism with Communism. During the war, Ho Chi Minh worked closely with the CIA's forerunner (the OSS) in a combined battle against Japanese occupation. He even helps to rescue downed American pilots. Then in the fall of '45, Ho Chi Minh proclaims the "Democratic Republic of Vietnam" independent.

A year later in 1946, communist leader Ho Chi Minh writes Harry Truman a series of letters looking for U.S. aid and assistance. He doesn't turn to the Soviet Union for help against his colonial oppressor, nor to the Chinese, but to the United States—the country with the best historic ideals and rhetoric when it comes to self-determination. Ho Chi Minh legalizes labor unions, establishes voting rights for men and women. He's attempting to mount a basic democracy within the confines of Marxist ideology. Ho Chi Minh is progressive compared to what the Vietnamese have known under French colonial rule.

Surely, the United States could see this.

By 1950, as part of Harry Truman's Containment Policy, Washington is financing more than 70 percent of France's war against Vietnamese independence. Also by 1950, China "has fallen" to the Communists—and Joe McCarthy is ready for his walk down Witch Hunt Road. Unfortunately, the writing is thick on the wall: despite convincing evidence that Vietnamese independence has no direct ties with the Soviet Union, and despite the fact that before his death in 1945, Franklin Delano Roosevelt opposed returning Vietnam to the French, and despite Ho Chi Minh's constructive advances to the United States, the drama of the Cold War foolishly links Vietnamese independence with the Kremlin's alleged drive to take over the world as well as with the dreaded Red Chinese menace.

Ultimately, it's a very bad read of history.

By 1954, the French are toast. They lost a total of 170,000 men—with the Vietnamese losing three times that number... and yet the Vietnamese fight on. General Giap's guerrilla tactics cripple the French, who are decisively defeated and finally laid to rest at Dien Bien Phu. Giap proclaims: *"Give me an army that's willing to die and I'll defeat any army that's willing to kill."*

Cease-fire. Then the Geneva Accords are signed in Switzerland in the spring of 1954. The Accords call for the temporary division of Vietnam into the north and the south, and then after a two-year cooling off period, internationally supervised elections are to take place to reunify Vietnam. All the major nations of the world sign with one notable exception: the United States. *Why you might ask?* Because the United States knows that if Jesus Christ climbed down off the cross and ran in that election, Ho Chi Minh beats him with his eyes closed. The Eisenhower Administration is scared shitless that Vietnam (like China) will fall to the communists. And as we've seen, Ike calls it the "Domino Theory," and then does the honorable thing *and ignores* the Geneva Accords, instead installing a puppet government—one headed by Ngo Dinh Diem, who's a militant Roman Catholic in a country overwhelmingly Buddhist. Lyndon Johnson dubs him the "Winston Churchill of Southeast Asia."

We swear we're not making this shit up.

By 1960, South Vietnamese insurgents rise up against Diem's repressive regime. These insurgents are both communists and non-communists—the so-called Vietcong or National Liberation Front. The rebellion prompts Washington to significantly build up its military and economic presence in South Vietnam. So by the time Ike leaves office, the United States has poured several billion dollars into Diem's regime and there's about a thousand American "advisors" *just hanging around.* Now, here comes Mr. Kennedy and the advisors start multiplying— and multiplying fast. In fact, they have a ringside seat when Buddhist monks, responding to Diem's tyrannical regime, immolate themselves on the streets of Saigon.

By 1963, Diem's regime is utterly pigheaded when it comes to reforms the Kennedy Administration is strongly trying to suggest. And by the fall of '63, Kennedy has increased American "advisors" to 16,000—with economic and military aid skyrocketing. Clearly, Diem and his corrupt regime are out of control. In October of 1963, Diem's own generals inform the Kennedy Administration that they're going to *remove* Diem from office. On 3 November, three weeks before JFK's fateful trip to Dallas, Diem and his brother are apprehended and slaughtered in the back of a truck. The Kennedy administration knew about this ahead of time and did nothing to stop it. That's called being complicit in the assassination of a foreign leader.

So it's pretty clear that by the time wheels were down on Love Field, 22 November, 1963, John Kennedy had taken the United States several giant steps deeper into what Pete Seeger called the "Big Muddy."

> *Waist deep in the Big Muddy*
> *The big fool says to push on*
> *Waist deep, neck deep*
> *Soon even a tall man will be over his head*
> *We're waist deep in the Big Muddy*

A Coup Is not a Tea Party

Placed in power over a majority Buddhist population, and at the helm of a country that did not exist until France and the U.S. created it—with the complicity of peace talks in Geneva that called for "partition" pending the results of a national election to determine its political future—Diem was never elected by the people he was ostensibly representing, rather his position was meant to forestall an actual election that President Ho Chi Minh would have won in overwhelming fashion. To defeat Vietnamese democracy—the ability of the Vietnamese to vote for whom they wanted—the U.S. nudged its puppets to disavow elections, for Diem knew he couldn't win an election with Vietnamese voters. (Not full and fair elections, in any event.) Fortunately, all he really needed were American votes—those in the White House and those in Langley… and the rest was disaster.

Diem, like many false princes, began to believe in the myth of his power, and, seeing the carnage committed by his erstwhile allies (the Americans), so despaired of their indiscriminate destruction and killing, that he and his brother, Ngo Dinh Nhu, began to call for significant troop withdrawals from what they foolishly thought was their country. Nhu granted interviews with the Washington news media to press his case. And when Diem began speaking publicly about "national sovereignty" and the will of his "government" to decide such things as troop levels and their behavior in-country, the boys from Langley and throughout Washington had enough.

In *Killing Hope*, William Blum provides a trenchant telling of what befell the Diem brothers after they tried to exercise some semblance of sovereignty against the Empire. Writes Blum:

> When popular resistance to Ngo Dinh Diem reached the level where he was more of a liability than an asset he was sacrificed. On 1 November 1963, some of Diem's generals overthrew him and then murdered both him and his brother after they had surrendered. The coup, wrote *Time* magazine, "was planned with the knowledge of Dean Rusk and Averell Harriman at the State Department, Robert S. McNamara and Roswell Gilpatrick at the Defense Department and the late Edward R. Murrow at the U.S. Information Agency."
>
> Evidently Washington had not planned on assassinations accompanying the coup, but as General Maxwell Taylor, President Kennedy's principal military adviser, has observed: "The execution of a coup is not like organizing a tea party; it's a very dangerous business. So I didn't think we had any right to be surprised... when Diem and his brother were murdered."[2]

"A coup is not a tea party." While that may be so, it begs the question, why a coup? Because Diem—a conservative Catholic in a country awash in Buddhist tradition, headed a regime that waged a vicious campaign of repression, torture, and antagonism against its own people—was hated by the South Vietnamese with rare Buddhist passion.

At the time of Diem's assassination, Buddhist monks set themselves aflame to the death in protest against his corrupt and violent puppet regime. Broad swaths of the population bitterly opposed the racist, brutal, and arrogant treatment they received from their U.S overlords (excuse us, "allies"). Diem, raised in a western European French-dominated matrix, narrow-minded, scornful of his peasantry, alienated from the deep veins of Buddhist culture, was yet a Vietnamese politician, who, acting in sync with such a role, had to try to mollify his outraged and terrified (not to mention terrorized!) population, who genuinely detested the presence of these foreign devils, who sowed the seeds of death with every step they took on Vietnamese land.

Do we really believe that the Americans gave a green light to a coup without knowing its probable end? Or that Kennedy's key advisors did so on their own motion—or that of the CIA? In the, quite literally, madness of the age, this was how things were done. (How things *are* done in the present age.) And in Diem's case, it is how it was done. He dared to bare his teeth to his imperial masters and the Empire consumed him along with his brother using *his own* generals (dig that!) to do the deed.

The Lucchese Crime Family could not have done it any better.

"What I don't know about, it won't hurt me"

L. Fletcher Prouty, a retired colonel (USAF), and former Chief of Operations for the Joint Chiefs of Staff during the Kennedy years (not to mention a clandestine CIA attaché for nearly a decade), offers us an aerial, multi-focused view regarding the build up of the Vietnam War that is both challenging and provocative. Challenging in that Prouty presents intriguing facts of U.S. governmental actions well before Vietnam, which can only give one pause; and certainly provocative in that Prouty places much of the blame for the Vietnam fiasco on a seldom-blamed source: the CIA.

Further, Prouty, while not specifically intending to deliver an in-depth, bird's eye view of the Vietnam debacle (as his primary subject was CIA complicity in the assassination of President John Kennedy), offers us tidbits too tempting to ignore. Here, as World War II was creaking to a close, he describes U.S. maneuvers to set the stage for the next big battle. (Or, as we hinted above: How many of you knew that the U.S. armed the core of the forces that would one day emerge as the Army of North Vietnam, under Ho Chi Minh?) Consider Prouty's account:

> The inconclusive Korean War had ground to a halt. The battleground of the Cold War was being moved from one region to another. As we mentioned earlier, more than one-half of all the military material once stockpiled on Kinawa for the planned invasion of Japan had been reloaded in September 1945 and transshipped to Haiphong, the port of Hanoi, Vietnam's capital. This stockpile had amounted to what the army called a 145,000 "man-pack" or supplies, that is, enough of everything required during combat to arm and supply that many men for war.
>
> Once in Haiphong Harbor, this enormous shipment of arms was transferred under the direction of Brig. Gen. Philip E. Gallagher, who was supporting the OSS, and his associate, Ho Chi Minh.

They had come from China to mop up the remnants of the defeated Japanese army. Ho's military commander Co. Vo Nguyen Giap, quickly moved this equipment into hiding for the day when it would be needed. By 1954, that time had come.[3]

Prouty's account reads like a deleted chapter from Joseph Heller's novel *Catch-22*—it's so discordant as to be disconcerting. Yet, as do many of his other assertions, it makes sense, if one considers the sinister nature of the Military-Industrial Complex. Moreover, Prouty's account is considerably buttressed by his presence at, or active participation in, many of the affairs he names or uncovers.

His essential abiding theme is that the nation's intelligence apparatus is running things, largely for the corporate sector, and that the political circles are a mere hindrance to the powerful elites that both support them and subvert them.

Indeed, Prouty argues on occasion that many political figures subvert themselves, by firmly placing their heads in the sand, the better not to know things. Prouty recounts a clipped discussion with a U.S. Senator that succinctly communicated his will not to know what was happening:

> One of the prominent members of the U.S. Senate, a member of that select group which is always informed of such CIA activities before they take place, told me one day when I had been sent to tell him about one of these operations, "Keep it short. *What I don't know about, it won't hurt me.*" I had learned that by "short" he meant, "Don't tell me anything." That was Senate "oversight" in the 1950s. The JCS [Joint Chiefs of Staff] felt much the same way and had limited their own participation in both the planning and operation of such activities as much as possible.[4]

Oversight? Hell, they didn't even have under-sight! Ever the politicians, they clamor for plausible deniability, erecting bulwarks of blindness, while Babylon falls. Vietnam, Prouty argues, was also an exercise in intelligence and military power designed by those in service to huge flows of capital: the defense industries. He quotes former President Eisenhower to showcase his plea against an escalation of Vietnam into the maddening conflagration it became:

> It was January 8, 1954. Dwight Eisenhower had been President of the United States for one year and was presiding over a meeting of the National Security Council with twenty-seven top-echelon

national security advisors in attendance. When the subject turned to U.S. objectives and courses of action with respect to Southeast Asia, the President—our foremost World War II military commander—said, as recorded at the time, "with vehemence":

> The key to winning this war is to get the Vietnamese to fight. There is just no sense in even talking about United States forces replacing the French in Indochina. If we do so, the Vietnamese could be expected to transfer their hatred of the French to us. I cannot tell you how bitterly opposed I am to such a course of action. This war in Indochina would absorb our troops by divisions![5]

Strong words from a man regarded as a strong leader, strengthened by his almost legendary military prowess. And yet, this is precisely what happened—inch-by-inch, man-by-man, aircraft-by-aircraft, division-by-division! Absorbed, sucked-in, eaten alive.

To be clear, much of the expansion occurred under the Kennedy administration, but it illustrates how presidents can be trapped into courses of action not under their control—or how they can be held captive by an unforeseen flood of events. This was particularly true in Vietnam, where one of the world's reigning superpowers unleashed Armageddon-like destruction on a largely agricultural, pre-industrial state—literally killing millions in an orgy of violence that would make Rome blush, and yet failed to bend them to their imperial will.

Albeit for a brief moment, Vietnam taught the world—even taught the Empire—that there were limits to great power, limits of will.

Yet, this was not, nor could it be, the only story of a complex, interwoven imperial project: the subjugation of Indochina to the will of the Empire—because empires work through many conduits of its multifaceted power. Principally, they use any road to reach ultimate objectives: means to a vile end. For while Prouty reports that U.S. forces armed the Indochinese core of the armed forces, the better to repel the impositions of the Japanese Empire, it did not shrink from its white allies: the French. Freelance journalist, historian, and ex-State Department official William Blum has written block-busting books regarding the efforts of empire via the global crimes of the CIA, and most notably about the tragedy of Vietnam. Blum recounts the discussions at the highest levels of the U.S. government in support of their faltering allies in the region. As we referred to in our short historical discourse above, Blum details the point regarding the road not taken:

> In 1945 and 1946, Vietminh [Vietnamese Independence League] leader Ho Chi Minh had written at least eight letters to President Truman and the State Department asking for America's help in winning Vietnamese Independence from the French. He wrote that world peace was being endangered by French efforts to reconquer Indochina and he requested that the "four powers" (U.S., USSR, China, and Great Britain) intervene in order to mediate a fair settlement and bring the Indochinese issue before the United Nations. (This was a remarkable repeat of history. In 1919, following the First World War, Ho Chi Minh had appealed to U.S. Secretary of State Robert Lansing for America's help in achieving basic civil liberties and an improvement in the living conditions for the colonial subjects of French Indochina. This plea, too, was ignored.)

> Despite the fact that Ho Chi Minh and his followers had worked closely with the American OSS during the recently ended world war, while the French authorities in Indochina had collaborated with the Japanese, the United States failed to answer any of the letters, did not reveal that it had received them, and eventually sided with the French. In 1950, part of the publicly stated rationale for the American position was that Ho Chi Minh was not really a "genuine nationalist" but rather a tool of "international communism," a conclusion that could be reached only by deliberately ignoring the totality of his life's work. He and the Vietminh had, in fact, been long-time admirers of the United States. He trusted the U.S. more than he did the Soviet Union and reportedly had a picture of George Washington and a copy of the American Declaration of Independence on his desk. According to a former OSS officer, Ho sought his advice on framing the Vietminh's own declaration of independence. The actual declaration of 1945 begins with the familiar "All men are created equal. They are endowed by their Creator with certain inalienable rights, among these are Life, Liberty, and the pursuit of Happiness."[6]

Both friend and foe? Sure, what the hell...

But, Jesus, what does that tell us about an empire that can arm both sides of a conflict? Probably this: being an empire means never having to say you're sorry. And the imperial forces, despite Eisenhower's apparent concern, proceeded to instill in the Vietminh a hatred of Americans that may have exceeded their hatred of the French; for while the French were doubtless brutal and cruel overlords, they didn't have the sheer power at their disposal that the Americans had. Indeed, France lasted as long as they did precisely because the Americans, in an effort to checkmate the Chinese, bankrolled their efforts. According to Blum, at the end of the French effort to beat the Indochinese back into submission, "direct American military aid to the French war effort ran to about a billion dollars a year." Blum adds, "By 1954, the authorized aid had reached the sum of $1.4 billion and constituted 78% of the French budget for the war."[7]

Whenever the French contemplated negotiating with the Vietminh, the Americans threatened to cut off aid, without which the French military effort would simply collapse. As it happened, negotiations—never seriously attempted—were ultimately unnecessary, for the Vietnamese nationalists routed the French at the valley battle of Dien Bien Phu, crushing their hopes to reestablish their Asian empire and strengthening their Indochinese colony.

Shadows and Fog

Intriguing and enticing times, to be sure, as the American-funded French were crumbling, their control of Indochina withering by the day. From the ironworks of the OSS, the newly minted Central Intelligence Agency was ramping up their operation throughout Southeast Asia. Washington saw communist shadows lurking everywhere, shadows from Moscow, shadows from Beijing. In 1954, the Cold War was red hot and the CIA recognized a glorious opportunity for expansion. Colonel Prouty describes a pivotal moment in the CIA's strategy for this corner of the world.

A meeting of the President's Special Committee on Indochina took place on 2 January 1954 ostensibly "to discuss what would be done to aid the French," and utilizing the findings of a report that "was premised on U.S. action short of the contribution of U.S. combat forces." Prouty recounts how CIA Director, Allen Dulles, suggests counterinsurgency specialist, Colonel Edward Geary Lansdale, whom Prouty refers to as an "unconventional-warfare officer," to be part of the American liaison to the French in Saigon. (This is the same Lansdale who dubiously distinguished himself with psyop tactics in the Philippines.) Prouty explains:

The start of a new phase of the OSS/CIA activity in Indochina, this step marked the beginning of the CIA's intervention into the affairs of the government of Indochina, which at that time was French. It was not long before the reins of government were wrested from the French by the Vietminh, after their victory at Dien Bien Phu under the leadership of our friend of OSS days, Ho Chi Minh.

With this action, the CIA established the Saigon Military Mission (SMM) in Vietnam. It was not often in Saigon. It was not military. It was CIA. Its mission was to work with the anti-Vietminh Indochinese and not to work with the French. With this background and these stipulations, this new CIA unit was not going to win the war for the French. As we learned the hard way later, it was not going to win the war for South Vietnam, either, or for the United States.[8]

The fuse was lit. After 1954, Washington's involvement in Southeast Asia went from military liaisons on the ground to the most massive aerial bombardment in human history.

Orange Is the New Black (Death)

When the Americans entered the war in earnest, they brought with it a political and military ferocity that the French simply couldn't muster. They bombed and trampled with complete impunity—not just Vietnamese territory, but neighboring states, like Laos, Cambodia, and beyond. They tortured people and then blamed it on the Vietminh forces. (And the media was hopelessly, shamefully complicit.) American forces cut off body parts, burned villages, threw thousands of people out of planes and helicopters (under the CIA-sponsored Phoenix program), subverted the local press, and blamed the removal of vast numbers of Vietnamese on the communists to stir anti-communist propaganda and to excite fears of the communist threat.

And that's the tip of the iceberg. In a hellish effort named "Operation Ranch Hand," which lasted from 1962 through 1971 (with the heaviest execution between '67 and '69), U.S. military forces unleashed millions of gallons of poisonous herbicides laced with the deadliest, most toxic agent known to man: dioxin. According to the American Cancer Society, these herbicides (plant-killing chemicals) were sprayed "on lands in Vietnam, Laos, and other nearby areas to remove forest cover, destroy crops, and clear vegetation from the perimeters of US bases."[9] They drenched the country with these poisons, agents so deadly that, to this day—decades after the war—areas of Vietnam, a subtropical region known for its lush vegetation since time immemorial, only grows a stunted pale memory of grass: white grass. Today, those pockets of Vietnam are clusters of cancer, neurological disease, liver disease, and abnormally high rates of birth defects.

Mostly dropped from a fleet of C-123 planes (but also sprayed from boats and trucks), the U.S. military doused U.S. servicemen and women as well as the indigenous population with a deadly phenoxy cocktail, a mixture of two chemicals: 2,4-dichlorophenoxyacetic acid and 2,4,5-trichlorophenoxyacetic acid. The chemical mixtures were shipped in large drums marked with identifying colored stripes. "The most widely used mixture," reports the American Cancer Society, "contained equal parts 2,4-D and 2,4,5-T. Because this herbicide came in drums with orange stripes, it was called Agent Orange."[10]

Few people have endured war such as this—and we haven't even introduced the bombing: campaigns that unmercifully pounded and pounded and then pounded again and again for what seemed like forever every square inch of what Lyndon Johnson termed that "damn little pissant country."[11]

Complete Madness

But Vietnam was far more than a quaint name from the other side of the world. It was a real place, with real people, who lived in a real nightmare because of U.S. policies and politics.

Since its beginning, and the aftermath, a plethora of books have emerged telling various sides of a story that continues to bedevil Americans as they try to come to grips with the unthinkable: U.S defeat at the hands of a third world state. One such tale is that of Claude A. Thomas, who, in *At Hell's Gate*, tells of the easy ways to enter war and almost impossible ways out. Thomas, like many young, impressionable boys, freely enlisted in the conflict, prepped by a lifetime of war movies, old men's tales, and the warrior spirit of sports:

> I ended up joining the military because I didn't know what else to
> do. My father suggested it, and he was my father. Even an absent
> father remains a powerful figure in a family's life, particularly in
> a son's. He and his friends who fought in the Second World War
> would all sit around and get drunk and tell stories that made war
> seem glamorous, exciting, and romantic. I not only listened to these
> stories, I drank them in, longing to be a part of them.

So I believed the stories, without question, listened to my father, without question, and joined the army. But one doesn't need to grow up with a father who is an ex-soldier to hear romantic and misleading stories about war. Popular culture produces endless movies that romanticize and glorify war. They almost never portray the reality of this experience.

And war, whether real or in the movies, is not the only place where a warrior mentality is cultivated. It is also nurtured though sports. I was very talented in all the sports that were offered in school: baseball, football, and wrestling. The only thing that kept me in school was my athletic ability. And in every sport and on every team, I found this warrior mentality. I developed a romantic vision of what competition, fighting, and battle were like. I envision war as just another game.

At the same time, I was extremely insecure, shy, withdrawn, and untrusting. I had the notion that if I went into the military, fought in a war, and received a lot of medals, I would come home a hero, and I would be loved, admired, and cared for. That is how the stories went. It would just happen like that, and I wouldn't have to think about anything. "Go into the military," my father said, "it will help make a man out of you." And becoming a man, I thought, would mean being respected and being loved.[12]

To say the least, although he won a chest full of medals, principally for his role as a helicopter M-60 gunner, he didn't find love upon his return. Quite the opposite. The war made him a killing machine: from the air he killed hundreds of Vietnamese people. Did he limit his killing to enemy soldiers?

Hardly.

The days merged into one, and he concentrated on his position as crew chief of a helicopter squad—and on survival. Nothing else mattered. Humiliated during basic training, he learned to shut down his feelings and get the job done. What was his job? Killing. And he was very, very adept at it. Here, he describes just one encounter:

[T]he unit that our company supported began to receive heavy automatic weapons fire from a village, so they radioed us and asked for help. We flew in with a heavy-fire team (three B-model Huey gunships with rockets and 7.62 mm machine guns, one with a 40mm cannon), opened fire, and without thought destroyed the entire village. We destroyed everything. The killing was complete madness. There was nothing there that was not the enemy. We killed everything that moved: men, women, children, water buffalo, dogs, chickens. Without any feeling, without any thought. Simply out of this madness. We destroyed buildings, trees, wagons, baskets, everything. All that remained when we were finished were dead bodies, fire, and smoke. It was all like a dream; it didn't feel real. Yet every act that I was committing was very real.

My job in Vietnam was to kill people. By the time I was first injured in combat (two or three months into my tour), I had already been directly responsible for the deaths of several *hundred* people. And today, each day, I can still see many of their faces.[13] [Emphasis added]

"War," said former Union General Ulysses S. Grant, "is hell." It was surely hell for those countless Vietnamese peasants who fell under the curtains of fire, napalm, bullets, bombs, and poisonous sprays. But, for those who unleashed those years of desolation and destruction, hell was a boomerang. For, although more than 58,000 American military personnel lost their lives in the war, another 100,000 plus veterans of that war have committed suicide. At least half of America's homeless are Vietnam veterans. And countless thousands of marriages have ended in divorce, because men who have been taught to hate, to kill, and to entomb their human feelings could not be fully human, or intimate to those who were closest to them: wives, children, families.

As for Thomas, he wandered through an empty life of drunkenness, drugs, and jail, until a humane counselor exposed him to the teachings of Zen Buddhism. Today, he is a Soto Zen Monk, trying to balance his life and those of others from a foundation of peace and mindfulness. But for thousands of his brethren, really children (he joined the military at seventeen, straight from high school), the war never allowed them to truly come back home—in mind or in soul.

Journalist and scholar Chris Hedges, a long-time foreign correspondent for *The New York Times*, wrote a gripping series of essays on the worship of war that lies deep in the American soul. In *War Is a Force That Gives Us Meaning,* Hedges recounts his own addiction to war (as a journalist) and how the media often sells glorious lies to hide the horrors of war. He interviewed a veteran who revealed the other side of coming out of the war, in ways broken and not whole:

> John Wheeler, who graduated from West Point in 1966, went
> to Vietnam, where he watched his class take the highest number
> of dead and wounded of all the classes that fought there. "I was a
> witness to Vietnam," he told me. "I spent half my life in a helicopter
> traveling around the country. I was a witness to the decimation of
> my West Point class. And I knew we were decimated for a lie." He
> left the army as a captain in 1971, went to Yale Law School, and
> became an activist. He was the driving force behind the Vietnam
> Veterans Memorial wall in Washington. "When I left law school
> the full impact of the lies hit me," he said. "I have been thinking
> about those lies, meditating on them and acting on them ever since.
> The honor system at West Point failed grotesquely within the chain
> of command. The most senior officers went along with [Defense
> Secretary Robert S.] McNamara and [U.S. Pres. Lyndon B.] Johnson
> and were guilty. It was an abomination. If in order to do your duty
> as an Admiral or a General you have to lie, West Point should tell
> the new plebes."[14]

We have heard the recollections of several veterans of the Vietnam War. But their voices, no matter how harrowing, should not be central to our inquiry. For the Vietnamese people in their entirety, north and south, are the central players in this grotesque tragedy, one driven by imperial vanity. They bore the brunt of the Empire's rage (and insanity). They formed the resistance to imperial invasion. They suffered the mega-trauma of imperial war at the hands of the greatest military machine in the world since the Nazi *Wehrmacht*, or the legions of Rome.

It may seem that we are mingling diverse subjects in treating north and south somewhat indistinguishably, but, in point of fact, this mingling happened over a century ago, by the French imperial forces and later, by the U.S. Army—which operated on what one journalist described as the military acronym "MGR"—for "mere gook rule," the racist, imperial reductionism of all Vietnamese people as "mere gooks," and thus unworthy of human consideration or compassion.

Award-winning journalist, Nick Turse, in his recent work *Kill Anything That Moves,* takes that largely untrodden path as he writes a blistering and stunningly powerful account of the raw, ugly, and terrifying truth of what the Vietnam War really was: an imperial, racist, monstrous, and genocidal war against a semi-feudal, pre-industrial, agricultural small state—one that was simply seeking independence from French colonial domination.

Turse, initially utilizing government records from long-unexamined U.S. government war crime files, embarked on a journey to learn what Vietnamese peasants (primarily of the South) experienced under the U.S. and its puppet governments during wartime. Turse went to Vietnam and, with interpreters, listened to the accounts of the beleaguered survivors of U.S. military and allied atrocities and massacres. He talked to Vietnam veterans. He combed through government files and court martial records. In Turse's work, he privileges those voices largely absent in the plethora of American books on Vietnam: those of the Vietnamese peasants who saw death falling from the skies; those mangled, mutilated, napalmed, dismembered many, who withstood the mightiest onslaught this earth has ever felt—the American Empire's "technowar."

The accounts are terrifying and numbing at the same time: so ugly, so awful, and yet so commonplace, so everyday, that it is quite difficult to process the vast range of imperial violence visited upon the Vietnamese people—and to imagine how they found the will to continue to resist.

It began innocently enough, when a young graduate student researching post-traumatic stress disorder among Vietnam vets at the U.S. National Archives was asked by a fellow researcher the question, "Could witnessing war crimes cause post-traumatic stress?" Turse, then in grad school, couldn't believe his ears. "War crimes? What is he talking about?" Within the hour, he had in his hands hundreds of pages of yellowing documents, some faded by time. They were the filings of the War Crimes Working Group, a chilling record of allegations of U.S. Army massacres, rapes, murders, torture, mutilations, and bone-chilling atrocities—all of which were substantiated by army investigators. But the files were only a doorway—a portal into a world that was then a nightmarish reality of war for hundreds of thousands of U.S. Army, Navy, and Air Force personnel—and more importantly, to Vietnamese women and men of all ages, and suckling babes at their mothers' breasts. It mattered little whether they were combatants or non-combatants. It didn't even matter if they were loyal to the North, or card-carrying supporters of the puppet regime in the south. It didn't matter whether they were Christian or Buddhist. What mattered was if they were gooks or not. If so, the U.S. Army was there to push them out of existence. And this they did with astonishing ferocity and efficiency.

In the files, American soldiers were outspoken and blunt about their actions. That is the face of the war that Americans rarely see either in news accounts, in novels, or in movies. Most Americans, influenced by the mass media popular accounts of the 15 March 1968 "My Lai Massacre" were appalled (and rightfully so) at what they saw—the bodies, the death. But in the context of what was transpiring away from the cameras and brave reporting of journalists like Seymour Hersh (who broke the My Lai story), this massacre was, in fact, nothing special at all, given the ugly reality of other massacres that dwarfed the sensationalized, popular reports of occurrences like My Lai.

Indeed, Turse's reportage reveals that the infamous My Lai massacre served to obscure other, more monstrous massacres—and because the corporate media positioned the event (which, by the way, was itself quite skewed and muted as to its violence and destruction) as an exception, other atrocities never saw the light of day. There was even a meaner, more sinister effect of My Lai's episodic coverage: savvy veterans and their commanders learned to downplay atrocities, so as not to cause the My Lai syndrome. Turse writes:

> Sometimes there were even too many civilian corpses, leading to a different sort of statistical manipulation: body-count deflation. After the My Lai massacre, the American Division claimed only 128 enemy dead, when in actuality more than 500 civilians had been slaughtered. At nearby My Khe, American troops massacred from 60-155 civilians, according to U.S. sources, but a body count of only 38 was reported to headquarters. Similarly, at the village of Truong Khanh, where 63 civilians were massacred, only 13 of those bodies were counted as enemy KIAs due to combat action by ground troops, with another 18 reported as having been killed by subsequent air strikes. And when Marines massacred 16 unarmed women and children at Son Thang, they were reported as a body count of 6 enemy kills.[15]

One must wonder, how was this done? And what was the thinking behind such practices? Turse explains:

Soldiers realized that small groups of civilians could be killed with impunity and logged as enemy dead, but larger numbers might raise red flags if there were no U.S. casualties or few weapons captured. To avoid uncomfortable questions about skewed kills-to-weapons ratios, many patrols planted grenades, rifles, or other arms on dead civilians as a matter of standard operating procedure. They obtained these from weapons caches they discovered, or by taking arms from prisoners or enemy dead carrying more than one weapon, or sometimes even by repurposing U.S. weapons as enemy material. As one Marine explained, "When civilians got killed, no problem, just stick a chicom [Chinese communist] grenade on 'em or an AK[-47 assault rifle], they became VC."[16]

This was made possible by the long-standing American practice of using dehumanizing racial slurs against people of color, with the term "gook" coming into popular military and home usage during the Vietnam War to describe the Vietnamese (and later, anyone Asian). Somewhat surprisingly, the term is actually of long and deep vintage amongst military, with a wider spread of usage than initially assumed. Turse notes:

> The deeply ingrained racism that helped turn the Vietnamese countryside into a charnel house was summed up in a single word: the ubiquitous "gook." That epithet evidently entered the military vocabulary in an earlier conflict, the eerily similar campaign in the Philippines at the turn of the twentieth century, where American troops began calling the indigenous enemies "goo-goos." The pejorative term then seems to have transmuted into "gook" and was applied over the decades to radically dissimilar enemies in Haiti, Nicaragua, and Korea before returning into Southeast Asia.[17]

One can discern a good deal about people by their use of humor, for as the old adage states, "within a joke, the truth often hides." Consider the following joke among American GIs in Vietnam: "What you do is, you load all the friendlies [South Vietnamese] onto ships and take them out to the South China Sea. Then you bomb the country flat. *Then you sink the ships.*" Funny... The Greek tragedian Euripides once wrote: "Authority is never without hate." Was this a mere joke? Or was it guys being guys? The history of American involvement in Vietnam was many things, but a joke it wasn't. As we shall see, it was one of the most massive exercises in organized murder that the world has ever seen.

Turse's work assures us that we will never look at the Vietnam War as a "mistake" again. It was as we have suggested: murder on a rare human scale, meant to humiliate, humble, destroy, destabilize, and finally demonstrate U.S. superiority over the Asian peasant nation of Vietnam. They destroyed aplenty, turning the verdant hills, forests, and rural hamlets of Vietnam into a macabre moonscape of mega-death.

But, in the aftermath, the empire was humbled; not the nation of peasants. Not since the great Haitian Revolution of 1801—when a peasant-army of slaves beat *several* imperial armies to achieve independence—has the world seen what Vietnam accomplished. But in order to get there, the Asian country had to swim through the seas of blood and slosh through the valley of death to overcome.

It was neither easy, nor preordained.

"I said one...two...three...
And he was hitting the baby with the [rifle] butt!"

Let us not mince words about villagers versus guerillas, for the essence of guerrilla war is for the theoretically weaker side to avoid engagement in great battles where the militarily more equipped group can overwhelm a poorly armed foe. It is, as the saying goes, the "war of the flea." This frustrating hit-and-run tactic destabilized and harassed U.S. forces to the point where they both considered and treated villagers (who were, for the most part, like peasants since antiquity, not involved in either side of the battles) as enemies. It was in such a state of mind that American forces developed strategies that were designed to harass, overwhelm, and ultimately, transfer peasants away from their ancestral lands—something hellishly difficult for Asian families to conceive of, let alone even contemplate doing. To be transferred, or more accurately, forcibly relocated, meant leaving the graves of ones ancestors. This was complete anathema to the Vietnamese people. Turse describes how the Americans tried to resolve the issue—by making the richest agricultural region in the country, the Mekong Delta, a hell from which the peasants were forced to flee:

> In 1964, an American officer remarked, "we must terrorize the villagers even more, so they see that their real self-interest lies with us. We've got to start bombing and strafing the villages that aren't friendly to the Government." One reporter recalled an army captain in a heavily populated Mekong Delta province sweeping his hand

across a couple dozen hamlets on a map and remarking that refugees were streaming out of the area. The reporter asked why. "Because it's not healthy out there," the captain replied. "We're shelling the hell out of them."[18]

Let us pause for a moment, if only to ponder these words, for the regnant narrative offered by both the U.S. government and a cooperative, supportive press is that the United States went to Vietnam to "help" the suffering benighted Asian masses. Here, in the voice of a ranking officer of the invaders, we find a truth common to all invading armies throughout the bloody tableau of history, paraphrased thusly: "We came to terrorize the people of this country, *for their own benefit!*"

Because the rhetoric justifying the war was only an obfuscation to cloud an imperial imposition of a corrupt, alien, puppet regime designed to repress popular will for Vietnamese reunification, the Americans unleashed a perfect horror against both those who opposed these puppets and those who were loyal supporters as well. Turse writes of American attributes vis-à-vis loyal or disloyal Vietnamese and that it didn't affect their armed behavior toward them:

> They regarded most of the province [of Guang Ngai, in the country's northeast] as hostile, and hostile was how they acted in return. But "friendly" enclaves weren't necessarily spared. In July 1965, for example, after the revolutionary forces overran a government outpost in the majority Catholic village of Ba Gia, U.S. and South Vietnamese group troops entered the village—now a nightmare landscape of shattered stucco and torn-apart bamboo homes—the guerrillas had long since withdrawn. A reporter watched as four local residents carrying a pallet with a wounded man "stared banefully at American advisers accompanying the Vietnamese marines." When asked about the number of innocents killed, the villagers bitterly replied: "many." Afterward, a U.S. officer prophetically remarked, "there will be many more civilians killed that way as time goes on."[19]

It is relatively easy to speak in generalities, in how malevolent, or vicious, the sophisticated Americans were to this community of predominantly agricultural peasants, devoted more to their crops than to any ideology, either pro or con. But such discussion gets us nowhere. It doesn't tell anything definitive about one of the most ruinous wars of an especially brutal century. For that reason, please allow us to cite extensively from Turse's text, to provide some deep and definitive flavor of the waging of the war, against whom and by whom. Here, we turn to an account, which made its way into the popular press, via the magazine *Esquire* by reporter Norman Poirier. It was published in August 1969, some three years after the events described, also after the My Lai Massacre became ubiquitous news. Turse writes:

> On September 23, 1966, Poirier related, a unit of Marines descended on Xuan Ngoc hamlet and began their rampage by breaking into the home of sixty-one-year-old Nguyen Luu, a rice farmer and carpenter. They punched, kicked, and slashed the unarmed man, while a Marine yelled "veee-ceee" at him. The intruders tore up his civilian ID card and wrecked his home. As Luu's young nieces screamed in terror, his nearly seventy-year-old wife was manhandled and his sister mercilessly kicked.
>
> Soon after, the door to Nguyen Truc's home burst open. His wife bolted for their five children, but the Marines grabbed her and shoved her out the door. The thirty-eight-year-old rice farmer was then beaten until he could no longer stand. Next, two Marines grabbed him by the legs and held him upside down while another delivered a devastating kick to his face. Shrieks and sobs filled the air.
>
> The screams reached the home of sixteen-year-old Nguyen Thi Mai, who took shelter in the cellar with her mother and aunt. As the three cowered in the basement, the Marines peered in and motioned for them to come out. The two older women obeyed, but Mai froze in fear. A hand reached in, grabbed her leg, and yanked her out. The Marines tore up the women's civilian ID cards. Then one of the Americans grabbed Mai around the neck and clapped a hand over her mouth. Two others grabbed her legs, threw her to the ground, and roughly tore off her pants.
>
> Busting into five or six homes in similar fashion, the Marines terrorized the hamlet without finding any weapons or contraband, or even a single piece of information about the enemy. Then they smashed into the home of eighteen-year-old Bui Thi Huong and

her twenty-year-old husband, Dao Quang Thinh, a farmer too ill to serve in the army. Their three-year-old son also lived in the hut, as did Thinh's mother, his sister, and her five-year-old daughter. The Marines accused Thinh of being a VC and beat him nearly unconscious, then propped him up against the front of his home next to his terrified sister and mother and the two young children.

Huong was dragged to the side of the house. A Marine held his hand over her mouth; others pinned her arms and legs to the ground. They tore off her pants, ripped open her shirt, and groped her. Then the gang rape began. First one Marine. Then another. Five in all. Huong's sobs elicited more screams of protest from her husband, so the Marines began beating him again, after which a burst of gunfire silenced him. Her mother-in-law's sobs ended after another staccato burst, and her sister-in-law's after a third. Soon Huong could no longer hear the children. Then came a crack and a blinding flash, followed by searing pain that brought her to the ground.

The Marines exploded a grenade to make the scene "look good," then radioed in their results: three dead VC. But back at the command post, they told their lieutenant that the shootings had not taken place at the prearranged ambush site and that some civilians were accidentally killed. The officer had the men bring him to the hamlet and saw the carnage himself.

Though he was shocked by the killings, the lieutenant formulated a plan to cover up the crimes. Thinh's body was dragged to the originally planned ambush site, half a mile away, and the Marines faked a firefight there. They also doctored up the massacre site in Xuan Ngoc. When they lifted the naked, blood-streaked body of Thinh's five-year-old-niece, the child cried out. Somehow the girl had survived the shooting, but Private First Class John Potter saw to it that this time she wouldn't live. He told the other Marines to count, and kept time "mashing up and down with his rifle," according to a fellow unit member. Another recalled, "I said one... two...three... And he was hitting the baby with the [rifle] butt!"[20]

This was the especially horrific face of the American invaders that would have vanished into the ether had the young woman, Bui Thi Huong, not, incredibly, survived the attack, having been rendered unconscious by the gunshot wound. When she told her story of what the nine Americans did in her village, the U.S. military justice system went into action, but after the machine stopped turning, three men were acquitted, and four others received short jail terms.

No one story can encapsulate the decade of death delivered to the Vietnamese people by the Americans. But this tale of Xuan Ngoc hamlet tells us much about how the Americans regarded the everyday people of the land. They were the proverbial "Other." Non-white. Buddhists. Speaking a strange tongue. Possibly, Viet Cong. VC. *Gooks.* "Ya know, not like us." Not human. American army veteran Haywood Kirkland said as much in an interview excerpted in Turse's work:

> As soon as [you] hit boot camp… they tried to change your total personality… Right away they told us not to call them Vietnamese. Call everybody gooks, dinks. They told us when you go over to Vietnam, you gonna be face to face with Charlie, the Viet Cong. They were like animals, or something other than human… They wouldn't allow you to talk about them as if they were people. They told us that they're not to be treated with any type of mercy… That's what they engraved into you. That killer instinct.[21]

Of mindsets such as these, warriors are made, and wars are waged, and atrocities are born. Another veteran told Turse that his basic training left him with unmistakable certainty, when it came to the "enemy." It was, he said, "anything with slant eyes who lives in the village. It doesn't make any difference if it's a woman or child."

(First, notice he said any*thing*—not anyone.)

This came down from top to bottom, and was hardly a grunt's perspective alone. Turse cites an officer for the following insight: "So a few women and children get killed… Teach 'em a damned good lesson. They're all VC or at least helping them… You can't convert them, only kill them."[22]

One must wonder. Convert them to what? Christianity? Capitalism? Whiteness? Round-eyeness?

Mindsets like this made Xuan Ngoc, My Lai, and tens of thousands of other massacres all but inevitable. For it was bred into the American bones by a rigid, conservative, and fearful education, one designed to raise an unquestioning military class able to do their masters' bidding without question or qualm. It did not begin in Vietnam, but has a long, savage pedigree birthed at the advent of the American founding. But for those many young men and boys who took this tour into Hades, the doorway was surely basic training, an exercise in unmitigated brutality and madness that turns humans into human-killers. Claude AnShin Thomas' account of basic was a journey of humiliation, hatred, and despair:

> We would have a barracks inspection: the company XO (executive officer, or assistant commander) would come in with white gloves, and if there was the slightest bit of dust anywhere, he would be propelled into a tirade, screaming obscenities at the top of his lungs. He would knock over wall lockers and our bunks, randomly dump footlockers on the floor and scatter the contents around the barracks. When he was finished he would give us twenty minutes to be ready for reinspection.
>
> For no clear reason we would have to scrub the shower room floor with a toothbrush, or dry shave (without water or lubrication). We would be called out by a drunken drill sergeant at two in the morning with orders to stand formation in the freezing rain in our underwear, with our boots fully laced, our collar brass in one hand and our belt buckle in the other hand, all highly shined. The emotional, psychological, and spiritual cruelty of all this made no sense. What I didn't grasp then was that basic training was really about breaking me down. Breaking me down and building me up in the image that they wanted. I was resistant to this, so I had a very difficult time.[23]

But Thomas' account isn't remarkable for guys who experienced basic. The military establishment must go considerably further to render these men good military material. Thomas recalls what finally made him fit in with the managers and maniacs of massacre who made Southeast Asia an infernal necropolis:

> During basic training I was taught to hate. On the firing range we were shooting at targets that resembled people. We were learning to kill *human beings*. We had to be taught how to do that—that is the work of the military. This work is done in a variety of subtle and not-so-subtle ways. When we were done on the firing range, we were supposed to stack our weapons in a particular way. One day, as

I was preparing to place my rifle on the stack, I dropped it. The drill instructor, a sergeant first class, screamed and cursed that I wasn't looking after my rifle properly, that my rifle was the most important thing in my life, because whether I lived or died depended on it.

This guy was six feet three inches to my five feet eight and a half. He stood in front of me, his chest jammed up against my face, stabbing me with his finger and screaming obscenities down at me. Then he pulled out his penis and urinated on me, in front of everyone.

I wasn't allowed to wash for two days. I felt shame at such a deep level. I couldn't begin to handle it. Instead, all I felt was rage. I couldn't act it out on him because I would have gone to jail. So I focused my rage on *the enemy*. The enemy was everyone unlike me, everyone who was not an American soldier. This conditioning is an essential ingredient in the creation of a good soldier. Soldiers are trained to see anything other as dangerous, threatening, and potentially deadly. You dehumanize the enemy. You dehumanize yourself. My military training ultimately taught me to dehumanize a whole race of people. There was no distinction between the Vietcong, the regular Vietnamese army, and the Vietnamese general population.[24]

Humiliation. Hatred. Rage. All bubbled in the cauldron of consciousness and found that the only way out—the only place where relief lived—was in turning that energy outward, against the "Other." Basic training was essentially a process of nothing less than brainwashing, to push Thomas outside of himself and his normal frame of reference, into a being who would obey orders, think as he was told to think—or better yet, not think at all. To become a military robot.

Ours is not to question why; Ours is but to do or die.

From our dysfunctional families, often fathered by men who have themselves been formed and marred by the traumas of wars past, to the barbarous "training" inculcated into youths really too young to seriously question, immersed in a culture of celluloid glory, all the way to the horrors of a My Lai, there is an endless daisy-chain of repression, brutality, and meanness that runs like water down a gulley. For the malevolence of war makes men send ribbons of terror downwards, from presidents to generals, from generals to colonels to captains, from captains to sergeants, from sergeants to privates, and from privates to peasants.

This waterfall of woe sends a vibration of dehumanization further downward, by men trained to not feel, so that the lowest level soldier is able to enact countless atrocities upon those powerless and unarmed beneath him. The more brutal, the greater the body count, and the greater the opportunity for promotion and career advancement. Thus, privates became squad leaders, then sergeants, then lieutenants, then captains and commissioned officers, and the cycle of repression carries on. Brutalized men become man-like machines of others, who pass on their rage to those who are unable to resist them.

Vietnam was a dishonorable example of that principle, where the biggest bully on the block rained liquid fire, bombs, poisons, and mass destruction on millions of the poorest people on the planet, essentially because they refused to bow to the Emperor, and his satrap, the puppet that the U.S. installed on his throne of skulls.

"Creating a Nation" aka "A Fool's Errand"

We have intimated, and even suggested, that the entity history now records as South Vietnam did not exist as a nation, until that is, it was in the interests of foreigners to breathe life into its own creation. The "State of Vietnam" has endured for centuries—centuries continuously marked by invasions and imperial interventions. Yet, the south was not separate from the north—until the French and the Americans wanted to create a puppet state with which it could exploit, colonize, and steal the labor of the peasantry. The French were motivated by sheer colonialism; the Americans by the grand strategy of the so-called Cold War (well, cold for *some*, eh?).

L. Fletcher Prouty, from whom we learned that initially cautious quote from President Eisenhower (that if Americans entered the French-Vietnamese war, Vietnamese hatred of the French would transfer to the Americans), notes the history of that region:

> It must be added here that one of the great weaknesses in the approach to South Vietnam taken by the United States in those early days was an oversight that continues to this day. It has been the failure to recognize that the piece of real estate historically known as Cochin China but that we call South Vietnam was not, and never has been, a sovereign nation-state. It has never truly governed itself, despite the fact that Indochina has a history of thousands of years. This significant failure of perception made all attempts at "Vietnamization," while the Democratic Republic of

Vietnam to the north was held by Ho Chi Minh, little more than words. A new country was being created and being asked to fight a major war, both at the same time. That was impossible, as we learned too late.

At the time of Eisenhower's comment, the indeterminate region of "South" Vietnam was under French military control, and the French army was at war with Ho Chi Minh and his "Vietminh" government. During that period and under those conditions, there was no way that the Vietnamese of the south, without a government, without leadership, and without an army, could have fought for their independence against the Democratic Government of Vietnam, which we ourselves had armed so well after World War II.[25]

Seen from this light, in retrospect, notwithstanding the immense cost in treasure, lives lost, massive environmental and social destruction, the Vietnam War was clearly a fool's errand. And the tragedy: it didn't need to be this way. It began in the madhouse of American politics, where corporate parties leveraged for position as the greatest patriot. Where the "great game," trying to best the Soviets, was the ultimate prize.

The fiasco that was to be the Vietnam War was birthed in the fevered dens of the CIA, and the State Department, as evinced by the words of John Foster Dulles (then Secretary of State) in the aftermath of the Vietminh's triumph over the French at Dien Bien Phu. Before the ashes cooled, the CIA came under its Saigon Military Mission, presumably to carry out Dulles's view: "We could carry on effective guerrilla operations [in Vietnam]… and we can raise hell."[26]

And that is precisely what the CIA proceeded to do: "raise hell."

Then came the intervention of the interlopers of international law. At a conference in Geneva, ground rules were constructed, ostensibly to allow peaceful reunification of the two communities into one, sovereign nation. The conference was supposedly designed to create the conditions for a peaceful settlement between the former French territories, but behind the diplomatic shadow-game, the world's first superpower was angling for its own interests—which had little to do with the Vietnamese people (or international law, for that matter). Prouty describes the efforts of the CIA to frustrate and contravene such international accords:

Before the conclusion of the Geneva Conference, in the summer of 1954, the CIA's SMM [Saigon Military Mission] had begun its political, psychological, and terrorist activities against the native population in the northern regions. Using a well-equipped cadre of saboteurs, it performed many terrorist acts in Hanoi and surrounding Tonkin. SMM agents polluted petroleum supplies, bombed the post offices, wrote and distributed millions of anti-Vietminh leaflets, printed and distributed counterfeit money.

As was intended, these clandestine activities played right into the hands of the war makers by creating a growing rift between the Vietminh and the Tonkinese Catholics. No blame was laid upon the SMM until later, when SMM-trained Vietnamese turned themselves in to the Vietminh.[27]

Prouty cites the infamous Pentagon Papers released by Daniel Ellsberg in which files are found detailing the actual SMM mission: "unconventional warfare." This process of attacks on people, property, and infrastructure was designed to guarantee that no real peace would ever be made between the two divided sections of Vietnam—unless on American terms. Prouty further details the significance of SMM activity in another, quite amazing aspect. SMM, Prouty writes, "produced one of the most amazing, unusual, and important war-making events" of the 20th century. Prouty continues:

[T]he mass exodus of more than one million Tonkinese natives, presumably Catholics, who were caused to leave their ancestral homeland and pour into the disorganized, strange, and inhospitable southland of Cochin China... Without a doubt, this mass of Catholic northerners and its unwelcome impact upon the population of the south had more to do with the scope, severity, and duration of the American-made war in Vietnam than anything else. It was an astounding event, for many reasons. First of all, how was such an enormous movement of otherwise immobile people brought about, and how were so many motivated to move that far from their ancient ancestral homes, land, and villages? Had they been scared to death? And how was everything kept so secret? Most news sources and historical reviews have either avoided or neglected these subjects.

At the time this exodus began in mid-1954, the State of Vietnam as a government was all but nonexistent. Yet it had been placed in charge of all the real estate south of the 17th parallel and of its ancient, settled, and peaceful population, variously estimated at from 10 to 12 million.

There can be no denying the fact that the influx of these hundreds of thousands of strangers on the already war weary (from World War II under the Japanese, from the French battle to retake Cochin China, and from the nine years of war against the Vietminh) southern population pushed them both to the breaking point. They were not the victims of a civil war in the classic sense so much as they found themselves in a situation analogous to that of the American Indians, where hundreds of thousands of Europeans invaded their North American homeland and decided that they would take it over for themselves. With the Catholic Ngo Dinh Diem in power, these intruders actually thought they had that right.[28]

This vast undertaking, done with the support of the U.S. Navy, the CIA's planes, and other support, was what Prouty called "genocide by transfer," for this psychologically stunned and terrified population was expelled to a site where conflict was virtually guaranteed, and moreover, where their very real needs for survival would come under tremendous pressures. In an ancestral-centric culture, when strangers or foreigners enter a community, they are seen as interlopers, and conflict, in such instances, is inevitable. And without doubt, the CIA's SMM stoked those fears with their "psyops," and intended to populate the south with a critical mass of people who would be loyal to Diem—and thus good soldiers for this government.

CIA legend and spookmaster, Edward Lansdale, sent his clandestine team into action for, among other things, the following missions:

  • Encouraged the migration of Vietnamese from the North to the South through "an extremely intensive, well-coordinated, and in terms of its objective, very successful...psychological warfare operation. Propaganda slogans and leaflets appealed to the devout Catholics with such themes as 'Christ has gone to the South' and the 'Virgin Mary has departed from the North.'"

- Distributed other bogus leaflets, supposedly put out by the Vietminh, to instill trepidation in the minds of people in the North about how life would be under Communist rule. The following day, refugee registration to move South tripled. (The exodus of Vietnamese to the South during the "regrouping" period that followed the Geneva Accords was often cited by American officials in the 1960s, as well as earlier, as proof of the fact that the people did not want to live under communism—"they voted with their feet" was the catchphrase.) Still other "Vietminh" leaflets were aimed at discouraging people in the South from returning to the North.[29]

The long and short of it? The United States, one of then two superpowers on earth, spent untold treasure and exterminated millions of people, moving heaven, earth, and hell to create a nation-state to its liking—and failed.

Napalm Sticks to Kids

Rare are the wars where the winner suffers greater loss of life than the loser, but such was the war in Vietnam.

It is interesting to note that this phenomenon, that of undercounting (or not counting at all) the losses of nonwhite, post-colonial people, is not limited either to Vietnam or the period of its war. For here, during the opening years of the 21st century, decades after the carnage that was Vietnam, neither the Iraq nor Afghanistan wars have yielded casualties figures in which anyone can place any confidence. That is not to say "we" do not know how many Americans have perished there. We are able to recite, virtually to the exact number, such war dead. Yet we cannot, despite its recentness, cite with any degree of specificity, the numbers of dead Iraqis, nor Afghanis. Perhaps these features, like the wisdom of the wars themselves, per George W. Bush, Barack Obama, and the Orange Dumpster Fire, are best left to history.

Yet they must be stated. Nick Turse, citing various sources from the 1960s to the present, comes to an estimate of roughly three million Vietnamese dead: one million plus soldiers, and two million plus civilians. One estimate he cites is upwards to 3.8 million Vietnamese war dead, according to a 2008 Health Metrics and Evaluation Study conducted by the University of Washington. Even this, he argues, may prove an underestimation. It illustrates, unflinchingly, what the American people in arms are capable of, against bogeymen who today are its most treasured trading partners (we speak here of China, then called Red China, and seen as the *bête noir* behind Vietnamese intransigence).

Millions gone. Up in smoke.

We can only look back with a kind of anguished awe. What if the Geneva Conference had been allowed to act without interference? History (and the associated tragedy) may have been radically different, for, as William Blum writes:

> The Geneva Conference, on 20 July, 1954, put a formal end to the War in Vietnam. The United States was alone in refusing to sign the Final Declaration, purely because it was peeved at the negotiated settlement, which precluded any further military effort to defeat the Vietminh. There has been ample indication of American displeasure with the whole process well before the end of the conference. Two weeks earlier, for example, President Eisenhower had declared at a news conference: "I will not be a party to any treaty that makes anybody a slave; now that is all there is to it." But the U.S. did issue a "unilateral declaration" in which it agreed to "refrain from the threat of the use of force to disturb" the accords.[30]

We have seen, have we not, how good the word of the Americans were on signed agreements? Within days of the American "declaration," Lansdale's SMM was wrecking havoc on the parties to the accord.

Decades before, in the Philippines, American soldiers sang "The Water Cure," a disturbing ode to water boarding. This begs the question: what did American soldiers sing during the time of the Vietnam War? Here is the marching cadence song of the 1st Cavalry Division:

> *We shoot the sick, the young, the lame,*
> *We do our best to kill and maim,*
> *Because the kills count all the same,*
> *Napalm sticks to kids.*
>
> *Ox cart rolling down the road,*
> *Peasants with a heavy load,*
> *They're all VC when the bombs explode,*
> *Napalm sticks to kids.*[31]

It is said that music soothes the savage beast. Well, not always. Every national entity calls war by names of its own choosing. Although American journalists, politicians, and historians call it the "Vietnam War," it's actually referred to in the Democratic People's Republic of Vietnam as something else. There, they call it the "American War."

And there, in the lyrics of young American soldiers on the march, is the war, encapsulated.

All together now: *"Napalm sticks to kids!"*

Photo: Nick Ut, Associated Press

❖ ❖ ❖

6 East Timor: Empire's Playground
Or Kissinger Strikes Again

Genocide. Slaughter. Massacres. Butchering.

Call it what you want.

Violent death is not a stranger to the people of East Timor, an island nation about 400 miles north of Australia, separated only by the Timor Sea. The Indonesian archipelago (a massive collection of 17,500+ islands) surrounds the Democratic Republic of Timor-Leste like a giant umbrella, appearing ready to overwhelm and swallow it whole. In fact, when you study a map of the region, East Timor looks out of place, trapped by the scattering blows and upheavals of continental shifts. But when the dark and brutal human history of this mountainous and tropical paradise is laid bare, it becomes all too clear that other powerful forces have also been at work on this place—external forces likewise attempting to engulf and swallow it whole. The veiled genocide and subsequent massacres that have taken place in East Timor were the direct result of its unfortunate history under the thumb of European colonization and it was sordid political chess games that helped initiate the infamous and murderous 1975 invasion by Suharto and his Indonesian forces—an invasion fully sanctioned by Australia as well as by Gerald Ford, Henry Kissinger, and the United States of America.

A Linear Timeline of Colonization

The story remains the same, especially when it comes to the colonization and conquest by European powers over native peoples, usually living peacefully in their ancestral homelands. It's as if history begins—or is allowed to begin—when

European contact occurs. Such is the case of the Timorese: a simple fishing and agrarian population living in their own Eden for some 42,000 years[1] before "resource and behavior management" by a distant civilization took over the operation.

Prior to European traders arriving in the early part of the 16th century, Timor was centered on the Java and Celebes trading route. Indian and Chinese merchants traded gold, silver, porcelain, and other goods for sandalwood—the island's most popular offering. By 1515, the Portuguese wanted a piece of the lucrative sandalwood trade and decided to set up shop. By 1561, the Dominican Order of Preachers hit the shores to preach the gospel of Jesus Christ and, of course, to civilize the heathens. In fact this same group of friars, nuns, and lay people were influential actors in the Portuguese colonial empire throughout Asia. By the early 1600s, the Dutch were also muscling in on the action and Timorese traders were more than obliging, trading beeswax and slaves along with their prized sandalwood. It wasn't long before the Europeans introduced flintlock rifles into the mix and the weapons quickly became the most desired object for trade.[2]

Christian conversion of the Timorese people pushed the European presence deep into the countryside and throughout the agrarian interior. "Pacification" campaigns executed on the Timorese people ensured the European stranglehold. In 1749, the larger overall island of Timor was split following a battle between the two European powers with Portugal taking the eastern half and the Dutch claiming the western half of the island, as well as dominating the surrounding Indonesian archipelago over the next three centuries.[3]

The Portuguese occupation of East Timor (which lasted nearly four centuries), like all occupations, resulted in brutality for the indigenous population, followed by the raping of the host country's resources for foreign profit. Whether it's Rome, London, Lisbon, Madrid, or Washington, the story of colonialism and empire remains devastatingly similar. As the 20th century opened, Portugal's economy was in the shitter, forcing the powers in charge to begin hauling out more and more material goods from their colonies everywhere. This desperate action by the occupiers prompted rebellions by the occupied, which is exactly what happened in East Timor between 1910 and 1912. To quell the "natives," Portugal imported troops from their other colonies and crushed an uprising by the Timorese, killing thousands.[4]

During World War II, as the Pacific theatre heated up, the Japanese invaded both ends of the island in February of 1942 and fought pitch battles against Allied forces comprised of Australians, British, as well as troops from Netherlands East Indies. Portugal remained neutral but the East Timorese and European colonials fought side-by-side with the Allies. But the Japanese Empire prevailed and remained in control of the island until their surrender in 1945. Estimates vary, but somewhere between 50,000 and 70,000 East Timorese were killed during this new imperial invasion and occupation by the Japanese[5]—an occupation highlighted by labor at gunpoint, starvation, rape, and outright execution.[6]

Once the Japanese withdrew, the Portuguese reestablished their colonial control over East Timor and began rebuilding the war-devastated country, "often employing the same brutal methods and forced labor they'd used before the war."[7] The Portuguese also put the pedal to the metal when it came to Timorese civilian control by making good use of the Catholic Church and their innate ability to spread pro-Portuguese propaganda in their education and worship models aimed at soothing any Timorese tension with their colonial masters.[8] Portugal's colonial rule was well entrenched.

> *East Timor, under the Portuguese, seemed to sit still in history. The clock of development didn't tick there.*
>
> —José Ramos-Horta (former president of East Timor and Nobel Peace Prize winner)

Indonesia Revisited: A Thorn in the Side

Born in 1901, Kusno Sosrodihardjo was more commonly known as Sukarno—the first president of Indonesia. Prior to his presidency, Sukarno was an Indonesian nationalist who battled Dutch colonialism for years and, in return for his rebellion, spent time in jail and in exile until he worked closely with the Japanese during their World War II occupation. Tap dancing through the muck and mire of changing colonial powers as well as fledgling independence movements, Sukarno operated first as a cipher-like leader, and then later, upon acquiring real power, embraced autocratic rule. From the mid-1950s until the early-60s, Sukarno instituted what was called "guided democracy"—a system that attempted to blend various movements (and pacify such factions as: nationalists/the army, religionists/Islamic fundamentalists, and communists) through debate, dialogue, and compromise. How do you think that worked out?

Exactly. It was an ongoing shit show. Bedlam defined his despotic presidency—spiraling inflation, regional insurrections, numerous assassination attempts on Sukarno's life, crisis after constitutional crisis, parliaments disbanded, newfangled parliaments reconstituted, as well as ongoing internal battles and chess games with the Indonesian military. And all of this was constantly intermingled with his unstable personal life and wealthy hedonistic excesses. Clearly, stabilization of Indonesia was near impossible with a splintered country and its citizens existing in a constant state of turmoil. And yet, in spite of this political and social turmoil, Indonesia made impressive gains in healthcare, education, and cultural growth—a testament to the Indonesian people's desire for a better, more autonomous life.

Add to this mélange the intrigue of distant Cold War gamesmanship and we have a recipe for disaster. After Sukarno visited the Peoples Republic of China in the 1950s and came away duly impressed, both the United States and Soviet Union began to court the Indonesian leader like a prized date for the prom—both superpowers intent on keeping Indonesia in their own spheres. In 1956, the Eisenhower administration invited Sukarno to address Congress. Shortly thereafter, the Soviet Union wined and dined Sukarno on vodka and Beluga caviar fresh from the Caspian Sea. The Russians were on a roll. Nikita Khrushchev showed up in Jakarta to present Sukarno with the Lenin Peace Price. Clearly, the Soviets were desperate to win his favor as other historic recipients included Paul Robeson, W.E.B. Du Bois, and Indira Gandhi—individuals whose achievements greatly outshine Sukarno's modest advancements. The attention was working because as the 1960s unfolded, Sukarno embraced a great deal of Soviet Bloc military aid. But, not to be outdone, and with fears that Indonesia might be slipping further "to the left," U.S. presidents Eisenhower (and then Kennedy) increased American military aid to Sukarno. Then, as a way to politically atone for the CIA's involvement in the failed Permesta rebellion against Sukarno in 1958, the U.S. invited Sukarno to Washington and Kennedy floated millions his way for the Indonesian military as well as economic aid.

"Go to hell with your aid!"

As the sixties rocked forward and with Lyndon Johnson in the White House about a year, Sukarno must have been gorging himself on Wheaties and giant cans of Popeye's spinach as he famously told the United States to "Go to hell with your aid"[9]—aid that amounted to more than a billion dollars over the previous fifteen years.[10] In fact, Sukarno's growing distrust of the West, coupled with the West's increased political pressure on Indonesia (especially with the neighboring war in Vietnam adding to Cold War imperial angst in the region), spelled trouble for the man Indonesians called "Bung Karno." He then began directing his slings and arrows at Moscow as well. And then, to top it off, Indonesia withdrew from the United Nations primarily because of the UN's support of Malaysia, which Sukarno viewed as "an imperialist plot of encirclement."[11] Sukarno was clearly embracing political nationalism over his country's economic realities. But throughout this tornado, Sukarno remained a popular leader, and was often called the "Great Leader of the Revolution" for his battles against imperialism and capitalism.[12]

The downfall came quickly as Sukarno continued to align his support with (and threw his political capital behind) the Indonesian Communist Party—the PKI, which closely mirrored his own standard Marxist beliefs. At the time, the PKI was one of the largest communist parties in the world and Sukarno approved the creation and discharge of an independent Indonesian armed force consisting of peasants and workers. Suffice it to say, the military—especially the right-wing leaders—were not overjoyed with this development. By mid-1965 there was little doubt that Sukarno had become a true thorn in the side of not only western colonial powers but also the generals and the military in his own country. The writing for his demise was clearly on the wall.

Genocide: Part One

"A complex series of events," explains former U.S. State Department official, William Blum, "involving a supposed coup attempt, a counter-coup, and perhaps a counter-counter-coup, with American fingerprints apparent at various points, resulted in the ouster from power of Sukarno and his replacement by a military coup led by General Suharto."[13] The leaders of this power grab, along with their leader Suharto, pointed the finger at the PKI, charging the communists with being behind the original purported coup and the murder of six military officers. Blum continues, "[They] used the incident to incite violence and hatred that ended up in a slaughter of Indonesians suspected of or being communists as well as Indonesians of Chinese descent as Communist China was also charged with being behind the coup attempt."[14] It didn't stop there as Blum reports that, "Anti-Communist organizations and individuals, particularly Muslims, were encouraged to join in the slaying of anyone suspected of being a PKI sympathizer."[15]

Twenty years younger than Sukarno, Suharto fully understood that the first president of Indonesia still enjoyed significant support within the military as well as with the general public. The campaign to usurp the presidency and the power from Sukarno, as well as the bloodbath that accompanied this right-wing military coup, carried well into 1966. Suharto slowly stripped Sukarno of power while simultaneously gutting the country of any possible resistance. Blum concludes:

> The massacre that began immediately—of Communists, Communist sympathizers, suspected Communists, suspected Communist sympathizers, and none of the above—was called by the New York Times "one of the most savage mass slayings of modern political history." The estimates of the number killed in the course of a few years begin at half a million and go above a million.[16]

Some were calling it "the silent slaughter." Almost three months passed—along with hundreds of thousands of Indonesian bodies—before the American press reported on the slaughter (read: genocide). In her book, *Indonesia 1965: The Second Greatest Crime of the Century,* author Deirdre Griswold writes:

> October, November, and half of December passed before any story of the mass slaughter taking place in Indonesia broke in the American press… Was this because the U.S. press didn't have the story earlier? That is inconceivable. An event of earth-shaking importance had taken place with the right-wing coup. Even a cub reporter would understand how significant such a political turn was for the fortunes of the U.S. in Asia. The Viet Nam War was going on just across the South China Sea. Hundreds of reporters were stationed there from every major news agency. Did the new regime exclude foreign reporters? If so, there was never a word about it printed in any newspaper. It can only be assumed that the U.S. press, as well as Washington, were intimately aware of the reign of terror, but were keeping mum. When, after three months, the awful toll was finally brought out, it was with an air of a fait accompli. Hundreds of thousands had already been killed. It was too late to stop it.[17]

Finally, a month before *The New York Times* covered the story, *Time* magazine reported on the carnage. As Griswold sets up:

> [*Time*], which usually judges the virtue of governments by the number of communist scalps dangling from their belts, nevertheless

objectively reported on December 17, 1965, that: "Communists, red sympathizers and their families are being massacred by the thousands. Backlands army units are reported to have executed thousands of Communists after interrogation in remote jails. Armed with wide-bladed knives called 'parangs,' Moslem bands crept at night into the homes of Communists, killing entire families and burying the bodies in shallow graves. The murder campaign became so brazen in parts of rural East Java, that Moslem bands placed the heads of victims on poles and paraded them through villages. The killings have been on such a scale that the disposal of the corpses has created a serious sanitation problem in East Java and Northern Sumatra where the humid air bears the reek of decaying flesh. Travelers from these areas tell of small rivers and streams that have been literally clogged with bodies. River transportation has at places been seriously impeded."[18]

Decades later, reports were uncovered showing how the American embassy "had compiled lists of 'Communist' operatives, from top echelons down to village cadres, as many as 5,000 names, and turned them over to the Indonesian army, which then hunted those persons down and killed them."[19] The U.S. diplomats also kept score on a checklist of who had been killed or taken prisoner. One diplomat reported: "It really was a big help to the army. They probably killed a lot of people, and I probably have a lot of blood on my hands, but that's not all bad."[20] In fact the complicity of the American government in this genocidal rampage is well documented.[21] For instance, Blum reports that longtime CIA and State Department official Roger Hilsman wrote in 1963:

> [O]ne-third of the Indonesian general staff had had some sort of training from Americans and almost half of the officer corps. As a result of both the civic program and the training program, the American and Indonesian military had come to know each other rather well. Bonds of personal respect and even affection existed.[22]

Ain't that sweet? In fact, inside reports like this were also backed up by the House Committee on Foreign Affairs as well as from the American paper of record, *The New York Times*, reporting that the Central Intelligence Agency was "so successful at infiltrating the top of the Indonesian government and army that the United States was reluctant to disrupt CIA covering operations by withdrawing aid and information programs in 1964 and 1965. What was presented officially in Washington as toleration of President Sukarno's insults and provocations was in much larger measure a desire to keep the CIA fronts in business as long as possible."[23]

Fairness and Accuracy in Reporting (FAIR) released a report in 1990 entitled "The Year of Dangerous Reporting: Indonesia Bloodbath, New York Times Whitewash." In the report, FAIR cites the States News Service and reporter Kathy Kadane reporting that the U.S. government had "abetted the massacre of thousands of Indonesians in 1965-66." The report goes on to disclose: "In the massacre, directed by the Indonesian military in an effort to eliminate the Indonesian Communist Party and its perceived sympathizers among the ethnic Chinese minority, an estimated 250,000 to 1 million people died." Of course, *The Times*—even after running Kadane's story, as did the *Washington Post, Boston Globe,* and *Chicago Tribune* (among others)—attempted to discredit her detailed reporting. In fact, the puppet-masters in the White House and the Pentagon as well as out in Langley must have been working overtime on their newspaper cronies because it didn't stop with their classic "kill the messenger" routine. The revered *Times*-ownership family member, C.L. Sulzberger, offered his patty-cake take on the bloodbath, writing, "Almost everyone is pleased by the changes being wrought" (8 April 1966). In fact, *The Times* editorial staff kicked things off a few days before, writing that the Indonesian military was "rightly playing its part with utmost caution" (5 April 1966). FAIR concluded in scathing fashion:

> But perhaps the most enthusiastic of all the Times' writers was Max Frankel, then Washington correspondent, now executive editor (1990). "U.S. Is Heartened by Red Setback in Indonesia Coup," one Frankel dispatch was tagged (October 11, 1965). "The Johnson administration believes that a dramatic new opportunity has developed both for anti-Communist Indonesians and for United States policies" in Indonesia, Frankel wrote. "Officials… believe the army will cripple and perhaps destroy the Communists as a significant political force."
>
> After the scale of the massacre began to be apparent, Frankel was even more enthusiastic. Under the headline "Elated U.S. Officials Looking to New Aid to Jakarta's Economy" (March 13, 1966), Frankel reported that "the Johnson administration found it difficult

today to hide its delight with the news from Indonesia…" Frankel went on to describe the leader of the massacre, Gen. Suharto, as "an efficient and effective military commander."

The American press, led by the impeccable imperial apologist and nonpareil establishment scribe James Reston of the nation's "newspaper of record," infamously described the imperial ransacking and U.S.-backed murder binge with Suharto in Indonesia as a "gleam of light in Asia."[24] *Time* wasn't far behind Reston's poetic gibberish with their own cheerleading when the magazine described the bloodbath and subsequent takeover as "The West's best news for years in Asia."[25]

And just so they don't feel left out, here are a few more pom-pom waving shout-outs from other media cheerleaders:

- *The Economist* described Suharto as "at heart benign."[26]

- Once again, *The New York Times*—this time referring to Suharto's regime as "Indonesian moderates."[27]

- The *World Policy Journal* embraced the "stability" that Suharto offered the region.[28]

- And finally, in 1987, after all the shit had already hit the fan, *The Christian Science Monitor* defined Suharto as a "moderate leader."[29]

"Elated… Heartened… Benign… Moderate… Stable… Gleam of light… Best news." *Jesus be praised, genocide sounds so damn, well, healthy!*

Of course, who better to deliver another nail in the coffin of U.S. collusion with the Indonesian slaughter than the Secretary of Defense at the time, Robert McNamara, who knew a thing or two about eliminating Asians in cold-blooded murder. Here's a snippet from his Senate testimony:

SENATOR SPARKMAN:
At a time when Indonesia was kicking up pretty badly—when we were getting a lot of criticism for continuing military aid—at that time we could not say what that military aid was for. Is it secret any more?

MCNAMARA:
I think in retrospect, that the aid was well justified.

SPARKMAN:
You think it paid dividends?

MCNAMARA:
I do, sir.

Interesting that the southern Democrat, Alabama Senator John Sparkman, used the term "dividends" because beneath all the blood and gore and political machinations and theatre, the first Indonesian genocide—the one from the mid-to-late sixties—was all about bizness. Sure, when Suharto came to power (as dramatically documented in John Pilger's film *Death of a Nation*), books were burned and the chance for popular democracy was completely crushed, but the west viewed Indonesia "as an investor's paradise—a huge market rich in oil and other natural resources. Richard Nixon called Indonesia: 'The greatest prize in Southeast Asia.' Suharto and his generals, along with their brutality, were welcomed to the free world."[30] Dissident and historian Noam Chomsky agrees with this assessment:

> Since 1965, when the Indonesian military took power in a coup that
> led to the slaughter of perhaps half a million to a million people,
> mostly landless peasants, Indonesia has been a valued ally [of the
> U.S.]. *The military rulers have opened the country to western plunder,*
> hindered only by the rapacity and corruption of our friends in
> Jakarta... the country has been turned into a "*paradise for investors.*"[31]
> [Emphasis added]

Nixon's evaluation was juicy fodder for the captains of industry: "The richest hoard of natural resources, the greatest prize in southeast Asia." And Suharto set the table. Late in 1967, "the greatest prize was handed out at a remarkable three-day conference sponsored by the Time-Life Corporation in Geneva. Led by David Rockefeller, all the corporate giants were represented..."[32] The line-up of carpetbaggers included General Motors, U.S. Steel, Siemens, British American Tobacco, and of course the major oil companies and major banks.[33] When Suharto died in 2008, John Pilger wrote a piece in *The Guardian* reiterating the west's ignoble role in propping up this murderous regime:

> Across the table sat Suharto's U.S.-trained economists who agreed
> to the corporate takeover of their country, sector by sector. The
> Freeport company got a mountain of copper in West Papua. A U.S./

European consortium got the nickel. The giant Alcoa company got the biggest slice of Indonesia's bauxite. American, Japanese, and French companies got the tropical forests of Sumatra. When the plunder was complete, President Lyndon Johnson sent his congratulations on "a magnificent story of opportunity seen and promise awakened."[34]

And, as time would tell, the 1965 Indonesian coup and subsequent shift in power was a precursor to the 1975 genocide in East Timor—and more violent repression beyond. In *Acts of Aggression: Policing Rogue States,* Chomsky examines Suharto's penchant for massacre and murder (and the American Empire's acceptance and embrace of the killing, especially when it's good for business):

> Indonesia… shifted from enemy to friend when General Suharto took power in 1965, presiding over an enormous slaughter that elicited great satisfaction in the West. Since then Suharto has been "our kind of guy," as the Clinton administration described him, while carrying out murderous aggression and endless atrocities against his own people; killing 10,000 Indonesians just in the 1980s, according to personal testimony of "our guy," who wrote that "the corpses were left lying around as a form of shock therapy."[35]

Murder as "shock therapy," financed and supported by U.S. taxpayer dollars. Same as "Shock and Awe," same as Hiroshima and Nagasaki, similar in murderous spirit to Manson's "Helter Skelter" and "Political Piggies"—violent political commercials at their deadliest best. When historian Gabriel Kolko looked back on this dark period in paradise, he wrote: "No single American action in the period after 1945 was as bloodthirsty as its role in Indonesia, for it tried to initiate the massacre." When the dust settled in the late 60s and early 70s, the Indonesian communist party was demolished with Sukarno and his regime long gone. As Blum concludes, "It could not have worked out better for the United States and the new military junta if it had been planned."[36]

Genocide: Part Two

My sister went to look for her husband and son. On her way she met a friend crying who told her, "Don't bother going there. I have just seen my cousin being eaten by a dog. They are all dead. Only the dogs are alive there."

—Eloise, an East Timorese living in Dili, describing her life on 7 December 1975

On the morning of 16 September 1974 *The Sydney Morning Herald* quoted Australian Prime Minister Gough Whitlam at a Jakarta press conference saying that, "an independent Timor would be an unviable State and a potential threat to the area."[37] What kind of threat did Whitlam and his new buddy Suharto—a war crimes superstar—envision materializing from the East Timorese people? Indonesia's population (some 200 million) along with their vast military superiority (not to mention their neighborhood bully support from the Americans and Australians) were not panic-stricken and quivering at the might and wrath of East Timor. Why were they so threatened? And strange that Whitlam was so pushy for regime change in East Timor. He was generally considered a progressive leader, supportive of small nation independence elsewhere in the world; and most importantly, Richard Helms, William Colby, and the rest of the spooks at CIA did not embrace Whitlam's foreign policy.[38] Was this just another case in point of the dreaded "good example"? *Is independence that bad for business?*

Whitlam's purported plan was simple: after decolonization from Portugal, he thought it was logical, sensible, and best for all concerned (did someone ask the East Timorese?) that East Timor be integrated into Indonesia (ostensibly for geographic reasons: with the Indonesian archipelago surrounding East Timor, it might look more tidy on a map if it were all one consistent color—to hell with pointless and useless reasons like the self-determination of a people). He then recommended that this so-called "natural" integration be one of freewill by the East Timorese; of course after the population was marched through a massive re-education program (picture cubes of pork being pounded into a sausage maker). Whitlam also proclaimed that if the situation deteriorated (read: the East Timorese said, "no thanks") that force should not be used.[39] Let's give him a few points for lip service… but the bottom-line was crystal clear: East Timor and its population were in the crosshairs of a hostile takeover.

In Pilger's *Death of a Nation*, the Australian Consul in East Timor, James Dunn, was interviewed years later and candidly revealed:

> More than a year before the invasion took place, we did know that an organization had been formed which was designed to bring about the integration of East Timor regardless of the wishes of the people. [It was] a subversive operation.[40]

At the time, regime change in Portugal opened the door to Timorese independence. But Portuguese leaders (military and political), split over the amount of independence to be allowed as well as the transition process itself, were slow to act. The Timorese began to take matters into their own hands and three factions emerged: the UDT (Timorese Democratic Union—conservative, in favor of keeping ties with Portugal), the ASDT (Association of Timorese Social Democrats—later known as FRETILIN, dedicated to full independence over a 10-year transition), and APODETI (Timorese Popular Democratic Association—committed to complete integration with Indonesia).[41]

At the outset, the UDT was the most popular and even began to support a future independence for East Timor; but by March 1975, and because of a superior organizing structure, the ASDT became the leading party and was venturing out from the capital city of Dili, educating rural populations and organizing trade unions as well as agricultural cooperatives. In fact, as the Timorese people became more radically independent in their beliefs and desires, the ASDT evolved into "The Revolutionary Front for an Independent East Timor" or FRETILIN.[42]

The process for transition to independence was gaining traction. The UDT and FRETILIN formed a coalition in solidarity and then, together with the MFA (Portugal's Armed Forces), decided that a transitional government would be formed by October of 1975, with national elections held in October of 1976.[43] It sounded like a budding and healthy democracy was taking root. Surely, the United States of America, the shining city on a hill called "democracy" would be thrilled by such a development. Surely, Australia, once a thriving penal colony and by 1975 one of the world's strongest representative democracies, would likewise be tickled pink by their neighbor's embrace of Aristotle's observation that "the basis of a democratic state is liberty." And surely, Indonesia, one of America's main squeezes in the region would be supportive of liberty and freedom for all—the very benchmarks of American aid and comfort. (Excuse us if our facetiousness is riddled with bitterness, but we believe we have just cause.)

"Indonesia had different plans," writes Matthew Jardine in his book *East Timor: Genocide in Paradise.* "By mid-1974, [Indonesia] had developed Operation Komodo—named after the Komodo dragons, giant man-eating lizards that live on other Indonesian islands." So much for Aristotle and his bag of crap. The objective of Operation Komodo was straightforward: devastate East Timor's independence movement; grind it into the ground—forever.

Civil War

Early in 1975, Indonesia began flexing its military muscle (hardware and training courtesy of their Washington D.C. supply depot) by staging East Timor attack exercises in nearby Sumatra. "Soon thereafter," Jardine reports, "Indonesia began disseminating false reports of a planned coup by the MFA and FRETILIN, and of supposed persecution of APODETI members."[44] The strong coalition between FRETILIN and UDT began to unravel, because as journalist John Pilger reports, "Indonesian agents infiltrated the coalition, undermining it, and finally destroying it. This led to civil war."[45] As fighting broke out, the Portuguese left East Timor. "After two weeks of fighting," Pilger continues, "FRETILIN emerged the clear winner and commanded the support of the majority of the (Timorese) population."[46]

Once again, James Dunn, the former Australian Consul in East Timor, remembers the mood as FRETILIN mounted their interim government:

> [FRETILIN] had obvious shortcomings, but it clearly enjoyed widespread support or cooperation from the population, including many former UDT supporters… Indeed, the leaders of the victorious party were welcomed warmly and spontaneously in all main centers by crowds of Timorese. In my long association with the territory, I had never before witnessed such demonstrations of spontaneous warmth and support from the ordinary people.[47]

Many corroborate that East Timor during this interim FRETILIN period was moving in a very constructive direction. The country was open to observers from aid organizations, the International Red Cross, as well as foreign journalists. "The reactions were quite positive," explains Noam Chomsky. "They were impressed by the level of popular support and the sensible measures of agricultural reform, literacy programs, and so on."[48] James Dunn described FRETILIN at the time as "populist Catholic."

FRETILIN attempted to use their newfound political capital and positive interaction with their population base to move things ahead constructively and called for a Peace Conference between Indonesia, Australia, and Portugal, but they received little or no support. Instead, Indonesia began making violent raids into border towns as theatrics to help sell their manufactured story of an ongoing civil war—a story that would later be used as Indonesia's "security" pretext and justification for a massive invasion. "When the Indonesians began their intervention," James Dunn recalls, "there was no civil war, there was no contest of FRETILIN control in any part of East Timor. That was a lie that kept coming out from Jakarta."[49]

Clearly, forces with another agenda—one of violent overthrow and theft—were perverting the reality regarding a healthy and budding self-determination movement in East Timor.

Western nations, especially the United States, knew full well of Indonesia's plans to viciously invade the sovereign country of East Timor, but silence from the world's media outlets and various governments ruled the day. In fact, the CIA was abundantly aware of every move being made; typical of cables being sent to Washington (17 September 1975): "…Jakarta is now sending guerrillas to provoke incidents that provide an excuse to invade."[50]

While reporting in East Timor in 1991, journalist and *DemocracyNow!* anchor Amy Goodman, along with fellow journalist Allan Nairn, were badly beaten and their lives threatened. Goodman writes about the media silence, especially the American media silence, during the 1975 invasion:

> [A]t the peak of the slaughter, there was hardly a mention in
> *The New York Times* or *The Washington Post* about the tragedy.
> Compare that to Pol Pot's Cambodia, where the genocide was
> proportionately similar. Hundreds of articles exposing Pol Pot's
> atrocities appeared in the U.S. media. The difference? Cambodia
> was an official enemy of the United States. Indonesia was a close
> ally. The U.S. president and secretary of state regularly denounced
> Pol Pot's Cambodia, and the press echoed that criticism. But what
> about when the United States remains silent on atrocities and
> supports the regime in power?[51]

This spectacle of selective "morality" is usually divided between the possible guilty parties—those defined as "moderates" and those defined as "extremists"—and then the trick is to spin the "necessary" murder and mayhem in a way conducive to either one of those definitive labels. And then when it comes to Washington's propaganda, "The 'leaders' put in place to serve U.S. power are invariably labeled 'moderates' by the U.S. mass media," explains media analyst Edward S. Herman; of course, as Herman illustrates, these "leaders" are vital to protecting American (business) interests:

U.S. officials treat them as reasonable people we can "work with," and suggest that any little unpleasantnesses in which they may have recently indulged are under review and will be corrected soon, under our tutelage. That is, they will do our bidding, kill only the right people, and allow foreign investment and sales, even if at a heavy price in a "corruption drain."[52]

In October of 1975, five members of the Australian press were courageously attempting to expose the coming bloodbath. They were brutally murdered by Indonesian forces. All five of them—reporters Greg Shackleton and Malcolm Rennie, cameramen Gary Cunningham and Brian Peters, and sound recordist Tony Stewart, were killed on 16 October 1975. The five journalists were in the coastal town of Balibo, East Timor, just six miles from the Indonesian border. They had received reports that Indonesian ships were just off the coast. One day before the journalists were slaughtered, Greg Shackleton recorded his last report—an eerily iconic image of a reporter, microphone in hand, kneeling on one knee in front of a grass hut, invoking the pleas of the family that lives there:

> Why, they ask, are the Indonesians invading us? Why, they ask, if the Indonesians believe that FRETILIN is communist do they not send a delegation to Dili to find out? Why, they ask, are the Australians not helping us? When the Japanese invaded, they did help us. Why, they ask, are the Portuguese not helping us? We're still a Portuguese colony. Who, they ask, will pay for the terrible damage to our homes?[53]

Shackleton is then seen painting the word "Australia" as well as the Australian flag on the ramshackle house in the hopes that "it will afford us some protection." It did not. The "Balibo Five," as they were later named, were killed shortly thereafter. Greg Shackleton's wife Shirley discusses the horror of her husband's death:

> Witnesses... said they heard the Australian journalists shouting "Australian journalists, non-combat." Then they said they heard fire... The majority of them were hung up by their feet, their sexual organs were removed and pushed into their mouth, they were stabbed with the short throwing knives that the Indonesian soldiers carry, and it isn't known whether they asphyxiated, or whether they bled to death, or whether some of them got stabbed in the heart and died quickly... This is quite common way to punish people in East

Timor, bodies are often found this way, and so the Timorese have a fair idea that it takes a long time. They asphyxiate usually.[54]

Another Australian journalist, Roger East, began to investigate the murder of the five men. On 7 December 1975 he was apprehended by the Indonesian military and badly beaten with rifle butts. Eyewitness accounts say that the fifty-year-old reporter was taken bloody and in handcuffs to the harbor in Dili. He was thrown into a group of fifty or so men, women, and children on the water's edge. In his book, *Funu: The Unfinished Saga of East Timor*, José Ramos-Horta—the former president of East Timor and 1996 Nobel Peace Prize winner, wrote about his friend's execution:

> One after another, the women, men, and children were shot, their bodies falling into the sea. According to my informant, who is still in Jakarta, an Indonesian officer shot Roger point blank in the head from very close range. The officer was so close that Roger managed to spit in his face... The next day, the bodies washed up on the beaches. The murder of Roger was never investigated by the Australian government, nor by his fellow journalists.[55]

Ramos-Horta recalls that a couple of days before East's execution, he suggested to his friend that he take along a rifle for his own protection. Roger East smiled, declined the weapon, and then held up his pen, saying: "This is my gun. It's more powerful than this gun of yours."[56]

In March of 1973, the last U.S. military unit left Vietnam. America's long war of imperial narcissism (and its expensive handcrafted gift to the defense industry) was over (although years earlier, Allen Ginsberg, Phil Ochs, as well as John & Yoko had declared the "war over"). Now it was the Indonesian nation—which Washington and American corporations had been betting on and supporting since their break from Dutch colonial rule in the late 1940s—that was the number one recipient of American economic investment in the region, even more than the Philippines. With a minimum wage of less than $2 a day, manufacturing giants like Nike, Levi Strauss, Toys R Us, Tommy Hilfiger, General Motors, DuPont, and others loved the "warm climate."[57]

Richard Nixon, who envisaged tangerine trees and marmalade skies when drooling over his "greatest prize in southeast Asia," was gone, exiled in San Clemente, California, or Saddle River, New Jersey, wherever, pressing his head against the wall wondering what the hell went wrong. In his place, the unelected Jerry Ford took a stroll in the Rose Garden with General Alexander Haig, a week before Nixon resigned, and together they made the deal to pardon the 37th President of the United States of all crimes, domestic and foreign.[58] And, of course, what that overt move accomplished reached far into the Empire's future: it gave every president a "get out of jail free" card for almost anything—war powers, surveillance, torture, covert operations both domestic and foreign, anything. Illustrative case in point: the Bush/Cheney junta absolved of all crimes by the inaction of the like-minded criminals that followed.

Lunch at Shangri-La

The details of the following meeting are offered by George Washington University's National Security Archive, under the heading: "Ford and Kissinger Gave Green Light to Indonesia's Invasion of East Timor, 1975."

5 July 1975. It was a warm and clear day at Camp David, the Presidential mountain retreat in the Maryland woods some sixty miles northwest of the White House. The meeting at this isolated rural location, originally called Shangri-La and renamed after Ike's grandson, took place just a few months after the fall of the Thieu regime in South Vietnam. The communists won the war. A strong and allied Indonesia was of utmost importance to Washington powerbrokers and, they hoped, would help quell any growing communist ferment that might arise throughout Southeast Asia.

At 12:40pm, in the Laurel Cabin on the northeast edge of Camp David, there was a casual get-together attended by President Gerald Ford, President Hadji Mohamed Suharto, Lt. General Brent Scowcroft, Dr. Henry Kissinger, and Mr. Widodo—the Indonesian interpreter. Four killers, and to the best of our knowledge, one working stiff doing his job. The declassified transcript of the meeting is fairly uneventful and quite friendly—two leaders sharing their thoughts on the geopolitical issues of the day, especially in Asia; it has that rubber-stamp tone to it—going through the motions where the finish line is already known and recognized by everyone involved. Kissinger walks in late, says nothing. Scowcroft must be asleep, snoring in his medals as Ford and Suharto continue with additional staged pleasantries. They then agree on some anti-communist nonsense, followed by some banter about the future of Vietnam. The important shit is basically a fait accompli: continued and ever-growing economic aid along with significant corporate investment for Suharto's nation, some chitchat about bank investments, more chitchat about oil, and then of course some boiler plate agreement on the all-important extension of U.S.-military aid and war toys to bolster Indonesia's "national resilience."[59]

And then, with no warning, a major development from the American president—

FORD: *Lunch is ready.*

And then Scowcroft woke up.

The Big Wink

> *In the annals of crime in this terrible century, Indonesia's assault against*
> *East Timor ranks high, not only because of its scale—perhaps the greatest*
> *death toll relative to the population since the Holocaust—but because it would*
> *have been so easy to prevent.*[60]
> —Noam Chomsky

5 December, 1975. By the time Air Force One touched down on a rain-soaked tarmac in Jakarta, the fix was in on the people of East Timor. While the band played, Jerry and Betty Ford (along with Henry Kissinger) exited the Boeing C-137 Stratoliner and dutifully watched the marching Indonesian soldiers present the colors: their red and white flag flapping right next to Old Glory. The American visit was described by one State Department official as "the big wink."[61]

A couple of days before Gerald Ford and his entourage arrived, U.S. State Department officials learned through intelligence that "[r]anking Indonesian civilian government leaders have decided the only solution in the Portuguese Timor situation is for Indonesia to launch an open offensive against Fretilin."[62] At the time, the bulk of weapons and military hardware came from the United States. In fact, numerous estimates put the percentage of American weaponry used during the invasion at 90 percent. Forget Washington's culpability in the murderous assault and/or "morality" of the act, it is clearly against American law for U.S. arms to be used in acts of aggression. And if this wasn't an act of aggression, then nothing is.

In fact, as Ford and Kissinger were en route to Jakarta, U.S. intelligence reports informed them that Suharto would be anxious to secure their approval. C. Philip Liechty, a senior CIA officer in Indonesia, spoke about and revealed actions by his superiors that underlined "a certain knowledge of what was about to happen."

> The Embassy staff were taking unusual measures to plan as many photo and visual opportunities to present Ford and Suharto together, demonstrating unlimited support for Suharto and the Indonesian government. And I thought, wait a minute, something is seriously wrong here... What I saw was that my own government was very much involved in what was going on in East Timor and what was going on was not good. You can be one hundred percent certain that Suharto was explicitly given the green light to do what he did.[63]

The writing wasn't on the wall—it was spray-painted all over the goddamned place. Ford and Kissinger knew full well that their go-ahead nod and "big wink" with Suharto was tantamount to signing a death warrant on the people of East Timor. As was his trademark, historic muckraking journalist Jack Anderson burrowed deep beneath the surface of this gory chapter in Murder Incorporated's history:

> [I]t was essential to neutralize the United States... That Suharto succeeded is confirmed by Ford himself. The United States had suffered a devastating setback in Vietnam, leaving Indonesia as the most important American ally in the area. The U.S. national interest, Ford concluded, "had to be on the side of Indonesia." Ford gave his tacit approval on December 6, 1975.[64]

Liechty agrees that Suharto was "given the green light" and further notes that without massive American military wherewithal, resources, and training "the Indonesians might not have been able to pull it off."[65] Keep in mind that throughout all of this, Indonesia holds no historical or legal claim to East Timor.

Here's the political kicker, the smoking gun if you will: five days after the Indonesian military created a hell on earth for the Timorese people, the United Nations voted to condemn the invasion as an unmitigated act of aggression. *Washington abstained and declined to vote.* "Thereafter," writes Jack Anderson, "the U.S. delegate maneuvered behind the scenes to resist U.N. moves aimed at forcing Indonesia to give up its conquest."[66] John Pilger reports that, "On December the 7th, as the presidential jet climbed out of Indonesian air space, the bloodbath began."[67]

Ten days later, on 18 December, with Timorese blood flowing like water and their bodies piling up all over the island nation, Kissinger was back in Washington and wanted "to raise a bit of hell" about the State Department's behavior while he was jetting around the planet. America's Secretary of State was reeling about a State Department cable that was sent to the Indonesian government regarding the use of U.S. military hardware in their current invasion of East Timor. "Until last week I thought we had a disciplined group," Kissinger arrogantly laced into his staff with his throat-heavy German accent. "Now we've gone to pieces completely… It is a disgrace to treat the Secretary of State this way."[68] Obvious question: Why is Kissinger pissed off and throwing a hissy fit? Equally obvious answer: Because he's fearful that Congress and/or the press will uncover his collusion with Suharto and their ongoing bloody slaughter.

The State Department meeting continues:

> KISSINGER:
> There's this masochism in the extreme here. No one has complained that it was aggression.
>
> MONROE LEIGH (Legal Advisor):
> The Indonesians were violating an agreement with us.
>
> KISSINGER:
> The Israelis when they go into Lebanon—when was the last time we protested that?
>
> LEIGH:
> That's a different situation.

CARLYLE MAW (Undersecretary):
It is self-defense.

KISSINGER:
And why can't we construe a Communist government in the middle of Indonesia as self-defense? ...On the Timor thing, that will leak in three months, and it will come out that Kissinger overruled his pristine bureaucrats and violated the law. How many people in L [the Legal Advisor's Office] know about this?

MONROE LEIGH (Legal Advisor):
Three.

PHILIP BABIB (Assistant Secretary):
There are at least two in my office.

KISSINGER:
Plus everybody in the meeting so you're talking about not less than 15 or 20. You have a responsibility to recognize that we are living in a revolutionary situation. Everything on paper will be used against me.[69]

Kissinger then makes a very strange and curious statement: *"I don't care if we sell equipment to Indonesia or not. I get nothing from it. I get no rakeoff."*[70] The Secretary is answering a question no one asked. "How peculiar that Kissinger should deny an allegation that had not been made," comments the late journalist Christopher Hitchens in his scathing book *The Trial of Henry Kissinger.* Hitchens then extends another obvious thought:

> It isn't possible to state with certainty when Kissinger began to profit personally from his association with the ruling circles in Indonesia... there is a perfect congruence between Kissinger's foreign policy counsel and his business connections. One might call it a harmony of interests, rather than a conflict.[71]

Six years after Kissinger leaves office, he established "Kissinger Associates"—a very private (damn near undercover) consulting firm that specializes in connecting (guess what) multinational corporations with any government of your choice. Possibly you've heard of some of their corporate clients: American Express, Coca-Cola, Fiat, Volvo, Revlon, Union Carbide, Heinz, Lockheed, Arco, Lehman

Brothers, J.P. Morgan Chase… and guess who came with Hank when he hung his shingle out in the rarefied air of New York City's upper crust? Among many others, General Brent Scowcroft, Lawrence Eagleburger, and L. Paul Bremer. Most of the Kissinger Associates consulting staff were former employees on the government's payroll (read: your payroll).

After the dubious 18 December 1975 State Department meeting, Kissinger (quietly) ordered all current shipments of U.S. arms be halted, but then quickly rescinded the order and shipments secretly began again in January. It was a chess game. "In fact, as the killings increased," reports Pilger, "American arm shipments doubled" in the escalating invasion.[72]

As an interesting and instructive side note on the above-cited Kissinger transcript is the fact that the "note taker" was none other than "Jerry Bremer," more famous (or infamous) decades later as L. Paul Bremer—neocon war collaborator. "He would later go on to join the global consulting firm Kissinger Associates," explain journalists Amy and David Goodman, "and in 2003 he became the occupier-in-chief of a devastated Iraq."[73]

Kissinger Revisited

I've got to tell you, the dark side of Henry Kissinger is very very dark.
–Seymour Hersh

And then sometimes you find brilliance in the damnedest place, like this from the late American chef Anthony Bourdain:

Photo: Marsha Miller, LBJ Library

Once you've been to Cambodia, you'll never stop wanting to beat Henry Kissinger to death with your bare hands. You will never again be able to open a newspaper and read about that treacherous, prevaricating, murderous scumbag sitting down for a nice chat with Charlie Rose or attending some black-tie affair for a new glossy magazine without choking. Witness what Henry did in Cambodia—the fruits of his genius for statesmanship—and you will never understand why he's not sitting in the dock at The Hague next to Milošević.

The carnage and brutal overthrow that rocked East Timor starting in 1975, like the carnage and brutal coup that rocked Chile two years before, are both interlocked and eerily similar to the American involvement in Cambodia (and of course throughout all of Vietnam in the late 60s and early 70s). The man with his finger on the trigger, of course, is none other than mass murderer and war criminal Henry Kissinger—and before we continue with the sordid and sorrowful tale of East Timor, a brief primer on Killer Hank. "The statement 'Henry Kissinger is a war criminal' is a statement I've been making for many years," explains Christopher Hitchens, "It's not a piece of rhetoric or a metaphor, it's a job description."[74]

From the late 1960s and into the 1970s, when Kissinger's power reigned supreme, the annals of American history clearly illustrate how his obsession with Cold War scheming led to his Machiavellian behavior—a modus operandi that not only threw the human cost of war to the wind, but a tactical operation in which he actively used murder and mayhem as his diplomatic ace-in-the-hole when political conquests were in reach. For this Harvard-educated megalomaniac, sacrificing countless innocent lives for international policy victories—victories that in the end simply ensured more power, prestige, and girlfriends for Dr. Henry Alfred Kissinger—was not an obstacle. It was commonplace.

In 1968, during the Paris Peace Talks, Kissinger was an advisor to the Johnson administration and was privy to all sensitive information. As the presidential election grew near and the Hubert Humphrey/Lyndon Johnson Democrats were close to striking a peace accord with all parties involved (a peace that probably would have cost Nixon the election), Kissinger—playing both sides against each other—secretly informed Nixon of the Johnson strategy and how close the war was to actually being over. Nixon moved quickly and opened secret talks with South Vietnamese President Nguyen Van Thieu. A couple of days before the U.S. election, Nixon convinced the former general not to take part in the current peace talks and for Thieu to wait for a new administration (one that would insist on "Peace with Honor"). FBI surveillance records document this entire episode.[75]

Nixon wins the election by a slim margin and suddenly Henry Kissinger assumes tremendous power. Nixon appoints him National Security Advisor and later Secretary of State. In fact, the liberal establishment actually viewed Kissinger as a check on Nixon and were gushing in certain quarters. Historian Arthur Schlesinger proclaimed, "Excellent... very encouraging."[76] Longtime Democratic operative Adam Yarmolinsky prattled, "I'll sleep better with Henry Kissinger in Washington."[77]

Right from the get-go, Kissinger exercised remarkable influence over the Pentagon as well as the CIA; he was orchestrating and dictating both political and military policy out of Washington.[78] Richard Nixon's superficial and arcane mantra during this period was "Peace with Honor" and this fit perfectly with Kissinger's hawkish Cold War mentality (read: obsession). Together, this team united in the nether world, hell-bent on making sure that America did not look weak in the eyes of the world and, more importantly, in the eyes of the Soviet Union. Together, these two madmen went hog wild and medieval in the skies over Vietnam and Cambodia, trying desperately to find North Vietnam's "breaking point."[79] In 1969, Nixon and Kissinger began carpet-bombing neutral Cambodia in the hopes of "cleaning up" the North Vietnamese sanctuaries—bombings that were secret, illegal, and massive. Between 1969 and 1973, more than 500,000 were killed in Cambodia. Reports illustrate how Kissinger was intimately involved in executing the ongoing bombardment of Cambodia, even to the point of manipulating and altering military bombing records.[80]

In October of 1972, shortly before the presidential election, Kissinger had struck a secret deal for peace with North Vietnam's Le Duc Tho. Kissinger held a press conference in Washington and declared that, "peace is at hand." The media blasted the headline across America and the world. Kissinger's melodramatic statement ended any small chance that Nixon's antiwar opponent for president, Senator George McGovern, may have had and it sent South Vietnam's President Thieu into an uproar. On 18 December, three years to the day before Kissinger took his staff out to the woodshed over East Timor, he and Nixon announced the Vietnam War's most vicious bombing campaign—death from above—courtesy of nonstop B-52 raids. "Linebacker II" or the "Christmas Bombings" as they were called, unleashed more tonnage across the cities, hamlets, and villages of North Vietnam than the U.S. dropped on Japan during all of World War II—*all of World War II.*

And the reason for the assault and subsequent slaughter?

So Kissinger and Nixon could prove America's resolve to South Vietnamese leadership, forcing them to sign the peace treaty. "It was a demonstration bombing," explains Hitchens, "it was a public relations mass murder from the sky."[81]

In fact, when all parties did sign the agreement in 1973, the treaty and the terms were almost identical to the 1968 accord that Kissinger went to great lengths to sabotage. This fact points us to some other interesting facts—facts Henry Kissinger couldn't give a shit about: more than 21,000 Americans were put into the permanent meat grinder during Nixon and Kissinger's tenure (almost 40 percent of total U.S. killed in action during the war)[82] as well as an estimated 1.5 to 2 million Southeast Asians (about 50 percent of total casualties). The numbers of wounded in action for both sides was disturbingly off the charts. Meanwhile, Kissinger, for his oh so noble efforts in the 1973 Paris agreement, received the Nobel Peace Prize.

> *Kill one person, call it murder.*
> *Kill a million, call it foreign policy.*

When Nixon and Kissinger went cartwheeling into Cambodia, there was no war, there were no killing fields. No famine, starvation, or genocide. It was their private and public war that laid the foundation and set the framework for the rise of the Khmer Rouge and their subsequent reign of absolute terror. By 1975, the Americans rotated back to amber waves of grain and left the Cambodians in a world of shit. By 1979, another 3 million more Cambodians lost their lives.[83]

Chile 1970: The Murder of General René Schneider

As the sixties turned into the seventies, major American corporations such as International Telephone & Telegraph (ITT) and PepsiCo were skittish regarding the political developments in Chile and the rise of the democratically elected Marxist and socialist leader Salvador Allende. They were openly wary of Allende's intention to nationalize Chile's copper industry as well as the fact that Allende could not be bought off with American aid. And everyone was, of course, suspicious of his close ties to Fidel Castro.

ITT pressured Kissinger to take action against Allende, while Pepsi's president Donald Kendall—a valued and old Nixon compadre—pressured the Commander-in-Chief. It was clear: Kendall and other potential big campaign contributors wanted Chile handled and handled quickly.[84] Bottom-line: Santiago under Allende's control was unacceptable to Washington and Wall Street.

Edward Korry, the U.S. Ambassador to Chile at the time, remembers a meeting with Nixon in the White House when Nixon went into a rant, pounding his fist, referring to Allende as "that bastard, that SOB," promising to smash him economically.[85] On 4 September 1970 Salvador Allende of the Popular Unity

Party won the election by a very close plurality. What happened next didn't take long to unfold.

On 12 September 1970—at twelve o'clock high—there was a phone call between National Security Advisor Henry Kissinger and CIA Director Richard Helms. The transcript of the phone call reveals immediate pressure from the Pepsi guy. The call also reiterates Henry's love of those working around him—obviously no one is as good or as smart as the boy from Fürth, Bavaria, Germany—the boy with his many degrees from Harvard.

> TELCON
> Helms/Kissinger
>
> H: We live in trying times. Have you heard from Don Kendall?
>
> K: He has been trying to get me but my moronic people turned him off.
>
> H: He talked to me last night... There's a problem here.[86]

The problem, of course, was Salvador Allende and the people of Chile. More specifically, their independence. His presidential victory still needed to be confirmed by a Congressional vote—and that's when the U.S. intelligence community went into high gear with Hank as the quarterback. Peter Kornbluh of the National Security Archives, studying the declassified secret memos, emphatically calls Kissinger the "general manager" of the operation aimed at preventing Allende's victory.[87] Like the secret bombing of Cambodia, Kissinger assumed a very hands-on approach. And for good reason, according to Kissinger's top aide, co-conspirator, and former U.S. general, Alexander Haig: "What brought about the changes in Chile were the facts that it was being communized by Allende... another Marxist regime in the hemisphere? No."[88] Communized? Fuck that says Hammerin' Hank: "I don't see why we need to standby and watch a country go communist due to the irresponsibility of its people."[89]

Prior to the election, the "40 Committee"—the Kissinger-led secret oversight panel that supervised American covert ops "directed CIA to carry out 'spoiling operations' to prevent an Allende victory," this according to the Central Intelligence Agency themselves.[90] This was easy for the U.S. and Kissinger since Washington was already using propaganda, disinformation, and dirty tricks to influence political outcomes and infiltrate Chilean political circles for years. But Allende still won the election, so a two-pronged approach was introduced to sink the newly elected president, as described by the CIA:

> As part of a "Track I" strategy to block Allende from taking office after the 4 September election, CIA sought to influence a Congressional run-off vote required by the Constitution because Allende did not win an absolute majority.

> As part of a "Track II" strategy, CIA was directed to seek to instigate a coup to prevent Allende from taking office.[91]

Kissinger knew a major obstacle when he saw one. General René Schneider was the leader of the largest segment of the Chilean armed forces and was strongly committed to acknowledging the will of the people and their Constitution. Schneider was a popular figure and well respected throughout the military. With this in mind, the CIA intensified their efforts, recruiting officers within the Chilean armed forces to undermine Allende's election and push the country back in a pro-American, pro-capitalist direction—but they needed more. They needed Schneider gone.

Together, the White House and the CIA pulled the trigger on initiating a coup, also referred to as Project FUBELT. At the heart of the plan was the kidnapping of General Schneider. Washington directly supplied the weaponry for the mission and the CIA directly supplied the high stakes payments to purchase the kidnappers and assassins. CIA Director Richard Helms reported directly to Kissinger. The plan was hidden from the American embassy in Santiago, as well as from both State and Defense.[92] According to the International Campaign Against Impunity:

> The first two attempts to kidnap Gen. Schneider failed. After each attempt, the U.S. not only encouraged the coup-plotters to keep trying, but also provided more gas masks and gas grenades. On October 22, 1970, six hours after the U.S. had delivered sub machine guns to one of the groups, Gen. René Schneider was shot on his way to work. The bullets perforated his liver and he had to undergo open heart surgery. After three days of agonizing, he died on October 25, 1970. He and his wife had five young children.[93]

Of course, (surprise, surprise) Kissinger denied his involvement. But the

CIA and Richard Helms, in open testimony before Congress, testified to the Church Committee that the CIA kept Kissinger completely up to date and in the loop—even after 15 October, the day Kissinger testified that he abandoned the coup operation. In fact, Kissinger has consistently and vigorously denied any involvement after 15 October.

Yet, on 16 October 1970, just days before Allende was to be confirmed and after Kissinger insists the coup plot was dead, the CIA cabled their Santiago station:

> It is firm and continuing policy that Allende be overthrown by a coup. It would be much preferable to have this transpire prior to 24 October but efforts in this regard will continue vigorously beyond this date. We are to continue to generate maximum pressure toward this end utilizing every appropriate resource. *It is imperative that these actions be implemented clandestinely and securely so that the USG and American hand be well hidden.*[94] [Emphasis added]

If the coup plot was truly dead, that's one hell of an obituary. In the devastating documentary, *The Trials of Henry Kissinger,* investigative journalist Seymour Hersh fills in the blanks of covert ops and plausible deniability:

> If you're Henry Kissinger, everybody knows what you want. Does he know they know what he wants? Sure. Does he know what they're going to do or how they're going to do it? Are you kidding? Anyone that would tell him what's going to happen is never going to do a briefing again. Do you really think somebody would take a piece of paper into the White House that says the consequence of this may be the death of somebody? Do you really think so? No.[95]

Two days later, another action-oriented cable from CIA to Santiago:

> Sub-machine guns and ammo being sent by regular courier leaving Washington 0700 hours 19 October. Due arrive Santiago late evening 20 October or early morning 21 October. Preferred use regular courier to avoid bringing undue attention to operation.[96]

If Kissinger had killed the coup plot, then he forgot to tell people because the CIA was rock-solid in their actions and communications. There wasn't a hint of pulling back. The agency reports that they briefed Kissinger's top aide, Alexander Haig, regarding coup plans on 19 October. The CIA also reports that on 20 October,

Kissinger himself requested a briefing on their attempts to eliminate General Schneider.[97] Once again, from the film *The Trials of Henry Kissinger*, Colonel Paul Wimert, the American Military attaché in Chile, a man intricately involved in the plot against Schneider, responded to Kissinger's denial:

> He's a liar.

U.S. Ambassador Edward Corry also responded to Kissinger's denial:

> He lied.

Followed by Seymour Hersh:

> He knew Schneider was certainly going to get killed, but not by us—you see? (with a smile) So therefore it's okay. That's the way it works.[98]

After the murder of General René Schneider, the CIA's own internal investigation uncovered that $35,000 was paid by the United States government to one of the killers.[99]

At the time, the death of René Schneider galvanized the Chilean military and helped to unite the people. Salvador Allende took the reins of power and began to govern—but the United States was just warming up. More secret declassified documents reveal Kissinger (just 10 days after Schneider was purged) briefing Nixon during a 5 November 1970 National Security Meeting. He begins with this opening statement and it's underlined: "The election of Allende as President of Chile poses for us one of the most serious challenges ever faced in this hemisphere." Kissinger, of course, links the rise of Chile's independence, along with Washington's response to this Marxist movement, as being the very essence of the Cold War. He rails against socialism and Chile's right to limit and/ or eliminate "U.S. influence in Chile." He then concludes by reminding Nixon about the real reason Allende's coalition should scare the hell out of them: "US investments (totaling some one billion dollars) may be lost."[100]

There is no doubt that the declassified secret documents from this episode paint an extraordinarily dark and diabolical picture of America's ongoing actions in the world. Peter Kornbluh, from the National Security Archive, concludes that, "There's a paper trail right up to Kissinger's office that help us revisit this history and understand our efforts to overthrow covertly the democratically-elected government in Chile."[101]

It was only a matter of time. On 11 September 1973, Salvador Allende's government was overthrown in a full-blown coup d'état—one that ushered in years of death, torture, and terror at the hands of Augusto Pinochet. Before capture, Allende put an AK-47 under his chin and pulled the trigger.

"Book 'em, Danno"

One of the world's leading human rights attorneys is Geoffrey Robertson, author of the epic tome *Crimes Against Humanity*. He outlines the basis for guilt when looking at the résumé of war criminals. "Crimes against humanity," he explains, "are crimes that comprise genocide, or torture, or mass murder, committed on a widespread and systematic basis against innocent civilian populations."[102]

Henry Kissinger: Vietnam, Cambodia, Chile, East Timor.

Robertson explains the foundation as to why American leaders consistently get away with murder: "It's a facet of American exceptionalism… to think that international law is a very fine thing for other countries. That international law applies to everyone except Americans."[103]

And where was the vaunted, pedigreed American press, the Fourth Estate in all of this? Hersh takes this question to heart: "That this man could operate at such a horrible level and not get exposed for year after year after year after year—how many people came out against him? It's an embarrassment to my profession."[104]

So make no mistake about it: while Kissinger was hosing the blood off his Nobel Peace Prize and frolicking around with the likes of Candice Bergen, Liv Ullman, Diane Sawyer, Jill St. John, and other sycophants, his U.S. supplied Bronco aircraft were crisscrossing East Timor, wiping out people who wanted little more than self-determination.

Dili, East Timor: 7 December 1975

RED CROSS RADIO TRANSMISSION FROM EAST TIMOR:
… a lot of people are being killed, I repeat, indiscriminately.

Historian Howard Zinn once wrote, "Until Noam Chomsky brought up the name of East Timor into public discussion nobody had even heard of it. The CIA had heard of East Timor."[105] Senior CIA officer C. Philip Liechty concurs: "We were providing most of the weaponry, helicopters, logistical support, food, uniforms, ammunition—all the expendables that the Indonesians needed to conduct this war."[106] And it wasn't just U.S. military aid, training, and those Hollywood-iconic helicopter gunships that "kept flowing into the hands of the Indonesian military" from their American friends, it was also warm, tactical bodies: "Fretilin reported on a number of occasions that American advisors were directing and even participating in the combat."[107]

From its very outset, the invasion was a savage operation, one that resembled Sherman's scorched earth policy on his 1864 devastating march to the sea. It was total war. Anything goes. "The Indonesian troops had been told that the East Timorese were communists and primitives who threatened the very existence of Indonesia itself," reports John Pilger. "The strategy was clearly to terrorize an entire nation."[108] The CIA was monitoring breaking updates as the invasion unfolded "from hard, firm reports from people on the scene in East Timor," Liechty recalls. "Reports of people being herded into school buildings by Indonesian soldiers with the building set on fire and anyone trying to get out being shot—most of the people being burned alive; people being herded into fields and machine-gunned; people being hunted down in the mountains. So anyone out there was in what amounted to a free fire zone."[109] A FRETILIN radio broadcast (frankly more of a dire plea) during the first few hours of the invasion cried out for help:

> Women and children are being shot in the streets. We are all going
> to be killed. I repeat, we are all going to be killed… This is an appeal
> for international help. Please do something to stop this invasion.[110]

The invasion began with the naval bombardment of Dili, followed by paratroopers blanketing the sky. Before long, Dili was under complete siege. One can imagine a whimsical cash register working overtime, calculating the huge American investment in this worthwhile endeavor. It was a mission that Henry Kissinger was very specific about, instructing Suharto on the eve of the invasion, "It is important that whatever you do succeeds quickly."[111] Suharto heard his American paymaster loud and clear. In fact, the Catholic bishop in Dili, Martinho da Costa Lopes recalls the murderous raid: "The soldiers who landed started killing everyone they could find. There were many dead bodies in the streets—all we could see were soldiers killing, killing, killing."[112] Death happened in the blink of an eye and it spread out everywhere—people shopping, people in their homes, in schools, even in a hospital. "Live grenades were thrown into houses," Pilger reports. "Women and girls were raped in front of their families."[113] Journalists Amy and David Goodman forcefully reiterate that 90 percent of the weapons used in the attack were courtesy of the United States of America. They then describe the horror:

> Thousands of people were killed in the first few days of the invasion. Indonesian troops would drag people out of their houses and shoot them as their family members were forced to count them as they fell into the harbor. The sea was red with blood.[114]

As previously described, this was the same terror that cost Australian journalist Roger East, his life tragically over in Dili's "sea of blood." John Pilger reports, "There was also a systematic pattern to the terror. People were brought here to die in groups, and as in Cambodia, often the first to die were the educated, public officials, teachers, students, nurses."[115] A Timorese man who was spared, possibly to spread the Indonesian "message" painfully recalled sheer terror:

> My brothers killed and executed in front of my eyes by the Indonesian military… after they killed, they pulled out their heart and showed to us and said "that's a dirty heart," now you must agree to integration.[116]

Invasion of the Body Snatchers

FRETILIN forces battled back but Indonesian military might proved overwhelming. East Timor's urban populations fled for the countryside seeking asylum and cover, but the Indonesian army hunted them down. The bottom-line for Indonesia and their western supporters was to gain control of the Timorese population and absorb them into the fold. It was the "Indonesianization" of East Timor, yet the East Timorese were a very different populace, speaking a completely different language, living in a much different culture. In fact, Indonesia is the largest Muslim nation in the world, whereas the vast majority of people in East Timor were Catholic or Animist. It was an invasion of the body snatchers. It was the British Empire colonizing and force-civilizing India. It was the Euro-American Empire colonizing and force-civilizing the indigenous people of the Americas—chock full of the same religious fanaticism and xenophobic rage. And to accomplish a civilizing undertaking, the colonizer must first control the colonized population. Matthew Jardine reveals Indonesia's method:

As early as April 1976, FRETILIN'S underground radio network reported the existence of "guarded camps" in Indonesian-controlled areas. According to a July 1979 report by the Australian Council for Overseas Aid, there were fifteen camps with a population of 318,921 "displaced persons."[117]

As the months unfolded—with Indonesian forces herding East Timor's population into camps and resettlement villages, combined with ongoing military operations still aimed at erasing FRETILIN and the so-called Timorese "terrorists"—malnutrition and famine wreaked havoc throughout the country. The Timorese language was outlawed. It was the domino effect racing downhill—one that started in hell and then got worse. "The invasion was bloody and brutal," writes Noam Chomsky. "Indonesia extended its aggression to other parts of the territory, and by 1977–78 was engaged in a program of wholesale destruction of villages and crops, and all the familiar techniques used by modern armies to subjugate a resisting population."[118]

Gerald Ford and Henry Kissinger left office in January of 1977, succeeded by "the self-proclaimed champion of human rights," Jimmy Carter.[119] The Carter administration actually increased military aid to Suharto and by the end of the century, in 1999, Washington supplied their friends in Indonesia with more than $1 billion worth of killing toys.[120]

Cone of Silence

One of the more outrageous aspects of this massive invasion and slaughter by the world's fifth largest nation was that it basically happened under a cone of silence. By 1989, Amnesty International estimated that Indonesian forces slaughtered at least 200,000 Timorese. That's "200,000 people out of a population of between 600,000 and 700,000, a death rate which is probably one of the highest in the entire history of wars."[121]

And the western media was AWOL.

As a bona fide news organization, how do you miss genocide of historic proportions? What kind of twisted priorities and what kind of inside deal with the devil must you be a part of to miss the genocide of 200,000 human beings—one that is being sanctioned, supported, and significantly financed by the United States of America? Author William Blum described the American media's blackout of what was transpiring in East Timor as akin to building "the Berlin Wall" around the truth—the hidden truth. Chomsky refers to the media's disappearing act as a "curtain of silence," and suggests that the four-year self-imposed gag order "hardly demonstrates the success of Indonesian arms, though it does stand as a remarkable testimonial to the effectiveness of Western propaganda systems."[122]

But sometimes voices get out; voices that cry from the wilderness; voices that transcend news blackouts and government strangleholds on free expression; voices that deliver the truth. Such is the case when two Catholic nuns in Portugal received a letter from a priest in East Timor. His words are chilling:

> The invaders have intensified their attacks in the three classic ways: from land, sea, and air. The bombers do not stop. Hundreds die everyday. The bodies of the victims become food for carnivorous birds. Villages have been completely destroyed. The barbarities—understandable in the Middles Ages, justifiable in the Stone Age—are an organized evil that has spread deep roots in East Timor. The terror of arbitrary imprisonment is our daily bread. I am on the persona non grata list and any day I could disappear... Genocide will come soon.[123]

In 1979, four brutal years after the invasion began, Bernard Nossiter—the United Nations reporter for *The New York Times*, was invited to a press conference regarding the situation in East Timor. He turned down the opportunity because the subject, he said, was "rather esoteric." After the press conference and U.N. debate that featured Timorese witnesses and refugees testifying about the horrors they experienced as well as America's role in these atrocities, Nossiter and *The Times* printed nothing.[124]

You might also ask, "Where the hell was the United Nations?" As we discussed earlier, the United Nations immediately voted to condemn the invasion as an unmitigated act of aggression. But America abstained and refused to vote. Chomsky chronicles their subsequent inability to stop the bloodshed:

> The reasons are explained by U.N. Ambassador Daniel P. Moynihan (U.S.) in his memoirs: "The United States wished things to turn out as they did, and worked to bring this about. The Department of State desired that the United Nations prove utterly ineffective in whatever measures it undertook. This task was given to me, and I carried it forward with no inconsiderable success."[125]

Well, bully for you. In fact, Moynihan was proclaiming success and pounding his chest knowing full well that by February of 1976 more than 60,000 Timorese had been killed by Indonesian forces, some 10 percent of the population. Moynihan himself notes that this is "almost the proportion of casualties experienced by the Soviet Union during the Second World War."[126] Chomsky suggests that Moynihan is "claiming credit for 'success' in helping to cause a massacre that he compares to the consequences of Nazi aggression, not to speak of the growing number of victims in the subsequent period."[127]

But it's not just about the numbers. In the end it's about the human toll, the flesh and blood, and the terror that resonates for years among the victims, those brutalized by distant invisible killers—as well as killers not so distant and not so invisible. Ines Almeida was a Timorese survivor. She knows the pain first hand. She can touch the terror:

> The people of East Timor themselves have suffered so much that
> you can see it through their eyes. There is a fear. The eyes say it all.
> You don't have to talk to the people of East Timor. Even the little
> children—it shows in their eyes, in their face. They never smile.[128]

Historian Howard Zinn knows exactly who the distant invisible killers were. He lived among them for eighty-seven years, and Zinn, of course, pulls no punches:

> There were the death squads in Latin America and the decimation
> of the population of East Timor, with our government actively
> collaborating. Our churchgoing Christian Presidents, so pious in
> their references to the genocide against the Jews, kept supplying the
> instruments of death to the perpetrators of these atrocities.[129]

Carter, Reagan, Bush, Clinton: The Beat (Up) Goes On

In 1997, journalist Allan Nairn questioned former Assistant Secretary of State, Richard Holbrooke, about his years as Jimmy Carter's point man on Indonesia and East Timor:

> RICHARD HOLBROOKE:
> I have nothing to hide about my own role... No one is error-free
> here. But just for the purpose of everyone else in the room, this is
> not an accurate description of the administration's policy or my
> own role in it... You're welcome to disagree. But I am interested in

consequences of policy. I'm interested in solving the problem and not—

ALLAN NAIRN:
The consequences in this case were genocide, a third of the Timorese population killed.[130]

Holbrooke attempted to deftly duck the questions altogether. Nairn persisted, reminding Holbrooke that during the Carter years (1977 through 1980) the killing in Timor "rose to a peak." Nairn also reminded Holbrooke that under Carter's watch, U.S. military aid—including low-flying OV-10 Bronco aircraft used to strafe the population—continued unabated. Nairn cited testimony from Catholic Church sources regarding the ongoing genocide, and then finally reminded Holbrooke that while all this was taking place, Washington was "blocking the U.N. Security Council from taking enforcement action on the two resolutions, which called on Indonesia to withdraw its troops without delay." Again, Holbrooke attempted to play it off: "I do not accept most of your statements… I tell you here for the benefit of everyone else that the Timor issue is not as simple as (you) described just now."[131]

Watching the replay of the tape, Brad Simpson—head of the National Security Archive and a professor at the University of Maryland, just shook his head and said: "Well, Richard Holbrooke is simply lying through his teeth."[132]

Simpson went on to specify exactly what the Carter policy amounted to during those years and not Holbrooke's denial of history. "The policy," Simpson forcefully explained, "was to accept Indonesia's occupation of East Timor and in fact to characterize the resistance of the Timorese as an assault on Indonesian sovereignty."[133] Simpson identified Holbrooke and National Security Advisor Zbigniew Brzezinski as two forces constantly frustrating "the efforts of congressional human rights activists" to halt American military aid. "[I]n fact," Simpson stressed, they "accelerated the flow of weapons to Indonesia at the height of the genocide."[134] In 1978, Vice President Walter Mondale visited Jakarta and Indonesian military leaders strongly lobbied the American veep for fighter planes; it seems they were "having trouble hunting down the Timorese in the rugged terrain of East Timor's mountains."[135] Mondale was an efficient bagman and rushed a shipment of A-4 attack planes to Suharto.

As well, during the Carter administration, Washington's partner in crime working out of 10 Downing Street was selling Indonesia hundreds of Hawk ground attack aircraft manufactured by British Aerospace. The remnants of the British Empire were quite chummy with the Suharto regime and continued to increase military hardware sales including missiles, helicopters, naval vessels, armored vehicles, as well as advanced associated technology.[136] In fact, Margaret Thatcher received an award from the Indonesians for her help increasing their technological capabilities. Thatcher told the Indonesian audience: "I am proud to be one of you." And regarding Suharto, she called him "an immensely hard-working and effective ruler."[137]

The man from Plains, Georgia, was swept out of office by the so-called Reagan Revolution, one bolstered by the shiny new neocons that were now calling the shots. Typical of these conservative hardliners was Paul Wolfowitz, well known as a major Bush/Cheney chickenhawk that helped orchestrate and engineer the destruction of Iraq. At the time, Wolfowitz was Reagan's ambassador and main squeeze in Jakarta; he would later become Donald Rumsfeld's ax man as well as President of the World Bank, but during Reagan's decade he was a major cheerleader for Suharto. In *Failed States*, Noam Chomsky's 2006 book, he writes, "The head of Indonesia's state-sponsored National Human Rights Commission reported that 'of all former US ambassadors, he was considered closest to and most influential with Suharto and his family. But he never showed any interest in issues regarding democratization or respect for human rights.'"[138] Chomsky stresses that other human rights activists said, "Wolfowitz 'remained a defender of the Suharto regime through the 1990s.'"[139] In fact, even when it seemed inevitable to the entire world, including the United States, that Indonesia was going to leave East Timor and support independence in 1999, Wolfowitz continued to lobby for Indonesian rule—rolling out the age-old argument about the Timorese being uncivilized and that the island would once again break out into civil war.[140] Plain and simple, Paul Wolfowitz and his neocon collaborators are fucking psychopaths.

Throughout the Reagan and Bush years, Suharto and his regime were embraced as an important safeguard against the dreaded scourge of communism possibly taking root between the South China Sea and the Indian Ocean. Looking back on Reagan shortly after his death (while American media outlets were waxing poetic and whitewashing a grim reality), Yayasan HAK human rights leader, Jose Luis Oliveira, set the record in his country straight: "The world must not forget that under his leadership, America helped the Indonesian military commit genocide in East Timor... Reagan was a key supporter of the Indonesian military"[141]—a military, lest we forget, that Amnesty International estimates butchered 200,000 East Timorese.

Historical fact remains clear: Ford and Kissinger... Carter, Mondale, Holbrooke, and Brzezinski... Reagan, Bush, and Wolfowitz—through all of them, the Empire's insidious and murderous game bolstering hegemony remained firmly intact. The names may have changed in Washington but the policy continued unabated, one of uninterrupted "corporatocracy" protected by the hammer of U.S. Empire. And then the next guy, William Jefferson Clinton, did not let the gods of the kingdom down.

Independence Day

> When I think of Indonesia—a country on the equator with 180 million people, a median age of 18, and a Muslim ban on alcohol—I feel like I know what heaven looks like.
> —Donald Keough, President of Coca-Cola, 1992[142]

On 20 May 2002—looking like two suburban real estate moguls opening a strip mall in San Diego—former President Bill Clinton, along with his final U.N. Ambassador, Richard Holbrooke, were on hand to commemorate East Timor's long awaited independence and open the new U.S. Embassy. George W. Bush put down his favorite book, *The Pet Goat*, just long enough to ask his predecessor to represent Washington at the celebration and do the ribbon cutting. The title of Vassar professor Dr. Joseph Nevins' critical article on the irony of the day said it all:

First the Butchery, Then the Flowers

In the late 1990s, American support for their long-standing friends in Indonesia weakened—not because Washington (specifically the White House and the State Department) had a change of heart and suddenly saw the light, but because real grassroots pressure from American and international citizens on congressmen and senators turned into pressure from Capitol Hill on the administration to limit U.S. complicity with Indonesian war crimes. During Clinton's administration, Washington "halted the sale of small and light arms, riot-control equipment, helicopter-mounted weaponry, and armored personnel carriers to Indonesia," writes Joseph Nevins, who then stresses, "[the Clinton administration] also provided over $500 million in economic assistance over its two terms in office and sold and licensed the sales of hundreds of millions of dollars in weaponry to Jakarta."[143] In fact, Clinton circumvented a Congressional ban on military training "by allowing Indonesia to buy the service instead of getting it gratis." Further, Washington clandestinely provided "lethal training to Indonesia's military (TNI)," Nevins reveals, also emphasizing that through the Pentagon's Joint Combined Exchange Training, "[a]t least 28 training exercises in sniper tactics, urban warfare, explosives, psychological operations, and other techniques took place between 1993 and 1998,"[144] courtesy of the Green Berets, U.S. Air Force Commandos, as well as the Marines. And who benefitted the most from this hardcore training? The Indonesian special-forces aka Kopassus—an outfit with a long history of brutal armed atrocities. And who felt the brunt? Obviously you know the answer.

In 1994, after Clinton approved the sale of F-16 fighter planes and assault equipment to Suharto, the *Boston Globe* suggested:

> The arguments presented by senators solicitous of Suharto's regime—and of defense contractors, oil companies and mining concerns doing business with Jakarta—made Americans seem a people willing to overlook genocide for the sake of commerce.[145]

Indeed.

Throughout the 90s, international activists, including Nelson Mandela, pushed hard against Indonesia, especially after Suharto resigned in 1998 and was replaced by B.J. Habibie. The Australian government, led by John Howard, also lobbied Jakarta strenuously to create a path toward East Timor's independence, which led to a U.N.-run referendum that was held in late August 1998 offering the Timorese a choice between independence or becoming an autonomous state within Indonesia. Almost 80 percent of the electorate voted for independence—even though the Timorese were being threatened and terrorized to vote against independence by groups loyal to the Indonesian military.

But the terror and violence didn't stop there. Pro-integration fighters in East Timor, who were strongly supported by the Indonesian military, continued to wreak even more havoc throughout East Timor, destroying more than 70 percent of the country's infrastructure—water, electricity, irrigation, even the schools.[146] In fact, prior to the referendum as well as after the vote and leading up to the near destruction of East Timor, Australia collected significant intelligence "proving that the TNI" continued to orchestrate attacks against the East Timorese and their infrastructure. Furthermore, Nevins draws a clear line to Washington's decision to "look the other way":

> Given the intense levels of intelligence cooperation between the two countries—in addition to Washington's own highly advanced intelligence-gathering capabilities—the Clinton White House undoubtedly had access to such information. Indeed, a U.S. National Security Agency liaison officer is always in the DSD headquarters in Canberra. Nevertheless, the administration failed to threaten a cut off of economic and military aid as a preventative measure. It even refused to issue a presidential statement warning Jakarta of the dangers of not complying with its obligations to ensure security for the U.N. ballot.[147]

While on the campaign trail in 1992, Bill Clinton actually allowed a hint of truth to sneak out when he was asked about cutting off aid to the Indonesian regime:

> I'm very concerned about what's happened in East Timor and I think we have to review it. I'm not prepared at the present time to say categorically we should cut off all aid... We have ignored it so far in ways that I think are unconscionable, and I think we have to engage the government on the question of how those people are being treated, and I certainly wouldn't rule out the prospect of cutting aid.[148]

Candidate Clinton may have offered a tiny glimmer of hope for the terrorized people of East Timor, but President Clinton followed the bloody footprints of previous residents living at 1600 Pennsylvania Avenue. In fact, Clinton offered ongoing military support to Suharto throughout his two terms in office, according to *DemocracyNow!*, "waiting until Indonesia's army had burned East Timor to the ground [in 1999] before finally cutting off military ties."[149]

Two years before Bill Clinton jumped on the Indonesian bandwagon of destruction, during his last days hangin' with Gennifer Flowers, Paula Jones, and a host of other below the waist "consultants," he should have been more aware of "current events" as they say, since Bubba wanted so much to be the most powerful man in the (so-called) free world. He should have focused his compassionate heart, the one so warmly influenced by a place called Hope, on a small southeast Asian island drenched in blood, courtesy of his country's weapons, military training, and their long-standing political support and cover regarding countless and ongoing atrocities. In fact, one of those atrocities happened right under Slick Willie's nose in late October of 1991.

Santa Cruz Cemetery: The Dili Massacre

It's really a very simple story. The United Nations sponsored a Portuguese delegation that was set to visit East Timor and investigate reported human rights abuses. The delegation would personally hear from the Timorese people themselves. "It would be the first real opportunity," write Amy and David Goodman, "that Timorese would have to let the outside world know what was happening to them."[150] Suddenly the Portuguese delegation cancelled "at the behest of the United States and Australia."[151] And who could blame them? It tends to be bad for PR when people find out you're complicit in genocide. So when the Indonesian military determined that the U.N.-sponsored event was cancelled, they surrounded the Motael Catholic Church where they discovered numerous young people seeking sanctuary inside, waiting for the delegation to hear their pleas. For the military, it was time to enact some payback against these Timorese who were courageous and ready to speak out regarding the iron fist of Indonesian rule.

A young man named Sebastião Gomes climbed up to the steeple of the church and began sounding the bell, a signal to all Timorese that the church was under siege. The troops rushed inside, apprehended Gomes and then executed him at close range. Amy Goodman remembers, "His dried blood was still on the church steps."[152] On the morning of 12 November 1991, a mass protest in response to the killing of Sebastião Gomes moved from the Motael Church through the streets of Dili toward their final destination—the Santa Cruz Cemetery. Goodman was there and writes:

> When the mourners arrived at the cemetery, the killing began…
> the soldiers beat us, fracturing Allan's skull [fellow journalist Allan
> Nairn]… But the experience for the Timorese was far, far worse…
> The soldiers went on killing for the entire morning. They chased
> unarmed men, women, and children into houses and through the
> cemetery and just kept shooting. The soldiers had dragged an old
> Timorese man into a sewer ditch behind us. Every time he put up
> his hands in a prayer sign, they would smash his face with the butts
> of their rifles.[153]

Max Stahl, a reporter from the UK's Yorkshire TV filmed the massacre, burying his videotapes in the cemetery for safety. After he was arrested, interrogated for nine hours, and finally released, he went back to the cemetery under the cover of night and retrieved his proof. One sequence in the footage is achingly beautiful and horrific at the same time. A young man is shot in the stomach and lays dying in his friend's arms. Blood is everywhere. As the young man nears death, he pleads with the reporter filming his death:

Show this to the world.[154]

7 Cannon Fodder...

Public Domain, United States Army

GUNNERY SERGEANT HARTMAN

Today is Christmas! There will be a magic show at zero-nine-thirty! Chaplain Charlie will tell you about how the free world will conquer Communism with the aid of God and a few Marines! God has a hard-on for Marines because we kill everything we see! He plays His games, we play ours! To show our appreciation for so much power, we keep heaven packed with fresh souls! God was here before the Marine Corps! So you can give your heart to Jesus, but your ass belongs to the Corps! Do you ladies understand?

—From Stanley Kubrick's tour de force Full Metal Jacket

...for Capitalism

I spent thirty-three years and four months in active military service as a member of this country's most agile military force, the Marine Corps. I served in all commissioned ranks from Second Lieutenant to Major-General. And during that period, I spent most of my time being a high class muscle-man for Big Business, for Wall Street and for the Bankers. In short, I was a racketeer, a gangster for capitalism.

—Excerpt from a speech delivered in 1933 by
Major General Smedley Butler, USMC

In fiscal year 2014, the Department of Defense budget for military recruitment and advertising was $1,868,700,000—that's $1.8 billion.[1] And like any other product bought and sold on the open market, major studies and focus groups were used to gather data that would later shape the public marketing assault—in this instance on the children being targeted for use as cannon fodder for the Empire and by the Empire—an Empire only as strong as the legs it stands on.

These studies have sterile, clinical names like "Evaluating Military Advertising and Recruiting: Theory and Methodology" and are conducted by equally sterile and clinical organizations like the "Board on Behavioral, Cognitive, and Sensory Sciences." Other studies include this gem: "Attitudes, Aptitudes, and Aspirations of American Youth: Implications for Military Recruitment" conducted by this same group of behavioral scientists dedicated (as their mission statement says) to drawing "attention to the significance of the behavioral, cognitive, and sensory sciences to national policy."[2] As their name and mission imply, they evaluate and report on the entire spectrum of the Department of Defense's efforts to recruit children and young adults all across the country.

But no matter how scientific and clinical these studies are, and no matter how savvy and incredibly well funded these marketing campaigns continue to be, the recruiting process is not unlike, and nothing more than, Mephistopheles stealing souls in an overpopulated Faustian bargain—the proverbial "deal with the devil."

> [Please note: throughout this chapter on American military recruitment, we felt it imperative to concentrate on the Empire's systems and strategies of recruitment at the height of imperial conflict—in this case the post-9/11 American invasions in the Middle East and Africa—when the dogs of war are most in need of fresh meat for the sausage grinder.]

Cannon Fodder, Part One:
Propaganda, Patriotism, and the Advertising that Kills

The disillusionment comes swiftly. It is not the war of the movies. It is not the glory promised by the recruiters. The mythology fed to you by the church, the press, the school, the state, and the entertainment industry is exposed as a lie.

—Chris Hedges, "War Is Betrayal"

What follows is a classic commercial/recruitment video for the United States Army, a piece of manipulation for the ages, one that marks a seminal work of marketing and scheming brilliance. Faustian indeed. In fact, the copywriter could have been Satan himself, banging away on his brand-new Dell, howling delightfully at the moon.

Throughout the transcript below, there are SHORT POETIC STATEMENTS that fade on- and off-screen, intercut with cinematic slow-motion imagery—a kaleidoscope narrative of demographic selling points (identified no doubt by the battery of behavioral scientists carefully crafting this diabolical, soul-sucking operation). It's a wily message hatched inside their climate controlled office towers, glass structures with impressive addresses throughout the District of Columbia. The example below is from the 2007 "Army Strong" campaign. Here's how the spot unfolds:

FADE IN

Cue music—which is noble and epic, and builds to a triumphant climax (and, of course, in the end the good guys win).

ONSCREEN COPY:

> **—WEBSTER DEFINES STRONG AS HAVING GREAT PHYSICAL POWER**

> **—AS HAVING MORAL OR INTELLECTUAL POWER**

> **—AS STRIKING OR SUPERIOR OF ITS KIND**

> **—BUT WITH ALL DUE RESPECT TO WEBSTER,**

> **—THERE'S STRONG.**

> **—AND THEN THERE'S ARMY STRONG.**

Followed by a stunning collection of stylized and vivid images that capture the adventure and glory of war—all very sexy.

> **—IT IS A STRENGTH LIKE NONE OTHER.**

More images: camaraderie, success.

> **—IT IS A PHYSICAL STRENGTH.**

Soldiers in training, dropping from silhouetted helicopter gunships set against a dramatic amber sky… followed by more helicopters airborne across a blazing and setting sun.

> **—IT IS AN EMOTIONAL STRENGTH.**

A returning soldier hugs his wife… followed by a soldier in his fatigues and helmet walking through Middle Eastern desert landscape surrounded by three brown kids holding hands, smiling.

> **—IT IS A STRENGTH OF CHARACTER.**

Medals are pinned on a young female soldier… then cut to an older Vet, maybe Korea or possibly Vietnam, saluting during a Fourth of July-like parade.

> **—AND STRENGTH OF PURPOSE.**

Images of soldiers standing watch—sentinels protecting us from an unseen enemy.

—THE STRENGTH TO DO GOOD TODAY.

Action shots of soldiers calling the shots—they're confident, in charge.

—AND THE STRENGTH TO DO WELL TOMORROW.

An African-American male looking out from a corporate tower high above the 99%, quickly followed by another African-American male fishing with his young son, sitting on the dock of the bay—it's golden hour. Miller time.

—THE STRENGTH TO OBEY.

Strong salutes from proud soldiers.

—AND STRENGTH TO COMMAND.

A rock-solid chiseled white dude from Central Casting, carrying all of Manifest Destiny on his shoulders… then, led by a crisp flag, a platoon of soldiers run like the wind.

—THE STRENGTH TO BUILD.

Slick camera shots capture a platoon literally moving earth with massive machines.

—AND THE STRENGTH TO TEAR DOWN.

Haloed in a cloud of dirt and smoke, a tank rumbles right at us.

—THE STRENGTH TO GET YOURSELF OVER.

A soldier climbs hard up the side of an obstacle course.

—AND THE STRENGTH TO GET OVER YOURSELF.

More climbing on the obstacle course… soldiers help a fellow climber make it over the top, brothers and sisters in arms.

—THERE IS NOTHING ON THIS GREEN EARTH

Fast shots of an engaged ARMY moving forward…

(Bet they wanted to say "God's green Earth"—also bet the audience mentally fills in the "God" part and then naturally absorbs the sentiment: Christendom, Soldiers for Christ.)

—THAT IS STRONGER THAN THE US ARMY.

Helicopters join the fight.

—BECAUSE THERE IS NOTHING ON THIS GREEN EARTH

Silhouetted against another brilliant amber sky, a soldier salutes a passing helicopter gunship that transitions into Old Glory—antique and flapping rhythmically with the crescendo of Hollywood's war music.

—THAT IS STRONGER THAN A US ARMY SOLDIER.

The camera slides past soldiers with their right hands raised taking an oath in front of a giant American flag… music ramps up faster, building to a big finish and ushered along by another sexy motherfucker of a shot—last title:

—STRONG. (Fade in) ARMY—ARMY STRONG.

Hard out on music: US Army logo.

FADE TO BLACK.

It's enough to make Helene Bertha Amalie "Leni" Riefenstahl blush with professional pride.

The infamous German actress, dancer, and film director who created *Triumph of the Will*—the 1934 Adolf Hitler commissioned film about Germany's return to world dominance—would stand in awe of Madison Avenue's ability to sell the American military machine to our children. They position a career in the military as the magic potion necessary to succeed in almost any walk of life. In reality, for some, it's the last ditch panacea for the frustration of unemployment; for others, those caught in a de facto poor people's draft, it's the nostrum for poverty; and for many more, it's the "trigger" moment for a generation of Manchurian candidates who have been slowly but dramatically brainwashed by a well-designed system of propaganda aimed at mass jingoistic indoctrination.

It starts in grade schools in all fifty states with a robotic pledge that's repeated daily for years: *"I pledge Allegiance to the flag of the United States of America and to the Republic for which it stands, one nation under God, indivisible, with Liberty and Justice for all."* To dissect this myth using the reality of American history would be child's play and unnecessary in this narrative. The substantive reality of the "pledge" falls smack dab in the crosshairs of Nazi Propaganda Minister Dr. Joseph Goebbels' oft-quoted suggestion: "The bigger the lie, the more it will be believed." Supplemental religious schools like traditional Sunday schools and Catholic Catechism classes supply coloring books for impressionable young minds so they can artistically connect resurrection pictures and the Annunciation of Mary with U.S. presidents carved on Mount Rushmore; add in Old Glory flapping above a Rockwell-esque Pleasantville and, well, you get the picture. The programming begins early and continues in similar forms and in varying degrees throughout the arc of one's American life.

Perhaps most conspicuously on game day—be it the NFL, NHL, NBA, MLB, college and high school sports, Little League baseball, Pop Warner football, as well as local crap games in dark alleyways. Besides the ad nauseam and completely pointless and superfluous playing of the National Anthem, Americans are forced to endure a ghastly song with bizarre lyrics—and then many times following the anthem fans are also forced to religiously suffer through additional patriotic hijinks. (Let us give props to Colin Kaepernick for his courage and steadfastness against this beast.)

In November 2015, U.S. Senators Jeff Flake (R-AZ) and John McCain (R-AZ) released a joint oversight report exposing that the Department of Defense budgeted $53 million for *staged* patriotic displays at sporting events—aka buying blind devotion and patriotism with taxpayer dollars. The menu of patriotic flaunts and struts included numerous events, from on-field performances and enlistment ceremonies, to ceremonial first pitches and puck drops. The $53 million did not include NASCAR sponsorships, which could total $100 million.

Let us set the scene: opening day, Dodger Stadium, 56,000-plus fans cheering hysterically... not for a walk-off blast deep in the right field bleachers, but for a military flyover of killing machines usually reserved for dropping their own blasts and bombs: F-18 fighter jets and a massive Stealth Bomber roar by overhead, lest anyone forget who the hell is in charge. The mass hysteria erupts in unison at this dramatic display of military hardware—much like the "queen of diamonds" in Richard Condon's *The Manchurian Candidate,* which triggers the guiltless assassin Sergeant Raymond Shaw... and then "The Pledge" comes roaring back from grade school with a vengeance: *"I pledge Allegiance to the flag of the United States of America..."* Look around the stadium: eyes wide open with movie blockbuster-like wonderment, locked on a crystal blue sky as the wave of bombers continues to rock Chavez Ravine. *"And to the Republic for which it stands..."* Hands clapping feverishly, arms waving like an Elmer Gantry tent revival. *"One nation, under God..."* There it is, Jesus and America, forever linked by bombs bursting in air... and then finally a giant American flag unfurls over the outfield grass—God's green Earth. *"With Liberty and Justice for all."* 'Nuff said. The roar dissipates into the distance of a warm Los Angeles afternoon. The crowd slowly comes down off of their patriotic crack high. The flag is folded up and carted away for another big day down the road. The aroma of Dodger Dogs, popcorn, and watered-down beer now replaces the smell of jet fuel. *Play ball!*

And then up in the sky, overlooking this spectacle, we freeze frame on Leni Riefenstahl's all-knowing grin, ghosted back in the far reaches of one's imagination, beaming from ear to Nazi ear.

Philosophizing Disgrace

We offer an alternative version of the all-too-familiar patriotic fly-over—simple and to the point. We start with a small prop plane creeping noisily along. The plane tows two massive banners. The first placard reads: *"Former U.S. Secretary of State Madeline Albright says 500,000 Dead Iraqi Children Was Worth It,"* followed by a second enormous banner boasting this image:

No credit

The stadium public address announcer accompanies the first flyover:

> *The Los Angeles Times reports that a deadly NATO airstrike in Afghanistan has killed a mother and her five children in the Sangin district.*[3]

Next, a second noisy prop plane rumbles out over the golden hills of Chavez Ravine pulling this banner:

No credit

Once again, accompanied by the stadium public address announcer:

A resident of Ishaqi shot this cell phone photograph of bodies Iraqi police said were children executed by U.S. troops after a night raid. A State Department cable obtained by WikiLeaks quotes the U.N. investigator of extrajudicial killings as saying an autopsy showed the residents of the house had been handcuffed and shot in the head, including children under the age of five. A U.S. diplomatic cable made public by WikiLeaks provides evidence that U.S. troops executed at least 10 Iraqi civilians, including a woman in her 70s and a 5-month-old infant, then called in an airstrike to destroy the evidence.[4]

And then this next image can be handed out as a four-color flyer, a souvenir to take home from the ballpark with a Dodger cap and a giant "We're #1" foam hand, courtesy of Farmer John Dodger Dogs… the extra long pork weiners:

Photo: Carolyn Cole, Los Angeles Times

With the caption:

An Iraqi family mourns the death of three relatives in Baghdad—a father, his teenage son, and another male relative. All were shot and killed by U.S. Marines after the car they were driving allegedly did not stop while passing a building occupied by the Marines.[5]

No, the photo isn't missing; the book printer didn't screw up. We attempted to clear the rights in good faith but the *Los Angeles Times* would not grant us permission to reprint the photo here. Why? We're not sure but we have our suspicions. Some guy at the paper that handles these things, Ralph something or other, let's call him Ralph Malph, asked for an overall synopsis of *Murder Incorporated* so they could review where the photo was going to be used. Fair enough—so we emailed the *Times* this synopsis:

Murder Incorporated: Empire, Genocide and Manifest Destiny is a searing critique of the American Empire, a diagnosis of a corrupt pathology. This dramatic three-book series strives to educate, to enlighten and enliven the people against the corruptions of empire—corruptions that stretch from Columbus's first steps on Hispaniola through yesterday's murderous drone attack. More than a history book, Murder Incorporated is a lively, irreverent, and spirited alternative to the orthodoxy of American exceptionalism.

Then Ralph Malph came back with this response:

Unfortunately due to the sensitive and graphic nature of the image (young children, mourning family), that particular photo is not authorized or available for licensing from the Los Angeles Times.

Let's review. (1) The photograph and the story was published in the paper back in 2003, at the height of the American bombardment and slaughter in Iraq. This major U.S. paper already published the photo for all the world to see. The image will live on the Internet probably until the planet spins out of orbit. *Sensitive?* (2) The photograph is not *graphic*—as you will see, it is the honest reaction to the graphic violence carried out by the United States Marine Corp. Semper Fidelis. (3) And here's the obvious bullshit: If their response above was true and accurate, why did they ask for a synopsis? What matter would a description of any kind make if this was their stated policy? Obviously none. In fact, if this were the policy they would have sent us their response before asking us for a synopsis. Clearly, this bastion of the Fourth Estate scampered back into the dense cowardly forest that obfuscates their chummy relationship protecting power—their usual knee-jerk and lock step reaction forever loyal to manufacturing consent. (We explore the mainstream media's cozy relationship to power in Book Three in the chapter titled *Tribune of the People or Servant to Power?*)

To view the image the *Los Angeles Times* decided was too *sensitive and graphic* for you to see, go here:

https://www.worldpressphoto.org/collection/photo/2004/people-news/carolyn-cole

Or here:
https://www.pinterest.com/pin/352336370818578622/?lp=true

Or why not go right to the *Los Angeles Times*:
http://www.latimes.com/world/la-041103cole-gallery-photogallery.html

PLAY BALL!

Photo: Robert Hanashiro, USA TODAY Sports

In fact Marine Corporal Nicholas Kimmel wanted desperately to play ball. But instead found himself hobbling out to the mound, waving to a cheering crowd before throwing out the ceremonial first pitch prior to Game 2 of the 2012 World Series in San Francisco. Kimmel, a former high school baseball star, lost both legs and his left arm during his second tour of duty in Afghanistan.[6] (Dalton Trumbo warned us well: ~~Johnny~~ *Nicholas Got His Gun.*)

Kimmel might disagree but this once fully whole person was thrown into a meat grinder by an empire that doesn't give a rat's ass about his life, nor his soul, and used him as a tool in their geopolitical and economic intrigues. Cannon fodder for Capitalism… and in San Francisco, the crowd roared.

Call it philosophizing disgrace.

Historian Howard Zinn passionately frames how unbridled patriotism distorts, manipulates, and finally allows for gruesome acts to be carried out in the name of God and country—a foundational element that encourages and bolsters military recruitment:

> What struck me as I began to study history was how nationalist fervor—inculcated from childhood on by pledges of allegiance, national anthems, flags waving and rhetoric blowing—permeated the educational systems of all countries, including our own. I wonder now how the foreign policies of the United States would look if we wiped out the national boundaries of the world, at least in our minds, and thought of all children everywhere as our own. Then we could never drop an atomic bomb on Hiroshima,

or napalm on Vietnam, or wage war anywhere, because wars, especially in our time, are always wars against children, indeed our children.[7]

Let's take Zinn a step further: history also illustrates that wars are always waged against children, *by* children. Or as former United States Senator and staunch antiwar presidential candidate George McGovern brusquely said, "I'm fed up to the ears with old men dreaming up new wars for young men to die in."

Engineering Consent

The indoctrination begins early and the manufacturing of the patriotic lie—chock full of demonization, xenophobia, and lockstep conditioning—becomes systemic and universal in almost every institutional framework: school, church, corporation, mass media, as well as the all-important drive of market forces. Edward Bernays, a pioneer in the scientific approach to shaping and then manipulating mass public opinion, famously wrote in his jarringly prophetic 1928 book *Propaganda*:

> The conscious and intelligent manipulation of the organized habits and opinions of the masses is an important element in democratic society. Those who manipulate this unseen mechanism of society constitute an invisible government which is the true ruling power of our country.[8]

Clearly, Bernays knew a thing or two about the "engineering of consent" (a term he coined). As an integral member of the U.S. Committee on Public Information during World War I, Bernays experienced firsthand, and actively participated in, the powerful propaganda apparatus that was mobilized by the American government to package, advertise, and sell the war to the American people—and they sold it like Corn Flakes.

"Make the World Safe for Democracy" became the rallying cry, the pitch, the slogan, the big sell. In fact, the overarching model hatched by the U.S. Committee on Public Information became the blueprint marketing strategy for all future U.S. wars. The potency of this propaganda gem can be easily measured by its longevity: it's been almost one hundred years and counting since American president Woodrow Wilson uttered the words to a joint session of Congress when seeking a Declaration of War against Germany so that the world would "be made safe for democracy."[9]

To this day the phrase remains a brawny and essential element in America's propaganda arsenal. And, of course, forgotten in Wilson's words regarding democracy was the carnage unleashed by the war's savagery. World War I, with its introduction of the modern machine gun, was a human garbage disposal grinding young bodies in shocking fashion. In his plea for war to the young (American cannon fodder he needed to fight and die by the droves), Wilson warned: "It is a fearful thing to lead this great peaceful people into war, into the most terrible and disastrous of all wars, civilization itself seeming to be in the balance." Unfortunately, Wilson was not exaggerating as he ushered more than 116,000 Americans into an early grave. Another 204,000 were wounded in action.[10] France lost half its male population between the ages of twenty and thirty-two. Casualties for Germany, Austria, and Hungary—the so-called enemy— were staggering: approximately three million killed and nine million wounded.

So, Mr. Wilson, as you once said, it was "the war to end all wars." How did that work out for you? How did that work out for the rest of us?

Regarding *Propaganda* the book and "propaganda" the practice, Mark Crispin Miller—author and Professor of Media, Culture and Communication at New York University, wrote the new introduction to the book's current reprint. In it he frames the powerful paradigm of mass manipulation, especially with regard to how the practices employed during World War I cast a long, dark, and influential shadow over all the war-mongering campaigns of the 20th and now 21st centuries.

> Although the practice had, albeit unnamed, been variously used by governments for centuries (Napoleon was especially incisive on the subject, as well as an inspired practitioner), it was not until 1915 that governments first systematically deployed the entire range of modern media to rouse their populations to fanatical assent. Here was an extraordinary state accomplishment: mass enthusiasm at the prospect of a global brawl that otherwise would mystify those very masses, and that shattered most of those who actually took part in it. The Anglo-American drive to demonize "the Hun," and to cast the war as a transcendent clash between Atlantic "civilization" and Prussian "barbarism," made so powerful an impression on so many that the worlds of government and business were forever changed.[11]

Bernays' career somersaulted through the 20th century and his services were well used by the U.S. Government and American corporations alike. He helped orchestrate General Electric's stranglehold on the electric power industry. He manipulated the truth and created dangerous outright lies that helped U.S. power brokers carry out their massive slaughter during World War I. In 1953, Bernays was employed by the United Fruit Company and worked closely with the Eisenhower Administration and the CIA to overthrow the democratically elected government of Jacabo Arbenz by spreading lies and legends about communist subversion and their associated hobgoblins.[12] Miller offers a trenchant warning regarding the undermining and manipulative power of systemic propaganda by concluding, "That propaganda easily seduces even those whom it most horrifies is a paradox that Bernays grasped completely; and it is one that we must try at last to understand, if we want to change the world that Edward Bernays, among others, made for us."[13]

> *"Patriotism is a superstition artificially created and maintained through a network of lies and falsehoods; a superstition that robs man of his self-respect and dignity, and increases his arrogance and conceit."*
> —Emma Goldman, "Patriotism: A Menace to Liberty" (1908)

The onslaught of propaganda designed to promote American exceptionalism has been ubiquitous over the past two centuries plus. From sea to shining sea, the tentacles of this mass hysteria reach every level of society. For Americans in the 21st century, it is the opiate of exceptionalism that rules the roost. In an interview with *ZNet*, political dissident, philosopher, and historian Noam Chomsky discusses the complexities of patriotism. "To begin with," Chomsky states, "we have to be clear about what we mean by patriotic feelings. For a time when I was in high school, I cheered for the school athletic teams. That's a form of patriotism—group loyalty. It can take pernicious forms, but in and of itself it can be quite harmless, maybe even positive."[14] Chomsky shifts the discussion of patriotism to how it intersects with the political landscape. "At the national level, what 'patriotism' means depends on how we view the society. Those with deep totalitarian commitments identify the state with the society, its people, and its culture. Therefore those who criticized the policies of the Kremlin under Stalin were condemned as 'anti-Soviet' or 'hating Russia.' For their counterparts in the West, those who criticize the policies of the U.S. government are 'anti-American' and 'hate America.' Those are the standard terms used by intellectual opinion, including left-liberal segments, so deeply committed to their totalitarian instincts that they cannot even recognize them, let alone understand their disgraceful history."[15] Chomsky then envisions a form of patriotism that puts the welfare of people above the commonplace practice of fear mongering. It's a viewpoint seldom shared.

> For those whose instincts are democratic rather than totalitarian, "patriotism" means commitment to the welfare and improvement of the society, its people, and its culture. That's a natural sentiment and one that can be quite positive. It's one all serious activists share, I presume; otherwise why take the trouble to do what we do? But the kind of "patriotism" fostered by totalitarian societies and military dictatorships, and internalized as second nature by much of intellectual opinion in more free societies, is one of the worst maladies of human history, and will probably do us all in before too long.[16]

Facing the truth has never been a strong suit for Americans or their leaders. Just a cursory look at the wide divide between the myth and reality of American history offers more than enough evidence of this ongoing problem. In fact, one of the great indicators of America's inability to acknowledge the stains on the canvas of their bloody history can be found in the language of the culture. Along with the spin-doctors and marketing gurus hired by the power brokers to sell death and destruction like dish detergent, Americans love to invent a soft language aimed at peddling the harsh realities in a polite and acceptable manner—euphemistic language that disguises the truth, evades fundamental facts, and ultimately "positions" the unthinkable as "normal."

SHELL SHOCK!

George Carlin offers this denunciation from his 1990 HBO Comedy Special *Doin' It Again.*

> There's a condition in combat. Most people know about it. It's when a fighting person's nervous system has been stressed to its absolute peak and maximum. Can't take anymore input. The nervous system has either snapped or is about to snap. In the First World War that condition was called "shell shock"—simple, honest, direct language. Two syllables: "shell shock." Almost sounds like the guns themselves. That was seventy years ago. Then a whole generation went by and the Second World War came along and that very same combat condition was called "battle fatigue"—four syllables now.

Takes a little longer to say. Doesn't seem to hurt as much. "Fatigue" is a nicer word than "shock." [yells] SHELL SHOCK! [now gentle] *Battle fatigue...* Then we had the war in Korea, 1950. Madison Avenue was riding high by that time and the very same combat condition was called "operational exhaustion." Hey, we're up to eight syllables now! And the humanity has been squeezed completely out of the phrase. It's totally sterile: "Operational exhaustion." Sounds like something that might happen to your car. Then of course, came the war in Vietnam, which has only been over for about sixteen or seventeen years, and thanks to the lies and deceits surrounding that war, I guess it's no surprise that the very same condition was called "post-traumatic stress disorder." Still eight syllables, but we've added a hyphen! And the pain is completely buried under jargon. "Post-traumatic stress disorder." I'll bet you if we still called it shell shock, some of those Vietnam veterans might have gotten the attention they needed at the time. I betcha. I betcha.

The manipulation runs hard and it runs deep.

It must, because what the oligarchy is actually asking mothers and fathers to embrace is the very real and tangible experience of giving birth to a child, raising that child, educating that child, loving that child, and then delivering that child to the overlords running the giant military sausage apparatus to then be converted into killing machines that are then launched out into hell—killing fields camouflaged by sexy mission names like "Operation Desert Storm," "Operation Enduring Freedom," and the Disney-like "Operation New Dawn," which summons up Bambi scampering through a dewy meadow.

Some recruits train and then transition to become enlisted personnel—and one day can become officers, who might be fortunate enough to spread liberty and democracy as valiant warriors lounging in comfortable office complexes stateside, working keyboards and joy sticks during the day and then home by six for supper and backyard time with the kids. The next morning it's back for more bloodless video war games, orchestrated from places like the CIA's complex in northern Virginia or Nevada's Creech and Nellis Air Force bases near Las Vegas, or Hurlburt Field on the Gulf of Mexico in Florida where segments of the Paramount/Hasbro film *Transformers 3* was fittingly filmed. Hollywood and a toy company—perfect partners working in a drone command center responsible for the sanitized murder taking place on the ground in places like Pakistan,

Afghanistan, Libya, Iraq, Somalia, and Yemen. Casually forgotten, of course, is this: the drones at the killing end of the video joy sticks are called "hunter-killers" and are loaded with Hellfire missiles and satellite-guided bombs that rip human beings to shreds. Their bloody entrails and shattered dreams are conveniently never felt and never witnessed. Sanitized killing is cost-effective and clean. No fuss, no muss. Of course, military recruiters pitch these cushy assignments as distinct, even likely possibilities and the associated marketing materials do more than hint at recruits landing these virtual experience gigs far from the bloody frontlines.

Bug-Splats

Back in 2011, Tara McKelvey, a correspondent for *Newsweek*, wrote this intro to an article entitled "Inside the Killing Machine," a chronicle that outlines how bureaucrats and CIA lawyers authorize and carry out drone attacks with less so-called "legal" wrangling than it takes to obtain permission in the United States to wiretap someone.

> It was an ordinary-looking room located in an office building in northern Virginia. The place was filled with computer monitors, keyboards, and maps. Someone sat at a desk with his hand on a joystick. John A. Rizzo, who was serving as the CIA's acting general counsel, hovered nearby, along with other people from the agency. Together they watched images on a screen that showed a man and his family traveling down a road thousands of miles away. The vehicle slowed down, and the man climbed out. A moment later, an explosion filled the screen, and the man was dead. "It was very businesslike," says Rizzo. An aerial drone had killed the man, a high-level terrorism suspect, after he had gotten out of the vehicle, while members of his family were spared. "The agency was very punctilious about this," Rizzo says. "They tried to minimize collateral damage, especially women and children."[17]

"Businesslike" indeed—bureaucrats and lawyers assassinating suspects at will. It's this cold, calculating, legalistic, and sterile approach that trickles down to the American body politic (with the unwavering support of the corporate media) and assures them that cold-blooded murder is okay because "we're" ridding the world of bad guys—the demons, terrorists, and savages who just want "to kill us because of our freedoms." This trickle down indoctrination also assures the body politic that the killing can be carried out in their name and financed by their immense tax dollars and it's all just hunky-dory—the ends justify the means. In a U.S. Government statement that underscores the axiom "law is politics by other means," McKelvey continues:

> In defense of a hard-nosed approach, administration officials say the aerial-drone strikes are wiping out Qaeda militants and reducing the chances of another terrorist attack. They have also been careful to reassure the public that the killings are legal. When NEWSWEEK asked the administration for comment, a U.S. official who declined to be identified addressing such a sensitive subject said: "These CT [counterterrorism] operations are conducted in strict accordance with American law and are governed by legal guidance provided by the Department of Justice."[18]

And the fox watches the hen house. McKelvey's article casually illustrates how the men ordering the kills clearly acknowledge that their actions are tantamount to murder.

> The broad outlines of the CIA's operations to kill suspected terrorists have been known to the public for some time—including how the United States kills Qaeda and Taliban militants by drone aircraft in Pakistan. But the formal process of determining who should be hunted down and "blown to bits," as Rizzo puts it, has not been previously reported. A look at the bureaucracy behind the operations reveals that it is multilayered and methodical, run by a corps of civil servants who carry out their duties in a professional manner. Still, the fact that Rizzo was involved in "murder," as he sometimes puts it, and that operations are planned in advance in a legalistic fashion, raises questions.[19]

Raises questions? Okay, *Newsweek*, here's one: why aren't these killers being prosecuted for murder? Oh, that's right—

Kill one person, call it murder
Kill a thousand, ten thousand, a million or so, call it foreign policy

Human rights lawyer Shahzad Akbar, who works for Pakistan's Foundation for Fundamental Rights and the British human rights charity Reprieve, released a damning dossier with extensive research that offers stunning evidence of the deadly impact of U.S. drone attacks in Pakistan. The *Daily Mail* in the UK reports on the new evidence, writing:

> [Exhaustive research] sets out in heartbreaking detail the deaths of teachers, students and Pakistani policemen. It also describes how bereaved relatives are forced to gather their loved ones' dismembered body parts in the aftermath of strikes.[20]

Court cases were filed in Pakistan aimed at producing murder investigations against two U.S. officials who were named for ordering the strikes inside Pakistan—Jonathan Banks, the former head of the CIA's Islamabad station, and the abovementioned John Rizzo. The plaintiff in the Islamabad case was Karim Khan, a journalist and translator and also the father of two sons: Asif Iqbal, 35, and Zahinullah, 18, who were both killed by a Hellfire missile fired from a Predator drone. The missile slammed into the family's dining room on New Year's Eve in 2009. Asif was an English teacher who liked to quote the Pakistani national poet, Iqbal. Zahinullah was working his way through college. "We have never had anything to do with militants or terrorists," Khan said, "and for that reason I always assumed we would be safe."[21]

Speaking further about the murder of his sons, Khan said, "Zahinullah had a wound on the side of his face and his body was crushed and charred. I am told the people who push the buttons to fire the missiles call these strikes 'bug-splats.' It is beyond my imagination how they can lack all mercy and compassion, and carry on doing this for years. They are not human beings."[22]

Obama Killed a 16-Year-Old American in Yemen. Trump Just Killed His 8-Year-Old Sister.

The headline above is from a 2017 report at *The Intercept* and underscores the U.S. government's long-standing tradition of passing the killing baton from one administration to the next. Obama—the so-called antiwar candidate in 2008—was elected and then quickly grabbed the truncheon from the Bush Crime Family and suddenly became "presidential" as he started his trigger-happy foreign policy in the Middle East and Africa; and it was drone homicide, courtesy of the AGM-114 Hellfire air-to-surface missile, that was his preferred big stick (produced for about $120,000 a piece by the good church-going folks at Lockheed Martin, Boeing, and Northrop Grumman). When Obama and his slick lawyers at the Justice Department decided to try their hand at killing American citizens without trial, they used as justification the Authorization to Use Military Force (AUMF)—the 14 September 2001 congressional act that sanctioned the indefinable global war against al-Qaida. Very similar to the freewheeling murderous spirit of the 1964 Gulf of Tonkin Resolution with regard to American military operations in Vietnam, recent administrations and the DOJ use this act to give U.S. presidents legal cover to strike and kill wherever and whomever they believe poses "a continued and imminent threat to U.S. persons or interests."[23] What a great bit of Washington wizardry and legal legerdemain: no real limitations—it's the "legal" authority to wage perpetual war on a global scale.

A license to kill… and that's exactly what Obama used as camouflage when he ordered the assassination of Anwar al-Awlaki, an American citizen living in Yemen. The imam and Islamic cleric was born in Las Cruces, New Mexico, and graduated from Colorado State University and then studied for his Ph.D. at George Washington University. The U.S. government believed he was a central planner for terrorist operations by Al-Qaeda—and this American citizen was killed in a September 2011 drone attack that hit a car he was stepping into "despite the fact that he had never been charged with (let alone convicted of) any crime,"[24] journalist Glenn Greenwald stresses.

Prior to and after the killing of al-Awlaki, the ACLU sued Obama in federal court on due process grounds, as characterized by a *Mother Jones* headline: *ACLU to Obama—You Can't Just Vaporize Americans Without Judicial Process*. And then weeks later, Obama killed his son, 16-year-old Abdulrahman. Greenwald offers the details:

> Two weeks after the killing of Awlaki, a separate CIA drone strike in Yemen killed his 16-year-old American born son, along with the boy's 17-year-old cousin and several other innocent Yemenis. The U.S. eventually claimed that the boy was not their target but merely "collateral damage." Abdulrahman's grief-stricken grandfather, Nasser al-Awlaki, urged the Washington Post "to visit a Facebook memorial page for Abdulrahman," which explained: "Look at his pictures, his friends, and his hobbies. His Facebook page shows a typical kid."[25]

When pressed on the killing, Obama's press secretary, Robert Gibbs, offered this glib and snarky comebacker, clearly blaming Abdulrahman for his own murder, saying the innocent teenager should have "had a more responsible father."[26]

Along with the United Kingdom and Saudi Arabia, Nobel Peace Prince Obama continued his thuggish and criminal mugging on Yemen and its population over the next five years—five years drone-driving an already destitute population to the brink of starvation. And then here comes this orange "insane clown president"— the physical manifestation of the American Empire's afterbirth, all entrails and viscera. Trump takes the oath of office, pulls his hand off Lincoln's Bible as well as his own comic book version, and then in the great tradition of American presidents, picks up where his predecessor left off, and joyously steps hog-wild into the Yemeni killing fields. Days later his Navy SEAL Team 6 commandos, along with Reaper drones, take out a compound sheltering members of Al-Qaeda. Trump laments the death of a U.S. soldier and U.S. wounded in the operation but (of course) there is no mention of civilian casualties. "But reports from Yemen quickly surfaced that 30 people were killed," Greenwald reports, "including 10 women and children."[27] One of the children was an eight-year-old girl named Nawar—the daughter of Anwar al-Awlaki. Greenwald rightly calls it "a hideous symbol of the bipartisan continuity of U.S. barbarism."[28]

Some of the SEALS, along with the Captain Video drone pilots, should take a long hard look at this photo of Nawar.

Yemeni Media/Via Twitter

Clearly, the Corporation's hierarchy—those bureaucratic and legal henchmen skulking around Pentagon and CIA hallways—need video pilots (just like they need cannon fodder on the ground) to carry out their dirty work. And let's not mince words here: it's dirty work that they themselves (like John Rizzo above) clearly recognize as murder. For public consumption and military recruitment, the mission is cloaked in euphemistic language suggesting feel-good ideas like nation building, eradicating despots and their associated tyranny, don't forget democracy building, and of course the old standby: protecting American interests abroad—but they always forget to add in the all-important word between "American" and "interest"— "BUSINESS."

Unfortunately, every generation falls for the ruse, the deception, the masterful sleight of hand—or as Nicholas von Hoffman calls it: "The Hoax." War has been a lie since man crawled out of that proverbial swamp. But the ruling class in every society manages to repackage the bullshit and convince another group of unsuspecting children to pick up arms and agree to kill and die for someone else's power and wealth. Perhaps Arundhati Roy gets to the heart of the matter best when she writes:

> Colorful demonstrations and weekend marches are vital but alone
> are not powerful enough to stop wars. Wars will be stopped only
> when soldiers refuse to fight, when workers refuse to load weapons
> onto ships and aircrafts, when people boycott the economic
> outposts of Empire that are strung across the globe.[29]

Initiated by George W. Bush in 2004, Washington's drone program expanded and matured into a full-blown Air Force operation under Barack Obama with most of the actions delegated to the Central Intelligence Agency. The story Americans occasionally hear from the U.S. government megaphone (through their PR partners in mainstream corporate newsrooms) is that drone strikes designed to kill alleged terrorists are vastly successful in their ability to surgically assassinate the terrorists but miraculously spare nearby family, friends, and small dogs. The U.S. military also orders what is known as "double-tap" drone strikes, a particularly heinous action where missiles are launched from a first drone—killing and maiming people, and then moments later when other locals rush in to help the wounded, wham-bam the double-tap: another round of missiles arrive courtesy of drone number two. If you love war, it's the old one-two punch.

On his podcast *Intercepted,* journalist Jeremy Scahill offers another odious and greasy method in which U.S. war-makers spin the LIE that drone warfare is meticulous and exact. Let's first hear from U.S. President Barack Obama as he spins some slick bullshit:

> OBAMA: It is not true that it has been this sort of willy-nilly, you know, let's bomb a village. That is not how folks have operated. And what I can say with great certainty is that the rate of civilian casualties in any drone operation are far lower than the rate of civilian casualties that occur in conventional war.

Scahill then responds to the American president:

> SCAHILL: The reality, though, was that in some so-called targeted killing operations, as many as nine out of ten people killed were not the intended target, and they were, as a matter of policy, labeled EKIA, or enemies killed in action. It was basically a macabre mathematical formula that was used by the Obama White House widely to claim that no civilians, or only a limited number of civilians, were being killed. The idea was: Well if we don't know who they are, let's first label them an enemy that we killed, unless someone posthumously proves that they were a civilian or an innocent bystander. It's pretty sick.[30]

Funny how the mainstream media conveniently forgets to broadcast these little tidbits when they're shilling for the White House or Pentagon about how precise U.S. drone strikes are for killing "bad guys" or how the math is cooked when counting the dead.

And what happens? Young military recruits hear these PR fairytales as well and accept them as truth—first and foremost (and for obvious "sales" reasons) because military recruiters LIE and paint rosy pictures of military life rather than expose the reality of bloodshed, amputated limbs, as well as the gratuitous death on both sides.

In their book, *Army of None,* authors Aimee Allison and David Solnit begin with a list of the hardcore recruitment falsehoods; and the list starts with the overarching commandment: *recruiters lie.* It continues:

> According to the New York Times, nearly one of five United States Army recruiters was under investigation in 2004 for offenses varying from "threats and coercion to false promises that applicants would not be sent to Iraq." One veteran recruiter told a reporter for

the Albany Times Union, "I've been recruiting for years, and I don't know one recruiter who wasn't dishonest about it. I did it myself."[31]

For the U.S. military, warfare is transitioning from boots on the ground and fierce firefights to a seemingly squeaky-clean high-tech videogame-like experience. It's warfare run by satellite imagery and carried out by drone execution 10,000 miles away from the trigger. The interaction with the bad guys sounds very attractive, sexy adventurous, and oh-so-cool to young recruits.

Video war games appear so appealing to young recruits considering the military because for the most part these kids have very few options anywhere else. They're eager to be convinced that this dramatic and life-altering decision will be a safe and sound decision—and who can blame them? It's the recruiters and their employer, the American Empire, who should shoulder the ugly blame for the lies and manipulation—along with one other guilty party: the Empire's various business partners; that wide array of multinational corporations, defense contractors, corrupt Wall Street shysters, and let's not forget the racketeers dressed up as oil men. Together, these good old boys urge, finance, and ultimately benefit reap grotesque profits from the military's ability to protect American BUSINESS interests everywhere on the planet—and now deep into space.

"No Blood For Oil" has been a popular antiwar rallying cry ever since George Bush I invaded Iraq in 1990 but that plea has fallen on deaf ears. American history continues to be defined by aggressive wars for power and profit. But in the crosshairs we find people—usually brown people. For centuries it was red people, black people, and then yellow people, but now a generalized cauldron of "brown people" are the ones in the way. This is best illustrated by the oft-quoted line: *"How did our oil get under their sand?"*

Win One for "The Gripper"

From a Syracuse, New York suburb, senior commander Colonel D. Scott "Gripper" Brenton (now retired) controlled a Reaper drone from his computer console somewhere inside Hancock Field Air National Guard Base. The Reaper crisscrossed Afghanistan looking for insurgents, or "bad guys" as the Empire likes to categorize the enemy living inside their own sovereign country. Brenton entered the Empire's Air Force as an ROTC recruit from the University of Notre Dame, where he earned his commission. Before controlling drone flights and strikes in the Middle East, Brenton flew thousands of hours in F-16 fighter jets and similar aircraft all across the globe.[32] "I see mothers with children, I see fathers with children, I see fathers with mothers, I see kids playing soccer," Colonel Brenton said in an article published in *The New York Times*.[33] Reporter Elisabeth Bumiller writes: "When the call comes for him to fire a missile and kill a militant—and only, Colonel Brenton said, when the women and children are not around—the hair on the back of his neck stands up, just as it did when he used to line up targets in his F-16 fighter jet."[34]

The Gripper became a benchmark for young recruits. He's a family man and cares for his wife and kids with all the passion in the world. He made a good living killing people, making the world safe for democracy. He's an iconic American hero. His retirement was read into the Congressional Record by New York Congressman John Katko. What recruit wouldn't want to be Colonel D. Scott "Gripper" Brenton? Well, maybe some kids might think twice about wanting to be "The Gripper" if they were exposed to another reality, the one where the absolute barbarism of war is right in their face. The bloody entrails running down a gutter may unlock their humanity—the humanity that's been shrewdly buried by the fear mongering, expert propaganda, and manipulation brought down on their heads in this wicked and calculating game known as predatory capitalism.

Luckily, we have Pulitzer Prize-winning journalist Chris Hedges to offer the unorthodox and heretical reality:

> War comes wrapped in patriotic slogans; calls for sacrifice, honor, and heroism; and promises of glory. It comes wrapped in the claims of divine providence. It is what a grateful nation asks of its children. It is what is right and just. It is waged to make the nation and the world a better place, to cleanse evil. War is touted as the ultimate test of manhood, where the young can find out what they are made of. From a distance it seems noble. It gives us comrades and power and a chance to play a bit part in the great drama of history. It promises to give us identities as warriors, patriots, as long as we go along with the myth, the one the war-makers need to wage wars and the defense contractors need to increase their profits.

> But up close war is a soulless void. War is about barbarity, perversion, and pain. Human decency and tenderness are crushed, and people become objects to use or kill. The noise, the stench, the fear, the scenes of eviscerated bodies and bloated corpses, the cries of the wounded all combine to spin those in combat into another

universe. In this moral void, naïvely blessed by secular and religious institutions at home, the hypocrisy of our social conventions, our strict adherence to moral precepts, becomes stark. War, for all its horror, has the power to strip away the trivial and the banal, the empty chatter and foolish obsessions that fill our days. It might let us see, although the cost is tremendous.[35]

The Vietnam War marked a watershed moment for the American people. For the first time in history, television networks beamed gruesome battlefield realities into America's living rooms and that transparency had an enormous effect on energizing the antiwar movement as well as helping to end the monstrous American murder-spree taking place in Southeast Asia. It was warfare upfront and personal. Social critic and human rights activist, Dick Gregory, frames this phenomenon when he states, "Take the camera out of Vietnam. It's just another war." Gregory then discusses his own experience and ties it to Vietnam:

> Let me tell you why I was willing to go into the military: *John Wayne.* I was born October 12, 1932, so my war was the movies. It was romantic. Dude get shot, he'd spit up some blood and then say to his best friend, "Tell Susie I love her." You don't hear anybody hollering and screaming for their mama... And so when I left the movies, I walked home talking like John Wayne, mad I didn't have a uniform. Then all at once Vietnam hit and there's something coming in my house on the TV and these guys don't look like John Wayne and they're hollering and screaming. And you hear folk cussing, man: "Get that motherfucking helicopter over here." We never heard this before... and then Americans made the mistake to sit and look at it with their children. Little children looking at Vietnam—there was no bad guy or good guy. They were looking and they were seeing people get killed.[36]

After a constant diet of these moments, this historic transparency, large segments of the American people turned against the war as well as their own country's imperial vanity. The "think tanks" that dot Washington's landscape as well as their kith and kin inside the Pentagon went into a full-blown panic. The brass started jumping up and down, pissing their pants like excited schoolboys: *"Jesus Harold Christ, don't let that shit happen again! Who the hell is Seymour Hersh? Who the hell is Morley Safer? Fuck these fucking Jews... and fuck Cronkite!"*

Flash-forward and indeed the schoolboys made sure that this shit would not happen again. Goodbye transparency. Hello embedded reporters, which reminds us of the sentiment often attributed to Mr. Orwell: "Journalism is printing what someone else does not want printed; everything else is public relations."

Lives in the Balance

Drone warfare, like all warfare, is a monumental lie—but it's a very effective lie when luring young minds to consider the military as a life choice. For most recruits it's the old bait and switch—tempt them with the super cool joystick office job but then wham-bam-thank-ya-man, Johnny Redblood is knee-deep in gore in some Baghdad shithole. It's the same game that offered kids heroism battling evil abroad but yielded the actual evil nightmare of sucking Agent Orange into their lungs; or trudging through pools of blood and brains trying to hit the beachhead at Normandy; or finding their way through a maze of bodies on the smoky battlefield known as Antietam; or lying in a rat-infested VA hospital learning how to walk on prosthetic limbs; or how about roaming the streets of New York, Los Angeles, Chicago, Newark, New Orleans, DC, Philly, Cleveland, anywhere—homeless, shattered, and delusional?

Obviously it's difficult to attract new raw meat when the bait is murder, mayhem, broken lives, and broken minds. But good clean fun, like these children are already enjoying with high-tech video games, is a safe and sound bet for military honchos and their Svengali-like recruiters. But even the reality of drone warfare is a much different story than the narrative coming out of Washington. The joystick warrior might crumble if he or she truly contemplates what is happening at the killing end of their launch. A painstaking study compiled by Stanford and New York universities entitled "Living Under Drones" illustrates that Washington, as muckraking journalist I.F. Stone so courageously warned all of us, is lying—and they're lying all the time.

> In the United States, the dominant narrative about the use of drones in Pakistan is of a surgically precise and effective tool that makes the U.S. safer by enabling "targeted killing" of terrorists, with minimal downsides or collateral impacts.
>
> The narrative is false.
>
> Following nine months of intensive research—including two investigations in Pakistan, more than 130 interviews with victims,

witnesses, and experts, and review of thousands of pages of
documentation and media reporting—this report presents evidence
of the damaging and counterproductive effects of current U.S.
drone strike policies.[37]

In the end, the study found that only two percent of drone strike casualties in
Pakistan are the top, so-called, militants hunted by the U.S. military. The study
goes on to reveal that the number of civilian casualties was far higher than the
aggressors acknowledged. Not surprising. The report concludes with this obvious
but sadly ignored deduction: "U.S. targeted killings and drone strike practices
undermine respect for the rule of law and international legal protections and may
set dangerous precedents."[38]

The truly depressing part of this giant lie is that the truth is sitting right there for
mainstream corporate journalists to pounce on, an act which would ultimately
allow their massive news organizations the ability to report these soul-sucking
stories far and wide; and yet, for the most part, they remain silent, choosing
instead the safe company line, proving once again that they are forever reverent
to their masters. In fact, throughout modern history, the press has been willing
and cooperative accomplices in helping to shield the public from the horrors of
war—and there's plenty of blame to go around: the policy-making warmongers
who wage war and their cohorts in the press who enthusiastically regurgitate the
selling points and bang the drums for war.

And their deceit always overlooks the obvious: there are lives in the balance.

Locking on Target: America's Teenagers

To illustrate the drone mentality taking over the military recruitment of America's
youth, one need only look at some interesting polls that show Xbox game users
overwhelmingly support American drone attacks. During the final debate of
the 2012 presidential election, an estimated 30,000 viewers watching on their
Xbox 360 consoles participated in a live poll. They were asked, *"Do you support
more use of drone aircraft to attack suspected terrorists?"* Seventy-two percent of the
viewers answered "yes." Xbox Live polling was conducted in partnership with
the company YouGov to provide "cutting-edge interactive television and polling
techniques" that will be "instrumental in both entertainment and information
gathering in the future," wrote David Rothschild, at the time the Xbox head
pollster and member of Microsoft Research NYC.[39]

Clearly, the trickle-down effect of Washington's drone message works like a charm, whether back in the old days of 2012 or right now.

For instance, Ubisoft's *Ghost Recon* has been an immensely popular video game series. Stuart White, a senior game producer, studied military technology at length. He has asserted a strong relationship with various defense contractors and the United States military. In fact, White was lucky: he was offered an inside track on advances in real military toys well before the American public. At one point, he came across a .50 caliber gun turret mounted on a Humvee that was controlled by a very recognizable device—an Xbox 360 controller. White recounts, "I pointed that out to them and they said 'Well, of course. We're not going to reinvent a new way because we get all these kids into the military, they already know how to use a 360 controller, they're already familiar with it. So we're just going to use that in how we're building the technology.'"[40]

Numerous games like *Ghost Recon, Sniper Elite,* and *Battlefield* continue to have a dramatic impact on both the minds of America's children as well as on defense contractors who build the "way cool" death machines. In fact, one game, *Call of Duty: Advanced Warfare takes* place in a world where private military contractors, and not countries, are in charge of protecting the world ("Calling Erik Prince"). Technology journalist from *The Guardian*, Keith Stuart, labeled the game "Activision's billion-dollar shoot-'em-up cash cow."[41] The series has sold more than 140 million units. "Since its arrival in 2003, the titles have relied on flashy hyper-violence, Michael Bay explosions and ludicrous plotlines," writes Stuart, who stresses that the *Call of Duty: Modern Warfare* titles have "reveled in post-9/11 paranoia."[42] Stuart reports that Sledgehammer Games (such an apropos name), the creative producer of the game, sought and received strong support from U.S. military advisers and a scenario planner from the Department of Defense "who is active in the Pentagon." The team studied private military contractors (PMCs), with of course Blackwater's operations in the spotlight. "Founder, Erik Prince, is surely a model for Jonathan Irons," suggests Stuart—the character Irons is the leader of the game's largest PMC—"played with obvious relish by Kevin Spacey."[43] Ultimately, and bolstered with Hollywood star power, these games help to push the LIE of war on a semi-literate young American demographic—one that embraces *Call of Duty*, this "big, bloody spectacle of a game series; a gung-ho celebration of military might."[44] And death.

And, of course, let's not forget the makers of Xbox and PlayStation—don't look now, but there's blood on your hands as well.

During the height of the U.S. invasions in Iraq and Afghanistan, *The Christian Science Monitor* reported that, "the military has aggressively expanded its marketing campaign targeting teenagers. Efforts included the release of Version 3 of the taxpayer-sponsored video game *America's Army*, two graphic novels that look and read like comic books, and a unique 14,500-sq.-ft. arcade—or 'Army Experience Center'—in a Philadelphia mall that is filled with simulators and shooter video games."[45] It should be noted that protests by parents and peace activists opposed to the U.S. military's campaign of targeting children too young to be legally recruited closed down the Philadelphia "experience." Pat Elder, from the National Network Opposing the Militarization of Youth, reports on *Common Dreams*:

> A ninth grader in a suburban Washington DC classroom is delighted to be excused from Algebra class to spend a half hour shooting a life-like 9 MM pistol and lobbing explosive ordinance from an M1A2 Abrams tank simulator. At the same time 3,000 miles away in La Habra, California, a 15 year-old girl is released from English class to squeeze off rounds from a very real looking M-16 rifle. The kids thoroughly enjoy the experience, especially the part about getting out of class.[46]

What these two students experienced along with thousands upon thousands of other high school students across America was the Army's "Adventure Van," a huge 18-wheeler jammed packed with interactive exhibits and toys that glorify battlefield combat along with some really cool weapons. And once again, as always, the murder, mayhem, blood, guts, and psychological trauma were nowhere to be found. In fact, the Army produced a large national fleet of these mobile pleasure palaces designed to generate an adrenaline rush that would hopefully translate into a decision to enlist. And then in a strategic attempt to entice the kids to jettison themselves into the wild blue yonder, the military also offered Aviation Recruiting Vans that contained an AH 64 helicopter simulator along with an interactive air warrior and weapons display.[47]

Enacted in 2001 and repealed in 2015, the "No Child Left Behind Act" allowed military recruiters equal access to high school students—the same access given to college and career recruiters. Elder's report highlighted their nefarious effort:

> Despite protests by parents and civic groups across the country, the Army defends its right to enter high school campuses with their high-tech mobile cinemas. Kelly Rowe, public affairs officer for

the Baltimore Recruiting Battalion, compared the Army Adventure Van to efforts by colleges to recruit students. "I don't think it's any different from an athlete who gets 10 letters saying, 'Come play for us.'"[48]

Rated "T" for Teen, *America's Army* is the official video game produced by the U.S. Army, offering teens the chance to be a tactical first-person shooter. Here's how they position and sell the game:

> The *America's Army* game provides civilians with an inside perspective and a virtual role in today's premier land force: the U.S. Army. The game is designed to provide an accurate portrayal of Soldier experiences...

> The Army's game is an entertaining way for young adults to explore the Army and its adventures and opportunities as a virtual Soldier. As such, it is part of the Army's communications strategy designed to leverage the power of the Internet as a portal through which young adults can get a first-hand look at what it is like to be a Soldier.[49]

In the product marketplace, most advertising claims stretch the truth. We know that. It's an accepted "wink" in the culture: eating *Special K* cereal will not turn the American female population into a legion of Jennifer Anistons and driving a Corvette will not transform balding, overweight, fifty-year-old males into a cadre of intoxicating Don Juans. We know the claims are a stretch but we don't mind the psychobabble. But then there are some advertising claims that amount to boldface lies. Military recruitment falls into this category. Starting with, of course, two giant overarching lies: (1) The American Empire is an instrument of good and fights for liberty and justice; and (2) The use of violence is a successful and useful tool for humans to embrace when settling conflict. And what makes the boldface lie of military recruitment even more diabolical is that the lie is ultimately responsible for death and destruction. Remember, we're not talking about Colgate toothpaste failing to get our teeth as white as a newly painted picket fence. The military recruitment lies go much deeper when you drill down into the details.

In their aforementioned scorching book, *Army of None* [2007], Aimee Allison and David Solnit have documented a world of deceit perpetrated by military recruiters as well as the Armed Services' increasing and oftentimes unchecked access to the halls and cafeterias of U.S. schools. Their exposé targeting the military recruitment complex reads like a depiction of the used car business. The authors make a compelling case that the U.S. clearly cannot sustain its empire without enough soldiers. And as we've seen, the budget for military recruitment is significant and bloated and the Department of Defense needs every penny. How else could they make murder, destruction, and death so appealing? Allison and Solnit underscore the leading lies:

> **The military contract guarantees nothing.** The Department of Defense's own enlistment/re-enlistment document states, "Laws and regulations that govern military personnel may change without notice to me. Such changes may affect my status, pay allowances, benefits and responsibilities as a member of the Armed Forces REGARDLESS of the provisions of this enlistment/re-enlistment document."

> **Advertised signing bonuses are bogus.** Bonuses are often thought of as gifts, but they're not. They're like loans: If an enlistee leaves the military before his or her agreed term of service, he or she will be forced to repay the bonus. Besides, Army data shows that the top bonus of $20,000 was given to only 6 percent of the 477,272 enlistees who signed up for active duty.

> **The military won't make you financially secure.** Military members are no strangers to financial strain: 48 percent report having financial difficulty, approximately 33 percent of homeless men in the United States are veterans, and nearly 200,000 veterans are homeless on any given night.

> **Money for college ($71,424 in the bank?).** If you expect the military to pay for college, better read the fine print. Among recruits who sign up for the Montgomery GI Bill, 65 percent receive no money for college, and only 15 percent ever receive a college degree. The maximum Montgomery GI Bill benefit is $37,224, and even this 37K is hard to get: To join, you must first put in a nonrefundable $1,200 deposit that has to be paid to the military during the first year of service. To receive the $37K, you must also be an active-duty member who has completed at least a three-year

service agreement and is attending a four-year college full time. Benefits are significantly lower if you are going to school part-time or attending a two-year college. If you receive a less than honorable discharge (as one in four do), leave the military early (as one in three do), or later decide not to go to college, the military will keep your deposit and give you nothing.

Job training. Vice President Dick Cheney once said, "The military is not a social welfare agency; it's not a jobs program." If you enlist, the military does not have to place you in your chosen career field or give you the specific training requested. Even if enlistees do receive training, it is often to develop skills that will not transfer to the civilian job market. (There aren't many jobs for M240 machine-gunners stateside.)

War, combat, and your contract. First off, if it's your first time enlisting, you're signing up for eight years. On top of that, the military can, without your consent, extend active-duty obligations during times of conflict, "national emergency," or when directed by the president. This means that even if an enlistee has two weeks left on his/her contract (yes, even Guard/Reserve) or has already served in combat, she/he can still be sent to war.[50]

A Suggestion for Recruiters: Get to Know Your Enemy

Here's an idea that recruiters might like. It's a way for them to help recruits realize exactly what they're signing up for by honestly teaching them about the people they're about to maim, terrorize, and kill. It's a fun video game we call "Get To Know Your Enemy."

> *Here's how this exciting new game works: you, the future recruit, will see brief dossiers pop up on screen offering intel on persons recently removed by American military operations. You, as the player, will get to reenact these thrilling hits. Remember, your targets are completely disposable brown people—they will all look the same, and remember, they're probably not adding much value to their shithole society anyway. We call a lot of these killings "collateral damage" or "Hey, shit happens."*

> *Now here's the beauty part: based on the intel and back story, you get to select and execute the final kill shot against our enemies, aka the bad guys—whether they had it coming or not. Get your game face on, BillyBoy666! Let 'er rip! Here are some choice targets:*

Abu Hassan, 48

Abu worked in a restaurant called the Nasser on Abu Taleb Street in Baghdad. He was making lunch for customers with his buddy Malek Hammoud when a missile hit the westbound carriageway. Both men were killed.[51]

Very nice... clean, two Hodgies with one shot. Well done, BillyBoy666. Cue AC/DC. Go claim your virgins in heaven, Hassan!

Mohammed al-Awrawi, 35

Mohammed stayed on in Baghdad after his family and relatives fled the city for the countryside. He left to join them on the day of the first U.S. incursion, on April 5. His family said he was travelling alone and unarmed. He was approaching a bridge over the Tigris at about 3pm when a U.S. tank opened fire.[52]

Man, you are one goddamn good shot. It's tough to hit a moving target, you gotta lead 'em just right. Give that boy a cigar. Okay, BillyBoy666, here's your third target, this one's a kid because kids can be fun targets, too. Let's see if you have the stomach.

Ali Nasaf, 6

Ali Nasaf was killed in a missile attack on the Bab al Muadan telephone exchange in Baghdad on March 31. His mother, Lamia, 31, told the Daily Mail: "Even the doctors and nurses cried when he died. They remember him as the boy who played football in the streets and always laughed."[53]

Football? You mean that soccer shit? Get out of here, kid, ya bother me. Bam. You nailed little Ali Baba, BillyBoy666. You're a goddamn American hero.

Now here's the denouement: after winning the game, the recruits are treated to a quick wrap-up feel-good commercial brought to you by the U.S. Army:

ANNOUNCER:
Whether it's firing sidewinder missiles into crowded cafés... or maybe incinerating unarmed towel heads driving reentry vehicles through the dust, or maybe your thing is launching cruise missiles into neighborhoods full of cute little street urchins wearing Adidas, remember one thing:

—THERE IS NOTHING ON THIS GREEN EARTH
—THAT IS STRONGER THAN THE U.S. ARMY.
—BECAUSE THERE IS NOTHING ON THIS GREEN EARTH
—THAT IS STRONGER THAN A U.S. ARMY SOLDIER.
—STRONG. (Fade in) ARMY—ARMY STRONG.

Cannon Fodder, Part Two:
Lies, Lies, and More Lies

Dear President Bush:

I kissed my son goodbye today. He is a 21-year-old Marine. You have ordered him to Saudi Arabia. The letter telling us he was going arrived at our vacation cottage in northern Wisconsin by Express Mail on Aug. 13. We left immediately for North Carolina to be with him. Our vacation was over. Some commentators say you are continuing your own vacation to avoid appearing trapped in the White House, as President Carter was during the Iran hostage crisis. Perhaps that is your reason.

—Alex Molnar's Letter to George Bush, August 23, 1990[54] (Part 1)

Just like any marketing campaign, it's all about positioning the sale—and the sale to young minds (as we've discussed) is crafted with a video game mentality: high tech wizardry that wipes out bad guys. In fact it's the identical false narrative that is used on the general population when selling the efficacy of drone warfare.

In another preposterous recruitment campaign for the U.S. Air Force, slick high-end filmmaking walks the promising recruit audience down the Yellowbrick Road of sexy technology—video cyberspace that makes *Grand Theft Auto* look like the 1981 release of Donkey Kong. Either the voice of God or onscreen graphics dramatically informs us: "It's not science fiction. It's what we do everyday." One airman in a "Remotely Piloted Aircraft" recruitment video from the same series utters this Orwellian masterpiece: "This is going to save someone's life today." The next video tells the recruit audience that joining the military is "similar to a civilian trade school." Of course that's true if you remove the brainwashing, demonization, terrorism, guns, blood, psychological and physical trauma, death, and mass murder. Sure, it's just like the DeVry Institute.

A pillar of the military recruitment-marketing scheme has been to push education as the bait to lure the poor and disenfranchised to trade their soul along with their physical and mental well being for an education. One recruitment spot promises "one on one personalized care" when learning a trade. The mantra is straightforward and obvious: "Listen, you really have no choice. It's either the shit highway into oblivion, prison, or working at McDonald's until you drop dead—or you can team up with Uncle Sam. Advance your career. Learn a job. Earn a degree. BE ALL YOU CAN BE."

Well, as Cheech Marin once satirized with stinging wit in his film *Born in East LA*:

> *In the Army… I wanted to be all I could be, except all they let me be was a mechanic.*

Chicken Hawks:

> *Those who strongly support war yet actively avoid military service.*

In fact, there's a perversion inherent in this deal with the devil: the perversion of the mercenary. Not only are these ruling class robber barons using America's poor and disenfranchised children as cannon fodder, as killers, as triggermen and women to fight wars they themselves won't fight in nor will they send their privileged children to fight in, but they entice your children with a golden carrot of false promises that signing up will deliver them from the poverty and squalor they've known since birth; poverty and squalor, by the way, that's been caused and perpetrated against them by the very same ruling class robber barons. It's a vicious and predetermined cycle. The late Dick Gregory framed the insidious deal in no uncertain terms, especially for African-Americans (but the formula holds true for any child no matter their heritage because the game here is really about class oppression):

> It's kind of sad… I remember when I was a little boy, a woman
> would get pregnant and I'd hear my mother and them good
> Christians say, "Oh, Tony went in the Army so he can get married
> and take care of the baby. She's getting an allotment check." And so
> you had black folk who went into the Army not because we loved
> America but because of the G.I. Bill. "Now, I can go to college and
> get me an education." So, when you go to war to fight for their
> country, that's called being a mercenary. There ain't nothing nastier
> in the eyes of God than a mercenary. And if you don't believe it,
> check out the French Foreign Legion… the French government
> never let them thugs come to France. They put them on remote
> islands and then sent whores, drugs, and whiskey. They'll rape

their mama, they'll rape their daughter. They go mad. That's the mentality of a mercenary. And that's what we black folks are going to have to realize one day.[55]

Poverty Draft

> However, as I sat in my motel room watching you on television, looking through my son's hastily written last will and testament and listening to military equipment rumble past, you seemed to me to be both callous and ridiculous chasing golf balls and zipping around in your boat in Kennebunkport.
>
> **—Alex Molnar's Letter to George Bush (Part 2)**

In his uncompromising book, *War is a Lie*, author David Swanson suggests that every recruiting device and scheme used by the U.S. military is a smoke screen to hide the fact that America is avoiding instituting a draft by filling the ranks of its armed forces with working class men and women who turn away from poverty's harsh face and embrace the military. Here, he distills down the process:

> (S)pend billions of dollars on recruitment, increase military pay, and offer signing bonuses until enough people "voluntarily" join by signing contracts that allow the military to change the terms at will. If more troops are needed, just extend the contracts of the ones you've got. Need more still? Federalize the National Guard and send kids off to war who signed up thinking they'd be helping hurricane victims. Still not enough? Hire contractors for transportation, cooking, cleaning, and construction. Let the soldiers be pure soldiers whose only job is to kill, just like the knights of old. Boom, you've instantly doubled the size of your force, and nobody's noticed but the profiteers. Still need more killers? Hire mercenaries... Not enough? Spend trillions of dollars on technology to maximize the power of each person. Use unmanned aircraft so nobody gets hurt. Promise immigrants they'll be citizens if they join. Change the standards for enlistment: take 'em older, fatter, in worse health, with less education, with criminal records... promise students they can pursue their chosen field within the wonderful world of death, and that you'll send them to college if they live... put military games in shopping malls. Send uniformed generals to kindergartens to warm the children up to the idea of truly and properly swearing

allegiance to the flag. Spend 10 times the money on recruiting each new soldier as we spend on educating each child. Do anything, anything, anything other than starting a draft.

But there's a name for this practice of avoiding a traditional draft. It's called a poverty draft.[56]

Journalist Chris Hedges has written extensively on the Empire's thirst for war as a business model for running the planet. In his searing indictment of America's war mentality, "War Is Betrayal: Persistent Myths of Combat," Hedges states:

> We condition the poor and the working class to go to war. We promise them honor, status, glory, and adventure. We promise boys they will become men. We hold these promises up against the dead-end jobs of small-town life, the financial dislocations, credit card debt, bad marriages, lack of health insurance, and dread of unemployment. The military is the call of the Sirens, the enticement that has for generations seduced young Americans working in fast food restaurants or behind the counters of Walmarts to fight and die for war profiteers and elites.
>
> The poor embrace the military because every other cul-de-sac in their lives breaks their spirit and their dignity. Pick up Erich Maria Remarque's *All Quiet on the Western Front* or James Jones's *From Here to Eternity*. Read *Henry IV*. Turn to the *Iliad*. The allure of combat is a trap, a ploy, an old, dirty game of deception in which the powerful, who do not go to war, promise a mirage to those who do.
>
> …Any story of war is a story of elites preying on the weak, the gullible, the marginal, the poor.[57]

I also met many of my son's fellow soldiers. They are fine young men. A number told me that they were from poor families. They joined the Marines as a way of earning enough money to go to college. None of the young men I met are likely to be invited to serve on the board of directors of a savings and loan association, as your son Neil was. And none of them have parents well enough connected to call or write a general to ensure that their child stays out of harm's way, as Vice President Dan Quayle's parents did for him during the Vietnam War.

—Alex Molnar's Letter to George Bush (Part 3)

As the Empire unleashed its imperial tentacles post-9/11, it found itself sinking into classic colonial quagmires throughout the Middle East and Africa—imperial occupations that quickly eat away at troop strength. Couple this with the way America's allies began holding Washington at arm's length—because of its aggressive and thug-violent foreign policy—and it's easy to see why the American military urgently ramped up and expanded its recruitment efforts, especially in the decade following the massive invasions into Iraq and Afghanistan. Expanding the poverty draft was an effective way to replenish the ranks. In his article at the time for *The Guardian* in the UK, Robert Burns explained the poverty draft this way:

> Due to the memory of Vietnam as well as a high level of resistance
> to America's colonial and unpopular wars at home, a general draft is
> a thorny proposition and would prove to be very unpopular hoisted
> on the middle class/working class all at once.[58]

Burns also reported that the U.S. military increased the number of recruiters by more than 30 percent and National Guard recruiters by more than 50 percent.[59] Using high-powered, expensive, and slick ad agencies (like Leo Burnett USA), the military historically pushes Madison Avenue to better sell the Armed Forces by thinking outside the box to find less conventional ways to attract recruits. At the height of post-9/11 Mephistopheles-like heist of bodies and souls, the *Chicago Tribune* reported that, "Recruiters are hitting NASCAR events, rock concerts, rodeos, and rib festivals, using custom-painted Humvees and other gimmicks to attract the masses like old-fashioned traveling salesmen."[60]

In his article "The Battle Over Military Recruitment," history professor Justin Akers Chacón concurs:

> In one stealth campaign at the University of Illinois at Chicago,
> recruiters teamed up with concert promoters to zero in on Latino
> students with a highly deceptive campus music festival called
> the "iCarumba Tour." Promoted as "music, step shows, games,
> movies and 'the hottest After-parties,'" the tour is sponsored by
> the U.S Army who supplies recruiters to participate and promote
> recruitment "amidst the fun."[61]

As we've unfortunately witnessed, the history of America has been characterized by consistent war and brutal violence. It is a society that has always been militarized, always defined with an "Old West" mentality—but the arc of that story has been growing exponentially since 11 September 2001. David Swanson encapsulates the growth when he writes: "We are more saturated with militarism than ever before. The military and its support industries eat up an increasingly larger share of the economy, providing jobs intentionally across all congressional districts. Military recruiters and recruitment advertising are ubiquitous."[62]

Unsurprisingly, the military has a short-term as well as a long-term strategy. The short-term strategy focuses on increasing the all-volunteer force by using economic incentives to draw more working class recruits into the war machine. The long-term strategy involves foundational indoctrination and propaganda. Akers continues:

> By popularizing war and normalizing conquest and colonization,
> far-sighted hawks hope to cultivate the next generations of
> working-class youth to be more apt to enlist and see fighting wars
> as a necessary form of national service.[63]

And now you have ordered my son to the Middle East. For what? Cheap gasoline? Is the American "way of life" that you say my son is risking his life for the continued "right" of Americans to consume 25 percent to 30 percent of the world's oil?

—Alex Molnar's Letter to George Bush (Part 4)

Infiltrating America's Schools

The goal is school ownership that can only lead to a greater number of Army enlistments.[64]
—U.S. Army School Recruiting Program Handbook

Plain and simple, the objective for military recruiters is to "own the schools."

Speaking about army recruiting and the draft, Dick Gregory railed against military service in a 1974 concert (not a rare occurrence), suggesting he wouldn't join "even if they was fighting in my living room." When talking about the government zeroing in on his children for conscription, he suggested:

> I got three sons, ten kids, three boys. I know they're never gonna
> get drafted. I'm gonna take care of that. I wish they would come by
> my house with an induction notice. "Yeah, what do you want, fella?
> Induction notice for my son? Gimme that... let me fill that out for

you. What do you mean I can't write on it… shut up and take this back to the Draft Board and give it to your boss. WHATEVER'S WRONG WITH DUPONT'S BOYS IS ALSO WRONG WITH MINE." I don't know where the DuPont's go during wartime but they better make room for three more![65]

When the "No Child Left Behind" legislation was in force, Justin Akers Chacón suggested that the act should, in reality, be characterized "No Child Left Unrecruited."[66] Buried deep in the No Child act was a requirement (Section 9528) that orders public secondary schools to provide military recruiters the contact information for all students. What was the penalty for noncompliance by a school district? An immediate cutoff of all federal aid. The act also guaranteed complete access to America's public schools, which allowed recruiters to "own the schools" as their handbook instructed. Prior to the enactment of No Child Left Behind, one-third of America's high schools openly refused access to their students by recruiters, believing that it was clearly improper. Justin Akers concluded that, "No Child Left Behind amounted to not only an open-door policy for the military in our schools, but a full-scale invasion and occupation of classrooms, playgrounds, and lunchrooms."[67]

In order to "own the schools," (i.e., plunder them for cannon fodder) recruiters need to deeply penetrate (pun intended) the high school and college markets. Like selling any piece of crap, it's a numbers game: how many children must you intrigue in order to steal their soul? Akers writes:

> Like any other psy-ops (psychological operations) program, the
> military seeks to become a permanent presence on campus and
> establish a system by which they collaborate with educators for the
> "hearts and minds" of students.[68]

Even if parents object, many U.S. military recruiters are ravenous in their aggressive and malevolent pursuit of "fresh souls" (as Gunnery Sergeant Hartman likes to call them). Back in 2002 when the Empire was ramping up their Middle East slaughter, journalist David Goodman in *Mother Jones* magazine reported that, "'The only thing that will get us to stop contacting the family is if they call their congressman,' says Major Johannes Paraan, head U.S. Army recruiter for Vermont and northeastern New York. 'Or maybe if the kid died, we'll take them off our list.'"[69]

Of course, military recruiters parachuting behind educational lines is nothing new. Howard Zinn remembers the Marine Corps infiltrating the campus of Boston University in 1972. "John Silber," Zinn writes, "had hardly settled into the presidential mansion—a twenty-room house, rent-free, only one of the many fringe benefits adding up to perhaps $100,000 a year which augment his $100,000 salary—when he embarked on the process the Germans call Gleichschaltung—'straightening things out.' He quickly made it clear that he would not tolerate student interference with military recruiting at BU for the war in Vietnam." When Silber's office invited Marine recruiters on campus, students staged a peaceful sit-in. Silber called in the cops and the anticipated arrests and then the beatings commenced at what Silber himself called "an open university." Zinn continues: "The university that was 'open' to the Marine Corps turned out to be closed to the campus chapter of Students for a Democratic Society (SDS), which lost its charter and its right to meet on campus because a scuffle had taken place during an SDS demonstration. The logic was established: SDS was a violent organization, while the Marine Corps had a well-known record for pacifism."[70]

> The "free market" to which you are so fervently devoted has a very high price tag, at least for parents like me and young men and women like my son... The troops I met deserve far better than the politicians and policies that hold them hostage. As my wife and I sat in a little cafe outside our son's base last week, trying to eat, fighting back tears, a youngMarine struck up a conversation with us. As we parted he wished us well and said, 'May God forgive us for what we are about to do.' President Bush, the policies you have advocated for the last decade have set the stage for military conflict in the Middle East. Your response to the Iraqi conquest of Kuwait has set in motion events that increasingly will pressure you to use our troops not to defend Saudi Arabia but to attack Iraq. And I'm afraid that, as that pressure mounts, you will wager my son's life in a gamble to save your political future.
>
> **—Alex Molnar's Letter to George Bush (Part 5)**

Kids R Us

U.S. military operations around the globe—especially in the Middle East—have necessitated the continued rise of aggressive recruitment tactics aimed at America's children. According to recruiters themselves, guys like Christopher Raissi—a former Marine recruiter in Georgia—the process includes deception, coercion, and the offering of false promises. Raissi states that, "Recruiters are trained to work everyone in a high school, from freshmen to seniors. From my experience, the schools don't give any notification to the parents about dissemination of students' personal information to recruiters. If parents ignore their phone calls, recruiters are trained to track down every kid on the list, either at school or at home."[71] In fact, authors Azadeh Shahshahani and Tim Franzen believe that this deceptive behavior nullifies the voluntary nature of recruiting young people and is in breach of the United States' international human rights obligations. The authors continue, "The U.S. ratified the Optional Protocol to the Convention on the Rights of the Child on the involvement of children in armed conflict in 2002. The Protocol is therefore binding on the U.S. government and state and local government entities and agents."[72]

[Note: Even though the United States had an active role in drafting the Convention on the Rights of the Child, and indeed signed it in 1995, no U.S. president has submitted the treaty to the U.S. Senate for ratification. During his first presidential campaign in 2008, then Senator Barack Obama called the U.S. failure to sign "embarrassing" and assured the American people that he would review this embarrassment. But he never did.

The United Nations General Assembly adopted the Convention in 1989 and it was ratified in September of 1990. Every member of the United Nations is a ratified party to the Convention on the Rights of the Child except the United States of America.]

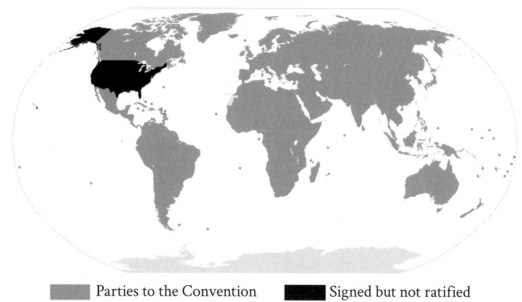

Parties to the Convention   Signed but not ratified

The minimum age for military recruitment under the Optional Protocol is seventeen years of age, although 89 of 128 countries that ratified the Protocol abide by eighteen years of age. Shahshahani and Franzen note that, "the American Civil Liberties Union submitted a report to the Committee on Rights of the Child (CRC), the United Nations body that monitors compliance with the Optional Protocol, detailing the government's failure to comply with its obligations under the Optional Protocol. The ACLU found that the U.S. military continues to engage in tactics designed to recruit students under the age of 17, and fails to protect 17-year-old students from aggressive and abusive recruitment."[73]

This passage from the actual report entitled "Soldiers of Misfortune" is a clear-cut indictment of practices by the U.S. military and its recruiters:

> Public schools serve as prime recruiting grounds for the military, and the U.S. military's generally accepted procedures for recruitment of high school students plainly violate the Optional Protocol. In its initial report to the U.N. Committee on the Rights of the Child, the U.N. body charged with monitoring compliance with the Optional Protocol, the U.S. Government claims that "[n]o one under age 17 is eligible for recruitment." In practice, however, the U.S. armed services regularly target children under 17 for military recruitment, heavily recruiting on high school campuses, in school lunchrooms, and in classes. Department of Defense instructions to recruiters, the U.S. military's collection of information on hundreds of thousands of 16-year-olds, and military training corps for children as young as 11 reveal that students are targeted for recruitment as early as possible. By exposing children younger than 17 to military recruitment, the United States military violates the terms of the Optional Protocol.[74]

The ACLU went on to report that recruitment tactics employed by the U.S. armed forces disproportionately target low-income children and also students of color. The report states that, "protections for students against abusive recruitment tactics remain weak. Recruiters threaten serious penalties to 17-year-old youth who have signed Deferred Entry contracts and subsequently changed their minds about enlisting, in some cases forcing these youth to report to basic training against their will."[75] The ACLU report drew a sharp conclusion: "Heavy-handed recruitment tactics and misconduct by recruiters often render recruitment involuntary."[76]

Based on this scathing report, the Committee on Rights of the Child called on the United States to halt military training in public schools and, as Shahshahani and Franzen state, "stop targeting racial minorities and children of low-income families and other vulnerable socioeconomic groups for military recruitment, as such activities run counter to the object and purpose of the Optional Protocol."[77]

> *In the past, you have demonstrated no enduring commitment to any principle other than the advancement of your political career. This makes me doubt that you have either the courage or the character to meet the challenge of finding a diplomatic solution to this crisis. If, as I expect, you eventually order American soldiers to attack Iraq, then it is God who will have to forgive you. I will not.*
>
> **—Alex Molnar's Letter to George Bush (Part 6)**

I saw heaven standing open and there before me was a white horse, whose rider is called Faithful and True. With justice he judges and wages war.
—Revelation 19:11

Indeed, Jesus Christ has become one mighty warrior. At one time many embraced Jesus as the "Prince of Peace," but when "fresh souls" are needed for battle he's been spotted helping zealots rally the young as an über recruiter for the U.S. military—and goddamnit he's good at it.

But this isn't new.

Barbara Ehrenreich, in her book *Blood Rites: Origins and History of the Passions*, discusses the marriage of religion and nationalism:

> It is in times of war and the threat of war that nationalism takes on its most overtly religious hues. During the temporary enthusiasms of war, such as those inspired by the outbreak of World War I, individuals see themselves as participants in, or candidates for, a divine form of "sacrifice." At the same time, whatever distinctions may have existed between church and state—or more precisely, between church-based religions and the religion of nationalism— tend to dissolve. During World War I, for example, secular authorities in the United States devised propaganda posters in which "Jesus was dressed in khaki and portrayed sighting down a gun barrel." For their part, religious authorities can

usually be counted on to help sacralize the war effort with their endorsements.[78]

Now defunct, but vastly popular during America's Iraq and Afghanistan war frenzy, was a Christian right-wing fundamentalist movement known as "BattleCry" (aka Acquire The Fire). The parachurch, supported by the likes of Pat Robertson and Chuck Colson, hunted for American youths in their targeted demographic to "acquire the fire" and become committed Christian soldiers. According to their website, if teens gave them 27 hours they would "encounter God in a total revolution of the heart." In fact, according to Teen Mania (the organization that created BattleCry), "over 2.7 million teens have been reached and will never be the same!"

Soldiers for Christ today. Soldiers for the Empire tomorrow.

In her three-part essay entitled "Battle Cry for Theocracy," Sunsara Taylor warned, "If you've been waiting to get alarmed until the Christian fascist movement started filling stadiums with young people and hyping them up to do battle in 'God's army,' wait no longer."[79]

BattleCry was chock-full of military rhetoric and obvious military similes all designed to usher manipulated young minds (and oftentimes troubled youth) straight into the U.S. military. Ron Luce was the leader and hails from the land that time forgot—also commonly known as the lunatic far-right-wing fringe of Christianity. His co-conspirators in this drive to demolish young souls included fellow psychopaths Robertson, Colson, Joyce Meyer, and none other than George W. Bush who gave Luce a White House Advisory Commission on Drug-Free Communities.

Nothing says "God's love" like an elite killing machine.
                              —Navy Seal on stage to a BattleCry crowd in Philadelphia[80]

Luce's maneuverings included giant youth gatherings in arenas and stadiums around America where thousands and thousands of young kids filled venues ready to experience "BattleCry." War was center stage and glorified at every turn. Hummers acted as props and were adorned with red revolutionary flags. Dog tags were everywhere as were posters advertising various teens carrying automatic weapons. Luce would glorify U.S. military atrocities and then embrace Navy Seals on stage to give Christian testimony. Then together they offered "BattlePlans"—a so-called strategy to put these warped ideas of violence and psychotic behavior into motion. A glowing endorsement of BattleCry sent by mass murderer and well-known war criminal, George W. Bush, was then read to the cheering throngs.[81] Sunsara Taylor's disturbing report continues, "While in the bathroom, I saw something equally unsettling—a preteen girl wearing a shirt being sported by many attendees that night: Jesus on the cross, robes waving, and emblazoned across the front the words 'Dressed to Kill.'"[82]

Clearly underscoring military propaganda and the indoctrination of unsuspecting children, Luce and the leaders of BattleCry would use biblical passages as rallying cries. Psalms 144:1 was a classic example: "Praise be to the Lord my Rock, who trains my hands for war, my fingers for battle." Luce offered a million of these gems.

> This is war. And Jesus invites us to get into the action, telling us that the violent—the "forceful" ones—will lay hold of the kingdom.[83]

> The devil hates us, and we gotta be ready to fight and not be these passive little lukewarm, namby-pamby, kum-ba-yah, thumb-sucking babies that call themselves Christians. Jesus? He got mad! I want an attacking church![84]

At the time, BattleCry was a dangerously large and growing force where military dogma ran hard and ran deep. Current and former members of the U.S. armed forces played a prominent role during events, constantly encouraging young people to become warriors in this epic battle. On stage, Luce passionately urged his young "Soldiers for Christ" to declare with power: "I will keep my eyes on the battle, submitting to Your code, even when I don't understand."[85]

In the second installment of Sunsara Taylor's essay, entitled "Fear and Loathing in Philadelphia," she expressed a personal note of horror:

> Throughout the three and a half hours of BattleCry's first session, I thought of only one analogy that fit the experience: This must have been what it felt like to watch the Hitler Youth, filled with self-righteous pride, proclaim the supremacy of their beliefs and their willingness to shed blood for them. And lest you think this is idle paranoia, BattleCry founder Ron Luce told the crowds the next morning that he plans to launch a "blitzkrieg" in the communities,

schools, malls, etc. against those who don't share his theocratic vision of society. Blitzkrieg. Nothing like a little Nazi imagery to whip up the masses.[86]

Many reports concur that organizations and movements like BattleCry are not only promoting war—and by extension military recruitment—but also an aggressive message that fosters raging homophobia as well as relentless sexism by rejecting the right of sovereignty by women over their own bodies. This theocratic creed hidden inside this military framework also denounces sexual diversity. Taylor reports "Luce's followers staged a protest... on the steps of San Francisco's City Hall because gay weddings had taken place there. Their answer to the scourge of rape and violence against women is to end the right of divorce, spread ignorance and insist on virginity—the very things that will entrap more women in these nightmares."[87] The entire movement can only be described as medieval—once again, from the land that time forgot.

Throughout history, the U.S. military—working at the behest of the American Empire—has been a battering ram for both Christianity and capitalism. The controversy at the U.S. Air Force Academy in Colorado Springs (during the height of America's slaughters in Iraq and Afghanistan), in which evangelical Christianity permeated the chain of command, is a perfect example of the evangelical Jesus factor and how it engulfs, pressures, and motivates the U.S. military: from the recruitment of children to the murder carried out to protect American *business* interests.

According to the Military Religious Freedom Foundation (MRFF) and Veterans for Common Sense (VCS), Christian proselytizing is common in the U.S. military along with the hatred of Muslims. But as we have seen, this is an old story—as old as the European invasion of the Americas. "They were trying to de-heathenize the local population and replace their religions with a trinity," Gore Vidal explains. "We had Jesus to hide behind. We had an occupying white race, killing for Jesus."[88]

The concept of eradicating the savage in the name of Jesus remains intact except that the unfortunate assemblage of targeted human beings changes as time and geography shift. Flash-forward to America's current boogeyman: Muslims. The problem has become so widespread that active duty soldiers as well as returning veterans are reporting the blatant Christian proselytizing at an alarming rate—so alarming that Mikey Weinstein (Founding President of MRFF) and Paul Sullivan (former Executive Director of VCS) sent a joint letter to then Secretary of Defense Robert Gates. "The Military Religious Freedom Foundation," the letter begins, "has learned on numerous occasions over the past several years about blatantly sectarian Christian religious programs and Christian proselytizing in the military. The proselytizing is unconstitutional and we demand you issue an order to stop it now."[89] The letter continues:

> Perhaps the most alarmingly repugnant stories are those coming in from our recent war veterans regarding the widespread practice of "battlefield Christian proselytizing." When, on active duty, our service members sought urgently needed mental health counseling while on the battlefield and with the gun smoke practically still in their faces, they were instead sent to evangelizing chaplains, who are apparently being used with increasing frequency to provide mental health care due to the acute shortage of mental health professionals. Chaplains are not certified, professional mental health experts.

> According to the reports of these veterans, the chaplains they were sent to for evaluation and treatment had the unmitigated temerity to urge, as a medicinal cure, a conversion to evangelical Christianity, and sometimes even went as far as disgustingly lacing their "counseling" with the soldiers' need to stay on the battlefield to "kill Muslims for Christ."[90]

Young men go to war. Sometimes because they have to, sometimes because they want to. Always, they feel they are supposed to.

This comes from the sad, layered stories of life, which over the centuries have seen courage confused with picking up arms, and cowardice confused with laying them down.[91]

—Mitch Albom

Helter Skelter

Empire-building is a zero-sum game. Not only do the conquered continue to suffer under the heel of military occupation, so too the victims who must finance it and serve as its foot soldiers.
—Justin Akers Chacón, "The Battle Over Military Recruitment"

In the final analysis it is crystal clear: the Empire recruits men and women who will carry out the necessary dirty work, pulling the trigger or jerking their joystick, whichever works… and when it comes to murder, it's identical to how the ruthless serial killer Charles Manson operated from his perch high atop the Santa Susana Mountains overlooking Los Angeles: sending in the "troops" to wipe out those Manson considered to be the guilty insurgents, or as he claimed the guilty "little piggies." It was all part of his insane Helter Skelter race war against the white establishment. Manson had *Helter Skelter*… George W. Bush drooled over *Shock and Awe*… Barack Obama elegantly embraced *Operation Enduring Freedom*… and then Donald J. Trump was stuffing his face with "the most beautiful piece of chocolate cake that you've every seen" while unleashing American death from above—all four operations equally insane, but the last three infinitely more murderous.

As I write, highly civilized human beings are flying overhead, trying to kill me.

They do not feel any enmity against me as an individual, nor I against them. They are 'only doing their duty', as the saying goes. Most of them, I have no doubt, are kind-hearted law-abiding men who would never dream of committing murder in private life. On the other hand, if one of them succeeds in blowing me to pieces with a well-placed bomb, he will never sleep any the worse for it. He is serving his country, which has the power to absolve him from evil.

—George Orwell
The Lion and the Unicorn: Socialism and the English Genius
Part 1: England Your England
1940

8 No

Battlefields.

Those wretched places where Mother Earth is soaked to the core—soaked with blood and soaked with the abject failure of the human species. The unincorporated community of Shiloh, in Tennessee, witnessed the destruction of 23,746 persons (killed or injured) over two gruesome days in the spring of 1862. Bordered to the east by the deep cut of the Tennessee River, the battlefield is encircled by Owl and Snake Creeks to the north and west, and Lick Creek to the south. If you stand on a ridge there today, any ridge, say the one overlooking Peach Orchard (and you have the right kind of eyes), you will suffer the fleeting wisps of death. It lingers, this insanity of war.

It lingers on similar ridges in Yanggu County in South Korea, ridges with names like Heartbreak and Bloody, and if you climb these infamous ridges in Gangwon Province you'll experience the same wisps of death—wisps soaked with the viscera of nearly 30,000 Americans, French, Chinese, and North Koreans.

It lingers everywhere—from Wounded Knee to Waterloo, from the Argonne Forest to Antietam, from Hastings on the south coast of England to the Ia Drang Valley in the central highlands of Vietnam. From Panzer Divisions rolling through Stalingrad to the open air concentration camp and battlefield of Gaza…

It lingers.

It also lingers on personal battlefields—theatres of war in places like the Cobbs Creek neighborhood in West Philadelphia or on streets hard between the Estación Central railway station and Alameda Avenue in Santiago, Chile—where certain individuals have stood up to the same vicious war-like insanity and said, "No, HELL NO… I refuse with every molecule in my body to be a part of your madness."

These next two heroic individuals, both in their own unique way, said "NO" to the demented machine.

One died a brutal death. The other survived a brutal attack.

❖ ❖ ❖

"Sing now... you bastard!"

Photo: Patricio Guzmán

The infamy of the date "September 11" actually began twenty-eight years earlier, in 1973, far from the black wind that thundered through lower Manhattan on a crystal clear late summer day. "9/11/1973" featured another thundering black wind—this one roaring down from the imposing Andes that loom over Chile, whipping across the Central Valley in this long and narrow coastal country where most of the Chilean population lives. This viento negro zigzagged through the capital city of Santiago, bouncing viciously off the various 19th century neo-classical edifices that shape this South American metropolis. (In actuality, this black wind, more a devil wind, a viento Diablo, began well north of the Andes, in a city well known for orchestrating distant coups, a city hard by the Potomac—a city named after a famous slave owner.)

It was Santiago, Chile, in 1952, where Alberto Granado and Ernesto Guevara de la Serna finally abandoned their broken-down motorcycle. And it was Santiago, in 1973, where Augusto Pinochet—backed by the full faith and credit of the United States government, its president, Richard Nixon, its Secretary of State, Henry Kissinger, and its international goon squad, the Central Intelligence Agency—violently overthrew the democratically elected government of President Salvador Allende.

It was a bloody coup... one for the ages. It was a coup that ferociously ensured that the opposition (that is the people's democracy, known as the Popular Unity government) would be sadistically and completely eliminated by a military junta headed by Commander Pinochet—Washington's corporate strong man and Margaret Thatcher's warm and cuddly teddy bear.[1] But hell, the dreaded "good example" that was quickly developing in Chile under the direction of the elected Marxist, Salvador Allende, was sending shock waves through wealthy foreign corporate elites and their Cold War partners. Allende and Popular Unity were well liked among Chile's working class, like the rank and file copper miners who toiled to extract the country's most valuable export, and this obviously didn't sit well with the power structure headed by Kennecott Copper, Anaconda, as well as the telecommunications giant ITT (who funded the right-wing Chilean newspaper *El Mercurio*).

Allende envisioned his nation's resources being directed toward the common good: ease the poverty, and then build health care and education. But the foreign corporations, along with U.S. government muscle, had a much different idea. In the book, *The Lawless State,* authors Morton Halperin, Jerry Berman, Robert Borosage, and Christine Marwick underscore America's interference:

> Since the early 1960s, American policy in Chile was directed at
> one objective—to keep Salvador Allende from coming to power.
> To accomplish this, Presidents Kennedy, Johnson, and Nixon,
> with the willing cooperation of the CIA, were prepared to destroy
> constitutional government in Chile.[2]

Allende died in the coup, committing suicide in La Moneda, the presidential palace under attack by opposition fighter jets. Determined not to be taken alive, Allende placed an AK-47 (given to him by Fidel Castro) under his chin and blew the top of his head off. He died instantly.[3]

But the 11 September assault was just the beginning. In the days and months immediately following, thousands of so-called "leftists" were killed or "disappeared." Some have defined Pinochet's reign of terror as "politicide" or "political genocide," but the many (not only tortured but murdered) may disagree with terms so clinical and clean—for this bloodbath was anything but clean. Many of the victims were slaughtered by the *Caravana de la Muerte* or Caravan of Death—formed by Pinochet and carried out with ruthless efficiency by his compañero Brigadier General Sergio Arellano. The mass political assassination plan was carried out with coldblooded precision, as assassins would dash around the countryside in Puma helicopters, visit an army installation where prisoners were held, and then summarily execute them. It resembled the final moments of *The Godfather.*

The National Stadium, or Estadio Nacional, was used as a makeshift concentration camp where some 40,000 political prisoners were held hostage. Book burning dotted the Santiago landscape. But it was the shrieks and cries of tortured prisoners deep inside the bowels of the stadium that forever etched horror into the memories of the survivors... and it was the constant bursts of machine gun fire—for days—that ushered in moments of ghastly silence. One of those brutally murdered by machine gun fire was Chilean poet and folksinger, Victor Jara, ripped apart just a few days before celebrating his forty-first flight around the Sun.

Victor Lidio Jara Martinez was born in September of 1932 in the tiny farming village of Lonquén, about fifty miles southwest of Santiago. Like many in Chile, Victor grew up navigating rural poverty. His father, Manuel, suffered from alcoholism and, of course, the family in turn suffered as well. Manuel beat his wife Amanda, Victor's mother, and the folksinger never forgot; from his song "La Luna Siempre Es Muy Linda"—

> *I remember the face of my father*
> *like a hole in the wall,*
> *mud-stained sheets,*
> *an earthen floor,*
> *my mother worked day and night*
> *crying and screaming.*

In her biography of her slain husband, Joan Jara writes about Victor as a young boy, living on the plantation-like farm of an "immensely rich" and powerful family, part of the Chilean oligarchy. The relationship between rulers and peasants was clearly feudal, with the *patrón* paying little while demanding blood, sweat, and tears. Joan Jara recalls Victor's vivid memories:

> Under a brilliant starry sky at the end of a long, hot summer, flames
> from a huge bonfire lit up the group of men, women, and children

squatting on the ground. They were peeling the husks off the golden maize cobs, piling them into great heaps, ready for spreading out to dry on the low, tiled roofs of the adobe houses... This was Victor's earliest childhood memory. He told me how he would lie on the ground, looking up at the stars, and how his mother sitting on one of the piles of maize, singing and playing her guitar, talking and joking with the people around her. He would fall asleep to the sound of her singing.[4]

There was no radio in the house, nothing to connect the family to an evolving outside world. But there was a large wooden cross that hovered above the village, placed there to ward off evil spirits, the adults in the village passing down the religious superstitions for generations, stories of "La Calchona," a half-woman half-goat who demanded their possessions, and of course the Devil himself, Satan, who demanded their souls. All of this was perfect fodder for the Church, who also demanded—and received—payments to the Virgin Mary. Once paid, she would dismiss these evil visitations. Of course this money was sorely needed for silly and useless things like food, clothing, and shelter.[5] Victor Jara never forgot, again from "La Luna Siempre Es Muy Linda"—

> *Candles always burning,*
> *One must take refuge in something.*
> *Where will the money come from*
> *to pay for the faith?*
> *They frighten the poor so much*
> *so that they will swallow their suffering,*
> *so that they will cover their misery*
> *with the images of saints.*

It's an old story and a common one in underdeveloped agrarian cultures, but Victor's father Manuel, who was illiterate, wanted the children to be nothing more than extra hands working the land. But Victor's mother Amanda had different plans. Unusual for a woman in her world, Amanda could read and write and knew how important education was for her children and she demanded their attendance and focus as students. Victor excelled in school and was twice voted "El mejor compañero" by his fellow students, "a term which meant not just most popular classmate," writes Joan Jara, "but the person most likely to stand up for them."[6] History proved the children correct.

In a dramatic move, one inspired by every human's quest for a better life, Amanda moved with her children to Santiago where she picked up a job in a small restaurant... and Victor picked up a guitar. Manuel lived a short distance away growing melons on a tiny plot of land purchased by Amanda's restaurant earnings, but Victor barely saw his father as the teenager was building his life with school, the guitar, and a group called Acción Católica—a church society dedicated less to Catholicism's hierarchy and population control and more to social consciousness as well as involving young people in the community. Victor continued playing his guitar, singing in the choir, listening to classical music, and becoming more involved with the church and his community. The teenager was also showcasing his talent as an artist and a singer in the local theatre world. At the same time, both his brother, Lalo, and his sister, Coca, left school far behind; Lalo became a father at sixteen, Coca was pregnant and attempted suicide. Both siblings were hanging and gang banging. Very concerned for them, Victor envisioned a much different future for himself. "His secret dream was to become a priest," recounts Joan Jara. "That seemed to him to be the highest ideal to which he could aspire."[7]

When Victor was fifteen he was summoned from his classroom to be told that his mother died working in the market. She suffered a massive stroke. Joan Jara writes:

> It was the end of an epoch. It was a profound shock for him. He
> loved her deeply and had always felt that one day he would be able
> to help her more, to relieve her of the need to work so hard. Now
> he was left with a sense of desolation and emptiness, almost of
> guilt.[8]

Living on his own, Victor made a living hauling freight and also worked with a furniture maker, but it was (at least he thought at the time) the voice of God calling him home as he entered the seminary toward the end of 1950. Vulnerable and compensating for the sudden loss of his mother's love, he turned to the spiritual. In 1973, Victor talked about his choice:

> It was a very serious decision for me to enter the seminary.
> Looking back now, from a more mature point of view, I think
> it was for very intimate and personal reasons; it was loneliness
> and the disappearance of a world which until then had been solid
> and enduring, with a home and maternal love. I already had a
> relationship with the church and at that moment I found refuge
> in it.[9]

Eighteen months later it was clear: celibacy was kicking Victor's ass. The Redemptorist Order in San Bernardo was a cloistered religious sect, cut off from everything. Full of life, Victor was wilting. Seminary students were forced to flog themselves in a cold shower if they experienced any sexual desires. Victor explained to Joan: "Everything healthy, that implied a state of physical well-being, had to be put aside. Your body became a sort of burden that you were forced to bear."[10] By mutual consent, Victor left the seminary. Ten days later he was drafted into the Chilean army.

The budding poet and revolutionary singer comported himself well in the military, rising to Sergeant and earned a glowing final report. The Chilean army saw Victor as officer material but he wanted nothing to do with a career in the military. In fact, once he left the seminary, "Victor never again went to mass," reports Joan Jara, "and on his return from military service he cut all links with Acción Católica."[11] From this moment forward, Victor Jara dedicated himself to music and theater as he attended the University of Chile in Santiago. Music became his lifeblood; he was exposed to actors, directors, and other musicians, as well as worldly folksingers like Violeta Parra, who had just recorded Chilean folk songs for the BBC, and who Victor spent time with at the Café São Paulo. He was becoming an integral part of the creative fabric of Chile as he was exposed to the political left movement in Santiago, one growing against the backdrop of the 1958 presidential election when Salvador Allende—representing a broad coalition of the left—lost to Jorge Alessandri, who was backed by Chile's wealthy and entrenched power. "The Chilean Communist Party was just coming out of hiding after being banned for almost a decade," Joan Jara remembers, "To the mass of working people who made up its membership and support, it had a heroic image."[12]

Victor's creative work was growing in leaps and bounds in both theatre and music. He wrote and recorded a comic folk song entitled "La beata," about a sanctimonious woman confessing her sins to a priest. "Some rather mischievous person played it on the radio at a time when there was a link-up of the whole national network," Joan Jara remembers. "It caused an uproar," she continues, "Victor found himself at the centre of a scandal."[13] In fact, the record was banned throughout Chile. Of course, there's always the law of unintended consequences: Jara's reputation as a rebel grew large in leftist and progressive circles.

Clearly, the right wing in Chile was similar to reactionaries everywhere and Jara was quickly identified with Allende, the socialist and Marxist leader, and with good reason: Victor's constant connection with the poor and their daily experience with hardship and deprivation affected him "in a very direct and personal way." As was true almost everywhere on Planet Earth in the 1960s, urgency was in the air in Chile: Victor was an artist and activist demanding change from the oppressive status quo.

> [It] motivated Victor to write several songs which had one common thread running through them: the dire consequences of poverty on human relationships, its capacity to destroy even the fundamental love of parents for their children, and the necessity of ending, once and for all, "this dark and bitter sea."[14]

His burgeoning art pushed him hard and it sharpened his political insight. He traveled to the Soviet Union and to Cuba and was forever changed by the people he met and their struggle he felt. Back in Chile, Victor joined the Communist Party. Like Guthrie and Seeger before him, along with contemporaries like Phil Ochs and Bob Dylan, and future travelers like Dead Prez and Public Enemy, the personal met the political; the art transformed itself into a powerful voice—a voice that was spreading throughout Chile and the world. A journalist asked Victor why he sings:

> I am moved more and more by what I see around me... the poverty of my own country, of Latin America... I have seen with my own eyes memorials to the Jews in Warsaw, the panic caused by the Bomb, the disintegration that war causes to human beings and all that is born of them... But I have also seen what love can do, what real liberty can do, what the strength of a man who is happy can achieve. Because of all this, and because above all I desire peace, I need the wood and strings of my guitar to give vent to sadness or happiness, some verse, which opens up the heart like a wound, some line which helps us all to turn from inside ourselves to look out and see the world with new eyes.[15]

Joan Jara reflects that, "The mid-sixties was a bad time for people on the left in Chile."[16] But Victor was growing the heart of a lion as the State—fronted by President Eduardo Frei—suggested economic and social reforms in every walk of Chilean life but delivered little, instead bowing to the demands of the U.S. government protecting the interests of American and foreign businesses—an old, tiresome, but effective oppression. Throughout Chile, classic instances of the State using their police forces to break up strikes, quell dissent, crack heads, even killing miners and their wives who dared to speak up for better wages and a better way of life, were commonplace. "The US government," Joan Jara laments, "saw Frei as a dyke against a real revolution."[17]

In 1969, Victor truly hit his soulful stride. His music and "unplugged" approach was not the formula for popular "top ten" music, which called for electric guitars, catchy melodies, and full studio production. His music was considered non-commercial and "Chilean-sounding,"[18] yet the people were embracing his revolutionary passion and organizers and promoters were booking him all over Chile—from big city clubs to the mines in the northern desert, from the oil fields in Tierra del Fuego to distant peasant villages. "An artist must be an authentic creator and therefore in very essence a revolutionary." Victor made his personal definition clear: "[He is] a man as dangerous as a guerrilla because of his great power of communication."[19] See John Winston Lennon.

Later in 1969, the political dam broke: some ninety homeless peasant families were living in muddy shit-fields near the city of Puerto Montt in southern Chile. A wealthy family owned the land but the peasants occupied the land in order to help bring attention to their plight (not unlike the occupiers of Zuccotti Park near the shit-fields of Wall Street). "They were tired of waiting for the right to live better than animals," remembers Joan Jara. But Pérez Zújovic—a universally disliked wealthy magnate with control over various elements of state security—ordered the peasants evicted and personally approved the use of force with firearms. A massacre ensued as tear gas along with shoot-to-kill orders unleashed heavily armed police on the completely unarmed peasants. Seven adults were killed, one baby, and another sixty people were critically wounded. Joan Jara recalls Victor's reaction:

> He became enraged and hurt as though it had been his own family
> which had been attacked and ravaged by the police. Immediately, he
> took his guitar and began to compose a song of accusation against
> Pérez Zújovic, seeing him as a symbol of the distorted values of the
> society we were living in.[20]

The next day violent clashes broke out all over Santiago between students and police. The fuse of political change was lit as a huge crowd of more than 100,000 gathered for a funeral march and protest through the capital city. "Speakers and artists were on the platform to express their condemnation of the horrible crime," Joan Jara recalls, and it was here that Victor Jara "took a decisive turn toward political confrontation with his song 'Preguntas por Puerto Montt' (Questions About Puerto Montt, 1969)."[21] That day Victor sang his searing new entreaty to the masses, a song "which took direct aim at a government official who had ordered police to attack squatters in the town of Puerto Montt."[22] In fact, from this flashpoint moment on, the entire landscape of Chilean politics began to boil over. Victor sang:

Usted debe responder	*You have to answer*
Señor Pérez Zujovic	*Mr. Pérez Zujovic*
porqué al pueblo indefenso	*why were defenseless people*
contestaron con fusil.	*replied to with guns.*
Señor Pérez su conciencia	*Mr. Pérez your conscience*
la enterró en un ataúd	*you buried in a coffin*
y no limpiarán sus manos	*and all the southern rains*
toda la lluvia del sur.	*won't clean your hands.*

In late 1970, the winds of change helped to elect the physician turned politician and leader, Salvador Allende, into office as Chile's Marxist president. By now, Victor and Joan were cultural icons in Chile and contributed greatly to Allende's campaign—Victor writing and performing "Venceremos" (We Will Triumph), which became the theme song for Allende's "Unidad Popular" or Popular Unity movement. Joan Jara recalls a "gigantic demonstration" in support of Popular Unity, "800,000 people there… It was the biggest, most festive, most combative ever, stretching the length of the Alameda, from Plaza Italia, past the Santa Lucia Hill, on down towards the Central Station… It was incredible to hear all those people singing 'Venceremos.'"[23]

Consabiente de nuestra bandera	*Underneath our banner*
La mujer ya se ha unido al clamor	*The women have joined in our call*
La Unidad Popular vencedora	*Victory for the Unidad Popular*
Será tumba del yanqui opresor	*Will be the defeat of the Yankee oppressor*

Throughout the early 1970s, Victor Jara dedicated himself to bringing Chile's diverse population together using music, theatre, dance, and art as the vehicles to help create a cohesive people's front. "Gigantic puppets, used in street theatre, were useful to make grotesque figures of the 'enemy,'" Joan Jara recalls. "[R]ight-wing politicians, ITT and other multi-nationals"[24] were depicted for their oppressive power and control over Chile's poor working class as well as their outright theft of natural resources.

In 1972, Pablo Neruda was awarded the Nobel Prize for Literature. "There can be few Nobel Prize awards that have ever been celebrated in urban slums and shanty-towns,"[25] writes Joan Jara, and indeed it was celebrated when the Chilean poet who was famous, not only for his erotic love poems, but for his explicitly political work, won the honor. Victor set selections of his poetry to music and performed at the ceremony honoring the Chilean artist at Estadio Nacional. Little did Victor know that the national stadium would soon be a house of death. Nor did he know that another stadium, the nearby Estadio Chile, would soon be his own tomb. It was there, in this makeshift sepulcher during the final hours of his life, that he would frantically scribble his last, unfinished and untitled poem, which begins:

> *There are five thousand of us here*
> *in this small part of the city*
> *We are five thousand.*
> *I wonder how many we are in all*
> *in the cities and in the whole country?*

On the morning of 11 September 1973, Victor was driving to work where he taught at the Technical University. He quickly realized that the center of Santiago was completely shut down. He managed to take a detour, through the tanks and the troops, heard the gunfire, saw the smoke, and still managed to get to campus. Suddenly, jets dedicated to the unfolding coup began their attack on La Moneda. Victor called home and told Joan he was safe at the school.

> *Here alone*
> *are ten thousand hands which plant seeds*
> *and make the factories run.*
> *How much humanity*
> *exposed to hunger, cold, panic, pain,*
> *Moral pressure, terror and insanity?*

The military junta orchestrating the coup, their terror sponsored by their U.S. allies, enforced a curfew on the city, which forced hundreds of students and teachers to be locked-down in numerous campus buildings for the night. "It was then that Victor must have phoned me for the second time," Joan Jara remembers. "He didn't tell me that the whole campus was surrounded by tanks and troops." People who attempted to bolt from the campus "under cover of darkness were shot outright."[26] The next morning, in broad daylight, the military began shelling buildings with tanks as well as firing haphazardly into buildings. There was no return fire since the students and teachers were unarmed. Once in control, the troops rounded up the campus population in one large area and "using rifle butts and boots" forced everyone face down to the ground. A short time later, as they were marching their "prisoners" off campus to another location, probably the national stadium, a non-commissioned officer recognized Victor: "You're that fucking singer, aren't you?"[27] The officer then beat Victor to the ground and isolated him with the so-called "dangerous" or "important" prisoners. Victor was brought to Estadio Chile, a small indoor arena. Hours of hell dripped by. Among the screams and agony of torture, Victor was spotted by some who later report that he was bloody and badly beaten. It is here that he wrote his final words.

> *Six of us were lost*
> *as if into starry space*
> *One dead, another beaten as I could never have believed*
> *a human being could be beaten.*
> *The other four wanted to end their terror –*
> *one jumping into nothingness,*
> *Another beating his head against a wall,*
> *but all with the fixed stare of death.*

Rolling Stone magazine wrote: "The love and justice songs of Chilean folk singer Victor Jara were apparently so threatening to the military leaders who staged the nation's 1973 coup that they had to murder him."[28] Joan Jara received a final message from Victor before he was taken away by guards for more medieval brutality—"a message for me brought out by someone who was near him for hours, down in the dressing rooms, converted now into torture chambers, a message of love for his daughters and for me," Joan writes.[29]

What horror the face of fascism creates!
They carry out their plans with knife-like precision.
Nothing matters to them.
To them, blood equals medals,
slaughter is an act of heroism.

From the *BBC*: "He was tortured, electrocuted and had his wrists and hands broken. On 16 September, he was machine-gunned to death."[30]

From *Rolling Stone*: "Taken prisoner with thousands of others in a stadium that now bears his name, Jara was tortured; after they broke his hands, guards mocked the singer, ordering him to play guitar."[31]

From Joan Jara: "...the officer nicknamed the Prince shouting at him, on the verge of hysteria, losing control of himself, '**Sing now, if you can, you bastard!**' and Victor's voice raised in the Stadium after those four days of suffering to sing a verse of the hymn of Popular Unity, 'Venceremos.' Then he was beaten down and dragged away for the last phase of his agony."[32]

From *Rolling Stone*: "Defiant, he sang a political anthem that translates as 'We Will Win.' For his insubordination, Jara was machine-gunned to death, his body dumped on a street outside Santiago."[33] Victor Jara was 41.

"Nothing of very great consequence"

On the morning of 16 September 1973 Henry Kissinger was relaxing at home, chatting on the phone with his boss, the well-known fellow mass murderer and big time pro football fan, Richard Milhous Nixon. (Go Redskins!)

Nixon: *Hi, Henry.*

Kissinger: *Mr. President.*

Nixon: *Where are you, in New York?*

Kissinger: *No, I am in Washington. I am working. I may go to the football game this afternoon if I get through.*

Nixon: *Good. Good. Well it is the opener. It is better than television. Nothing new of any importance or is there?*

Kissinger: *Nothing of very great consequence. The Chilean thing is getting consolidated and of course the newspapers are bleeding because a pro-Communist government has been overthrown.*

Nixon: *Isn't that something. Isn't that something.*

Kissinger: *I mean instead of celebrating—in the Eisenhower period we would be heroes.*[34]

"Nothing of very great consequence." And it was at this moment that the cold, dark wind that began in Washington years before, completed its mission thousands of miles away... and then quickly circled back and withdrew behind the Potomac, past Foggy Bottom, 17th Street NW, and finally disappearing into the subterranean vault deep beneath 1600 Pennsylvania Avenue—the large white house built by terrorized black slaves.

As a small group of people from Santiago came upon six machine-gun riddled bodies in the working class district of San Miguel, someone noticed that one of the mangled, ripped apart carcasses was that of Victor Jara.[35] Behind those six bodies, there were six more, ten more, twenty more, one hundred more, one thousand, two-three-four thousand more.

Indeed, *"Nothing of very great consequence."*

How hard it is to sing
when I must sing of horror.
Horror which I am living,
Horror which I am dying.

In 2004, the National Security Archive released the declassified transcripts of these chats between Nixon and Kissinger. Later in the conversation Kissinger states: "we helped them… created the conditions as great as possible." Nixon responded: "That is right." The 16 September 1973 "telcon" was discovered by the Archive's Chile specialist, Peter Kornbluh, who commented, "damning proof, in Kissinger's own words, that the Nixon administration directly contributed to creating a coup climate in Chile which made the September 11, 1973, military takeover possible."[36]

To see myself among so much
and so many moments of infinity
in which silence and screams
are the end of my song.

A few months later, in 1974, Phil Ochs—who performed with Jara on a South American tour, organized a benefit concert known as "An Evening with Salvador Allende." Bob Dylan, Pete Seeger, Arlo Guthrie, as well as Phil Ochs himself headlined a New York City benefit in Jara's name at Madison Square Garden. In 2003, the stadium where Victor spent his last days and hours was renamed "Estadio Victor Jara." In that last message smuggled out from the stadium to Joan, Victor asked that his work be carried on… and for sure it lives. "They could kill him, but they couldn't kill his songs," Joan told the BBC.[37]

Victor Jara's last song, last poem, last plea remains unfinished. "The lyrics literally stop mid-sentence as he was led away to the changing rooms of the stadium," reports the BBC, "and was shot repeatedly through the chest."

What I see, I have never seen
What I have felt and what I feel
Will give birth to the moment...
—Victor Jara, Estadio Chile
September 1973

"Attention MOVE: This is America!"

Many years ago, decades in fact, a young woman wanted to become a lawyer. She was a good student, very smart, and with the loving support of her mother and family, all of her dreams seemed within reach. Her mother was a hairdresser, and as such, in the Black community of West Philadelphia, this meant a good living, for Black women (then, as now) spent a good sum to tame their locks, to relax those rebellious, tempestuous kinks and curls.

Courtesy of Street Legal Cinema

The young woman was in pre-law classes at Temple University's North Philadelphia campus, where perhaps the majority of the city's lawyers made their foundation to a life lived in the law (perhaps the private school, University of Pennsylvania posed some challenge, but as Temple was a state-supported college, it lured more of the city's up-and-coming working-class kids).

Her road was set, and before her seemed few obstacles, except for the usual presented for Black women in a society marked by racial and sexual animus. She studied the U.S. Constitution and read treatises by law professors waxing wise and eloquent on the rights and privileges of American citizenship. Perhaps she dreamed of representing the poor and underprivileged in the courts of the land, with a bold, white-lettered nameplate on her desk: "RAMONA JOHNSON, ESQ." Her office would be a tony downtown address, where she would mingle with the wealthy and the famous; or perhaps she dreamed of representing corporations (for that is where the money is) in a high-rise office in Center City, maybe part of a small, but lucrative law firm where she was both a partner and a rainmaker: "WILSON & JOHNSON LAW OFFICES, P.C."

But dreams are, after all, but dreams. They are bridges that get us through the night. They live in a dominion all their own, on the twinkling twilight of consciousness. Yet although such dreams were as possible for her as they were for tens of thousands of young women in the 1970s, for Ramona, they were not to be.

Her path changed forever when she discovered MOVE—a small, but spirited commune in West Philadelphia, comprised of Black, Latino, Asian, and White young rebels fiercely committed to the radical change of the American system and an immediate move back to nature. But MOVE didn't extinguish her dreams.

The City of Philadelphia did.

They did it by trying nine MOVE members in a 1978 courtroom where all those precious rules that Ramona studied were turned into little more than dust. They took her from the soft and comfortable schoolroom of theory, and hurled her into a courtroom charade in Philadelphia's City Hall, where she witnessed things that took her breath away. She learned, by the very living of it, what real law was—and was not. It transformed her from a bookish, somewhat naïve young college student into a revolutionary. And it sent her and the city into a spiral that would transform both forever.

MOVE was a small but loud group of naturalists famous (or infamous, depending on your point-of-view) for, above all else, *resisting*. It seemed like they resisted everything. Industry. The Philadelphia Zoo. Celebrities. The cops. The courts. The media.

Everything.

On 8 August 1978, after a yearlong standoff juiced by the media, police had erected barricades around a West Philadelphia two-story home near Powelton Avenue, with an assembled domestic police force almost unprecedented in modern U.S. history. This blockade was manned by hundreds of cops, many armed with automatic weapons. Police snipers were situated at key access points. Philadelphia's then mayor was the bombastic former Police Commissioner, Frank Lazarro Rizzo, a man who kindled both love and hate (again, depending on your perspective). In South Philly, Rizzo was loved and honored, and his image—proud, strong, and with his prominent iconic chin leading the way—radiated from more than a few homes. As a man of working-class origins (not to mention high-school dropout) and its first Italian mayor, he was lionized by the city's white ethnic community. Among Black Philadelphians, however, another perspective reigned.

Older Blacks knew of his practical persona, as a vicious, brutal cop who beat and demeaned them. Black neighborhoods envisioned Rizzo as a walking nightstick. For some, especially those from the South who spoke in Ebonics, they used the emphasized term "Rizzio" to name him. They remembered him as an armed bully, who rose into the highest circle of politics on their backs, a rise based on coercion and force, as exemplified by the 1969 raids on the Black Panther offices—his police armed with submachine guns. Philadelphia Black Panther captain, Reggie Schell, remembers Rizzo well. "I knew of Rizzo when I was a kid," Schell's eyes still burning with pain. "He was a brute. He would beat the shit out of you. The man was a brute and we had to deal with this guy."[38]

New York *Daily News* investigative reporter, Juan Gonzalez, contends that throughout Rizzo's tenure, "He gave the police department carte blanche to do whatever his men needed to do to keep the natives of Philadelphia under control.[39] In 1979, Rizzo framed his view of the world to NBC's Tom Snyder this way: 'You're dealing with criminals, with barbarians, you're safer in the jungle.'" Rizzo boasted that his men in blue "could invade Cuba and win... we are now trained and equipped to fight wars."[40] Former U.S. Attorney General, Ramsey Clark, said that he "tangled with him a few times when he was Chief of Police." Clark described "Rizzio" as "an unprincipled person with compelling prejudices that caused abuse of police power and harmed good people."[41]

Rizzo or "Rizzio," the name mattered less than the man, for he energized his victims to act in the realm of politics and to transform the power relations between white and Black Philadelphia.

Enter MOVE.

Led by the charismatic John Africa, its adherents were trained in confrontation and armed with a steel of the spirit that allowed them to withstand atrocities that would—and did—break lesser organizations. Led by Rizzo's bombast and bellicosity, the police opened urban warfare against MOVE in the early morning hours of 8 August 1978. It was a dire attempt to bring an end to an almost yearlong and bitter standoff between MOVE and the City. MOVE members built a stage-like platform on their property that allowed them to speak to the masses of assembled media—and their message spread across the Delaware Valley and around the world. They spoke of their numerous conflicts with police, the brutality they suffered, and offered their message to the world. The actions and military assault by the Philadelphia Police Department that hot August day were meant to put an end to MOVE, once and for all. Firefighters, cops, MOVE members, and bystanders were injured in the crossfire. One cop, Officer James Ramp, was shot in the back of the head. (Later, nine MOVE members were found guilty of third-degree murder.)

Enter Ramona. As a student of the law, she felt the trial would be real-life insight into the ways that jurisprudence worked. She learned far more than she reckoned for. In an interview with your co-authors, she explained her experiences in the courtroom of Judges Merna Marshall and, later, Edwin Malmed of the Philadelphia court system:

> When I was going to college I intended on becoming a lawyer. I had a pre-law curriculum. My mother kept telling me, "you can be whatever you want to be, be a doctor, be a lawyer." Well I wasn't into the blood and guts so I leaned toward the law. What turned me around was in early 1979 I met Pam Africa and some other MOVE supporters at a meeting to plan a MOVE demonstration. Pam gave me a lot of information. She gave me literature about MOVE, and knowing I was headed to becoming a lawyer, she encouraged me to come down to City Hall and sit in on the "MOVE 9" trials. And that's what I did.[42]

Ramona attended several pre-trial hearings before the late Judge Merna Marshall of the city's Municipal Court. What did she see that impacted her?

> Nothing that I was taught in those classrooms at Temple was happening in the courtroom. Nothing the professors said or that the textbooks laid out led me to believe this was how the legal system operated—none of it was happening in the actual courtroom. I was shocked and appalled. But beyond that, I was totally impressed with how the MOVE people represented themselves, not shouting a bunch of legalities, but pointing out the inconsistencies of the American legal system, the inconsistencies of the prosecution witnesses, the police witnesses. They weren't intimidated at all by the courtroom atmosphere or the judge, the sheriff, or the prosecutors. No intimidation whatsoever by how bad and unjust MOVE was being treated. I was just thoroughly impressed by their courage.[43]

Ramona makes several key observations at this juncture that create a turning point not just in her consciousness, but in her life's trajectory as well. For, as a pre-law student, we can suppose that she aspired not just to becoming a lawyer, but actually "lawyering" in some capacity to make a difference. The very essence of the lawyer function is the legal representation of others, either individual or corporate. As such, she had already accepted the lawyer's function. In a sense, lawyers look to courts as priests look to church: they are a part of it, a functionary, at some level. That she sees, senses, and identifies, not with the court, nor the peripheral entities of the court, but looks to the accused—MOVE people representing themselves—is nothing short of remarkable. In one sense, of course, it shows her identifying herself with the oppressed, and as such, reflects a depth of Black Identity; yet, it must have forced her to choose which persona would prevail: Ramona, the lawyer—or Ramona, the activist. But, like a good pre-lawyer, she didn't jump in the pool willy-nilly. She did abundant research. She studied the problem. She examined the trial process, telling us:

> I finally started going up to the prison with other supporters to
> visit imprisoned MOVE people and to talk with them face-to-face.
> They never tried to influence me one way or the other in terms
> of whether or not to go ahead to law school that fall of '79. After
> being in and out of those courtrooms so much and learning so much
> about—not only about the case of the MOVE 9 but a number of
> other cases where people were railroaded—I made a decision that
> there was no way I wanted to be like the judge, like the prosecuting
> attorney, or like the so-called defense attorneys. I didn't want
> anything to do with that utter compromise, so I decided not to go to
> law school. I didn't want to be like those lawyers. I wanted to be like
> MOVE, like John Africa, a revolutionary.[44]

The break was complete, and yet…

What if the legal system was indeed fair and impartial and existed as it was written in the treatises and law books she read and spoken of in the lectures to which she listened? What if the judges of the Court of Common Pleas were actually truthful and just, instead of political hacks known for their smoky backroom deals? What if MOVE actually could get justice in the courts of the land and were acquitted on the basis of their factual innocence in relations to the killing of James Ramp on 8 August 1978?

Such a supposition seems downright silly in light of how history has actually played out. But history is, among other things, a tableau of "ifs." And if this were so, Ramona "Africa" may not have been born, for, absent that tension, that sense of "shock," that deeply felt sense of betrayal by teachers, professors, scholars and the like, she would not have needed to come forth. She would have earned her

Juris Doctor, joined the Public Defenders office, or opened her own practice, or joined a mega-firm, or...

In the Black Panther Party's newspaper, at the height of the 1960s, a motto appeared on the pages of the weekly newspaper, reading: "Repression Breeds Resistance." If Ramona hadn't seen what she had seen, the world—and perhaps her world—would be a profoundly different place. But she did; and it isn't. We live in the world that we live in—and judges aren't fair, and the System is overtly corrupt. And cops are more brutal today than they were thirty years ago. And Ramona took the revolutionary road.

Several years after the MOVE trial, which resulted in the framing of nine MOVE men and women, all of them sent to brutal, malicious, and unjust 30-to-100–year prison sentences, Ramona continued her support and advocacy for MOVE. As a member of MOVE, she began representing herself in court, fighting the inevitable arrests and harassments by the Philadelphia PD that accompany MOVE membership. It was baptism by fire as she looked the monolith square between the eyes and said, "C'mon, Philly, give me your best corrupt and racist shot."

"Attention MOVE: This is America!"
—Loudspeaker Warning by Philadelphia Police Commissioner Gregore Sambor

It was 13 May 1985—seven years after the massive assault by Frank Rizzo and Philadelphia's finest on the MOVE organization. On this day, smack dab in the middle of the Reagan regime, the Philadelphia Police, now under orders from Mayor Wilson Goode, returned to West Philadelphia to carry out another—this time full-out—military assault on the MOVE row house. Clearly, they came looking to finish the job: tear gas barrage, water cannons, and a then a hail of gunfire as Brotherly Love storm-troopers launched 10,000 rounds of ammunition into the MOVE dwelling. And then finally, as a coup de grâce, a police helicopter drops an FBI-supplied C-4 plastique bomb onto the roof of the MOVE home. A raging fire engulfed the neighborhood. The cops decided to "let the fire burn" (Police Commissioner Gregore Sambor to Fire Commissioner William Richmond[45]), which destroyed more than sixty homes and murdered eleven MOVE members—five of them children, some babies. A subsequent commission and grand jury investigated the actions and determined that city officials along with Wilson Goode's soldier-cops were completely at fault, "responsible for this disaster,"[46] but (surprise-surprise) no criminal charges were ever filed. The cops and their superiors triggered mass murder, holocaust in a major American city, and not one of the culprits were ever charged with a crime. Only Ramona Africa, guilty only of surviving, spent time in prison.

Ultimately, it was authoritarian alchemy: it was—the Philadelphia Police Department, together with the state government of Pennsylvania, bolstered by the Federal Bureau of Investigation and the Bureau of Alcohol, Tobacco, and Firearms of the U.S. Government—who bombed MOVE people on 13 May 1985. But no one would call any of those organizations or their employer, the U.S. Government, terrorists. But why not? The conspirators fit any and all definitions of terrorist. "No, no, no, it's not acceptable to bomb your own citizens," implores poet Aya de Leon. "You shouldn't bomb anybody, but it's extra crazy in your own city to bomb your own citizens, you just don't get to do that!"[47]

11 murders... including 5 children.

The twisted mentalities at work in the grim corridors of Philadelphia power were akin to those of My Lai and the broader Vietnam War (or more recently the various American assaults on the Middle East)—the spirit behind the mindlessly murderous mantra that echoed out of DaNang: *"We had to destroy the village in order to save it."*

Although perhaps best known for representing herself during the trial following her miraculous survival of the ferocious state bombing of MOVE's home on 13 May 1985, Ramona represented herself several times before the headline trial, but the press neglected to mention this in their demeaning critique of her ability and constitutional right to defend herself. In her interview with us, she addressed the issue of self-representation:

> I began representing myself after encountering MOVE and understanding John Africa's position when it came to self-representation. A lawyer can stand up there and shout legalities, but at the end of the trial, if you lose, who's going to jail? You or the lawyer? And who knows the truth of what really happened better than you? The lawyer wasn't there. So John Africa taught MOVE people to represent themselves. Now, on civil matters and on appeals where it's massive paperwork and briefs, yeah a lawyer can do that, but in terms of an actual trial, where you're either guilty or innocent of the charge, no one can represent you but you... who will go the whole nine yards for you but you?

Many legal experts disagree. But Ramona suggests an interesting counterpoint, especially when discussing political cases and political prisoners:

> Some folks, particularly with the case of the MOVE 9, have said to me, "Don't you think the MOVE 9 would have made out better if they had experienced and well-known attorneys?" And we're saying "no" because MOVE people aren't in prison because they lacked a legal argument. MOVE people are in prison for being committed disciples of John Africa, for being revolutionaries who don't believe in the system, and we fight the system on every level. It has nothing to do with criminality or being guilty of anything. The system knows this full well. Look at the more than 2.5 million people in prisons across the United States. I would venture to say that ninety-nine percent of them had lawyers. So, what kind of argument is that? "If you had a good lawyer, you would've beat the case." We put our freedom in our own hands and conducted ourselves according to the truth, you can't go wrong there. I'm not saying you won't end up in prison, but you always have the power of righteousness on your side.[48]

MOVE people, like Ramona, tend to be self-effacing. She did not detail nor boast that when she represented herself at trial (as the sole adult survivor of the city's bombing, incineration, and shooting of eleven MOVE people) that she actually did quite well, having several of the charges against her dismissed. She was sentenced to a minimum and maximum that ran to 7 years; if she renounced MOVE—that is, said that she would no longer associate with them, and left the group—she would've been eligible for immediate release. Ramona declined the offer.

She served her complete sentence and walked out free (or as free as a Black woman could be in modern-day America). It certainly indicates that MOVE membership, as she has noted, was more important to the state than any notion of criminality. When she emerged from Muncy State Women's Prison, a well-known Black Philadelphia talk show host (known by the radio name Mary Mason) sent her own limousine to fetch her, and bring her back to the very city that tried unsuccessfully to kill her back in 1985.

Of her years in the joint, Ramona became close with several MOVE women (Janine, Merle, Janet, and Debbie Africa), imprisoned on the spurious 1978 case following Philadelphia's initial attack on MOVE. Ramona remembers:

Fortunately, I had my sisters up there. You have to stand strong and set a strong example because if they pick up any kind of weakness in you, anything that would indicate they might be able to break you, they will come down on you like a ton of bricks. But they finally realized they would never be able to break MOVE people, and with that, the staff and the prison guards started getting close to us, started talking to us about their personal problems—their children, their marriages, their health situations. When you are right, you are strong, and when you're strong you're setting a life example. I don't care what kind of background people reveal—whether it's racism, classism, or whatever—they cannot help but respect and be attracted to that kind of strength, in spite of themselves.[49]

Ramona Africa literally walked through fire to become the freedom fighter that she is today. When the City of Philadelphia dropped a bomb on her and her family, it is fair to say that no one was expected to survive that terrible conflagration. It is also a marker for our era that of all the people involved in this horrid attack—the politicians who ordered it, the minions who followed their orders, as well as other social forces that played a role in making it happen—only Ramona Africa—the sole adult survivor, spent any time in prison; and as we have seen, she could have walked away immediately if only she renounced her belief. This, she would not—could not—do.

Since her imprisonment, Ramona lectures at colleges and universities across the country, and around the world, about the nightmarish attack on Osage Avenue in Southwest Philadelphia. She didn't just say NO—she has lived NO—and continues to do so to this very day. She faced the hatred, the enmity, and the monstrous violence of the system—and lived still to make evident *resistance*. What she learned about the nature of the system, she passes on, word-of-mouth, person-to-person, day-by-day. And among those lessons?

America and Philadelphia, particularly the cradle of independence and all that—it's a lie, *it's all a lie*. These people do whatever they want to do. The people that framed government, the scriptwriters— their aim was never freedom, justice, equality. When they were talking about "We hold these truths to be self-evident, that all men were created equal"—who the hell were they talking about? They weren't talking about women, they weren't talking about the African slaves they brought over here, they weren't talking about the indigenous people they were slaughtering, they weren't even talking about white men who didn't own land. So who the hell were they talking about, "all these men created equal, endowed by their creator with certain inalienable rights?" It was all a lie. And it's still a lie.[50]

Ramona Africa. Revolutionary.

AFTERWORD

If you've just read this whole book, pause and let it sink in a little. Set it down and go glance at a U.S. newspaper or television "news" network. You'll see complete and utter acceptance, and sometimes enthusiastic promotion, of organized crime, of Murder Inc.

War is banned by the Kellogg-Briand Pact, and—with narrow exceptions not met by any recent wars—by the United Nations Charter, not to mention by the most basic conception of morality, namely that one ought not to engage in mass murder. Yet war truly is the favorite pastime of the U.S. government. With very little debate it swallows up well over half of the money that the U.S. Congress votes on each year.

Three percent of the money that the United States dumps into war could end starvation on earth. A little over one percent could end the lack of clean drinking water everywhere. A fraction of war spending could transform the United States, the rest of the world, and the chances of slowing climate destruction. War kills first and foremost by this choice of where to dump resources—something in which the United States leads the world and just about equals the rest of the world combined. More than three-quarters of world military spending is by the United States and its allies/weapons customers. The U.S. government gives or facilitates the sale of weapons to almost three quarters of the world's dictatorships, by its own definition of dictatorship, and gives military training to most of them. The United States has troops in over 175 countries, and some 1,000 bases outside its own borders, compared to a couple of dozen foreign bases belonging to the rest of the world's nations combined.

There must be some advantage to this scheme, some upside, some pay off? Is there? Not only is military spending the one place with the funds that could address environmental collapse, but the military is also the top destroyer of the environment. It is the justification for nuclear arsenals that risk eliminating human life before environmental collapse can get around to it. It is the central justification for government secrecy, for the erosion of civil liberties (in the name of "freedom!"), for clampdowns on journalism and activism and on petitioning governments for a redress of grievances. It militarizes local police and trains them in warfare—brings them to understand as enemies those they claim to "protect and serve." It feeds off and simultaneously fuels racism, religious bigotry, and xenophobia. It directly kills millions, injures millions more, turns millions more into refugees, traumatizes whole generations, fuels lasting hostility, destabilizes whole regions, and creates mass migrations. And in so doing, it makes the residents of the imperial homeland, whether they like it or not, less safe, not more safe.

This key fact is blurted out by dozens of just-retired top U.S. officials. The drone murders, the non-drone murders, the bombs, the occupations—they create more enemies than they kill. They create them by killing. Just as I'm writing this there was a former U.S. Navy SEAL on Fox News asked about recent wars, and he proposed that the U.S. was going to need to "stop bombing people and creating terrorists," that the United States would need to try something different because that wasn't working. His segment ended very soon thereafter. Policing the globe for its own good whether the globe likes it or not runs up against the solidity of the problem—the world doesn't like it nor wants it. A Gallup poll of 65 countries in 2013 found that the U.S. was widely viewed as the greatest threat to peace. A Pew survey in 2017 found similar results.

War is the worst thing humanity does, and it has no up side. Yes, it makes a buck for some profiteers. It allows politicians to justify antidemocratic measures. It satisfies, ever so temporarily, irrational and sadistic urges. But there's nothing valuable to actually weigh in the balance against its downsides. It's not even an economic boon, as Congress members like to claim with such practiced sociopathy. Military spending means fewer and worse paying jobs than other types of spending, or even never taxing the money from working people.

In contrast, the upside to abolishing the institution of war would be almost too good for many to believe. Even life as it currently exists in some European and Asian countries is too good for most people in the United States to believe. Principally because of its war addiction, the United States trails many other countries in quality of life, in happiness, in education, in sustainability, in security, in life expectancy, in health. Despite leading the world in patriotism, belief in superiority, and flags per capita, the people of the United States are worse off in many ways than are people in other wealthy countries. Poor people in the United States are far worse off than poor people in other wealthy countries, and yet they are more patriotic than people in other countries or than wealthy Americans.

The USA is number one in exactly nothing to be proud of, but is number one in war spending, war making, incarceration, and various other measures to be much regretted, including various sorts of environmental destruction.

Simply by curing this one little sickness called warlust, the United States could have things it doesn't dare dream of, and help provide much of the rest of the world with the same: education, healthcare, retirement, clean energy. But how does one cure such a thing? The majority in the United States would reduce war spending right now if we had a representative government or a direct democracy. So, democratic reforms instead of bombing campaigns to "spread democracy" would be a start. But the majority in the United States would not abolish war entirely. To accomplish that, it would be necessary to advance by steps, to spark a reverse arms race, to close foreign bases, to end foreign weapons sales, to negotiate nuclear weapons reductions, and to have people's understanding evolve with the facts on the ground. Meanwhile, most people remain susceptible to bursts of war fever, and oblivious to the risks involved in parroting propaganda that demonizes potential new enemies.

If we want to overcome deficiencies in democracy, if we want to systematically move toward abolition, we are going to need activism beyond simply giving the right answers in a poll. We are going to need millions of people to recognize and grow outraged by the lies, the damn lies, the recruitment lies, and the $1.8 billion advertising budget for war exposed in this book. We are going to need public educational events organized around this book and others that make the case to end all war. We are going to need this truth of the matter taught in our schools, displayed in our public monuments, conveyed in our popular culture.

As you talk to others about the case for ending war, you'll discover that a particular section of this book is crucial. Virtually every person in the United States who defends the possibility of there being a just and necessary war someday—which is to say, virtually every person in the United States—focuses their argument on World War II. We should recognize this practice as absurd. Nobody goes back 75 years to find the most recent justifiable example of any other common practice; why is that permitted for our largest public expense? World War II happened in a pre-nuclear age of conquest and colonialism at which time knowledge of the tactics of nonviolent activism was virtually nonexistent. Despite the absurdity of the past 75 years of spotting new Hitlers and selling more weapons, we must face head-on the need to reject World War II mythology. Read that section of this book again. Read it to others out loud. Nothing is more needed.

Give young people the usual books and movies about Anne Frank. Let them build up the usual sense of righteous indignation. Then add one sentence: The U.S. State Department turned down Anne Frank's family's visa request. Then maybe one more: The U.S. Coast Guard chased a ship of Jewish refugees away from Miami, Florida. Then maybe a whole discussion of the fact that the U.S. public and its government did not want to save the Jews until after they had not been saved. Peace activists asked the U.S. and U.K. governments to evacuate the Jews and were told they couldn't be bothered with such things, that they had a war to fight.

On the evening of the attack on Pearl Harbor, President Franklin Roosevelt drafted a declaration of war against two countries, Japan and Germany. Then he decided he couldn't get away with it, and took to Congress only a declaration of war on Japan. The United States government wanted to dominate the post-war world. And the nation it least wanted to share in that domination was the Soviet Union. From the moment the U.S. entered the war, the Soviets spent two-and-a-half years pleading with the United States to attack the Germans from the West. Before the United States had even entered the war, the Soviets had turned the tide against the Nazis outside of Moscow. Nazi defeat was understood, but the losses continued to be heavy. The U.S. priority, however, was a weakened Russia.

Immediately upon German surrender, Winston Churchill proposed using Nazi troops together with allied troops to attack the Soviet Union, the nation that had just done the bulk of the work of defeating the Nazis. This was not an off-the-cuff proposal. The U.S. and British had sought and achieved partial German surrenders, had kept German troops armed and ready, and had debriefed German commanders on lessons learned from their failure against the Russians. Attacking the Russians sooner rather than later was a view advocated by General George Patton, and by Hitler's replacement Admiral Karl Donitz, not to mention Allen Dulles and the OSS. Dulles made a separate peace with Germany in Italy to cut out the Russians, and began sabotaging democracy in Europe immediately and empowering former Nazis in Germany, as well as importing them into the U.S. military to focus on war against Russia.

U.S. hostility toward Russia did not begin as a distraction from Democratic Party emails discussing how to help Hillary Clinton defeat Bernie Sanders in the 2016 primaries. It began, as this book explains, but most people in the United States do not know, with the 1918 U.S.-and-allies invasion of Russia in a failed attempt to undo its revolution. But the past 100 years of anti-Russian warmongering grew out of the deeper desire to dominate the globe, which flowed directly out of the genocidal desire to dominate North America. The commitment to dominating others will have to end before the tactic of warfare can be ended.

The alternative is to restrain nationalism, to identify locally and globally with humanity, to allow the United States to be one nation among others, among equals, to allow the world to be run by representatives of its peoples in proportion to their numbers, and to understand that 96 percent of humanity is outside of the United States. The alternative to war is respect, cooperation, the rule of law, diplomacy, and actual aid—not "military aid" but actual assistance or reparations that cost less and benefit more than militarism.

As this book reveals, there have always been wise resisters to warmongering. Over the years, their tools have improved, just as have the weapons of war. Unarmed civilian protectors, nonviolent peaceforces, skilled negotiators, engineers of economic conversion—these are our allies who we should thank for their service. We are up against skilled propagandists and misguided loyalties. When people in the United States opposed George W. Bush's wars because Bush was a Republican, and then accepted Barack Obama's wars because he was a Democrat, one might have thought that a Donald Trump White House would fill the streets with peace demonstrations. Not at all. The Democratic Party's leadership has not opposed the wars, and so neither have their followers. War has been made so acceptable, that we've seen a rehabilitation of the reputation of Bush. Monuments to a half-dozen more wars, including the "war on terrorism" are being planned and built in Washington, D.C.

What we need is a burst of pacifism on the scale of the never-yet-undone burst of militarism that accompanied World War II. Such a thing is perfectly possible. Even with what weak powers we've had, we have prevented and ended wars, blocked weapons production and sales, and educated millions to facts unmentioned by corporate media. What we might soon do is vastly more significant. This book gives us a new tool to use in our struggle—a struggle we have a moral duty to engage in, and a struggle in which we can find all the solidarity, sacrifice, courage, and commitment once associated with participation in mass murder.

David Swanson

Charlottesville, Virginia

Fall, 2018

David Swanson *is an author, activist, journalist, and radio host. He is director of WorldBeyondWar.org and campaign coordinator for RootsAction.org. Swanson's books include* **War Is A Lie** *and* **When the World Outlawed War**. *He blogs at DavidSwanson.org and WarIsACrime.org. He hosts Talk Nation Radio. He is a 2015, 2016, 2017 Nobel Peace Prize Nominee.*

Endnotes

Prologue

1 Mark Zepezauer, *The CIA's Greatest Hits*, Soft Skull Press, New York, 1994, 2011-12, p. 35.

Chapter 1

1 Howard Zinn, *A People's History of the United States*, Harper-Collins, New York, 2003, p. 360.

2 Helen Keller, as quoted in Lois Einhorn, *Helen Keller, Public Speaker: Sightless But Seen, Deaf But Heard*, Greenwood Publishing, Westport, CT, 1998, pp. 100-101.

3 Zinn, p. 363.

4 John Reed, "The Traders' War," *The Masses*, Vol. 5, Issue 12, September, 1914, p. 16.

5 Ibid.

6 Lance Selfa, *The Democrats: A Critical History*, Haymarket Books, Chicago, 2008, p. 129.

7 Emma Goldman, as quoted in María DeGuzmán, *Spain's Long Shadow: The Black Legend, Off-whiteness, and Anglo-American Empire*, University of Minnesota Press, Minneapolis, MN, 2005, p. 154.

8 Selfa, p. 130.

9 William Pfaff, *The Irony of Manifest Destiny: The Tragedy of America's Foreign Policy*, Walker Publishing, New York, 2010, pp. 70-71.

10 Ibid., pp. 71-72.

11 Justin Raimondo, "Gang of Democracies," *The American Conservative*, October 6, 2008. http://www.theamericanconservative.com/articles/gang-of-democracies/ (Retrieved Jan 14, 2015)

12 Pfaff, p. 72.

13 Barack Obama, "Remarks by the President in Address to the Nation on the Way Forward in Afghanistan and Pakistan", delivered at West Point, December 1, 2009.

14 Tariq Ali, *The Obama Syndrome: Surrender At Home, War Abroad*, Verso, New York, 2010, pp. 71-22.

15 Ibid., p. 73.

16 Selfa, p. 130.

17 Woodrow Wilson, as quoted in Selfa, p. 130.

18 Gore Vidal, interview with Erik Lundegaard, "Time-Traveling with Gore Vidal," *The Seattle Times*, November 15, 1999.

19 Gary Gerstle, "Race and Nation in the Thought and Politics of Woodrow Wilson," in *Reconsidering Woodrow Wilson: Progressivism, Internationalism, War, and Peace*, John Milton Cooper, Jr., editor, Woodrow Wilson Center Press, Washington D.C., 2008, p. 94.

20 Michael Kazin, "The Forgotten President," *The New Republic*, June 4, 2013. http://www.newrepublic.com/article/113365/woodrow-wilson-liberal-president-most-similar-obama (Retrieved Jan 14, 2015)

21 Ibid.

22 William Pfaff, "A Question of Hegemony," *The Japan Times*, January 1, 2001.

23 Zinn, p. 363.

24 Richard Hofstadter, *The American Political Tradition (and the Men Who Made It)*, Vintage Books, New York, 1989, p. 341.

25 Zinn, p. 361.

26 Noam Chomsky, *Media Control: The Spectacular Achievements of Propaganda*, Seven Stories Press, New York, 2002, p. 11.

27 Zinn, p. 362.

28 Ibid.

29 Woodrow Wilson, "Flag Day Address, Washington D.C., June 14, 1917," *War Reprint: War Supplement to the History Teacher's Magazine, Issues 1-7*, No. 6, McKinley Publishing, Philadelphia, 1918, p. 12.

30 Elihu Root, as quoted in "Shoot Our Traitors At Home," *The New York Times*, August 16, 1917.

31 Chomsky, p. 11.

32 Ibid.

33 Ibid.

34 Ibid.

35 Margaret A. Blanchard, quoting from a *New York Times* article published June 6, 1917 in *Revolutionary Sparks: Freedom of Expression in Modern America*, Oxford University Press, New York, 1992, p. 99.

36 Noam Chomsky, *The Culture of Terrorism*, South End Press, New York, 1999, p. 2.

37 Frederic L. Paxson, as quoted in Peter Novick, *That Noble Dream: The "Objectivity Question" and the American Historical Profession*, Cambridge University Press, UK, 1988, p. 128.

38 Zinn, p. 364.

39 David Swanson, *War is a Lie*, davidswanson.org, Charlottesville, VA, 2010, p. 21.

40 Ibid., p. 26.

41 Jeanette Keith, *Rich Man's War, Poor Man's Fight: Race, Class, and Power in the Rural South during the First World War*, University of North Carolina Press, Chapel Hill, 2004, pp. 58-59.

42 Buffalo Soldiers Research Museum Newsletter, Vol. 4, Issue 4, October 2006.

43 Ibid.

44 Keith, pp. 57-58.

45 R.B. Quinn, as quoted in James C. Juhnke, "Mob Violence and Kansas Mennonites in 1918," *Kansas Historical Quarterly*, Vol. 43, No. 3, Autumn, 1977, pp. 334-350.

46 Ben Salmon, as quoted in Torin R. T. Finney, *Unsung Hero of the Great War: The Life and Witness of Ben Salmon*, Paulist Press, Mahwah, NJ, 1989, p. 118.

47 Finney, p. 48.

48 University of California Regents, *The Emma Goldman Papers*, "War Resistance, Anti-Militarism, and Deportation, 1917-1919," Berkeley Digital Library SunSITE, 2003. http://sunsite.berkeley.edu/Goldman/Exhibition/deportation.html (Retrieved Jan 16, 2015)

49 Emma Goldman, *Transcript of Record: Supreme Court of the United States, October Term 1917. Emma Goldman and Alexander Berkman, Plaintiffs-in-Error vs. The United States,* pp. 452-453. http://catalog.hathitrust.org/Record/002019946 (Retrieved Jan 16, 2015)

50 Lance Selfa, "Emma Goldman: A Life of Controversy," *International Socialist Review*, Issue 34, March-April 2004.

51 University of California Regents, *The Emma Goldman Papers*, http://sunsite.berkeley.edu/Goldman/Exhibition/deportation.html.

52 J. Edgar Hoover, as quoted in Richard Drinnon, *Rebel in Paradise: A Biography of Emma Goldman*, University of Chicago Press, Chicago, 1961, p. 215.

53 Emma Goldman, as quoted in Zinn, p. 372.

54 University of California Regents, *The Emma Goldman Papers*, http://sunsite.berkeley.edu/Goldman/Exhibition/deportation.html.

55 Selfa, "Emma Goldman: A Life of Controversy".

56 Duane C.S. Stoltzfus, "Standing in chains at Alcatraz," *The Mennonite*, August 1, 2012, p. 16.

57 Ibid.

58 Ibid., p. 17.

59 Ibid., p. 18.

60 Ibid.

61 Eugene Debs, "The Canton, Ohio, Anti-War Speech, 1918," from *The Gilded Age and Progressive Era: A Documentary Reader*, William A. Link and Susannah J. Link, editors, Wiley-Blackwell, West Sussex, UK, 2012, p. 310.

62 John Kiriakou, "Obama's use of Espionage Act is modern-day McCarthyism," *The Guardian*, August 6, 2013. http://www.theguardian.com/commentisfree/2013/aug/06/obama-abuse-espionage-act-mccarthyism (Retrieved 15 Jan 2015)

63 Geoffrey R. Stone, "Mr. Wilson's First Amendment," in *Reconsidering Woodrow Wilson...*, Cooper, Jr., ed., pp. 192-194.

64 Zinn, p. 366.

65 Smedley D. Butler, *War is a Racket!*, Feral House, Los Angeles, 2003 (1935), p. 24.

66 Ibid., p. 23.

67 Ibid., pp. 27-31.

68 Ibid., p. 33.

69 Ibid., pp. 33-34.

70 Ibid., p. 35.

71 Ibid., p. 23.

72 Ibid., pp. 39-40.

73 Pfaff, "A Question of Hegemony".

74 Ibid.

75 Woodrow Wilson, as quoted in Pfaff, "A Question of Hegemony".

76 Butler, p. 43.

77 Walter Hines Page, as quoted in Swanson, p. 176.

78 Robert Lansing, as quoted in Michael Parenti, *The Terrorism Trap*, City Lights Books, San Francisco, 2002, p. 87.

79 Michael Parenti, *Contrary Notions*, City Lights Books, San Francisco, 2007, p. 353.

80 Ibid., p. 357.

81 Ibid.

82 Richard Nixon, as quoted in Elizabeth Sirimarco, *American Voices from the Cold War*, Benchmark Books, 2005, Tarrytown, NY, p. 66.

83 Ronald Reagan, as quoted in David S. Foglesong, *America's Secret War Against Bolshevism: U.S. Intervention in the Russian Civil War, 1917-1920*, The University of North Carolina Press, Chapel Hill, 1995, p. 7.

84 Ibid., also *Khrushchev in America*, Crosscurrents Press, New York, 1960, p. 112; accessed from Archive.org, https://archive.org/stream/khrushchevinamer006997mbp/khrushchevinamer006997mbp_djvu.txt (Retrieved Jan 25, 2015)

85 Parenti, *Contrary Notions*, p. 354.

86 Ibid.

87 Robert Lansing, as quoted in Parenti, *Contrary Notions*, p. 355.

88 Vladimir Lenin, as quoted in Bill Keach, "International Law: Illusion and Reality," *International Socialist Review*, Issue 27, January-February 2003.

89 Ibid.

90 Lenin, as quoted in Keach, "International Law: Illusion and Reality".

91 Keach, "International Law: Illusion and Reality".

92 Tony Cliff citing Marx biographer Franz Mehring in the Introduction to *Rosa Luxemburg: Ideas in Action*, by Paul Frölich, Pluto Press, London, 1994, p. 9.

93 Rosa Luxemburg, "Peace Utopias," *Leipziger Volkzeitung*, May 6 & 8, 1911. Translation from the Marxists Internet Archive, http://www.marxists.org/archive/luxemburg/1911/05/11.htm (Retrieved Jan 21, 2015)

94 Ibid.

95 John Reed, undelivered speech written for the First Congress of the Peoples of the East, 1920, originally published as an appendix in *Baku: Congress of the Peoples of the East*, New Park, London, 1977. http://www.icl-fi.org/english/wv/970/reed.html (Retrieved Jan 25, 2015)

96 Ibid.

97 Ibid.

98 Leon Trotsky, "The Programme of Peace," pamphlet originally published June 1917. "This translation by John G. Wright is an unexpurgated text based on the Russian text as given in the 1923 edition of Trotsky's *Collected Works*, vol. II, pp. 462-82, issued by State Publishers in Moscow."

http://www.marxists.org/archive/trotsky/works/britain/ch11.htm (Retrieved Jan 21, 2015)

99 Joel Martin and William J. Birnes, *The Haunting of the Presidents: A Paranormal History of the U.S. Presidency*, New American Library/Penguin, New York, 2005, pp. 69-72.

Chapter 2

1 Justin Lewis-Anthony, "The new archbishop of Canterbury should be a disciple rather than a leader," *The Guardian*, February 4, 2013. http://www.theguardian.com/commentisfree/belief/2013/feb/04/archbishop-canterbury-justin-welby-disciple (Retrieved Jan 21, 2015)

2 Howard Zinn, "Private Ryan Saves War," *The Progressive*, October 1998. Archived at HowardZinn.org, http://howardzinn.org/private-ryan-saves-war/ (Retrieved Jan 21, 2015)

3 Ibid.

4 Ibid.

5 Ibid.

6 Claire Suddath, "Why Did World War I Just End?" *Time*, October 4, 2010. http://content.time.com/time/world/article/0,8599,2023140,00.html (Retrieved Jan 21, 2015)

7 David Swanson, *War is a Lie*, 2010, davidswanson.org, Charlottesville, VA, p. 115.

8 Ibid., pp. 115-116.

9 Johann Hari, "Not his finest hour: The dark side of Winston Churchill," *The Independent*, October 28, 2010. http://www.independent.co.uk/news/uk/politics/not-his-finest-hour-the-dark-side-of-winston-churchill-2118317.html (Retrieved Jan 21, 2015)

10 Winston Churchill, as quoted in Hari, "Not his finest hour".

11 Gary Younge, "Churchill—the truth," *The Guardian*, September 29, 2002. http://www.theguardian.com/world/2002/sep/30/race.politics (Retrieved Jan 21, 2015)

12 *The New York Times*, "How Lieut. Churchill Escaped From Boers," December 13, 1900.

13 Hari, "Not his finest hour".

14 Ralph Raico, "Rethinking Churchill," published in *The Costs of War: America's Pyrrhic Victories,* John V. Denson, editor, Transaction Publishers, New Brunswick, NJ, 1999, p. 325.

15 Richard Burton, "To Play Churchill Is to Hate Him," *The New York Times*, November 24, 1974.

16 Howard Zinn, *On War*, Seven Stories Press, New York, 2001, p. 107.

17 Swanson, p. 117.

18 Ibid., p. 116.

19 Theodore Roosevelt, as quoted in James Bradley, *The Imperial Cruise: A Secret History of Empire and War,* Little, Brown, and Company, New York, 2009, p. 1.

20 Ibid., p. 3.

21 Ibid., p. 4.

22 Ibid., p. 8.

23 Ibid.

24 Ibid.

25 Ibid.

26 Howard Zinn, *A People's History of the United States*, Harper Collins, New York, 2003, pp. 410-411.

27 Bruce Russett, *No Clear and Present Danger: A Skeptical View of the U.S. Entry into World War II*, Harper & Row, New York, 1972, p. 19.

28 Gore Vidal, "Pearl Harbor: An Exchange," *The New York Review of Books*, May 17, 2001; http://www.nybooks.com/articles/archives/2001/may/17/pearl-harbor-an-exchange/ (Retrieved Jan 26, 2015)

29 Ibid.

30 Robert Stinnett, *Day of Deceit: The Truth About FDR and Pearl Harbor*, Touchstone/Simon & Schuster, New York, 2000, p. 259.

31 Ibid., p. 9.

32 Ibid.

33 Ibid.

34 Franklin D. Roosevelt, as quoted in Stinnett, p. 9.

35 Gore Vidal, *Dreaming War*, Thunder Mouth Press/Nation Books, New York, 2002, p. 74.

36 Admiral Husband Kimmel, as quoted in Stinnett, p. 9.

37 Russett, p. 45.

38 Howard Zinn, *A People's History of the United States*, p. 410.

39 Ibid.

40 Vidal, "Pearl Harbor: An Exchange".

41 Howard Zinn, *A People's History of the United States*, p. 410.

42 Russett, p. 56.

43 Vidal, "Pearl Harbor: An Exchange".

44 Russett, p. 58.

45 Robert Higgs, "How the U.S. Economic Warfare Provoked Japan's Attack on Pearl Harbor," *The Independent Review*, May 1, 2006; http://www.independent.org/newsroom/article.asp?id=1930#1

(Retrieved Jan 26, 2015)

46 Vidal, "Pearl Harbor: An Exchange".

47 Ibid.

48 Higgs, "How the U.S. Economic Warfare Provoked Japan's Attack on Pearl Harbor".

49 Henry Stimson, as quoted in George Morgenstern, "The Actual Road to Pearl Harbor," from *Perpetual War for Perpetual Peace: A Critical Examination of the Foreign Policy of Franklin Delano Roosevelt and its Aftermath*, Harry Elmer Barnes, editor, Ostara Publications, 2013 (1953), p. 343.

50 Vidal, "Pearl Harbor: An Exchange".

51 Henry Stimson, as quoted in Morgenstern, p. 384.

52 Russett, p. 54.

53 Ibid.

54 Ibid.

55 Ibid., p. 56.

56 Herbert Hoover, as quoted in Donald W. Whisenhunt, *President Herbert Hoover*, Nova Science Publishers, New York, 2007, p. 129.

57 Vidal, "Pearl Harbor: An Exchange".

58 Swanson, p. 116.

59 Ibid., p. 35.

60 United States Holocaust Memorial Museum, Holocaust Encyclopedia, "Emigration and the Evian Conference," http://www.ushmm.org/wlc/en/article. php?ModuleId=10005520 (Retrieved Jan 26, 2015)

61 Arnold A. Offner, *American Appeasement: United States Foreign Policy and Germany, 1933-1938*, Harvard University Press, Cambridge, 1969, p. 81

62 Simon Wiesenthal Center, Museum of Tolerance Learning Center, "What was the response of the Allies to the persecution of the Jews?"; http://motlc.wiesenthal.com/site/ pp.asp?c=gvKVLcMVluG&b=394663#20 (Retrieved Jan 26, 2015)

63 United States Holocaust Memorial Museum, "Emigration and the Evian Conference".

64 Ronnie S. Landau, *The Nazi Holocaust: Its History and Meaning*, I.B. Taurus & Co., New York, 2006, p. 137.

65 Arthur Morse, *While Six Million Died: A Chronicle of American Apathy*, Random House, New York, pp. 203-204.

66 Adolf Hitler, as quoted in Morse, p. 204.

67 United States Holocaust Memorial Museum, Holocaust Encyclopedia, "Life After the Holocaust: Thomas Buergenthal," http:// www.ushmm.org/wlc/en/media oi.php?ModuleId=10007192&MedId=5603 (Retrieved Jan 26, 2015)

68 Landau, pp. 137-138.

69 Helen Fein, as quoted in Landau, p. 138.

70 Helen Fein, *Congregational Sponsors of Indochinese Refugees in the United States, 1979-1981*, Fairleigh Dickenson University Press, London, 1987, p. 36.

71 Ibid., p. 37.

72 Laurel Leff, *Buried by the Times: The Holocaust and America's Most Important Newspaper*, Cambridge University Press, 2005, p. 28.

73 Ibid.

74 Ibid., p. 341.

75 Ibid.

76 Ibid., p. 344.

77 Ibid., p. 339.

78 Stuart Eizenstat, writing praise for Leff, *Buried by the Times.*

79 Deborah E. Lipstadt, *Beyond Belief: The American Press and the Coming of the Holocaust, 1933-1945*, The Free Press/Simon & Schuster, New York, 1986, p. 277.

80 David S. Wyman, *The Abandonment of the Jews: America and the Holocaust, 1941-1945*, Pantheon Books, New York, 1984, p. 316.

81 Richard Becker, *Palestine: Israel & the U.S. Empire,* PSL Publications, San Francisco, 2013, pp. 51-52.

82 Henry Morgenthau, Jr., as quoted in Becker, pp. 49-50.

83 Lipstadt, p. 277.

84 Ibid.

85 Ibid.

86 Ibid., p. 278.

87 Charles Higham, *Trading with the Enemy: The Nazi-American Money Plot 1933-1949*, Delacorte Press, New York, 1983, p. Xv.

88 Bradford Snell, as quoted in Michael Dobbs, "Ford and GM Scrutinized for Alleged Nazi Collaboration," *The Washington Post*, November 30, 1998; http://www.washingtonpost.com/wp-srv/national/daily/nov98/nazicars30.htm (Retrieved Jan 26, 2015)

89 Ibid.

90 Edwin Black, "IBM's Role in the Holocaust - What the New Documents Reveal," *Huffington Post,* February 27, 2012; http://www.huffingtonpost.com/edwin-black/ibm-holocaust_b_1301691.html (Retrieved Jan 26, 2015)

91 Edwin Black, *IBM and the Holocaust: The Strategic Alliance Between Nazi Germany and America's Most Powerful Corporation,* Dialog Press, Washington, D.C., 2011, p. 10.

92 Ibid., p. 8.

93 Ibid.

94 Ibid.

95 Ibid.

96 Edwin Black, "IBM's Role in the Holocaust - What the New Documents Reveal".

97 Ibid.

98 Ibid.

99 "Children of the Camps: Internment History," *PBS*, 1999; http://www.pbs.org/childofcamp/history/ (Retrieved Jan 26, 2015)

100 The Commission on Wartime Relocation and Internment of Civilians, *Personal Justice Denied*, The Civil Liberties Public Education Fund & the University of Washington Press, Seattle, 1997, pp. 2-3. (Originally published in two volumes by the U.S. Government Printing Office in 1982 and 1983.)

101 Ibid., p. 3.

102 Ibid.

103 The Civil Liberties Public Education Fund, "Prologue" to *Personal Justice Denied*, p. xxii.

104 Michi Weglyn, *Years of Infamy: The Untold Story of America's Concentration Camps*, Morrow Quill Paperbacks, New York, 1976, p. 7.

105 John DeWitt, as quoted in Frank Wu, "Profiling in the Wake of September 11: The Precedent of the Japanese American Internment," *Criminal Justice Magazine*, Volume 17, Issue 2, Summer 2002.

106 Peter Irons, "Politics and Principle: An Assessment of the Roosevelt Record on Civil Rights and Civil Liberties," from *At War with Civil Rights and Civil*

Liberties, Thomas E. Baker and John F. Stack, editors, Rowman and Littlefield Publishers, Lanham, MD, 2006, p. 68.

107 Ibid.

108 Ibid.

109 "Why Japan *Really* Lost The War," citing Paul Kennedy, *The Rise and Fall of the Great Powers*, Vintage, New York, 1989; http://www.combinedfleet.com/economic.htm (Retrieved Jan 26, 2015)

110 Frank Wu, "Profiling in the Wake of September 11".

111 Ibid.

112 "Children of the Camps: Internment History," *PBS*.

113 Keiho Soga, "Experiencing Internment," *Digital History*, ID 46, 2013; http://www.digitalhistory.uh.edu/disp_textbook.cfm?smtid=3&psid=46 (Retrieved Jan 26, 2015)

114 Ibid.

115 Ibid.

116 Guide to the Records of the United States War Relocation Authority Central Utah Project, 1941-1945, University of Washington, February 27, 2009; http://digital.lib.washington.edu/findingaids/view?docId=USWarRelocation AuthorityUtah56.xml (Retrieved Jan 26, 2015)

117 Ibid.

118 Japanese American Veterans Association, "Topaz Relocation Center, Utah," citing Americans of Japanese Ancestry World War II Military Alliance, *Echoes of Silence: The Untold Stories of the Nisei Soldiers Who Served in WWII*; CD_ROM, 2007; http://www.javadc.org/topaz_relocation_center.htm (Retrieved Jan 29, 2015)

119 Ibid.

120 Ibid.

121 *The Economist*, "The Consequences of Terror," September 20, 2001; http://www.economist.com/node/788126 (Retrieved Jan 26, 2015)

122 Smithsonian National Museum of American History, "A More Perfect Union: Japanese Americans and The U.S. Constitution"; http://amhistory.si.edu/perfectunion/non-flash/removal_crisis.html (Retrieved Jan 26, 2015)

123 Congressman John Rankin, as quoted in Maisie Conrat & Richard Conrat, *Executive Order 9066: The Internment of 110,000 Japanese Americans*, UCLA Asian American Studies Center Press, Los Angeles, p. 34.

124 Robert Sherrod, as quoted in James Bradley, *Flyboys: A True Story of Courage*, Little, Brown and Company, New York, 2006, p. 253.

125 Kurt Vonnegut, *Palm Sunday*, Delacorte Press, New York, 1981, p. 302.

126 Kurt Vonnegut, *Slaughterhouse-Five*, Dell, New York, 1969, p. 101.

127 Franklin D. Roosevelt, as quoted in Howard Zinn, *The Bomb*, City Lights Books, San Francisco, 2010, p. 38.

128 Zinn, *A People's History of the United States*, p. 421.

129 Ibid.

130 Andrew J. Rotter, *Hiroshima: The World's Bomb*, Oxford University Press, UK, 2008, p. 53.

131 Marshall De Bruhl, *Firestorm: Allied Airpower and the Destruction of Dresden*, Random House, New York, 2006, p. xi.

132 Ibid.

133 *BBC*, "1945: Thousands of Bombs Destroy Dresden," from database, *ON THIS DAY* (14 February 1945); http://news.bbc.co.uk/onthisday/hi/dates/stories/february/14/newsid_3549000/3549905.stm (Retrieved Jan 26, 2015)

134 Kurt Vonnegut, as quoted in Richard Rhodes, *The Making of the Atomic Bomb*, Simon & Schuster, New York, 1986, p. 593.

135 Zinn, *The Bomb*, p. 39.

136 De Bruhl, p. xii.

137 Louis Fieser, as quoted in G. Wayne Miller, *The Xeno Chronicles: Two Years on the Frontier of Medicine Inside Harvard's Transplant Research Lab*, Public Affairs/Perseus Books, Cambridge, MA, 2013, p. 69.

138 Robert McNamara, as quoted in Errol Morris, *The Fog of War,* Sony Pictures Classics, 2003. From transcript, http://www.errolmorris.com/film/fow_transcript.html (Retrieved Jan 26, 2015)

139 John F. Ptak, "The Most Lethal Number: M-69 vs. U-235 (Japan, 1945)," *JF Ptak Science Books*, Post 695, July 24, 2009; http://longstreet.typepad.com/thesciencebookstore/2009/07/the-most-lethal-number-m69-vs-u235-japan-1945.html (Retrieved Jan 26, 2015)

140 Joseph Coleman, "1945 Tokyo Firebombing Left Legacy of Terror, Pain," Associated Press, March 10, 2005.

141 Noam Chomsky, "Memories," *Z Magazine*, July-August, 1995; http://www.chomsky.info/articles/199508--.htm (Retrieved Jan 26, 2015)

142 Truman Nelson, as quoted in Dick Gregory, *No More Lies*, Harper & Row, New York, 1971, pp. 9-10.

143 John Pilger, "The Lies of Hiroshima are the Lies of Today," *johnpilger.com*, August 6, 2008; http://johnpilger.com/articles/the-lies-of-hiroshima-are-the-lies-of-today (Retrieved Jan 26, 2015)

144 Zinn, *The Bomb*, p. 43.

145 Curtis LeMay, as quoted in Zinn, *The Bomb*, p. 43.

146 Gar Alperovitz, *The Decision to Use the Atomic Bomb*, Vintage Books, New York, 1995, p. 524.

147 Rhodes, p. 715.

148 Alperovitz, p. 416.

149 Rhodes, pp. 717-718.

150 Rhodes, p. 726.

151 Harry Truman, as quoted in Greg Mitchell and Robert Jay Lifton, "When Truman Announced Attack on Hiroshima 65 Years Ago: The Beginning of a 'Cover-Up,'" *The Nation*, August 6, 2010; http://www.thenation.com/blog/153919/when-truman-announced-attack-hiroshima-65-years-ago-beginning-cover# (Retrieved Jan 26, 2015)

152 Malcolm Boyd, *Are You Running With Me, Jesus*, Holt, New York, 1965, p. 27.

153 Zinn, *The Bomb*, p. 26.

154 John Pilger, "The Lies of Hiroshima are the Lies of Today".

155 Mikki Smith, "Hiroshima was no longer a city," *International Socialist Review*, Issue 13, August-September 2000.

156 Gar Alperovitz, *Atomic Diplomacy: Hiroshima and Potsdam*, Pluto Press, London, 1994, p. 155.

157 Zinn, *The Bomb*, pp. 43-44.

158 Ibid., p. 44.

159 Ibid., p. 46.

160 William Blum, "Hiroshima: Needless Slaughter, Useful Terror," from *Covert*

Action: The Roots of Terrorism, Ellen Ray, William H. Schaap, editors, Ocean Press, New York, 2003 p. 244.

161 Alperovitz, *Atomic Diplomacy: Hiroshima and Potsdam*, p. 156.

162 Dwight Eisenhower, as quoted in Alperovitz, *The Decision to Use the Atomic Bomb*, p. 4.

163 William Leahy, as quoted in Alperovitz, *Atomic Diplomacy: Hiroshima and Potsdam*, p. 19.

164 Curtis LeMay, speaking to the press, as reported by the *New York Herald Tribune*, September 20, 1945, cited in Alperovitz, *The Decision to Use the Atomic Bomb,* p. 336.

165 Admiral Chester Nimitz, as quoted in Gar Alperovitz, "The Decision to Bomb Hiroshima," Counterpunch, August 5, 2011; http://www.counterpunch. org/2011/08/05/the-decision-to-bomb-hiroshima/ (Retrieved Jan 26, 2015)

166 United States Strategic Bombing Survey, *Summary Report (Pacific War)*, United States Government Printing Office, Washington, D.C., July 1, 1946, p. 26; https://archive.org/details/ summaryreportpac00unit (Retrieved Jan 26, 2015)

167 Amy Goodman and David Goodman, "The Hiroshima Cover-Up," *The Baltimore Sun*, August 5, 2005; http:// articles.baltimoresun.com/2005-08-05/ news/0508050019_1_atomic-bombings-bomb-on-hiroshima-george-weller (Retrieved Jan 26, 2015)

168 Ibid.

169 Ibid.

170 Ibid.

171 Ibid.

172 Ibid.

173 Hanson Baldwin, as quoted in Dennis D. Wainstock, *The Decision to Drop the Atomic Bomb: Hiroshima and Nagasaki— August 1945*, Enigma Books, New York, p. 122.

174 Alperovitz, *The Decision to Use the Atomic Bomb*, pp. 466-467.

175 Gore Vidal, interview with Paul Jay, *The Real News*, July, 2007; "Gore Vidal on the Cold War" YouTube video, uploaded by TheRealNews, Sept 4, 2007; https:// www.youtube.com/watch?v=IkugyGdJLy8 (Retrieved Jan 29, 2015)

176 Blum, from *Covert Action: The Roots of Terrorism*, p. 243.

177 Ibid.

178 John Pilger, "The Lies of Hiroshima are the Lies of Today".

179 General Leslie Groves, as quoted in Pilger, "The Lies of Hiroshima are the Lies of Today".

180 Henry Stimson, as quoted in Blum, from *Covert Action: The Roots of Terrorism*, p. 243.

181 Charles L. Mee, Jr., *Meeting at Potsdam*, M. Evans & Company, New York, 1975, p. 239.

182 Alperovitz, "The Decision to Bomb Hiroshima".

183 Harry Truman, *Letters of a Nation*, Andrew Carroll, editor, Broadway Books, 1999, p. 163.

184 Ibid.

185 Peter Kuznick, interviewed by Dave Lieberson, "Oliver Stone's Secret History: An Interview with Peter Kuznick," George Mason University, *History News Network*, March 10, 2010; http://www.hnn.us/ article/124005 (Retrieved Jan 26, 2015)

186 Noam Chomsky, *American Power and*

the New Mandarins, Pantheon Books, 1969, Paperback, The New Press, 2002, p. 192.

187 A.J. Muste, as quoted in Chomsky, *American Power and the New Mandarins*, p. 194.

Chapter 3

1 Gore Vidal, "National Security Act and the Constitution," speech to the National Press Club; broadcast on C-Span, March 18, 1998; http://www.c-span.org/video/?c37969/clip-national-security-act-constitution (Relevant quote at 18:14:13)

2 Garry Wills, *Bomb Power: The Modern Presidency and the National Security State*, Penguin Books, London, 2001, pp. 2-3.

3 Gore Vidal, *Dreaming War: Blood for Oil and the Cheney-Bush Junta*, Thunder's Mouth Press/Nation Books, New York, 2002, p. 122.

4 Leonard Lewin, *Report from Iron Mountain: On the Possibility and Desirability of Peace*, Dial Press, New York, 1967, p. 26.

5 Ibid.

6 Michael J. Hogan, *A Cross of Iron: Harry S. Truman and the Origins of the National Security State, 1945-1954*, Cambridge University Press, New York, 1998, p. 26.

7 George Kennan, *Telegram, George Kennan to George Marshall ["Long Telegram"]*, February 22, 1946, Harry S. Truman Administration File, Elsey Papers; https://www.trumanlibrary.org/whistlestop/study_collections/coldwar/documents/pdf/6-6.pdf (Retrieved Jan 28, 2015)

8 U.S. Department of Defense, "James V. Forrestal, 1st Secretary of Defense," http://www.defense.gov/specials/secdef_histories/SecDef_01.aspx (Retrieved Jan 28, 2015)

9 Gore Vidal, "The Scholar Squirrels and the National Security Scare," from *Conversations with Gore Vidal*, Richard Peabody and Lucinda Ebersole, editors, University Press of Mississippi, 2005, p. 122.

10 Ibid.

11 Noam Chomsky, *Deterring Democracy*, Hill and Wang, New York, 1991, p. 10.

12 Ibid., p. 10.

13 Ibid., p. 58.

14 Ibid., p. 59.

15 Gore Vidal interview with the authors, "Murder Incorporated Sessions," Street Legal Cinema, 2007, transcript.

16 Vidal, *Dreaming War*, p. 12.

17 William Blum, *Killing Hope: U.S. Military and C.I.A. Interventions Since World War II*, Common Courage Press, Maine, 2004, pp. 7-8.

18 Ibid., p. 8.

19 Ibid., pp. 9-10.

20 Noam Chomsky, interviewed by David Barsamian, *How the World Works*, Arthur Naiman, editor, Soft Skull Press, Brooklyn, NY, 1986-2011, pp. 66-67.

21 Ibid., p. 67.

22 Ibid., p. 67.

23 Tim Weiner, *Legacy of Ashes: The History of the CIA*, First Anchor Books, New York, 2008, p. 3.

24 Ibid., p. 3.

25 Ibid., p. 3.

26 Ibid., p. 3.

27 Louis Menand, "Wild Thing," *The New Yorker*, March 14, 2011; http://www.newyorker.com/magazine/2011/03/14/wild-thing-3 (Retrieved Jan 28, 2015)

28 Weiner, p. 4.

29 William Donovan, as quoted in Weiner, p. 4.

30 Allen W. Dulles, "William J. Donovan and the National Security," CIA Library, Center for the Study of Intelligence, Sept 22, 1993; https://www.cia.gov/library/center-for-the-study-of-intelligence/kent-csi/vol3no3/html/v03i3a07p_0001.htm (Retrieved Jan 28, 2015)

31 Weiner, p. 4.

32 Menand, "Wild Thing".

33 Ibid.

34 Jonathan Rauch, "Firebombs Over Tokyo," The Atlantic, July 1, 2002; http://www.theatlantic.com/magazine/archive/2002/07/firebombs-over-tokyo/302547/ (Retrieved Jan 28, 2015)

35 Jennet Conant, "Swashbuckling Spymaster," The New York Times Book Review, February 11, 2011; http://www.nytimes.com/2011/02/13/books/review/Conant-t.html?pagewanted=all&_r=0 (Retrieved Jan 28, 2015)

36 Weiner, p. 5.

37 Douglas Waller, Wild Bill Donovan: The Spymaster Who Created the OSS and Modern American Espionage, Free Press, New York, 2011, p. 4.

38 Weiner, p. 7.

39 National Security Act of 1947 (as originally enacted), Section 102(a); http://www.intelligence.senate.gov/nsact1947.pdf (Retrieved Jan 28, 2015)

40 Christopher J. Fuhrmann, Policing the Roman Empire: Soldiers, Administration, and Public Order, Oxford University Press, New York, 2012, p. 152.

41 Waller, p. 4.

42 Waller, p. 389.

43 Ibid.

44 Elaine Sciolino, "Mailer Visits C.I.A. and Finds He's in Friendly Territory. Really," The New York Times, February 3, 1992.

45 Saul Landau, "Norman Mailer will not R.I.P.," Counterpunch, November 24, 2007; http://www.counterpunch.org/2007/11/24/norman-mailer-will-not-r-i-p/ (Retrieved Jan 28, 2015)

46 Charles Michaud, "Harlot's Ghost," Book review, Library Journal, September 1, 1991, Vol. 116, Issue 14, p. 231.

47 Norman Mailer, Harlot's Ghost, Random House, New York, 1991, pp. 399-400.

48 Federal Research Division, Library of Congress, "A Country Study: Iran," see SAVAK; http://lcweb2.loc.gov/frd/cs/irtoc.html (Retrieved Jan 28, 2015); also Library of Congress, Iran: a country study, Glenn E. Curtis and Eric Hooglung, editors, 2008, pp. 276-277; http://lcweb2.loc.gov/frd/cs/pdf/CS_Iran.pdf (Retrieved Jan 28, 2015)

49 Ibid.

50 Craig Smith, "Eastern Europe Struggles to Purge Security Services," The New York Times, December 12, 2006.

51 Jeremy Scahill, "Notorious Mercenary Erik Prince is Advising Trump from the Shadows," The Intercept, January 17, 2017; https://theintercept.com/2017/01/17/notorious-mercenary-erik-prince-is-advising-trump-from-the-shadows/

52 Chris Hedges, "The War in the Shadows," Truthdig, August 20, 2012; http://www.truthdig.com/report/item/the_war_in_the_shadows_20120820/ (Retrieved Jan 28, 2015)

53 Ibid.

54 Ibid.

55 Michael Parenti, interview with the authors, "Murder Incorporated Sessions," Street Legal Cinema, 2012, transcript.

56 Ibid.

57 William Blum, *Rogue State: A Guide to the World's Only Superpower*, Zed Books, London, p. 1.

58 William Blum, "A Brief History of U.S. Interventions: 1945 to the Present," *Z Magazine*, June, 1999.

59 Dick Gregory, *Caught in the Act*, Poppy Records, 1974.

60 Summary of Blum, *Killing Hope*, from author website; http://williamblum.org/books/killing-hope, 2008 (Retrieved Jan 28, 2015)

61 Blum, *Killing Hope*, p. 392.

62 James Bradley, *Flyboys*, Little, Brown and Company, New York, 2003, p. 93.

63 Howard Zinn, *A People's History of the United States*, Harper Collins, New York, 2003, p. 427.

64 Noam Chomsky, "On the Backgrounds of the Pacific War," *Liberation*, September-October, 1967; http://www.chomsky.info/articles/196709--.htm#36 (Retrieved Jan 28, 2015)

65 Jonathan Fenby, *Chiang Kai Shek: China's Generalissimo and the Nation He Lost*, Carroll and Graf, New York, 2003, p. 43.

66 Blum, *Killing Hope*, pp. 21-22.

67 Blum, *Killing Hope*, p. 23.

68 Zinn, *A People's History of the United States*, p. 427.

69 Dennis Dayle, as quoted in Peter Dale Scott and Jonathan Marshall, *Cocaine Politics: Drugs, Armies, and the CIA in Central America*, University of California Press, Berkeley, 1991, pp. x-xi.

70 Wilda Williams, "The Politics of Heroin: CIA Complicity in the Global Drug Trade," Book review, *Library Journal*, July, 1991, Vol. 116, Issue 12, p. 115.

71 Alfred McCoy, interviewed by Paul DeRienzo, *ThePeoplesVoice.org*, October 23, 2008, transcript; http://www.thepeoplesvoice.org/TPV3/Voices.php/2008/10/23/the-politics-of-heroin-cia-complicity-in (Retrieved Jan 28, 2015)

72 Alexander Cockburn and Jeffrey St. Clair, *White Out: The CIA, Drugs and the Press*, Verso, New York, 1998, p. 215.

73 Ibid.

74 Tim Weiner, "F. Mark Wyatt, 86, C.I.A. Officer, Is Dead," *The New York Times*, July 6, 2006.

75 Ibid.

76 Blum, "A Brief History of U.S. Interventions: 1945 to the Present".

77 Olive Sutton, *Murder Inc. in Greece*, Prism Key Press, New York, 2013 (1948), p. 8.

78 Ganser Daniele, *NATO's Secret Armies: Operation GLADIO and Terrorism in Western Europe*, Frank Cass, New York, p. 218.

79 Ibid.

80 Sutton, p. 8.

81 Blum, *Killing Hope*, p. 43.

82 William McKinley, as quoted in Michael Parenti, *The Sword & The Dollar*, St. Martin's Press, New York, 1989, p. 86.

83 Ibid.

84 James Bradley, *The Imperial Cruise: A Secret History of Empire and War*, Little, Brown and Company, New York, 2009, p. 131.

85 Marc D. Bernstein, "Ed Lansdale's Black

Warfare in 1950s Vietnam," *HistoryNet*, February 16, 2010; http://www.historynet.com/ed-lansdales-black-warfare-in-1950s-vietnam.htm (Retrieved Jan 28, 2015)

86 Blum, "A Brief History of U.S. Interventions: 1945 to the Present".

87 Jonathan Nashel, *Edward Lansdale's Cold War*, University of Massachusetts Press, Amherst, Massachusetts, 2005, p. 38.

88 Ibid.

89 Gore Vidal, as quoted in Robert McCrum, "Gore Vidal: The lion in winter," *The Guardian*, June 16, 2007; http://www.guardian.co.uk/books/2007/jun/17/culture.features (Retrieved Jan 28, 2015)

90 Bethany Lacina and Nils Petter Gleditsch, "Monitoring Trends in Global Combat," *European Journal of Population*, 2005, pp. 145-166.

91 L. Fletcher Prouty, *JFK: The CIA, Vietnam, and the Plot to Assassinate John F. Kennedy*, Carol Publishing Group, New York, 1996, p. 17.

92 Ibid., p. 18.

93 Ibid.

94 Ibid.

95 Weiner, *Legacy of Ashes*, p. 61.

96 Ibid.

97 David Swanson, War is a Lie, davidswanson.org, Charlottesville, VA, 2010, pp. 74-75.

98 Ibid.

99 Blum, *Killing Hope*, p. 55.

100 Swanson, p. 76.

101 Ibid.

102 Blum, *Killing Hope*, p. 55.

103 A. Ross Johnson, "Then And Now: Free Media In Unfree Societies," Radio Free Europe/Radio Liberty; http://www.rferl.org/info/history/133.html (Retrieved Jan 28, 2015)

104 Arch Puddington, *Broadcasting Freedom: The Cold War Triumph of Radio Free Europe and Radio Liberty*, University Press of Kentucky, 2000, p. 24.

105 L. W. Gluchowski, "The Defection of Jozef Swiatlo and the Search for Jewish Scapegoats in the Polish United Workers' Party, 1953-1954," *InterMarium*, Columbia University electronic journal, 1999; http://ece.columbia.edu/files/ece/images/gluchowski-1.pdf (Retrieved Jan 28, 2015)

106 Carl Bernstein, "The CIA and the Media," *Rolling Stone*, October 20, 1977.

107 *Final Report of the Select Committee to Study Government Operations with Respect to Intelligence Activities*, Book 1, "Foreign and Military Intelligence," U.S. Government Printing Office, Washington, D.C., April 1976, p. 455; http://www.intelligence.senate.gov/pdfs94th/94755_I.pdf

108 Alex Constantine, *Virtual Government: CIA Mind Control Operations in America*, Feral House, Los Angeles, 1997, p. 36.

109 Bernstein, "The CIA and the Media".

110 Ibid.

111 Ibid.

112 Ibid.

113 Ibid.

114 Peter R. Prifti, *Socialist Albania Since 1944: Domestic and Foreign Developments*, MIT Press, Cambridge, MA, 1978, p. 252.

115 Helga Turku, *Isolationist States in an Interdependent World*, Ashgate Publishing, Burlington, VT, 2013, p. 109.

116 Gordon Carera, "Tinker, Tailor, Soldier, Spy: John le Carre and Reality," *BBC News Magazine*, September 10,

2011; http://www.bbc.co.uk/news/magazine-14846154 (Retrieved Jan 28, 2015)

117 Encyclopedia Britannica, "Kim Philby," updated June 5, 2014; http://www.britannica.com/EBchecked/topic/455901/Kim-Philby (Retrieved Jan 28, 2015)

118 The National Security Archive, George Washington University, "The CIA and Nazi War Criminals: National Security Archive Posts Secret CIA History Released Under Nazi War Crimes Disclosure Act," National Security Archive Electronic Briefing Book No. 146, Tamara Feinstein, editor, February 4, 2005; http://www.gwu.edu/~nsarchiv/NSAEBB/NSAEBB146/index.htm (Retrieved Jan 28, 2015)

119 Elizabeth Holtzman, as quoted in Douglas Jehl, "C.I.A. Said to Rebuff Congress on Nazi Files," *The New York Times*, January 30, 2005; http://www.nytimes.com/2005/01/30/international/europe/30nazis.html (Retrieved Jan 28, 2015)

120 Blum, "A Brief History of U.S. Interventions: 1945 to the Present".

121 Blum, *Killing Hope,* pp. 62-63.

122 Noam Chomsky, *Interventions*, The New York Times Syndicate/City Lights Books, San Francisco, p. 182.

123 Ibid.

124 Chomsky, *How the World Works*, p. 19.

125 Stephen Kinzer, *All the Shah's Men*, John Wiley & Sons, Hoboken, NJ, 2003, p. 80.

126 Ibid., p. 158.

127 Ibid., p. 163.

128 M. S. Vassiliou, *Historical Dictionary of the Petroleum Industry, Vol. 3*, Scarecrow Press/Rowman and Littlefield, 2009, p. 269.

129 James Risen, "SECRETS OF HISTORY: The C.I.A. in Iran - A special report: How a Plot Convulsed Iran in '53 (and in '79)," *The New York Times*, April 16, 2000; http://www.nytimes.com/2000/04/16/world/secrets-history-cia-iran-special-report-plot-convulsed-iran-53-79.html; (Retrieved Jan 28, 2015)

130 Donald Wilber, as quoted in Risen, "SECRETS OF HISTORY: The C.I.A. in Iran".

131 Sasan Fayazmanesh, "In Memory of August 19, 1953: What Kermit Roosevelt Didn't Say," *Counterpunch*, August 18, 2003; http://www.counterpunch.org/2003/08/18/what-kermit-roosevelt-didn-t-say/ (Retrieved Jan 28, 2015)

132 Chomsky, *How the World Works*, p. 22.

133 "Journey to Banana Land: 1950 Agricultural & Food Production Educational Documentary," YouTube video, uploaded by "Val73TV," Sept. 17, 2012; https://www.youtube.com/watch?v=lrhotfmGSXk (Retrieved Jan 28, 2015)

134 Blum, "A Brief History of U.S. Interventions: 1945 to the Present".

135 Ibid.

136 Piero Gleijeses, *Shattered Hope: The Guatemalan Revolution and the United States, 1944-1954*, Princeton University Press, 1992, p. 365.

137 Chomsky, *How the World Works*, p. 19.

138 U.S. Department of State, Office of the Historian, "Milestones: 1953–1960: The Eisenhower Doctrine, 1957"; http://history.state.gov/milestones/1953-1960/eisenhower-doctrine (Retrieved Jan 28,

2015)

139 Robert Dreyfus, *Devil's Game: How the United States Helped Unleash Fundamentalist Islam*, Metropolitan Books, Henry Holt and Company, New York, 2005, pp. 3, 90-91.

140 Blum, "A Brief History of U.S. Interventions: 1945 to the Present".

141 Spartacus Educational Online Encyclopedia, "David Wise"; http://www.spartacus.schoolnet.co.uk/JFKwiseD.htm (Retrieved Jan 28, 2015)

142 David Wise and Thomas B. Ross, *The Invisible Government*, Random House, New York, 1964, p. 145.

143 Norm Dixon, "The Genocidal Beginning of President Suharto," *Green Left*, December 10, 1991; http://www.greenleft.org.au/node/70 (Retrieved Jan 28, 2015)

144 Edward S. Herman, "Good and Bad Genocide," *Fairness & Accuracy in Reporting* (*FAIR*), September 1, 1998; http://fair.org/extra-online-articles/good-and-bad-genocide/ (Retrieved Jan 28, 2015)

145 Ibid.

146 Blum, "A Brief History of U.S. Interventions: 1945 to the Present".

147 Robert Kennedy, as quoted in Arthur M. Schlesinger, Jr., *Robert Kennedy and His Times*, Houghton Mifflin Company, New York, 1978, p. 696.

148 Blum, "A Brief History of U.S. Interventions: 1945 to the Present".

149 Lyndon B. Johnson Library, Tape WH6602.01, Conversation 9602, February 1, 1966; http://millercenter.org/presidentialrecordings/lbj-wh6602.01-9602 (Retrieved Jan 28, 2015) (Pertinent quote begins 02:15)

150 Prouty, p. 250.

151 Douglas Valentine, *The Phoenix Program*, William Morrow and Co., 1990, Re-printed by iUniverse.com, Lincoln, NE, 2000, p. 13.

152 Ibid., p. 13.

153 Ibid., p. 85.

154 Ibid., p. 307.

155 Bart Osborn, as quoted in Valentine, p. 347.

156 Prouty, pp. 327-328.

157 Ibid., p. 328.

158 George McGovern, interviewed in *One Bright Shining Moment: The Forgotten Summer of George McGovern,* documentary film, Stephen Vittoria, director, Street Legal Cinema, 2005.

159 Valentine, p. 11.

160 Blum, "A Brief History of U.S. Interventions: 1945 to the Present".

161 Mark Zepezauer, *The CIA's Greatest Hits,* Soft Skull Press, 1994, 2011-12, p. 46.

162 David M. Barrett/CIA Library, "Sterilizing a 'Red Infection,' Congress, the CIA, and Guatemala, 1954"; https://www.cia.gov/library/center-for-the-study-of-intelligence/kent-csi/vol44no5/html/v44i5a03p.htm (Retrieved Jan 28, 2015)

163 Norodom Sihanouk, *My War with the CIA: Cambodia's Fight for Survival*, as related to Wilfred Burchett, Penguin Books, Middlesex, England, 1974, p. 22.

164 Zepezauer, p. 46.

165 Ibid.

166 Taylor Owen and Ben Kiernan, "Bombs Over Cambodia," *The Walrus,* October, 2006; archived by Yale University, http://www.yale.edu/cgp/Walrus_CambodiaBombing_OCT06.pdf

(Retrieved Jan 29, 2015)

167 Ibid., citing U.S. Air Force Report.

168 Richard Nixon, as quoted in Owen, Kiernan, "Bombs Over Cambodia".

169 Henry Kissinger, as quoted in Owen, Kiernan, "Bombs Over Cambodia".

170 John Pilger, "The Long Secret Alliance: Uncle Sam and Pol Pot," *Covert Action Quarterly*, No. 62, Fall 1997, pp. 5-9.

171 Owen, Kiernan, "Bombs Over Cambodia".

172 Ibid.

173 William Shawcross, *Sideshow: Kissinger, Nixon, and the Destruction of Cambodia*, Simon & Schuster, New York, 1979, p. 396.

174 "The Senate Select Committee to Study Governmental Operations with Respect to Intelligence Activities" (Church Committee), "Alleged Assassination Plots Involving Foreign Leaders," U.S. Government Printing Office, Washington, D.C., 1975, p. 13; http://www.intelligence. senate.gov/pdfs94th/94465.pdf (Retrieved Jan 29, 2015)

175 Adam Hochschild, "An Assassination's Long Shadow," *The New York Times*, January 16, 2011; http://www.nytimes. com/2011/01/17/opinion/17hochschild. html (Retrieved Jan 29, 2015)

176 Ibid.

177 Ibid.

178 Blum, "A Brief History of U.S. Interventions: 1945 to the Present".

179 Hochschild, "An Assassination's Long Shadow."

180 George H.W. Bush, "Remarks Following Discussions with President Mobutu Sese Seko of Zaire," June 29, 1989, The American Presidency Project; http://

www.presidency.ucsb.edu/ws/?pid=17223 (Retrieved Jan 29, 2015)

181 Noam Chomsky, *Year 501: The Conquest Continues*, South End Press, Cambridge, MA, 1993, pp. 162-163.

182 The National Security Archive, "Brazil Marks 40th Anniversary of Military Coup," Peter Kornbluh, editor; link includes audio tape of President Johnson; http:// www.gwu.edu/~nsarchiv/NSAEBB/ NSAEBB118/index.htm (Retrieved Jan 29, 2015)

183 Blum, "A Brief History of U.S. Interventions: 1945 to the Present".

184 Chomsky, *How the World Works,*" p. 26.

185 Clara Nieto, *Masters of War: Latin America and U.S. Aggression*, Seven Stories Press, New York, p. 155.

186 Blum, "A Brief History of U.S. Interventions: 1945 to the Present".

187 Chomsky, *How the World Works,* p. 27.

188 Nieto, p. 155.

189 Tim Mansel, "'I Shot the Cruelest Dictator in the Americas,'" *BBC News*, May 27, 2011; http://www.bbc.com/news/ world-latin-america-13560512 (Retrieved Jan 29, 2015)

190 Ibid.

191 George Smathers, as quoted in Howard Zinn, *Postwar America, 1945-1971*, South End Press, Cambridge, MA, 1973, pp. 66-67.

192 Blum, "A Brief History of U.S. Interventions: 1945 to the Present."

193 Zinn, *Postwar America, 1945-1971*, p. 67.

194 John Bartlow Martin, as quoted in Zinn, *Postwar America, 1945-1971*, p. 67.

195 Zinn, *Postwar America*, p. 67.

196 *New York Citizen-Call* article excerpt

reprinted in Joy James, "Review/Harlem Hospitality and Political History: Malcolm X and Fidel Castro at the Hotel Theresa," from *Contributions in Black Studies*, Vol. 12, Ethnicity, Gender, Culture, & Cuba, University of Massachusetts Amherst, Jan 1, 1994, p. 108.

197 Nieto, p. 68.

198 Blum, "A Brief History of U.S. Interventions: 1945 to the Present".

199 Ibid.

200 Isabelle Allende, *My Invented Country, A Memoir,* Harper Collins, New York, 2003, p. 148.

201 CIA Library, "CIA Activities in Chile," General Report, September 18, 2000; https://www.cia.gov/library/reports/general-reports-1/chile/ (Retrieved Jan 28, 2015)

202 Allende, p. 150.

203 CIA Library, "CIA Activities in Chile".

204 Allende, p. 150.

205 Blum, "A Brief History of U.S. Interventions: 1945 to the Present".

206 Nieto, p. 299.

207 "Highest Level Vatican Concern Over Propaganda On Chile," *Wikileaks*, Public Library of US Diplomacy, Classification: Secret, Executive Order 11652 GDS; From American Embassy, Rome, To Secretary of State, Washington, Oct 18, 1973; https://www.wikileaks.org/plusd/cables/1973ROME11385_b.html (Retrieved Jan 30, 2015)

208 "Flashback: Caravan of Death," *BBC News*, July 25, 2000, http://news.bbc.co.uk/2/hi/americas/850932.stm (Retrieved Jan 30, 2015)

209 *Human Rights Watch*, "Chile: Government Discloses Torture Was State Policy," November 30, 2004; http://www.hrw.org/news/2004/11/29/chile-government-discloses-torture-was-state-policy (Retrieved Jan 30, 2015)

210 Nima Shirazi, "The Ironic Lady: Margaret Thatcher, Supposed Champion of Freedom and Democracy, and Her Dictator Friends," *Wide Asleep In America*, April 8, 2013; http://www.wideasleepinamerica.com/2013/04/the-ironic-lady-margaret-thatcher.html (Retrieved Jan 30, 2015)

211 Ibid.

212 Ibid.

213 John Dinges, *The Condor Years: How Pinochet and His Allies Brought Terrorism to Three Continents*, The New Press, New York, 2012, p. 2.

214 Patricia Sullivan, "CIA Agent Gust L. Avrakotos Dies at Age 67," *The Washington Post,* December 25, 2005; http://www.washingtonpost.com/wp-dyn/content/article/2005/12/24/AR2005122400871.html (Retrieved Jan 30, 2015)

215 George Crile, *Charlie Wilson's War,* Grove/Atlantic, New York, 2003, p. 52.

216 Fidel Castro, as quoted in Michael Ratner and Michael Steven Smith, *Who Killed Che? How the CIA Got Away With Murder*, OR Books, New York, 2011, p. 20.

217 Ratner, Steven Smith, *Who Killed Che?*, p. 42.

218 Ibid.

219 Ernesto "Che" Guevara," *che guevara reader: writings on politics and revolution*, Ocean Press, Melbourne, 2007 (2003), p. 330.

220 Blum, *Killing Hope*, p. 222.

221 Ratner, Steven Smith, p. 33.

222 Ibid.

223 Che Guevara, as quoted in Ratner, Steven Smith, p. 33.

224 Ibid.

225 Dick Gregory, interview in *One Bright Shining Moment: The Forgotten Summer of George McGovern*, documentary film, Stephen Vittoria, director, Street Legal Cinema, 2005.

226 Ratner, Steven Smith, p. 34.

227 Blum, *Killing Hope*, p. 225.

228 Ibid., p. 226.

229 James W. Douglas, *JFK and the Unspeakable: Why He Died and Why It Matters*, Touchstone/Simon & Schuster, New York, 2008, p. 33.

230 H.W. Brands, *The Devil We Knew: Americans and the Cold War*, Oxford University Press, New York, 1993, p. 62.

231 Ratner, Steven Smith, p. 32.

232 Ibid., p. 25.

233 Ibid.

234 Peter Kornbluh, "CIA Debriefing of Felix Rodriguez, June 3, 1975," from "The Death of Che Guevara: Declassified," *National Security Archive*, George Washington University; http://www2.gwu.edu/~nsarchiv/NSAEBB/NSAEBB5/ (Retrieved Jan 30, 2015)

235 Ratner, Steven Smith, p. 32.

236 Ibid., p. 27.

237 Will Grant, "CIA man recounts Che Guevara's death," *BBC News*, October 8, 2007; http://news.bbc.co.uk/2/hi/7027619.stm (Retrieved Jan 30, 2015)

238 Michéle Ray, "In Cold Blood: The Execution of Che by the CIA," *Ramparts*, March, 1968, p. 33.

239 Paul G. Pierpaoli, Jr., "Operation CHAOS," *The Encyclopedia of the Vietnam War*, Spencer C. Tucker, editor, ABC-CLIO, Santa Barbara, CA, 2011, p. 186.

240 Ibid., p. 187.

241 Ibid.

242 Chris Hedges, "Murder Is Our National Sport," *Truthdig*, May 12, 2013; http://www.truthdig.com/report/item/murder_is_our_national_sport_20130512 (Retrieved Jan 30, 2015)

243 Blum, "A Brief History of U.S. Interventions: 1945 to the Present".

244 "NICARAGUA: Somoza's Reign of Terror," *Time*, March 14, 1977.

245 Zinn, *A People's History*, p. 572.

246 Noam Chomsky, interviewed by David Barsamian, *Imperial Ambitions: Conversations on the Post-9/11 World*, Metropolitan Books, New York, 2005, pp. 93-94.

247 *American Experience: Reagan*, "The Iran-Contra Affair," *PBS*, http://www.pbs.org/wgbh/americanexperience/features/general-article/reagan-iran/ (Retrieved Jan 30, 2015)

248 Blum, "A Brief History of U.S. Interventions: 1945 to the Present".

249 Robert Parry, "America's Debt to Gary Webb," *FAIR*, March 1, 2005; http://fair.org/extra-online-articles/americas-debt-to-gary-webb/ (Retrieved Jan 30, 2015)

250 Mike Davis, endorsement of Nick Schou, *Kill the Messenger*, Nation Books,

New York, 2006.

251 Jeff Cohen, "R.I.P. Gary Webb—Unembedded Reporter," *Common Dreams*, December 13, 2004; http://www.commondreams.org/views/2004/12/13/rip-gary-webb-unembedded-reporter (Retrieved Jan 30, 2015)

252 Tom Hayden, endorsement of Schou, *Kill the Messenger*.

253 Gary Webb, as quoted in Bill Forman and Melinda Walsh, "Gary Webb remembered," *Sacramento News & Review*, Dec 16, 2004; http://www.newsreview.com/sacramento/gary-webb-remembered/content?oid=32816 (Retrieved Jan 30, 2015)

254 Michael Levine, as quoted in Forman and Walsh, "Gary Webb remembered".

255 Robert Parry, "Gary Webb's Death: American Tragedy," *Consortium News,* December 9, 2006; http://www.consortiumnews.com/2006/120906.html (Retrieved Jan 30, 2015)

256 George Sanchez, "The Life and Times of Gary Webb," *The Narco News Bulletin*, January 25, 2005; http://www.narconews.com/Issue35/article1154.html (Retrieved Jan 30, 2015)

257 Parry, "Gary Webb's Death: American Tragedy".

258 Bill Bigelow, "Grenada: Remembering 'A Lovely Little War,'" The Zinn Education Project, *Common Dreams*, October 22, 2013; http://www.commondreams.org/views/2013/10/22/grenada-remembering-lovely-little-war (Retrieved Jan 30, 2015)

259 Ibid.

260 Ibid.

261 Ibid.

262 Ronald Reagan, as quoted in Bigelow, "Grenada: Remembering 'A Lovely Little War'".

263 Bigelow, "Grenada: Remembering 'A Lovely Little War'".

264 Ibid.

265 Chomsky, *How the World Works*, p. 233.

266 Zinn, *A People's History*, p. 577.

267 Chomsky, *How the World Works*, p. 233.

268 Blum, "A Brief History of U.S. Interventions: 1945 to the Present".

269 Edward Herman, "The New York Times on Libya-Pan Am 103," *Z Magazine*, October 1, 2007; https://zcomm.org/zmagazine/the-new-york-times-on-libya-pan-am-103-by-edward-herman/ (Retrieved Jan 30, 2015)

270 Ibid.

271 Ibid., citing Paul Foot, "Lockerbie: The Flight From Justice," *Private Eye*, May/June 2001, p. 10.

272 Ibid.

273 Juan Cole, "Qaddafi was a CIA Asset," *Informed Comment* (juancole.com), September 3, 2011; http://www.juancole.com/2011/09/qaddafi-was-a-cia-asset.html (Retrieved Jan 30, 2015)

274 Yvonne Bell, "CIA, MI6 helped Gaddafi on dissidents: rights group," *Reuters*, September 3, 2011; http://www.reuters.com/article/2011/09/03/us-libya-usa-cia-idUSTRE78213Y20110903 (Retrieved Jan 30, 2015)

275 Ben Hubbard, "Moammar Gaddafi's CIA Ties: Documents Suggest Libya and Washington Worked Together," *Huffington Post*, September 3, 2011; http://www.huffingtonpost.com/2011/09/03/

moammar-gaddafi-cia-ties-_n_947769.
html (Retrieved Jan 30, 2015)

276 Robert E. Bauman, *Panama Money Secrets*, The Sovereign Society, Delray Beach, FL, 2007, p. 24.

277 Zepezauer, p. 82.

278 Frederick Kempe, *Divorcing the Dictator: America's Bungled Affair with Noriega*, G.P. Putnam, New York, 1990, p. 59.

279 Holliston Perni, *A Heritage of Hypocrisy,* Pleasant Mount Press, Union Dale, PA, 2005, p. 127.

280 *Frontline*, "Thirty Years of America's Drug War: a Chronology," *PBS*; http://www.pbs.org/wgbh/pages/frontline/shows/drugs/cron/ (Retrieved Jan 30, 2015)

281 Encyclopedia of World Biography, "Manuel Noriega," http://www.notablebiographies.com/Ni-Pe/Noriega-Manuel.html (Retrieved Jan 30, 2015)

282 Bauman, *Panama Money Secrets*, p. 24.

283 Perni, p. 128.

284 Ibid.

285 Mark Tran, "Manuel Noriega—from US friend to foe," *The Guardian,* April 27, 2010; http://www.theguardian.com/world/2010/apr/27/manuel-noriega-us-friend-foe (Retrieved Jan 30, 2015)

286 Kempe, p. 244.

287 Los Angeles Times Wire Services, "Signs of Occult Found in Abandoned Noriega Office," December 22, 1989; http://articles.latimes.com/1989-12-22/news/mn-948_1_abandoned-office (Retrieved Jan 30, 2015)

288 Phil Gasper, "Afghanistan, the CIA, bin Laden, and the Taliban," *International Socialist Review*, November-December 2001.

289 Amy Goodman and David Goodman, *The Exception to the Rulers*, Hyperion Books, New York, 2004, p. 24.

290 Michael Moran, "Bin Laden comes home to roost," *NBC News*, August 24, 1998; http://www.nbcnews.com/id/3340101/t/bin-laden-comes-home-roost (Retrieved Jan 30, 2015)

291 Ibid.

292 Zbigniew Brzezinski, interview for *Le Nouvel Observateur,* January 15-21, 1998, translated by William Blum, posted on *Global Research*, http://www.globalresearch.ca/articles/BRZ110A.html (Retrieved Jan 30, 2015)

293 Amy and David Goodman, p. 25.

294 Noor Ahmad Khalidi, "Afghanistan: Demographic Consequences of War, 1978-1987," *Central Asian Survey*, Vol. 10, No. 3, 1991, pp. 101-126.

295 Michael Parenti, *Against Empire*, City Lights Books, San Francisco, 1995, p. 39.

296 Arthur Goldberg, as quoted in John Loftus and Mark Aarons, *The Secret War Against the Jews: How Western Espionage Betrayed The Jewish People*, St. Martin's Press, New York, 1994, p. 71.

297 Loftus and Aarons, *The Secret War Against the Jews*, pp. 61-71.

298 David Talbot, *The Devil's Chessboard: Allen Dulles, the CIA, and the Rise of America's Secret Government,* Harper Collins, New York, 2015, p. 4

299 Ibid.

300 Ibid., p. 33

301 Ibid., pp. 4-5

302 Ibid., p. 198

303 John Foster Dulles, as quoted in

Stephen Kinzer, *The Brothers: John Foster Dulles, Allen Dulles, and Their Secret World War*, Times Books, Henry Holt and Company, New York, 2013, pp. 320-321.

304 William Blum, "The Anti-Empire Report #118," June 26, 2013; http://williamblum.org/aer/read/118 (Retrieved Jan 30, 2015)

305 Blum, *Killing Hope*, p. 20.

Chapter 4

1 David Greenberg, "Beware the Military-Industrial Complex," *Slate*, January 14, 2011; http://www.slate.com/articles/news_and_politics/history_lesson/2011/01/beware_the_militaryindustrial_complex.html (Retrieved Feb 3, 2015)

2 Ibid.

3 Ibid.

4 Dwight Eisenhower, as quoted in Mike Gravel and Joe Lauria, *Political Odyssey: The Rise of American Militarism and One Man's Fight to Stop It*, Seven Stories Press, New York, 2008, pp. 112-113.

5 Dwight Eisenhower, as quoted in Ira Chernus, "The Real Eisenhower: Planning to Win Nuclear War," *Common Dreams*, March 18, 2008; http://www.commondreams.org/views/2008/03/18/real-eisenhower-planning-win-nuclear-war (Retrieved Feb 3, 2015)

6 Ira Chernus, "The Real Eisenhower: Planning to Win Nuclear War".

7 Ibid.

8 Dwight Eisenhower, as quoted in Ira Chernus, "The Real Eisenhower".

9 George Lee Butler, as quoted in Louis Menand, "Nukes of Hazard," *The New Yorker*, September 30, 2013; http://www.newyorker.com/magazine/2013/09/30/nukes-of-hazard (Retrieved Feb 3, 2015)

10 Dwight Eisenhower, as quoted in Noam Chomsky, *Fateful Triangle: The United States, Israel, and the Palestinians*, Pluto Press, London, 1999, p. 15.

11 President Dwight Eisenhower, "Special Message to the Congress on the Situation in the Middle East," January 5, 1957, *The American Presidency Project*; http://www.presidency.ucsb.edu/ws/?pid=11007 (Retrieved Feb 3, 2015)

12 William Blum, "A Brief History of U.S. Interventions: 1945 to the Present," *Z Magazine, June 1999*.

13 Al Stewart, "(A Child's View) The Eisenhower Years," *Sparks of Ancient Light*, Appleseed Records, 2008.

14 Gore Vidal, "Truman," *The Independent Magazine*, October 3, 1992.

15 *Milestones: 1945-1952*, "NSC-68, 1950," U.S. Department of State, Office of the Historian; https://history.state.gov/milestones/1945-1952/NSC68 (Retrieved Feb 3, 2015)

16 Ibid.

17 Noam Chomsky, "Is the World Too Big to Fail?", *Al Jazeera*, September 29, 2011; http://www.aljazeera.com/indepth/opinion/2011/09/201192514364490977.html (Retrieved Feb 3, 2015)

18 James Ledbetter, *Unwarranted Influence: Dwight D. Eisenhower and the Military-Industrial Complex*, Yale University Press, New Haven, CT, 2011, p. 4.

19 Greenberg, "Beware the Military-Industrial Complex".

20 Ibid.

21 Ibid.

22 Andrew Bacevich, "The Tyranny of Defense Inc.," *The Atlantic*, January/

February 2011; http://www.theatlantic.com/magazine/archive/2011/01/the-tyranny-of-defense-inc/308342/ (Retrieved Feb 3, 2015)

23 Ibid.

24 Ibid.

25 David Halberstam, *The Fifties*, Random House, New York, 1993, p. 625.

26 Ledbetter, p. 88.

27 Ibid., p. 91.

28 Greenberg, "Beware the Military-Industrial Complex".

29 Ledbetter, p. 91.

30 Chernus, "The Real Eisenhower: Planning to Win Nuclear War".

31 Ibid.

32 Dwight Eisenhower, as quoted in Chernus, "The Real Eisenhower".

33 Chernus, "The Real Eisenhower".

34 Greenberg, "Beware the Military-Industrial Complex".

35 Ibid.

36 Ibid.

37 Dwight Eisenhower, as quoted in Greenberg, "Beware the Military-Industrial Complex".

38 Marjorie Cohn, "Daniel Ellsberg: United States Nearly Used Nukes During Vietnam War," *Truthout*, June 9, 2014; http://truth-out.org/news/item/24245-daniel-ellsberg-united-states-nearly-used-nukes-during-vietnam-war (Retrieved Feb 3, 2015)

39 Lyndon B. Johnson Conversation with Dwight Eisenhower, Feb 19, 1968, WH6802.02; http://millercenter.org/presidentialrecordings/lbj-wh6802.02-12723 (Retrieved Feb 3, 2015)

40 Nicholas von Hoffman, *Hoax*, Nation Books, New York, 2004, p. 25.

41 Ibid., p. 26.

42 Smedley Butler, as quoted in David Talbot, *Devil Dog: The Amazing True Story of the Man Who Saved America*, Simon & Schuster, New York, 2010, p. 125.

43 von Hoffman, p. 29.

44 Ibid.

45 James A. Huston, "The Military-Industrial Complex," *Encyclopedia of the American Foreign Relations*; http://www.americanforeignrelations.com/E-N/The-Military-Industrial-Complex.html; (Retrieved Feb 3, 2015)

46 Sidney Lens, *The Military-Industrial Complex*, Pilgrim Press, Philadelphia, 1970, p. 4.

47 Talbot, *Devil Dog*, p. 28.

48 Gravel and Lauria, pp. 101-102.

49 Calvin Coolidge, as quoted in *Serving America's Veterans: A Reference Handbook*, Greenwood Publishing Group, Santa Barbara, CA, 2009, p. 22

50 Gravel and Lauria, p. 101.

51 Ibid.

52 Ibid.

53 Robert Higgs, "World War II and the Military-Industrial-Congressional Complex," *The Independent Institute*, May 1, 1995; http://www.independent.org/publications/article.asp?id=141 (Retrieved Feb 3, 2015)

54 Ibid.

55 Franklin D. Roosevelt, as quoted in Gravel and Lauria, p. 101.

56 Gravel and Lauria, p. 101.

57 Ibid, p. 102.

58 Clifford Powell, as quoted in Burton W. Folsom, Jr. and Anita Folsom, *FDR Goes to War*, Threshold/Simon & Schuster, New York, 2011, p. 55.

59 Henry Stimson, as quoted in Folsom Jr. and Folsom, p. 55.

60 Gravel and Lauria, p. 102.

61 Henry Stimson, as quoted in Peter Trubowitz, *Defining the National Interest: Conflict and Change in American Foreign Policy*, University of Chicago Press, Chicago, 1998, p. 126.

62 Gravel and Lauria, p. 102.

63 Ibid., p. 103.

64 Gore Vidal, "Decline of the Empire," (1986), *Gore Vidal's State of the Union: Nation Essays 1958-2005*, Richard Lingeman, editor, Nation Books, New York, 2013 (NP).

65 Lens, p. 22.

66 Harry Truman, as quoted in Lens, p. 22.

67 Ibid.

68 Vidal, "Decline of the Empire".

69 Ibid.

70 Ibid.

71 Herbert I. Schiller, "The Use of American Power in the Post-Colonial World," *The Massachusetts Review*, Volume 9, No. 4, Autumn, 1968, p. 634.

72 Samuel Huntington, as quoted in Schiller, "The Use of American Power," Ibid.

73 Lens, p. 31.

74 Ibid.

75 Schiller, p. 635.

76 Lens, p. 32.

77 Ibid., p. 1.

78 Ibid.

79 Ibid., pp. 1-2.

80 John Prados, *Operation Vulture: America's Dien Bien Phu*, iBooks, DCA, Inc., 2014, Preface, (NP). (Originally published as *The Sky Would Fall*, Dial Press, 1983)

81 Ibid.

82 John Prados, "Geneva Ends U.S. Action in French Indochina," johnprados. com, July 21, 2014; http://johnprados. com/2014/07/21/geneva-ends-u-s-action-in-french-indochina/ (Retrieved Feb 3, 2015)

83 Ibid.

84 Ibid.

85 Gareth Porter, "From Military-Industrial Complex to Permanent War State," *Common Dreams*, January 17, 2011; http://www.commondreams.org/views/2011/01/17/military-industrial-complex-permanent-war-state (Retrieved Feb 3, 2015)

86 Oscar Guardiola-Rivera, *Story of a Death Foretold: The Coup Against Salvador Allende, September 11, 1973*, Bloomsbury Press, New York, 2013, p. 228.

87 Michael D. Yates, "Oliver Stone, Obama, and the War in Vietnam," *Counterpunch*, January 10, 2013, citing Oliver Stone and Peter Kuznick, *Untold History of the United States*, documentary series, Showtime, 2012; http://www. counterpunch.org/2013/01/10/oliver-stone-obama-and-the-war-in-vietnam/ (Retrieved Feb 3, 2015)

88 Kallie Szczepanski, "Napalm and Agent Orange in the Vietnam War," *About Education*; http://asianhistory.about. com/od/warsinasia/fl/Napalm-and-Agent-Orange-in-the-Vietnam-War.htm (Retrieved Feb 3, 2015)

89 Ibid.

90 "Records of U.S. Military Casualties, Missing in Action, and Prisoners of War from the Era of the Vietnam War," *National Archives*, http://www.archives.gov/research/military/vietnam-war/electronic-records.html; also "Vietnam War Statistics," http://www.statisticbrain.com/vietnam-war-statistics/; also Michael Ip, "Looking Back: The End of the Vietnam War," *ABC News*, Mar 29, 2013, http://abcnews.go.com/blogs/headlines/2013/03/looking-back-the-end-of-the-vietnam-war/; also Steve Bentley, "A Short History of PTSD: From Thermopylae to Hue," *The VVA Veteran*, March/April, 2005, http://www.vva.org/archive/TheVeteran/2005_03/feature_HistoryPTSD.htm; also U.S. Department of Veterans Affairs, "Veterans' Disease Associated with Agent Orange," http://www.publichealth.va.gov/exposures/agentorange/conditions/index.asp (All retrieved Feb 3, 2015)

91 Stephen Daggett, "Costs of Major U.S. Wars," Congressional Research Service, (prepared for members and committees in Congress), June 29, 2010; https://www.fas.org/sgp/crs/natsec/RS22926.pdf (Retrieved Feb 3, 2015)

92 Stuart W. Leslie, *The Cold War and American Science: The Military-Industrial Complex at MIT and Stanford*, Columbia University Press, New York, 1993, p. 12.

93 Robert Parry, "Profiting Off Nixon's Vietnam 'Treason,'" *Consortium News*, March 4, 2012; https://consortiumnews.com/2012/03/04/profiting-off-nixons-vietnam-treason/ (Retrieved Feb 3, 2015)

94 Ibid.

95 William J. Astore, "The Business of America is War: Disaster Capitalism on the Battlefield and in the Boardroom," *TomDispatch*, October 20, 2013; http://www.tomdispatch.com/blog/175762/ (Retrieved Feb 3, 2015)

96 Parry, "Profiting Off Nixon's Vietnam 'Treason'".

97 Ibid.

98 Gravel and Lauria, p. 18.

99 William Blum, "The Anti-Empire Report #114," Mar 11, 2013, citing the introduction to *Rogue State* and Bin Laden's appropriation of his text; http://williamblum.org/aer/read/114 (Retrieved Feb 3, 2015)

100 William Hartung, "Profits of War, The Fruits of the Permanent Military-Industrial Complex," *Multinational Monitor*, January/February, Vol. 26, No. 1, 2005.

101 Ibid.

102 "A Byte Out of History: The Lasting Legacy of Operation Illwind," *FBI.gov*, June 14, 2013; http://www.fbi.gov/news/stories/2013/june/a-byte-out-of-history-the-lasting-legacy-of-operation-illwind (Retrieved Feb 3, 2015)

103 Hartung, "Profits of War".

104 Ibid.

105 George F. Kennan, from the Foreword to Norman Cousins, *The Pathology of Power*, W.W. Norton & Company, New York, 1987, p. 11.

106 Gore Vidal, interviewed by David Barsamian, *The Progressive*, October 25, 2006; http://www.progressive.org/mag_intv0806 (Retrieved Feb 3, 2015)

107 Howard Zinn, *Terrorism and War*, Seven Stories Press, New York, 2002, p. 48.

108 Astore, "The Business of America is War".

109 Gravel and Lauria, p. 18.

110 Chris Hedges, "The Menace of the Military Mind," *Truthdig*, February 3, 2014; http://www.truthdig.com/report/item/the_menace_of_the_military_mind_20140203 (Retrieved Feb 3, 2015)

111 Gravel and Lauria, p. 18.

112 Hartung, "Profits of War".

113 Noam Chomsky, *Failed States*, Metropolitan Books/Henry Holt and Company, New York, 2006, p. 56.

114 Porter, "From Military-Industrial Complex to Permanent War State".

115 Dr. Helen Caldicott, *The New Nuclear Danger: George W. Bush's Military-Industrial Complex*, The New Press, New York, 2002, 2004, p. xxi.

116 Ibid.

117 Ibid., p. xxiv.

118 Ibid., pp. xxii-xxiii.

119 Dr. Hunter S. Thompson, "Fear & Loathing in America," *ESPN Page 2*, September 12, 2001; http://proxy.espn.go.com/espn/page2/story?id=1250751 (Retrieved Feb 3, 2015)

120 Astore, "The Business of America is War".

121 Ibid.

122 Greg Palast, *The Best Democracy Money Can Buy*, Penguin, New York, 2004, pp. 359-360.

123 "The Budget and Economic Outlook: Fiscal Years 2010 to 2020," Congressional Budget Office, Jan 28, 2010; http://www.cbo.gov/sites/default/files/01-28-testimony_senate.pdf (Retrieved Feb 3, 2015)

124 Winslow Wheeler, "America's $1 Trillion National Security Budget," *Counterpunch*, March 14, 2014; http://www.counterpunch.org/2014/03/14/americas-1-trillion-national-security-budget/ (Retrieved Feb 10, 2015)

125 Straus Military Reform Project, "Total U.S. National Security Spending, 2014-2015," Center for Defense Information at the Project on Government Oversight (POGO), March 13, 2014; http://www.pogo.org/our-work/straus-military-reform-project/defense-budget/2014/total-us-national-security-spending.html (Retrieved Feb 10, 2015)

126 Raed Jarrar, "B is for Billion: What Military Cuts?," *Common Dreams*, February 2, 2015; http://www.commondreams.org/views/2015/02/02/b-billion-what-military-cuts (Retrieved Feb 10, 2015)

127 Ibid.

128 von Hoffman, p. 99.

129 "Who Pays the Pro-War Pundits? Conflicts of Interest Exposed for TV Guests Backing Military Action," *DemocracyNow*, September 15, 2014; http://www.democracynow.org/2014/9/15/who_pays_the_pro_war_pundits (Retrieved Feb 3, 2015)

130 Robert Greenwald and Melanie Sloan, "The Real Scandal Involving Generals," Huffington Post, November 19, 2012; http://www.huffingtonpost.com/robert-greenwald/once-a-soldier-always-a-s_b_2161490.html (Retrieved Feb 3, 2015)

131 "Jeremy Scahill on Obama's Orwellian War in Iraq: We Created the Very Threat We Claim to be Fighting," *DemocracyNow*, October 3, 2014; http://www.democracynow.org/2014/10/3/jeremy_scahill_on_obamas_orwellian_war (Retrieved Feb 3, 2015)

132 John Steinbeck, as quoted in Paul Fussell, *Wartime: Understanding and Behavior in the Second World War*, Oxford University Press, New York, 1989, p. 285.

133 Eric Boehm, "Defense Contractors Spend Millions Lobbying Congress, Get Billions in New Budget," *Watchdog. org*, January 22, 2014; http://watchdog.org/124909/defense-spending/ (Retrieved Feb 3, 2015)

134 Michael Parenti, *Profit Pathology and Other Indecencies*, Paradigm Press, Boulder, CO, 2015, (NP).

135 Porter, "From Military-Industrial Complex to Permanent War State".

136 Dennis Kucinich, "The Real Reason We Are Bombing Syria," *Huffington Post*, September 23, 2014; http://www.huffingtonpost.com/dennis-j-kucinich/syria-isis-war_b_5869964.html (Retrieved Feb 3, 2015)

137 Lens, p. 138.

138 Hedges, "The Menace of the Military Mind".

139 Carl Boggs, *Imperial Delusions: American Militarism and Endless War*, Rowman & Littlefield Publishers, Lanham, MD, 2005, p. 1.

140 Hedges, "The Menace of the Military Mind".

141 Astore, "The Business of America is War".

142 Lens, p. 161.

143 Bertrand Russell, *The Basic Writings of Bertrand Russell, 1903-1959*, Routledge, London/New York, 2003 (1961), p. 459.

Chapter 5

1 Commodore Matthew Perry, as quoted in James Bradley, *The Imperial Cruise*, Little, Brown and Company, New York, 2009, p. 171.

2 William Blum, *Killing Hope: U.S. Military and CIA Interventions Since World War II*, Common Courage Press, Monroe, ME, 2004, p. 128.

3 L. Fletcher Prouty, *JFK: The CIA, Vietnam, and the Plot to Assassinate John F. Kennedy*, Skyhorse, New York, 2011, pp. 37-38.

4 Ibid., p. 224.

5 Ibid., p. 51.

6 Blum, p. 123.

7 Ibid., p. 123.

8 Prouty, pp. 39-40.

9 American Cancer Society, "Agent Orange and Cancer," January 27, 2014; http://www.cancer.org/cancer/cancercauses/othercarcinogens/intheworkplace/agent-orange-and-cancer (Retrieved Jan 26, 2015)

10 Ibid.

11 *PBS*, "LBJ: Foreign Affairs," from *American Experience* series; http://www.pbs.org/wgbh/americanexperience/features/general-article/lbj-foreign/ (Retrieved Jan 26, 2015)

12 Claude AnShin Thomas, *At Hell's Gate: A Soldier's Journey from War to Peace*, Shambhala, Boston, MA, 2004, pp. 10-11.

13 Ibid., p. 20.

14 Chris Hedges, *War Is a Force That Gives Us Meaning*, Anchor/Random House, New York, 2002, p. 11.

15 Nick Turse, *Kill Anything That Moves: The Real American War in Vietnam*, Picador, New York, p. 48.

16 Ibid.

17 Ibid., p. 49.

18 Ibid., p. 64.

19 Ibid., p. 128.

20 Ibid., pp. 129-131.

21 Ibid., p. 28.

22 Ibid., p. 29.

23 AnShin Thomas, pp. 12-13.

24 Ibid., pp. 6-7.

25 Prouty, pp. 50-51.

26 Ibid., p. 70.

27 Ibid., p. 71.

28 Ibid., p. 72.

29 Blum, pp. 125-126.

30 Ibid., p. 125.

31 Turse, pp. 48-49.

Chapter 6

1 Sue O'Connor, Rintaro Ono, Chris Clarkson, "Pelagic Fishing at 42,000 Years Before the Present and Maritime Skills of Modern Humans," *Science*, Nov 25, 2011, Vol. 334, no. 6059, pp. 1117-1121.

2 Christopher Shepherd, *Development and Environmental Politics Unmasked: Authority, Participation, and Equity in East Timor*, Routledge, New York, 2014, p. 6.

3 "East Timor Profile," *BBC News Asia*, July 22, 2014; http://www.bbc.com/news/world-sia-pacific-14919009 (Retrieved Feb 4, 2015)

4 Adam Schwarz, *A Nation in Waiting: Indonesia's Search for Stability*, Westview Press, Oxford, 2000, pp. 198-199.

5 "East Timor Profile," *BBC News Asia*.

6 Matthew Jardine, *East Timor: Genocide in Paradise*, Common Courage Press, Chicago, 1995, p. 21.

7 Ibid., p. 22.

8 Ibid.

9 Alastair M. Taylor, "Sukarno: First United Nations Dropout," *International Journal*, Vol. 20, No. 2, Spring, 1965, p. 206.

10 Willard Hanna, "Sukarno," *Encyclopedia Britannica*; http://www.britannica.com/EBchecked/topic/572207/Sukarno/6967/Indonesian-independence

11 Ibid.

12 Ibid.

13 William Blum, "A Brief History of U.S. Interventions: 1945 to the Present," *Z Magazine*, June 1999.

14 Ibid.

15 Ibid.

16 Ibid.

17 Deirdre Griswold, *Indonesia 1965: The Second Greatest Crime of the Century*, Worldview Publishers, 1970, Chapter 1, "The Bloodbath," (NP).

18 Ibid.

19 William Blum, *Killing Hope: U.S. Military and C.I.A. Interventions Since World War II*, Common Courage Press, Monroe, ME, p. 194.

20 Ibid.

21 "CIA Stalling State Department Histories," *The National Security Archive*, George Washington University, Electronic Briefing Book No. 52, Thomas Blanton, editor, July 27, 2001; http://www2.gwu.edu/~nsarchiv/NSAEBB/NSAEBB52/ (Retrieved Feb 4, 2015)

22 Roger Hilsman, as quoted in Blum, *Killing Hope*, pp. 195-196.

23 Blum, *Killing Hope*, citing *The New York Times*, p. 196.

24 James Reston, "Washington: A Gleam of Light in Asia," *The New York Times*, June 19, 1966.

25 Robert Cribb, "The Indonesian Massacres," citing *Time* ("Vengeance," 1966) from *Century of Genocide: Critical Essays and Eyewitness Accounts*, Samuel Totten and William S. Parsons, editors, Routledge, New York, 2009, p. 200.

26 Edward S. Herman, *Beyond Hypocrisy: Decoding the News in an Age of Propaganda*, South End Press, Boston, 1992, p. 38.

27 Jardine, p. 9.

28 Herman, *Beyond Hypocrisy*, p. 38.

29 Ibid.

30 John Pilger, *Death of a Nation*, documentary film, written/directed by John Pilger, ITV Central Production, 1994.

31 Noam Chomsky, "The United States and East Timor" from *The Essential Chomsky*, Anthony Arnove, editor, The New Press, New York, 2008, p. 195.

32 John Pilger, "Our Model Dictator," *The Guardian*, January 27, 2008; http://www.theguardian.com/commentisfree/2008/jan/28/indonesia.world (Retrieved Feb 4, 2015)

33 Ibid.

34 Ibid.

35 Noam Chomsky, "Rogue States," from *Acts of Aggression: Policing Rogue States* (with Edward Said), Seven Stories Press, New York, 1999, pp. 34-35.

36 Blum, *Killing Hope*, p. 195.

37 Gough Whitlam, as quoted in Peter Hastings, "Whitlam treads dangerous grounds on Timor," *The Sydney Morning Herald*, September 16, 1974.

38 Richard C. S. Trahair, Robert L. Miller, *Encyclopedia of Cold War Espionage, Spies, and Secret Operations*, Enigma Books, New York, 2009, p. 423.

39 Pilger, *Death of a Nation*.

40 James Dunn, as interviewed in Pilger, *Death of a Nation*.

41 Jardine, pp. 24-26.

42 Ibid., pp. 26-27.

43 Ibid., p. 28.

44 Jardine, p. 28.

45 Pilger, *Death of a Nation*.

46 Ibid.

47 Jardine, p. 30

48 Noam Chomsky, "The United States and East Timor," p. 188.

49 James Dunn, as interviewed in Pilger, *Death of a Nation*.

50 Pilger, *Death of a Nation*.

51 Amy Goodman and David Goodman, *The Exception to the Rulers*, Hyperion, New York, 2004, p. 218.

52 Herman, *Beyond Hypocrisy*, p. 38.

53 Greg Shackleton, from Pilger, *Death of a Nation*.

54 Shirley Shackleton, from Pilger, *Death of a Nation*.

55 José Ramos-Horta, *Funu: The Unfinished Saga of East Timor*, Red Sea Press, Lawrenceville, NJ, 1997, pp. 101-102.

56 Ibid., p. 101.

57 Jardine, p. 37.

58 "Did Ford Agree to Nixon Pardon Before Taking Office? The Nation's Victor Navasky on Ford's Memoirs and the Lawsuit that Followed," *DemocracyNow*, December 29, 2006; http://www.democracynow.org/2006/12/27/did_gerald_ford_agree_to_nixon (Retrieved Feb 4, 2015)

59 "East Timor Revisited: Ford, Kissinger and the Indonesian Invasion, 1975-76,"

The National Security Archive, George Washington University, Electronic Briefing Book No. 62, William Burr and Michael L. Evans, editors, December 6, 2001; http://www2.gwu.edu/~nsarchiv/NSAEBB/NSAEBB62/ (Retrieved Feb 4, 2015)

60 Noam Chomsky, "An Island Lies Bleeding," *The Guardian*, July 5, 1994.

61 Pilger, *Death of a Nation*.

62 Jack Anderson, "Another Slaughter," *San Francisco Chronicle*, November 9, 1979.

63 C. Philip Liechty, interviewed in Pilger, *Death of a Nation*.

64 Jack Anderson, "300,000 Died as America Stood By," *Sarasota Herald-Tribune*, November 10, 1979.

65 C. Philip Liechty, as quoted in Christopher Hitchens, *The Trial of Henry Kissinger*, Verso, New York, 2002, Ch. 8, "East Timor," (NP).

66 Anderson, "Another Slaughter".

67 Pilger, *Death of a Nation*.

68 Henry Kissinger, as quoted in Hitchens, *The Trial of Henry Kissinger*, (from a Declassified State Department Memorandum of Conversation, December 18, 1975), Ch. 8, "East Timor," (NP).

69 Ibid.

70 Ibid.

71 Hitchens, *The Trial of Henry Kissinger*, Ch. 10, "Afterword: The Profit Margin," (NP).

72 Pilger, *Death of a Nation*.

73 Amy and David Goodman, *The Exception to the Rulers*, p. 218.

74 Christopher Hitchens, interviewed in *The Trials of Henry Kissinger*, documentary film, directed by Eugene Jarecki, *BBC*, 2002.

75 Jarecki, *The Trials of Henry Kissinger*.

76 Arthur Schlesinger, as quoted in William Shawcross, *Sideshow: Kissinger, Nixon, and the Destruction of Cambodia*, Simon & Schuster, New York, 1979, p. 79.

77 Adam Yarmolinsky, as quoted in Shawcross, *Sideshow* , p. 79.

78 Jarecki, *The Trials of Henry Kissinger*.

79 Ibid.

80 Ibid.

81 Christopher Hitchens, interviewed in Jarecki, *The Trials of Henry Kissinger*.

82 Colin Shultz, "Nixon Prolonged Vietnam War for Political Gain," *Smithsonian.com*, March 18, 2013; http://www.smithsonianmag.com/smart-news/nixon-prolonged-vietnam-war-for-political-gainand-johnson-knew-about-it-newly-unclassified-tapes-suggest-3595441/?no-ist (Retrieved Feb 4, 2015)

83 Jarecki, *The Trials of Henry Kissinger*.

84 Ibid.

85 Ibid.

86 "Kissinger and Chile: The Declassified Record," *The National Security Archive*, George Washington University, Briefing Book #437, Document 1: Telcon, Helms – Kissinger, September 12, 1970, Peter Kornbluh, editor, September 11, 2013; http://www2.gwu.edu/~nsarchiv/NSAEBB/NSAEBB437/ (Retrieved Feb 4, 2015)

87 Peter Kornbluh, interviewed in Jarecki, *The Trials of Henry Kissinger*.

88 Alexander Haig, as quoted in Jarecki, *The Trials of Henry Kissinger*.

89 Amy Goodman, "Ask Kissinger About Pinochet," *DemocracyNow*, December 14, 2006; http://www.democracynow.org/blog/2006/12/14/ask_kissinger_about_

pinochet_http_seattlepinwsourcecom_ opinion_295792_amy14html (Retrieved Feb 4, 2015)

90 "CIA Activities in Chile," CIA Library, Sept 18, 2000; https://www.cia.gov/ library/reports/general-reports-1/chile/#4 (Retrieved Feb 4, 2015)

91 Ibid.

92 Jarecki, *The Trials of Henry Kissinger*.

93 "The Murder of General Rene Schneider," Kissinger Watch #1 – 03, International Campaign Against Impunity; http://www.icai-online. org/56282,46136.html (Retrieved Feb 4, 2015)

94 Hitchens, *The Trial of Henry Kissinger*, p. 60.

95 Seymour Hersh, interviewed in Jarecki, *The Trials of Henry Kissinger*.

96 Jarecki, *The Trials of Henry Kissinger*.

97 Ibid.

98 Ibid.

99 Ibid.

100 "Kissinger and Chile: The Declassified Record," *The National Security Archive*, Briefing Book #437, Document 4: White House, Kissinger, Memorandum for the President, "Subject: NSC Meeting, November 6-Chile," November 5, 1970.

101 Peter Kornbluh, interviewed in Jarecki, *The Trials of Henry Kissinger*.

102 Geoffrey Robertson, interviewed in Jarecki, *The Trials of Henry Kissinger*.

103 Ibid.

104 Seymour Hersh, interviewed in Jarecki, *The Trials of Henry Kissinger*.

105 Howard Zinn, *Just and Unjust Wars, Failure to Quit: Reflections of an Optimistic Historian*, South End Press, Cambridge, MA, 2002 (1993), p. 108.

106 C. Philip Liechty, interviewed in Pilger, *Death of a Nation*.

107 Blum, *Killing Hope*, p. 198.

108 Pilger, *Death of a Nation*.

109 C. Philip Liechty, interviewed in Pilger, *Death of a Nation*.

110 Jardine, p. 31.

111 Henry Kissinger, as quoted in "East Timor Revisited: Ford, Kissinger and the Indonesian Invasion, 1975-76," *The National Security Archive*, Burr and Evans, editors.

112 Martinho da Costa Lopes, as quoted in Jardine, pp. 34-35.

113 Pilger, *Death of a Nation*.

114 Amy and David Goodman, *The Exception to the Rulers*, pp. 217-218.

115 Pilger, *Death of a Nation*.

116 Ibid.

117 Jardine, p. 59.

118 Chomsky, "The United States and East Timor" from *The Essential Chomsky*, pp. 188-189.

119 Stephen R. Shalom, Noam Chomsky, and Michael Albert, "East Timor Questions & Answers," Z Magazine, October 1999; http://www.chomsky.info/ articles/199910--02.htm (Retrieved Feb 4, 2015)

120 Ibid.

121 William Blum, "The Anti-Empire Report #41," January 12, 2007; http:// williamblum.org/aer/read/41 (Retrieved Feb 4, 2015)

122 Chomsky, "The United States and East Timor" from *The Essential Chomsky*, p. 190.

123 Pilger, *Death of a Nation*.

124 Chomsky, "The United States and East Timor" from *The Essential Chomsky*, p. 196.

125 Ibid., p. 189.

126 Daniel P. Moynihan, as quoted in Chomsky, "The United States and East Timor" from *The Essential Chomsky*, p. 189.

127 Chomsky, "The United States and East Timor" from *The Essential Chomsky*, pp. 189-190.

128 Pilger, *Death of a Nation*.

129 Howard Zinn, "Respecting the Holocaust," *The Progressive*, November 1999.

130 "The Democrats & Suharto: Bill Clinton & Richard Holbrooke Questioned on Their Support for Brutal Indonesian Dictatorship," *DemocracyNow*, January 28, 2008; http://www.democracynow. org/2008/1/28/the_democrats_suharto_bill_clinton_richard (Retrieved Feb 4, 2015)

131 Ibid.

132 Ibid.

133 Ibid.

134 Ibid.

135 Amy and David Goodman, *The Exception to the Rulers*, p. 220.

136 Pilger, *Death of a Nation*.

137 Margaret Thatcher, as quoted in Mark Phythian, *The Politics of British Arms Sales Since 1964: To Secure Our Rightful Share*, Manchester University Press, 2000, p. 154.

138 Noam Chomsky, *Failed States: The Abuse of Power and the Assault on Democracy*, Metropolitan Books/Henry Holt, New York, p. 135.

139 Ibid.

140 Ibid., pp. 135-136.

141 Jose Luis Oliveira, as quoted in "Reagan 'behind East Timor genocide,'" *Al Jazeera*, June 6, 2004; http://www.aljazeera.com/archive/2004/06/20084914410753603. html (Retrieved Feb 4, 2015)

142 Donald Keough, as quoted in Jardine, p. 37.

143 Joseph Nevins, "First the Butchery, Then the Flowers," *Counterpunch*, Vol. 9, No. 10, May 16-31, 2002.

144 Ibid.

145 *Boston Globe* article cited in Howard Zinn, *A People's History of the United States*, Harper Collins, New York, 2003, p. 655.

146 Nevins, "First the Butchery, Then the Flowers".

147 Ibid.

148 "Journalists Allan Nairn and Amy Goodman Confront Bill Clinton, Richard Holbrooke, and Henry Kissinger Over U.S. Military Support to Indonesia," *DemocracyNow*, May 17, 2002; http://www.democracynow.org/2002/5/17/journalists_allan_nairn_and_amy_goodman (Retrieved Feb 4, 2015)

149 Ibid.

150 Amy and David Goodman, *The Exception to the Rulers*, p. 219.

151 Ibid., p. 220.

152 Ibid., p. 221.

153 Ibid., p. 222.

154 Ibid., p. 225.

Chapter 7

1 Department of Defense 2016 Fiscal Year Budget.

2 "Overview of Board on Behavioral, Cognitive, and Sensory Sciences Activities," http://sites.nationalacademies. org/DBASSE/BBCSS/DBASSE_071390 (Retrieved Feb 5, 2015)

3 "Afghans: NATO airstrike kills mother, 5 children, 3 Western troops die," May 7, 2012; http://latimesblogs.latimes.com/world_now/2012/05/afghanistan-nato-airstrike-kills-mother-children.html (Retrieved Feb 5, 2015)

4 Matthew Schofield, "WikiLeaks: Iraqi children in U.S. raid shot in head, U.N. says," *McClatchyDC*, August 31, 2011; http://www.mcclatchydc.com/2011/08/31/122789/wikileaks-iraqi-children-in-us.html#storylink=cpy (Retrieved Feb 5, 2015)

5 Carolyn Cole, "Mourning," *Los Angeles Times*, April 11, 2003, http://www.latimes.com/world/la-041103cole-gallery-photogallery.html (Retrieved Feb 5, 2015)

6 Steve Gardner, "Triple amputee war veteran throws first pitch," *USA Today*, Oct 26, 2012; http://www.usatoday.com/story/gameon/2012/10/25/triple-amputee-war-veteran-throws-first-pitch-world-series/1659149/ (Retrieved Feb 5, 2015)

7 Howard Zinn, *A People's History of the United States: 1492 to Present*, Harper Collins, New York, 2003, p. 685.

8 Edward Bernays, *Propaganda*, IG Publishing, Brooklyn, New York, 2005 (1928), p. 37.

9 Woodrow Wilson, "Address delivered at Joint Session of the Two Houses of Congress," April 2, 1917, U.S. 65th Congress, 1st Session, Senate Document No. 5.

10 Nese F. DeBruyne and Anne Leland, "American War and Military Operations Casualties: Lists and Statistics," Congressional Research Service, January 2, 2015, p. 2; http://www.fas.org/sgp/crs/natsec/RL32492.pdf (Retrieved Feb 5, 2015)

11 Mark Crispin Miller, Introduction to Bernays, *Propaganda*, pp. 11-12.

12 Ibid.

13 Ibid.

14 Noam Chomsky interview, *ZNet* Magazine, November, 2002.

15 Ibid.

16 Ibid.

17 Tara McKelvey, "Inside the Killing Machine," *Newsweek*, February 13, 2011; http://www.thedailybeast.com/newsweek/2011/02/13/inside-the-killing-machine.html (Retrieved Feb 5, 2015)

18 Ibid.

19 Ibid.

20 David Rose, "CIA chiefs face arrest over horrific evidence of bloody 'video game' sorties by drone pilots," *The Daily Mail*; http://www.dailymail.co.uk/news/article-2220828/US-drone-attacks-CIA-chiefs-face-arrest-horrific-evidence-bloody-video-game-sorties.html (Retrieved Feb 5, 2015)

21 Ibid.

22 Ibid.

23 Spencer Ackerman, "US Cited Controversial Law in Decision to Kill American Citizen by Drone," *The Guardian*, June 23, 2014; https://www.theguardian.com/world/2014/jun/23/us-justification-drone-killing-american-citizen-awlaki

24 Glenn Greenwald, "Obama Killed a 16-Year-Old American in Yemen. Trump Just Killed His 8-Year-Old Sister," *The Intercept*, January 30, 2017; https://theintercept.com/2017/01/30/obama-killed-a-16-year-old-american-in-yemen-trump-just-killed-his-8-year-old-sister/

25 Ibid.

26 Ibid.

27 Ibid.

28 Ibid.

29 Arundhati Roy, *Public Power in the Age of Empire*, Seven Stories Press, New York, 2004, p. 39.

30 Jeremy Scahill, "A Nation Addicted to War," *The Intercept, (Intercepted Podcast)*, April 11, 2018; https://theintercept.com/2018/04/11/a-nation-addicted-to-war-syria-trump/

31 Aimee Allison and David Solnit, *Army of None*, Seven Stories Press, New York, 2007, p. 3.

32 Joe Pappalardo, "Inside the War Games for Air Force Fighter Pilots," *Popular Mechanics*, Sept 30, 2009; http://www.popularmechanics.com/military/a12350/4311433/ (Retrieved Feb 5, 2015)

33 Elisabeth Bumiller, "A Day Job Waiting for a Kill Shot a World Away," *The New York Times*, July 29, 2012; http://www.nytimes.com/2012/07/30/us/drone-pilots-waiting-for-a-kill-shot-7000-miles-away.html (Retrieved Feb 5, 2015)

34 Ibid.

35 Chris Hedges, "War is Betrayal," July 13, 2012; http://www.truthdig.com/report/item/war_is_betrayal_20120713/ (Retrieved Feb 5, 2015)

36 Dick Gregory, interviewed in *One Bright Shining Moment: The Forgotten Summer of George McGovern*, documentary film, Stephen Vittoria, director, Street Legal Cinema, 2005.

37 International Human Rights and Conflict Resolution Clinic of Stanford Law School & Global Justice Clinic at New York University School of Law, "Living Under Drones," June 12, 2012; http://www.livingunderdrones.org/executive-summary-recommendations/ (Retrieved Feb 5, 2015)

38 Ibid.

39 Melissa Melton, "Conditioning? Xbox Poll Shows Overwhelming Game Support For "More" Drone Strikes," *Infowars*, Oct 24, 2012; http://www.infowars.com/xbox-live-poll-shows-overwhelming-support-for-more-drone-strikes/ (Retrieved Feb 5, 2015)

40 Stuart White, as quoted in Greg Voakes, "How Do Video Games and Modern Military Influence Each Other?" *Forbes*, May 30, 2012; http://www.forbes.com/sites/gregvoakes/2012/05/30/how-do-video-games-and-modern-military-influence-each-other/ (Retrieved Feb 5, 2015)

41 Keith Stuart, "Call of Duty: Advanced Warfare: 'We worked with a Pentagon adviser,'" *The Guardian*, August 28, 2014 https://www.theguardian.com/technology/2014/aug/28/call-of-duty-advanced-warfare-pentagon-adviser

42 Ibid.

43 Ibid.

44 Ibid.

45 Jamie Holmes, "US military is meeting recruitment goals with video games—but at what cost?" *Christian Science Monitor*, Dec. 28, 2009; http://www.csmonitor.com/Commentary/Opinion/2009/1228/US-military-is-meeting-recruitment-goals-with-video-games-but-at-what-cost (Retrieved Feb 5, 2015)

46 Pat Elder, "Military Recruiting Vans Draw Fire," November 26, 2007, *Common Dreams*; https://www.commondreams.org/archive/2007/11/26/5440 (Retrieved Feb 5, 2015)

47 Ibid.

48 Ibid.

49 U.S. Army, *America's Army 3*, video game, 2009; http://aa3.americasarmy.com/documents/AA3_Knowledge_Center_FAQ.pdf (Retrieved Feb 5, 2015)

50 Allison and Solnit, pp. 3-6.

51 "Iraq: A memorial to those who died in the 2003 war," *The Guardian*; http://www.guardian.co.uk/Iraq/memorial/0,,952862,00.html (Retrieved Feb 5, 2015)

52 Ibid.

53 Ibid.

54 Alex Molnar, as quoted in *Voices of a People's History of the United States*, Howard Zinn and Anthony Arnove, editors, Seven Stories Press, New York, 2004, pp. 544-546.

55 Dick Gregory, interview outtakes from Vittoria, *One Bright Shining Moment: The Forgotten Summer of George McGovern*.

56 David Swanson, *War is a Lie*, davidswanson.org, Charlottesville, VA, 2010, pp. 147-148.

57 Hedges, "War is Betrayal".

58 Robert Burns, "Army Likely Won't Meet Recruiting Goals," *The Guardian*, March 23, 2005.

59 Ibid.

60 Michael Kilian and Deborah Horan, "Enlistment drought spurs new strategies," *Chicago Tribune*, March 31, 2005; http://articles.chicagotribune.com/2005-03-31/news/0503310286_1_military-aptitude-test-national-guard-recruiter-army-secretary-francis-harvey (Retrieved Feb 5, 2015)

61 Justin Akers Chacón, "The Battle Over Military Recruitment," *International Socialist Review*, May-June 2005.

62 Swanson, p. 10.

63 Akers Chacón, "The Battle Over Military Recruitment".

64 United States Army Recruiting Command, "School Recruiting Program Handbook," USAREC Pamphlet 350-13, September 1, 2004; https://www.grassrootspeace.org/army_recruiter_hdbk.pdf

65 Dick Gregory, *Caught in the Act*, Poppy Records, 1973.

66 Akers, "The Battle Over Military Recruitment".

67 Ibid.

68 Ibid.

69 David Goodman, "No Child Unrecruited," *Mother Jones*, November/December 2002; http://www.motherjones.com/politics/2002/11/no-child-unrecruited (Retrieved Feb 5, 2015)

70 Howard Zinn, "To Disagree Is to Be Put on the Enemies List," from *The Historic Unfulfilled Promise*, City Lights Books, San Francisco, 2012, pp. 16-17 (article originally published in *The Progressive*, June 1980).

71 Christopher Raissi, as quoted in Azadeh Shahshahani and Tim Franzen, "Georgia Law Will Safeguard Children from Abusive Military Recruitment," *Huffington Post*, April 3, 2010; http://www.huffingtonpost.com/azadeh-shahshaani/georgia-law-will-safeguar_b_444974.html (Retrieved Feb 5, 2015)

72 Shahshahani and Franzen, "Georgia Law Will Safeguard Children from Abusive Military Recruitment".

73 Ibid.

74 *Soldiers of Misfortune: Abusive U.S. Military Recruitment and Failure to Protect Child Soldiers*, ACLU report, May 13, 2008, pp. 2-3; https://www.aclu.org/files/pdfs/humanrights/crc_report_20080513.pdf (Retrieved Feb 5, 2015)

75 Ibid., p. 3.

76 Ibid.

77 Shahshahani and Franzen, "Georgia Law Will Safeguard Children from Abusive Military Recruitment".

78 Barbara Ehrenreich, *Blood Rites: Origins and History of the Passions of War*, Virago Press, London, 1998, p. 205.

79 Sunsara Taylor, "Battle Cry for Theocracy," *Truthdig*, May 11, 2006; http://www.truthdig.com/report/item/20060511_battle_cry_theocracy (Retrieved Feb 5, 2015)

80 Sunsara Taylor, "Fear and Loathing at Philadelphia's BattleCry," *Truthdig*, May 13, 2006; http://www.truthdig.com/report/item/20060513_battlecry_philadelphia (Retrieved Feb 5, 2015)

81 Taylor, "Battle Cry for Theocracy".

82 Taylor, "Fear and Loathing at Philadelphia's BattleCry".

83 Ron Luce, *Battle Cry for a Generation: The Fight to Save America's Youth*, Cook Communication Ministries, Colorado Springs, CO, 2005, p. 57.

84 Ron Luce, as quoted in Jeff Sharlet, "Teenage Holy War," *Rolling Stone*, April 19, 2007.

85 Ibid.

86 Taylor, "Fear and Loathing at Philadelphia's BattleCry".

87 Taylor, "Battle Cry for Theocracy".

88 Gore Vidal, interview with the authors, "Murder Incorporated Sessions," Street Legal Cinema, 2007, transcript.

89 Chris Rodda, "Chaplains and Religion Substituted for Professional Mental Health Care in the Military," *Huffington Post*, August 15, 2010; http://www.huffingtonpost.com/chris-rodda/chaplains-and-religion-su_b_678779.html (Retrieved Feb 5, 2015)

90 Ibid.

91 Mitch Albom, *The Five People You Meet in Heaven*, Hyperion, New York, 2003, p. 57.

Chapter 8

1 BBC, "UK Thatcher Stands by Pinochet," March 26, 1999; http://news.bbc.co.uk/2/hi/304516.stm (Retrieved Feb 12, 2015)

2 Morton Halperin, Jerry Berman, Robert Borosage, & Christine Marwick, *The Lawless State*, Penguin Books, 1976, p. 16.

3 Associated Press, "Chilean president Salvador Allende committed suicide, autopsy confirms," *The Guardian*, July 19, 2011; http://www.theguardian.com/world/2011/jul/20/salvador-allende-committed-suicide-autopsy (Retrieved Feb 12, 2015)

4 Joan Jara, *An Unfinished Song: The Life of Victor Jara*, Ticknor & Fields, New York, 1984, pp. 23-24.

5 Ibid., pp. 27-28.

6 Ibid., p. 29.

7 Ibid., p. 34.

8 Ibid., pp. 34-35.

9 Victor Jara, as quoted in Jara, *An Unfinished Song*, p. 35.

10 Ibid., p. 36.

11 Jara, p. 37.

12 Ibid., p. 41.

13 Ibid., p. 87.

14 Ibid., p. 88.

15 Victor Jara, as quoted in Jara, p. 98.

16 Jara, p. 97.

17 Ibid., p. 97.

18 Ibid., p. 124.

19 Victor Jara, as quoted in Jara, p. 124.

20 Jara, p. 125.

21 Encyclopedia of World Biography, Victor Jara Bio; http://www.notablebiographies.com/supp/Supplement-Fl-Ka/Jara-Victor.html (Retrieved Feb 12, 2015)

22 Ibid.

23 Jara, p. 147.

24 Ibid., p. 204.

25 Ibid., p. 205.

26 Ibid., p. 246.

27 Ibid., p. 247.

28 "15 Rock and Roll Rebels," Rolling Stone; http://www.rollingstone.com/music/lists/15-rock-roll-rebels-20130603/victor-jara-19691231 (Retrieved Feb 12, 2015)

29 Jara, p. 249.

30 "Victor Jara murder: Chile arrests ex-army officers," BBC News, January 3, 2013 http://www.bbc.co.uk/news/world-latin-america-20897545 (Retrieved Feb 12, 2015)

31 "15 Rock and Roll Rebels," Rolling Stone.

32 Jara, p. 249.

33 "15 Rock and Roll Rebels," Rolling Stone.

34 "The Kissinger Telcons: Kissinger Telcons on Chile," The National Security Archive, Electronic Briefing Book No. 123, Peter Kornbluh, editor, May 26, 2004; http://www.gwu.edu/~nsarchiv/NSAEBB/NSAEBB123/chile.htm (Retrieved Feb 12, 2015)

35 Jara, p. 249.

36 "Kissinger Telcons on Chile," The National Security Archive.

37 "They couldn't kill his songs," BBC News, September 5, 1998; http://news.bbc.co.uk/2/hi/americas/165363.stm (Retrieved Feb 12, 2015)

38 Reggie Schell, interviewed in Long Distance Revolutionary, documentary film, Stephen Vittoria, director, Street Legal Cinema, 2013.

39 Juan Gonzalez interviewed in Long Distance Revolutionary, documentary film, Stephen Vittoria, director, Street Legal Cinema, 2013.

40 Frank Rizzo, from NBC interview with Tom Snyder as featured in Vittoria, Long Distance Revolutionary".

41 Ramsey Clark, interviewed in Vittoria, Long Distance Revolutionary.

42 Ramona Africa, interview with the authors, September, 2013.

43 Ibid.

44 Ibid.

45 William Stevens, "Grand Jury Clears Everyone In Fatal Philadelphia Siege," The New York Times, May 4, 1988; http://www.nytimes.com/1988/05/04/us/grand-jury-clears-everyone-in-fatal-philadelphia-siege.html (Retrieved Feb 12, 2015)

46 Ibid.

47 Aya de Leon, interviewed in Vittoria, Long Distance Revolutionary.

48 Ramona Africa, interview with the authors, September, 2013.

49 Ibid.

50 Ramona Africa, interviewed in Vittoria, *Long Distance Revolutionary*.

Index

recruitment of Nazi war criminals, 171–172

Saigon Military Mission, 163, 302–303, 319–321

against Salvador Allende, 351–353

in Southeast Asia, 302

support for Contras, 215–218

Vietnam, 153, 184–187, 268, 297–298, 302–303, 319–322

CIA's Greatest Hits, The (Zepezaur), 190

Cienfuegos, Camilo, 197

"City on the hill," 33, 247–249

Civilian casualties, of war
Cambodia, 190, 191, 349, 350
Chile, 202
Dresden firebombing, 108–111
of drone attacks, 383–390
East Timor, 362–363, 366
Hiroshima and Nagasaki, 111–113, 114–132
Iraq, 225, 375–377
Korean War, 168
MOVE bombing, 439
Panama, 224–225
Soviet-Afghan conflict, 229
Tokyo firebombing, 111–113
Vietnam War, 184–187, 265–266, 322–323
World War II, 77, 108–113, 114–132, 257–258

Civil War, 250

Clark, Ramsey, 435

Class struggle, war and, 61–62

Clinton, Bill
budget surplus under, 282
East Timor genocide and, 363–364, 365–366
speech to the CIA, 230

Clinton, Hillary, 222–223

Coca-Cola, 363

Cohan, George M., 36

Cohen, Jeff, 216–217

Cohen, Leonard, 291

Cohn, Marjorie, 247

COINTELPRO, 140

Colby, William, 148, 185, 186, 336

Cold War
beginning of, 126–127, 240
fear as basis for, 139–141
financing of, 241–242
"good *versus* evil" mentality of, 137–138, 145
Korean War during, 165–169
National Security Act and, 134
origin of term, 251
propaganda of, 139–141
Truman and, 140–141, 240

U. S. nuclear strategy during, 236–238

Cole, Juan, 222

Coleman, Joseph, 112–113

Colonialism
Spanish-American War and, 31–32
Woodrow Wilson on, 34
World War I and, 29–30

Colson, Chuck, 413

Commerce, war as, 270–271

Commission on Wartime Relocation and Internment of Civilians, 101

Committee on the Present Danger, 271

Communism
Christian ideology use by, 151–152
containment policy for, 240
in Vietnam, 187–188

Communist Party
Brazilian, 194–195
Chilean, 199, 424, 425
Chinese, 158–159, 160
Filipino, 164
Greek, 162
Indonesian, 180–182, 329, 330–335
Italian, 160

Communists, Suharto's massacre of, 330–335

Concentration camps
in East Timor, 357–358
IBM's involvement with, 97, 98
for Japanese-Americans, 99–108
transportation to, 97

Condor Years, The (Dinges), 202–203

Congo/Zaire, 192–194, 205

Conscientious objectors, 46–48
in World War I, 36, 41

Conservative Party (U. K.), 202

Contras, 159, 215–218, 224

Convention on the Rights of the Child, 410–412

Conversations with Gore Vidal, 137

Coolidge, Calvin, 254

Copley, James, 170

Corporations. *See also names of specific corporations*
CIA's services to, 154–155
control of the media, 141
in defense industry, 252
involvement in Chile, 350, 420
involvement in Indonesia, 334–335, 342

Iraq War-related profits, 278–280, 281, 282
as Kissinger Associates clients, 346–347
with land holdings in Cuba, 205
multinational, 137
opposition to Allende, 201
partnerships with Nazi Germany, 95–99
in post-war Iraq, 278–279
socialism's threat to, 142
Vietnam war-related profits, 268–269

Corry, Edward, 354

Cortez, Julia, 211–212

Costa Rica, 274

Coup d'etats
against Allende, 199–203, 350–355, 419–421
against Arbenz, 189
Brazil, 194–195
Dominican Republic, 196–197
against Estenssoro, 205–206
fictional depiction of, 133
against Mossadegh, 174–176
National Security State as, 134
in South Vietnam, 149
against Sukarno, 180–182, 329–330

Court martials, during World War I, 41, 42, 66

Cousins, Norman, 274

Creel, George, 37, 40

Creel Commission, 37

Crile, George, 203–204

Crimes Against Humanity (Robertson), 355

Criminal Justice Magazine, 104

Crowder, Enoch, 41

Cuba, 197–199
agrarian reform in, 205
Bay of Pigs invasion, 197, 198, 208, 238, 250
Bolivia's relations with, 205–206
Operation Mongoose, 163
U. S. blockade, 205
U. S. control of, 63

Cuban Revolution, 205

Cunningham, Gary, 340

Curzon, Lord, 128

Cyprus, 26

D

Daley, Richard, 271

Darbyshire, Norman, 175

"Dark Alliance" (Webb), 216–218

Davis, Deborah, 170

Davis, Mike, 216

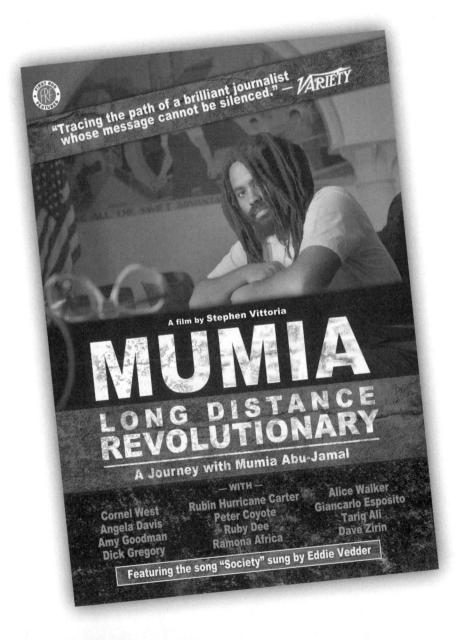